PRAISE FOR *FORGING AMERICA*

"By placing American events in a global context, Steven Hahn has written a remarkably inclusive narrative. It puts people first, not government systems. It places working people and others on the periphery at the center of the story. The result is a refreshing and new interpretation of American history."

—**Justin Behrend,** *The State University of New York, Geneseo*

"In *Forging America* Steven Hahn weaves a remarkable variety of threads into a lively, engaging, and challenging history of North America. Masterfully recapturing a sense of contingency, Hahn raises thought-provoking questions, offers insightful explanations, and illuminates a complex and multi-faceted story."

—**Cara Shelly,** *Oakland University*

"Steven Hahn's *Forging America* has the appealing double-benefit of communicating to students the necessary information to understand America's history, while also prompting students to think like historians in their own right."

—**John William Nelson,** *Texas Tech University*

"Many of our students now get their information through podcasts instead of print. The *Forging America* audiobook, with its professional narration and music, will help draw students into the reading and give them two ways to remember the material."

—**Mary Lyons-Carmona,** *Metropolitan Community College*

About the Cover

Left. In *Girl in a Green Turban* (1913), William James Glackens shows a "New Woman" of the early twentieth century. Her loose clothing contrasts sharply with the style of dress worn by women of the preceding generation, while her Asian-looking headwrap attests to the mixing of cultures in a rapidly globalizing world.

Right. Artist Andrew Wyeth painted this compelling portrait of Ojibwe activist Nogeeshik Aquash in 1972, the same year Aquash participated in the Trail of Broken Treaties, a cross-country protest that culminated in Washington, DC, where a number of protestors occupied the Bureau of Indian Affairs building in order to draw attention to Native American rights. The following year Aquash, his wife, and other members of the American Indian Movement occupied Wounded Knee at the Pine Ridge Reservation in South Dakota for seventy-one days.

Forging America

Forging America

A CONTINENTAL HISTORY
OF THE UNITED STATES

VOLUME TWO: SINCE 1863

Steven Hahn
New York University

OXFORD
UNIVERSITY PRESS

OXFORD
UNIVERSITY PRESS

Oxford University Press is a department of the University of Oxford.
It furthers the University's objective of excellence in research, scholarship,
and education by publishing worldwide. Oxford is a registered trade mark
of Oxford University Press in the UK and in certain other countries.

Published in the United States of America by Oxford University Press
198 Madison Avenue, New York, NY 10016, United States of America.

© 2024 by Oxford University Press

For titles covered by Section 112 of the US Higher Education Opportunity
Act, please visit www.oup.com/us/he for the latest information about
pricing and alternate formats.

Library of Congress Cataloging-in-Publication Data
Names: Hahn, Steven, 1951- author.
Title: Forging America : a continental history of the United States /
  Steven Hahn, New York University.
Other titles: Continental history of the United States
Identifiers: LCCN 2023017322 (print) | LCCN 2023017323 (ebook) | ISBN
  9780197540190 (v. 1 ; paperback) | ISBN 9780197540206 (v. 2 ; paperback)
  | ISBN 9780197540251 (v. 1 ; epub) | ISBN 9780197540268 (v. 2 ; epub)
Subjects: LCSH: United States—History—Textbooks.
Classification: LCC E178.1 .H15 2024 (print) | LCC E178.1 (ebook) | DDC
  973—dc23/eng/20230419
LC record available at https://lccn.loc.gov/2023017322
LC ebook record available at https://lccn.loc.gov/2023017323

Printed by Quad/Graphics, Inc., Mexico

To history's students, who know that forging a just and humane

future demands a serious and honest encounter with the past

Brief Contents

Contents

PERSPECTIVES
Remembering the Battle of
Little Big Horn/The Battle of
Greasy Grass *704*

MAPPING AMERICA
Peoples on the Move *716*

CHAPTER 18 **Cauldrons of Protest, 1873–1896** *733*

CHAPTER **19** **Constructing Progressivism, 1886–1914**   *779*

CHAPTER 24 Flames of Global War, Visions of Global Peace, 1940–1945 *999*

CHAPTER **25** Cold War America, 1945–1957 *1041*

PART SIX   **Conservatism, Neoliberalism, and Militarism**

> **WHAT IF** Martin Luther King, Jr., and Robert F. Kennedy Had Not Been **Assassinated?** *1133*

CHAPTER 27 | Destabilizations, 1969–1979 *1139*

CHAPTER 28 A New Conservatism and Its Discontents, 1980–1989   *1185*

Maps, Tables, and Figures

Maps

Tables

Figures

Features

Sources for *Forging America, Volume Two: Since 1863*

Edited by Felicia A. Viator and Stefan Lund

The primary sources listed below are found in this volume's e-book as well as well as in the print and e-book companion sourcebook, *Sources for Forging America.*

Preface

Not long after I began to teach, I went to see a special exhibition of the works of Pablo Picasso. Picasso's art always spoke to me in powerful ways, with his use of color and his edgy depictions of objects and people. As a college freshman I had a poster of his *Three Musicians* on the wall in my dorm room, and it remained with me for years. But this time, I looked at his paintings with the new eyes of a historian, and suddenly I had a much deeper understanding of what he was offering us. It was not simply his interpretation of a world in the throes of change and turmoil. It was also his attempt to have us see the world from multiple perspectives *simultaneously*, from the inside out as well as the outside in. Picasso was doing on a canvas what historians struggle to do in their research and writing; he was trying to capture the world in its many dimensions, recognizing that no single one of them could represent the truth.

Artists like Pablo Picasso have great license to represent their subjects and to invite us to look at the world as they do. Historians have more constraints. We need to base our representations of the past on the words and signs that people at many different times produce. But, like artists, we also learn very quickly that historical events are many layered and that historical actors have different understandings of what is happening. This is a challenge because it leaves us with few hard truths however deep we dig in the sources. Yet it is also exciting because we realize that all sorts of people—rich and poor, prominent and obscure, female and male—play roles in historical change, and because we recognize that history is a continuous process of discovery: and that we can be the discoverers.

A history of the United States is a daunting undertaking for readers and writers alike. It covers well over 400 years and involves people and places from all over the globe. It also requires that we transport ourselves into worlds very different than our own and try to see those worlds through the eyes of the people we study. It requires that

Pablo Picasso, *Three Musicians* (1921)

we acknowledge the "pastness" of the past and do what we can to reckon with it. At the same time, we must also acknowledge the "presentness of the past," that the past is always living within us, is being carried by us even if we're not aware of it. "The past is never dead," a famous novelist once wrote. "It's not even past." History is our companion and our teacher. History is a way of learning and thinking. History is something we cannot escape nor should we want to.

I wrote *Forging America: A Continental History of the United States* because, after many years of teaching and writing, I thought that there might be a way to envision US history that speaks both to the complexities of historical experience and to the meanings of the past for our present-day lives. And I've come to think that *perspectives* of many sorts can be the key. There can be perspectives on geography, social class or status, race and ethnicity, gender and sexuality. There can also be perspectives about power and how power is wielded, about how those who are empowered and those who are subject to power view their relationships. Perspectives are about the vantage points we choose to take and from which we make historical narratives. Should we, for example, approach the colonization of North America from the point of view of Europe and the settler-colonizers or should we approach it from the point of view of North America and the Indigenous peoples who already resided there? Or, Picasso-like, should we view colonization from both perspectives simultaneously? Should we accept the label of "Civil War" to capture the brutal conflagration that erupted between 1861 and 1865, suggesting as it does a struggle between parties with comparable perspectives and political standing; or, Picasso-like, should we speak of a "War of the Rebellion" because it captures, simultaneously, the view of the Lincoln administration, which regarded secession as a rebellion, and the view of rebel enslavers, who saw themselves rejecting the authority of the federal government in order to safeguard their slave system?

Perspectives are important springboards because they allow us to validate the ideas and experiences of many more people than usually find themselves in historical accounts. They remind us that people make history, and even if they do not get what they want or are defeated in their quests, we can see how they give shape to the outcomes. Perspectives are also important because they demand that we try to identify a very full range of human and social relationships—from household and home to the highest levels of the state—and explore how power operates within and between those relationships. In fact, perspectives do not simply permit us to gain a fuller and deeper sense of how social relationships and power operate: perspectives are relationships and forms of power. In the most basic sense, power is getting people to do what you want them to do whether they want to or not, and power reveals itself in who controls the wealth, who works for whom, who can enjoy life's opportunities. But power is also about whose ideas and values and interpretations gain support, about whose notion of the public good is validated, whose construction of gender and sexuality is privileged, whose vision of what is beautiful and ugly or of what are acceptable or unacceptable aspirations come to prevail. In short, power is about whose perspectives are privileged, consulted, and spread about and whose are not.

Forging America uses multiple and shifting perspectives to narrate the history of the United States and to focus the readers' attentions on those moments when historical change occurs. In effect, we tell the story from the inside out as well as the outside in, from the West to the East as well as the East to the West, from the South to the North as well as the North to the South, and from below to above as well as above to below. In order to do this, we use a number of distinctive methods and devices:

Geography

Histories of the United States generally move from Europe and the Atlantic westward. They usually begin with an Atlantic world taking shape in the fifteenth and sixteenth centuries as a context for the European colonization of North America and its eastern interior. The Pacific and its world appear much later in the story and as a product of American "expansion" and "conquest." *Forging America* does something different. We start from Asia and the Pacific, China in particular, and thereby make the Pacific world as much a part of United States history as the Atlantic world has been. After all, China was the globe's greatest empire during the fifteenth and sixteenth centuries and both the Pacific and trans-Mississippi West produced formidable societies and empires in their own right. *Forging America* is the story of the collision of these powers and how the collision transformed everyone, sometimes in unexpected ways. Emphasizing the Pacific also helps explain why leaders of the early American republic saw the country's destiny as taking hold of the Pacific coast, why the question of slavery's fate in the American West proved so convulsive, why the search for foreign markets in the late nineteenth century looked to East Asia, why American entry into World War II was triggered by a Japanese attack on Pearl Harbor in the Hawaiian Islands, and why the United States became embroiled militarily in Vietnam during the 1960s. *Forging America*, logically, ends with the reemergence of China on the world stage as the new and leading rival of the United States.

The maps in *Forging America* support the book's multifocal approach to geography. Textbooks usually follow standard geographical conventions in their depiction of events and developments, and many of the maps in *Forging America* will be familiar to most readers. But *Forging America* breaks from convention by striving, whenever possible, to map continuity and change from the perspectives of the people who lived through them. Instead of relying exclusively on standard projections that show the United States with an east-west and north-south orientation, some maps in *Forging America* show events from a south-north or west-east perspective. For example, when discussing the borderlands of the Southwest, maps that show a south-north view better reflect the experiences of local peoples than ones that take a north-south orientation. In addition, each chapter includes a "Mapping America" feature that juxtaposes two different ways cartographers might document the same event or development. For instance, the "Mapping America" feature in Chapter 11 (which looks at the 1830s and 1840s) contrasts a standard view of westward expansion with one that offers a different spatial geography, namely, a view from a Comanche perspective.

Visuality

Perspectives can be presented in written form, but they also appear visually in paintings, displays, parades, demonstrations, protests, cartoons, and ceremonies. Eventually they appear in photographs and film. *Forging America* uses a variety of images to convey the substance and meaning of differing perspectives. Maps and charts are especially interesting because they help us understand how people envisioned the world around them: do they focus on changes in the land, on the flora and fauna? Do they focus on borders and boundaries that are imposed by those in power? Do they focus on the groups of people who populate the landscape? Do they focus on the ways that people gain their subsistence and engage in trade? These are the many ways in which we can attempt to capture different perspectives and suggest how those who are long gone *saw* themselves and their societies. To give students opportunities to engage visually with different perspectives, each chapter in *Forging America* offers a "Perspectives" feature that compares multiple images. For example, Chapter 15 pairs two images that contrast the different ways the Civil War was remembered by the North and South. By asking students to consider different ways of looking at the same event or place—as well as to consider the audience for, and purpose of, the arguments made by visual sources—the "Perspectives" features encourage visual literacy as well as historical thinking.

Contingency

Many people assume that history is pretty much preordained. They assume that what happened in the past was destined to have happened, that alternative outcomes were extremely unlikely to have occurred. Yet those who lived at times when important historical events took place did not themselves know what the outcome would be; after all, we don't know how the challenges we face will play out. One of the important themes of *Forging America* that relates to the issue of perspective is the contingency of history: the idea that at any one point several outcomes may be possible, and a confluence of events—some personal decisions, some impersonal forces—usually determines what happens in the end. This is not, of course, to say that anything is possible. Far from it. Contexts limit the range of possibilities and do make certain outcomes more likely than others. Yet highly unexpected developments such as a major storm, a chance encounter, or a small error of judgment can shift history's balances in one direction or another, and, in some cases, have huge repercussions.

What If?

To bring added emphasis to the phenomenon of contingency, *Forging America* has another distinctive feature. Every chapter ends with a "What If?" section: an alternative outcome accompanied by original source materials that bear on the case for students to consider, discuss, and debate. The purpose is not to construct a parallel universe of history-making but rather to sharpen student's perspectives on the past and the questions they ask of it. The alternative outcomes are not far-fetched; they reflect the specific struggles and ideas of that moment, and are the sort of things that observers at the time and scholars since have speculated about. In Volume One, the "What If?" feature for Chapter 8 looks at what the consequences might have been if the slave rebellion on Saint Domingue/Haiti had been defeated. In Volume Two, Chapter 29 explores the different trajectory that would have unfolded for the United States if 9/11 had never happened.

As Americans struggle over how to envision and construct their future, history is more than ever at the center of their discussions and concerns. History is continuously invoked to frame political debates, to fashion public policy, to consider the nature of American identity, and to decide what is taught in our schools. This has not made the process easier; if anything, it has shown that historical interpretation is no less contested than our politics. But the process also suggests that historical thinking and understanding are crucial resources for all of us. They not only offer critical perspectives on the relation of past and present; they are our best defenses against manipulation and repression. The ambition of this textbook is to promote the historical thinking and understanding we so desperately need.

Digital Learning Resources for *Forging America*

Oxford University Press offers instructors and students digital learning resources that increase student engagement and optimize the classroom teaching experience.

Enhanced E-book

The enhanced e-book delivers learning experiences that empower students to actively engage in course content. It includes an integrated audio book narrated by professional actors, "What If?" videos, "Check Your Understanding" assessments, and note-taking guides. The enhanced e-book also includes all of the primary sources from the two-volume sourcebook (see page xxxi for the list of sources), a significant savings for students. E-books are available for purchase directly at www.oup.com as well as at Vital Source, RedShelf, Perusall, and other vendors.

Oxford Learning Link (OLL)

The online resource center www.learninglink.oup.com is available to adopters of *Forging America*, and it offers a test-item file, a computerized test bank, an instructor's resource manual, quizzes, PowerPoint slides, videos, handouts, and primary sources. The digital learning resources for *Forging America* can be embedded directly in an LMS via a one-time course integration, or instructors may choose to assign the resources in OUP's user-friendly, cloud-based platform.

Acknowledgments

Writing a book such as this is a lengthy process that depends upon the help, comments, and criticisms of many people. Some are historians and instructors of history who have been asked for responses to many of the chapters, but who have submitted them in a way that remained anonymous to me. Therefore, since I can't thank them individually, I'd like to offer my thanks to them collectively for their insights, judgments, and sometimes dissatisfactions. These were not always easy to read, but together they improved the book in organization, style, and substance. Nonetheless, a number of friends who were not anonymous agreed to review sections of the book, and their reactions and ideas have been invaluable. My sincere thanks go to Greg Downs, Rachel Klein, Jonathan Prude, and Amy Dru Stanley.

I also benefitted from the extraordinary resources of the Huntington Library, where I was a Rogers Fellow for the 2016–2017 academic year, and where I wrote a great deal of the first draft. Special thanks to Steve Hindle and Roy Ritchie of the Huntington Library and fellows John Demos, Woody Holton, Scott Heerman, and Beth Sayler.

Charles Cavaliere of Oxford University Press has been a remarkable editor. A close student of American and European history in his own right, he has been insightful, encouraging, demanding when necessary, and committed to the project I was hoping to complete. I could not have asked for more wisdom or textbook sense. At Oxford, too, I was helped in important ways by Meg Botteon, Elizabeth M. Welch, Ann West, Sukwinder Kaur, Julia Wray, Nicholas Ashman, Stefan Lund, Sheryl Adams, and by fact-checker Hannah Craddock. Copyeditor Leslie Anglin polished my prose and Senior Production Manager Cheryl Loe juggled with great dexterity a schedule that was both compressed and complex. I also thank Samara Naeymi at Brick Shop Studio for coordinating the production of the audio book.

Forging America took shape over quite a number of years, more than I had initially expected, and the process necessarily takes a toll on loved ones surrounding you. I would like to offer a special thanks to my partner, Susan Wishingrad, and my—now grown—children, Declan and Saoirse, for putting up with my writing obsessions and, most important, for reading much of the book manuscript and discussing it with me. I know they share my pleasure in finally seeing it done.

The book's dedication is a measure of the crisis our society faces and the importance of history teaching, learning, and thinking to any positive resolutions that may be found. History has come to the forefront of contemporary political struggles, and their outcome will determine whose values will prevail, whose vision of the future will guide us, and who will wield power and how. History instructors at all educational levels are embattled if not outright threatened in their efforts to help us understand worlds very different than our own as well as recognize how the past resonates in our daily lives. Their determination is inspiring and we must do our best to stand with them.

Expert Reviewers

Justin Behrend	SUNY Geneseo
William Bolt	Francis Marion University
Kyle Bulthuis	Utah State University
Kevin D. Butler	University of Arkansas at Pine Bluff
Mylynka Cardona	Texas A&M University—Commerce
Brad Cartwright	University of Texas at El Paso
Colt Chaney	Tyler Junior College
Christopher Childers	Pittsburg State University
Dawn Ciofoletti	Florida Gulf Coast University
Michael Leonard Cox	San Diego Mesa College
Christine Dee	Fitchburg State University
Brian Dempsey	University of North Alabama
Gregory P. Downs	University of California, Davis
Jeff Ewen	Ivy Tech Community College
Joshua Farrington	Bluegrass Community and Technical College
Andre Fleche	Castleton State University
Jeffrey Fortney	Florida Gulf Coast University
Alison Gough	Hawaii Pacific University
Jennifer Grohol	Bakersfield College
Evan Haefeli	Texas A&M University
Ian Hartman	University of Alaska Anchorage
David Head	University of Central Florida
Kenneth Heineman	Angelo State University
Jennifer Heth	Tarrant County College
Karlos K. Hill	University of Oklahoma
Brady L. Holley	Middle Tennessee State University

Michael Holm	Boston University
Maya Lisa Holzman	Oregon State University–Cascades
James Hrdlicka	Arizona State University
Katherine Jenkins	College of Charleston
Benjamin Johnson	Loyola University Chicago
Katherine Johnson	Montana State University
Sarah Keyes	University of Nevada, Reno
Rachel Klein	UC San Diego
Gary Lee	Georgia State University–Perimeter College
Leslie Leighton	Georgia State University
Lawrence M. Lipin	Pacific University
George Lloyd Johnson	Campbell University
Camilo Lund-Montaño	Whitman College
Mary Lyons-Carmona	Metro Community College
Scott C. Martin	Bowling Green State University
Thomas Massey	Cape Fear Community College
Lindsay Maxwell	Florida International University
Daniel Murphree	University of Central Florida
Jennifer M. Murray	Oklahoma State University
Sarah Naramore	Northwest Missouri State University
Benjamin Park	Sam Houston State University
Robert Parkinson	Binghamton University
Brian Peterson	Shasta College
Christopher Pieczynski	Tidewater Community College
Jonathan Prude	Emory University
Ansley Quiros	University of North Alabama
Mervyn Roberts	Central Texas College
Sarah Robey	Idaho State University
Joseph A. Rodriguez	University of Wisconsin–Milwaukee
Cara Shelly	Oakland University
Suzanne E. Smith	George Mason University
Robert S. Smith	Marquette University

Marie Stango	Idaho State University
Amy Dru Stanley	University of Chicago
Rowan Steineker	Florida Gulf Coast University
Michael Stout	University of Texas at Arlington
Tom Summerhill	Michigan State University
Julie Anne Sweet	Baylor University
Matthijs Tieleman	Arizona State University
Evan Turiano	Queens College, CUNY
Felicity Turner	Georgia Southern University
Felicia Viator	San Francisco State University
Robert Voss	Northwest Missouri State University
William Wantland	Mount Vernon Nazarene University
Jamin Wells	University of West Florida
John William Nelson	Texas Tech University
Lee B. Wilson	Clemson University
Jonathan Wilson	Rowan University
Thomas Wirth	SUNY Cortland

About the Author

Steven Hahn earned his BA at the University of Rochester and his MA and PhD at Yale University. He is a specialist on the social and political history of the nineteenth-century United States, on the history of the American South, on slavery, emancipation, and race, and on the development of American empire on the North American continent, in the Western Hemisphere, and in the Pacific world. His books include the Pulitzer Prize–winning *A Nation Under Our Feet: Black Political Struggles in the Rural South from Slavery to the Great Migration* (2003); *The Political Worlds of Slavery and Freedom* (2009); *A Nation Without Borders: The United States and Its World in an Age of Civil Wars, 1830–1910* (2016); and most recently, *Illiberal America: A History* (2024).

Hahn has held fellowships from the John Simon Guggenheim Foundation, the National Endowment for the Humanities, the American Council of Learned Societies, the Center for Advanced Study in the Behavioral Sciences at Stanford, and the Cullman Center for Scholars and Writers of the New York Public Library. He has taught at the University of Delaware, the University of California San Diego, Northwestern University, and the University of Pennsylvania, and is currently Professor of History at New York University, where he is also actively involved in the NYU Prison Education Program.

Forging America

15

Ending the Rebellion and (Re)constructing the Nation
1863–1865

≡ **"Bread or Blood!"**   With a threat of famine hanging like a dark cloud over the Confederacy, a large crowd of women ransack bakeries and dry goods stores in Richmond on April 2, 1863.

On April 2, 1863, a crowd of more than 200 women, mostly the wives of Confederate soldiers and local iron workers, marched on the Virginia governor's mansion in Richmond, then the Confederate capital. Led by Mary Jackson and Minerva Meredith, the latter described as "tall, daring, and Amazonian looking," they had met the day before amid growing hardship that food shortages, Confederate policies, and spiraling inflation had brought upon them and their families. Their plan was to meet with the governor and demand action. But when the time came, the governor refused to see them, and so the women—soon joined by many hundreds more, some carrying knives, axes, and other weapons—took to the streets shouting, "We celebrate our right to live! We are starving!" and, more ominously, "Bread or Blood!" Quickly, they turned their wrath on the symbols of their plight, on the government warehouses and the dry goods stores that were hoarding supplies and asking highly inflated prices

Timeline

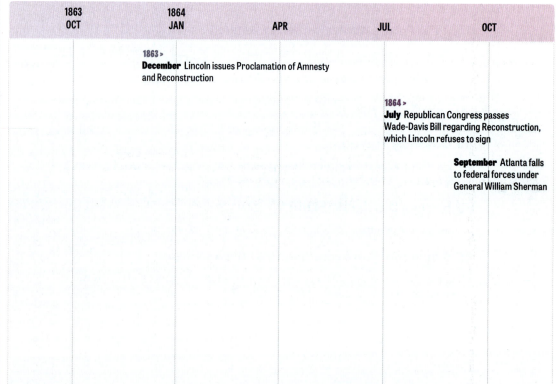

1863 OCT	1864 JAN	APR	JUL	OCT

1863 ›
December Lincoln issues Proclamation of Amnesty and Reconstruction

1864 ›
July Republican Congress passes Wade-Davis Bill regarding Reconstruction, which Lincoln refuses to sign

September Atlanta falls to federal forces under General William Sherman

for their sale. The women sacked them, seizing food, clothing, and other necessities. It was a classic food riot of the sort that exploded in many societies when starvation loomed and some profited off the miseries of most others.

Arriving on the scene, Richmond's mayor demanded that the women withdraw, but to no avail. The governor finally appeared, to little effect. And then came Jefferson Davis, the Confederacy's president and commander in chief. Climbing on a wagon, Davis begged the women to disperse, emptied his pockets of coins, and tossed them their way. He then warned that an artillery unit would arrive and fire upon them if they persisted. Slowly, the women moved off; their food riot was at an end.

Richmond was not alone. Food riots led by women occurred in other parts of the Confederacy in March and April 1863, and they testified to the internal crises that

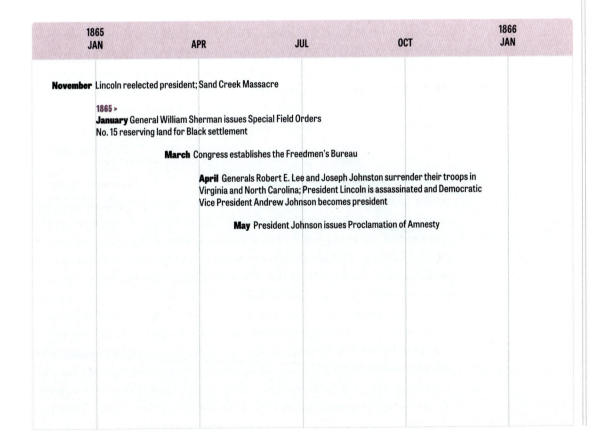

1865 JAN	APR	JUL	OCT	1866 JAN

November Lincoln reelected president; Sand Creek Massacre

1865 ▸
January General William Sherman issues Special Field Orders No. 15 reserving land for Black settlement

March Congress establishes the Freedmen's Bureau

April Generals Robert E. Lee and Joseph Johnston surrender their troops in Virginia and North Carolina; President Lincoln is assassinated and Democratic Vice President Andrew Johnson becomes president

May President Johnson issues Proclamation of Amnesty

afflicted the Confederacy as its troops struggled to hold their lines on the battlefields. The War of the Rebellion, as would be true of other modern wars, wreaked havoc on civilian as well as military populations. Both the federal government and the Confederate rebels needed to contain social tensions and conflicts within their own sides. How these conflicts were managed would play an important role in the outcome of the war and in ways in which the peace might be imagined.

15.1   The Problem of Confederate Territory

||| Explain the challenges of reunification once the Civil War ended.

Even before federal armies marched into the rebellious slaveholding states in 1861, new Republican policymakers began to think about how and in what form the country might be reunified. The rebels had met in special conventions, broken their ties with the United States, formed what they called the Confederate States of America, and vowed to resist federal coercion in a fight for their independence. But what did this really mean in political and constitutional terms, and what powers did the federal government have to act? How was the rebellion to be interpreted, and how would the interpretation shape a process of reconstruction? And which branches of government—the president, Congress, or the courts—had the authority to make the rules?

Republican Perspectives

At the outset, the prevailing view of Lincoln and fellow Republicans was that secession was constitutionally impossible. There was simply no basis in the Constitution to permit a state to leave the union of states. As a result, secession and the Confederacy—Lincoln always referred to it as the "so-called Confederacy"— were regarded as nothing more than the work of rebels who had taken control of their respective states and determined to wage war against the federal government to achieve their ends. The Confederacy could not be diplomatically recognized because it had no legal existence and, as it turned out, no other country in Europe or the Western Hemisphere lent the Confederacy formal recognition. The Republicans optimistically imagined that the Confederate rebels composed only a minority of the population and that loyalty to the United States remained widespread though temporarily pushed below the surface of public opinion. Therefore, from the perspective of the Lincoln administration, the task was to suppress the rebellion, find people loyal to the United States, and return control of the affected states to them. Under these circumstances, the position of the states in the Union would not have changed and their laws and institutions—as well as the status of their citizens who had not engaged in rebellion—would still be in place.

This perspective, of course, was based on the expectation that the rebellion would be defeated quickly and unionism again would rise to the surface of political life. "The States have their *status* in the Union," Lincoln told Congress in July 1861, "and they have no other *legal status*." Yet, as it became clear that the rebellion would not be rapidly subdued and that Republicans couldn't count on much of a base of loyalty among whites in the rebellious states, such thinking appeared misguided. New thinking was necessary.

Republicans, mainly from the radical wing of the party, began to devise a very different argument and perspective. They did not deny that the United States was perpetual or that secession was constitutionally impossible. What they did deny was that nothing fundamental had happened. Radical Republican leaders claimed that the "treasonably civil organization" created in those states effectively forfeited "*their* powers and rights as States," and Massachusetts Senator Charles Sumner went so far as to insist that by the act of secession the states had committed constitutional "suicide." They had ceased to exist. Many of Sumner's colleagues, though rejecting his specific analogy, nonetheless came to a similar conclusion: that the rebel states had been returned to the condition of territories subject to the jurisdiction of the federal government.

This argument was called **territorialization**, though it didn't bring with it any specific plan for reorganizing those states politically. As Congress began to debate the question in early 1862, all sorts of ideas and approaches were offered, some involving the very heavy hand of the Republican-dominated government and a lengthy road to reunification. Lincoln was more hesitant and was not among those Radical Republicans who embraced the concept of territorialization. In principle, he remained committed both to the notion that secession was constitutionally impossible and that loyal state governments should be established as soon as feasible. Even so, his thinking had evolved. More than a year into the war and with little prospect of an end to the rebellion, he could hardly have expected those states to rejoin the United States on their own. Instead, the federal government through its military arm would have to step in and take charge, providing for elections and identifying eligible voters. And, as the Lincoln administration and Congress committed the war to emancipation, the issue of abolition as a prerequisite to any reunification now defined the process.

In this context, Lincoln, shortly after his address at Gettysburg, issued in December 1863 a **Proclamation of Amnesty and Reconstruction**. More of a

THE WAR IN THE SOUTHWEST...ADJUTANT GENERAL THOMAS ADDRESSING THE NEGROES IN LOUISIANA ON THE DUTIES OF FREEDOM.

≡ **Freed African Americans**   A large crowd of African American men, women, and children, some wearing federal military uniforms, listen to General Lorenzo Thomas speak "on the duties and responsibilities of freedom," in Louisiana in 1863.

framework than a clear-cut plan and designed to end the war as soon as feasible, the proclamation set out guidelines for the establishment of new state governments in those parts of the South occupied by federal troops. Offering pardons to all rebels who would now pledge allegiance to the United States, with the exception of top Confederate leaders, Lincoln determined that when such loyalists made up at least one-tenth of all those who voted in the 1860 presidential election, they could adopt a new state constitution and seek representation in Congress. Since the proclamation began by declaring that "treason" had been committed by "many persons" in those states, Lincoln's terms were remarkably generous; that is, save for enslavement.

Lincoln's pardon would carry the "restoration of all rights of property, *except as to slaves*," and he expected the new state governments to provide for the "permanent freedom" of enslaved people. Nothing at all was said about the civil or political status of the formerly enslaved, and Lincoln accepted the likelihood of arrangements "consistent with their present condition as a laboring, landless, and homeless class." Thus, as the problem of enslavement moved toward resolution, the problem of freedom for the formerly enslaved increasingly reared its head. Still, Lincoln had embarked on a course that he had once considered unconstitutional. He asserted the supremacy of the federal government over the states and required them to abolish slavery as a condition for regaining their place in the Union.

The proclamation has become known as Lincoln's "ten-percent plan," and it initially enjoyed support among most Republicans because of its insistence on emancipation. Then, much of that support evaporated as the policy played out in Louisiana, where the federal army had gained a significant foothold in 1862 and loyalist factions—wealthy sugar planters among them—were jockeying for advantage. Some of those who took oaths of allegiance still hoped to be compensated for the chattel property that had been taken from them and to resume their familiar stations in civil and political life. As the Boston-born radical reformer Wendell Phillips saw it, Lincoln's policy "leaves the large landed proprietors of the South still to domineer . . . and makes the negro's freedom a mere sham." Those pardoned under the ten-percent plan, men like Phillips feared, could be of dubious loyalty and, if quickly readmitted to Congress, threaten Republican power.

Clashing Perspectives and Policies

Republicans in Congress increasingly embraced two perspectives that brought them into conflict with Lincoln. One was that Lincoln's plan was too hasty and lenient, and something much tougher was needed. After all, by Lincoln's own telling, the Confederate rebels had committed treason. The other perspective was that, in their view, the Constitution gave Congress, not the president, the power to determine whether a state had an appropriate form of government.

By the early summer of 1864, congressional Republicans put together an alternative policy that reflected their views. It was called the **Wade-Davis Bill** (for co-sponsors Ohio Senator Benjamin Wade and Maryland Representative Henry Winter Davis), and although it made no move in the direction of Black citizenship or suffrage, it did demand that a majority of "white male citizens" (not 10 percent of 1860 voters) pledge their loyalty to the United States before any reorganization of state governments could go forward. Then, only those who never held military or political office under the Confederacy or never "voluntarily" took up "arms against the United States" could participate in the process. They would, furthermore, have to abolish slavery, disfranchise top Confederate leaders, and extend to "all persons," including the formerly enslaved, the right to justice before the law. Until these conditions were met—and they would not be easy to meet—the states would remain under the control of a provisional governor appointed by the president with the consent of the Senate.

Passed with overwhelming support in Congress, the Wade-Davis Bill went to Lincoln's desk for his signature. There it sat. Lincoln didn't fundamentally oppose the bill's requirements and had no problem if any rebellious state chose, of its own accord, to follow them. But he feared that if the bill became law, it would derail the process already underway as a result of his ten-percent plan (in Arkansas, Tennessee, and Virginia, as well as Louisiana) and perhaps lengthen the war. Consequently, he refused to sign the bill (an action known as a "pocket veto") and deeply angered his Republican colleagues. It was the first of many struggles that would play out for another decade between the executive and legislative branches of the federal government over basic questions of constitutional power and between warring elements of the Republican Party over the pace and extent of Reconstruction policy. But a momentous shift nonetheless was taking place. After seven decades of confusion, struggle, and compromise over the question of political sovereignty—over whether the states or the central government was ultimately in charge—the War of the Rebellion enabled the Republicans to begin defining the character of a new and different entity: not a union but a nation.

15.2   The Future of the Formerly Enslaved

||| Identify the issues that emancipation raised for the future of Black people.

For all of their sweep and political drama, the laws and decrees abolishing slavery said nothing about the civil or political rights of those men, women, and children who had been enslaved. Nothing about citizenship, nothing about the right to vote, nothing about the ability to sue or testify in court or to sit in judgment of those who allegedly violated the law. As a result, enslaved people who had been liberated would enter a world still governed by the Supreme Court's *Dred Scott* decision of 1857 and the racially discriminatory practices widespread at the state and local levels. This was a world in which people of African descent had "no rights that whites were bound to respect" and could not be citizens of the United States. At best, policymakers imagined them, much like Lincoln did, as laboring people who would now work for wages. This was true of most abolitionists as well, even the full-throated William Lloyd Garrison.

Limits of Change

The assumption that freedmen and women would continue to endure a life of labor, chiefly on the agricultural lands of the southern states, had a powerful logic. No one could deny that the cotton plant had fueled the engine of antebellum (prewar) economic growth, and most political leaders in the United States envisioned a revitalized cotton economy as crucial to the future prosperity of the country. Some saw the opportunity to demonstrate the superior efficiency and productivity of free, as opposed to enslaved, labor. Others were eager to cash in on the high prices cotton fetched on the international market. In all cases, the availability of Black labor was seen as critical to ending the war and shaping the peace.

The federal government embarked upon or encouraged a series of initiatives during the war itself that paved the road to such an end. Through the auspices of the military, it first introduced, in parts of the occupied South, what was called the "**contract labor system**." Enslaved people who had fled to federal army lines—becoming contrabands—and were not needed by the military could be hired out to southern landowners who had taken the loyalty oath or to the thousands of northerners who had leased or purchased agricultural lands in the South. They would receive small monthly wages and basic subsistence while being subject to close supervision and limited mobility. At the same time, organizations like the American Missionary Association, which had been involved in the antislavery movement since the late 1840s, mobilized missionaries and teachers to go into areas occupied by the federal troops both to lend aid to the contrabands and to prepare them for the new world of freedom. Worried that the formerly enslaved might not yet be "ready" for freedom, they hoped to tutor them in freedom's demands and responsibilities. They instructed them in literacy, sexual propriety, the values of thrift and industry, the proper roles for men and women, and the nature of Christian worship.

The Lincoln administration took its own measures of the condition of the freedpeople in 1863 by appointing the **American Freedmen's Inquiry Commission**. The Commission toured the occupied South and interviewed military officials, former slaveholders, and missionaries as well as the previously enslaved and free people of color to learn about the conditions and prospects for African Americans in a post-emancipation South. When they completed their work, the commissioners recommended the creation of a federal organization to supervise the transition out of enslavement, provide for education and the administration of justice, and ensure that the now freedpeople received wages for their work. In March 1865, the Congress implemented the recommendation when it established the **Freedmen's Bureau** (formally known as the Bureau of Refugees, Freedmen, and Abandoned Lands) for one year, hoping that contract rather than coercion would organize new labor relations and that avenues to redress grievances would be made available for Black laborers and white employers alike.

Aspirations of the Freedpeople

For all of the paternalistic concerns about whether the once enslaved were "ready" for freedom, African American men and women demonstrated, in a variety of settings across the South, that they were indeed prepared for freedom and had well-developed perspectives as to what their freedom might entail. Along the coast of South Carolina and Georgia and in southwestern Mississippi, where plantation owners and enslavers had fled in the face of federal troops, they continued to cultivate lands they had tended as enslaved people and established their own forms of self-governance, including constitutions, elected officials, and local courts. In the Mississippi Valley, some groups pooled their meager resources to rent plots of land either from the federal government or from northern lessees and made an

Teachers and Relief Workers Ten teachers, all women, from the American Missionary Association of New York pose in front of their mission house in Port Royal, South Carolina, in 1862. Two African American children stand at left, hiding their faces with their caps.

impressive go of it. In occupied portions of North Carolina and Virginia, the formerly enslaved gradually turned contraband camps and the immediately surrounding countryside into what one federal official could call "African villages," constructing their own shelters, farming for themselves, building churches and schools, and running stores. Where territory was still controlled by Confederate rebels, those still enslaved attempted to renegotiate the rhythms and rules of their captivity, demanding small wages and greater leverage over their working conditions.

As Black people struggled to make their aspirations known and to pursue them as best as they could, they showed that the transition from enslavement to freedom would be deeply contested. They also showed that they could win allies among the federal officials, teachers, and missionaries they encountered in contraband camps, leased plantations, and army units, some of whom came to discover that, even as enslaved people, African Americans held complex "notions of liberty," were often familiar with the Bible, were "shrewd" and understood "compensation received for work," and, more than anything else, wished "to possess land, if it only be a few acres." It seemed, in short, for those willing to see, that Black people had constructed relations and expectations as to family, work, and community that had a lot in common with those of whites but did not easily accord with the type of nation-building many Republican leaders wished to pursue.

15.3 Indigenous People and the Future of the West

||| Describe how the war between the federal government and the Confederates came to involve Indigenous peoples in the West.

The eyes of the developing American nation looked West as well as South and on Indigenous people as well as newly emancipated Black people. The threads of a policy toward Indigenous people had, as we have seen, been in place since the founding of the republic, mixing the carrot of assimilation with the stick of expulsion and confinement on reservations. Reformers who viewed Native Americans, much as they viewed African Americans, as culturally backward though potentially redeemable urged that efforts be made to promote "civilization." They imagined that white teachers could encourage literacy, missionaries could spread Christianity, Indigenous men could turn from hunting to agriculture, and communal forms of property could be discarded.

Treaties and Reservations

But the reformers offered little to challenge the designs of white settlers and their political allies, who hungered for the land that Indigenous people claimed and had no interest in the goal of assimilating them. In general, the settlers saw Indigenous people as barbaric obstacles in the way of "progress" who had to be reduced and pushed out of the way. Even those like the mixed-blood faction of the Cherokees, who tried to reorganize their lives and politics in the ways of the whites (as we saw in Chapter 9), learned that the stick of retribution was unavoidable. Since the reformers mostly accepted the settlers' distinction between "progress" and "barbarism" and wished to advance the former at the expense of the latter, they could only limit the worst effects of a process whose objectives—economic development and evangelicalism—they largely shared. This is what scholars now term **settler colonialism** to suggest the goals and power involved in the process.

As a result, the reservation became the means to resolve the tensions between coercion and civilization. Indigenous people would agree to give up lands that white settlers desired, move to tracts of land set aside for them by the government, and there, with the help of federal Indian agents, annuities, and missionaries, embrace the ways of the whites. On reservations, as white officials saw it, the "wild energies" and "haughty pride" of the Indigenous people could be "subdued" and they could be "trained in the pursuits of civilized life." Beginning with a series of arrangements covering 139 small tribes in California in the early 1850s, such reservations soon became the policy orientation of choice among those in the federal government charged with supervising "Indian affairs."

The centerpiece of this process was, as it had previously been, the treaty, very much a reflection of the multiple forms of sovereignty that defined the American union and empire before the War of the Rebellion erupted. As we saw in Chapter 9, in the 1830s the Supreme Court had ruled that Native Americans were members of "domestic dependent nations," something less than full-fledged sovereigns but distinctive political entities neither to be counted for purposes of congressional apportionment nor subject to taxation. But treaty-making almost invariably created divisions among the Native Americans who entered into it, and the onset of civil warfare in 1861 unhinged the relations and understandings that supported the treaties.

Civil Warfare and Indigenous Warfare

Almost immediately, the Five Civilized Tribes in Indian Territory made formal alliances with the Confederacy that simultaneously recognized their sovereignty and encouraged their political and military participation in the Confederate rebellion (as discussed in Chapter 14). By mid-May 1861, Chickasaws and Choctaws were sending troops and, before long, pro-Confederate Cherokees were driving pro-Union Cherokees, Creeks, and Seminoles into neighboring Kansas. By November 1861, the Confederacy defined Indian Territory as one of its military departments, and Cherokee leaders gained commissions in the Confederate Army—one chief, Stand Watie, even achieved the rank of general. For his part, Lincoln stopped annuity payments and withdrew all federal troops from the area, and Congress soon permitted him to terminate treaties with any tribe "in actual hostility to the United States."

Then Lincoln thought better of abandoning Indian Territory and determined to reoccupy it. A decisive federal victory at Pea Ridge in northwestern Arkansas in March 1862 against a combined Confederate-Indigenous force opened the way and symbolized the militarization of federal Indigenous policy. The ball was now in the court of federal army commanders who had little patience for diplomacy and more interest in dealing with Indigenous people through force. In Minnesota, General John Pope, sent to suppress the Sioux rebellion of that summer (discussed in Chapter 14), scorned treaty-making and the entire "Indian system" more generally. He wanted authority over Indigenous matters shifted from the Interior to the War Department and sizeable military posts established that would control tribes once they had been defeated and confined to reservations.

Out in the territory of New Mexico, federal Brigadier General James Carlton, who had marched his troops from California to intercept Confederate advances in the Southwest, took a similar view after encounters with Navajos and Apaches. Acknowledging the objective of getting the Indigenous people onto a reservation where they could acquire "new habits" and "modes

≡ **Indigenous Fighters at the Battle of Pea Ridge**   Confederate cavalry and infantry, assisted by mounted Cherokee and Chickasaw warriors, attack a line of Union cannon and infantry at Pea Ridge.

of life," he nonetheless insisted that the "application of force" could never be "relaxed." Like Pope, he scoffed at signing treaties and instead believed that hostile Indigenous people had to be pursued without mercy and beaten into submission. Mangas Coloradas, one of the powerful Apache leaders, felt the lethal brunt of this policy. Lured into a trap by soldiers waving a flag of truce, Coloradas was brutally tortured and shot to death. His body was then decapitated and his large head sent east to the Smithsonian Institution in Washington, DC, where it found a place among a growing collection of Indigenous bones and artifacts: museum pieces testifying to the superior culture of white Americans.

The aggressiveness of Carlton and Pope in the apparent service of "civilization" and the United States was indicative of an increasingly iron-fisted and violence-ridden politics that spread across the Plains beginning in 1862 (see Map 15.1). Carlton

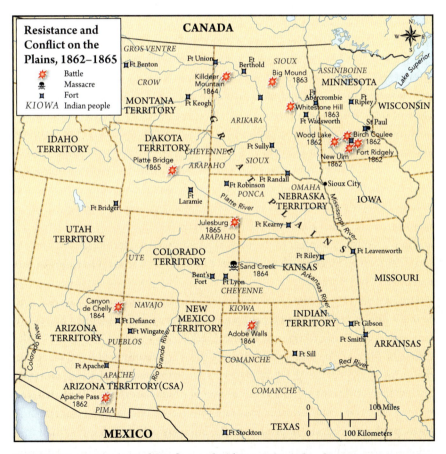

≡ **MAP 15.1 Resistance and Conflict on the Plains, 1862–1865** In response to increasing belligerence from the United States, Cheyennes, Arapahos, Kiowas, Comanches, and Sioux began a general uprising across the Plains.

not only put several thousand Apaches and Navajos (themselves enemies) onto the small reservation of Bosque Redondo in eastern New Mexico but ruled them in a dictatorial fashion. An equally autocratic regime took shape in the Colorado Territory under Governor John Evans, a railroad promoter originally from Illinois (where he was one of the founders of Northwestern University, located in the town renamed for him, Evanston). Less concerned about Confederate sympathizers than about the hunting and raiding of the Cheyenne and Arapaho, Evans believed that suppressing Indigenous resistance was the key to attracting a transcontinental railroad through Denver, a potential financial windfall. In John Chivington, who commanded a regiment of Colorado volunteers, he found a kindred spirit.

But if Evans and Chivington assumed that the Indigenous people could easily be forced into submission, they miscalculated. Indeed, by the summer of 1864, Cheyennes, Arapahos, Kiowas, Comanches, and Sioux had begun a general uprising across the Plains and interrupted traffic and communication along the Santa Fe and Overland Trails. Frustrated that federal officials seemed to ignore his warnings about a "terrible war" taking place, Evans then urged white Coloradans to take matters into their own hands and exterminate hostile Indigenous people "wherever they may be found." Chivington was ready to go. In late November 1864, he and a force of some 700 soldiers marched to Sand Creek, southeast of Denver, attacked an encampment of Cheyenne and Arapaho who had already submitted to military authorities, and massacred them.

News of the **Sand Creek Massacre** spread quickly, intensifying the outrage of Plains Indians who expanded their attacks while horrifying many congressional policymakers who saw Chivington's actions as savagery in their own right. Serious questions were raised about the army's ability to rein in its own forms of terror, and new credibility was lent to the ways of humanitarian reformers. Even Lincoln was disturbed and pledged that "if we get through this war and I live, this Indian system shall be reformed."

But Lincoln also accepted the image of Indigenous people as "savages" and found it difficult to envision them as part of the "people of the United States." In language very similar to what he offered Black leaders visiting him at the White House in 1862—"You and we are different races"—Lincoln told tribal leaders in the spring of 1863 of the "great difference between the pale-faced people and their red brethren both as to numbers and the way in which they lived." "The pale-faced people," he explained, "are numerous and prosperous because they cultivate the earth, produce bread, and depend upon the products of the earth rather than wild game for subsistence." Thus, just as he once concluded that colonization was the proper solution to the dilemmas of white and Black, so he regarded "the plan of concentrating Indians and confining them to reservations" as the "fixed policy of the government."

Reinforcing this "fixed policy" was Lincoln's perspective on the relation of the civil warfare to the development of the trans-Mississippi West. Noting the "steady expansion of the population," the "great enterprise" of connecting the Atlantic and Pacific by rail and telegraph, and the discovery of gold and silver mines, he hoped to provide a "proper government of the Indians" to make the West "secure for the advancing settler." "That portion of the earth's surface which is owned and inhabited by the people of the United States is well adapted to be the home of one national family,"

Delegation of Plains Indians at the White House This March 1863 photograph shows a delegation of leaders from the Kiowa and Cheyenne nations during a visit to the White House. Eighteen months after this photo was taken all four men in the front row were dead, including two who were killed at Sand Creek. The woman in the back row on the far right has been identified as Mary Todd Lincoln.

Lincoln observed, "and it is not well-adapted for two or more." It was a strange and ominous twist on the concept of the "house divided."

15.4 Making Freedom

Summarize what did and didn't change in the status and experiences of formerly enslaved people.

The question of who the "people of the United States" were, of how membership in the "national family" would be determined, was not only raised by Indigenous people reluctant to live like whites. It was also raised by people of African descent already in rebellion against their enslavers and enslavement. Ever since the 1820s and 1830s, fugitives from enslavement together with free Black allies had been pressing state and federal authorities to end their cooperation with slaveholders and reject the markers of subordinate status that African Americans were forced to bear. Increasingly they demanded civil equality, access to education and other public institutions, and the right to vote on the same basis as whites. But it was the arming of enslaved men to aid in crushing the Confederacy that shifted the nature of discussion and the horizon of possibility.

Black Men in Blue

The military recruitment of African Americans—enslaved and free—came in the face of deep traditions of exclusion and then wartime rebuffs from federal officials despite their need for thousands of volunteers. Indeed, it was the enslaved who accomplished what free Black leaders like Frederick Douglass failed to do by fleeing the sites of their captivity in numbers never anticipated by the federal government and flooding into contraband camps and other military sites. A chaplain in the Army of the Tennessee could compare the volume of enslaved people who had abandoned neighboring cotton plantations and headed to federal lines to an "army in themselves." Contract labor and other leasing arrangements offered one means of alleviating the pressure, but as manpower shortages challenged the goals of the Lincoln administration, Black recruitment emerged as an option that could no longer be ignored. In July 1862, Congress passed a Militia Act and soon thereafter the War Department permitted the establishment of the **First South Carolina Volunteers**, a regiment made up of formerly enslaved men from the state that had led the secession process.

But full-scale mobilization had to await the Emancipation Proclamation of January 1, 1863. Only then did the Lincoln administration allow northern governors to begin enrolling Black men living in their states (many were fugitives from enslavement and their children). Nearly three-quarters of those between the ages of eighteen and forty-five came forward (about 33,000), a much higher proportion than was true among eligible white men. By far the greatest number, however, were recruited in the slave states, especially those of the Confederacy. Totaling over 140,000, they would come to compose over 10 percent of the US Army and, in some departments, nearly half of it. Emancipation, therefore, not only came as a war measure but was directly tied to the military recruitment of Black men who gained freedom for themselves as well as for their mothers, wives, and children. It thereby embedded a gender hierarchy—the men were the prime political movers and liberators—that was central to the political and cultural vision of the developing nation.

Initially federal officials imagined that Black troops would serve mainly behind the lines as laborers, enabling more of the white troops to do the fighting. But before long African Americans could be found armed and in the heat of battle. Behind their own lines, however, Black soldiers faced an assortment of challenges. Their units were segregated from those of white troops and, with a few exceptions, they were denied the opportunity to become commissioned officers (sergeant was the highest rank they could attain). They were put to work doing the most degrading work in camp and, as a consequence of their presumed status, paid less than one-half of their white soldiering counterparts. Many of the white officers and enlistees treated them with derision and contempt, believing that Black bodies were more expendable than white ones.

But these were only some of the special liabilities that defined the Black experience of military service. Although many Black men who had been enslaved relished the opportunity to help defeat the Confederacy and the system of enslavement on which it rested, they were vulnerable to a retribution not shared by white soldiers. Simply put, the Confederacy regarded them as slaves "in flagrant rebellion." According to the Confederates, they were not to be recognized as soldiers "subject to the rules of war" but rather as "slaves in armed insurrection," meriting, by order of Jefferson Davis, the punishment of re-enslavement or execution. "It was understood among us," a Confederate soldier wrote in 1864, "that we take no negro prisoners." Small wonder that Black people fought with a special ferocity. "There is death to the rebel in every black man's eyes," one northerner reported.

THE GALLANT CHARGE OF THE FIFTY FOURTH MASSACHUSETTS (COLORED) REGIMENT.
On the Rebel works at Fort Wagner, Morris Island near Charleston July 18th 1863, and death of Colonel Robt G. Shaw.

Storming Fort Wagner The print dramatizes the 54th Massachusetts' assault on the parapets of Fort Wagner. Colonel Robert Gould Shaw, the regiment's white leader, clutches his chest as he is mortally struck by a bullet. The soldier holding the American flag is William Harvey Carney, who was awarded the Congressional Medal of Honor for his gallantry in guarding the regimental colors.

That ferocity and determination had significant effect. Black people steadily dispelled doubts among federal policymakers that enslavement had rendered them too cowardly and undisciplined to fight. In major engagements at Milliken's Bend and Port Hudson in the lower Mississippi Valley and at Fort Wagner in South Carolina—all during the spring and summer of 1863—they faced down enemy fire and performed valiantly. They would soon appear in most theaters of warfare, especially in Virginia, as the army commanded by General Ulysses S. Grant battled to defeat rebel forces under Robert E. Lee. The arming of African American men came at a time of military stalemate and low morale in much of the North. Thus, their participation proved to be a tipping point in the war, fortifying the United States and weakening the Confederacy, while challenging the racial attitudes of many white northerners.

The Political Significance of Black Soldiering

The political significance of Black soldiering may have been as great as the military. Contraband camps and army units drew African Americans together in numbers that dwarfed the size of plantations and farms. Here they met enslaved and free

Black people from near and far as well as white officers who had spent years in the antislavery movement or had fled as political refugees from failed midcentury (1848) republican revolutions in Europe. Here they could also follow the progress of the war, learn of federal policies, discover forms of authority and loyalty other than those prescribed by their enslavers or small communities, and achieve basic literacy. "The general aim and probable consequences of this war," Thomas Wentworth Higginson, an abolitionist who commanded Black troops, observed, "are better understood in my regiment than in any white regiment."

The political consciousness that so impressed Higginson could be seen on a number of fronts. Within the army, Black soldiers soon mobilized to protest discrimination in combat status, pay, and promotion, eventually forcing the Congress to equalize pay scales. In a series of important assemblies in the Northeast, Midwest, and occupied South, they demanded not only the "immediate and unconditional" abolition of slavery everywhere in the United States but, citing their military role in the service of the country, the "full measure of citizenship." "If we are called on to do military duty against the rebel armies in the field," one group of them asked, "why should we be denied the privilege of voting?" Now the world defined by *Scott v. Sandford* (1857), which denied citizenship or rights to Black people, was under direct attack by those who were its intended victims.

But the repercussions could go even further. In January 1865, after marching his troops from Atlanta to Savannah, Georgia, federal army General William T. Sherman organized a meeting of local Black ministers, many of whom had been enslaved, to take the temperature of Black aspirations. He learned that the ministers understood slavery as "receiving by *irresistible power* the work of another man" and freedom as "placing us where we could reap the fruit of our labor, [and] take care of ourselves." He learned, too, that they believed "the way we can best take care of ourselves is to have land, and to turn it by our own labor." Sherman was no revolutionary, but he despised the Confederate rebels and had been getting bad press back at home for his treatment of the enslaved people who left their plantations and followed in his wake across Georgia. So, to meet what he termed "the

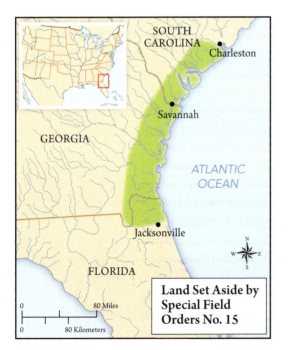

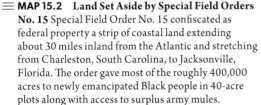

≣ **MAP 15.2 Land Set Aside by Special Field Orders No. 15** Special Field Order No. 15 confiscated as federal property a strip of coastal land extending about 30 miles inland from the Atlantic and stretching from Charleston, South Carolina, to Jacksonville, Florida. The order gave most of the roughly 400,000 acres to newly emancipated Black people in 40-acre plots along with access to surplus army mules.

pressing necessities of the case," he stepped into the radical role that only such a war made possible. On January 16, 1865, Sherman issued **Special Field Orders No. 15**, which set apart, for exclusive Black settlement, the islands and coastal rice fields south from Charleston to the St. John's River in Florida, to be subdivided into 40-acre plots. It was 400,000 acres of the richest plantation land in the southern states, effectively destroying the haughty coastal ruling class and possibly laying the foundation of a new social order. Black people in the United States would long commemorate this event by speaking of the reward of "forty acres and a mule" that the federal government had provided for their forced captivity and military service to the country (see Map 15.2).

15.5   When Did the War End?

III Analyze the complexities of bringing the Civil War to a conclusion.

As revolutionary as Special Field Orders No. 15 was, Sherman would not have been able to issue it if he did not have the rebels on the run and their defeat in sight. It was a dramatic shift in the course of events. Before the summer of 1863, the military outcome of the war seemed in serious doubt. Robert E. Lee and his troops, fresh from stunning victories at Fredericksburg and Chancellorsville in Virginia, readied themselves for another offensive across the Potomac and into Maryland and Pennsylvania. A military triumph on northern soil might deflate Union morale beyond repair, release pressure on besieged Confederates at Vicksburg, and force Lincoln to seek a truce that would place the sweeping Emancipation Proclamation in jeopardy. Then, in fairly quick succession, Lee suffered a devastating defeat at Gettysburg, exhausted Confederates surrendered to Grant at Vicksburg, and Sherman pushed rebel troops out of Tennessee and into northwest Georgia. What would this mean for the objectives of the Lincoln administration?

Confederates on the Defensive

An important change in the dynamics of warfare accompanied all of this. The arming of enslaved African Americans indicated a new resolve to defeat the Confederate rebellion and destroy its base of enslavement. At the same time, the resources available to the Lincoln administration in railroad transportation, armaments manufacture, and manpower slowly made their significance felt. The federal armed forces would be able to mobilize twice as many men as their Confederate counterparts, and they would be able to feed, clothe, and provision troops in ways that the rebels simply could not. Eventually, men of foreign birth and African descent would

≡ **Lincoln's Generals**   In Grant (*left*) and Sherman (*right*) Lincoln finally found military leaders who shared his vision of how the war needed to be fought, and they battled relentlessly to crush the rebel armies.

compose more than half of the federal army. Equally important, Lincoln finally found in Grant and Sherman military leaders who shared his vision of how the war needed to be fought, and they battled relentlessly to crush the rebel armies.

Yet it was one thing to put the Confederate rebellion on the defensive and quite another to fully end the rebellion in ways that both sides recognized. Lincoln sought "unconditional surrender," but of whom and to what effect? Clearly, he wanted Confederate troops to lay down their arms and the Confederate government to be disbanded, but since he never acknowledged the Confederacy and insisted that the rebellion was one of individuals in the states, what would have to happen before the rebellion could be regarded as over and the authority of the federal government accepted?

There was no getting around the fact that the Confederates were in deep trouble. By 1864 they were under enormous strain on the home front as well as on the battlefield. Desperate for soldiers, supplies, and workers behind the lines, they had enacted a draft, imposed a tax-in-kind on agricultural produce (seeking goods rather than money), and authorized provision officers to take (impress) needed supplies from private citizens. No one in the Confederate states was unaffected, but it was the nonslaveholders and their families who suffered most grievously. With adult men and even teenage boys off in the army, women, children, and the elderly were left to bring in the crops and provide for themselves. Growing numbers experienced deprivation and, given rampant inflation (by this time the Confederate government was pretty much just printing money), were unable to purchase necessities in town. Some women, like those organized by Mary Jackson and Minerva Meredith in Richmond, rioted against merchants and planters who hoarded supplies, but many others wrote to their husbands and sons about their plight and encouraged them to desert. By early 1864 somewhere between one-third and one-half of the Confederate troops may have been absent from their units: many had deserted, taking the advice of their wives and mothers, and others had granted themselves leave from the fighting to aid their families.

The prospect of defeat could lead even those who remained loyal to the rebel cause in opposing directions. Patrick Cleburne from Arkansas, who had supported secession and risen to the rank of major general, came to the conclusion that the only way Confederates could hope to prevail was by recruiting the enslaved to fight with a promise of freedom for those who remained loyal. Enlist the enslaved and abolish slavery to salvage the Confederate rebellion? The initial response from Cleburne's superiors was nothing short of outrage, though over time the idea did win a small following—including Lee and Davis—but not enough of one to initiate a genuine policy. All that rebels were left to do was assume a defensive posture, drag out the war for as long as possible, and hope that the political winds might shift in a more favorable direction.

Military and Political Turning Points

There was still some reason for Confederate hopefulness. In the fall of 1864, the United States would hold regular elections for the presidency and the Congress, and Lincoln was in trouble. Radical members of the Republican Party had been angered by his moderation, and one of them, Secretary of the Treasury Salmon P. Chase, contemplated challenging him for the nomination; he soon thought better of it when Lincoln called both for a "complete suppression of the rebellion" and a constitutional amendment abolishing slavery. In an unprecedented move, Lincoln, the Republican, also took Tennessee Democrat, Andrew Johnson, as his vice president on what was now called a Union ticket. Johnson was widely lauded for his stance against secession and the rebels, and Lincoln expected that such a ticket would find more votes among soldiers in the field and Democrats at home than a Republican one.

He seemed to need all the votes he could get. Lincoln faced a formidable opponent in the election who pledged to follow a very different set of political goals. For the Democrats nominated the popular federal General George B. McClellan, whom Lincoln had sent into retirement months before, and they approved a platform that

MAPPING AMERICA

Contrabands and Refugees

All wars displace civilian populations. After World War II, millions of refugees moved across the borders of Eastern Europe as ethnic groups fled or were expelled from their homes. Since Russia's invasion in February 2022, over thirteen million people in Ukraine have been displaced. Though the

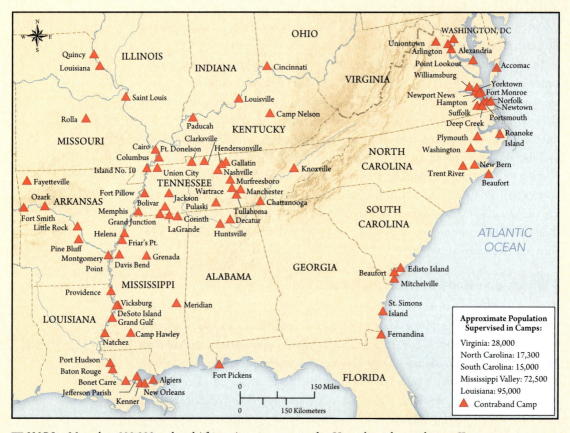

≡ **MAP 1**   More than 500,000 enslaved African Americans escaped to Union lines during the war. Known as "contrabands," about a third of the escapees lived for varying amounts of time in camps. For many freedpeople, the camps were the first step in the transition to freedom.

condemned Lincoln's "usurpation" of power. Instead, despite federal advances on the battlefield and the Emancipation Proclamation, they called for an immediate armistice with no mention of enslavement or abolition. In other words, the Democrats appeared ready to abandon the goal of ending slavery if they could reach an agreement

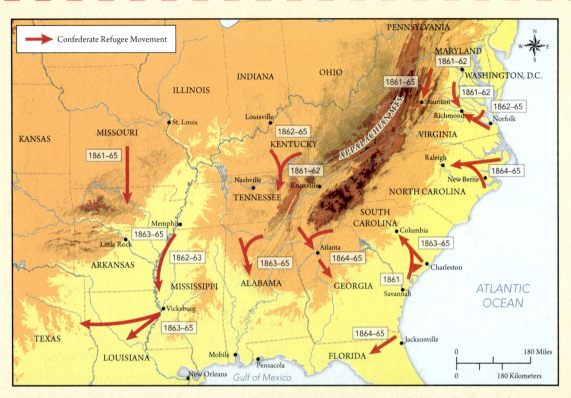

≡ **MAP 2**   Beginning with the wealthy planters of the South Carolina Sea Islands who fled their plantations when Union ships captured Port Royal in November 1861, thousands of white Confederates fled before advancing Union armies. Some relocated to secondary homes not far from the places they were fleeing. Others traveled greater distances, bringing their enslaved workers with them in the hopes of maintaining their old way of life in a different setting. Most poor white people, however, simply stayed where they were and hoped for the best.

magnitude of the displacements caused by the War of Rebellion was not as great as these other conflicts, the effect they had on free and unfree civilian populations was just as profound.

Thinking Geographically

1. Examine the two maps. Is there a correlation between the locations of contraband camps and the movements of Confederate refugees? If so, what is the likely reason for this correlation?

2. Which geographical features influenced the movements of contrabands and refugees?

to stop the war. So convinced was Lincoln that the contest was lost that he pledged to work with McClellan to "save the Union between the election and the inauguration" because it would be impossible to "save it afterward." "I am a beaten man," Lincoln concluded in late August, "unless we can have some great victory."

Almost miraculously, the "great victory" Lincoln looked for did come—and only two days after he had pronounced himself a "beaten man." The miracle maker was none other than William Sherman. While Grant's Army of the Potomac was mired in the blood-soaked Virginia soil battling Lee and his rebel soldiers, Sherman and his troops, after a protracted struggle in north Georgia, marched into the strategic rail center of Atlanta on September 3, 1864. The city had been torched by retreating Confederates, but Sherman stood triumphant while the rebels were in disarray.

The political effect was nothing short of electric. By the time voters cast their ballots in early November, the electoral landscape had been transformed, and Lincoln and the Republicans won an overwhelming victory: 55 percent of the popular vote and every state in the Union except Kentucky, Delaware, and New Jersey. Especially gratifying for Lincoln was the soldier vote, which went for him by nearly 80 percent despite McClellan's standing with the troops. Especially consequential, the Republicans would also control three-quarters of the seats in Congress and all of the governorships and legislatures in the states Lincoln carried.

For the rebels, the effect of Sherman's "great victory" was nothing short of disastrous. "Since Atlanta I have felt as if it were all dead within me," South Carolina's Mary Chesnut, an ardent rebel from the first, wrote. "We are going to be wiped off the earth." In Virginia, morale among Lee's besieged units began to sink so fast that hundreds of his men were deserting each week. By late January 1865 Lee was suggesting to Davis that his army could not hold out very much longer (see Map 15.3).

Confederates Begin to Surrender

Davis was determined to fight on, even at the price of arming enslaved men on the Confederacy's behalf and accepting some plan of gradual emancipation. Perhaps this would bring English and French recognition and the economic and military aid bound to come with it. Perhaps, too, Davis could negotiate a peace based on an implicit recognition of the integrity and independence of the Confederacy. But in this Davis seems to have taken the wrong message from a conciliatory meeting Lincoln had held with a small Confederate delegation at Hampton Roads, Virginia, in early February 1865. Whatever olive branches were extended, he had no intention of recognizing the Confederacy and would only accept an "unconditional surrender." Much of the rebel political leadership, both within Davis's cabinet and among the war governors, saw the options more clearly than Davis did, and they were ready to admit defeat. Their main interest was no longer in sustaining the rebellion militarily but in cutting a deal that would allow them to hold onto power in their states and localities, maintain their political rights, protect their property from confiscation, and avoid prosecution for secession- and war-related offenses,

≡ **MAP 15.3   Major Battles and Campaigns, 1864–1865**   Sherman's capture of Atlanta and his ensuing "march to the sea" demonstrated the ability of Union forces to cut straight through the center of the Confederacy. His army then moved north to join Ulysses S. Grant in trapping the two remaining Confederate armies.

particularly for treason. After four years of fighting and hundreds of thousands of casualties, it was a lot to ask.

Lee had also foreseen defeat, and although some of the rebels—including Davis—hoped he might disperse his own forces to fight on in guerilla fashion, Lee decided otherwise. To that end, Lee agreed to meet with Grant on April 9, 1865, at Appomattox Court House in Virginia, and, as painful as it might have been for him to give up, he could not have hoped for better terms. Rebel officers and their men would be paroled (not taken as war prisoners), their arms stacked and turned over to Grant, and they would all be permitted to return home with their sidearms and horses, not to be "disturbed by United States authority so long as they observe their paroles and the laws in force where they reside." No one was taken into custody—not Lee or anyone else—and nothing was said of arrests, charges of treason, or punishments of any sort.

Sherman, the bane of the rebel armies, unaccountably offered even more generous terms to Joseph Johnston and his rebel troops in North Carolina. They would

PERSPECTIVES

Martyrdom and Defeat

The memorialization of the war began immediately after the fighting ended, but the North and South remembered the war in different ways. A Memorial Day speech Frederick Douglass gave in 1878, in which he paid homage to "the heroic deeds of and virtues of the brave men who volunteered, fought, and fell in the cause of Union and freedom" is representative of the way northerners remembered the war. In contrast, a Lost Cause ideology took hold among defeated southerners, idealizing the slave system and righteous martyrs overwhelmed by the ruthless

≡ **George Washington, Abraham Lincoln, and a Choir of Angels**

Yankee war machine. In the popular poem, "The Conquered Banner," published right after Appomattox, the Confederate flag is sacralized: "yet 'tis wreathed around with glory, / And 'twill live in song and story / though its folds are in the dust!" The South occupied the moral high ground and had no cause for shame.

After Lincoln's death, northerners gathered to hear sermons preached to their martyred president. An estimated seven million people—one in every four Americans—watched his funeral train over the course of its thirteen-day trip to Springfield, Illinois; and more than one million paid respects to his remains as he lay in state in the cities the train passed through. In this 1866 engraving, we see George Washington and a choir of angels welcoming the victorious martyr to paradise.

The Lost Cause was constructed quite sometime after the war ended, in the late 1870s and 1880s, when women played a prominent role. Believers in the Lost Cause had their own martyr: Robert E. Lee. While Lee was not felled by an assassin's bullet, Confederate armies had been mercilessly crushed by heartless Union armies. Despite overwhelming odds, Confederate generals like Lee fought valiantly to the end. They were righteous and blameless. This undated print casts a warm glow on Lee's Farewell Address to his troops. Set amid scenes of his life, the Address extols Confederate "valor and devotion" that ultimately was "compelled to yield to overwhelming numbers and resources." For many white southerners, Lee's Farewell Address held layers of meaning.

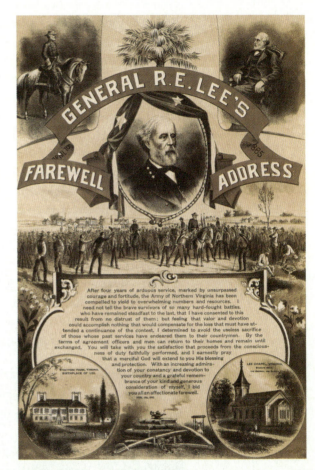

≡ **Robert E. Lee's Farewell Address**

CONSIDER THIS

In the different ways the North and South remembered the war, which side viewed America's best days in the past? Is this viewpoint still prevalent in American society today?

have to disband militarily rather than formally surrender and would be permitted to take their arms home, supposedly to be deposited in their state arsenals. Their existing governments would be recognized as soon as elected officials took oaths of loyalty to the United States, and inhabitants of the rebellious states would be guaranteed their civil, political, and property rights as long as they abstained from acts of armed hostility. It was a far cry from Special Field Orders No. 15 and far more lenient than the Lincoln administration ever had in mind. Grant immediately stepped in. He traveled to North Carolina and insisted that Johnston accept the same terms presented to Lee at Appomattox.

Both Lee and Johnston seemed to think that their surrenders amounted to the end of the Confederacy. But was this, in fact, the end of the slaveholders' rebellion? Jefferson Davis and his cabinet had fled Richmond in early April and headed south with the intent of reestablishing their government. Even when Davis learned of the surrenders, he still believed that Confederate troops could be rallied and looked to the trans-Mississippi West, where he might link up with forces there under General Edmund Kirby Smith, who hadn't yet laid down their arms. Davis could then seek an alliance with the Mexican state, now in the hands of French-imposed monarch Maximilian. Perhaps there was still life to the rebellion.

The Assassination of Lincoln

In the meantime, the federal government sustained a tragic and unprecedented blow at the hands of a Confederate sympathizer and conspirator. On the night of April 14, 1865, four years to the day after federal troops at Fort Sumter had themselves surrendered, Abraham Lincoln was assassinated by actor John Wilkes Booth at Ford's Theater in Washington, DC. Maryland-born and the son of a famed theatrical actor, Booth regarded Black enslavement as "one of the great blessings that God ever bestowed" and detested Lincoln as a tyrant, particularly when he heard Lincoln suggest that political rights might be conferred on some of the previously enslaved men. Indeed, like Davis, Booth thought that the fortunes of the Confederacy might be turned around by "something decisive and great," and so he plotted with a small group to murder Vice President Andrew Johnson and Secretary of State William Seward as well. The plot very nearly succeeded. Although Johnson escaped unharmed, Seward was brutally assaulted and, for a time, lingered near death. Never before had a president of the United States fallen victim to an assassin.

And never before or since, had a president from one political party served with a vice president from another. Initially, the problems that this might pose were not apparent. From a humble background, Johnson was also an experienced politician in the tradition of Jacksonian Democrats, who saw themselves representing the interests of small landholders and laboring people. He seemed to have a special animosity for the southern planter class, remained loyal to the United States, and promised to make treason "odious" and have "traitors punished."

Jefferson Davis blanched when he heard of Lincoln's assassination. Knowing of Johnson's temperament and sensibilities, he thought the results would be "disastrous for our people." That fear was widely shared. Would the federal government now move to arrest and punish the rebel leaders and wreak vengeance on the rebellious South? For their part, some Radical Republicans seemed heartened by the turn of events. Whereas Lincoln had spoken a language of generosity and reconciliation, Johnson spoke one of punishment and retribution. "I believe that the Almighty continued Mr. Lincoln in office as long as he was useful," one of the radicals explained, "and then substituted a man better suited to finish the work."

Although some Confederates were still holding out, Johnson could have lowered the boom. He could have imposed martial law, arrested the rebel leadership (Davis was captured in Georgia in early May), set strict terms, such as the Wade-Davis Bill did, for the restoration of the states, allowed the Freedmen's Bureau to subdivide confiscated and abandoned land, and extended civil equality to people of African descent and the franchise to at least some of them. With that, the Confederate rebellion would have been at an end.

15.6   Reunification According to Andrew Johnson

Explain the emerging clash between President Andrew Johnson and congressional Republicans over Reconstruction policy.

Andrew Johnson was in no hurry to remove federal troops from the rebellious South or to declare the rebellion officially over. But when he did become president after Lincoln's death, he suddenly had a great deal of power at his disposal. The Congress was out of session until December, so he stepped onto the contested ground that Lincoln had earlier occupied. Who was tasked with the authority to set the terms of reunification? Was it Johnson, the president, or was it Congress, the federal legislature? Or was the authority to be shared? Johnson could have called Congress into emergency session, as Lincoln did in the summer of 1861, and worked with both houses to craft the necessary legislation. But he didn't. Instead, he seemed to follow Lincoln's earlier lead and issued orders and proclamations of his own devising. It was the beginning of a major political struggle with the outcome of the War and the fate of the nation in the balance.

Presidential Reconstruction

In late May 1865, when President Johnson issued proclamations outlining his policy, the tone and requirements were very different from what radicals and rebels had expected. He granted blanket amnesty and pardons to all but an elite cut of Confederates—restoration of their property, excluding enslaved people, and their civil and political rights—once they took an oath of loyalty to the United States. He went on to appoint a provisional governor for each of the states from the ranks of the population who did not actively support secession, and they, in turn, would oversee the rewriting of state constitutions that had been the political foundations of slave societies. All that Johnson required was that the states acknowledge the abolition of slavery, renounce secession, and void all state debts contracted to aid the rebellion. He also only hinted that he would look favorably on a limited enfranchisement of Black men. No African Americans either voted for delegates to constitutional conventions or took part in the rewriting of the constitutions under what is generally called Johnson's **Presidential Reconstruction**.

What happened? Had Johnson lost his nerve? Did radicals and rebels alike misunderstand him? It's easy to exaggerate what appears to have happened, at least from Johnson's point of view. On the one hand, Johnson's policy was not much different from what Lincoln had suggested before his death: establishing the authority of the federal government and the illegitimacy of secession, securing the end of enslavement, offering most former rebels the opportunity to demonstrate their loyalty and responsibility, and enabling the rebellious states to rejoin the Union quickly. On the other hand, Johnson singled out the rebel leadership for possible punishment to a far greater extent than Lincoln ever had. His refusal to grant blanket pardons to those Confederates who owned $20,000 or more of property—they had to apply to him for special pardons—threatened a potential political earthquake, weakening the wealthy planter class and strengthening smaller landowners who were less beholden to enslavers and the rebellion.

Johnson, in short, could have used his power to work a political transformation in the rebel South. But Democrat that he was (he couldn't count on Republican support for the presidential nomination in 1868), he chose instead to seek powerful allies there. Although Jefferson Davis and Alexander Stephens, the president and vice president of the Confederacy, were in custody, Johnson decided not to press a legal case against them for treason. As individual applications for pardon swamped his desk—mostly from rich planters—he granted almost all of them. Furthermore, Johnson moved to restore landed property that had been abandoned or confiscated to its original owners, even if the formerly enslaved had already begun cultivating it as under Sherman's Special Field Orders No. 15. And when Freedmen's Bureau officials sympathetic to the formerly enslaved tried to drag their feet in carrying out his orders, Johnson pressured them to obey.

Confederate Defiance and a Reset

Needless to say, Confederates were relieved to hear of Johnson's moves. Some had been predicting a world turned upside down of the sort they imagined when Lincoln was elected president in 1860. But instead of breathing a sigh of relief and showing a measure of gratitude and compliance, they turned brazen and defiant. Now it seemed that they could turn the clock back rather than suffer as victims of defeat.

Their response was quite remarkable given their surrenders only weeks before. When delegates of the rebellious states met to rewrite their constitutions, they often thumbed their noses at the Johnson administration. Mississippi and Alabama would only acknowledge that enslavement had been abolished. Mississippi, Georgia, and Florida refused to nullify (invalidate) their secession ordinances. The state legislatures elected under Johnson's policy included large numbers of active rebels, and they quickly began to pass laws that would limit the new freedom of the previously enslaved. Known as **Black Codes**, these included vagrancy laws that required gainful employment by a certain date at the risk of arrest; game and fence laws that prohibited customary hunting and fishing on unenclosed land; laws narrowing the rights of freedpeople to gain justice in the courts, especially the right to testify against white people; and laws restricting their ability to rent or purchase land. In localities where the plantation order had prevailed, planters and their clients resumed their places as sheriffs, treasurers, and magistrates. And although most of the congressional representatives chosen by the states had opposed secession even if they then supported the rebellion, the Georgia legislature sent none other than Alexander Stephens, former Confederate vice president, to take a seat in the US Senate.

≡ **Slavery Is Dead?**   Perhaps not. Cartoonist Thomas Nast juxtaposes the sale of enslaved people (on the left) with the whipping of freedpeople (on the right) after the war, suggesting that conditions had not really changed all that much for African Americans in the South.

When the duly elected members of Congress returned to Washington, DC, in December 1865, they were in no mood to offer welcomes to their recent enemies. Many were shocked at the results of Johnson's policies and the chaos it produced in the states of the former Confederacy. They were especially aghast at how the freedpeople, many of whom supported their efforts to defeat the Confederates, were being treated by their one-time enslavers. They could reasonably ask whether the rebellion had truly been suppressed or whether it had taken new form. But now they had the opportunity to set reunification terms of their own.

Conclusion: How to Secure the Peace?

From the start of the War, the Lincoln administration faced two massive challenges: how to defeat the Confederate rebellion militarily and how to reunify the country as a whole. Both posed great problems, though in effect they were interconnected. Not long after ordering an invasion of the South, Republicans had to determine what secession really meant in constitutional terms and how that meaning would shape policy. They also had to determine who held the power—Congress or the president—to make policy. In the process, they not only embraced emancipation and the arming of Black men; they also had to decide the terms on which Indigenous people in the trans-Mississippi West would have a place in a reunified country, the signs marking the defeat of the Confederate rebellion, and the future status—and possible punishment—of the rebels themselves.

For a time, it was unclear whether the Lincoln administration would accomplish either of its major goals. The war dragged on, with little end in sight. As it did, great strains were placed on civilian populations across the country, especially in the rebellious states, and Confederates faced explosions of violent resistance to their policies, particularly from the ranks of nonslaveholders and their families. Eventually the combination of federal military and economic power—greatly strengthened by Black soldiers—and social tensions within the Confederate rebellion itself enabled federal forces to prevail on the battlefield and to move forward with plans for peace. Setting the terms of peace would not, however, be easy, not only because differences between Congress and the president had already erupted in the midst of civil warfare but also because Lincoln was felled by an assassin's bullet and Andrew Johnson became president. The issue that hovered had yet to be resolved. How would the Union be restored or reconstructed? Out of the ashes of civil warfare would a new nation be forged?

WHAT IF Lincoln Hadn't Been Assassinated?

No counterfactual question is more commonly asked of this period than what might have happened if Lincoln escaped assassination and served out his second term. The question is a good one. It reflects the very high regard in which Lincoln is held and a somber sense about what his death meant for the future of the country. Since Lincoln commanded the struggle that saved the Union and eventually abolished enslavement and since his words still speak powerfully to us, it's not surprising that many Americans feel that he would have continued to guide the United States along a righteous path. Perhaps so. But what we know of the policies he was developing toward the end of his presidency and of his perspectives on a postwar South raise some cause for doubt. Lincoln was clearly committed to upholding the abolition of enslavement and strongly supported a Thirteenth Amendment to the Constitution that would make abolition nearly impossible to overturn. Yet he was less clear about the status that the formerly enslaved would occupy in the post-emancipation South, about whether they would become full citizens or claim the political rights that free white people enjoyed. And although he regarded the slaveholders' rebellion as an act of treason—and called it that

by name—he seemed more interested in healing wounds than in punishing traitors. He had already clashed with more radical members of his own party over Reconstruction policy, and he would likely clash again now that the war was ending and more policies had to be implemented.

To be sure, unlike Johnson, Lincoln was a Republican and not in search of renomination. He might have developed a closer working relationship with the congressional Republicans and avoided antagonizing them as Johnson would do. During the war itself, Lincoln had shown a capacity for growth on the questions of enslavement and emancipation, and there is evidence that he was extremely impressed by and grateful for the heroism of Black soldiers. At the same time, Lincoln may well have formed an alliance with more moderate Republicans, and either the position of the formerly enslaved could have been weakened or Lincoln could have struggled and lost the political fight with the radicals in his party, in which case the position of the formerly enslaved might have been placed on a firmer social and political footing.

Had Lincoln lived to oversee postwar Reconstruction until his term ran out, would we have come to think less or more of him?

DOCUMENT 15.1: Lincoln's Second Inaugural Address

On March 4, 1865, only forty-one days before his assassination, Lincoln was sworn in for a second term and gave the following address to the nation. What does it portend for the character of Reconstruction on his watch and for the policies of his second term more generally?

Fellow countrymen: at this second appearing to take the oath of the presidential office there is less occasion for an extended address than there was at the first. Then a statement somewhat in detail of a course to be pursued seemed fitting and proper. Now, at the expiration of four years during which public declarations have been constantly called forth on every point and phase of the great contest which still absorbs the attention and engrosses the energies of the nation little that is new could be presented. The progress of our arms, upon which all else chiefly depends is as well known to the public as to myself and it is I trust reasonably satisfactory and encouraging to all. With high hope for the future no prediction in regard to it is ventured.

On the occasion corresponding to this four years ago all thoughts were anxiously directed to an impending civil war. All dreaded it—all sought to avert it. While the inaugural address was being delivered from this place devoted altogether to saving the Union without war insurgent agents were in the city seeking to destroy it without war—seeking to dissolve the Union and divide effects by negotiation. Both parties deprecated war but one of them would make war rather than let the nation survive, and the other would accept war rather than let it perish. And the war came.

One eighth of the whole population were colored slaves not distributed generally over the union but localized in the southern part of it. These slaves constituted a peculiar and powerful interest. All knew that this interest was somehow the cause of the war. To strengthen perpetuate and extend this interest was the object for which the insurgents would rend the Union even by war while the government claimed no right to do more than to restrict the territorial enlargement of it. Neither party expected for the war the magnitude or the duration which it has already attained. Neither anticipated that the cause of the conflict might cease with or even before the conflict itself should cease. Each looked for an easier triumph and a result less fundamental and astounding. Both read the same Bible and pray to the same God and each invokes His aid against the other. It may seem strange that any men should dare to ask a just God's assistance in wringing their bread from the sweat of other men's faces but let us judge not that we be not judged. The prayers of both could not be answered—that of neither has been answered fully. The Almighty has His own purposes. "Woe unto the world because of offenses for it must needs be that offenses come but woe to that man by whom the offense cometh." If we shall suppose that American slavery is one of those offenses which in the providence of God must needs come but which having continued through His appointed time He now wills to remove and that He gives to both North and South this terrible war as the woe due to those by whom the offense came shall we discern therein any departure from those divine attributes which the believers in a living God always ascribe to Him. Fondly do we hope—fervently do we pray—that this mighty scourge of war may speedily pass away. Yet, if God wills that it continue until all the wealth piled by the bondsman's two hundred and fifty years of unrequited toil shall be sunk and until every drop of blood drawn with the lash shall be paid by another drawn with the sword as was said three thousand years ago so still it must be said "the judgments of the Lord are true and righteous altogether."

With malice toward none with charity for all with firmness in the right as God gives us to see the right let us strive on to finish the work we are in to bind up the nation's wounds, to care for him who shall have borne the battle and for his widow and his orphan—to do all which may achieve and cherish a just and lasting peace among ourselves and with all nations.

Source: Library of Congress.

DOCUMENT 15.2: President Andrew Johnson's Proclamation of Amnesty

On May 29, 1865, the new president, Andrew Johnson, issued his own Proclamation of Amnesty to set the stage for his Reconstruction policies. How different are his views from those expressed in Lincoln's second inaugural address?

To the end, therefore, that the authority of the government of the United States may be restored, and that peace, order, and freedom may be established, I, ANDREW JOHNSON, President of the United States, do proclaim and declare that I hereby grant to all persons who have, directly or indirectly, participated in the existing rebellion, except as hereinafter excepted, amnesty and pardon, with restoration of all rights of property, except as to slaves, and except in cases where legal proceedings, under the laws of the United States providing for the confiscation of property of persons engaged in rebellion, have been instituted; but upon the condition, nevertheless, that every such person shall take and subscribe the following oath, (or affirmation,) and thenceforward keep and maintain said oath inviolate; and which oath shall be registered for permanent preservation, and shall be of the tenor and effect following, to wit:

I, _____ _____, do solemnly swear, (or affirm,) in presence of Almighty God, that I will henceforth faithfully support, protect, and defend the Constitution of the United States, and the union of the States thereunder; and that I will, in like manner, abide by, and faithfully support all laws and proclamations which have been made during the existing rebellion with reference to the emancipation of slaves. So help me God.

The following classes of persons are excepted from the benefits of this proclamation: 1st, all who are or shall have been pretended civil or diplomatic officers or otherwise domestic or foreign agents of the pretended Confederate government; 2nd, all who left judicial stations under the United States to aid the rebellion; 3d, all who shall have been military or naval officers of said pretended Confederate government above the rank of colonel in the army or lieutenant in the navy; 4th, all who left seats in the Congress of the United States to aid the rebellion;

5th, all who resigned or tendered resignations of their commissions in the army or navy of the United States to evade duty in resisting the rebellion; 6th, all who have engaged in any way in treating otherwise than lawfully as prisoners of war persons found in the United States service, as officers, soldiers, seamen, or in other capacities; 7th, all persons who have been, or are absentees from the United States for the purpose of aiding the rebellion; 8th, all military and naval officers in the rebel service, who were educated by the government in the Military Academy at West Point or the United States Naval Academy; 9th, all persons who held the pretended offices of governors of States in insurrection against the United States; 10th, all persons who left their homes within the jurisdiction and protection of the United States, and passed beyond the Federal military lines into the pretended Confederate States for the purpose of aiding the rebellion; 11th, all persons who have been engaged in the destruction of the commerce of the United States upon the high seas, and all persons who have made raids into the United States from Canada, or been engaged in destroying the commerce of the United States upon the lakes and rivers that separate the British Provinces from the United States; 12th, all persons who, at the time when they seek to obtain the benefits hereof by taking the oath herein prescribed, are in military, naval, or civil confinement, or custody, or under bonds of the civil, military, or naval authorities, or agents of the United States as prisoners of war, or persons detained for offenses of any kind, either before or after conviction; 13th, all persons who have voluntarily participated in said rebellion, and the estimated value of whose taxable property is over twenty thousand dollars; 14th, all persons who have taken the oath of amnesty as prescribed in the President's proclamation of December 8th, AD 1863, or an oath of allegiance to the government of the United States since the date of said proclamation, and who have not thenceforward kept and maintained the same inviolate.

Provided, That special application may be made to the President for pardon by any person belonging to the excepted classes; and such clemency will be liberally extended as may be consistent with the facts of the case and the peace and dignity of the United States.

Source: U.S. Congress, *United States Statutes at Large* (Washington, DC: U.S. G.P.O., 1937), vol. 13, pp. 758–760.

Thinking About Contingency

1. What does Lincoln's Second Inaugural portend for the character of Reconstruction on his watch and for the policies of his second term more generally?
2. How different are Johnson's views from those expressed in Lincoln's second inaugural address?

REVIEW QUESTIONS

1. How did Republicans understand the nature of secession and the Confederate rebellion, and how did this understanding shape their wartime approaches to reunifying the country?

2. Why did Lincoln and the Republican-dominated Congress struggle over Reconstruction policy?

3. How did the Civil War shape relations between the federal government and Indigenous people as well as between the Confederates and Indigenous people?

4. What sort of future did Republican policymakers imagine for previously enslaved people and for Native Americans?

5. In what ways were Black people, previously enslaved and free, politicized during the war, and how did their developing political consciousness give shape to the war and its meaning?

6. How could the Confederate rebellion be ended, and what would be the fate of those who carried on the rebellion?

7. What did Confederates expect from President Andrew Johnson?

8. Should we accept the label of "Civil War" to capture the brutal conflagration that erupted between 1861 and 1865, or should we speak of it as a "War of the Rebellion"?

KEY TERMS

American Freedmen's Inquiry Commission (p. 617)

Black Codes (p. 639)

contract labor system (p. 616)

First South Carolina Volunteers (p. 624)

Freedmen's Bureau (p. 617)

Presidential Reconstruction (p. 638)

Proclamation of Amnesty and Reconstruction (p. 613)

Sand Creek Massacre (p. 622)

settler colonialism (p. 619)

Special Field Orders No. 15 (p. 627)

territorialization (p. 613)

Wade-Davis Bill (p. 615)

RECOMMENDED READINGS

Ira Berlin, et al., eds., *Freedom: A Documentary History of Emancipation: The Black Military Experience* (Cambridge University Press, 1982).

Eric Foner, *Reconstruction: America's Unfinished Revolution, 1863–1877* (Harper and Row, 1988).

Thavolia Glymph, *The Women's Fight: The Civil War Battles for Home, Freedom, and Nation* (University of North Carolina Press, 2020).

Steven Hahn, *A Nation under Our Feet: Black Political Struggles in the Rural South from Slavery to the Great Migration* (Harvard University Press, 2003).

Chandra Manning, *What This Cruel War Was Over: Soldiers, Slavery, and the Civil War* (Vintage 2008).

David A. Nichols, *Lincoln and the Indians: Civil War Policy and Politics* (Minnesota Historical Society Press, 2012).

Michael Perman, *Reunion Without Compromise: The South and Reconstruction, 1865–1868* (Cambridge University Press, 1973).

Lawrence N. Powell, *New Masters: Northern Planters During the Civil War and Reconstruction* (Yale University Press, 1980).

Joseph P. Reidy, *Illusions of Emancipation: The Pursuit of Freedom and Equality in the Twilight of Slavery* (University of North Carolina Press, 2020).

Willie Lee Rose, *Rehearsal for Reconstruction: The Port Royal Experiment* (Bobbs Merrill, 1964).

16

The Promise and Limits of Reconstruction

1865–1877

Chapter Outline

≡ **Suffragists**   By 1870, when this photo was taken, Elizabeth Cady Stanton and Susan B. Anthony were household names. The two women are seated around a circular desk similar to the ones where Stanton penned the 1848 "Declaration of Sentiments." Contrary to popular belief, Anthony was not present at the famous gathering of women at Seneca Falls in 1848.

In the late summer of 1865, both Elizabeth Cady Stanton and Susan B. Anthony, antislavery and woman suffrage activists, were deeply disturbed by the news that was leaking out of Congress. Concerned about the status of the formerly enslaved people in the South and by President Andrew Johnson's conciliatory policies toward the former Confederate rebels, Republicans were drafting a Fourteenth Amendment to the Constitution, which would grant citizenship to African Americans, effectively overturning the *Dred Scott* decision of 1857. Further, it would encourage the states of the former Confederacy to grant African American men the franchise (right to vote) by taking congressional representation from them if they failed to do so.

Stanton and Anthony had collected thousands of names on a petition to Congress in 1864 calling for a Constitutional Amendment to abolish enslavement, hoping, too, that as part of this remarkable—indeed, revolutionary—era, emancipation would be linked to the enfranchisement of women as well as Black men. But what they learned

Timeline

1865	1866	1867	1868	1869	1870	1871	1872	1873

1865 >
January Congress passes Thirteenth Amendment abolishing enslavement
May President Johnson issues Proclamation of Amnesty
December Congress returns to session and rejects new members from former Confederate states; states ratify Thirteenth Amendment

1866 >
March Civil Rights Act and Freedmen's Bureau Act passed by Congress over President Johnson's vetoes
June Congress passes Fourteenth Amendment granting birthright citizenship
November Republicans increase congressional majorities in fall elections

1867 >
March Military Reconstruction Acts imposing federal military rule on the South passed by Congress over President Johnson's vetoes

1868 >
March House of Representatives passes Articles of Impeachment against President Andrew Johnson
May President Johnson acquitted by the Senate
July Fourteenth Amendment ratified by the states

1869 > Congress passes Fifteenth Amendment prohibiting discrimination on account of race, color, or previous condition of servitude for the right to vote

1870 > Fifteenth Amendment ratified by the states

1870–1871 > Congress passes Enforcement Acts to combat attacks on the voting rights of African Americans from state officials or paramilitary groups like the Ku Klux Klan

was that the Fourteenth Amendment would require universal adult "male" suffrage, for the first time marking a distinction in constitutional rights based on gender. Stanton sensibly worried that, "if the word 'male' be inserted it will take a century at least to get it out." And so, she and Anthony sent another petition directly to Congress arguing that, "as you are now amending the Constitution [and] placing new safeguards round the individual rights of four million of emancipated ex-slaves, we ask that you extend the right of Suffrage to Women and thus fulfill your constitutional obligation 'to guarantee to every State in the Union a Republican form of Government.'"

They made a powerful argument, using broad rights language with a basis in the Constitution. Yet male abolitionists had already indicated that woman suffrage would have to take a back seat to the civil and political rights of freed*men*. The Republicans were deeply concerned about holding on to power and safeguarding their achievements, and they recognized that Black male suffrage, alone, was bound to provoke

1874	1875	1876	1877	1878	1879	1880	1881	1882

1874 ▸ Democrats take control of House of Representatives

1876 ▸ Contested presidential election between Rutherford B. Hayes (Republican) and Samuel Tilden (Democrat)

1877 ▸ Compromise of 1877 gives Hayes the presidency with concessions to the Democrats that effectively end Reconstruction; Hayes withdraws last US troops from the South

opposition in the North as well as in the South. Nonetheless, they viewed Black suffrage as essential to their success in building up their party in the rebellious states and in maintaining their hold on Congress and the presidency. As Radical Republican Wendell Phillips saw it, "in time" he hoped he could be bold enough to demand suffrage for women as well as men, but "this hour belongs to the Negro."

Stanton responded bitterly, asking Phillips if he "believe[d] the African race is composed entirely of males?" There was, however, little that she or her suffrage movement could do since women did not have the right to vote and could not sit in Congress debating legislation and amendments. When Congress subsequently drafted the **Fifteenth Amendment**, in 1869, they again chose not to add "sex" to "race, color, or previous condition of servitude" as unlawful exclusions from voting rights. Thus, seeing that their antebellum (pre–Civil War) alliances were now at an end, Stanton and Anthony turned their attention to building a new, independent woman suffrage movement. They were, it appeared, on their own.

The defeat of woman suffrage and the victory of Black male suffrage reveal much about American Reconstruction. Before the War of the Rebellion, there were few places where even free people of African descent could vote and little interracial support for Black voting rights. Now, a majority of Republicans in Congress, through the Military Reconstruction Acts (1867) and the Fifteenth Amendment (1870), supported the enfranchisement of Black men. It was a remarkable and controversial move. But the failure of woman suffrage suggested the limits to the changes that Reconstruction would usher in. In understanding both the promise and limits of Reconstruction, we might begin by asking why it was so much more difficult for Republicans—even the Radicals among them—to end gender discrimination in political rights than it was to end discrimination based on "race or previous condition of servitude."

16.1   The Black Struggle for Rights and Independence

Describe the aspirations of the formerly enslaved and free people of color in their struggles during Reconstruction.

The unexpected course of President Andrew Johnson's Reconstruction policies was contested from the first by African Americans across the rebellious states. Stepping into the public light in the occupied South and owing to enlistment in the federal armed forces, they advanced a very different perspective on a post-emancipation world than either Lincoln or Johnson had offered. In meetings and processions, they called for civil rights, full citizenship, the right to vote, land to cultivate, and community independence. In the process, they brought on intense conflict with their former enslavers and recently disbanded Confederate soldiers in what would prove to be the final battles of the rebellion. As a result, they paved the way for a new settlement and political order.

Opening Forays

The earliest mobilizations of African Americans came in southern cities and in adjacent districts where federal troops had arrived before Confederate forces began to surrender. They occurred in New Orleans; Memphis; Mobile, Alabama; Norfolk, Virginia; and the coastal districts south of Charleston, South Carolina. Political organizations connected with the Republican Party, such as the Union League, became vehicles of a new political presence. They organized meetings, introduced leaders from near and far, and celebrated the role of Black troops in destroying enslavement and defeating the enslavers. They also protested discriminatory treatment by federal officials and Confederates alike, framed aspirations and grievances, taught thousands of Black people about the workings of the government, and pressed for entrance into civil and political society.

Nothing better exemplified the alternatives to Johnson's Reconstruction policies devised by African Americans than the **freedmen's conventions** held in most of the rebellious states in the summer and fall of 1865. Led mainly by free people of color from the North and South, they met in the states' capitols or largest cities and insisted that "we are part of the American republic." Often anticipating or coinciding with the whites-only constitutional conventions held under Johnson's plan, they effectively cast doubt on the legitimacy of Presidential Reconstruction. In the resolutions that virtually all of the freedmen's conventions passed, they emphasized their desire for education, loyalty to the United States, courage in the country's "darkest hour," and "right to carry their ballot to the ballot box." "Any attempt to reconstruct the states without giving to American citizens of African descent all the rights and immunities accorded to white citizens," the Virginia freedmen's convention declared, "is an act of gross injustice." In an important sense, these conventions followed the precedents of those that took place in the North before the war erupted (discussed in Chapter 12).

The Land Question

Things were different in the rural areas where the freedpeople still overwhelmingly resided. There, what circulated at the very time the freedmen's conventions were demanding "equal rights" were rumors of a massive redistribution of land accomplished either by the federal government or by armed Black insurrection. A powerful logic was at play, at least for the freedpeople. The idea of land reform reflected both their sense of what a just and meaningful emancipation would involve and their expectations of what the federal government would do. Much like their emancipated counterparts in other slave-plantation societies of the Western Hemisphere, they associated land with subsistence, independence, and community stability. As formerly enslaved people, they were well aware that their labor had given the lands their value and the slaveholders their prosperity. Some even recognized their contributions to the economic growth of the entire country. "Didn't we clear the land and raise the crops? And then didn't them large cities in the North grow up on the cotton and the sugars and the rice that we made?" a Virginia freedman asked, insisting, "we have a right to [that] land."

Such ideas about a "right to land" were reinforced by the actions of the federal government. Owing to the Confiscation Acts of 1861 and 1862 as well as Sherman's Field Orders No. 15, the government controlled more than 900,000 acres of rebel land with authority to divide it into 40-acre tracts for distribution among the freedpeople. Land reform appeared to loom as a real possibility, and even President Johnson's efforts to restore confiscated land to white owners failed to dim the fires of expectation. As a result, starting in the summer of 1865, talk of a general, government-sponsored property division began to spread among the freedpeople, especially in areas where they could be found in largest numbers. One Freedmen's Bureau official stationed in the lower Mississippi Valley reported that "a majority of the colored population positively believe that the government would take the plantations, cut them up into forty acres parcels and give them to the colored people." Although some imagined that the great day might arrive at any time, more and more looked to the Christmas season, especially to Christmas or New Year's Day: the time when gifts were customarily exchanged and the slaveholders' paternalism was most fully on display.

Yet the very prospect of land reform and the Black power it would promote sparked reorganizations of disbanded rebel troops. Planters and white landowning supporters just home from the battlefields told one another of "extravagant ideas of freedom" that the formerly enslaved entertained and of plans devised by the freedpeople to stage an "insurrection" to take the land by force if the federal government refused to act. Much of the blame, they insisted, could be placed on the shoulders of African American troops in the army of occupation, who "emboldened" the freedpeople politically and "demoralized" them at their work.

Here the fatal weaknesses of Johnson's policies became apparent. Alarmed white landowners brought their concerns to the attention of the state provisional governors selected under Presidential Reconstruction. Although the governors may have opposed secession and kept a low profile during the war, they usually sympathized with the fears of fellow property owners. The provisional governors in turn contacted federal officials and, if necessary, Johnson himself to tell of the alleged insurrectionary activities and demand both the removal of Black troops and the authority to mobilize militia companies to maintain order. Johnson and the Freedmen's Bureau commissioner then sent Bureau agents into the rural districts to "disabuse" the freedpeople of the "false impression" they had about land redistribution and urge them to make labor contracts. At the same time, Johnson gave the governors the green light to reorganize the militias, which were little more than disbanded Confederate units and slave patrols.

Why did Johnson do this? Why did he allow defeated Confederates to rearm and threaten the lives of the formerly enslaved? Johnson despised the antebellum southern elite, the big plantation owners, but he had no love either for the enslaved or the freedpeople. He imagined—much like Lincoln—that the post-emancipation

≡ **Power Conflicts**   In this allegorical representation of the Freedmen's Bureau from 1868, a Union soldier keeps the peace between unruly groups of Black people and white men.

MAPPING AMERICA

The Changing Landscape of the South

The War of the Rebellion rearranged human relations in the South—between white people and Black people, and between men and women—and it also transformed the built environment. The environmental costs of four years of war were staggering. Sherman's march through Georgia and the Carolinas was particularly devastating, with tens of thousands of horses, mules, and livestock killed, and millions of pounds of corn, grain, and other foodstuffs destroyed. On a smaller scale, the war also rearranged the way people lived in the places they called home. We can see this change by looking at the Barrow Plantation in central Georgia before and after the war.

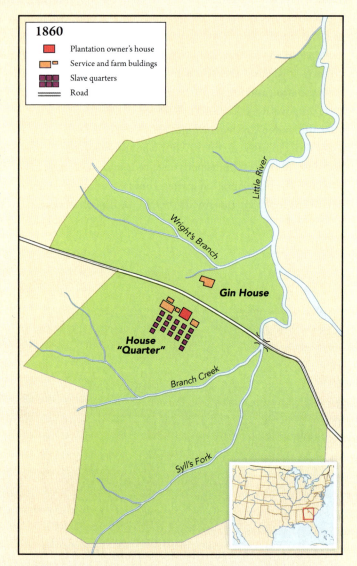

1860

- 🟥 Plantation owner's house
- 🟧 Service and farm buldings
- 🟥🟥 Slave quarters
- ▭ Road

Little River

Wright's Branch

Gin House

House "Quarter"

Branch Creek

Syll's Fork

≡ **MAP 1**   In 1860, the ninety-four enslaved workers on the Barrow Plantation lived in quarters near the owner's house. They were subject to strict control, but they also could build a tightly knit community.

Thinking Geographically

1. How would you describe the built environment of the Barrow Plantation in 1860? How does this landscape reflect the cultural values of the people who lived there?

2. How would you describe the built environment of the Barrow Plantation in 1881? How does this new landscape reflect the economic priorities and cultural values of the people who lived there? What patterns of continuity and change do you see when you compare the two maps?

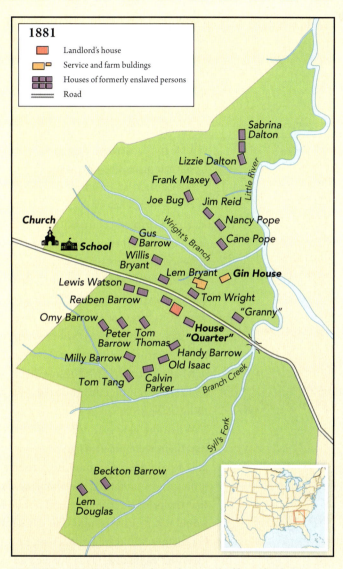

≡ **MAP 2**   Twenty-one years later, the estate had been divided into small plots worked by the formerly enslaved people as sharecroppers. The croppers had also constructed a church where they could worship and a school where their children could learn to read and write. Only the gin house, where picked cotton was cleaned, remained in the same position as before the war, evidence of the crop's continuing economic importance.

world would be run by and for white people with Black people as a subordinate laboring class. He also wanted to restore self-government rapidly in the rebellious states through policies that would allow one-time rebels to show their newfound loyalty and demonstrate to the country that the rebellion was truly at an end. But Johnson's willingness to allow former Confederates to police their states and localities only demonstrated that the spirit of rebellion was very much alive. Using the threat of insurrection as a rationale, the planters and their allies brazenly launched campaigns to disarm, disperse, and intimidate rural Black people. When away from their posts, even Black federal soldiers fell victim to vigilante violence.

White fears of an imminent Black insurrection were unwarranted; there was never any evidence of such a plot. But the fears did spotlight the early political activities of freed communities and the contests for power that developed in the wake of emancipation. Indeed, just as white landowners spread rumors of Black violence to reassert their local prerogatives, so did the freedpeople use rumors of land redistribution to strengthen their own bargaining positions. Wrestling with landowners over the terms of their pay or over claims to the land, some freedpeople refused to enter into labor agreements for 1866, not only out of worry that they might be coercive but also because the prospect of land would provide the opportunity to farm for themselves. "The Negroes are not inclined to make any contracts until after Christmas," a Tennessee landowner complained that October. "They seem to expect something to take place about that time, a division of land or something of the kind."

When the new year did arrive, these Tennessee freedpeople and many others like them were able to sign contracts for better terms than they had originally been accorded: higher monthly pay or larger shares of the crop, access to provision grounds, lower rents on their housing. But in signing contracts, they acknowledged that the promise of land would not be fulfilled and the threat of an insurrection would not be carried out. The Christmas season brought them not land reform but further rounds of harassment, floggings, and late-night searches by white militias and vigilantes. Black people had learned the hard lesson that the promise of sweeping change that granted them freedom and independence could be painfully limited and even withdrawn.

The Collapse of Presidential Reconstruction

For their part, rebels who had briefly been humbled by the official surrender of their armies and the prospects of being punished as traitors reorganized their resistance to federal authority and started to carve out a post-emancipation order that was favorable to them. Johnson granted most of them amnesty and the return of their property that had fallen into federal hands. Federal army commanders agreed to planters' demands to remove Black soldiers from trouble spots in rural areas.

Freedmen's Bureau agents tried to convince the formerly enslaved that land would not be distributed and they had to sign labor contracts. And southern legislatures elected under Johnson's plans—with no African Americans in them—quickly enacted Black Codes, which, as we saw in Chapter 15, restricted Black opportunities for either economic independence or civil equality, enforced labor contracts, and punished those deemed "vagrants." These were the first official signs of the coercive measures that former enslavers would deploy against the formerly enslaved.

Presidential Reconstruction was clearly in tatters, and the support Johnson once received from Republicans in Congress was collapsing. The Radicals in the party had been worried that Johnson's pardons to individual rebels and his conditions for the readmission of rebel states were too lenient. But nothing angered more northerners or pushed more moderate and conservative Republicans toward disenchantment with, if not outright opposition to, his policies than the epidemic of violence against Black people and white loyalists that exploded amid rumors of federal land reform. Together they seemed to threaten the results of the war and to rupture the boundaries of northern tolerance. "The most favorable opportunity was afforded to the southern people," a Cincinnati newspaper editorialized in December 1865, "but the spirit in which this was responded to was a rebellious one."

Congress agreed. When the House and Senate reconvened the first week of December 1865, their members acted with dispatch. They refused to seat the representatives elected by the rebellious states; they formed the Joint Committee on Reconstruction to investigate conditions in the South; and they began to challenge Johnson's policies and authority. Recognizing that rebels who had been defeated militarily might claim victory on terrain of their own choosing, the Republican Congress determined to seize the initiative and bring the rebellion to a different sort of end.

16.2   Toward Radical Nationhood

Explain the political vision of the Reconstruction Republicans and how they understood the nation they were trying to forge.

Even while Lincoln was alive, the federal government, through its executive and legislative branches, had assumed powers and envisioned a reconstructed government that moved well beyond the boundaries established by the original Constitution. In good part, this was the result of fighting a war on a scale that could not have been imagined in 1861. But it also grew out of the challenges that Republicans faced once the shooting stopped. Many worried that the results of the bloody war might be undermined or reversed and that the party itself might be driven from power once the rebellious states had been readmitted to the Union. Andrew Johnson's behavior was a warning sign, and Republicans determined that having won the war they would not lose the peace. In the process a new nation was forged.

The Thirteenth Amendment

Congress took a dramatic step in asserting its authority and extending the reach of federal power, though much of the initiative came from outside its walls. Pressure had been building among abolitionists and other antislavery activists to secure an emancipation that was universal and permanent. As early as the spring of 1863 the **Women's Loyal National League** led by Elizabeth Cady Stanton and Susan B. Anthony launched the massive petition drive noted at the start of this chapter; they would collect about 400,000 signatures. By the end of that year, congressional Republicans and a small number of Democratic colleagues were ready to act. They saw the limits of the Emancipation Proclamation, which did not abolish slavery in all of the states, only in those that had rebelled against the federal government. Further, its reach was dependent on the arrival of the federal army both to announce the Proclamation and to enforce its authority. In east Texas, the ending of slavery was not officially decreed until June 19, 1865, when US General Gordon Granger arrived in Galveston with his troops and publicly read the Emancipation Proclamation. This important event has since been commemorated as **Juneteenth**, now observed as a national holiday.

Abolitionists, congressional Republicans, and antislavery Democrats also feared that, as a war measure, the Emancipation Proclamation might be overturned by hostile courts once the war had ended. Although they first considered the idea of passing a statutory law to end enslavement in the United States, they ultimately decided to craft an abolition amendment to the Constitution—the "Supreme Law of the Land" and therefore preeminent over all other federal laws, not contained in the Constitution.

A constitutional amendment did, however, raise a great many questions. What should such an amendment include, and how far should it go? Should the amendment's language be confined to the abolition of enslavement within the borders of the United States, or should it also address the civil status of those who had been emancipated? Influenced by what had happened in France in 1794 as a result of the Haitian Revolution, Radical Republican Charles Sumner of Massachusetts proposed that the amendment not only abolish enslavement but also stipulate that "all people are equal before the law," a move in the direction of citizenship that the French had pioneered. But Sumner couldn't get enough support for his proposal, and the result was an amendment that adopted the language of the Northwest

Ordinance of 1787 (discussed in Chapter 7) and said nothing about equality or citizenship: "Neither slavery nor involuntary servitude except as a punishment for crime whereof the party shall be duly convicted, shall exist within the United States, or any place subject to their jurisdiction." The amendment did thereby prohibit enslavement in any future territory of the United States (quite the opposite of the Confederate constitution), and it granted Congress the "power to enforce [it] by appropriate legislation."

Although the congressional power of enforcement might appear to be a bureaucratic add-on, it worried most northern Democrats as well as former enslavers, and for good reason. It gave the federal government sovereign power beyond anything previously enjoyed under the Constitution and opened the door for an assortment of initiatives as to the civil and political status of the freedpeople. If enslavement and involuntary labor were prohibited, what type of legislation would be necessary "to enforce" the prohibition? Would the Black Codes invite federal intervention, and would the Republican majority use the enforcement power to press the matters of African American citizenship and voting rights? More than a few southern legislators feared that it would. But with the Republicans in control of all branches of the federal government and of most legislatures in the North and West, the **Thirteenth Amendment** was passed by Congress in January 1865 and ratified by the requisite number (three-fourths) of states by the following December.

≡ **The Black Codes in Action**   The services of a freedman, unable to pay a fine, are sold to the highest bidder in Monticello, Florida, in 1867. The scene does not look all that different from a prewar slave auction.

Civil Rights and the Fourteenth Amendment

The fears of white southerners were justified. While President Johnson, Secretary of State William Seward, and loyal Democrats were quick to argue that the Thirteenth Amendment would end rather than spark conflicts over Black rights, most Republicans did see the opportunity to demonstrate that freedom meant more than, in the words of Ohio congressman and future president James A. Garfield, "the bare privilege of not being chained." Citing the enforcement clause, Republicans moved quickly to give freedom substance. In early 1866 they drafted and passed bills extending the life of the Freedmen's Bureau—and authorizing agents to protect freedpeople in the "civil rights belonging to white people"—and prescribing that "all persons born in the United States and not subject to any foreign power, excluding Indians not taxed, are hereby declared to be citizens of the United States." The latter is known as the **Civil Rights Act of 1866**. Their passage reflected Republicans' insistence that slavery's end required a new civil status for the formerly enslaved, that citizenship would be defined and granted by the federal government, and that *Dred Scott* was no longer the law of the land. It also suggested that Indigenous people would continue to be excluded even in this radical redefinition of rights.

President Johnson vetoed both bills. He called them "strides toward centralization," and he appeared interested in isolating Radical Republicans and building support for himself among Democrats and Republican conservatives. If this was his motivation, however, he blundered again. His vetoes served only to unify Republicans in an effort to defend their own power and remove Johnson's hands from their policy objectives. It would mean another constitutional amendment, but this time they were following the lead of African Americans who had struggled to put Black political rights on the table for decades and now were making strong arguments about the relation of soldiering and political citizenship. A growing number of Republicans, for reasons of principle as well as opportunism, came to embrace their cause. After all, the Republican Party was barely organized in the former slave states, and the end of enslavement meant that the federal ratio, which counted an enslaved person as three-fifths of a free person for apportioning congressional seats and electoral votes, would no longer prevail. Now freedpeople would count five-fifths, and their former enslavers would have even more power regardless of the civil and political status of Black people. It was a recipe for Republican defeat.

But if Republicans were to push forward with a political revolution, how far should it go? What would citizenship mean in the new nation that was under construction? Woman suffrage activists, with deep ties to abolitionism, had fought spirited but losing battles for the vote for years and then put aside their aspirations to support the federal government and the emancipation of the enslaved. Now a moment for extending the revolution seemed to have arrived, a moment, as Elizabeth Cady Stanton put it, "to bury the woman and the negro in the citizen."

As Cady Stanton indicated, woman suffrage advocates hoped to maintain and strengthen, not break, their alliance with the formerly enslaved. But the case that African American men made to support their enfranchisement demonstrated the vulnerability of women's position. By arguing that military service had revealed their courage and manhood, they embraced the gendered political culture of the nineteenth century that masculinized claims for citizenship and political rights. Republicans, who mostly aligned with the culture of evangelical Protestantism, saw male-headed households as the basis of social stability, with "separate spheres" (for women in the home and men in the outside world, as discussed in Chapter 10) the organizing principle of public and private life. As slavery collapsed during the war, they looked for assurances that the formerly enslaved were acquainted with middle-class values, could respond to market incentives, and would construct their family relations in a morally acceptable hierarchy. Thus, while Radical Republican Wendell Phillips hoped that "in time" the franchise could be extended to women, for him "this hour belongs to the negro."

The **Fourteenth Amendment** that came out of Congress in June 1866 showed both the reach and limits of this revolutionary moment. Building on the Civil Rights Act of 1866, it established a **birthright citizenship** ("All persons born or naturalized in the United States") that offered the same "privileges and immunities" and the "equal protection of the laws" wherever citizens resided in the United States. A more direct and ringing rejection of the world of *Dred Scott* could hardly be found. The amendment also disfranchised any political or military office holder who had joined the Confederate rebellion after taking an oath of allegiance to the Constitution, though Congress could remove this disqualification by a two-thirds vote.

But the second section of the amendment revealed the barriers that were still in place. Congress could have taken up the franchise question by establishing a broad principle of political citizenship that did not allow state tampering and that held open the door for more expansive political participation. Instead, Congress took the indirect route on federal authority and the direct route on the matter of gender. It would now count five-fifths of all persons for apportionment and penalize any state that denied voting rights to any of its "inhabitants" over twenty-one years of age by reducing congressional representation proportionally; thus, if Black people were not enfranchised and composed 40 percent of the population, the state would lose 40 percent of its congressional seats. Yet, in a move that put a dagger into the heart of women's suffrage, the amendment also designated those "inhabitants" as "male," making explicit the exclusion of women. So ended an alliance that had helped defeat the Confederate rebellion and drive the revolution of emancipation.

16.3   Political Revolution and Its Limits

Assess the extent of political change that occurred in the Reconstruction South as well as in the nation as a whole.

It was one thing for Congress to pass the Fourteenth Amendment; it was another to get the requisite three-fourths of states to ratify it. Ratification was now the requirement for readmission to the United States, yet all but one of the rebellious states—Tennessee, Johnson's home state, being the ironic exception—refused to ratify the Fourteenth Amendment during the fall and early winter of 1866–1867, citing both the threat of Black suffrage and the exclusion of former Confederates. For Radical Republicans the lesson was obvious. The rebellious states could not be left to their own devices; they had to be subject to federal authority.

Advent of Military Reconstruction

The Radical Republicans saw an important opening. Congressional elections would take place in the fall of 1866, and Radicals turned them into a referendum on the Fourteenth Amendment. They were aided in this effort by Andrew Johnson himself, who set out on an extended speaking tour to mobilize Democratic opposition but behaved so erratically—often haranguing Republican adversaries in the most bitter and demeaning terms and occasionally appearing intoxicated—that even potentially sympathetic voters abandoned him and his party in droves. When the ballots were counted, the Republicans won handily. They increased their control of Congress to more than two-thirds of the seats (making it veto-proof). Johnson was now the one who appeared isolated.

The radicalism that emerged from what one newspaper called "the fiery ordeal of a mighty revolution" was now at the height of its influence and would meet the last phase of the Confederate rebellion with terms far different from those considered by Lincoln, Johnson, or moderate Republicans. In the **Military Reconstruction Acts**, passed overwhelmingly in March 1867, Congress decisively rejected Johnson's approach of encouraging rebels to show their loyalty and permitting them to rebuild their political institutions as they saw fit. Instead, the rebellious states were now divided into five military districts, each under the command of a US Army general, who would supervise still another reorganization of state constitutions. Constitutional conventions would again be held, popular ratifications of their work would occur, and elections for local, state, and national offices would take place. But this time Black men, most of whom had been enslaved, would participate as voters and delegates. And this time the constitutional conventions would have to enfranchise African Americans on the same basis as whites and rat-ify the Fourteenth Amendment as a condition of readmission.

Over the following months, the US Army carried out the first voter registration in American history. Although a daunting undertaking, it proved a remarkable success. By the fall of 1867, the rolls of eligible voters had been compiled, and they included an astonishingly high proportion of eligible Black men: over 90 percent everywhere except Mississippi, where 83 percent had registered. Even more conse-quentially, Black voters now made up a substantial portion, if not a majority, of the total electorate in the rebellious states, especially in the localities where slavehold-ing planters had long ruled.

The rebellion now appeared to be at an end, with the elements of a new politi-cal order in the South seemingly in place. The federal government proclaimed its sovereign authority over the territorial United States. The leading rebels, though avoiding arrest and punishment, were penalized politically, and a once-powerful southern bloc in Congress and national political life was subdued. A national citi-zenship had been established, and universal manhood suffrage advanced as a princi-ple of American political culture. The formerly enslaved and other people of African descent won access to power where they resided in largest numbers. And Radical Republicans were in a position to shape the country's future. What had begun as a battle to quell a rebellion of slaveholders had turned into a social and political rev-olution that gave rise to a new nation (see Table 16.1). Nowhere else in the world of Atlantic enslavement, not even in Haiti, did emancipation lead to such potential empowerment for the formerly enslaved who, just a few short years earlier, cultivat-ed acres of crops under threat of the lash and had no rights that whites needed to respect. For all of these reasons, the War of the Rebellion and the Reconstruction that followed may be considered one of the greatest and most sweeping revolutions in all of modern history.

Indigenous People in a New Nation

Still, the full meaning of that revolution had yet to be determined. Land reform in the South and woman's suffrage in the nation at large had tested the limits of change and been repelled. Questions about money, banking, tariffs, and railroads hovered over Congress, asking whose interests the great transformations of war and emancipation would serve. But the signs of the future may have been revealing themselves most consequentially in the trans-Mississippi West. With the slave-holders' rebellion defeated, the federal government was more determined than ever to suppress Indigenous rebellions that continued to erupt across the Plains, the Southwest, and the Northwest. Only a few months after the last Confederate armies surrendered, the tribes in Indian Territory were made to pay for their

		Table 16.1 Reconstruction Amendments, 1865–1870	
Amendment	**Main Provisions**	**Congressional Passage (two-thirds majority in each house required)**	**Ratification Process (three-quarters of all states including ex-Confederate states required)**
Thirteenth	Slavery and involuntary servitude prohibited in the United States	January 1865	December 1865 (twenty-seven states, including eight southern states)
Fourteenth	1. Birthright citizenship for anyone born or naturalized in the United States	June 1866	Rejected by twelve southern and border states, February 1867
	2. State representation in Congress reduced proportionally to number of male voters disfranchised		Radicals make readmission of southern states hinge on ratification
	3. Former high-ranking Confederates denied right to hold office until Congress removes disabilities		Ratified July 1868
	4. Confederate debt repudiated; validity of US public debt not to be questioned		
Fifteenth	Denial of franchise because of race, color, or previous condition of servitude explicitly prohibited	February 1869	Ratification required for readmission of Virginia, Texas, Mississippi, and Georgia; ratified March 1870

alliances with the rebels. They would have to forfeit all annuity payments, make new treaties, set aside lands for tribes that had been friendly to the United States, and grant railroads rights-of-way through their lands. They would also have to accept the emancipation of all the enslaved Black people they held as well as the inclusion of those formerly enslaved into their tribes "on an equal footing with original members."

Earlier that summer of 1865, Secretary of the Interior James Harlan instructed his agents to impress upon the Indigenous people, "in the most forcible terms," that white settlement would be spreading rapidly, that the government had no intention of slowing it down, and that Indigenous people would be well advised to "abandon [their] wandering life" and settle upon reservation lands. Nearly three years later, as the first elections under Military Reconstruction were taking place, General William Tecumseh Sherman—he who had practiced "total warfare" against the Confederate rebels and issued Field Orders No. 15 to confiscate and redistribute their lands—traveled out to Wyoming with an Indian Peace Commission to negotiate an agreement with the previously rebellious Sioux and their allies. Known as the Treaty of Fort Laramie and drafted in the spring of 1868, it defined the boundaries of their reservation and demanded that they no longer resist the construction of railroads then being built on the Plains (see Map 16.1).

Not all the Sioux signed the treaty, and some of the most militant, led by Lakota chief Sitting Bull, continued to raid federal forts along the upper Missouri River. Elsewhere on the Plains and in the Southwest and Northwest, the summer months of 1868 saw Kiowas, Comanches, Cheyenne, Apaches, and Paiutes engage in warfare against the flood of white settlement. By October, the Indian Commission was ready to take further stock of the situation and urge a dramatic shift in federal policy. The Commissioners recommended that Native American tribes no longer be recognized by the federal government as "domestic dependent nations" and instead be held subject to the laws of the United States. Three years later, Congress

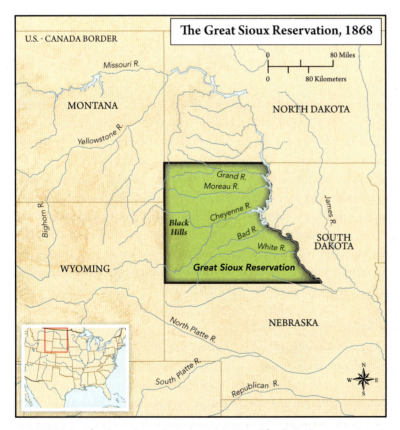

≡ **MAP 16.1   The Great Sioux Reservation, 1868**   The Great Sioux Reservation defined by the Treaty of Fort Laramie encompassed more than 48,000 square miles of land between the Missouri River and the Black Hills.

made official what a new nation would demand of those who resided within its borders: "hereafter no Indian nation or tribe . . . shall be acknowledged or recognized as an independent nation, tribe, or power with whom the United States may contract by treaty." The Reconstruction of the South and the Reconstruction of the West thereby formed part of a sweeping national project.

16.4 Building a Republican Base in the South

||| Summarize how Republicans tried to build bases of political support in the formerly rebellious states of the South.

The Military Reconstruction Acts showed the determination of Radical Republicans to win the peace as well as the war, to make sure that the Confederate rebellion was defeated and a new nation based on expanded freedom and citizenship came in its place. But the Military Reconstruction Acts also highlighted the politically precarious situation that Republicans found themselves in as the War of the Rebellion ended and the formerly rebellious states were being restored to the American Union.

When the war broke out, the Republican Party had little basis in the states where enslavement remained legal. Outside Maryland, Delaware, Kentucky, and Missouri, Lincoln didn't even make it onto the ballot. Although Lincoln's wartime "ten-percent plan" (discussed in Chapter 15) created openings for the party in Virginia, Arkansas, Tennessee, and Louisiana, had the rebellious states been readmitted to the Union under Johnson's policies—before freedmen gained the vote—the Democrats would have taken full control of them. The Republicans would have had their congressional initiatives, including the Fourteenth and Fifteenth Amendments, blocked, if they were not driven from national power entirely. The destiny of the Republican Party and the new nation they intended to forge teetered in the balance.

The Challenge and the Allies

When the Military Reconstruction Acts passed in March 1867, General Philip H. Sheridan was appointed governor of the newly created Fifth Military District, encompassing Louisiana and Texas (see Map 16.2). One of five army generals selected to impose martial law and oversee the reconstruction and restoration of the rebellious states, he was a particularly good choice. Sheridan had run roughshod over Confederates in the Shenandoah Valley of Virginia, and he was just as tough minded now that hostilities had ceased. He insisted on establishing the authority

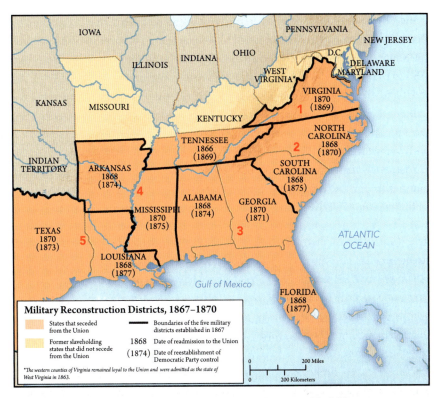

≡ MAP 16.2 **Military Reconstruction Districts, 1867–1870** The Military Reconstruction Acts divided the South into five districts commanded by a military governor, usually, as in the case of Philip H. Sheridan, a former Union army general.

of the federal government, had no interest in appeasing defeated rebels and their collaborators, and believed that the freedom of the formerly enslaved had to be placed on a secure basis. He knew what he was up against. Witnessing rampant "lawlessness" in his district and finding "more disloyalty now than in '61," Sheridan removed officials who had been empowered under Johnson's policies—including the governors of both states—and conducted a massive registration of newly enfranchised Black voters.

Neither Sheridan nor any of the other military governors had great resources at their disposals. The Army of Occupation had been dwindling in size since the spring of 1865; roughly 20,000 soldiers were left to enforce the Military Reconstruction Acts, most of whom were stationed in or near the larger towns and only scattered about across the countryside. The Freedmen's Bureau, authorized to take charge of abandoned rebel lands and supervise the implementation of a free labor system, was already having its operations curtailed. And despite hopes that there would be supportive people in the southern white population, few such allies could be found. Indeed, hostility to the Republican reconstruction project and to Black suffrage in particular continued to simmer if not boil over in many parts of the South. It assumed deadly incarnation in white paramilitary organizations like the Ku Klux Klan, which came to life with the Reconstruction Acts.

Congressional Republicans did have some allies in their effort to turn the rebellious South and its new Black citizens into components of the nation-state they were building. Many were northern missionaries and social reformers, often filled with evangelical zeal, who set up schools and churches designed to advance literacy, Christianity, the values of thrift and industry, and the formation of patriarchal families among the freedpeople. Many others were US Army officers, often serving in the Freedmen's Bureau and locally based detachments, who offered freedmen and women an opportunity to have their grievances redressed and to find measures of justice and protection against the retribution of defeated rebels. Some were entrepreneurial types from the northern states, still fired by antislavery fervor, who leased or purchased plantations with hopes of tutoring freedpeople in the ways of contracts while demonstrating the economic superiority of free over enslaved labor.

But the most important allies the Republicans had were organizers who traveled into the South to give the party its first real footing along with the Black constituents they mobilized to turn that footing into political power. And no organization was more important to the undertaking than the **Union League**.

Emerging in 1862 and 1863 to rally public support for the Lincoln administration and the war, the League followed the federal army into the occupied South and, once the fighting formally ended, did political work mainly among white Unionists who resided in the hill and mountain districts, outside the plantation belt. But once the Reconstruction Acts provided for a Black male franchise and voter registration, League organizers fanned out into the countryside, particularly into the plantation counties, where African Americans lived in greatest numbers. Associated with the national Republican Party, the League attracted a diverse lot of activists. Some were northern Republicans with experience

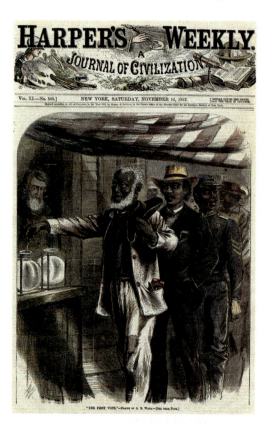

≡ **"The First Vote"**   In this sympathetic portrayal of Black men casting their first vote in 1867, the artist has represented individuals who symbolize respectable, responsible citizens worthy of the vote, including an artisan (note the tools in his pocket) and a Union soldier.

in the military and Freedmen's Bureau, and some were southern white Unionists who had already helped establish Leagues in white-majority counties. But more and more important were African Americans who had served in the federal army, attended freedmen's conventions, or preached the gospel, especially ministers of the African Methodist Episcopal (AME) Church. The work of these Union League organizers was especially difficult and dangerous. Intent on mobilizing freedpeople, they often fell victim to swift and deadly retaliation at the hands of white landowners and vigilantes. Secrecy and armed self-defense were crucial.

The success of Union League organizers could hardly have been predicted. Although more than a few Republicans worried that new Black voters might be manipulated by their employers, freedmen confounded these fears. Building on communications networks and spiritual communities they had forged while enslaved, they not only registered to vote in overwhelming numbers; they also resisted the threats of white Democrats, marched to the polls in legions, participated in the writing of new state constitutions, and, with few exceptions, gave their support to the Republican Party. Without question, at a very critical moment, they enabled the Republicans to consolidate their regime.

Black People and Republicans: A Complex Alliance

The developing alliance between Republicans in Washington, DC, and the formerly enslaved, mediated at the grassroots by the Union League and party activists, was logical, necessary, and deeply problematic. Beyond question, they had a shared interest in emancipation, the military defeat of the enslavers, birthright citizenship, Black male suffrage, and the establishment of the Republican Party in the South. Without Black votes, the Republicans had little chance to move forward with their projects of nation building: very few southern whites were willing to join them, and most saw the Black vote and the political mobilizations it made possible as an illegitimate outrage. And without Republican support, the freedpeople would have faced much difficulty in exercising their new rights or adequately protecting themselves from vigilante violence.

But the alliance was as tense as it was extraordinary. Although they may have shared a commitment to free labor, civic equality, and political democracy, Republican leaders and freedpeople occupied very different social stations. Republicans had put together a complex coalition, but their policymaking heart increasingly beat for the interests of manufacturers, financiers, and other propertied producers; they were concerned mainly with advancing industrialization, stabilizing money and credit, reviving the cotton economy, and drawing more and more of the United States into the capitalist marketplace. The freedpeople, by contrast, were overwhelmingly working people who owned very little property and had to labor for employers in the fields as well as on docks, on railroads, in mines, in forests, and in towns and cities. Their aspiration was to escape economic dependency and provide for themselves. Short of that, they struggled to limit their exploitation, improve their material conditions, rebuild their communities, and use the political process to improve their prospects. Never before or since has a section of the American working class been as closely aligned with a political party as freedmen were with the Republicans. But it was not "their" party.

Black Power in the South

For a time, especially in the early phases of Military Reconstruction, the alliance not only held but offered participants political rewards well beyond what any of them anticipated. African American activism was the key. Despite dangers and direct threats, they organized their communities, rallied to the Republican banner, and turned out to vote in stunning numbers (80 to 90 percent of those eligible), drawing as they often did on forms of communication and self-defense that they had fashioned when enslaved. Indeed, politics was for African Americans very much a collective undertaking and one in which lines of age and gender could become blurred. It is true, of course, that the franchise was extended only to Black men, and without doubt it tipped the balances of community power and authority further in their direction at a time when all sorts of social relations were being renegotiated. But participation and important forms of decision-making were more widely dispersed, connecting the electoral sphere with other arenas of social and political life. Black women not only attended rallies and meetings and registered their views; they became so deeply involved with the expression of party loyalties that the vote itself could be seen as something of a family property. Some of them gathered and transmitted necessary information (as did children); some taught in rural schools; and some helped defend public assemblies from attack. Where possible, Black women accompanied voting-age men to the ballot box, providing added cover and steeling men's nerves.

Black electoral support allowed the Republican Party to strengthen its hold on the national government and to extend its reach into the South. In 1868, Black ballots gave Republican presidential candidate Ulysses S. Grant the majority of popular votes cast—he won only a minority of the white vote—and, owing to African American turnout in the rebellious states, a comfortable margin in the electoral college as well. Grant won six of them (see Map 16.3). As these states began to hold elections under their new constitutions, which enfranchised Black men and disfranchised some of the rebels, the Republicans then won control of the governorships and legislatures most everywhere (Virginia was the exception) and took charge of county and municipal governments in many places, especially in the plantation districts. It was a political revolution of the sort that few modern societies have ever witnessed, displacing a wealthy and formidable elite that had claimed local sovereignty with far more humble officials directly tied to the newly proclaimed sovereignty of the nation.

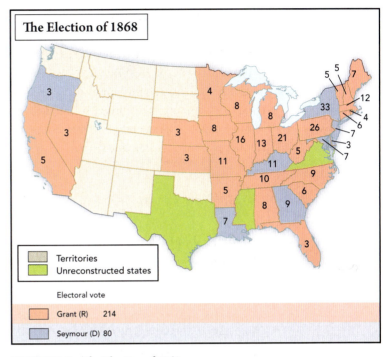

The Election of 1868

Territories	
Unreconstructed states	

Electoral vote

	Grant (R)	214
	Seymour (D)	80

≡ **MAP 16.3** **The Election of 1868**

In no way was the political revolution more striking or consequential than in the election of African Americans, most of whom had recently been enslaved, to office. Two Black men—Hiram R. Revels and Blanche K. Bruce, both from Mississippi—were elevated to the US Senate. Sixteen Black men, many from the secessionist stronghold of South Carolina, would sit in the House of Representatives. But as dramatic as election to Congress was, Black officeholding in the states and localities counted for even more. Nearly 300 Black people served in constitutional conventions called under Military Reconstruction, where they helped move state governments in far more inclusive and democratic directions. More than 100 won election or appointment to posts having jurisdiction over entire states, including one as lieutenant governor of Louisiana—P. B. S. Pinchback, who would briefly serve as governor when the sitting governor was impeached. And nearly 800 took seats in state legislatures, in some cases forming majorities (South Carolina and Mississippi) or near majorities (Louisiana), where they battled to create new post-emancipation societies. One northern journalist, observing the changes in the South Carolina statehouse, saw "the spectacle of a society turned bottomside up."

Yet such a "spectacle" was most evident in the rural counties, where freedpeople composed the majority of the population. There, in the one-time realm of enslavers, Black men—maybe as many as 1,400 or 1,500 of them—now held

≡ **African American Office Holders** Along with the many other African Americans who held public office in the 1860s and 1870s, the Black men pictured were elected to Congress, disproving critics who charged that Black officeholding during the Reconstruction era led to irresponsible government.

the levers of power: as jurors, magistrates, county commissioners, tax assessors, school superintendents, coroners, constables, and even as sheriffs. It was an unprecedented political transformation that directly threatened the social order that southern whites had known. As Georgia's Black Republican leader Henry McNeal Turner explained, white Democrats "do not care so much about Congress admitting negroes to their halls but they don't want negroes over them at home."

Republican Rule

It surely was a world "turned bottomside up." Aghast, white Democrats howled about the onset of "Negro rule." In point of fact, however, it was whites, not Black people, who predominated among Republican leaders and officeholders during this period, especially among those who took the most visible and formidable seats of power. National offices, like senators and congressmen, as well as statewide offices, were filled overwhelmingly by white men. Governorships (except for Pinchback's brief reign) were filled exclusively by white men, and outside of South Carolina, Mississippi, and Louisiana, Republican legislative delegations were majority white. Even on the local level, most of the offices—especially those with police or taxing power—were held by whites. It was, more accurately, "Republican rule," in which the predominant base of support was Black.

So, why the alarm? What the idea of "Negro rule" did capture was the significant shift in political power that Military Reconstruction made possible: from the former slaveholding elite toward a number of groups who had previously been outsiders to southern politics. In addition to the freedmen, they included white northerners, known derisively as **carpetbaggers**, who had served in the US Army and Freedmen's Bureau, had taken up planting or merchandising, or had engaged in teaching and missionary work; white southerners, known even more derisively as **scalawags**, who had been Unionists or unenthusiastic rebels, had been non-slaveholders or small slaveholders, or who had lived beyond the immediate orbit of the planter class; Black northerners, some having escaped enslavement, who had been educated and had come South with the army or the church; and some Black southerners who had been free before the war. Together they were substantially less wealthy, less experienced politically, and less committed to perpetuating the old plantation order than the antebellum elite while, for the most part, owing their positions to Black votes.

Although their programs and achievements varied some from place to place, the Republican regimes that took charge of the rebellious states in 1868 began to carry out sweeping reforms and innovations. They rebuilt the region's infrastructure, reorganized its political life, adjusted the balances of local power, and tied the fortunes of its new governments closely to the national state. Republicans were responsible for creating the first systems of public education in the South (serving white as well as Black people, though in a segregated fashion) while establishing or significantly increasing the resources of public institutions such as hospitals, asylums, orphanages, and penitentiaries. They raised taxes and shifted the burden from individuals (head taxes) to landed and personal property owners, in some cases forcing plantation land onto the market for nonpayment. In alliance with railroad developers, they repaired lines destroyed during the war and constructed new ones that reached into areas previously on the edge of the market economy and linked the South more directly to the Northeast and Midwest.

Republicans generally centralized the power of political appointments, putting it in the hands of the governors, blocked planter attempts to enforce the dependency of Black laborers, outlawed corporal punishment, and reduced both the number of capital offenses and the penalties for minor crimes. They liberalized women's ability to get a divorce, granted new property rights to women who were married, and enabled African Americans to sue and testify in court as well as sit on juries. It was a far cry from the old order, when enslavers ruled over their sovereign domains, rail and river transportation mainly connected the plantation belt with southern ports, and the public sector was scarcely more than a shell.

Paramilitary Counterrevolution

Not surprisingly, this Republican political revolution provoked turmoil. Former enslavers, most of whom supported the Democratic Party, recognized that power and authority were changing hands and that their ability to enforce the submission of Black workers was seriously compromised. And when their efforts to convince freedpeople to follow their leads came to little, they turned very quickly to methods of battle that had long maintained order under slavery: paramilitarism and vigilante

≡ **"Worse Than Slavery"**   Some imagined that the harassment and violence that many African Americans suffered in the Reconstruction was less tolerable than slavery, as shown in this 1874 illustration by Thomas Nast.

violence. Paramilitary organizations like the local units known as the **Ku Klux Klan** were generally composed of rebel officers and other young war veterans who had been paroled or allowed to desert without surrendering their arms, ammunition, and horses. They began to police the countryside—much as slave patrols had once done—harassing and punishing freedpeople who took advantage of their freedom, showed signs of economic independence, or behaved in ways regarded as insubordinate.

But more than anything else, the paramilitaries moved against local Black leaders and their allies: Union League organizers, Black grassroots activists and candidates for office, sympathetic teachers and ministers, and African Americans determined to vote for the Republican Party. Many Black leaders were assassinated or driven away, families and communities were terrorized, and schools and churches were torched. So fierce and successful could the paramilitaries be that in 1868 they enabled the Democrats to carry the presidential electoral votes of Georgia and Virginia.

The big question was whether the federal government together with the loyal state governments in the South would use the political and military means at their disposal to protect Republican voters and officeholders and secure the power of their regimes. For a time, the answer was "yes." The Grant administration dispatched federal troops to quell serious disturbances and suppress the most outrageous examples of vigilantism. Congress, in turn, launched an investigation of the Klan that resulted in legislation known as the **Enforcement Acts** of 1870 and 1871, which outlawed "conspiracies" that deprived Black people of their civil and political rights. Closer to the ground, some of the Republican governors reorganized state militias—sometimes with Black troops heavily represented—and put them to good use in Klan-infested areas.

16.5   The Weakening of the Radicals and the Ending of Reconstruction

❙❙❙ Explain how and why the Reconstruction experiment came undone.

But the political temper of the times was shifting away from the Radical faction of the Republican Party and toward the more numerous Moderates, thereby favoring a retraction of federal involvement in southern affairs. In part, it was the empowerment of the formerly enslaved and in part the impeachment of President Andrew Johnson by the House of Representatives for violations of federal laws that provoked a backlash against the Radicals. It was also the growing influence of financial and industrial interests in Republican policymaking circles. What would a Radical agenda in the South mean for the governance and economy of the nation? Reconstruction was first hobbled by those who were supervising it, and then it was overthrown by those who had once been Confederate rebels.

The Impeachment of Andrew Johnson

The Constitution of the United States allows for the **impeachment**, conviction, and removal of a sitting president for "treason, bribery, or other high crimes and misdemeanors" (Article II, Section 4), but as of 1868, no sitting president had ever been so charged. There was a high bar for removal. The House of Representatives first had to impeach—effectively indict—the offending president by a majority vote, and then the Senate—effectively sitting as a jury—had to convict by a vote of at least two-thirds of its members. Once removed from office, according to the Constitution, the convicted president could never again run for public office.

But after several years of fighting with Andrew Johnson, the Republicans were fed up. He was continually tampering with their Reconstruction policies and, even though Congress overrode his vetoes, he retained the power to replace officials acceptable to the Republicans with those Johnson believed were more loyal to him and might sabotage the Republican projects. Finally, they determined to act and brought articles of impeachment against Johnson for doing just this sort of thing—specifically for violating the recently passed **Tenure of Office Act**, which required Senate approval for the filling of certain federal posts.

The House of Representatives quickly supported the articles and voted to impeach Johnson. The case then went to the Senate, where the Republicans were in the majority but divided between Radical and Moderate factions. And although the Radicals and some of the Moderates were ready to convict, other Moderates had serious doubts. Should Johnson be removed, he would be replaced, not by a sitting vice president—there was none, Johnson having been Lincoln's vice president—but by the president pro tempore of the Senate, Ohio's Benjamin Wade. Wade was a prominent leader of the Radical faction at a time when the winds were shifting away from the Radicals in the Republican Party. He strongly supported Military Reconstruction in the South as well as policies more favorable to labor and small producers than the industrialists and financial interests who were becoming more and more powerful in the Party and the nation.

A President Wade was too much for the Moderates to allow, and so, after receiving assurances from Johnson that he would no longer trouble them, they helped find the votes to prevent his conviction and removal. Johnson survived, the first and last president to suffer impeachment (or threat of impeachment) for another century, and the Radicals sustained a blow from which they would never really recover.

Economic and Political Turbulence

The hobbling of Reconstruction was accompanied and influenced by the painful impact of an economic panic in 1873 (discussed in Chapter 17) and by the widespread retrenchments it ushered in. Not only were the financial and manufacturing sectors of the Republican coalition hard hit, but the labor unrest that quickly erupted shook their confidence. Hundreds of textile, railroad, and mine workers went out on strike to oppose the wage cuts their employers imposed, and many thousands were thrown out of work in the deepening economic depression that followed. Together these workers took part in massive demonstrations in industrializing cities of the Northeast and Midwest that called upon state and municipal governments to help mitigate their suffering, perhaps by initiating public works projects to provide needed employment.

As a result of the social unrest spreading around them, northern employers and financiers felt a growing sympathy for southern planters who had been complaining about the insolence and political insubordination of their Black laborers. Further, the Grant administration had less and less enthusiasm for coming to the aid of embattled Republicans at any level in the South. When, in such an atmosphere, the Democratic Party reclaimed control of the House of Representatives in 1874, the arms of the Republican state were further weakened and their ability to guide a variety of ambitious projects hatched during the War of the Rebellion was placed in jeopardy.

While the Panic and its aftermath aggravated tensions between Republican leaders at the national level and Black constituents in the South, they also aggravated tensions among Republicans within the South. Well before the economic panic, Black Republicans were feeling ill at ease with the leadership that white Republicans were willing to provide. They feared their status as junior partners to the whites was too deeply etched, their aspirations and concerns poorly understood or ignored, their claim to a fair share of offices rejected, and their vulnerabilities to violence insufficiently addressed. One Black South Carolinian bitterly complained about white Republicans who made "loud and big promises to the freedmen till they got elected to office, then did not do one single thing," who refused to support the nomination of "a colored man" for major office, who "removed a number of black trial justices," and who "disarmed a number of black militia companies." "The first duty of any race," he insisted, "is to see to their own interests specially."

Black discontent soon forced white Republican officeholders, especially governors, to make a critical choice. They could attend more fully to the interests of their Black supporters and risk alienating white ones, or they could curry the favor of moderate Democrats by cutting taxes and spending, decrying "corruption," championing "reform," and offering Democrats a share of the patronage and offices. Most chose the latter, but even that was to little avail. Democrats had no inclination to join hands with white Republicans. They preferred to rally southern whites against the threat of "Negro rule" and rely on paramilitaries to achieve what ballots might fail to do: drive the Republicans and their Black supporters from political power.

Redemption

The Ku Klux Klan may have been targeted by the federal government, but its place was soon taken by a variety of rifle clubs known as the White Leagues or Red Shirts—closely tied to the Democratic Party and fixed upon dismantling and destroying the opposition. Using networks of kinship, patronage, and military service that crossed county lines, they brought a reign of terror into the plantation districts and

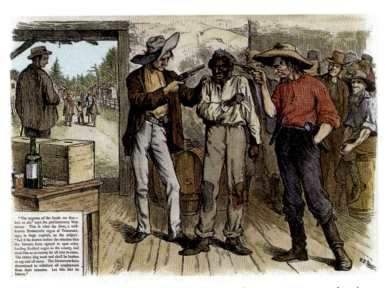

≡ **Voter Intimidation**   In 1875 and 1876, paramilitary units connected with the Democratic Party helped topple the last Republican governments in Mississippi, Louisiana, and South Carolina.

eventually to the doors of the state legislatures. Rifle club members (who, unlike Klansmen, did not bother with disguises and therefore did not technically violate the Enforcement Acts) attacked Republican meetings and incited riots that claimed the lives of many Black people in attendance. They beat and murdered local Black and white Republican leaders, threatened prospective voters, and then menaced them at the polls. Even if Republicans managed to win elections, the rifle clubs tried to prevent successful candidates from taking office or to drive them off once they did.

More and more counties were redeemed in this way, undermining Republican state and local regimes or isolating them in a rising sea of paramilitarism. In Louisiana, while several thousand White Leaguers brazenly attempted to oust the Republican governor and legislature in 1874 (failing only because of the last-minute intervention of federal troops), their rural counterparts did them better. They crippled or overthrew Republican officials in at least eight parishes in a wave of bloody violence. Red River Parish was particularly gruesome. There, in August, the duly elected sheriff, tax collector, and justice of the peace together with a registrar, a Republican attorney, and several Black supporters were summarily slaughtered near the county seat of Coushatta.

Remarkably, African Americans maintained their loyalty to the Republican Party, and as white Republicanism shrank in the face of paramilitarism and Black assertiveness, they became the mainstays of the party. Their support in states like South Carolina, Mississippi, Louisiana, and Florida enabled Republican regimes to hold on. Black officeholding in the South grew during the early 1870s. It may have peaked around 1874 and, in some localities, Black militants effectively stared the rifle clubs down. For all of their saber-rattling, night-riding, and terrorism, the Democrats, without massive electoral fraud, would have remained on the losing end, out of power, especially in the Deep South, where Black political strength was greatest.

The Contested Election of 1876

Yet the reach of the Republican state would extend only so far. Republicans had crushed the slaveholders' rebellion, abolished enslavement, fortified the power of the federal government, established a national citizenship, and organized the party in the rebellious states with a social base that had previously been enslaved. They had imposed martial law and prescribed a raft of political and social conditions that had to be met before those states could regain their status in what was now a nation. And they also succeeded, to the benefit of Black men both inside and outside of the rebellious states, in enacting the last of the Reconstruction Amendments, the Fifteenth (1870), which guaranteed that the "right to vote," would not be denied on account of "race, color, or previous condition of servitude" (though not on account of "sex" as woman suffrage activists had demanded).

This was the political and social revolution that had been made, and for that revolution to continue or to be fully preserved the force of federal arms would have to be flexed for some time to come. But the long-term interests of the Republican Party were increasingly aligned with property and capital, not with the Black laborers who had made the revolution possible and whose lives and rights were most in jeopardy. As a result, little by little, in the halls of Congress and on the ground in the South, the revolution was being rolled back, pushing the Radicals to the margins nationally and leaving Republican Party supporters in jeopardy in the former rebellious states. How would this end? And who would the winners be?

The die was finally cast in 1876. That year a presidential election set Republican Rutherford B. Hayes of Ohio against Democrat Samuel J. Tilden of New York, and when all the ballots were counted, no winner could be declared. Tilden, it seemed, had bucked the trend of the previous four election cycles. He won the popular vote and was within one vote of having a majority in the electoral college. But the returns of South Carolina, Florida, and Louisiana were in dispute, owing to charges of fraud and harassment at the polling places (see Map 16.4). For a time, tempers were so frayed that it appeared hostilities might again erupt. At the very least it was unclear whether a victor could be determined by inauguration day, then March 4, making for an unprecedented political and constitutional crisis. In the meantime, the disputed vote also brought dual state governments in South Carolina and Louisiana, one Democratic and one Republican, each claiming to be the rightful authority. In this tense atmosphere, Democratic rifle clubs made the first move. They surrounded the Republican governors and legislators in the state capitals and demanded that they surrender their offices.

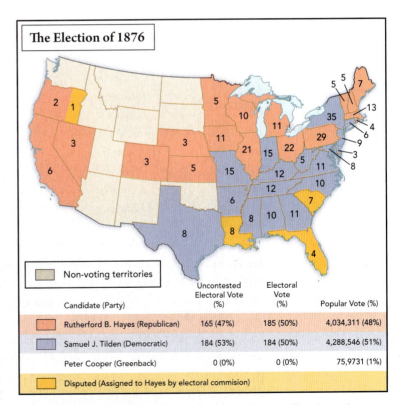

The Election of 1876

Candidate (Party)	Uncontested Electoral Vote (%)	Electoral Vote (%)	Popular Vote (%)
Rutherford B. Hayes (Republican)	165 (47%)	185 (50%)	4,034,311 (48%)
Samuel J. Tilden (Democratic)	184 (53%)	184 (50%)	4,288,546 (51%)
Peter Cooper (Greenback)	0 (0%)	0 (0%)	75,9731 (1%)

Non-voting territories

Disputed (Assigned to Hayes by electoral commision)

☰ **MAP 16.4   The Election of 1876**   The election was marred by white violence and vote-rigging, and Congress deadlocked on choosing a victor. An Electoral Commission eventually determined that Rutherford B. Hayes would be sworn in. As a bow to Democrats, Hayes then withdrew the last federal troops from the South.

Contrasting Views of Reconstruction

Reconstruction is widely regarded as comprising a revolution in American society and politics, but revolutions often have their limits as well as promises. On the one hand, Reconstruction fundamentally changed the South. The Thirteenth, Fourteenth, and Fifteenth Amendments established limited economic and political equality, the Freedmen's Bureau protected African Americans, and, perhaps most obviously, the federal government divided the defeated Confederacy into military districts under direct army supervision. As a result, hundreds of Black people served in state legislatures, and sixteen served in Congress. Therefore, the postwar South showed the beneficial effects of Congressional Reconstruction.

THE "STRONG" GOVERNMENT 1869—1877.

≡ Political Cartoon (Part 1): "Strong" Government.

On the other hand, although the federal government made limited attempts to expand equality for freedpeople, it was unable to achieve real equality. Relatively few African Americans won federal elections, tenants and sharecroppers enjoyed few rights, and vigilantes terrorized free Black people and their supporters (see Chapter 17). As a result, **Redeemers** quickly retook control over southern Democrats, ensuring an end to Reconstruction.

This two-part cartoon from 1890 shows how many southerners viewed Reconstruction. In the first image, "The Solid South" is seen struggling under the "Carpet Bag and Bayonet Rule" of the "Strong" US government, led by President Ulysses S. Grant, who is seen riding among bayonets with an escort of two federal soldiers. In the background, we see a destroyed and occupied South.

We see a different picture in the second image. Under the presidency of Rutherford B. Hayes, the "Carpet Bag and Bayonet Rule" is being plowed under by the president's "Let'em Alone Policy." Under this "Weak" government, the South flourishes amid factories and fertile fields. A white man, presumably a landowner, gives orders to an African American tenant farmer.

THE "WEAK" GOVERNMENT 1877–1881.

≡ **Political Cartoon (Part 2): "Weak" Government.**

CONSIDER THIS

According to the cartoonist, why did southern states desire a "weak" government? How would an African American living in the South in 1890 have viewed these two time periods?

Seeking to find a settlement and defuse the crisis, Congress appointed an independent electoral commission and, with a thin majority of Republican members, the commission determined that all the disputed electoral votes would go to Rutherford Hayes, giving him the presidency. In the process, however, Hayes made a devil's bargain of his own, known as the **Compromise of 1877**. To appease the Democrats, he agreed to give them some important posts in his cabinet and, far more important, he ordered the remaining US Army troops in the rebellious states to return to their barracks rather than aid the besieged Republicans of South Carolina and Louisiana. As a result, just as Hayes took his oath of office the last of the Republican governments fell. The Reconstruction experiment was over.

Conclusion: The Limits of Revolution

The War of the Rebellion and Reconstruction are widely regarded as comprising a revolution in American society and politics: a second American revolution, some have called it. And, indeed, it was revolutionary in the nineteenth-century world to abolish slavery without any compensation to enslavers and on the backs of their military defeat. Along with this, the political power of the former enslavers and of the big southern landowners was dramatically curtailed in national politics while the civil and political rights of the people they had enslaved were established. No one, in any part of the United States at the beginning of 1861, would have imagined such a country four years later. Only the Haitian Revolution (1791–1804, discussed in Chapter 8) is comparable in its reach and reverberations, and even it did not go so far in shifting political power to the formerly enslaved.

But revolutions often have their limits as well as promises, and this one did on the matters of private property, economic growth, race, and gender. Only a small group of Radical Republicans dared suggest that Confederate rebels be punished for treason, have their lands confiscated and redistributed to Black people and white yeoman farmers, and subject the rebellious South to a lengthy period of federal supervision. The Republican Party, more generally, was too committed to private property to confiscate and redistribute land, even the land of traitors to the republic. It was too committed to the country's economic growth to risk the future of the cotton economy of the South by enabling Black laborers to become landowners. It was too committed to developing the trans-Mississippi West into a commodity-producing region to permit Indigenous people to be incorporated into the country on a basis of citizenship and maintain their ways of life and culture. And it was too committed to patriarchy and the nuclear family to disrupt the gender hierarchy of households and the country at large by awarding women the right to vote. We still live with the consequences of what they did and didn't do.

WHAT IF the Confederate Rebels Had Been Punished as Traitors?

In many respects, the leniency of the federal government toward the Confederate rebels was astonishing. During the American Revolution, loyalists were driven off and sometimes killed by the patriots, and once the Revolution ended, many were forced into exile and had their property confiscated. They were regarded as traitors, and nothing was more damning in political life.

President Lincoln, moderate though he was, nonetheless called the Confederates traitors and their rebellion treasonous. Some Radical Republicans thought that, in order to prevent another such rebellion, the leadership should be severely punished and the basis of their wealth and power destroyed by confiscating their lands and redistributing them to the formerly enslaved and to humble white people who did not support the Confederacy. They were not alone. Many people in the northern states, especially those whose husbands and sons fought and died in the bloody war, worried that without an iron hand crushing down on the rebels the war would have been fought in vain.

What if, upon the surrender of Confederate armies, the top political and military leaders of the rebellion—Jefferson Davis, Alexander Stephens, Robert E. Lee, the war governors, members of the Confederate congress, the secessionist delegates who precipitated the war—were taken into custody, charged with treason, and made to stand trial? Most would have been convicted and sentenced either to long prison terms or execution, the usual punishment for treason. What if the richest slaveholding planters were sent into exile—a version of colonization, as Frederick Douglass once suggested to Lincoln—and their allies disfranchised for at least a decade? What if the plantations owned by people who had participated in the rebellion were confiscated by the federal government and—in the manner of Sherman's Field Orders No. 15—redistributed to formerly enslaved families in 40-acre plots, enough for them to grow not only subsistence but some market crops? And what if the federal government chose to protect white family farmers, too, and used its resources to enable them, as well as freed farmers, to get necessary credit at low rates of interest, so that they would not fall into debt and lose their land?

These are not pipe dreams. In one form or another they were all proposed at the time either by political leaders or ordinary citizens. What would the postwar United States have looked like if there was "malice" toward some and "charity" for those who were loyal to and helped save the country from the Confederate rebellion?

Document 16.1: Committee of Freedmen on Edisto Island, South Carolina, to the Freedmen's Bureau Commissioner, October 20 or 21, 1865

In the fall of 1865, under orders of President Johnson, land that had been confiscated and distributed for exclusive Black settlement along the South Carolina coast and its Sea Islands (in accordance with Sherman's Field Orders No. 15) was returned to its former owners. A committee of freedmen then wrote to the commissioner of the Freedmen's Bureau, General Oliver Howard, to protest the president's decision.

[Edisto Island, S.C., October 20 or 21, 1865]

General   It Is with painfull Hearts that we the committe address you, we Have thorougholy considered the order which you wished us to Sighn, we wish we could do so but cannot feel our rights Safe If we do so,

General we want Homestead's; we were promised Homestead's by the government, If It does not carry out the promises Its agents made to us, If the government Haveing concluded to befriend Its late enemies and to neglect to observe the principles of common faith between Its self and us Its allies In the war you said was over, now takes away from them all right to the soil they stand upon save such as they can get by again working for *your* late and thier *all time ememies.*–If the government does so we are left In a more unpleasant condition than our former

we are at the mercy of those who are combined to prevent us from getting land enough to lay our Fathers bones upon. We Have property In Horses, cattle, carriages, & articles of furniture, but we are landless and Homeless, from the Homes we Have lived In In the past we can only do one of three things   Step Into the public *road or the sea* or remain on them working as In former time and subject to thire will as then. We can not resist It In any way without being driven out Homeless upon the road.

You will see this Is not the condition of really freemen

You ask us to forgive the land owners of our Island, *You* only lost your right arm. In war and might forgive them. The man who tied me to a tree & gave me 39 lashes & who stripped and flogged my mother & my sister & who will not let me stay In His empty Hut except I will do His planting & be Satisfied with His price & who combines with others to keep away land from me well knowing I would not Have any thing to do with Him If I Had land of my own.–that man, I cannot well forgive. Does It look as If He Has forgiven me, seeing How He tries to keep me In a condition of Helplessness

General, we cannot remain Here In such condition and If the government permits them to come back we ask It to Help us to reach land where we shall not be slaves nor compelled to work for those who would treat us as such

we Have not been treacherous, we Have not for selfish motives allied to us those who suffered like us from a common enemy & then Haveing gained *our* purpose left our allies In thier Hands   There Is no rights secured to us there Is no law likely to be made which our Hands can reach. The state will make laws that we shall not be able to Hold land even If we pay for It Landless, Homeless. Voteless. we can only pray to god & Hope for *His Help, your Infuence & assistance* With consideration of esteem your Obt Servts In behalf of the people

	Henry Bram
Committe	Ishmael Moultrie
	yates Sampson

Source: Henry Bram et al. to Major General O. O. Howard, [October 20 or 21, 1865], B 53 1865, Letters Received, ser. 15, Washington Hdqrs., RG 105.

Document 16.2: Speech of Representative Thaddeus Stevens (PA) to Congress, March 1867

This speech was delivered by Radical Republican Thaddeus Stevens of Pennsylvania in March 1867 in support of legislation that would punish Confederate rebels and offer necessary rewards to Black and white loyalists in the South.

The fifth section [of the 1862 Confiscation Act] enacts that—"To insure the speedy termination of the present rebellion, it shall be the duty of the President of the United States to cause the seizure of all the estates and property, money, stocks, credits, and effects of the persons hereinafter named in this section, and apply and use the same and the proceeds thereof for the support of the Army of the United States."

The cause of the war was slavery. We have liberated the slaves. It is our duty to protect them, and provide for them while they are unable to provide for themselves. Have we not a right . . . "to do ourselves justice respecting the object which has caused the war," by taking lands for homesteads [for] these "objects" of the war?

Have we not a right, if we chose to go to that extent, to indemnify [compensate] ourselves for the expenses and damages caused by the war? . . .

We could be further justified in inflicting severe penalties upon this whole hostile people as "a fierce and savage people," as an "obstinate enemy," whom it is a duty to tame and punish. Our future safety requires stern justice. . . .

I must earnestly pray that [the provision granting land to freedmen] may not be defeated. On its success, in my judgment, depends not only the happiness and respectability of the colored race, but their very existence. Homesteads to them are far more valuable than the immediate right of suffrage, though both are their due.

Four million of persons have just been freed from a condition of dependence, wholly unacquainted with business transactions, kept systematically in ignorance of all their rights and of the common elements of education, without which none of any race are competent to earn an honest living, to guard against the frauds which will always be practiced on the ignorant. . . . Make them independent of their old masters, so that they may not be compelled to work for them upon unfair terms, which can only be done by giving them a small tract of land to cultivate for themselves, and you remove all this danger. You also elevate the character of the freedman. Nothing is so likely to make a man a good citizen as to make him a freeholder. Nothing will so multiply the productions of the South as to divide it into small farms. Nothing will make men so industrious and moral as to let them feel that they are above want and are the owners of the soil which they till. It will also be of service to the white inhabitants. They will have constantly among them industrious laborers, anxious to work for fair wages. How is it possible for them to cultivate their lands if these people were expelled? If Moses should lead or drive them into exile, or carry out the absurd idea of colonizing them, the South would become a barren waste.

Source: Speech of Hon. T. Stevens, of Pennsylvania, delivered in the House of Representatives, March 19, 1867: on the bill (H.R. no. 20) relative to damages to loyal men, and for other purposes.

Thinking About Contingency

1. How did the Edisto Island freedmen justify their right to the land?
2. Besides the formerly enslaved people themselves, who might have supported an alternative Reconstruction plan such as the one proposed by Stevens?
3. What were the challenges to the plan to severely punish Confederate leaders and to turn a plantation-based society into one based on small yeoman farms?
4. To what extent would this plan have changed the socioeconomic and political history of the United States or shaped relations between Black and white Americans?

REVIEW QUESTIONS

1. What visions did the formerly enslaved and free Black people have for a post-emancipation South, and why did those visions stir fears among many white southerners?

2. Why was President Johnson so strongly opposed to Republican Reconstruction plans, and how far were Republicans prepared to go to transform the South?

3. Why did the Republican-controlled Congress extend voting rights to Black men but refuse to do so for any women?

4. How did the Republican Party build a base of support in the southern states, and how much political power did formerly enslaved people gain in the process?

5. What did Republican Reconstruction governments try to accomplish in the southern states, and how were they driven from power?

6. How much of a revolution did Republican Reconstruction carry through?

KEY TERMS

birthright citizenship (p. 661)

carpetbaggers (p. 672)

Civil Rights Act of 1866 (p. 660)

Compromise of 1877 (p. 682)

Enforcement Acts (p. 674)

Fifteenth Amendment (p. 650)

Fourteenth Amendment (p. 661)

freedmen's conventions (p. 651)

impeachment (p. 675)

Juneteenth (p. 658)

Ku Klux Klan (p. 674)

Military Reconstruction Acts
  (p. 662)

Redeemers (p. 681)

scalawags (p. 673)

Tenure of Office Act (p. 675)

Thirteenth Amendment (p. 659)

Union League (p. 668)

Women's Loyal National League
  (p. 658)

RECOMMENDED READINGS

Justin Behrend, *Reconstructing Democracy: Grassroots Politics in the Deep South After the Civil War* (University of Georgia Press, 2017).

Gregory Downs, *After Appomattox: Military Occupation and the Ends of War* (Harvard University Press, 2019).

W. E. B. Du Bois, *Black Reconstruction in America, 1860–1880* (1936; Free Press, 1998).

Ellen Dubois, *Feminism and Suffrage: The Emergence of an Independent Women's Movement in America, 1848–1869* (Cornell University Press, 1978).

Carole Emberton, *Beyond Redemption, Race, Violence, and the American South After the Civil War* (University of Chicago, 2015).

Eric Foner, *Reconstruction: America's Unfinished Revolution, 1863–1877* (Harper and Row, 1988).

Eric Foner, *The Second Founding* (W.W. Norton, 2020).

Steven Hahn, *A Nation Under Our Feet: Black Political Struggles in the Rural South from Slavery to the Great Migration* (Harvard University Press, 2003).

Edward Magdol, *A Right to the Land: Essays on the Freedman's Community* (Praeger, 1977).

Alaina Roberts, *I've Been Here All the While: Black Freedom on Native Land* (University of Pennsylvania Press, 2021).

Julie Saville, *The Work of Reconstruction* (Cambridge University Press, 1994).

Capitalism and the Gilded Age
1873–1890

Chapter Outline

☰ **The Dynamics of Capitalism**   In this *Puck* cartoon from May 1882, oppressed workers pull a carriage carrying Jay Gould and other Gilded Age magnates.

In November 1882, a remarkable banquet took place at Delmonico's in New York City, well known as a watering hole for the city's elite. The occasion was a celebration of Englishman Herbert Spencer, who had just completed a seven-week tour of the United States and was widely known for his philosophical theories, resonating with those of fellow Englishman, scientist Charles Darwin, of a struggle for existence in the social world in which the naturally talented had risen to the top. "Survival of the fittest," he termed it.

As one might expect, some of America's most important intellectuals and cultural leaders were in attendance—journalists E. L. Godkin and Charles Dana, writer and diplomat Charles Francis Adams, historian and philosopher John Fiske, clergyman and social reformer Henry Ward Beecher—but they were joined by a veritable who's who of the country's new industrial age. These included iron manufacturer Abram Hewitt, railroad executive Chauncey Depew, telegraph pioneer Cyrus Field, and

Timeline

1869	1871	1873	1875	1877	1879

1869 > Completion of first transcontinental railroad

1872 > *New York Sun* breaks the story of the Credit Mobilier scandal

1873 > Financial panic ushers in nationwide economic depression; in *Slaughterhouse Cases* Supreme Court begins to undercut the Fourteenth Amendment

1875 > Andrew Carnegie establishes first steel mill

1876 > Custer's cavalry killed by Sioux forces in the Battle of Little Bighorn; in *U.S. v. Cruikshank* the Supreme Court rules that voting rights remain a state prerogative

steel magnate Andrew Carnegie, who worshipped Spencer (in his correspondence Carnegie addressed Spencer as "dear master"). Over an extravagant meal, they feted Spencer in the grandest terms, as both a visionary and a scientist. He appeared to validate the authority they had come to hold, offering them a way to understand themselves as the products, not of corrupt or exploitative practices, but of natural laws of evolutionary change and immutable progress. One speaker even suggested that the Civil War might have been avoided if southern elites had been familiar with Spencer's writings.

American capitalism was on full display at the banquet at Delmonico's. Capitalism as a system, that is, which is not just about the exchange of goods and services with an eye toward profit, evidence of which can be found over many centuries. Modern capitalism is much more. It is a massive web of social, economic, and political relationships

1881	1883	1885	1887	1889	1891

1883 ▸ In *Civil Rights Cases* Supreme Court further limits protections of the Fourteenth Amendment

1886 ▸ In *Santa Clara County v. Southern Pacific Railroad* Supreme Court rules that corporations have rights of personhood under the Fourteenth Amendment

that depend upon and support one another, as the attendees at Delmonico's suggest. Its development requires that most people lose the ability to provide for themselves, deprived of access to land and other productive resources, and must work for others in order to earn their daily bread. It requires that land, labor, and other forms of property become commodities, capable of being bought and sold. It requires new technologies that enable mass production and distribution and link economic actors across great geographical spaces. And it requires that states, through their legislative and judicial arms, secure the means by which essential transactions can take place: contracts, financial obligations, patents, money and banking, property rights, and the relative distribution of power in the marketplace. Capitalism had to be forged.

All of this took time and faced a good deal of skepticism and resistance. Capitalism represented a novel and radical force, providing both new opportunities for enrichment and new conditions of dependence. Although features that we associate with capitalism and capitalist societies could be observed from early on in the settlement of colonial North America and even more so with the market expansions and intensifications of the first half of the nineteenth century, capitalism truly took hold in the United States during the War of the Rebellion. This was not so much because the demands of war gave a great boost to manufacturers and financiers alike, though they certainly did, but because the needs of wartime finance forged a new relationship between rising capitalists—industrialists and financiers in particular—and the federal government. It would be a bumpy but transformational ride, and it would take some time after the war for that relationship to gain traction. Yet, owing to the accumulations of wealth and power that occurred and the forms of corruption and exploitation that were also involved, the period between 1873 and 1890 would come to be called, in a phrase coined by the writer Mark Twain, "the **Gilded Age**."

17.1   A New World of Finance Capital

Describe how a new class of financiers gained power and wealth as a result of the Civil War.

Ever since the founding of the American republic, the greatest sources of wealth were to be found among large landowners—especially slaveholding planters—and merchants who were involved in the export trade. The production and sale of staple crops like cotton served as an engine of American economic growth and as the best means of accumulating significant personal wealth. Cotton planters of the Deep South, their agents in cities like New Orleans, Mobile, and Charleston, and commission merchants in the Northeast—especially in New York City—served as the vital links driving much of the American economy. Manufacturers were only beginning to gain stature and produce for consumers beyond local markets; not surprisingly, among the most prominent of them were owners of textile mills that turned southern cotton into yarn and cloth.

The demands of fighting the War of the Rebellion, however, began to accelerate an important transformation in the power structure undergirding the country's economy. Manufacturers would gain new advantages both from government contracts and protective tariffs newly placed on imports, and investment bankers and other financiers would have new opportunities to enrich and empower themselves by helping the government raise the money to fight the war. This was part of a larger process by which cities and industries came to dominate rural areas and agriculture economically, undermining the once powerful planters and merchants and ultimately pushing yeoman farmers to the wall. But the tipping point was a financial panic in the midst of Reconstruction.

The Panic of 1873

One of the most prominent economic beneficiaries of the War of the Rebellion was Jay Cooke. A Philadelphia banker with a modest portfolio when the shooting started in 1861, Cooke used his connections and creative energies to make a fortune marketing the federal bonds that paid for much of the war effort. By the late 1860s he was flush. He presided over the sprawling Philadelphia-based banking house of Jay Cooke and Company, which counted more than $1 million in profits each year (about $22 million in today's dollars), while maintaining close ties to the Republican administration in Washington, DC.

Then, to the shock of the financial community in the United States, on September 18, 1873, Cooke and Company suddenly had to close its doors and declare bankruptcy. The New York Stock Exchange, in turn, was shaken to its core, briefly closing its own doors. A domino effect of bank failures quickly spread across the country, ushering in an economic depression the likes of which Americans had never seen before. We call it the **Panic of 1873.**

The immediate source of Cooke's troubles was his gamble on investing in the Northern Pacific Railroad, intended to link Duluth, Minnesota, and the Puget Sound of Washington State, which Congress had chartered in 1864 as part of its efforts to build rail lines across the trans-Mississippi West. Although Cooke had some doubts about the project, he soon imagined himself sitting at the helm of a great northwestern rail corridor that could possibly include much of western Canada, too. Cooke probably should have been concerned that the European market for

≡ **Spanning the Continent** Representatives of the Central Pacific and Union Pacific shake hands on May 10, 1869, at Promontory Summit in Utah, in a ceremony marking the completion of the first transcontinental railroad.

American railroad bonds— necessary to finance construction—was drying up, but he was so successful at marketing wartime bonds to small investors in the United States that he most likely ignored the warning signs.

That was a big mistake. The weak European bond market was an indication of serious troubles in the world of international finance, and when flows of capital (resources for investment, trade, and business operations) were interrupted in the early 1870s by a glut of grain coming onto the international commodity market, there was a chain reaction of collapse. Banks and stock markets teetered, and the Bank of England—titan of the global economy— had to raise its discount rate (interest rate for borrowers) to the highest levels of the nineteenth century. The ripple effects soon crossed the Atlantic and washed up on the shores of the United States.

The "Money Question"

For American financiers like Jay Cooke, this was a shocking jolt in what had been a relatively smooth ride to wealth thanks to help from Congress and the Treasury Department. When major hostilities in the War of the Rebellion ended, the federal government had a number of important decisions to make about the initiatives it had taken in the midst of battle. Would policies and institutions that had dramatically expanded the reach and authority of the federal government be maintained, augmented, or scaled back, and whose interests would be privileged in the decision-making?

Some of the most pressing issues concerned wartime finance because a new banking system had been created and over $400 million in greenbacks (the first national currency of the United States, named for the paper money's distinctive color) were now in circulation. Would the banking system be preserved and continue to favor the urban and manufacturing sectors of the economy? Would greenbacks remain a circulating medium, the volume increased or decreased as the times demanded? Or would the greenbacks be retired (not recirculated once they were collected for payments) in favor of a currency based on specie (coin made of precious metals, largely gold), fixed in volume? And would the many millions of dollars in government bonds, whose interest payments were coming due, be settled in greenbacks (favoring debtors because they had inflated in value) or only in gold (favoring creditors)?

≡ **Greenback** This ten-dollar note from 1861 shows Abraham Lincoln on the left and an allegorical representation of art on the right.

The Republican Party had substantial majorities in Congress and was in a position to put its stamp on the postwar economy. But there were serious divisions in its own ranks over the speed and direction of any readjustments. Eastern banking and financial interests hoped to scale back government initiatives, reduce protective tariffs, withdraw greenbacks from circulation, and have bondholders paid off in gold. Western agricultural producers (farmers and ranchers), however, favored monetary inflation, protectionism to bolster the national economy, debt repayment in greenbacks, and federal support for rail and other infrastructure projects. Across the manufacturing belt that linked New England and the Midwest, there were additional fractures between those who looked to the domestic and those who looked to the Atlantic economy. In many ways, it was a defining moment in the unfolding of Reconstruction, with Radical Republicans, who hoped to transform the former slave South, supporting greenbacks and protectionism and with more moderate and conservative Republicans, who were eager to resurrect the plantation economy of the South, favoring low tariffs and the return to sound, specie-based money.

For the next three decades, the **money question** would embroil American politics like no other issue. But by the late 1860s, signs of the outcome could be glimpsed. President Andrew Johnson's Treasury Secretary Hugh McCulloch, himself a banker and advisee of Jay Cooke, struck the first blow (with considerable Republican support) by retiring greenbacks as they came into the federal treasury and promoting a mildly deflationary course. Then, in 1869, with the strong backing of eastern Republicans, Congress determined that the government's debt obligations would be paid in specie rather than greenbacks. These were victories, on both matters, for the larger financial interests.

Seeds of Corruption

Bankers and investors like Jay Cooke could flex their political muscles because they were accumulating political friends almost as fast as they were accumulating capital. To be sure, most Republicans had long favored federal support for infra-structure and manufacturing that would bring the sprawling territories of the United States under the authority of a new nation-state. But financing railroad projects required more than land grants and start-up loans; they required almost endless borrowing to keep projects afloat during extended periods of construc-tion. For financiers and builders, winning the favor of congressional legislators with handouts of various sorts and finding their way into many federal money tills proved essential. Seats on railroad boards of directors were offered up, watered (artificially inflated) railroad stock was sold, and dummy (fake) building corpora-tions were invented.

The net of corruption and bribery reached well into the national government, as the **Credit Mobilier scandal** did during the administration of President Ulysses S. Grant. Credit Mobilier was one of the dummy corporations that dramatical-ly inflated the costs of railroad construction—in this case, of the Union Pacific Railroad. Although the railroad cost only $50 million to build, Credit Mobilier billed $94 million and Union Pacific executives pocketed the excess, $44 million. They used part of the money to bribe key Republican congressmen for legislation, funding, and regulatory rulings favorable to the Union Pacific. The *New York Sun* broke the story in 1872, and for decades partisan newspapers used the scandal to stir widespread distrust of Republicans and the federal government.

For Jay Cooke corruption was a family affair. In 1870 he purchased controlling interest in the Northern Pacific Railroad, which included 50 million acres in land grants. But when the federal government failed to stand behind the debt he had piled up and construction of his railroad slowed, Cooke turned for help to his brother Henry, who had become finance chairman of the Freedmen's Savings Bank, established by Congress in March 1865.

The Freedmen's Savings Bank was designed to encourage the creation of bank accounts by men and women newly liberated from enslavement; it was not a com-mercial investment house. Yet Henry Cooke was soon loaning out the bank's mon-ey and sank over $500,000 of its deposits into brother Jay's operations. Without knowing it, that is, poor Black working people became investors in the House of Cooke and, by extension, in the Northern Pacific Railroad.

Unfortunately for the Black depositors the fate of the Northern Pacific was in-creasingly dubious. Not only was Cooke running short of cash, but as the railroad inched along toward Puget Sound, it had to pass through lands in eastern Montana claimed by militant Sioux bands led by the Lakota chief Sitting Bull. Although hun-dreds of US soldiers were sent—at federal expense—to protect Northern Pacific crews, the Sioux decided to fight it out regardless of the consequences. Word of hostilities soon filtered back, and when the news became public in the late summer of 1873, the bottom fell out of Cooke's railroad operations. The insurgent Sioux thereby sealed the doom of haughty financier Jay Cooke, and in the Panic of 1873 he took the Freedmen's Savings Bank down along with him.

Railroads and a New Capitalist Alliance

It was a telling historical moment, bringing a period of dramatic economic change to an abrupt close and setting the foundation for a new system of social and political relations. And the railroads were the emblems of what had happened and where things were likely to go. Beginning with the first great boom of the late 1840s and early 1850s, railroad construction brought about the emergence of large private companies, supported by state and municipal governments, which sold bonds and related financial instruments, took corporate form, created administrative hierarchies, and depended on a huge supply of wage workers who fired the engines, handled the brakes, connected the cars, drove the locomotives, and staffed the repair shops. Whatever the political course of the country, the railroads would have been powerful pacesetters for an American capitalism that was beginning to take hold around midcentury.

But the War of the Rebellion and the rise of a nation-state lent the process new scope, scale, direction, connections, and personnel. At the center was an alliance between the financiers and industrialists who had benefitted from government business, the legislative and executive wings of the federal government, and the higher reaches of the US military; eventually the alliance would include federal and state courts. Finance capital was positioning itself to play an increasingly important role not only in the construction of the great transcontinental railroads but also in the building of many other rail lines that would traverse the United States and help power American industrialization. The men at the helm sought to accumulate resources, remove obstacles, and draw upon the muscle of laborers who had been driven off the land and were moving around the globe in search of livelihoods. Their eyes were trained especially on the trans-Mississippi West and, with the aid of political allies on both sides of the border, on Mexico, Canada, and perhaps the rest of the Western Hemisphere (see Map 17.1).

When the speculative bubble finally burst in 1873 and the railroad boom collapsed, the consequences were deep, wide ranging, and long lasting. Credit dried up, factories and shops closed or dramatically cut their workforces, wages were slashed, unemployment and underemployment spiraled, bankruptcies exploded in number, and household economies unraveled. More than two decades of political struggle began to erupt, threatening social upheaval and calling into question many of the basic ways in which the national economy worked. But the capitalist alliance that came out of the war would endure and, in many respects, become stronger.

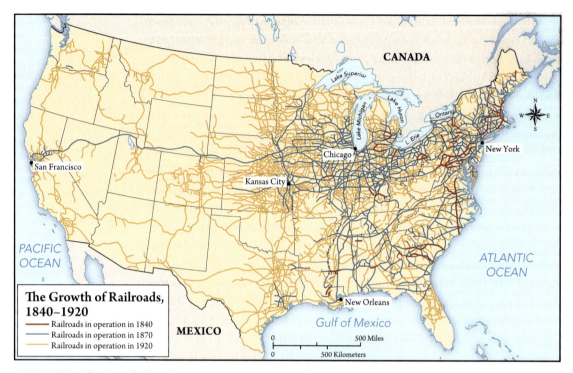

☰ MAP 17.1   The Growth of Railroads, 1840–1920   Railroads were powerful pacesetters for an American capitalism that took hold around the middle of the nineteenth century.

17.2   Remaking the Countryside: The South

||| Explain the capitalist transformation of the postbellum South.

Although the development of capitalism is generally associated with cities and industries, the transformation of the countryside in the United States and around the globe was the necessary foundation for capitalism's rise and sustenance. Until land became a commodity that could be bought and sold, and until the ties that bound the great mass of humanity to the soil by means of enslavement, servitude, and community obligation were severed, no mass market in goods or labor could emerge. While the transformation unfolded over several centuries, it gained great speed in the nineteenth century when enslaved people and peasants were emancipated in Europe and the Western Hemisphere. Many millions of men, women, and children were turned loose to earn their keep, often moving across huge distances in what became history's largest migrations.

By far the greatest number would come to the United States, where they found work on docks and construction sites, on canals and railroads, and in mines, mills, and factories. But the American countryside also reverberated with change during and immediately after the war, further contributing to the advance of capitalism. Nowhere was this more apparent than in the South and the trans-Mississippi West. Let's turn first to the South.

The Plantation South

The plantation economies of the southern states were of deep concern to Republican policymakers from the start of the war, and it was there that some of the most convulsive and consequential transformations occurred. The stakes were high because cotton and sugar planters were among the wealthiest and most powerful of all Americans on the eve of the fighting, and the crops that their enslaved workers cultivated were critical to the economic growth of the whole country. Although a handful of Radical Republicans wished to take the plantation sector apart and promote small-scale white and Black family farming, most Republicans believed that resurrecting the cotton economy was crucial to the future prosperity of the nation. That meant resurrecting the plantations.

Federal policies toward this end rolled out during the War of the Rebellion itself, and they aimed to promote the development of a loyal class of white cotton and sugar growers while envisioning formerly enslaved people mainly as wage laborers on reorganized plantations. The contract lease system, initiated in the lower Mississippi Valley in 1862, was one such example. It permitted northerners and loyal white southerners to lease plantations that had been abandoned by their owners and hire formerly enslaved men and women to work them for small wages. This would become the model for a new agricultural order whose creation would be supervised by the Freedmen's Bureau beginning in the spring of 1865: it would now revolve around labor contracts entered into voluntarily, the payment of wages or shares of the growing crop, and mutually agreed-upon obligations. Coercion or corporal punishment could no longer be used to motivate or discipline laborers, as had been the case under slavery.

That, at least, was the theory and intention. But implementation proved extremely difficult. Why? Because neither former enslavers nor the formerly enslaved wanted this for their future. Former enslavers did not believe that newly freed people would work without the use of the coercive mechanisms they had long deployed, and many were outraged at the prospect of bargaining with men and women they had been accustomed to ordering around. The formerly enslaved had little interest in going back to work for their former enslavers and hoped instead to work for themselves on lands they could purchase or rent.

It was a recipe for conflict as the former enslavers tried to preserve as much of slavery as possible and newly freed men and women tried to hold onto the gains they had made during their enslavement while limiting the coercive authority to which they previously had been subjected. In the end, neither side got what it most wanted. In some places, like the sugar parishes of lower Louisiana or the general farming areas of the border South, a system of wage labor took hold. In others, like the cotton and tobacco belts of the lower and upper South, the hard-fisted vestiges of coercion survived most tenaciously, as planters and freedpeople fought their way toward a system known as **sharecropping**. Under it, landowners would supply housing, tools, draft animals, and seed but also divide their plantations into smaller plots that would be cultivated by individual Black families in return for a share of the crop instead of for cash wages, since cash was very scarce (see Map 17.2).

What all of these arrangements had in common was a new set of social relations that linked farms and plantations across the southern states to proliferating towns and villages nearby and then to centers of finance and political power in the Northeast. Although coercions and repression persisted, they did not formally

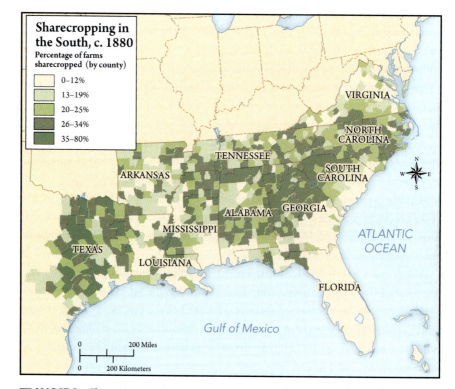

≡ **MAP 17.2   Sharecropping, c. 1880**   Sharecropping was most common in the inland areas of the South, where cotton and tobacco primarily were grown.

bind Black laborers to the land or to the direct authority of property holders as had been true under slavery. Instead, a class of workers gradually took shape who, while claiming ownership of their persons, lacked the means to produce or subsist on their own account and thus were left with few alternatives—in good part because of the police powers of state and local governments—to laboring in the fields for the landowners. State and locally passed **vagrancy laws** required them to have "gainful employment" by a certain date or be subject to arrest. **Anti-enticement laws** prohibited employers from luring laborers away from their jobs with the promise of higher wages and better working conditions. And **fence and game laws** restricted the use of unenclosed land for hunting or raising livestock. Already by the 1870s, southern courts determined that, for all intents and purposes, "sharecroppers" were the same as "wage laborers."

Unmaking the Southern Yeomanry

Formerly enslaved workers and former enslavers were not alone in experiencing a rapid transformation of the agricultural economies in which they worked. White yeoman farmers, who had depended chiefly on household labor and mixed subsistence agriculture with limited market production, felt the effects as well. Very quickly, new rail lines—often with the support of Reconstruction governments—pushed into the regions where they lived in greatest numbers and drew them into national and international markets. Towns multiplied along the railroad routes, and merchandisers soon offered means for selling staple crops like cotton as well as credit instruments for encouraging their production. Before long, yeomen had to give merchants liens, or mortgages, on their crops (generally known as **crop liens**), land, and other property as collateral for their debts while they moved deeper and deeper into cotton cultivation. For their part, the merchants began to accumulate land and increasingly claimed power in local and state political life.

Had the cotton economy of the South returned to its antebellum strength, this process of commercialization could well have had wide benefits, at least for white landowners. If the cotton they produced fetched high prices, their material conditions would have improved. But this was not to be. The federal wartime blockade of the rebellious southern states took them out of the international cotton market and provided incentives for cotton production in other parts of the world—especially in China, India, Egypt, and Brazil, where growing cotton had previously been pursued on only a limited scale. At war's end, the world cotton supply was increasing rapidly while demand for the fiber in the industrial hubs of Europe and North America was beginning to flatten.

By the early 1870s, the international price for cotton—and for other agricultural commodities—began to slip. The Panic of 1873 and its aftermath only worsened

≡ **Children Picking Cotton**   With bags nearly as big as themselves, children near Bells, Texas, strain to haul their pickings.

a downward spiral that brought more and more producers down with it. Before the century was out, most of the South's cotton would be raised by white labor, tenancy and sharecropping would be rampant among them, and growing numbers of white farmers would be looking to textile mills and other forms of regular and seasonal employment to subsist.

Witnesses to the dramatic transformation of the southern countryside began to think that the South had become something of a colony of the Northeast. Its economy was organized mostly around agriculture and the extraction of other raw materials (coal, lumber, minerals), the products of which were shipped North for processing and manufacture. The prices obtained for the South's exports were declining while the interest charges paid for necessary credit were increasing. And the South had come to occupy a subordinate position in the structure of national politics: a far cry from the power the region had wielded before the war. At the very least, the idea of a "colonial South" spoke to the new balances of power in the United States that the War of the Rebellion brought into being.

17.3   Remaking the Countryside: The Trans-Mississippi West

‖‖‖ Explain the capitalist transformation of the postbellum West.

But it was in the trans-Mississippi West that the transformations most closely approximated a colonial relationship and ultimately became a proving ground for later colonial projects elsewhere in the world. Here the federal government played a large role both in encouraging the exploitation of the land and in exercising direct political authority over the many territories it had created. And here new relations of economic power increasingly subordinated the West to the Northeast.

The driving forces of western development were the railroads that pushed across the vast interior, especially into mineral-rich districts from the northern Plains and Rockies into the desert Southwest. They were energized by the marriage of the government (at federal, state, and local levels) and finance capital, and they drove the expansion of mining and lumbering not least because they became enormous consumers of wood (for track and cars) and coal (for firing engines). Railroads would be of great benefit to the iron and steel industries as well. But much of this land was still claimed by Indigenous people, and they were prepared to fight to keep it.

The Mineral Boom and the Defeat of Indigenous Peoples

The mineral boom that spread across the West during the last four decades of the nineteenth century exemplified these connections as well as the challenges of dispossessing Indigenous people. Gold and silver rushes took place in Colorado, Nevada, Idaho, Montana, South Dakota, and Arizona during the 1870s and 1880s before moving northwest to Canada and Alaska around the turn of the twentieth century. And, especially early on, they provided the context for the US Army to wage war against Indigenous people across the West, none more so than the Sioux, who refused to sell or lease the gold-laden Black Hills of South Dakota.

The military high command claimed to be ready for a "campaign of annihilation," driving Indigenous people from their winter camps, destroying their access to subsistence (most notably the already declining buffalo herds), and pursuing them relentlessly until they surrendered. But such haughtiness was no guarantee of success, and while the army did force many of the tribes on the southern Plains (Comanche, Cheyenne, and Arapaho) to give up, in the Black Hills it was not at all easy to do.

Troops attempting to attack the militant Sioux bands intent on defending their lands were greeted with sniper fire and ambush. "They are brave and ready to fight for their country," Oglala chief Red Cloud said of them. "They are not afraid of the soldiers." Failing to heed the message, the soldiers continued to arrive in the spring and summer of 1876. Overconfident commanders like General George Armstrong Custer pressed ahead into what turned into a lethal ambush: "Custer's last stand" it was called when his entire Seventh Cavalry was cut down at the **Battle of Little Bighorn**—the Battle of Greasy Grass as the Sioux named it—that July. But it was a temporary setback. Crazy Horse and Sitting Bull, two of the leading militants, eventually gave up, and the mineral excavation of the sacred Black Hills—as was true elsewhere—moved ahead with seemingly inexorable speed.

Gold and silver were not the only metals to be found under the surface in many parts of the trans-Mississippi West. Copper strikes occurred in the southwestern

PERSPECTIVES

Remembering the Battle of Little Big Horn/The Battle of Greasy Grass

Within six months of Custer's "last stand," Frederick Whittaker published *A Complete Life of General George A. Custer*. Whittaker's biography established the image of Custer as a dashing cavalier, a superb frontiersman undone by the cowardice of his supporting officers and the insurmountability of Indigenous force. In Whittaker's account, Custer was a "great man, one of the few really great men that America has produced." Custer, according to historian Pekka Hämäläinen, "was elevated into an exemplary Christian knight, and the hill of his Last Stand became a Golgotha."[1]

≡ 1896 Lithograph from Anheuser-Busch Brewing Company.

[1]Pekka Hämäläinen, *Lakota America: A New History of Indigenous Power* (New Haven, CT: Yale University Press, 2019), 372.

Custer's martyrdom is celebrated in this 1896 lithograph that Anheuser-Busch Brewing Company used as an advertising promotion for Budweiser Beer. Over 150,000 copies were distributed to saloons and restaurants across the United States. As they sipped their beer, patrons in dining establishments gazed at the scene of the buckskin-fringed hero's ultimately futile effort to defy the demonic savagery of the red-skinned Sioux.

In contrast, this pictograph, created in 1881 by Red Horse, a Lakota Sioux who fought in the battle, shows a different version of events. Instead of the mythic images of the Last Stand that position Custer in the center of the action, Red Horse's pictographic account emphasizes the battle's chaos and indiscriminate carnage. "It was as if they were driving buffalo to a good place to slaughter," remembered one Lakota Sioux woman.

≡ **1881 Pictograph drawn by Red Horse.**

CONSIDER THIS

How did acts of misrepresentation, such as the lithograph used by Anheuser-Busch in its marketing, serve to erase the Sioux and their history from American memory? Why was it necessary to portray Custer as heroic and the Sioux as treacherous?

borderlands as well as in Montana in the 1880s. The exploitation of the great iron ore ranges in Wisconsin, Minnesota, and Michigan began in the 1880s and 1890s. What all these mineral sites had in common were the railroads as sources of transportation and investment capital, the rise of small urban centers, the appearance of multicultural and multiethnic wage labor forces, and the rapid move toward corporate organization—all of this as the Indigenous inhabitants were confined to proliferating reservations (see Map 17.3).

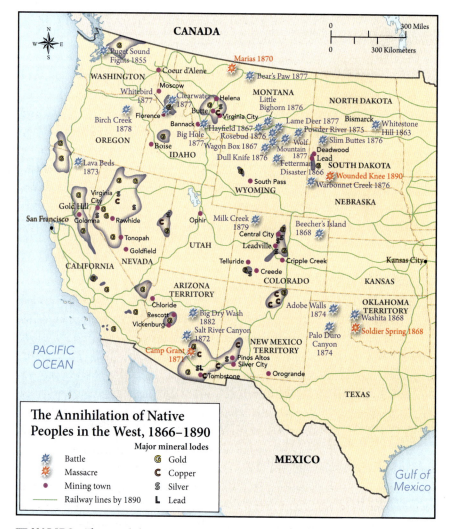

The Annihilation of Native Peoples in the West, 1866–1890

Major mineral lodes

- ✳ Battle
- ✴ Massacre
- • Mining town
- — Railway lines by 1890

- Ⓖ Gold
- C Copper
- S Silver
- L Lead

≡ **MAP 17.3   The Annihilation of Indigenous Peoples in the West, 1866–1890**   The mineral boom that spread across the West during the last four decades of the nineteenth century went hand in hand with the dispossession of Indigenous peoples.

The miners who initially established individual or group claims were, for the most part, small operators who worked close to the surface panning (sluicing) for minerals. But when the surface (placer) deposits became exhausted, deeper, hard-rock mining required shafts or pits that were far more expensive to construct and operate. The original miners were steadily pushed out, replaced by mine workers with hierarchies based on skill and ethnicity. Experienced colliers (coal miners), often from England and Ireland, sat atop a pyramid that included less-skilled and unskilled workers from Central and Eastern Europe, the Mediterranean, Scandinavia, and Mexico, along with a small number of African Americans and Chinese. Few of the workers, other than the African Americans, were native born, and ethnic rivalries frequently roiled the camps.

As for the investors and owners, it was the northeastern financial houses (particularly in New York and Boston), many already involved in western railroading, that provided most of the capital. In the 1880s, new rail hubs like El Paso, Albuquerque, and Tucson became gateways to mineral exploitation in the arid hinterlands. Oftentimes, new corporate mine owners became lords of all they surveyed, buying up huge tracts of land, establishing **company towns**, and taking control of local governments. Names like E.H. Harriman, Jay Gould, J.P. Morgan, and Harry Guggenheim dominated the landscape. PhelpsDodge Corporation, with mines, refineries, and railroad lines, held sway in Arizona. The Rockefeller-owned Anaconda copper corporation effectively ruled Montana. Capitalism and colonialism appeared to go hand in glove.

Western Ranching and Agriculture

Much the same could be said for the open-range cattle industry, which exploded across the Great Plains and into the Great Basin west of the Rockies in the 1870s and 1880s as the US Army completed its defeat of Indigenous people, railroads pushed across the landscape, and the once immense bison herds disappeared. Texas cattlemen began the **long drives** to Abilene and other western Kansas towns soon after the War of the Rebellion was over. Between 1865 and 1885, over five million head of cattle made the trek out of Texas on their way to stockyards in Chicago and, to a lesser extent, St. Louis, Omaha, and Kansas City. But as rail access increased and conflicts between cattle drovers and farmers intensified, a new economic arrangement came into being. Using the barbed wire that had been newly patented (1874) to contain the livestock and financed by investment capital from the Northeast and Great Britain, large ranches multiplied across the Plains to the foothills of the Rockies (a young Theodore Roosevelt bought two of them). Organized as land and cattle companies, they engrossed thousands of acres and could ship directly to stockyards and meatpacking plants.

≡ **Western Ranching and Agriculture**   Two views of capitalist agriculture in the West, c. 1900: A cowboy with lasso gets ready to round up his cattle on a Kansas ranch.

Large-scale capitalist agriculture, which dwarfed the plantations of the slave South, was also a product of the postwar western economic scramble. The most formidable could be found in California, where sizable Mexican land grants and the high costs of irrigation paved the way for huge wheat farms. Heavily mechanized from the outset, with combines (machines that combined the harvesting operations of reaping, threshing, gathering, and winnowing into a single process) and steam-powered tractors in the fields, they had a small corps of managers and full-time employees supplemented by the work of **migrant laborers** (Mexicans, Chinese, southern Europeans) during the harvest. By the 1880s California ranked second only to Minnesota as an American wheat producer, and the organization of the estates clearly anticipated the agribusinesses that would dominate California's central valley in the twentieth century.

Even more spectacular were the **bonanza farms** of the Dakotas that rose from the ashes of the 1870s depression as the bankrupt Northern Pacific disposed of almost 3 million acres of its land, much of it to investors from the Northeast and Britain. Quickly, farms averaging 7,000 acres in size (and up to 100,000 acres) began operations, much like those in California, with expensive machinery, managers, and gangs of migrant laborers. While the subsequent depression of the 1890s threw these highly profitable bonanza farms into crisis, most were parceled off and either sold or rented to farmers who maintained, on a smaller scale, the capitalist relations that successful agricultural operations on the Great Plains required.

Still, most of the corn and wheat continued to be raised by farm families whose search for breathing space moved the center of production west from Indiana, Illinois, Wisconsin, and Missouri onto the prairies of Kansas, Nebraska, Minnesota, and the Dakotas. These farmers generally hoped to cultivate grains destined for national and international markets along with a

≡ **Western Ranching and Agriculture**   A harvester rolls across wheat fields in Walla Walla, Washington.

host of other crops and livestock that might be sold locally or consumed by the farm household itself, much as they had done for decades. But after the War of the Rebellion, and especially after the Panic of 1873, they faced a new world of exchange and credit that tied them to more distant financial institutions and increasingly disrupted the strategies they had long followed. Somewhat like the white yeomen of the southern states, these western farmers needed to devote more and more of their farms to market crops, whether wheat, corn, or dairy.

The result was that grains and other agricultural commodities began to flood the market. It was a global, not only a national, story. Just as the Great Plains were drawn into the vortex of international trade, so, too, were the Russian and Austro-Hungarian steppes, the Argentine pampas, the Canadian prairies, and the Australian outback—evidence of land grabs and greatly increased crop production throughout the world. World wheat production more than doubled during the second half of the nineteenth century and grew especially fast between 1870 and 1890 (see Map 17.4). Compared to earlier examples of agricultural expansion, this one was both far greater in its geographical reach and far more tenacious in its social grip. It did not just involve the extension of the market economy; it also involved the fastening of capitalist social relations.

17.4 Industrialization

Summarize the complex road of postbellum industrialization in the United States.

Economic historians differ widely over when American industrialization truly began. Did it start with the rise of textile mills in New England in the early nineteenth century or with the economic boom following the Panic of 1837? Or were the government-supported projects of the Civil War era crucial to industrialization's launch? The debate has gone on for decades, and it will likely go on for decades more. But some things are certainly true. Industrialization is a process by which the manufacture and distribution of goods assumes a large-scale and continuously expanding character, provides employment for a growing segment of the labor force, and involves machinery that makes mass production possible. And in the United States, an important shift in the composition of industry took place between 1860 and 1900.

Pace and Direction of Change

On the eve of the War of the Rebellion, the country's leading industries were oriented to what are known as **consumer goods**: goods that are mainly eaten, worn, or used to build houses, such as flour, ready-made clothing, and lumber.

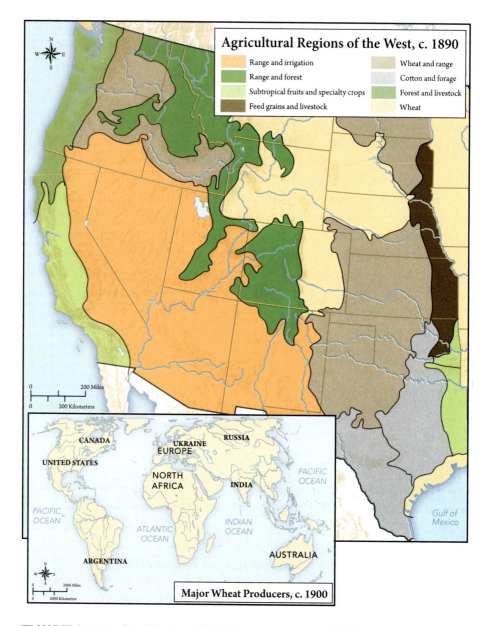

≡ MAP 17.4   Agricultural Regions of the West, c. 1890   As world wheat production more than doubled during the second half of the nineteenth century, the Great Plains were drawn into the vortex of international trade.

Where mechanization or the division of labor had become most advanced (such as in textiles and the garment trades), the workforce was composed mostly of women and children. Otherwise, male artisans, journeymen, and skilled craftsmen working in relatively small shops predominated.

By the end of the nineteenth century, however, a very different industrial economy had taken shape. Consumer goods had been equaled if not surpassed in importance by **capital goods**: goods used to make other goods, such as iron and steel, machine tools, rubber, petroleum, and chemicals. The proportion of the labor force involved in industrial production had also tripled. Artisan shops had been marginalized, and semiskilled operatives did the greatest share of the work. This was the industrial America that emerged as the leading economic powerhouse in the world (see Map 17.5).

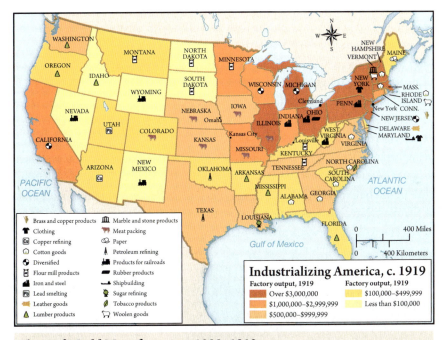

Industrializing America, c. 1919

Factory output, 1919
- Over $3,000,000
- $1,000,000–$2,999,999
- $500,000–$999,999

Factory output, 1919
- $100,000–$499,999
- Less than $100,000

Legend:
- Brass and copper products
- Clothing
- Copper refining
- Cotton goods
- Diversified
- Flour mill products
- Iron and steel
- Lead smelting
- Leather goods
- Lumber products
- Marble and stone products
- Meat packing
- Paper
- Petroleum refining
- Products for railroads
- Rubber products
- Shipbuilding
- Sugar refining
- Tobacco products
- Woolen goods

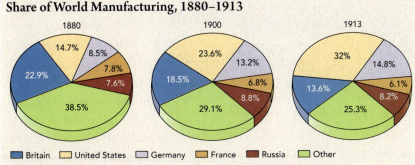

Share of World Manufacturing, 1880–1913

1880: 14.7%, 8.5%, 7.8%, 7.6%, 22.9%, 38.5%
1900: 23.6%, 13.2%, 6.8%, 8.8%, 18.5%, 29.1%
1913: 32%, 14.8%, 6.1%, 8.2%, 13.6%, 25.3%

Legend: Britain | United States | Germany | France | Russia | Other

≡ **MAP 17.5 Industrializing America, c. 1890** By the end of the nineteenth century, the new industrial economy helped make the United States the world's leading industrial power, but the pace of change was neither smooth nor incremental.

Even so, the pace of change was neither smooth nor incremental. New factories often absorbed rather than transformed more traditional methods of production even as they became more and more mechanized, and skilled craftsmen struggled to hold onto their technical expertise and control over operations even as their workplaces moved from small shops to factory floors. Many battles would occur before a new industrial order could be consolidated. But whatever the form of organization and management, the wage relation had greatly enlarged its reach and now lay at the heart of manufacturing.

Wage Labor and Industrial Diversity

Although working for wages had once been regarded as a relatively temporary condition, a stepping stone on the path to working for oneself, to economic independence, as early as 1870, two-thirds of the nonagricultural labor force were wage workers. In part, this was the result of the expansion of the market economy that had swept through the Northeast, Middle Atlantic, and Midwest during the antebellum decades and brought more and more people into the cash and credit networks. Farm families came to raise more for sale, and their sons and daughters began to look elsewhere for work as household production dramatically declined in importance. Rural-to-urban migrations flowed, first to smaller towns and then to larger cities along the East Coast and near interior. New York and Philadelphia grew in size but not as much as Chicago, Pittsburgh, St. Louis, and Buffalo. Some of the most rapid growth took place in still-modest commercial and manufacturing towns like Milwaukee, Minneapolis, Grand Rapids, Michigan, Toledo, Ohio, Syracuse, New York, Bridgeport, Connecticut, and Jersey City, New Jersey. In all of these locations, migrants mostly worked for wages: whether as clerks, skilled tradesmen, seamstresses, domestic servants, or members of construction crews.

Yet the spread of wage labor occurred in an industrial economy marked by great diversity. On one end of the spectrum were the country's largest cities

≡ **Altoona, Pennsylvania in 1895** The pace of industrial development was most robust, not in the largest cities or the one-industry towns, but in smaller urban centers, such as Altoona, Pennsylvania, which was an important manufacturing hub for the Pennsylvania Railroad.

boasting the most complex economies. There a wide range of manufacturing establishments developed, some small and some large, some powered by machines and some still dependent on skilled hands. Alongside them, sprawling railroad yards and docks could also be found. At the other end of the spectrum were one-industry towns such as the textile and shoe centers of New England, the coal-mining districts of northeastern Pennsylvania, the iron- and steel-making hubs of western Pennsylvania, and the lumber and mining camps of the South and trans-Mississippi West.

But in the 1870s, the pace of industrial development was most robust, not in the largest cities or the one-industry towns, but in smaller urban centers that usually combined manufacturing and transportation with important ties to the surrounding countryside. These were towns like Wilmington, Delaware; Trenton, New Jersey; Providence, Rhode Island; Rochester, New York; Altoona, Pennsylvania; Pueblo, Colorado; and Virginia City, Nevada. Here, a significant portion of America's postwar industrial workforce resided.

The dynamism of small industrial towns reflected the continuing importance of craft organization, the limited authority of employers over the production process, and the social composition of the labor force. Unlike textile mills, which were often seen as symbols of the industrial revolution, most manufacturing establishments in the 1860s and 1870s were small in size, owned by men who probably had been artisans and master craftsmen, and staffed by skilled workers who were mainly native born and from the town or nearby rural areas. The great influx of Irish immigrants in the 1840s and 1850s had only begun to tip the balances of industrial workplaces, and then chiefly in the largest cities. Some of the factories were little more than enlarged artisan shops; some had more extensive divisions of labor, mixing skilled and semiskilled workers; and some were tied to forms of outwork, often finishing jobs performed away from the workplace, usually where the workers (customarily women) lived.

The result was a labor market that was anything but uniform. It was more of a patchwork in which variations as to region, gender, and place of birth abounded. Highly skilled male workers could shape the conditions of their labor as well as their wages and benefits. Foreign-born men could be found in certain sectors of the industrial economy (iron and steel, textiles, mining) but less so in others (printing, lumbering, milling). Females, whatever their nationality, were mostly in sex-segregated trades (garment and shoe) and even there consigned to certain jobs. Native-born men who lacked skills were often on the move, with varying prospects for steady employment. And African Americans, nearly all of whom lived in the South, had few employment opportunities outside agriculture, owing to local legislation, informal understandings, and racist practices.

≡ **Diverse Workforce** This 1899 photograph of a cotton gin in Dahomey, Mississippi, shows both African American workers and white overseers engaged in the challenging and stifling work of processing raw cotton.

Industrial Organization

But change was on the horizon, especially once the smoke cleared after the Panic of 1873 and the subsequent depression. The impetus often came from owners and managers who started careers outside the particular industry or trade but had acquired a larger view of the economy, had an awareness of technological advances, and were familiar with new bureaucratic forms of administration. Not surprisingly, more than a few had experience working in the offices of railroad companies or in merchandising; some had trained as engineers. They came to see the customary practices of manufacturing as chaotic and inefficient and believed that factories needed to be run by managers from above rather than by skilled workers from below. And they increasingly viewed competition as a major cause of their woes, cutting into profits and creating instabilities across the economy.

As organizational innovators, they tried to do several things. They sought to mechanize more and more of the labor process to undercut the control exercised by skilled workers and craftsmen. They attempted to add specialized tasks so that semiskilled operatives could replace craft workers. They wanted to shift supervisory responsibilities away from foremen on the shop floor and into the hands of their own hired staff. They attempted to implement cost accounting and related bookkeeping methods. And they moved to take charge of as much of the market for their goods as possible.

It was not easy to do. Skilled workers dug in their heels to protect their places and prerogatives, making for an era of unprecedented labor conflict, as we will see in Chapter 18. Smaller manufacturers and shippers also pushed back against the new concentrations of wealth and power being created and undermining their ability to compete. Reformers worried deeply about the social and political price that was being paid.

So, for the next two decades, the changes would be haphazard and difficult to measure. But by the end of the nineteenth century the balances clearly tilted toward the organizational dynamics of the new industrialism. The size of factories and plants more than doubled. The pace of work grew exponentially. Craft workers were being replaced by machine operatives. And the struggle to install more rational and efficient management and to reorganize the marketplace for labor and products was steadily being won by owners and their allies.

From Railroads to Steel Production

The steel empire built by Andrew Carnegie in the 1870s, 1880s, and 1890s well illustrates what was happening. A Scottish immigrant from humble roots, Carnegie had no firsthand experience making iron or steel (an alloy of iron and carbon stronger and more flexible than iron). But he did get his start in the offices of the Pennsylvania Railroad (owing to local patronage), where he not only learned enough about business and investing to accumulate a fortune during the War of the Rebellion, but he was also alerted to the industry on which the railroads fundamentally depended: iron and steel.

Carnegie initially got involved with an iron mill and bridge construction company that enabled him to see the long-term prospects as well as the sorry state of the industry. Despite the enormous demand for iron and steel goods, there was little integration in the production process, poor coordination between producers and merchants, and outright ignorance when it came to assessing costs. Well aware of the latest technologies, especially Bessemer converters that would allow steel to supplant iron, he constructed one of the nation's first steel mills in 1875 by raising capital through political connections and selling rails to his old employer, the Pennsylvania Railroad. But Carnegie also insisted on new accounting techniques and a new hierarchy of management run by men of his choosing who were devoted to cutting costs, holding down wages, and substituting machines for skilled workers. Over the next several decades, Carnegie expanded his facilities, integrated his operations, diversified his product line, and took control of the flow and processing of raw materials by purchasing iron ore mines and the latest steelmaking technologies.

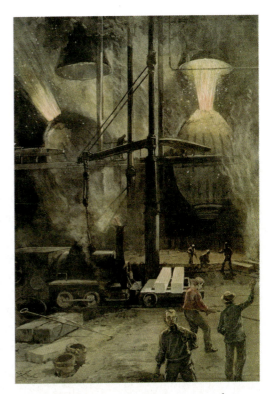

≡ **Steel Production**   This 1886 engraving of Andrew Carnegie's Pittsburgh steelworks captures the magic-like brilliance of the Bessemer converter. The workers are dwarfed by the glittering sparks.

MAPPING AMERICA

Peoples on the Move

The massive migrations of the late nineteenth century reshaped the world's labor force, but no country felt the impact of the movement of peoples more than the United States. Between 1890 and 1920, migration brought a net gain of 18.2 million people to the shores of the United States—more than in the entire previous history of the country. In combination with industrialization, this new source of workers turned the United States into a major world power.

Thinking Geographically

1. What perspective on immigration do you gain when you compare these two maps? How do the different scales—in terms of time span and geographical area—affect the "story" that each map tells?

2. What types of networks do you see in each map?

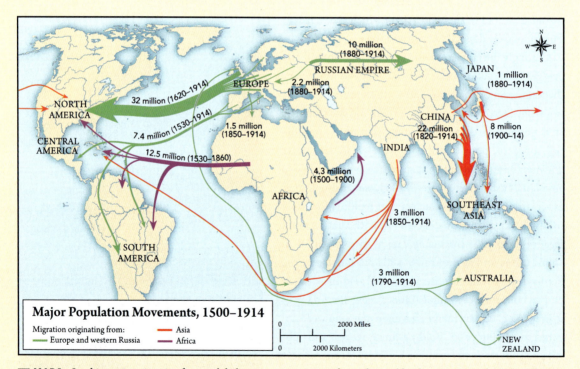

Major Population Movements, 1500–1914

Migration originating from:
— Asia
— Europe and western Russia
— Africa

≡ **MAP 1** Looking at immigration from a global perspective puts into focus the worldwide movement of peoples. This map shows major population movements over four centuries.

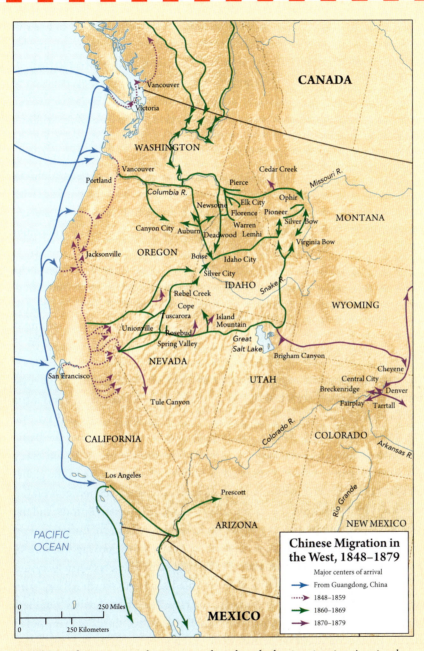

Chinese Migration in the West, 1848–1879

Major centers of arrival
From Guangdong, China
1848–1859
1860–1869
1870–1879

≡ **MAP 2** If we narrow our lens, we can take a closer look at immigration. A regional perspective, such as this map showing Chinese migration throughout the West during the period 1848–1879, allows us to see migrant communities at a local level.

Andrew Carnegie loved competition because he expected to win. But few of his counterparts in the industrial world of the later nineteenth century shared his view. They considered competition destructive and inefficient, a threat to their investments, and a nasty inconvenience. So just as owners and managers began to experiment with new ways to transform production, they also began to explore new avenues of consolidation. One was **incorporation**, the process of constituting a company as a legal entity, which permitted them to raise capital by selling stock, protect investors from excessive liability for debt, separate ownership and management, and provide long-term stability. Another avenue, exemplified by John D. Rockefeller in the new petroleum industry, was to buy out rivals and cut deals with railroad companies to reduce the rates paid for shipping. Still another—pioneered by the railroads—was to create **pools**, agreements among rival railway companies to divide up traffic and to fix freight and passenger rates.

Greed definitely inspired creativity, but in these cases, it was of limited help. Pools were difficult to enforce and, together with other forms of consolidation, provoked public hostility. By the 1880s a number of powerful industrialists and financiers had begun to recognize that further experimentation would be required.

New Sources of Workers

What gave industrialists more and more leverage was immigration on a scale the country had never seen before. The migrants came mainly from rural areas in southern and eastern Europe and Asia. They came from Russia and Poland, Hungary and the Balkans, Greece and Italy, the Iberian Peninsula and the Baltic states, Scandinavia and southeastern China. They were the products—in many cases, the refugees—of forces creating new economies across much of the globe: the expansion of empires and international trade, the emancipation of enslaved people and servile peasants, the industrialization of northwestern Europe, and the construction of new nation-states. Well over half the population of Europe was on the move over the course of the nineteenth century, mostly looking for work in the countryside or in rapidly expanding cities. But somewhere between forty and fifty million of them left the continent entirely and headed to North Africa, Latin America, the Caribbean basin, or Australia and New Zealand; in greatest numbers by far, however, they came to North America. Roughly two-thirds of them ended up in the United States, either permanently or temporarily (more than the entire population of the country in 1860), joining thousands more from the hinterlands of Guangdong, China.

The most organized of these migrations, managed by a group of San Francisco–based Chinese merchants known as the Six Companies, brought nearly 200,000 overwhelmingly male workers from various parts of southeast China between the late 1840s and the early 1880s. They would end up in mining camps and on railroad construction crews, as well as on farms and ranches and in factories and laundries. By 1870 they may have made up 10 percent of California's total population and perhaps 20 percent of all those gainfully employed in the state.

Immigration from Europe was much larger in scale and far more extended in duration; it was also less tightly orchestrated. The many millions of southern and eastern Europeans who arrived after the early 1870s swelled the size of industrializing American cities and of the ethnic enclaves within them. Much like the Irish immigrants of the 1840s and 1850s, they had few skills associated with manufacturing and cultural traditions (language, religion) that stood them apart from the native-born mainstream. Most of them had been peasants or had lived in agricultural communities disrupted by the spread of market relations. Many imagined short stays in the United States before accumulating the re-

≡ **Eadweard Muybridge**   Eadweard Muybridge is known today for his photographs from the 1870s and 1880s of animal locomotion, but in the 1850s Muybridge lived in Sacramento, California, close to the gold fields, where he sold and published prints, including this photo showing two miners, one Chinese, panning for the precious metal.

sources to return to their countries of origin. What all of them had, irrespective of their ethnic and cultural roots, was the muscle and determination to labor long hours at tasks that could be quickly learned and tend the machines that were replacing skilled workers and craftsmen.

17.5   The Culture of Capitalism

Assess the role of the courts and the military, as well as of new ideas, in securing the hold of American capitalism.

By the early postbellum era, if not before, American capitalism had attracted the intellectual and cultural supports that both inspired and sustained its development. Most important were liberal ideas, hatched by political theorists and abolitionists, which imagined a world of autonomous individuals pursuing their self-interest to the benefit of everyone. The groundwork had been established decades earlier by Adam Smith, David Ricardo, Thomas Malthus, and John Stuart Mill, all from Scotland and England, who were offering alternatives to the fixed hierarchies of the monarchical states and the mercantilist policies that harked back to the early modern era. Their ideas, which circulated widely, were then taken up and advanced by social reformers who challenged enslavement and other forms of coercive power and who advocated a freedom based upon self-ownership and exchange in the marketplace, foundational to the rise of nineteenth-century capitalism. But liberal ideas gained even greater traction in the 1870s, owing to social and political conflicts on both sides of the Atlantic.

Social Darwinism

In some ways, the War of the Rebellion and, especially, Reconstruction were emblematic of the conflicts buffeting the entire Atlantic world. No society witnessed more of a direct, and successful, challenge to an entrenched elite (the enslavers) or as great an empowerment of a section of the working class (the formerly enslaved). Yet in Britain and particularly on the European continent there were similar dynamics at play. These included the expansion of trade unionism, the organization of the International Workingmen's Association (1864), and the brief rule of the Paris Commune, when the workers and poor of the French capital seized power for two months in the spring of 1871.

Together these developments seemed to suggest, even to one-time social reformers, the dangers that class consciousness and state activism could bring. Liberal intellectuals in the United States like Edwin L. Godkin, editor of *The Nation*, who once had been firmly in the antislavery camp, began to sour on the prospects of the freedpeople in the southern states and question their readiness for the rights that had been granted to them. He and other liberals believed that the federal government had overextended its reach on behalf of Black people and should be pulled back regardless of the consequences for the formerly enslaved. They also objected to the inflationary schemes being pushed by workers and farmers and to the practices of new urban political machines (party organizations that offered basic necessities like housing, food, and jobs in exchange for votes) in allying with recently arrived European immigrants—all involving interventions by the state in economic and political life. Some went so far as to question whether popular democracy was the best method for governing an industrial society.

In this atmosphere, the works of Englishman Herbert Spencer and American William Graham Sumner won an increasingly warm reception, especially, as we saw at the start of this chapter, among industrial and financial elites. Trained as an engineer, Spencer had little but scorn for those reformers who hoped to use legislation for the purpose of social improvement. He staunchly opposed government interference in either the economy or in civil society, particularly if it proposed to benefit the poor. It was he, not the famed British scientist Charles Darwin, who wrote of the "survival of the fittest." And during the last decades of the nine-teenth century, Spencer's ideas became intellectual touchstones not only for many American thinkers but for a wider public as well. By one estimate, Spencer's books may have sold 400,000 copies in the United States by 1900, a remarkable number for the time.

Among those influenced by Spencer was Sumner, the son of an English artisan who instructed his family in the values of hard work and self-reliance. Twenty years younger than Spencer, Sumner would acquaint students with Spencerian ideas in the sociology course he taught at Yale University, a position he took up in the early 1870s after he quit the Episcopalian ministry. He, too, spoke and wrote of a social "struggle for existence," which has generally given him and Spencer alike the label of being social Darwinists, meaning that they appeared to apply Charles Darwin's ideas about evolution and the struggle for existence in the natural world to the social world, although the influence was less direct than it seemed. "The State," Sumner argued, owed nothing to anybody except "peace, order, and the guarantee of rights."

Neither Spencer nor Sumner regarded himself as an advocate for the new class of big capitalists coming to power. Yet both were embraced wholeheartedly by them. In their understanding of **social Darwinism**, the success of huge industries and great industrialists was a sign of their superiority and therefore inevitable and to be welcomed. This belief fortified the perspectives of these men of wealth and pow-er, and encouraged them to neglect the poor in the name of progress. And when the poor were of a different race or ethnicity from the wealthy—as they so often were—social Darwinism fueled their racism. Social Darwinist thinking lent "sci-entific" and intellectual heft to the notion of Anglo-Saxon superiority.

Social Darwinism was tailor-made for late nineteenth-century capitalism. Railroad magnate James J. Hill and oil tycoon John D. Rockefeller exulted that their fortunes and those of other large businesses were "determined by the law of the survival of the fittest" and showed their "superior ability, foresight, and adapt-ability." But it was Andrew Carnegie whose worldview was most transformed. He found in the works of Darwin and Spencer "lights that came in as a flood," reveal-ing "the truth," perspectives that represented progress as being both moral and ma-terial and industrial society as an improvement over whatever came before. Small wonder that when Spencer visited the United States in 1882, he was feted not only by Carnegie, who had already showered him with gifts, but also by many more luminaries of the new world of capitalism, satisfied with the cultural authority they seem to have been offered.

Sumner and Spencer became household names among the educated middle and upper classes across the United States. But their ideas would be bitterly opposed by others, especially by working people and small producers in rural and urban areas

≡ **Andrew Carnegie** Carnegie saw progress as being both moral and material, and industrial society as an improvement over whatever came before.

who sought to hold the market at bay or to construct alternatives to it. There is, in fact, no way to measure how widely or deeply this culture of capitalism became implanted in the United States.

The Courts and the Law

Yet ideas favorable to the growth of capitalism took hold in consequential sectors of US society during the second half of the nineteenth century. How? With enormously important effect through the state and federal judiciary. Why? Because of the legal traditions that governed the world of work and the class orientations of the jurists themselves. At the federal level, judicial appointees were overwhelmingly Republican, with strong ties to the moderate and conservative wings of the party, and they came overwhelmingly from upper-middle-class and upper-class social backgrounds. Their perspectives would have been shaped by commerce, manufacturing, or finance, and their educations would have acquainted them with social Darwinian ideas, the common law, and the economic orientations of antebellum courts.

At the state level, the playing field would seem to have been more level. There most judges were elected rather than appointed, and Democrats as well as Republicans filled these positions. But if we except local courts, the social profiles and legal thinking of state and federal judges were more alike than different. They both came from privileged families or were supported by them. They were eager to expand their jurisdictional authority. They rallied around freedom of contract. And they generally held workers at fault for resisting their employers' demands.

The actions of the US Supreme Court, now dominated by Republican justices from the Northeast and Midwest, are best known though not fully appreciated in these terms. In a series of landmark decisions—the *Slaughterhouse Cases* (1873), *U.S. v. Cruikshank* (1876), the *Civil Rights Cases* (1883)—the Court narrowed the reach of the Thirteenth and Fourteenth Amendments, limited federal citizenship rights, and left freedpeople in the South vulnerable to the violence and discrimination of individuals who, in the justices' opinions, were subject only to the laws of the states in which they lived. In doing this, the Court strengthened the hands of employers (often former enslavers) who needed Black labor and were accustomed to using methods of coercion to enforce discipline.

At the same time, the Court began to sketch out new doctrines of contract and, especially, what is known as substantive due process—a legal principle that protects certain fundamental rights from government interference—to give corporations legal personhood under the Fourteenth Amendment (established by the Supreme Court in *Santa Clara v. Southern Pacific Railroad* in 1886) and thereby protection from workers, small business people, and the political institutions that might try to rein in their power.

But in many ways, it was the lower federal and state courts that proved most effective in naturalizing relations of the marketplace and enhancing the power of employers. On the one hand, judges saw the legal world of labor as still defined by the centuries-old common law tradition of **master and servant**. This meant that even when workers entered into contracts voluntarily, employers had what was deemed a "property interest" in the worker's labor over the course of the entire contract: that is to say, while on the job, wage workers were under the thumbs of their employers and could be deprived of their wages if they quit without "legal cause" before the contract expired. And it also meant that employers had very little liability for an injury or death suffered by an employee in a workplace accident. Employers would be responsible only if it could be shown that they were personally at fault and that the fault was not shared by the worker. During the postbellum era, when the United States had the highest incidence of industrial accidents in the world and workers in some sectors (like agriculture) entered into annual contracts, these rules gave employers great leverage and left employees with great vulnerabilities.

On the other hand, when it came to the marketplace, courts continued to move away from common law precedent and toward a set of doctrines that was more flexible and pragmatic. A "rule as you go" mentality took hold when it came to commercial activities, and federal courts began to provide business interests with a haven in the face of state and local lawsuits. When state legislatures, which were more subject to popular influence, intervened in the contracting process, say, by limiting the hours of the legal workday, the courts were quick to step in on the side of the employers.

Where the laws of labor and the marketplace most clearly intersected was in the arena of collective actions—strikes, boycotts, picketing—on the part of workers (which we will discuss further in Chapter 18). Beginning in 1877, federal courts first stepped into large labor disputes, issuing injunctions (orders to cease activities) against workers who were striking railroad lines between Baltimore and St. Louis. Over the next two decades, railroad strikes would be the main sites of court injunctions, although judges also made use of them to combat the growing frequency of citywide boycotts and "sympathy strikes" (strikes in support of other striking workers), which could mobilize whole communities. These were found to be "combinations of irresponsible cabals or cliques" that sought to bring "an end to government."

At times injunctions exposed the close relations between members of the judiciary and railroad companies. Some judges, quite simply, were on the payroll, having represented railroad companies in court, served on their boards, or invested in the lines. But more generally, injunctions showed a meeting of the minds on the social relations of capitalism, on who was "responsible" and who "irresponsible," on private property and freedom of contract. Although some judges worried about the size and power of new industrial interests, they tended to see labor mobilizations, especially when organized by unions, as far more menacing and destructive, possible signs of "communistic" influences that were spreading across the Atlantic. When necessary, the judges had no objection to seeing the troops called in.

Capitalism's Heavy Hands

The railroad strike of 1877 was the largest and most destructive labor conflict in all of the nineteenth century (see Chapter 18). But it also witnessed, for the first time, federal troops deployed to support the interests of capital. Local militia units were ineffective in getting the trains rolling and, in some cases, had even fraternized with the strikers. State officials therefore turned to the national government and received a favorable reply. "The Army is to the United States what a well-disciplined and trained police force is to a city," President Rutherford B. Hayes's secretary of war proclaimed, and top US Army generals like William T. Sherman and Philip Sheridan thrilled at the prospect that labor unrest could bolster the armed services.

Congress was less interested in expanding the size and reach of the US Army, however, so the initiative in dealing with striking workers fell to state and local governments. Some were already prepared. Large cities like New York and Philadelphia had begun to establish uniformed police forces during the 1840s as their populations expanded with Irish Catholic immigrants. The new urban police, often recruited among native- or British-born Protestant artisans, were instructed in the use of coercion rather than persuasion, carrying billy clubs and showing an intimidating bearing. As one police chief instructed his men, "Never arrest a man until you have licked him in a fair fight first." Over the next three decades, the number of police in cities across the United States grew rapidly, and some took over a number of activities of interest to municipal authorities, including surveillance of working-class organizations.

Yet the most important developments may have occurred among the state militias. In the aftermath of the railroad strike of 1877, the National Guard Association was established "to promote military efficiency throughout the active militia of the United States." Over the next decade and a half, states—especially in the industrial belt stretching from the Northeast well out into the West—revised their military codes to provide for newly organized national guard units, greatly increased their funding, and began to require regular training. New armories were soon being built in industrial cities across the country to house, train, and supply what were now called national guardsmen. Countrywide, the number of guardsmen grew to over 100,000, and everywhere their main purpose was to serve as state police officers in the control and suppression of labor unrest.

Although most of the new national guard troops—like most of the country's total population—could be found east of the Missouri River, nowhere did capitalists rely more heavily on the use of force than in the West. This was because federal, state, and territorial officials alike had deep interests—often financial in nature—in western developmental projects. Federal troops were sent to defeat the resistance of Indigenous people to railroad building and to the white settlement that accompanied it, and then were left to protect the lines, which were in private hands. National guardsmen were of-

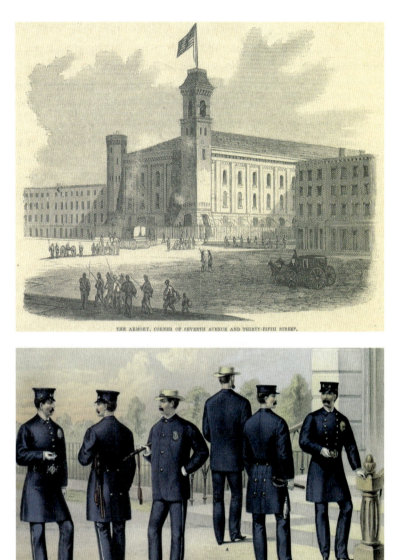

THE ARMORY, CORNER OF SEVENTH AVENUE AND THIRTY-FIFTH STREET.

≡ **Organizing Force**   These views of New York City in the 1870s show two ways cities and states organized force: uniformed police (such as these officers sporting nightsticks) and armories (such as this arsenal, built in 1858).

ten called in by state and territorial governors to suppress labor disputes on the railroads and in the mines of the interior West, in which they might have been personally invested. And when these military forces were insufficient or unavailable, a variety of cattle ranchers, mine owners, and agricultural operators turned to hired gunmen, vigilantes, and private armies (like the notorious Pinkertons) to enforce their rules and punish their adversaries.

This was an approach quite to the liking of former enslavers who neither wanted to see federal troops on the ground nor pay for an expanded state militia. Vigilantes who either served as their families' clients or were directly attached to the Democratic Party thus played a central role in patrolling freedpeople and defeating hostile Reconstruction regimes on the local and state levels. By the 1880s, when the geographical expansion of the cotton and timber economies brought a westward surge of migration on the part of young Black laborers, lynch parties looked to enforce the submission that enslavement and its generational legacies no longer could. In more than a few cases, lynching victims had run afoul of their employers and were accused of murdering them or members of their employers' families. Sheriffs and magistrates generally looked the other way if they were not directly involved in the lynchings themselves.

Conclusion: The Dynamics of Capitalism

The role of the courts and the widespread use of state militias or legally sanctioned violence to manage labor conflict seemed emblematic of American capitalism's complex course during the postwar period. On the one hand, the War of the Rebellion served to energize those forces most committed to advancing a capitalist economy and defeat those who stood in the way. With enormous assistance from the federal government, capital accumulated rapidly in the hands of a new class of manufacturers and financiers who wished to expand the market to every corner of the United States and beyond, and the vital plantation economy of the Deep South was resuscitated and reorganized around labor relations that approximated wage labor. Liberal ideas now wedded to the logic of the marketplace gained influence in middle-class and elite circles, delivering blows to Radical Republicanism, to which they were once attached. Federal and state judiciaries, moreover, were increasingly staffed by judges who held freedom of contract dear and regarded workers as subject to the authority of employers while on the job and potentially dangerous while off of it.

On the other hand, manufacturers faced serious challenges in attempting to enlarge their workplaces and build new factories, as artisans and skilled workers were able to use their technical knowledge to control much of the process of production. Large landowners in the South were short of cash and credit and produced for an international commodities market that was sinking under the weight of grains and fibers being raised in new market economies around the globe. Even the farmers of the Midwest, Plains, and Far West were feeling the squeeze from mortgages on their land and low prices for their crops. The social and political explosions that followed would make for a still newer national and international economic order.

WHAT IF the Confederate Rebellion Had Not Been Defeated?

There can be little doubt that capitalism, as a system, was on the march across much of the Atlantic—and to a lesser extent the Pacific—worlds by the middle of the nineteenth century. But it is also clear that capitalism required significant help in order to keep advancing, especially from the institutions of government: protecting forms of property; validating the currency and instruments of exchange; establishing rules about contracts, employment, and ownership; investing in turnpikes, canals, and railroads; favoring certain sectors of the economy at the expense of others through taxation, banking, and tariffs; policing society to maintain order.

Capitalism would have continued to develop in the United States whatever the outcome of the War of the Rebellion, because the United States was already part of a globalizing system. But what would it have been like if the federal government side failed to subdue the Confederate rebellion and instead either reunified with the slave South or broke into several pieces? What would have been the fate of the financial and manufacturing sectors or of the big landed classes? What would have been the fate of the slavery system or the status and rights of African Americans, whether enslaved or free? How might the agricultural sector have fared and what might the future have held for yeoman farmers? Would Indigenous people of the trans-Mississippi West have had a different fate? Might the United States have remained more of an agricultural and small-town society rather than a rapidly urbanizing and industrializing one?

DOCUMENT 17.1: Excerpts from the Confederate Constitution

The Confederate Constitution, written and ratified in 1861, offers a glimpse of the Confederacy's perspective on the future of enslavement and people of African descent in their "country" and possibly beyond it.

Article 1, Section 3: Representatives and direct taxes shall be apportioned among the several States, which may be included within this Confederacy, according to their respective numbers, which shall be determined by adding to the whole number of free persons, including those bound to service for a term of years, and excluding Indians not taxed, three-fifths of all slaves. The actual enumeration shall be made within three years after the first meeting of the Congress of the Confederate States, and within every subsequent term of ten years,

Article 1, Section 9: No bill of attainder, ex post facto law, or law denying or impairing the right of property in negro slaves shall be passed.

Article 4, Section 2(1): The citizens of each State shall be entitled to all the privileges and immunities of citizens in the several States; and shall have the right of transit and sojourn in any

State of this Confederacy, with their slaves and other property; and the right of property in said slaves shall not be thereby impaired.

Article 4, Section 2(3): No slave or other person held to service or labor in any State or Territory of the Confederate States, under the laws thereof, escaping or lawfully carried into another, shall, in consequence of any law or regulation therein, be discharged from such service or labor; but shall be delivered up on claim of the party to whom such slave belongs,. or to whom such service or labor may be due.

Article 4, Section 3: The Confederate States may acquire new territory; and Congress shall have power to legislate and provide governments for the inhabitants of all territory belonging to the Confederate States, lying without the limits of the several Sates; and may permit them, at such times, and in such manner as it may by law provide, to form States to be admitted into the Confederacy. In all such territory the institution of negro slavery, as it now exists in the Confederate States, shall be recognized and protected be Congress and by the Territorial government; and the inhabitants of the several Confederate States and Territories shall have the right to take to such Territory any slaves lawfully held by them in any of the States or Territories of the Confederate States.

Source: Richardson, James D. A Compilation of the Messages and Papers of the Confederacy Including the Diplomatic Correspondence 1861–1865 (Nashville, TN: United States Publishing Company, 1905).

DOCUMENT 17.2: Frederick Douglass, "The Lessons of the Hour," January 9, 1894

In this speech delivered in Washington, DC, Douglass warns that the repression and exploitation of Black people in the South has implications for the nation as a whole, hinting at what an even more politically powerful white South would have had in store.

The land owners of the South want the labor of the negro on the hardest possible terms. They once had it for nothing. They now want it for next to nothing and they have contrived three ways of thus obtaining it. The first is to rent their land to the negro at an exorbitant price per annum, and compel him to mortgage his crop in advance. The laws under which this is done are entirely in the interest of the landlord. He has a first claim upon everything produced on the land. The negro can have nothing, can keep nothing, can sell nothing, without the consent of the landlord. As the negro is at the start poor and empty handed, he has to draw on the landlord for meat and bread to feed himself and family while his crop is growing. The landlord keeps books; the negro does not; hence, no matter how hard he may work or how saving he may be, he is, in most cases, brought in debt at the end of the year, and once in debt, he is fastened to the land as by hooks of steel. If he attempts to leave he may be arrested under the law . . .

The presence of eight millions of people in any section of this country constituting an aggrieved class, smarting under terrible wrongs, denied the exercise of the commonest rights of humanity, and regarded by the ruling class in that section, as outside of the government, outside of the law, and outside of society; having nothing in common with the people with whom they live, the sport of mob violence and murder is not only a disgrace and scandal to that particular section but a menace to the peace and security of the people of the whole country I have waited patiently but anxiously to see the end of the epidemic of mob law and persecution now prevailing at the South. But the indications are not hopeful, great and terrible as have been its ravages in the past, it now seems to be in—creasing not only in the number of its victims, but in its frantic rage and savage extravagance. Lawless vengeance is beginning to be visited upon white men as well as black. Our newspapers are daily disfigured by its ghastly horrors. It is no longer local, but national; no longer confined to the South, but has invaded the North. The contagion is spreading, extending and over-leaping geographical lines and state boundaries, and if permitted to go on it threatens to destroy all respect for law and order not only in the South, but in all parts of our country—North as well as South. For certain it is, that crime allowed to go on unresisted and unarrested will breed crime. When the poison of anarchy is once in the air, like the pestilence that walketh in the darkness, the winds of heaven will take it up and favor its diffusion.

Though it may strike down the weak to-day, it will strike down the strong to-morrow. Not a breeze comes to us now from the late rebellious States that is not tainted and freighted with negro blood. In its thirst for blood and its rage for vengeance, the mob has blindly, boldly and defiantly supplanted sheriffs, constables and police. It has assumed all the functions of civil authority. It laughs at legal processes, courts and juries, and its redhanded murderers range abroad unchecked and unchallenged by law or by public opinion. Prison walls and iron bars are no protection to the innocent or guilty, if the mob is in pursuit of negroes accused of crime. Jail doors are battered down in the presence of unresisting jailors, and the accused, awaiting trial in the courts of law are dragged out and hanged, shot, stabbed or burned to death as the blind and irresponsible mob may elect.We claim to be a Christian country and a highly civilized nation, yet, I fearlessly affirm that there is nothing in the history of savages to surpass the blood chilling horrors and fiendish excesses perpetrated against the colored people by the so-called enlightened and Christian people of the South.

Source: https://www.loc.gov/item/mss1187900481/

Thinking About Contingency

1. What would it have meant for the development of the country after the Civil War if the enslavement of African Americans continued into the early twentieth century or was subject to very gradual abolition?
2. Given the political power of southern enslavers during the first half of the nineteenth century, how would the maintenance or expansion of their power have shaped the country?
3. Who, aside from the enslavers, would have benefitted from an outcome to the War of the Rebellion if the Confederates had not been not defeated? Yeoman farmers? Indigenous people?
4. If the federal government had failed to defeat the Confederate rebellion militarily, what would have been the likely political results for the organization of the United States and how would American development have been affected?

REVIEW QUESTIONS

1. How did a new class of financiers gain power and wealth as a result of the Civil War? How did capitalists form a web of social, economic, and political relationships that strengthened their hold on power? Why did Mark Twain describe this period in American history as the "Gilded Age"?

2. Why does capitalism represent a radical new force, providing both new opportunities for enrichment and new conditions of dependence?

3. How did cities and industries come to dominate rural areas and agriculture economically? How were the South and West transformed after the War?

4. How did industrialization and immigration transform American society in the late nineteenth century?

5. How did the courts and the military, as well as new ideas like social Darwinism, help secure the hold of American capitalism?

KEY TERMS

anti-enticement laws (p. 701)

Battle of Little Bighorn (p. 703)

bonanza farms (p. 708)

capital goods (p. 711)

company towns (p. 707)

consumer goods (p. 709)

Credit Mobilier scandal (p. 696)

crop liens (p. 701)

fence and game laws (p. 701)

Gilded Age (p. 692)

incorporation (p. 718)

long drives (p. 707)

master and servant (p. 723)

migrant laborers (p. 708)

money question (p. 695)

Panic of 1873 (p. 693)

pools (p. 718)

sharecropping (p. 700)

social Darwinism (p. 721)

vagrancy laws (p. 701)

RECOMMENDED READINGS

Sven Beckert, *The Monied Metropolis: New York City and the Consolidation of the American Bourgeoisie, 1850–1896* (Cambridge University Press, 2001).

Nancy Cohen, *The Reconstruction of American Liberalism, 1865–1914* (University of North Carolina Press, 2002).

Richard Hofstadter, *Social Darwinism in American Thought* (University of Pennsylvania Press, 1944).

Jonathan Levy, *Freaks of Fortune: The Emerging World of Capitalism and Risk in America* (Harvard University Press, 2014).

Walter Licht, *Industrializing America: The Nineteenth Century* (Johns Hopkins University Press, 1995).

David Nasaw, *Andrew Carnegie* (Penguin, 2007).

Karen Orren, *Belated Feudalism: Labor, Law, and Liberal Development in the United States* (Cambridge University Press, 1992).

Rodman Paul, *The Far West and Great Plains in Transition, 1859–1900* (Harper and Row, 1988).

Amy Dru Stanley, *From Bondage to Contract: Wage Labor, Marriage, and the Market in the Age of Emancipation* (Cambridge University Press, 1998).

Richard White, *Railroaded: The Transcontinentals and the Making of Modern America* (W.W. Norton, 2011).

Harold D. Woodman, *New South, New Law: The Legal Foundations of Labor and Credit Relations in the Postbellum South* (Louisiana State University Press, 1995).

18

Cauldrons of Protest
1873–1896

Chapter Outline

18.1 Antimonopoly

||| Explain the meaning and significance of "antimonopoly."

18.2 Communities in Arms

||| Assess the community support that striking workers often received.

18.3 The Explosions of 1886

||| Describe the causes and impact of the massive social conflicts that erupted in 1886.

18.4 Recasting the Republic

||| Evaluate the efforts made by labor and independent political organizations to forge change at the ballot box.

18.5 A Cooperative Commonwealth

||| Consider how a cooperative commonwealth represented an alternative to the political and social order of industrialization.

18.6 A Social Democratic Legacy

||| Analyze how the popular protests of the Gilded Age contributed a historical legacy of social democratic ideas and projects.

≡ **Celebrating Labor**   The first Labor Day was celebrated in New York City in 1882. This ribbon from 1887 features the "arm and hammer" symbol that has long been identified with the labor movement.

Few Americans symbolized the political arc of late nineteenth-century popular protest better than Ignatius Donnelly. Born in Philadelphia, Pennsylvania, in 1826, he moved out to Minnesota in the 1850s where he became active in the antislavery politics of the Republican Party and was soon elected to Congress. Serving three terms in the midst of the War of the Rebellion, Donnelly aligned with the Radical Republicans both for the nationalism of their economic program and for their interest in advancing the rights and protecting the lives of the freedpeople in the South.

But by the early 1870s, Donnelly left Republican politics behind and joined the Saint Paul chapter of the Grange (officially named the National Grange of the Order of Patrons of Husbandry), an agricultural organization that fought against the power and privileges of railroad companies. Recognizing what farmers and workers were up against, he helped to establish the state's Anti-Monopoly Party while editing a weekly paper called the *Anti-Monopolist*. Both set their sights on "monopolies" of wealth and

Timeline

1868	1870	1872	1874	1876	1878	1880	1882	1884

1869 ▸ Knights of Labor organized in Philadelphia

1874 ▸ Greenback-Labor Party organized in Indianapolis

1877 ▸ Great Railroad Strike

1879 ▸ Henry George publishes *Progress and Poverty*

1882 ▸ Congress passes Chinese Exclusion Act

power, the control over economic and political life that large-scale businesses and the very rich could exercise at the expense of ordinary men and women. Before the decade was out, Donnelly aligned with the Greenback-Labor Party, which was mobilizing farmers and workers across the country in the interest of transforming the monetary system. He also headed up the Minnesota branch of the Farmers' Alliance, which scorned Eastern bankers and financiers and looked toward building agricultural cooperatives to raise the prices of crops and lower the interest for the credit that most farmers needed.

But in July 1892, Donnelly truly stepped forth on a new political stage. Indeed, on July 4, as hundreds of delegates meeting in Omaha, Nebraska, formed the People's or Populist Party, Donnelly took the stage to deliver the preamble, which he had crafted, to the Populist platform. "We meet in the midst of a nation brought to the verge of moral, political, and material ruin [where] corruption dominates the ballot box,

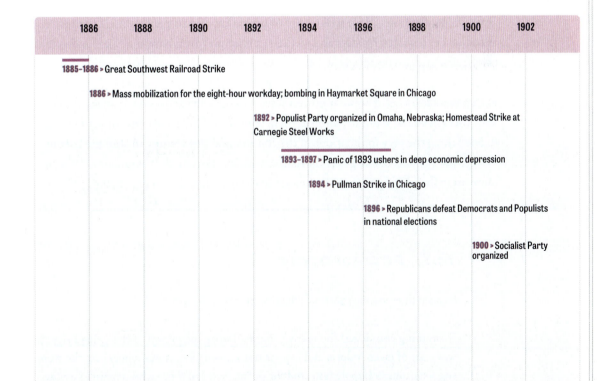

1886	1888	1890	1892	1894	1896	1898	1900	1902

1885–1886 › Great Southwest Railroad Strike

1886 › Mass mobilization for the eight-hour workday; bombing in Haymarket Square in Chicago

1892 › Populist Party organized in Omaha, Nebraska; Homestead Strike at Carnegie Steel Works

1893–1897 › Panic of 1893 ushers in deep economic depression

1894 › Pullman Strike in Chicago

1896 › Republicans defeat Democrats and Populists in national elections

1900 › Socialist Party organized

the Legislatures, the Congress, and touches even the ermine of the bench," he thundered. The press had been muzzled, labor had been pauperized, the money supply was controlled by bondholders and other private interests, and the "womb of government injustice" had produced "two great classes—tramps and millionaires." Instead, the Populists would offer a new vision in which "the power of government—in other words of the people—should be expanded to the end that oppression, injustice, and poverty shall eventually cease in the land." Thus launched, advocating a nationwide system of cooperatives (farm or popular business organizations owned and run jointly by their members, who share the profits and benefits), an inflationary currency in public hands, government ownership of the railroads and telegraph, and a graduated income tax, the Populists—feeding off the ideas of the Grange, the Greenbackers, and the Farmers' Alliance, as Donnelly had done—would become the largest third-party movement in American history.

In the three decades after 1870, as capitalism took hold in the United States, popular protest—so clearly embodied in Donnelly's personal history—took hold as well. It erupted in cities and rural areas, in almost all types of economic and political environments, and eventually touched all corners of the country. Protest involved street demonstrations, labor strikes, the organization of insurgent political parties, and alliances between farmers and workers; sometimes even between Black and white people. Protest also involved the development of political vocabularies and connections that were international in scope. Before long, elites became fearful of the advances that various forms of popular protest were making and used a variety of means to keep them in check, if not to suppress them entirely. By the 1890s, the unrest seemed to be shaking the very foundations of the country and threatening to shift the balances of power in efforts to forge an alternative path for the nation. It would be a defining moment in the making of modern American society. How did it come to be?

18.1 Antimonopoly

||| Explain the meaning and significance of "antimonopoly."

If anything connected the many protests during the period of the Gilded Age, it was a set of ideas, values, and aspirations known as "antimonopoly." As the term suggests, antimonopoly reflected the perspectives of those who remained wedded to a world that was being rapidly overrun. It was a world in which farmers, artisans, and small manufacturers—small-scale producers—still defined the social relations of the American economy, in which the distribution of wealth was not extremely skewed, in which power was widely dispersed, in which economic independence could still be achieved, and in which the government embodied the will of the people rather than that of the rich and powerful. Antimonopoly had deep roots in American political culture as well as in the wider Atlantic world. It found expression among labor reformers in the 1820s and 1830s, opponents of banks and paper money in the 1840s and 1850s, critics of enslavement, and European revolutionaries in 1848. But antimonopoly won special appeal in the postwar era as capitalism took hold.

Progress and Poverty

One man spoke with special power for antimonopoly. His name was Henry George, and he had come to California from Philadelphia in the 1850s to seek his fortune in the gold rush of 1849. Like many with this ambition, however, George failed and ended up in the bustling town of San Francisco. Fortunately, he had typesetting skills and found work editing a newspaper. Yet he was also unsettled by what he had been observing. Having grown up in a household of Jacksonian Democrats back east, George was both attracted by California's frontier character and shocked by the speculative mania that followed the gold rush. The social landscape seemed one of great mansions alongside miserable shanties. George was especially riled by the government land grants, particularly to railroad companies, that put large sections of the public domain into private hands. Why was it, he wondered, that "advancing wealth" brought "advancing poverty" along with it?

In the late 1870s, George decided to find an answer and sat down to write a book. He called it *Progress and Poverty*. It didn't make for light reading. At more than 500 pages, it was a hefty volume and engaged with the leading economic and political theorists of the time. As George saw it, the main problem for the country was that a few wealthy men had come to "monopolize" one of the basic means of production—land—and, as a result, were able to drive working people out of gainful employment and force their wages down. "The great cause of inequality in the distribution of wealth," George wrote, "is inequality in the ownership of land."

Although George was sympathetic to the idea of making land "common property," he did not really favor "restricting landownership." Instead, he called for a policy of taxation on land—it would be labeled the "**single tax**"—equivalent to the value of rent which, he believed, would discourage speculation and monopolization. Landowners would see no benefit in accumulating land because they

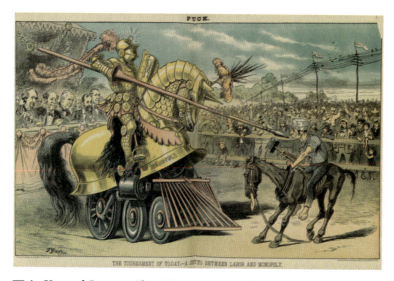

PUCK.

THE TOURNAMENT OF TODAY—A SET TO BETWEEN LABOR AND MONOPOLY.

An Unequal Contest   This 1883 print sums up the inequalities that Henry George identified. An enormous and gilded knight, representing capitalism, is about to spear a puny horseman who represents labor.

would have to pay the tax. Therefore, they would either put the land to productive use or sell it off to aspiring farmers.

Progress and Poverty was a spectacular success when it was published in 1879. In nineteenth-century America, only the Bible and *Uncle Tom's Cabin* sold more copies. How was that possible? George didn't tell riveting stories or use inflated language or include lots of illustrations. What he did do, however, was strike a familiar note of political concern that resonated across the country. He articulated what was on the minds of millions of people, addressing an issue that troubled them, and offering a way to think about it. What he articulated were antimonopoly sensibilities energized by the inequalities George saw and by the struggles that the advance of capitalism was provoking. One of the most important, along with the "land question," involved the "money question" and the fate of "greenbacks."

Greenbackers

Greenbacks, as we saw, were a paper currency issued by the federal government to help finance the War of the Rebellion. They were accepted for taxes and various forms of exchange but were not redeemable (you couldn't exchange them) for gold or silver coin. Their value was effectively backed up by the integrity of the federal government and the interest-bearing bonds the government sold. As long as greenbacks remained in circulation, the government was directly in control of the money supply, and smaller producers in towns and rural districts had more access to the cash they needed for their shops, farms, and debts.

The problem was that bankers and other financial interests wanted the greenbacks removed from circulation and replaced by specie-backed currency (gold preferably, or some combination of gold and silver) that privately owned banks holding charters in the National Banking system would issue. At first, as we saw in Chapter 17, the financial interests won out. The federal government, determined to gradually retire the greenbacks. But, especially after the Panic of 1873, greenback supporters rallied and attempted to organize their ranks. In late 1874, meeting in Indianapolis, Indiana, they launched the Greenback-Labor Party with the hope of winning political power.

What was this all about? **Greenbackers**, as they were known, had come to believe that the banking system was at the core of the economic troubles the country was facing: a version of Henry George's argument about land. Banks were privately owned and, if they had a national charter, could issue money. They therefore could control how much money was in circulation and manipulate interest rates to their own benefit. Bankers and lenders were in the driver's seat—just as land speculators were—"monopolizing" essential resources, and producers who needed credit were at their mercy.

The solution to this injustice, from the Greenbackers' perspective, was to put the federal government—an extension of the public in their view—in control of money and banking, and to make greenbacks. This meant that interest rates could be kept low, and the money supply could be increased or decreased as the needs of agriculture and industry demanded. The volume of currency, that is, would be adjusted to the requirements of economic growth rather than to those of bankers' profits.

Greenback ideas won the allegiance of many farmers and small manufacturers who felt exploited by railroad companies or creditors. They were especially numerous in New England, parts of the Middle Atlantic, the Upper Plains, the Rocky Mountains, and the Far West. But the strongest exponents of the greenback faith were labor reformers and unionists, some affiliated with the recently organized National Labor Union (1866) as well as with the Radical wing of the Republican Party. Beginning in 1876, they cast many votes for the Greenback-Labor Party, not only electing twenty members of Congress but also making strong showings on the local level, especially in industrial and mining towns like Toledo, Ohio. There the Greenbackers swept the city and some of the county offices and sent two of their candidates to the state legislature.

By the late 1870s, greenback and other antimonopoly perspectives were giving rise to a host of new organizations. The Patrons of Husbandry (the **Grange**) promoted the social and economic needs of farmers with education about advanced farming methods and cooperative economic efforts. Granges spread through the cash crop districts of the Plains, Midwest, and Southeast calling for railroad regulation and the creation of marketing and purchasing cooperatives to avoid the monopolizing hold of "middle men." The Farmers' Alliance emerged in Texas to "better the condition of the agricultural classes" and in some cases worked with

Greenbackers in local electoral contests. But the threads of antimonopoly came together with special strength in a labor union known as the Knights of Labor.

The Knights of Labor and the Eight-Hour Workday

The **Knights of Labor** was established in Philadelphia in the late 1860s but only began a period of growth in the 1870s. When the Knights met in the town of Reading, Pennsylvania, for their first national convention, they chose Terence V. Powderly, a machinist and the Greenback-Labor mayor of Scranton, as their president. Unlike previous labor organizations, built around skilled workers and artisans, the Knights opened their ranks to the unskilled as well and were happy to welcome sympathetic shopkeepers, merchants, and manufacturers. Only bankers, stockbrokers, lawyers, gamblers, and liquor dealers—associated with idleness, vice, and corruption—were barred.

The goals that inspired the Knights included the abolition of convict labor, the implementation of a graduated income tax, and land policies that favored settlers rather than speculators (like Henry George). Worried about the "alarming development and aggressiveness of great capitalists and corporations," they also called for a bureau of labor statistics, government protection of the health and safety of workers, cooperative institutions, and a greenback-based monetary system. But the issue with which the Knights would become most closely identified, and which brought forth their distinctive contribution to antimonopoly, was the eight-hour workday.

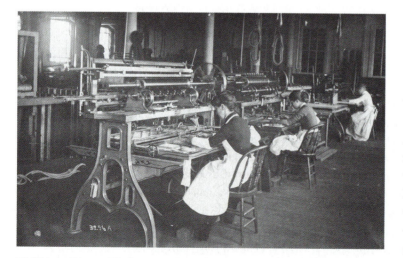

≡ **Women Factory Workers, c. 1885** The seeming tranquility of this scene of women working in a cloth factory should not belie the long hours on the job that they and other wage workers faced. After laboring ten, eleven, or twelve hours a day, there was little time for families, communities, or leisure.

The hours of labor are often regarded as "bread and butter" issues that speak mainly to the material interests of workers. In the postwar period, the norm was ten hours per day, though a great many workers labored for longer stints; reducing those hours would certainly lighten the burdens of their lives. But for workers who began to rally around the cause of the eight-hour workday, something much more was at stake. Indeed, supporters of the eight-hour workday had an expansive political vision. Like labor reformers who came before them, they believed that wage work threatened economic dependency, and that long hours on the job made for a type of slavery—"**wage slavery**" they termed it—in which employers "monopolized" all of the waking hours of their employees. After working ten, eleven, or twelve hours, wage workers had little time for families, communities, or themselves.

The eight-hour workday therefore not only improved material conditions, but it also strengthened working-class households and social institutions, and enabled workers to pursue education, culture, and the obligations of citizenship: to participate fully in political life. "Eight hours for work, eight hours for rest, eight hours for what we will!" was the great slogan. Together with monetary and land reform and the promotion of producers' cooperatives, the eight-hour workday was seen as striking a blow against the "**wages system**"—in which free laborers are hired by capitalists to do the productive work of society—and setting the basis for a new type of commonwealth.

The Chinese Question

How encompassing would this commonwealth be? The Knights claimed to open their organization to the "industrial masses . . . irrespective of party, race, and sex," and in this stated principle they were bold and pioneering. By the mid-1880s women and African Americans each accounted for about 10 percent of the Knights' membership. Yet women mostly established their own assemblies, and in no cases were assemblies integrated by race. Although President Powderly insisted that the order recognized no color line, the reality on the ground was very different. Segregated assemblies might join together in labor actions, but white members generally objected to "working in the same assembly with the negroes."

Even more powerful was the Knights' opposition to the Chinese. They were to be utterly excluded. In this the Knights embraced a perspective and movement that had been developing in California since the 1850s and traveled very rapidly eastward. Although the Chinese played an important role in the American industrial economy, especially on railroad crews out West, they confounded ideas of belonging that many Americans had come to accept. They were considered "semi-barbarians" and "heathens," an inferior race of people who were "incapable of assimilating." They had been brought to the United States in groups, and overwhelmingly male in number, did not form families or practice the Christian faith. The few women among them were thought (wrongly) to be disease-ridden prostitutes. Some observers compared the Chinese to Native Americans in their otherness, and when it came to civil and political rights, they, like Native Americans, were shut out.

Yet for many workers and their allies, the most unsettling thing about the Chinese was their apparent status as wage slaves, utterly dependent and submissive, able to survive on the lowest of wages. In an age of emancipation, the Chinese seemed to be reintroducing a form of bondage into American society. "It is slavery in another form," a California newspaper charged. The racist term for the Chinese was "coolie," and anti-coolie clubs demanded an end to Chinese immigration, prohibited them from some of the craft associations, and, on occasion, moved to drive them out by violent means. In the 1870s, a powerful Workingmen's Party took control of the San Francisco city government on a vicious anti-Chinese platform and helped write a new state constitution that denied Chinese the right to vote.

So strong did anti-Chinese sentiment become that it bridged political and social divisions and contemplated extreme measures. Although the Burlingame Treaty signed in 1868 had lent China most favored nation status with regard to trade and lifted restrictions on immigration, national political leaders soon moved toward a policy of outright exclusion. In May 1882, by overwhelming margins, Congress passed, and Republican President Chester A. Arthur signed, a bill banning the immigration of "all Chinese laborers" for a decade (the law was renewed until 1943). Not by accident did this **Chinese Exclusion Act** come at the very time that the federal government was also abandoning African Americans in the South, completing the confinement of Native Americans on reservations, and conferring on corporations the status of citizenship under the Fourteenth Amendment.

Henry George was among those who voiced his support for Chinese exclusion. Like others who shared his perspective, George believed the Chinese were "utter heathens, treacherous, sensuous, cowardly, and cruel . . . an infusible element." But George also feared that the Chinese would depress wages, promote the monopolies of railroad companies and land purchasers who hired them, and move coolieism (exploitation of workers at substandard wages) across the country. It was an exacerbated version of the social fate that *Progress and Poverty* was meant to expose. Yet on what basis could the Chinese—and other victims of monopolization—those who had been rendered dependent and submissive, be included in the struggle for an alternative America that

≣ **Anti-Chinese Riot** Anti-Chinese sentiment exploded into violence in Denver on Halloween night, 1880. An enraged mob of white people destroyed Chinese-owned property and killed one man.

George and his antimonopoly allies were seeking to forge? This was the challenge and dilemma at the heart of antimonopoly.

18.2 Communities in Arms

||| Assess the community support that striking workers often received.

During the 1870s and 1880s, the term "class" became an important part of the American political vocabulary. It reflected the significant social divisions that the postwar development of capitalism was creating and the increasingly antagonistic perspectives of employers and the men and women who labored for them. Antimonopoly offered a language to describe these divisions as well as a moral stance by which those divisions and their making could be judged. Especially revealing during this period was the community support workers could attract to aid them in their struggles. In many cases, that support was crucial to how those struggles played out.

The Great Railroad Strike of 1877

The Knights of Labor grew rapidly after an unprecedented strike against some of the nation's largest railroads. Provoked by a series of wage cuts, the strike began in mid-July 1877, spread rapidly from east to west, involved thousands of workers, and shut down lines of vital rail traffic for days. As great as this work stoppage was, the idea of "strike" doesn't quite capture the dynamics of the episode. Almost everywhere, striking railroad workers had the backing of local residents, whether craftsmen, shopkeepers, merchandisers, or laborers who sympathized with their

≡ **The Great Railroad Strike, 1877** Nothing on the scale of the Great Strike of 1877 had ever happened before. In the middle of that year, much of the nation's railroad system—the very symbol of American progress, wealth, and modernity—was shut down by angry employees. This engraving shows the destruction of Union Depot in Pittsburgh during the Great Railroad Strike.

struggle. In some places local sympathizers left their own jobs in solidarity; in some they created new political institutions; in some they and the strikers armed themselves and took control of the railroads; and in some they torched railroad yards. So convulsive and threatening did the Great Railroad Strike of 1877 become that officials described it as an "insurrection" and moved to crush it with military force.

Why could these striking workers depend on such strong public support? It was because community members, across class and ethnic lines, themselves had long-standing grievances against the railroads. They objected to the railroad corporations' size and arrogance, financial manipulations, political corruption, monopolistic power, and utter disregard for the welfare of the communities they traversed. Railroad tracks usually were laid directly through the main streets and neighborhoods of cities and towns, where working people lived in large numbers. The noise, smoke, congestion, and dangers to pedestrians had become worse and worse, and local governments seemed unable to hold the railroads accountable. That is why this strike—of workers who resisted the railroads' efforts to make them shoulder the burdens of economic downturns—unleashed popular outrage.

Sympathies for strikers not only mobilized local communities but, at times, reached into the local police and even the state militia, whose members could well be friends and neighbors. Instead of trying to break the strike and get the railroad cars moving, some police and militia fraternized with the strikers and came to their defense. As a result, frustrated state governors saw no alternative to requesting the sending in of US Army troops, who had no ties to the communities they occupied and were well armed. Tellingly as to the political direction of the country, the soldiers sent to put an end to the Railroad Strike of 1877 had previously been deployed in the Reconstruction South. "The strikers have been put down by *force*," Republican President Rutherford B. Hayes proclaimed.

But the strike's defeat only raised workers' interest in adjusting the balances of power in the Gilded Age. "The railroad strike of 1877 was the tocsin [alarm bell] that sounded a ringing message of hope to us all," labor leader Samuel Gompers (discussed in Chapter 19) later recalled. It did indeed. Strike activity increased rather than diminished after 1877. Over the next seven years more than 450 strikes involving well over 100,000 workers took place annually across the nation; in 1886 there were more than 1,400 strikes involving over 400,000 workers. Equally significant, only about half of all the strikes were called by unions and most were provoked by wage cuts—a pattern that had been in evidence since the early 1870s and one that testified to their community-based and politically rebellious nature.

In smaller towns and semirural areas, strikers continued to push back against what they considered the arbitrary power of employers who often had no ties, other than investments, to their communities, and they could usually depend on the support of nonstrikers to whom they were related or economically interdependent. In larger cities, striking workers could count on the assistance of central labor unions and trades assemblies that could offer a range of material and political resources.

Labor Conflict in the South

Similar dynamics were at play in parts of the plantation South where field hands still had local and state political allies. When rice workers along the South Carolina coast responded to pay cuts and remuneration in scrip (a form of payment that could only be redeemed at the company store) rather than cash with a massive strike in 1876, they held a better hand than might have been expected. They moved in squads from plantation to plantation rallying fellow workers and pressuring those still in the fields to join them. Alarmed, the planters sought a "strong hand" to restore "order." But they could not find one.

The Reconstruction regime in the state had not yet collapsed. Many of the local officials, including the trial justices, were Black Republicans. The state militia, tasked with imposing order, was composed mainly of coastal Black men who sympathized with the strikers. And the governor was a Republican who refused to intervene on the planters' side. Instead, the governor sent a formerly enslaved man and now a representative in the US Congress named Robert Smalls to negotiate a settlement. Before long, the planters yielded and strikers who had been arrested were released. The new power relations that Reconstruction brought into being made a great difference for the people most in need of political support.

Four years later, a similar sort of strike erupted in the sugar parishes of lower Louisiana, this one owing to price increases for necessities rather than wage cuts. Workers mobilized, drew up a "constitution," and resolved to hold out for "a dollar a day." The governor, who by this point was a white Democrat, immediately called out the state militia (no longer loyal to the Republicans), and white officials in some of the parishes had the strike ringleaders arrested for trespass. But another of the parish sheriffs was Black and he blocked them while the Black state senator stepped in as a mediator. The white state militia quickly backed down, many of the arrested strikers gained release, and a new workingmen's protective association was organized. With that, a foundation was established that enabled the Knights of Labor to move into the sugar parishes in the early 1880s, create its own network of assemblies, and play a significant role in a sugar strike later in the decade.

The Knights and the Decision to Strike

On the one hand, mobilizations such as these turned the Knights of Labor into the largest and most formidable labor organization of the era. By 1886, the Knights

≡ **Women Delegates to the 1886 Convention of the Knights of Labor** Elizabeth Rodgers, the woman in the center, holds her two-week-old daughter, Lizzie, on her lap. This photo demonstrated working women's allegiance to the labor movement.

could claim nearly 10,000 assemblies nationwide with roughly three-quarters of a million members. The assemblies stretched from the Northeast through the mid-Atlantic and Midwestern industrial belts, into the mining districts of the Rockies, and to the ports of the West Coast. Linking town and countryside, most of the Knights' new recruits were semiskilled and unskilled workers, a harbinger of the industrial organizing that would occur during the twentieth century.

On the other hand, for all of the strikes that erupted across the country, the Knights' national leadership, especially Terence Powderly, took a dim view of them. In part, this was because Powderly hoped to build a large organization with a committed rank and file, and he feared that strikes attracted members who would quickly leave the order if they were defeated. But the issue was also ideological. The antimonopoly views of the Knights' leaders, despite including a thunderous critique of postbellum capitalism, saw the world divided between "producers" and "non-producers," between those who created wealth and those who accumulated and manipulated it. Powderly "cursed the word class," set his sights on abolishing "wage slavery," and imagined that "thorough organization" and "arbitration" (private settlement of a dispute) would work more effectively than strikes.

As it turned out, "thorough organization" and "arbitration" could not ward off the assaults of employers who unilaterally cut wages or violated work rules. And, at the grassroots, members of the Knights generally recognized as much. Indeed, militancy and experimentation could be found among the rank and file despite Powderly's caution. Such was the case along railroad tycoon Jay Gould's sprawling "southwest system" where massive strikes broke out in 1885–1886. Gould was a good target for the workers' wrath. Like many other "monied men" of the late nineteenth century, Gould had made his fortune during the War of the Rebellion in financial speculation before turning his eyes to the railroads. By the early 1880s, he controlled a railroad empire that ran from Illinois out through Colorado and Texas and included at least seven lines with 15,000 miles of track. If that was not enough, Gould also took over the *New York World* and Western Union Telegraph. But when the economic crunch came, he was quick to reduce the wages and hours of his employees and risk a backlash. So confident was Gould in the power he wielded that he boasted he "could hire one half of the working class to kill the other half."

The workers proved him wrong. As in previous railroad strikes, they initially won the sympathy and support of the public and much of the press both because of the dire privations many of them suffered and because of Gould's reputation for greed and corruption. To many observers, Gould was the consummate "**robber baron**," enriching himself at the workers' expense and deserving little but scorn. Reading the public mood, Gould officials soon looked for an accommodation, and they agreed to restore wages that were cut and rehire the strikers even if they belonged to the Knights. But there was still skepticism about the company's intentions and more militance in the local Knights' assemblies than national leaders thought wise.

≡ **Webs of Power** This 1885 cartoon shows Jay Gould as a spider flitting across a web of Western Union telecommunication lines that ensnare the justice and political system.

18.3 The Explosions of 1886

Describe the causes and impact of the massive social conflicts that erupted in 1886.

The "Great Southwest Strike," as it was called, began in a context of nationwide agitation and expectation over the eight-hour workday. Although the federal government had enacted eight-hour legislation for mechanics and laborers it employed, and although some states and municipalities had done the same, the laws were generally ignored by employers and rarely enforced by public authorities. The courts, for their part, ruled that eight-hour laws violated what they regarded as the cardinal principle of the new industrial economy: **freedom of contract**. Workers,

MAPPING AMERICA

Immigration at National and Local Levels

In the late nineteenth century, the Chinese Exclusion Act was the lone form of immigration restriction in the United States. As a result, the United States led all nations in the Western Hemisphere in the admission of transatlantic immigrants, receiving from 1871 to 1914 nearly 25 million immigrants. By comparison, Canada received 4.6 million new arrivals, Argentina 4.5 million, and Brazil 3.2 million. The United States was also a leading destination for immigrants from Asia who were not legally excluded.

Thinking Geographically

1. What historical narratives can be read in Map 1? Which historical and economic developments explain the great diversity of some regions of the country and the lack of diversity in other regions?

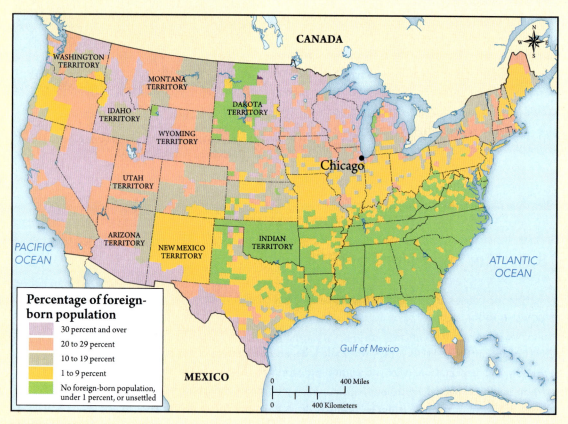

Percentage of foreign-born population

- 30 percent and over
- 20 to 29 percent
- 10 to 19 percent
- 1 to 9 percent
- No foreign-born population, under 1 percent, or unsettled

≡ **MAP 1** This map shows the foreign-born population of the United States in 1880. Regional differences are clearly visible, with the South far less diverse than the West, Southwest, or Upper Midwest.

2. Looking at Map 2, what inferences can you make about how the different ethnic groups living in Chicago in 1900 interacted with each other? Did they forge connections? Or did they confine themselves to their diasporic enclaves? How did they fit into wider American society?

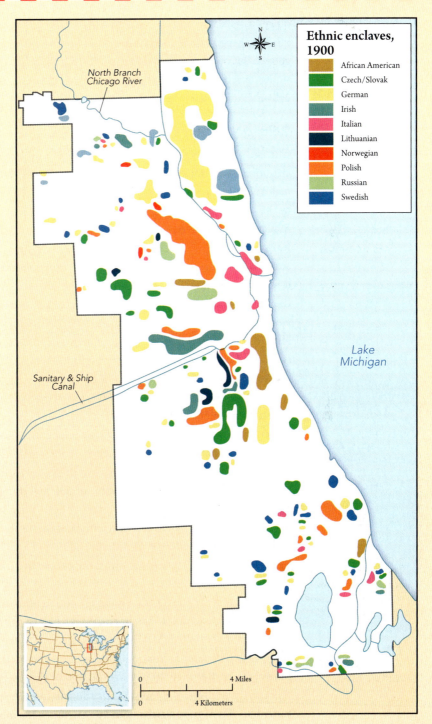

North Branch Chicago River

Ethnic enclaves, 1900

- African American
- Czech/Slovak
- German
- Irish
- Italian
- Lithuanian
- Norwegian
- Polish
- Russian
- Swedish

Sanitary & Ship Canal

Lake Michigan

≡ **MAP 2**   Tightening up our lens, we can see the new composite pattern of diversity on display in a particular locale: Chicago. This map shows a kaleidoscope of ethnic groups clustered into distinct neighborhoods, or enclaves.

0 ——— 4 Miles

0 ——— 4 Kilometers

judges insisted, should be "free" to enter into any contracts they chose to without inhibiting regulations, a legal argument that utterly ignored the power relations involved. But optimism had been growing in labor's ranks, and the Knights set their sights on achieving the goal in the spring of 1886. The city of Chicago became the epicenter of protest.

Chicago Seething

Chicago seemed an ideal setting. By the 1880s it had emerged as a major industrial city with a very rapidly growing population. It was the western terminus for all major railroads east of the Mississippi and the eastern terminus for many of those to the west. It had attracted pioneering manufacturers and retailers like Cyrus McCormick (farm equipment), George Pullman (train cars), Philip Armour (meatpacking), and Marshal Field (department store), as well as political radicals and revolutionaries from Europe and the United States who found a sympathetic audience among Chicago's enormous working-class base. About 40 percent of the city's population and nearly 60 percent of its workforce were immigrant—Germans, Poles, Slavs, Scandinavians, and Irish—who filled the large factories, formed ethnic organizations, engaged in urban politics, organized on the job, and subscribed to foreign-language and socialist newspapers. For nearly twenty years, they had been demanding an eight-hour workday.

Few if any cities in the United States seethed with the popular discontent of Chicago or benefitted from such committed radicals. Over time, political organizers in the working-class wards wove together threads of antimonopoly, greenbackism, Irish nationalism, and socialism as they challenged the power of the city's capitalists. Some called themselves **anarchists** because they saw government as the tool of capital, though their dreams of self-governing communities of producers had much in common with antimonopolists. The political air mixed the ideas of German philosopher Karl Marx, author of the 1848 pamphlet *The Communist Manifesto*, and revolutionary American and French republicanism. There was also a growing sense among the city's working people that an eight-hour workday was within their grasp.

May 1 was set as the day for concerted action both in Chicago and around the country, though agitation had begun weeks before and small-scale gains had already been made. When May 1 arrived, hundreds of thousands of workers joined demonstrations, and at least 350,000 nationwide participated in a coordinated general strike. Between 40,000 and 60,000 of them were in Chicago, where the *Chicago Tribune* reported "no smoke curled up from the tall chimneys of factories and mills." Then, quite suddenly and disastrously, the movement fell apart.

Bombing at the Haymarket

The first setbacks had nothing directly to do with the eight-hour mobilizations. They rather involved the collapse of the Great Southwest Strike owing to escalating violence and court injunctions, and a bloody encounter closer to home between striking workers and police outside the McCormick Reaper Works on Chicago's South Side. In response, anarchist leaders called a rally for Haymarket Square, not far from the city center, the next evening, May 4. As it turned out, attendance at the rally was disappointing and, according to a keen observer, the speeches were relatively tame despite the intensity of the moment. But the police determined to disperse the crowd and moved in. That was when someone threw a bomb and an explosion ripped the square. Guns were soon ablaze, and when the smoke cleared seven police officers and four workers lay dead. An additional sixty policemen and thirty to forty workers suffered injuries.

Accounts of the "Haymarket bombing" remain disputed to this day. Was there a conspiracy on the part of the anarchists? Was this a massacre carried out by the police? Who threw the bomb? We still do not know. What is not in dispute is the aftermath of the event. In an atmosphere of fear, eight anarchists—all but one of whom were foreign-born—were arrested, tried, and, with little but circumstantial evidence, hastily convicted of conspiracy in the bombing. Although they all denied the charges against them, seven were sentenced to death and one to a lengthy prison term. Four were hanged, and one committed suicide in jail before his scheduled execution. Two would have their death sentences commuted to life imprisonment before being pardoned in 1893 by Illinois reform Governor John Altgeld, who criticized the rush to judgment.

Working people and radical intellectuals in the United States and around the world were, like Altgeld, shocked and outraged by the trial's outcome. They had come to admire the Haymarket martyrs for their courage in the face of execution, and they denounced Chicago elites for

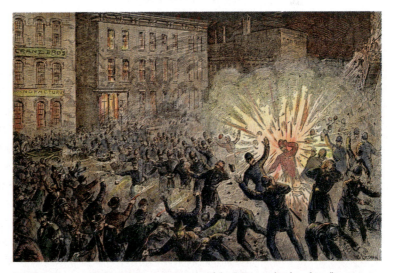

≡ **The Haymarket Bombing**   Accounts of the "Haymarket bombing" remain in dispute to this day. But the popular movements that had been growing for over a decade were dealt crippling blows.

cowardice and vindictiveness. The Haymarket anarchists would truly live on, becoming international symbols of the struggle for justice against the lethal arm of the state. But the popular movements that had been growing for over a decade would never fully recover from these blows, and what had appeared to be a vibrant and increasingly confident labor movement would have to lick its wounds and reassess its goals.

18.4   Recasting the Republic

Evaluate the efforts made by labor and independent political organizations to forge change at the ballot box.

In the shorter term, however, the consequences of what had happened in Chicago and on the Great Southwest Railroad lines were not nearly so apparent, and popular energies remained high. This was especially true when it came to politics. Elections across the country, especially at the local level, vibrated with working-class challenges to the power of urban and rural elites, often organized around newly independent political parties like the Greenbackers of the 1870s. The antimonopoly spirit coursed through their demands and aspirations, mobilizing working people who saw in the political arena a place to bring about change. It was a moment when clashing perspectives about the nature and fate of the American republic met at the ballot box and the boundaries of democracy would be defined and tested.

A Mayor for New York City

In New York City, the fall of 1886 saw a remarkable election for mayor. The large Central Labor Union organized a United Labor Party and chose Henry George as its candidate. It was something of a surprise because George had no real ties to the city; he was an easterner who had long lived in the west. But ever since the 1879 publication of *Progress and Poverty*, George had been winning an enthusiastic following and lecturing to local assemblies of the Knights of Labor across the country. He took his ideas to Europe as well, hitting resonant chords, especially in Ireland, where an impoverished peasantry had more than its fill of exploiting landlords. By 1886, as the Central Labor Union saw it, George's "name had become a household word to millions," and he had already argued that a land tax would help solve New York's problems of overcrowded tenements.

George did not run a single-issue campaign. As a measure of the social questions erupting across the country, his campaign demanded shorter hours, higher wages, municipal ownership of public transportation, and an end to police harassment of workers. The campaign also made a special effort to target the city's landlords, depicting them as wealthy parasites who fed off laborers and the poor. Needless to say, George quickly won the attention of working-class New Yorkers. Yet he also stoked the fears of the city's elite who imagined in George and his campaign the radical specters of the "French Revolution" and the Paris "Commune." Desperately, they tried to rally support against George and in defense of "property and order."

They nearly failed. When the election took place and the ballots were counted, George finished second behind Democrat Abram Hewitt and did particularly well in the New York's working-class wards. He even attracted a good many Irish Catholic votes that ordinarily would have gone Democratic. A distant third was the Republican Party candidate, a young Theodore Roosevelt, trying to make his way into New York political life.

Labor Politics

Among Henry George's supporters for mayor of New York City was Knights of Labor president Terence Powderly. It wasn't to be expected. Since the early 1880s, Powderly had spoken as strongly against the Knights' involvement in electoral politics as he did against their inclination to strike. Like some other labor leaders of the time, he was reflecting on the experience of his Greenback-Labor Party, which seemed to hold such promise in the 1870s before faltering in the late 1880s amid electoral defeats. Mainstream politics, he believed, was a distraction from the important task of "thorough organization." Yet, on the ground, Knights' assemblies marched to their own drummers, and although the organization did not formally establish political parties, they backed an assortment of independent tickets for municipal, county, and state offices. Between 1885 and 1888, the Knights of Labor ran tickets—called "Union Labor," "United Labor," "Workingmen," "Independents," and even "Knights of Labor"—in almost 200 cities and towns in thirty-four states and four territories and reported electoral victories in roughly one-third of them. Some were in major metropolitan centers like Chicago, New York, San Francisco, Pittsburgh, and Denver; others were in small towns like Eureka, California; Marion, Indiana; Boone, Iowa; Red Wing, Minnesota; Water Valley, Mississippi; and Gardiner, Maine.

No set platform or list of demands unified these labor tickets. Almost everywhere, they called for an eight-hour workday and looked to improve municipal and social services to benefit working-class communities. At times, they called for minimum daily wages, the extension of street car lines, producer cooperatives, or public works projects. Sometimes they simply wanted to run municipalities themselves and demonstrate that they could do so with greater reach and efficiency.

Noble Workers

The clashing political visions that reverberated throughout the United States in the late nineteenth century were part of a wider struggle that spanned both sides of the Atlantic. As American reformers sought to mobilize working people to bring about change, their counterparts in Europe were striking the same notes of political

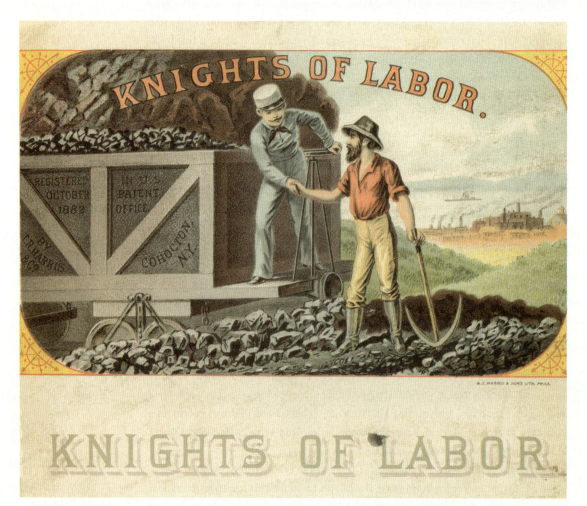

≡ **An American Perspective**   This cigar box from 1882 shows the two archetypal industrial laborers of the late nineteenth century—a miner and a railroad worker—shaking hands in solidarity. The illustration suggests that through their cooperative (and entirely masculine) effort the goals of the labor movement will be realized in a peaceful manner. The smoke-billowing factory in the background will be controlled, but it will not be destroyed.

concern, because similar issues—minimum wage, the eight-hour workday, and the distribution of wealth—troubled workingmen and workingwomen as much in Britain, France, Germany, and Italy as they did in the United States. On both continents, thinkers, artists, and advertisers promoted the inherent value of work. Workers were portrayed as noble and dignified despite the dreary grind of labor.

≡ **A European Perspective** This Italian painting from 1899 entitled *Il Quarto Stato* (The Fourth Estate) evinces a more revolutionary spirit. The crowd of grim workers advances like parts of a giant machine, with mechanical rhythm. Thirsty for justice, no obstacle can stand in its way—not even the woman who appeals to one of the leaders in the foreground. The triumph of the working class is inevitable.

CONSIDER THIS

Giuseppe Pelizza, the painter of *Il Quarto Stato*, believed that artists were workers who had a social responsibility to elevate and inspire other workers. What would he have thought of workers being used as an advertisement for cigars? What elements of *Il Quarto Stato* make it less suitable for representing the American labor movement?

But given the racial and ethnic complexities of working-class America, they put together winning coalitions in a remarkable range of places. They won in New England towns like Rochester, New Hampshire, that had customarily gone Republican and had a labor force made up of New Englanders, French-Canadians, Irish, and British. They won in Kansas City, Kansas, with a workforce of native whites, African Americans, Irish, Germans, and British that traditionally had gone Democratic. And they won in Milwaukee, Wisconsin, a growing city with a diverse industrial base and large contingents of Germans and Poles. Throughout, in pursuit of a more democratic republic, the ideas of antimonopoly and the mechanisms of the electoral arena went into the making of an increasingly self-conscious working class.

Political Insurgencies in the South

The pulse of political change could be felt in the former rebellious states of the South as well. The reestablishment of "home" or white Democratic rule was, of course, a process of great significance to the political history of the United States. It ended prospects for a Republican alliance that afforded freedmen an important position in party affairs and policy, and it showed how marginalized the Radical faction had become. It also indicated that the new governing coalition in American politics would link big financial and industrial interests in the Northeast with big landed, commercial, and mining interests in the South and West.

But the Compromise of 1877, which as we saw in Chapter 16, ended the Reconstruction experiment, did not wholly destroy the materials to construct political coalitions more favorable to small producers and working people. The freedmen themselves had not been vanquished politically. Despite losing vital allies in southern state governments and militant leaders on the ground, they continued to vote in substantial numbers, and, in some densely populated districts, continued to elect political officials and wield some power. So well organized did African Americans remain in some of the plantation counties that both conservative Democrats and especially white insurgents influenced by antimonopoly ideas sought to ally with them.

Nowhere did such an interracial alliance prove stronger than in Virginia. It was hardly a given. Alone among the formerly rebellious states, Virginia did not give rise to a Radical Republican regime. Instead, a "Conservative" coalition based mainly on urban railroad and banking interests came to power during the Reconstruction years. But in the Black-majority counties of the southeast, freedmen mobilized successfully and elected almost seventy African Americans to the state legislature, many of whom had skills, land, extensive kinship ties, and connections to local aid societies and churches. And when Conservatives decided to raise taxes and cut social services, including public education, in order to pay off the large debts incurred by the state, their own coalition fractured.

A broad front of opposition to the Conservatives took shape in the rural areas, especially in the western part of the state where there had been few enslaved people before the War of the Rebellion. In early 1879 they formed a party called the **Readjusters**. The Readjusters were committed to scaling down (readjusting) the state debt so it would not place a burden on ordinary people and to reclaiming power from the conservative elites.

From the first, white Readjusters reached out to Black Republicans because they knew that African Americans had strong bases in many counties and were increasingly dissatisfied with white Republican leaders. But the moment might have passed were it not for a shrewd and tireless politician who headed up the Readjuster party: William Mahone.

Mahone did not fit the mold of an insurgent. He had been a general in the Confederate army, a lifelong Democrat, and, of all things, president of a railroad. But he was also politically ambitious and, trained as an engineer, had a keen sense of how political bridges might be built. He quickly met with Black members of the state legislature and learned that only by paying close attention to their concerns could the Readjusters hope to win over the Black vote. The price of Black support was very specific: it would be a share of the state's patronage (state resources used to reward individuals for their electoral support), political offices at various levels, the abolition of the whipping post (a relic of enslavement), repeal of the state's poll tax as a prerequisite for voting (which made it difficult for poor Black people and poor white people to vote), and significant resources for public schools.

Mahone knew how best to pay. He made certain that these demands were included in the Readjuster platform and, as a result, Virginia Black people flocked to the party's standard. So impressive was the Readjuster mobilization that within two election cycles Mahone was elevated to the US Senate, the Readjusters won control of both the governorship and the state legislature, and most of the party's platform was enacted. It was the sort of outcome that Radical Republicans had initially hoped for throughout the rebellious South: a ruling coalition that joined freedmen with yeoman whites in the general interest of small producers.

Readjusterism was also a stunning example of insurgencies that began to erupt from Georgia to Texas in the 1880s, showing the fault lines in Democratic home rule. Aligned either with the Greenback-Labor Party or calling themselves "Independents," the insurgents had their main base of support outside the plantation districts—including in new mining districts—though they hoped also to win the votes of disgruntled Black Republicans. To that end, they called for an end to electoral fraud, the repeal of new poll taxes, the abolition of convict leasing (which

≡ **Convict Leasing**   Enchained Florida prisoners stare listlessly at the camera around 1900. The lumber industry throughout the Deep South employed Black convicts for the most grueling work.

mainly victimized Black people), and increased funding for public schools. "A free ballot and a fair count" was their cry and bid for a political biracialism.

Among these Deep South insurgencies none emerged more notably than in east-central Texas. There Republicans had first formed a coalition with Greenbackers in the late 1870s and then, in a number of counties, helped build interracial coalitions that took and held power, sometimes for years. Hard times for poor white and Black people alike proved to be the starting point for a course that appeared to defy Democratic cries for white supremacy, but strong local leadership and the experience of working together kept these extraordinary experiments in motion. It seemed indicative of a developing political culture in Texas, where the South met and became entangled with the West, where German and Mexican immigrants resided in large numbers, and where oppositional politics found fertile soil. No state gave a greater proportion of its votes in national elections to Greenbackers than Texas. Here the prospects for building a popular movement that linked town and country appeared auspicious indeed.

18.5   A Cooperative Commonwealth

Consider how a cooperative commonwealth represented an alternative to the political and social order of industrialization.

The antimonopoly sentiment that shaped popular protests in the 1870s and 1880s was not only a critique of postbellum capitalism or of the financial and industrial elites who had come to power and prominence. It also informed perspectives on alternatives to the social and political relations that had become entrenched in city and countryside across the United States. Those who hoisted the antimonopoly banner called into question the wages system for the impoverishment and dependency it imposed; the advent of large companies like railroads for the ways in which they were able to manipulate prices and freight rates; the power of middle men for profiting through the use of high interest rates; and the competitive market for the advantages it gave to capital at the expense of workers and other producers. Instead, they hoped to use the mechanisms of the state and federal governments to adjust the playing field for the benefit of small producers, especially through regulations of trade and control of the money supply, in part through the free and unlimited coinage of silver. But they hoped as well to offset the pressures of the market by organizing cooperatives for both the production and sale of goods. Their vision was something of a **cooperative commonwealth**.

The Farmers' Alliance

As we have seen, around 1875 the organization known as the **Farmers' Alliance** took root in east-central Texas, not far from Dallas. It emerged in the context of a bitter fence-cutting war that set small farmers and livestock raisers trying to keep use of the open range against large land syndicates and ranchers who erected barbed wire fences to protect their holdings. The ongoing dispute catalyzed antimonopoly sentiments. The area became a Greenback stronghold, and, before long, the Knights of Labor were also organizing farmers as well as miners and railroad workers.

Aided by traveling lecturers, the Alliance soon expanded across Texas and then, as the cotton economy continued to falter, across much of the Deep South. But it also cultivated close relations with the Knights and other antimonopoly leagues. Thus, when the Alliance met in Cleburne, Texas, in 1886, just after the collapse of the Great Southwest Strike, its demands included recognition of trade unions and cooperative stores, taxation of railroads and corporations, a laborers' lien law (making sure that employers paid their workers before satisfying other costs), the abolition of convict leasing and alien (noncitizen) landownership, the taxation of land held for speculation (like George's "single tax"), the removal of fences from public lands (so it could be used by all), the passage of an interstate commerce law, and a greenback-based monetary system.

Alliance organizations began to appear as well in the Upper Plains, the Rocky Mountains, and the Far West. Miners and railroad workers played a prominent part in the Rockies, mostly in association with the Knights, and they were often joined, especially in California, by followers of Henry George and Edward Bellamy, whose utopian novel of a cooperative commonwealth, *Looking Backward* (1888), won a large readership. What linked all these efforts—South and West—was the tumultuous experience of capitalist development, the powerful spirit of antimonopoly, and deep interest in cooperative alternatives to the competitive marketplace.

Cooperatives could come in many forms. Indeed, they had roots in the practices of mutuality that shaped the everyday lives of rural, village, and urban communities

≡ **A Cooperative, c. 1900**   Cooperatives, like this Wisconsin creamery, offset the pressures of the market by organizing both the production and sale of goods.

alike. They included cooperatives to sell crops, purchase supplies, mine coal, cobble shoes, construct machines, and make clothing. From the outset, the Knights of Labor encouraged "producer cooperatives" while the Grange and other agricultural societies often attempted to organize cooperatives for the purchase and sale of goods. The Farmers' Alliance established what it called "cooperative exchanges" on the local and state levels, most of which suffered from inadequate capital.

But the crowning idea, and one that potentially challenged the basic relations of the market economy, was the **subtreasury system**. The brainchild of Texan and Farmers' Alliance leader Charles Macune, the subtreasury was to be a federally financed and operated network of warehouses. Farmers, planters, and tenants could bring their crops to the warehouses, store them, and then have access to credit at very low rates of interest. The crops, in turn, could be held back until market conditions improved and brought higher prices than would otherwise be the case. Subtreasuries were, in essence, cooperatives on a massive scale. They would sidestep both unfavorable capital markets where interest rates spiked and cotton brokers who flooded the market after harvest, forcing commodity prices down.

Thus, in 1889, when the Farmers' Alliance met again, this time in St. Louis, to craft a national platform, the subtreasury was included together with five other planks that reflected greenback and antimonopoly ideas: abolition of national banks (which were privately owned), government ownership of the railroads and telegraph, prohibition of alien landownership, equitable taxation, and "free silver." By that point, the Alliance had well over half a million members and was growing at a rapid clip.

Tensions of Party, Race, and Class

Like the Knights of Labor, the Farmers' Alliance, especially in the South, was cautious about entering the political arena as an independent party. Partisan loyalties remained strong across the country, and Republicans and Democrats alike occupied formidable positions from which to fight antimonopoly. Both major parties were organized nationally, dominated most branches of government, and had very substantial resources at their disposals. What's more, the political balances differed from region to region. In the Plains and Far West, the Republicans were the strongest party; in the South, the Democrats were; and much of the Rocky Mountain West and Upper Plains were still federal territories. As a result, in one section of the country, political insurgents would have to break with Republicans. In another they would have to break with Democrats. And throughout, they would have to join hands across a threshold that the War of the Rebellion had created.

Equally important, the Farmers' Alliance, like the antimonopoly movement more generally, was beset by its own social tensions. The leadership was composed of well-to-do farmers and planters who were deeply involved in the commercial economy. The rank and file included smaller farmers, tenants, and even sharecroppers who either had been staple crop growers for some time or had more recently been caught in the rapid expansion of market relations. What they shared was an experience of exploitation in the sphere of exchange because of concentrations of control in finance, marketing, and transportation as well as limited access to policymaking in the federal government. Broad antimonopoly outlooks and interest in monetary inflation unified them, but various forms of social differentiation divided them.

Race was one source of division. The southern wing of the Farmers' Alliance excluded African Americans from membership. Black people formed their own Colored Farmers' Alliance in 1886, but although there was some talk of mutual support there was no talk of a merger and a great deal of suspicion on either side. The suspicions then exploded into fury in 1891 when the Colored Alliance supported a cotton pickers' strike and the white Alliance moved to crush it: not the best of prospects for breaking the hold of white supremacist Democrats.

At the same time, there was less enthusiasm for the subtreasury plan and for the possibility of an independent party in the South than in the West. Indeed, while the Southern Alliance planned to work through the Democratic Party, demanding that candidates for office publicly endorse the organization's platform, western Alliances were ready to take the first bold steps into the political arena. From the Dakotas to Colorado to Kansas, they fielded their own tickets—called Alliance, Independent, and People's Parties—and scored notable successes. In the congressional elections of 1890, People's Party candidates in Kansas won five of seven seats.

Rise of the Populists

What permitted an independent political movement to emerge nationally was the failure of the Southern Alliance strategy of working with the Democrats. On the one hand, they elected Alliance-endorsed candidates across the South, taking hold of governorships, state legislatures, and nearly twenty seats in Congress. On the other hand, they soon discovered that their newly elected Democratic representatives would do little to enact the Alliance program or even speak in its support. By 1892, there seemed little alternative to following an independent path, and in Omaha, Nebraska, that July a substantial portion of the Southern Alliance broke away and joined their counterparts from the Plains and Mountain West to form the **Populist (People's) Party**.

The Populist platform ratified in Omaha expressed, perhaps better than any other document of the period, the vision of antimonopoly politics. Populists, like the Alliance and Greenbackers, called for a "permanent and perpetual union of the labor forces of the United States" and demanded the abolition of national banks, a greenback currency, a graduated income tax, an end to alien landownership, and government ownership of the railroads and telegraphs. Like the Alliance, too, they called for the "free and unlimited coinage of silver" as well as the subtreasury plan. The Populists, according to their preamble drafted by Ignatius Donnelly, believed "that the power of the government—in other words of the people—should be expanded . . . to the end that oppression, injustice, and poverty shall eventually cease in the land."

New as the party was, the Populists did quite well in the national elections of 1892. They won the electoral votes of five western states (North Dakota, Kansas, Colorado, Idaho, and Nevada) and attracted more than one-third of the popular vote in five others, West and South (South Dakota, Nebraska, Wyoming, Oregon, and Alabama). Overall, the Populists received more than one million votes in the presidential election (about 9 percent of the total) and won congressional races, governorships, and legislative seats in states stretching from North Carolina to California. Two years later, they did better still, especially in some states of the Deep South where white farmers lent growing support. It was a major achievement since Democrats accused Populists of undermining white supremacy and often tried to prevent them from voting (see Map 18.1).

The Populists' success in 1894 owed in large measure to a panic on Wall Street in 1893 that touched off an economic depression—perhaps the deepest the nation had yet experienced—that would not lift until 1897. The Panic of 1893 put nearly half of the labor force out of work, and untold numbers of farmers lost their land to bank foreclosure. It's small wonder that the Populists' critique of the new industrial order gained resonance.

The fate of southern Populists would hinge on the party's ability to forge some sort of coalition with Black voters who ordinarily voted Republican. Only that way could they win solid majorities. They had a model in the Virginia Readjusters who

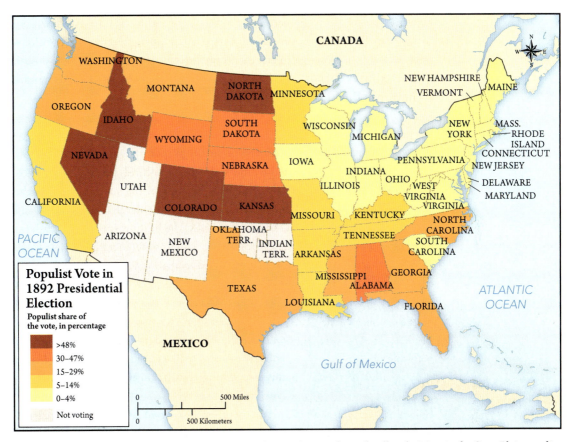

≡ **MAP 18.1** **Populist Vote in the 1892 Election** The Populists performed well in the West, in the Great Plains, and in pockets of the Deep South.

attempted to address the interests of African Americans in tangible ways. But the Populists had no William Mahone to lead the way, and they suffered accordingly. Some of their leaders, like Tom Watson in Georgia and H. S. P. "Stump" Ashby in Texas, embraced a language of protest in which Black and white people could be imagined as participants in the same political arenas, suffering similar problems, and having common stakes in political battle. Similarly, at the grassroots, some organizers could tell Black people that "your race today, like ours, is groaning," and that "to better our condition means to better yours."

It was enough to attract some Black votes, particularly from those who had experience working with white insurgents in previous years. It also helped cement a successful coalition between Populists and Republicans in North Carolina, where African Americans were able to win election to political office and the state legislature was taken out of Democratic hands. But, for the most part,

Populists ignored or were inattentive to Black concerns and rarely were willing to nominate them for office or provide them with important leadership positions. Populists were happy to get Black votes but reluctant to give Black people power, and so the Black support that Populists received tended to be lukewarm and it declined over time.

Finding a Way Forward

Given its character as a movement of small, property-owning producers, the Populists probably reached the limits of their political prospects in 1894. Misgivings about the role of the state, the meaning of the subtreasury, and the place of African Americans hampered their ability to enlarge their coalition and compete for genuine national power. Ironically, the best prospects for a path inspired by Populists were soon to be found in a changing Democratic Party. In some of the southern states, Democrats responded to the Populist challenge by moving in reform directions that the party had previously resisted. Many Democrats were, after all, Alliance members to begin with and shared antimonopoly views even if they did not fully embrace the Alliance program. A few also addressed issues of concern to Black constituents and pushed to increase funding for Black schools while denouncing lynch mobs.

But the most important developments occurred on the national level as the inflationist wing of the Democratic Party, based mainly in the South and West, challenged the gold wing based in the Northeast. It had been a long-standing struggle, but the Panic of 1893 strengthened their hand.

By 1896, pressured by Populists as well as by widespread labor unrest, the inflationist Democrats won out and, although they rejected both the subtreasury and government ownership of the railroads and telegraph, nonetheless showed the deep imprint of antimonopoly. Their platform lashed out at the national banking system, denounced the concentration of wealth in so few hands, and demanded the free and unlimited coinage of silver. To exemplify the changing of the party's guard, the national convention meeting in Chicago chose as its presidential candidate a young congressman and free silverite

≡ **William Jennings Bryan, 1896**   "The Great Commoner" represented the aggrieved in an era of capitalist rapacity.

from Nebraska who, in a ringing keynote speech, warned that "mankind" risked being crucified "upon a cross of gold." His name was William Jennings Bryan. Recognizing their affinities or bitterly swallowing their pride, most of the Populists reluctantly signed on and battled for the future of the country.

18.6   A Social Democratic Legacy

Analyze how the popular protests of the Gilded Age contributed a historical legacy of social democratic ideas and projects.

When social and political movements succeed in winning power or even a substantial share of it, we have a basis from which to judge their achievements and legacies. Did they carry out the changes they struggled and campaigned upon? How much were they forced to compromise? How true were they to their supporters? Did they make a real difference to their society and its history? During the 1880s and 1890s, antimonopoly movements struggled for power in most parts of the country, and by 1896 they competed for power nationally. In many ways, these movements made the 1890s a tipping point in the history of the United States, and although they suffered significant defeats, it is important to ask what they left us.

Defeats of the 1890s

The national election of 1896 was a critical moment in American political history—some call it one of only a few "critical elections"—and it was one that went badly for those who held antimonopoly perspectives and aspirations. After three decades of very close elections, numerous insurgencies, greenback-inspired platforms, and the organization of the largest third party in American history, the Republican Party completed the ascendancy it began in the 1850s. Although Republican standard bearer William McKinley only won 51 percent of the popular vote, he won big in the Electoral College (271 of 447 votes) by sweeping the states of the Northeast, Middle Atlantic, Midwest, and Far West. The South, the Plains, and the Rocky Mountain West were united in defeat (see Map 18.2).

McKinley was aided by the inventive campaign tactics of Ohio businessman and political strategist Mark Hanna, who helped raise $3.5 million (five times more than the Democrats and equivalent to about $127 million in today's dollars) from frightened members of the elite, setting a model for the advertised and monied politics so prevalent today. The Republicans would now be in control for the next three decades, the national banking system would be preserved, the railroads and telegraph would remain in private hands, and talk of greenbacks and free silver would

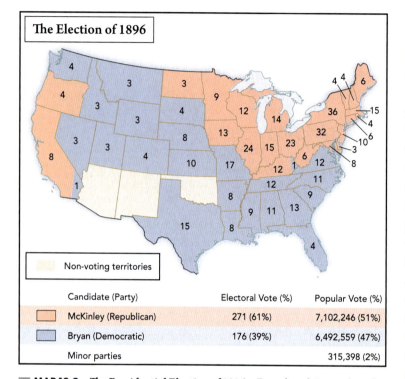

The Election of 1896

Candidate (Party)	Electoral Vote (%)	Popular Vote (%)
McKinley (Republican)	271 (61%)	7,102,246 (51%)
Bryan (Democratic)	176 (39%)	6,492,559 (47%)
Minor parties		315,398 (2%)

Non-voting territories

≡ **MAP 18.2   The Presidential Election of 1896**   Even though Bryan threw his heart and soul into the campaign, he lost to McKinley, who won in the Electoral College by a landslide.

end. In 1900, the McKinley administration put the United States officially on the gold standard.

Other antimonopoly defeats were smaller in scale but meaningful, nonetheless. The **Homestead Strike (1892)**, a showdown at Andrew Carnegie's Homestead Steel Works, just outside Pittsburgh, was particularly devastating. Intent on breaking the Amalgamated Association of Iron and Steel Workers, the union which had won a collective bargaining agreement, Carnegie's hard-nosed superintendent Henry Clay Frick imposed a 20 percent wage cut and locked the striking workers out. Pitched battles soon erupted between strikers and Pinkerton security guards brought in to protect strikebreakers. But the tide turned when Pennsylvania's governor, who sympathized with the workers but nonetheless yielded to pressure from Frick, ordered in 8,000 state troops to help the strikebreakers. In the end, the workers' resistance was crushed, and the Amalgamated Association never recovered.

Farther west, another struggle was brewing in the town of Pullman, just south of Chicago. There, sleeping car magnate George Pullman had built what he regarded as a veritable paradise for company workers: a town with stores, parks, banks, churches, and libraries meant to stand in contrast to the congestion and dangerous influences of the industrial city. But there was no democracy on the ground, just the paternalism of Pullman and his managers, and when the company cut wages—though not the dividends of investors—by 30–50 percent in the spring of 1894 without also reducing rents or prices at the stores, the workers rebelled. They had the support of the newly organized **American Railway Union** (ARU), which already had some success. Led by Eugene V. Debs, the ARU recruited unskilled as well as skilled workers and called a nationwide boycott of Pullman cars.

For a time, it appeared that the ARU might gain the upper hand. As many as 250,000 workers in twenty-seven states honored the boycott, and rail traffic between Chicago and the Pacific coast ground to a virtual halt. But Pullman still had cards to play. He might have looked to the Illinois governor for help like Henry Clay Frick did at Homestead, but the governor at the time, John Peter Altgeld—the same man who earlier had issued the Haymarket Bombing pardons—firmly supported the

≡ **Breaking the Pullman Strike**   The first meat train leaves the Chicago stockyards with a US Cavalry escort on July 10, 1894.

strikers. So Pullman instead turned to the federal government, where he had a powerful ally. President Grover Cleveland's Attorney General Richard Olney was a long-time railroad lawyer who continued to serve on several railroad boards, including one involved with the strike. Olney had no hesitation about responding to Pullman. Obtaining a blanket injunction against the ARU for interfering with the mails and commerce, Olney ordered the strikers to desist. When they refused, he sent in troops under the command of General Nelson A. Miles who had been spending much of his time fighting Native Americans in the West. The **Pullman Strike** was broken, trains were soon rolling, and Debs was hauled off to prison, where he served a six-month term for contempt of court.

Debsian Socialism

The outlook seemed grim for working people and agricultural producers. Yet, once the smoke of defeat settled, it was also clear that their political activities of the previous decades had lasting impact. Challenging the power of financial and industrial capital, insurgent workers and farmers helped shape a new conception of the role of government and the meaning of a civil society, a new compact involving an activist state and broader notions of social responsibility.

Combining features of populism and socialism, a new type of social democracy arose.

The political journey of ARU leader Eugene V. Debs is revealing here. Born in Terre Haute, Indiana, in 1855, Debs became a locomotive fireman and loyal Democrat who imagined a world in which capital and labor could cooperate and settle their differences amicably. Although he joined and rose to a position of leadership in the Brotherhood of Locomotive Firemen, Debs—like the Knights of Labor's Terence Powderly—was cool to the tactic of the strike. But the events at Homestead in 1892 helped move him to embrace the industrial unionism of the ARU—so long as members were white—and the subsequent battle at Pullman convinced him that Democrats and Republicans were both allied with big corporations. Workers, he believed, now had to chart an independent course.

Initially, Debs leaned to the Populists, but during the months he sat in an Illinois jail after the Pullman Strike had been defeated, Debs began to have another political conversion experience. He studied the works of major political theorists, including Karl Marx, talked socialism with a number of militant left-wing visitors, and read *The Coming Nation*, a newspaper published in Kansas by socialist J. A. Wayland. Once released from prison, Debs campaigned for William Jennings Bryan but then set out on a new political path. "The issue is Socialism versus Capitalism," Debs wrote. "I am for Socialism because I am for humanity . . . Money constitutes no proper basis of civilization. The time has come to regenerate society."

The socialism that Debs advocated had complex roots in the trans-Atlantic thought and movements of the nineteenth century: from the communitarians and utopians of the 1820s and 1830s, to the republican revolutions of 1830 and 1848, to the organization of the First International (or International Working Men's Association) in 1864. But socialism remained less a specific program or vision than a set of political counterpoints to liberal individualism, market competition, economic hierarchies, and elite rule. What socialists shared were commitments to the social good—mutual cooperation, political democratization, and worker empowerment. In Europe they pressed for the establishment of parliamentary regimes, for the expansion of the elective franchise, for workplace organization, and for constructing international networks of solidarity. Socialists built the largest mass party in Germany (the Social Democratic Party—SPD), and German immigrants figured significantly in the development of socialism in the United States.

The most zealous socialists not only threw themselves into the fight against capitalism but also battled among themselves over the best political path to follow. Should they focus on industrial organizing or build dual unions (that is, parallel unions as a strategy for winning political power) or mobilize for revolution or participate in the formal electoral arena? In the United States, several of these tendencies found an uneasy home in 1901, when Debs, Victor Berger, and Morris Hillquit helped found the **Socialist Party of America**. Over the next two decades, with Debs at the helm, the party would win hundreds of thousands of votes (over one million in 1912) and elect local officials and state legislators across the country (see Map 18.3). Organized socialism clearly found a place on the American political spectrum.

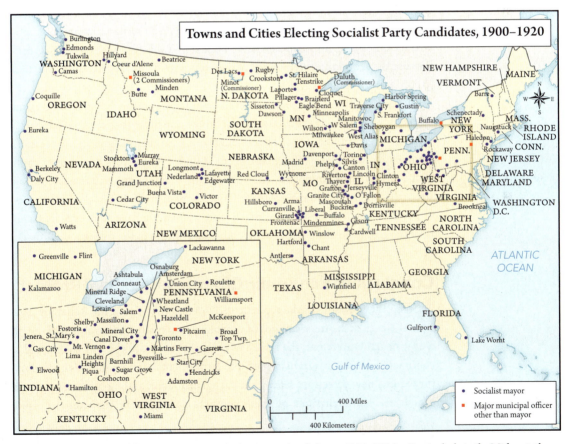

≡ **MAP 18.3   Towns and Cities Electing Socialist Party Candidates, 1900–1920**   Particularly in the Midwest, the Socialist Party flourished at the local level in the first decades of the twentieth century.

Perhaps more importantly, during the last two decades of the nineteenth century and the first decade of the twentieth, socialist ideals and ideas took hold among a broad range of producers as well as intellectuals and reformers who may never have aligned with the Socialist Party but nonetheless sought alternatives to or modifications in the "wages" system. Some became aware of European social democratic thought; some—like Henry George and Edward Bellamy—built on antimonopoly; and many felt the energies of moral revitalization that Christianity could provide.

A political culture of social democracy may well have been the most significant legacy that the great struggles of the late nineteenth century left to the country's future. And nowhere did social democracy assume a more distinctly American form than in the trans-Mississippi West. There among miners, lumberjacks, migrant farm laborers, railroad workers, radicalized members of the middle class, and social scientists, new sets of ideas—reflecting the inheritance of antimonopoly, trade unionism, greenbackism, and Populism—took special shape in good part because the economic development of the West was so rapid, exploitative, and tied to corporate power and greed.

There were some glimmerings, as well, of alliances across the lines of race and ethnicity, especially on the docks, in coal mines, and in lumber camps. To be sure, they involved limited social fraternizing and continued segregation; tensions could easily flare. But working people could find ways to struggle together, even in the face of their employers' efforts to divide them, to appreciate each other's strengths, and to imagine outcomes that might benefit all. In an age of Jim Crow segregation and repression it was much more than might have been expected, and it set the groundwork for social democratic possibilities in the future.

Conclusion: Economic Change and Social Protest

Between the founding of the republic in 1776 and the War of the Rebellion, the central conflicts in American politics involved two related issues: the making of a continental empire and the future of enslavement. Once the war ended, and a continental empire was transformed into a continental nation, the axis of conflict turned in a new direction, setting capital against labor, and monied men against producers. Although signs of these conflicts flared before the war, the rapid industrialization of the United States and the growing power of manufacturers and financiers turned the last three decades of the nineteenth century into a cauldron of change and protest.

The protests of the period, whether in cities or the countryside, in industry or agriculture were organized by antimonopoly perspectives, which made them more than just reform movements. They were movements that challenged the direction of the American industrial order and the power relations—social, economic, and political—that were driving it. During the 1880s, the US Senate convened a lengthy investigation of the relations between "labor and capital," and elites in many parts of the country feared a social revolution might be at hand. The fight was brutal. The United States had the most violent labor history in the world during the 1870s, 1880s, and 1890s, and, even elections were marked by the use of coercive methods as well as very high turnouts. By the early years of the twentieth century, new groups of reformers, intent on diffusing conflicts and finding social harmony, began to carry out reconstructions of sorts: nearly as sweeping though very different in their goals than the Reconstruction that commenced in 1865. We call them the Progressives.

WHAT IF Antimonopoly Movements Gained More Power?

After the defeat of the Knights, the Populists, and the free silver crusade, it was easy for the winners to regard rebellious farmers and workers as cranks and dreamers who offered up solutions to the crises of late nineteenth-century America that were unrealistic or outright dangerous. They all seemed to be looking backward to an earlier and simpler time while the victorious Republicans looked ahead to a modern and complex society.

In truth, it wasn't a struggle of the backward-lookers against the forward-lookers, but rather a struggle of competing visions over what a modern future should be and who should be in charge. The stakes, as all participants recognized, were very high. Could there have been a different outcome and what would that have meant? It would have been difficult though not impossible for insurgents to win a share of national power and implement some of the programs they had been rallying around: adjustments to the monetary and banking system to favor producers instead of creditors; greater public control over the means of transportation and communication to better balance the marketplace; a system of cooperatives designed to boost commodity prices and cut purchasing costs; a tax policy that penalized speculative investments and rewarded productive ones; and an eight-hour day for employees in all lines of work. A Populist-producerist political regime might have slowed the wheels of American industrialization, directed more resources to rural districts, small towns, and working-class wards, placed greater hurdles in the path of mounting inequalities of wealth, and perhaps discouraged American saber-rattling in the search for overseas markets.

DOCUMENT 18.1: The Omaha Platform of the People's Party (1892)

The People's Party Platform of 1892 touched on important political as well as economic issues shaping the power relations in American society, capturing many ideas of popular protest during the Gilded Age.

PREAMBLE

The conditions which surround us best justify our co-operation; we meet in the midst of a nation brought to the verge of moral, political, and material ruin. Corruption dominates the ballot-box, the Legislatures, the Congress, and touches even the ermine of the bench. The people are demoralized; most of the States have been compelled to isolate the voters at the polling places to prevent universal intimidation and bribery. The urban workmen are denied the right to organize for self-protection, imported pauperized labor beats down their wages, a hireling standing army, unrecognized by our laws, is established to shoot them down, and they are rapidly degenerating into European conditions. The fruits of the toil of millions are boldly stolen to build up colossal fortunes for a few, unprecedented in the history of mankind; and the possessors of those, in turn, despise the republic and endanger liberty. From the same prolific womb of governmental injustice we breed the two great classes—tramps and millionaires . . .

We have witnessed for more than a quarter of a century the struggles of the two great political parties for power and plunder, while grievous wrongs have been inflicted upon the suffering people. We charge that the controlling influences dominating both these parties have permitted the existing dreadful conditions to develop without serious effort to prevent or restrain them. Neither do they now promise us any substantial reform . . .

Assembled on the anniversary of the birthday of the nation, and filled with the spirit of the grand general and chief who established our independence, we seek to restore the government of the Republic to the hands of "the plain people," with which class it originated. We assert our purposes to be identical with the purposes of the National Constitution; to form a more perfect union and establish justice, insure domestic tranquility, provide for the common defense, promote the general welfare, and secure the blessings of liberty for ourselves and our posterity.

We believe that the power of government—in other words, of the people—should be expanded (as in the case of the postal service) as rapidly and as far as the good sense of an intelligent people and the teachings of experience shall justify, to the end that oppression, injustice, and poverty shall eventually cease in the land.

PLATFORM

We declare, therefore—

First.—That the union of the labor forces of the United States this day consummated shall be permanent and perpetual; may its spirit enter into all hearts for the salvation of the Republic and the uplifting of mankind.

Second.—Wealth belongs to him who creates it, and every dollar taken from industry without an equivalent is robbery. "If any will not work, neither shall he eat." The interests of rural and civic labor are the same; their enemies are identical.

Third.—We believe that the time has come when the railroad corporations will either own the people or the people must own the railroads, and should the government enter upon the work of owning and managing all railroads

FINANCE.—We demand a national currency, safe, sound, and flexible, issued by the general government only, a full legal tender for all debts, public and private, and that without the use of banking corporations, a just, equitable, and efficient means of distribution direct to the people, at a tax not to exceed 2 percent per annum, to be provided as set forth in the sub-treasury plan of the Farmers' Alliance, or a better system; also by payments in discharge of its obligations for public improvements.

1. We demand free and unlimited coinage of silver and gold at the present legal ratio of 16 to 1.

TRANSPORTATION.—Transportation being a means of exchange and a public necessity, the government should own and operate the railroads in the interest of the people. The telegraph, telephone, like the post-office system, being a necessity for the transmission of news, should be owned and operated by the government in the interest of the people.

LAND.—The land, including all the natural sources of wealth, is the heritage of the people, and should not be monopolized for speculative purposes, and alien ownership of land should be prohibited. All land now held by railroads and other corporations in excess of their actual needs, and all lands now owned by aliens should be reclaimed by the government and held for actual settlers only.

1. RESOLVED, That we demand a free ballot and a fair count in all elections and pledge ourselves to secure it to every legal voter without Federal Intervention, through the adoption by the States of the unperverted Australian or secret ballot system.

2. RESOLVED, That the revenue derived from a graduated income tax should be applied to the reduction of the burden of taxation now levied upon the domestic industries of this country.

3. RESOLVED, That we pledge our support to fair and liberal pensions to ex-Union soldiers and sailors.

4. RESOLVED, That we condemn the fallacy of protecting American labor under the present system, which opens our ports to the pauper and criminal classes of the world and crowds out our wage-earners; and we denounce the present ineffective laws against contract labor, and demand the further restriction of undesirable emigration.

5. RESOLVED, That we cordially sympathize with the efforts of organized workingmen to shorten the hours of labor, and demand a rigid enforcement of the existing eight-hour law on Government work.

6. RESOLVED, That this convention sympathizes with the Knights of Labor and their righteous contest with the tyrannical combine of clothing manufacturers of Rochester, and declare it to be a duty of all who hate tyranny and oppression to refuse to purchase the goods made by the said manufacturers, or to patronize any merchants who sell such goods.

Source: Edward McPherson, *A Handbook of Politics for 1892* (Washington D.C.: James J. Chapman, 1892), 269–271.

DOCUMENT 18.2: The Republican Party Platform (1896)

The Republican Party platform offered a very different perspective on the country's past and future. It would be the basis of national policy after 1896. These are the important planks.

The Republicans of the United States, assembled by their representatives in National Convention, appealing for the popular and historical justification of their claims to the matchless achievements of thirty years of Republican rule, earnestly and confidently address themselves to the awakened intelligence, experience and conscience of their countrymen in the following declaration of facts and principles:

Every consideration of public safety and individual interest demands that the government shall be wrested from the hands of those who have shown themselves incapable of conducting it without disaster at home and dishonor abroad and shall be restored to the party which for thirty years administered it with unequaled success and prosperity. We renew and emphasize our allegiance to the policy of protection, as the bulwark of American industrial independence, and the foundation of American development and prosperity. This true American policy taxes foreign products and encourages home industry. It puts the burden of revenue on foreign goods; it secures the American market for the American producer.

The Republican party is unreservedly for sound money. It caused the enactment of a law providing for the redemption [resumption] of specie payments in 1879. Since then every dollar has been as good as gold. We are unalterably opposed to every measure calculated to debase our currency or impair the credit of our country. We are therefore opposed to the free coinage of silver, except by international agreement with the leading commercial nations of the earth, which agreement we pledge ourselves to promote, and until such agreement can be obtained the existing gold standard must be maintained.

The Hawaiian Islands should be controlled by the United States, and no foreign power should be permitted to interfere with them. The Nicaragua Canal should be built, owned and operated by the United States. And, by the purchase of the Danish Islands we should secure a much needed Naval station in the West Indies.

We reassert the Monroe Doctrine in its full extent, and we reaffirm the rights of the United States to give the Doctrine effect by responding to the appeal of any American State for friendly intervention in ease of European encroachment.

For the protection of the equality of our American citizenship and of the wages of our workingmen, against the fatal competition of low priced labor, we demand that the immigration laws be thoroughly enforced, and so extended as to exclude from entrance to the United States those who can neither read nor write.

We demand that every citizen of the United States shall be allowed to cast one free and unrestricted ballot, and that such ballot shall be counted and returned as cast.

We proclaim our unqualified condemnation of the uncivilized and preposterous [barbarous] practice well known as lynching, and the killing of human beings suspected or charged with crime without process of law.

We favor the admission of the remaining Territories at the earliest practicable date having due regard to the interests of the people of the Territories and of the United States. And the Federal officers appointed for the Territories should be selected from the bona-fide residents thereof, and the right of self-government should be accorded them as far as practicable.

Source: Republican Party Platforms, Republican Party Platform of 1896 Online by Gerhard Peters and John T. Woolley, The American Presidency Project https://www.presidency.ucsb.edu/node/273316

Thinking About Contingency

1. How would you describe the differences in the Populist and Republican Party platforms?
2. How would you describe the Populist and Republican views of the "money question?"
3. If the antimonopoly forces gained national power, how do you think they would have transformed the United States and what would the politics and economy of the country have looked like?
4. Would the government have been more or less powerful under the rule of antimonopoly forces, and to what ends?

REVIEW QUESTIONS

1. Why did the rapid industrialization of the United States and the growing power of manufacturers and financiers turn the last three decades of the nineteenth century into a cauldron of change and protest?

2. How did the Knights of Labor and the Populists challenge the direction of the American political economy? Why is 1886 a turning point?

3. How would you evaluate the success of labor and independent political organizations to forge change at the ballot box?

4. How did organized socialism establish itself on the American political spectrum? In which regions did a political culture of social democracy take hold in the nineteenth century?

5. In what ways does a cooperative commonwealth represent an alternative to the political economy of industrialization? Can you think of forms of cooperative commonwealth in American society today?

KEY TERMS

American Railway Union (p. 766)

anarchists (p. 750)

Chinese Exclusion Act (p. 742)

cooperative commonwealth
(p. 759)

cooperatives (p. 759)

Farmers' Alliance (p. 759)

freedom of contract (p. 747)

Grange (p. 739)

Greenbackers (p. 739)

Homestead Strike (p. 766)

Knights of Labor (p. 740)

Populist (People's) Party
(p. 762)

Pullman Strike (p. 767)

Readjusters (p. 757)

robber baron (p. 747)

single tax (p. 737)

Socialist Party of America
(p. 769)

subtreasury system (p. 760)

wage slavery (p. 741)

wages system (p. 741)

RECOMMENDED READINGS

Leon Fink, *Workingmen's Democracy: The Knights of Labor and American Politics* (University of Illinois Press, 1985).

James R. Green, *Death in the Haymarket: A Story of Chicago, the First Labor Movement, and the Bombing That Divided Gilded Age America* (Pantheon, 2006).

Herbert G. Gutman, *Work, Culture, and Society in Industrializing America* (Knopf, 1976).

Beth Lew-Williams, *The Chinese Must Go: Violence, Exclusion, and the Making of the Alien in America* (Harvard University Press, 2021).

Robert McMath, *American Populism: A Social History, 1877–1996* (Hill and Wang, 1992).

Edward T. O'Donnell, *Henry George and the Crisis of Inequality* (Columbia University Press, 2017).

Charles Postel, *Equality: An American Dilemma, 1866–1896* (Farrar, Straus and Giroux, 2019).

Gretchen Ritter, *Goldbugs and Greenbacks: The Antimonopoly Tradition and the Politics of Finance in America, 1865–1896* (Cambridge University Press, 1999).

Nick Salvatore, *Eugene Debs: Citizen and Socialist* (University of Illinois Press, 1984).

19

Constructing Progressivism
1886–1914

Chapter Outline

≡ **Jane Addams** Jane Addams is best known for the work she did as a young woman at Hull House, but she strove tirelessly to construct a society based on a new set of principles and aspirations right until her death in 1935. Here she is shown in 1933, sitting with children on the front steps of Hull House.

Few Americans better captured the ways in which the reform movement known as Progressivism was constructed out of the crises of the Gilded Age than Jane Addams. Born to a family of local prominence and Quaker ethic in rural Illinois on the eve of the War of the Rebellion, Addams got the best education available to a white middle-class woman and then headed off to Europe for what was a customary tour for women like her. But rather than merely contributing to her cultural attainments, the tour wholly changed her social perspective. What she saw was the ugly face of the industrial age, its inequities and degradations, and the importance of an active life, a life of civic engagement. When Addams returned to the United States, therefore, rather than choose middle-class comfort, she decided to do "useful work."

Addams headed off to the west side of Chicago, teeming with recent immigrants of the working class who lived in crowded tenements and struggled for daily survival. There she established a settlement house in 1889—she called it Hull House after the original owner—something like the institutions she had witnessed in London. For Addams and the women who joined her, Hull House was both a teaching and

Timeline

1886	1888	1890	1892	1894	1896	1898	1900	1902

1886 › Founding of the American Federation of Labor; Supreme Court declares corporations to be persons under Fourteenth Amendment

1887 › Congress passes the Interstate Commerce Act

1889 › Hull House founded

1890 › Congress passes the Sherman Anti-Trust Act; constitutional convention in Mississippi disfranchises Black and poor white voters; founding of the National American Woman Suffrage Association; publication of Jacob Riis's *How the Other Half Lives*

1895 › In *United States v. E.C. Knight Co.* Supreme Court limits the federal government's power to pursue antitrust actions under the Sherman Anti-Trust Act

1898 › Frances Willard dies, led Women's Christian Temperance Union since 1879

1900 › National Civic Federation founded

1901 › President McKinley assassinated and Theodore Roosevelt becomes president

learning experience: it was a place that provided important social and educational services for the neighborhood and one in which she and her colleagues could learn more about the experiences of her working-class neighbors, women as well as men.

Hull House also put Addams at the center of the many currents and connections that would make up Progressivism. She witnessed young children at work rather than in school, terrible labor conditions, class conflict, and grinding poverty. Alongside other reformers like her, she threw herself into factory reform, child labor reform, working-hours legislation, court reform, temperance (limiting the drinking of alcohol), and woman suffrage. In the process, Progressives hoped to construct a society based on a new set of principles and aspirations. Addams's social and intellectual network included social scientists, educational leaders, and political reformers, often enlarged and refreshed at annual summer retreats held in Chautauqua, New York, where the great issues of the day, and the visions for a new one, were discussed before large, educated audiences. As a result, Addams helped to forge one of the most significant periods of social reform in US history, and in so doing, the character of modern American society.

1904	1906	1908	1910	1912	1914	1916	1918	1920

1905 ▸ Industrial Workers of the World (IWW) founded

1906 ▸ Publication of Upton Sinclair's *The Jungle*

1911 ▸ Triangle Shirtwaist fire kills 146 workers; in *Standard Oil Co. of New Jersey v. United States* and *United States v. American Tobacco Co.* Supreme Court establishes the rule of reason to determine antitrust cases; publication of Frederick Taylor, *The Principles of Scientific Management*

1912 ▸ Woodrow Wilson elected president

1913 ▸ Congress establishes Federal Reserve System

1914 ▸ Congress passes Federal Trade Commission Act; Congress passes Clayton Anti-Trust Act

1920 ▸ Passage of Nineteenth Amendment

19.1   Constructing a New Social World

||| Describe how Progressivism reimagined the relationship between individuals and the social order.

Over the course of the nineteenth century, many Americans, especially those of the middle and upper classes, believed that the fate of human beings rested in their own hands. Whether owing to the idea of moral free agency that evangelical Protestantism preached or the social Darwinism that depicted a massive struggle for existence in which the fittest won out, they insisted upon an individualism that could not be deterred even in a rapidly changing environment or by the interference of the government. Indeed, when they witnessed growing inequalities of wealth, poverty, and economic dependency, they easily blamed these results on personal failures and limited capacities that no institutional force could really aid.

But as popular protest mounted during the Gilded Age, some intellectuals and social thinkers began to have doubts about individualism and a limited role for the state. They began to imagine society as composed of groups rather than of disconnected individuals and reform as a collective process that required government support. Although Populism and other antimonopoly movements were defeated, their perspective gained wider traction among Progressives and helped forge a new social and political order.

Transatlantic Impulses

Few reformers showed the threads of new thinking better than Florence Kelley. Daughter of William D. "Pig Iron" Kelley, one of the founders of the Republican Party and a powerful congressman from the party's radical wing, she was exposed to abolitionism and women's rights early in her life and as a young woman set out in a direction that the great changes of the postwar period made possible. Taking advantage of new educational opportunities for middle-class white women, she attended Cornell University in Ithaca, New York. There she gravitated to the new social sciences, became interested in child welfare, and while she didn't complete her degree, ultimately finished a thesis on the subject that was published. Equally important was her four-year stay in Europe, much of it in Germany, where she was attracted to socialism, became involved with Germany's Social Democratic Party (SPD), married a Russian socialist, and returned to the United States as a wife and mother.

For a time, Florence Kelley mixed interests in the struggles of working women and children with the politics of the Socialist Labor Party, an American version of the German SPD spearheaded by German and other European immigrants. But she eventually broke with the party over organizing disputes and turned her attention more fully to the hardships of working people in general, and women and children in particular. She soon met up with Jane Addams, who had returned from her own trip to Europe to help launch the settlement house on the west side of Chicago. With a base in Addams's Hull House, Kelley hoped to train young women in domestic work. She was appointed a special agent of the Illinois Bureau of Labor Statistics, and, when fellow reformer John Peter Altgeld was elected governor, she became state factory inspector.

≡ **Factory Inspectors, 1914**   This photo by the muckraking photographer Lewis Wickes Hine shows a group of factory inspectors, including Florence Kelley, third from the left. It offers visual evidence of the central part that women played in constructing Progressivism.

The Road to Progressivism

Florence Kelley's lifelong attachment to socialism set her apart from many other reformers, but her political journey in striking ways marked the road from antebellum reform to what became known as **Progressivism**. It also exemplified the central part that women activists played in laying out that road. Building on the foundations of evangelicalism, abolitionism, and women's rights, they became immersed in the work of mobilizing, missionizing, and volunteering that moved through the upheavals of civil warfare and then the social traumas of industrial capitalism. Usually from white middle-class families of the Northeast, Midwest, and Pacific coast, often born in the 1850s and 1860s, many bridled at the limited expectations that midcentury American culture prescribed. Instead, they enrolled in institutions of higher learning that either sought out or agreed to admit women and then had shocking encounters with the poverty and deprivation that surrounded them. In the process, they came to reject the tenets of social Darwinism and liberal individualism, and advanced new ideas of social responsibility and the role of the government as a vehicle of reform.

In some respects, settlement house reformers, social workers, and teachers were carrying forward the work of antebellum predecessors who had "visited" poor women in neighborhood tenements or tried to "rescue" prostitutes, while nurturing their own middle-class sensibilities. But Progressive reformers' understanding of the problems and their developing sense of the necessary solutions had changed in significant ways.

Nothing was more important to this change than the massive conflicts that engulfed the United States and much of the Atlantic world during the second half of the nineteenth century. The revolutions that accompanied nation building on the European continent, the abolition of enslavement and serfdom, and the epic social consequences of the War of the Rebellion established new political connections across large geographical spaces and emphasized the transformative possibilities of an activist government. At the same time, the rapid advance of capitalism not only produced disruptions on a global scale, but led—across Europe, Latin America, and the United States—to new battles between labor and capital. Late nineteenth-century reformers like Kelley, Addams, and Lillian Wald were heirs to women who came before them: women who, in the many hundreds, tended to federal soldiers and the formerly enslaved during the war; signed petitions supporting the Thirteenth Amendment to the Constitution; headed South and West with church-related groups to minister to freedpeople and Native Americans; and organized unsuccessfully to have women, as well as African American men, gain the right to vote.

≡ **Tenement Yard, New York City**   Crowded tenements, such as this one photographed by reformer Jacob Riis in the late 1890s, shocked Progressives and inspired them to do "useful" work.

They were witnesses to the ways in which industrial capitalism was reshaping American cities, as unprecedented numbers of immigrants—mainly from southern and eastern Europe—fled the limited opportunities in their homelands and flooded into the urban United States between 1870 and 1914. They saw the crowded tenements and residential enclaves that Poles, Italians, Slavs, Germans, Jews, and Bohemians came to occupy, the rampant unemployment and underemployment that afflicted them, the lack of adequate lighting and sanitation, and the exploitation of women and children whose meager earnings were nonetheless vital to family and community economies. All of this shocked them out of their middle-class complacencies and inspired them to do "useful" work. They also saw bitter conflicts between employers and employees turning into pitched street battles. For Jane Addams and Florence Kelley, the Pullman Strike of 1894, which as we saw in Chapter 18 resulted in bitter defeat for labor, was especially arresting and revealing. "Americans are divided into two nations," Addams concluded.

Settlement Houses and the Social Gospel

Settlement houses, which spread across industrializing America between the late 1880s and the 1910s, provided many social services for the working-class neighborhoods in which they were located. They offered child care and kindergartens, lectures and adult education classes, job training and theatrical productions, shelters and public baths. Before long, Protestant and Catholic churches devised their own settlements and programs, as did the nondenominational (unaligned with any particular church) Young Men's Christian Association (YMCA) and the Salvation Army.

As this suggests, the **settlement house movement** and other urban social reforms of the late nineteenth and early twentieth century developed in close association with a new sense of social awareness, particularly among Protestants. Clergy from a number of denominations—most of whom grew up and continued to preach in industrializing cities—sought to apply what they regarded as Christian ethics to social problems, turning evangelicalism into a motor of social justice, often called the **social gospel**.

At the radical edge of the social gospel were men like Walter Rauschenbusch, who was born in Rochester, New York, and preached in Hell's Kitchen, a poor and working-class section of New York City. He attacked both the poverty and inequality that industrial capitalism was creating as well as the individualism that evangelicalism had once so forcefully advanced. "Capitalism set out as the opponent of privilege and the champion of freedom," Rauschenbusch wrote. "It has ended by being the defender of privilege and the intrenchment of aristocracy." Together with ministers Lyman Abbott, Josiah Strong, and Washington Gladden, he exhorted his listeners to embrace "association." "Our disorganized, competitive life must pass into an organic cooperative life," he urged, channeling the sentiments of Greenbackers, Knights of Labor, and Populists before him.

Rauschenbusch shared with many other advocates of the social gospel an interest in applying "the teaching of Jesus and the total message of Christian salvation" to society, a desire to join with like-minded intellectuals, political leaders, and reformers in the project of what Washington Gladden called "reconstruction." Rauschenbusch had supported the New York mayoralty campaign of Henry George in 1886 (discussed in Chapter 18), started a Christian socialist newspaper, *For the Right*, and had growing influence on social scientists, philosophers, and educators who were laying the groundwork of social democratic and progressive thought—reformers like Richard T. Ely, founder of the American Economic Association and author of numerous works on the labor movement and Christian socialism. The social gospel not only lent Progressive reform much of its moral fervor but also provided a language that spoke to the personal struggles and visions of many of the reformers themselves.

Frances Willard and the WCTU

Few movements saw the intersection of these cultural impulses with the project of "reconstruction" more directly than did the movement for temperance and the outright prohibition of the production and sale of alcohol. The movement already had a lengthy history, having won great popular appeal in the antebellum North where it made a dent in the consumption of alcoholic beverages. But earlier temperance supporters tended to see what they called "enslavement to demon rum" as a consequence of personal failings that the embrace of Christ and self-improvement were meant to overcome.

When the movement reignited in the 1870s, however, alcoholism was increasingly seen in a broad social context—as cause and consequence—and its eradication was understood as requiring a number of cultural and political interventions. This was especially true for the **Woman's Christian Temperance Union (WCTU)**, headed up for the last twenty years of the nineteenth century by Frances Willard, and easily the most powerful organization of its kind.

Born in Rochester, New York, Willard grew up in small-town Wisconsin, and was then educated at Northwestern Women's College in Evanston, Illinois (later Northwestern University). She came to temperance as a result of personal and family crises (her brother was an alcoholic), but Willard's ambitions were broadly based. Under her leadership, the WCTU adopted a "do everything" model, pressing for liquor laws, temperance education, and grassroots mobilizations while at the same time taking up labor reform, child welfare legislation, municipal sanitation, antipolygamy laws, and women's suffrage. Willard's feminism did not reject domesticity but instead saw it as a moral center for social change. Soon she was working with Jane Addams, Richard T. Ely, and Washington Gladden, most notably at the annual summer retreats in Chautauqua, New York described at the start of this chapter.

New Perspectives on Education

John Dewey had little interest in temperance, but, like Frances Willard, he did have a capacious sense of the work that needed to be done and, like Washington

≡ **Los Angeles Members of the WCTU, 1910**   The Los Angeles chapter of the WCTU was established in 1883. Note the two men in the back row.

Gladden, saw that work as "reconstruction." Dewey cannot easily be categorized into a single field: he was a philosopher, psychologist, political theorist, advocate for democracy, and educator. Best known for his foundational role in the philosophic theory of pragmatism—a way of understanding the world that breaks down the boundaries between intellect and experience, between thought and action, to deal with problems in a practical way—he took some of those ideas and used them to develop a new perspective on education.

His perspective was significant. Into the late nineteenth century, ideas about educational practice, about the nature and purpose of schooling, were still informed by a hierarchical notion of teaching and learning as well as a reliance on rote learning, the process of memorizing information based on repetition. The instructor was to disseminate knowledge and the students were to imbibe it. It was a model that comported well with the religious influences that had suffused educational practice since the seventeenth century and one that depicted knowledge as an assemblage of fixed truths.

Dewey's was a much more dynamic perspective, not only for the relation between instructor and student but also for that between the classroom and the world outside of it. He was very much influenced by the scientific method, by the ways in which experimentation and creativity were central to scientific discovery—and by extension to social progress. A frequent visitor at Hull House, Dewey was also deeply influenced by Jane Addams's social concerns. The purpose of education, as he saw it, was to produce citizens who were thoughtful, critically engaged, and ready to experience the active life. Rote learning resulted in apathy and social disconnection. Children, he argued, learned best by doing, by exploring.

As a measure of the trans-Atlantic framework of the period, Italian educator Maria Montessori also began developing new ideas about the classroom and educational process that resonated with some of Dewey's. She believed that

≡ **Education in the Fresh Air**   The Fresh Air movement was guided by the belief that spending time in a rural environment would alleviate the stress caused by inner-city living. In 1907, Camp Algonquin was established as a fresh air camp in Illinois, on 20 acres along the Fox River.

education should be child-centered, interconnected with the world around them, oriented to independent thinking, and open to experimentation. Classrooms, as she saw them, should be composed of children of different ages engaged in teaching each other under the instructor's guidance. By 1910, Montessori's ideas had spread well outside of Italy and were circulating in the United States. Before long, there were "Montessori" schools across the country, and they continue to appeal to parents and children, especially of the educated middle class, to this day.

So capacious was the educational orientation of Progressivism that it could even move in the direction of women and men with disabilities. One of them was southern-born Helen Keller who, owing to an illness (possibly scarlet fever) as an infant, lost her sight and hearing. Having the opportunity to work with an extraordinary teacher named Anne Sullivan, with whom she spent many years, Keller was able to eventually graduate from Radcliffe College (chartered in 1894 as a college for women with degrees countersigned by the president of Harvard College) and write extensively about blindness and deafness, subjects that had not previously been addressed to popular audiences. In the process, she became acutely attuned to the many ways in which disadvantage as well as disability afflicted many people and so was active in the Socialist Party and cofounded the **American Civil Liberties Union (ACLU)** in 1920.

Social Engineering and Eugenics

Still, the growing interest in confronting and seeking to overcome society's social ills—social engineering as it is often called—could lead in frightening directions. Many reformers of the period, especially those who sought to harness science in the service of social improvement, became attracted to "scientific breeding" later termed **"eugenics"** by Francis Galton, half-cousin to Charles Darwin, the British scientist best known for his theory of evolution. Rather than seeking to help those with disabilities, whether physical or mental, some Progressives thought that a better solution was to prevent them from reproducing. Referred to as the "feeble-minded" and generally "enfeebled," they were seen as a drag on society and a likely source of crime and moral decay. As a result, some of the most influential reformers began to entertain the idea of sterilization of those regarded as inferior beings. "Society has no business to permit degenerates to reproduce their kind," Theodore Roosevelt announced at the time. More and more states in the early twentieth century enacted legislation providing for eugenic sterilization, and in 1911 then New Jersey Governor Woodrow Wilson signed such a bill into law.

Prominent foundations such as the Carnegie Institution began to fund eugenic research, and Margaret Sanger—an early advocate of birth control—embraced eugenic perspectives as a way to convince Americans of the importance of population control and family planning. "The philosophy of Birth Control," she wrote, "points out that so long as civilized communities encourage unrestrained fertility they will be faced with the ever-increasing feeble-mindedness and lack of balance between the 'fit' and 'unfit.'" Attendees of the First American Birth Control Conference included *New Republic* editor Herbert Croly, Stanford University president David Starr Jordan, settlement house organizer Lillian Wald, and Britain's Winston Churchill. The eugenics connection would tarnish Planned Parenthood, which Sanger founded in 1921.

Progressives and Socialists

Progressive reformers were part of a trans-Atlantic network of activists and intellectuals who were redefining the terms and institutional bases of political and civic involvement. Like Rauschenbusch, Kelley, Ely, and Addams, many had studied and traveled abroad—especially in Germany and Britain—become familiar with new social democratic ideas, and witnessed experiments in welfare policy and city planning, including social insurance, missions to the poor, and architectural innovations. They had also been influencing the emergence of professional social science and economics in the United States, both largely devoted to the study of contemporary social problems.

Almost invariably, "socialism" formed part of their language and vision. They rejected models of societies organized around the individual in favor of new ones based on social groups and other collective entities. They cast critical eyes on free-market "competition" and emphasized the need for "cooperation." And they saw the government, at various levels, as an engine of transformation and construction, whether in its regulatory function for the workplace or in its ownership of public utilities. As Protestant theologian and editor Lyman Abbott put it, "individualism is the characteristic of simple barbarism, not of republican civilization." Many such critics and reformers supported long-standing issues like an eight-hour workday, but to this they added child-labor legislation, tenement house reform, the regulation of sweatshops, and progressive taxation (like the graduated income tax). Some backed the recognition of labor unions. When Florence Kelley helped establish the National Consumers' League with Jane Addams and Josephine Lowell in 1899, she hoped to promote safer and less exploitive working conditions through the power that consumers—mostly women in their view—could wield in the marketplace. It was a tactic that abolitionist forebears had used in boycotting goods produced by enslaved laborers.

What separated "progressive" reformers from the socialists whose perspectives and ideas they often borrowed, however, was a resistance to empowering the very people whose lives they seemed devoted to improving. For all of their

PERSPECTIVES

Muckraking and the Meatpacking Industry

Concerned with finding solutions to the problems created by industrialization, urbanization, and immigration, Progressives were particularly outraged at government and corporate corruption and irresponsibility. The desire to make cities better places to live and work connected progressivism with **muckraking**, the new genre of investigative journalism that emerged in the late nineteenth century. Muckraking was important, Progressives believed, because it could rouse public sentiment around an issue and create an impetus for political change. Ida Tarbell's *The History of the Standard Oil Company* (1904) and Upton Sinclair's *The Jungle* (1906) are among the best-known examples of muckraking, but many other books, articles, and reports exposed graft, corruption, and incompetence in both business and government.

Chicago's enormous Packingtown complex, where meatpacking was conducted on an industrial scale, was a natural target for muckrakers. Packingtown's boosters promoted its efficient assembly lines where workers disassembled hogs and cattle. This promotional lithograph from 1880 offers a sanitized view of the pork-packing process. Even the "killing benches" appear untainted by blood or entrails, while workers operate in safe conditions.

In contrast, in *The Jungle* Sinclair described "diseased cattle . . . covered with boils. It was a nasty job killing these, for when you plunged your knife into them they

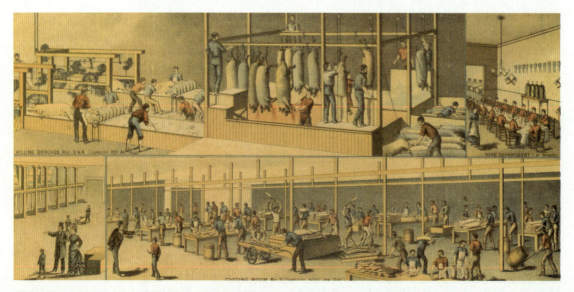

≡ **Packingtown: Promotional Lithograph from 1880**

would burst and splash foul-smelling stuff into your face and when a man's face was smeared with blood, and his hands steeped in it, how was he ever to wipe his face, or to clear his eyes so that he could see?"[1] This 1906 photo of the Swift and Company packinghouse in Chicago shows a similarly squalid scene.

≡ **1906 photo of the Swift and Company Packinghouse**

CONSIDER THIS

Theodore Roosevelt was no fan of muckrakers, but the angry letters sent to the White House by readers of *The Jungle* prompted Roosevelt to take action. In the aftermath of the uproar, the president endorsed the Pure Food and Drug Act and the Federal Meat Inspection Act, both of which became law in 1906. Can you think of other examples of journalism acting as a catalyst for change? Progressives were active on local, state, and national levels. Can you think of reform movements in your own community?

[1]Upton Sinclair, *The Jungle* (1906; Project Gutenberg ebook 2006). https://www.gutenberg.org/ebooks/140

efforts to improve the lives of the "other half"—as the photojournalist Jacob Riis termed people, mostly immigrants like himself, whom he met in New York City slums in the 1880s and documented in *How the Other Half Lives* (1890)— Progressive reformers spoke mainly to other members of the middle and upper class, upholding standards of comportment, aspiration, and respectability that were familiar to people like themselves. Some turned their subjects into "exotics" whose "primitive needs" would have to be reconstructed in the name of civic progress and social peace: a reconstruction that would be directed by educated experts such as themselves, not by the workers and immigrants who were supposed to benefit.

They also seemed ready to bring out heavier ammunition. Reformers of an earlier day looked to persuade, exhort, and convert those whom they perceived had fallen or succumbed to their darker selves. Progressives were instead more willing to compel change, to use the apparatus of the state to attack alcoholism, illiteracy, corruption, disease, exploitation, and physical and mental disability. In so doing, they began to lay the foundation of what, decades later, would become the welfare state, while at the same time they lent moral authority to projects of defining the destinies of peoples both in the United States and elsewhere in the world.

19.2   Constructing a New World of Business

‖‖‖ Identify how corporate reform came into being and distinguish it from earlier antitrust reforms.

Few Americans were more concerned about the class conflict of the late nineteenth century than members of the emerging industrial and financial elite. They were frightened. Quick to put strikes, political insurgencies, and critiques of capitalism in an international setting of revolutionary agitation and socialism, they worried that the tide of radicalism might soon be sweeping over them. Everywhere they looked, discontent seemed to be bubbling to the surface and then erupting. Movements for the eight-hour workday, a greenback currency, the regulation of railroads and other big businesses, and the nationalization of transportation and communication had been roiling the landscape and perhaps even threatening the sanctity of private property. Railroad president James J. Hill was not alone in being haunted by a "reign of terror [that] exists in the large urban centres." For some, Populism and the silver crusade of William Jennings Bryan were the last straws, "representative of anarchy, socialism, and a debased currency." The times seemed to demand new courses of action.

The Rise of the Corporation

Large employers and their political allies in legislatures and the courts had, as we saw in Chapter 18, inflicted major defeats on workers and farmers at the workplace, in municipal politics, and in the countryside. But these could be seen as only temporary. After all, strike activity continued to mount and socialist ideas gained popular traction. Under pressure from a variety of constituencies, Congress passed the **Interstate Commerce Act (1887)**, which was designed to monitor railroad rates, and then the **Sherman Anti-Trust Act (1890)**, which outlawed "any combination, in the form of trust [a large grouping of business interests with significant market power, effectively a monopoly] or otherwise, in restraint of trade"—signs of ongoing struggles over the shape and direction of the economy.

There was no single response to what was perceived as a crisis, and some members of the elite just chose to dig in their heels and fight off the challenges by any means necessary. But there also arose among some of the largest and most influential industrial and financial capitalists something that could be called a social movement in its own right: one devoted to constructing both new institutions of economic life and new relations between the economy and the government. The movement had no official leadership or set of demands. It rather took the form of private associations, lobbying groups, informal networks, and alliances among intellectual and political leaders. Although those who composed the movement disagreed about a number of issues and approaches, they could rally under a banner that might have read "Corporate Capitalism and the Administered Marketplace."

We tend to equate American industrialization with the corporation, but, in truth, until the very end of the nineteenth century the corporate form was not widespread among manufacturers, even those who were building large and increasingly integrated businesses. Firms were generally owned by individuals, families, and partnerships, and capital was raised by tapping personal resources, reinvesting profits, or borrowing from commercial lenders. The surge in incorporations did not begin until the late 1880s and early 1890s, owing to a number of developments: the limited usefulness of pools and trusts (informal means by which companies could set prices, reduce competition, and attempt to control the market) to expand power in the marketplace; the increasing ties between industrial and financial capital; and the encouragement given by the courts and some state legislatures to corporate ambitions. The growing centrality of the corporation to the American economy was not simply incremental; it was a qualitative leap and represented a new form of capitalism.

So what was new? The **corporation** embodied new forms of property and new sets of social relations. Ownership would no longer rest in only a few hands.

Management would no longer risk unlimited liability in case of debt or lawsuit. Company assets would no longer be tied to particular places or take mainly tangible form. And companies would no longer be barred from controlling other companies. Incorporation meant that formal ownership would be distributed among shareholders, liability would be limited and boards of directors vested with legal powers, and, at least in some states, corporations would be permitted to cast their nets very widely. At the same time, capital would increasingly be raised through the institutions that were strengthened by the outcome of the War of the Rebellion: stock and bond markets, brokerage houses, and investment banks.

This did not happen through the "invisible hand" of the competitive market. It happened because of precedents in the arena of incorporation, especially involving railroads, and because of political and legal interventions that made corporations "individuals" in the eyes of the law. Beginning in 1886 with the case of *Santa Clara County v. Southern Pacific Railroad*, the Supreme Court declared that corporations had the same rights of due process as "*natural* persons" under the Fifth and Fourteenth Amendments of the Constitution. Four years later, when Congress crafted the Sherman Anti-Trust Act, it followed suit. Congress not only outlawed combinations in restraint of trade but also explicitly stipulated that "the word 'person' or 'persons,' whenever used in this act, shall be deemed to include corporations and associations." With these rulings, the corporation would simultaneously enjoy protection from aggressive regulations imposed by government to which individuals were not subject and become a discrete form of property that individuals could not hold.

Consolidation

"Restraint of trade" raised many questions about the practices in which large firms could engage. To this day, the issue hovers over the corporate world and the quest for control over markets. But as "pools" and "trusts" came under public fire during the late nineteenth century—Standard Oil, John D. Rockefeller's massive petroleum corporation, used the device of a "trust" to harness both production and distribution—some states stepped in to increase the leverage corporations could have (incorporation took place in states because there was no federal incorporation law). New Jersey, in 1889, was especially generous. It allowed corporations to hold stock in other corporations even if they were located in different states and thereby gave legal standing to what was known as the "**holding company**": corporations that existed only for the purpose of gaining ownership rights in other corporations. Not surprisingly, by 1900, two-thirds of all firms valued at $10 million or more were incorporated in New Jersey no matter where they did their main business.

The question of what constituted an illegal restraint of trade was contested ground for the next two decades, and, for a time, a slim majority on the Supreme Court, led by Associate Justice John Marshall Harlan of Kentucky, ruled in favor of strict enforcement of the Sherman Anti-Trust Act. Only in 1911, in the *Standard Oil Co. of New Jersey v. United States* and *United States v. American Tobacco Co.* decisions (with Harlan in dissent), did the Court establish the "rule of reason," which holds that business practices are anticompetitive only if they work against the public interest. Pressure for such a ruling that distinguished between reasonable and unreasonable restraints of trade had been building among business and political leaders ever since the Sherman Act had passed, and at no point did the Court suggest that the size of a corporation was, in itself, grounds for regarding it an illegal combination. In 1895, in *United States v E.C. Knight Co.*, the Court ruled that the American Sugar Refining Company (also known as the "Sugar Trust") did not violate the Sherman Act even though it controlled 95 percent of the refining market. The idea that large-scale institutions were foundational to modern society was gaining more and more acceptance, especially among those who held power.

This was, in good part, because of a wave of corporate consolidation that had, by the late 1890s, become something of a tsunami. Between 1894 and 1897 alone, railroads with over 40,000 miles of track and over $2.5 billion in assets were aggregated in foreclosure sales, much of it financed by J. P. Morgan and a handful of other investment bankers. By 1906, two-thirds of the

Corporate King   In this 1901 cartoon from *Puck* magazine, John D. Rockefeller wears a huge crown and a kingly robe, standing on an oil storage tank labeled "Standard Oil." His crown is adorned with railroad cars, oil tanks, and the names of railroad companies that he owned.

nation's track mileage was controlled by only seven groups of investors, including Cornelius Vanderbilt, Jay Gould, E. H. Harriman, and Morgan. In the meantime, between 1895 and 1904, as the American economy emerged from the depths of the 1890s depression, Morgan and John D. Rockefeller presided over a "**Great Merger movement**" that restructured the metals, food products, petroleum, chemical, coal, machinery, and transportation industries. Almost 3,000 mergers occurred, and the 300 largest combinations controlled nearly half of the nation's manufacturing capital. Among them were U.S. Steel, Du Pont, General Electric, Standard Oil, and American Tobacco, all beginning their epic histories.

19.3   Constructing a New Industrial Workplace

||| Explain how scientific management attempted to reconfigure the industrial workplace.

Constructing a new world of business involved more than securing the corporate form and extending the corporation's reach. It also involved reconfiguring the internal structure of the corporate enterprise, especially at the workplace. The economic crises that stretched from the 1870s through the mid-1890s encompassed many aspects of economic activity: the flow of capital, the rise and fall of prices and wages, and the pressures of an intensely competitive market. All of these, in the view of many manufacturers, reduced or undercut profit margins. When the crunch came, as it did at various points during those years, they tried to keep their own heads above water by cutting costs (especially wages) and suppressing the resistance of their workers, sometimes through the use of paramilitary violence. Those who made it through might look to increase their market leverage by scooping up the losers and experimenting with new ways to manage the volatilities of pricing, production, and distribution. Pools, trusts, holding companies, and corporate consolidation represented some of what they came up with. But they were also interested in breaking a significant roadblock on the shop floor.

The Contested Shop Floor

As industrialization advanced, the shop floor proved to be highly contested terrain. There, skilled workers with the technical knowledge required to make the goods retained important power. This was the result of deeply rooted traditions of craft, which workers drew upon to exert control over the organization and pace of labor, as well as over the type of pay they received (by the hour, by the piece, etc.), even in new factory settings. **Mechanization**—in effect, increasing the role of machines in the production process—was one way for employers to undercut craft workers' power because it enabled semiskilled machine tenders with little experience of the craft to replace their skilled counterparts. **Specialization**, or breaking down production into smaller specialized units, was still another. Yet increasingly attractive to the larger enterprises was a more sweeping process known as "**scientific management**."

"Scientific" or "systematic" management showed the growing interconnections between science and industry, the growing sense among corporate managers that the capitalist crises of the late nineteenth century could be mastered only by bringing order to the ways in which business was done. A new cohort of engineers in the steel, electrical, and chemical industries was—like Andrew Carnegie before them—often shocked at the chaos and inefficiencies they saw in manufacturing plants. In their view, workers and foremen held too much power and authority and supervisors and managers too little. The production process, they believed, had to be organized from the top down rather than the bottom up.

No one was more important to scientific management than its pioneer, Frederick Winslow Taylor. Born to a wealthy family in Philadelphia in 1856, Taylor could easily have gone into law or finance since his father was involved both worlds. Instead, he apprenticed as a machinist and then went to work at the nearby Midvale Steel Company in 1878. Quickly rising in the ranks, he became foreman and eventually research director and chief engineer. By the time Taylor moved on from Midvale, he had well-developed ideas about how to "systematize shop management and manufacturing costs." He put them all together in his book, *The Principles of Scientific Management* (1911).

Taylor termed the craft practices skilled workers used to protect their control of the workplace "soldiering," a term that reflects the way conscripts may approach following orders, meaning that workers refused to labor as hard and as steady as they could, undermining efficiency and productivity. The solution, he felt, entailed the scientific study of all operations in a plant; the centralization of planning; the standardization of work, pay, and accounting; the close supervision and training of the workforce; and the use of wage incentives. Management needed to gather "all the great mass of traditional knowledge, which in the past has been in the heads of the workmen," and then closely examine each stage of the production process—including the use of "time and motion studies"—to expand their technical authority while routinizing work tasks. Taylor believed that "only through *enforced* standardization of methods" and "*enforced* cooperation" could industrial efficiency be assured.

Taylor's ideas were slow to take hold in part because

≡ **A New Industrial Workplace** This 1915 photo of Dodge Brothers Motor Car Company plant in Michigan shows the new shop floor as envisioned by Frederick Winslow Taylor. Workers assemble vehicles in an orderly, standardized fashion.

workers found new ways to resist them. But they were only the most comprehensive version of a new approach to management–labor relations that shared his goals of shifting technical control to the hands of employers and using that control to reorder manufacturing operations. And here, significant progress was made. By the early twentieth century, many metal, textile, and machine-making companies had constructed new plants designed to streamline the flow of materials while concern for "efficiency," "organization," and "standardization" became mantras for corporate capitalists, engineers, and social scientists alike.

Corporate Liberalism

These mantras were keywords of a developing ideology that began to take hold among business, political, and academic leaders who saw a new social compact as an alternative to the social conflict all around them. They had come to frown at the intense competition that seemed to cause cycles of economic volatility, as well as at the populist attachment to small-scale production in many parts of the country. They frowned, too, at much of mid-nineteenth-century liberalism, which postulated a world of atomized individuals who pursued their interests and independence.

Instead, they saw the rise of large corporations and financial institutions as the sign of modern times and the guarantors of economic stability. And they increasingly advocated a new ethic of partnerships and cooperation—involving capital, labor, and the state—as the best way to insure social peace. In the process, they began to create a new form of liberalism (some have called it corporate liberalism) that attempted to connect corporate capitalism with the mechanisms of democratic governance. In effect, this would prove to be the birth of what we would come to call "modern liberalism."

An example of this development was the **National Civic Federation (NCF)**, founded in Chicago in 1900. The NCF had a membership drawn from business, labor, and the "public," though bankers and industrialists dominated. Indeed, the NCF had representatives from many of the largest corporations in the United States, and its first president was Mark Hanna, an Ohio senator, President McKinley's closest strategist, and a major industrialist in his own right. What NCF members shared was an interest in meeting the challenges of industrialization and a willingness to experiment with new approaches, including the involvement of the government. They were concerned with popular discontent over the practices of big business and the uncertainties of regulation, especially antitrust regulation. They organized conferences, attempted to influence public opinion, worked with elected officials, and sometimes drew up legislation. Although the NCF saw false starts and defeats, its perspectives and lobbying contributed to the establishment of the Federal Reserve System (1913) and passage of the **Clayton Anti-Trust Act (1914)** and the Federal

Trade Commission Act (1914), measures that created a more centralized banking structure, strengthened the corporation, and implemented regulations acceptable to corporate capital (see Table 19.1).

Most of all, NCF members focused on the labor question because of the ongoing, bitter struggles between employers and employees. Some had come to accept the need for conservative unionism; others looked to informal means to resolve labor disputes and to reforms like workman's compensation and the regulation of child labor. There was a sense in the NCF that companies had to assume greater responsibilities for their labor force if they were to avoid prolonged conflict and the threat of political radicalization.

Samuel Gompers and the AFL

Among the members of the NCF was Samuel L. Gompers, head of the **American Federation of Labor (AFL)**, a national organization of trade unions founded in 1886 that included only skilled workers. His participation anchored labor's leg of the NCF tripod, and it was neither unexpected nor out of character. In many ways it reflected the construction of a new unionism that Gompers and the AFL were trying to carry out. But that direction seemed a long way from Gompers's political roots.

Table 19.1 The Progressive Era: Major Reforms		
Year	**Legislation**	**Action**
1887	Interstate Commerce Act	Regulated the railroad industry
1890	Sherman Anti-Trust Act	Allowed federal action against monopolies
1902	Newlands Reclamation Act	Gave the federal government the authority to build reservoirs and irrigation systems in the West in order to reclaim arid lands for farmng
1906	Pure Food and Drug Act	Required accurate labeling of food
	Federal Meat Inspection Act	Made it illegal to adulterate or misbrand meat and ensured that meat products were processed under sanitary conditions
	Hepburn Act	Allowed Interstate Commerce Commission to set freight rates
1910	Mann-Elkins Act	Regulated telephone, telegraph, and cable communications
1913	Federal Reserve Act	Reorganized banking system
1914	Clayton Anti-Trust Act	Strengthened antitrust enforcement
	Federal Trade Commission Act	Outlawed unfair methods of competition

A London-born immigrant, Gompers arrived in New York City in 1863, learned the cigar-making trade from his father, and was swept into the world of Marxian socialism on New York's Lower East Side. Gompers became a leader of the Cigar Makers' International Union and, despite sympathies for Henry George and the Knights of Labor (discussed in Chapter 18), was—like Terence Powderly before him—generally suspicious of electoral initiatives taken by organized working-men. Together with fellow cigar-maker Adolph Strasser, a Hungarian immigrant, Gompers instead focused on organization at the workplace, building trade unions, and augmenting their leverage with employers. He called it "pure and simple unionism." *Pure* referred to membership: strictly limited to workers, organized by craft and occupation, with no reliance on outside advisors or allies. *Simple* referred to goals: only those that immediately benefited workers, notably better wages, hours, and working conditions.

Given labor's thumping political defeats in the 1880s and early 1890s, Gompers's perspective did not seem misplaced. Intent on revitalizing working-class power when he helped organize the AFL in 1886, he had witnessed destructive court injunctions, lethal military interventions, and disheartening electoral losses. Even supporters of "independent labor politics" in the AFL soon gravitated toward Gompers's position. Unlike their counterparts during the 1870s and 1880s who, as we saw in Chapter 18, called for dismantling the wages system and formed alliances with antimonopolists, the leadership of the AFL increasingly accepted the permanence of a large-scale, corporate-dominated economy and fought to find a stable and secure place for unions within it.

This recognition helped bring Gompers and some other union leaders into association with the NCF and its corporate liberal vision. What Gompers didn't accept was the new reliance on the government. "**Voluntarism**," with its emphasis on collective bargaining and voluntary agreements between unions and employers without assistance from the state, remained central to his philosophy: except for

≡ **Mother Jones Leading a Strike, 1903** The Irish-born labor organizer, child-rights activist, and self-proclaimed "hell-raiser" is shown here with striking textile workers in Philadelphia in 1903.

immigration restriction, especially regarding the Chinese, which he happily left to the federal government.

Yet the pro-labor perspective of Gompers and others in the AFL leadership had ripple effects well beyond the AFL, especially when unemployment was low and workers had their best chance to organize. These ripple effects fueled the rise of the **Industrial Workers of the World (IWW)**, a labor union founded in Chicago in 1905. The Wobblies, as they were called, were fervent supporters of the class struggle and workplace organizing. In the spirit of the Knights of Labor, the Wobblies took special interest in unskilled workers, together with industry-wide mobilizations and collective control over the conditions of work as a response to scientific management.

The founding of the IWW was indicative of rising labor militance in the opening decades of the twentieth century. The **International Ladies' Garment Workers' Union (ILGWU)**, which represented hundreds of thousands of garment workers, mostly women, staged general strikes in New York City that brought thousands of female workers into the fray, including one in 1909 against the Triangle Shirtwaist Company. In 1911, disaster struck the same Triangle Shirtwaist Company when 146 young workers were killed in a fire, many of whom jumped from the upper stories of the factory to escape the flames. In response to the tragedy, New York City enacted fire safety regulations.

A massive textile strike in Lawrence, Massachusetts, in 1912, aided by the IWW, involved well over 20,000 laborers from as many as fifty different nationalities. Mine fields from northeastern Pennsylvania to southern Colorado to northern Idaho were ablaze with class warfare led by the **United Mine Workers (UMW)**, which had been founded in Ohio in 1890, and the even more militant Western Federation of Miners. By 1920, more and more workers were achieving an eight-hour workday, not as a result of legislation but as a product of workplace strikes. While the American economy was being constructed in a corporate image, new fields of struggle had been established and the balances of power had yet to be determined.

19.4 Constructing New Political and Economic Power

❚❚❚ Assess the differing political perspectives of Progressive reformers.

Samuel Gompers and other AFL leaders who wanted to steer labor away from reliance on the government were the exceptions rather than the rule in the larger political arena. By the end of the nineteenth century, a growing proportion of

Americans had come to see the government, at all levels, as central to resolving the problems of industrial capitalism. To a large extent, they had embraced the thinking of antimonopoly movements that blamed the troubles of producers on political corruption and believed that only an empowered government beholden to the will of the people could tame the excesses of big business.

Progressive Reform from the Grassroots

The ideas of the antimonopolists clearly lived on despite the political defeats they suffered. A great deal of energy remained at the state and local levels, much of it in a geographical arc stretching from the Midwest across the northern Plains and then down the Pacific coast. State legislatures, which were more responsive to popular pressure than the federal government, led the way in continued attempts to regulate railroads, mining companies, and other large industrial enterprises. The battles were especially intense in California as farmers, workers, and small business people mobilized against the power of the Southern Pacific Railroad, known as the "Octopus."

Coalitions of labor unions, progressive reformers, and socialists pushed for municipal regulation or outright ownership of utilities and public transportation—"gas and water socialism" some called it—in cities large and small. In North Dakota, the threads of Populism and socialism went into the making of the Nonpartisan League, which demanded public ownership of grain elevators, flour mills, and packing houses together with a state-operated bank. Many of these states led the way in establishing railroad commissions, workmen's compensation, and women's suffrage. Indeed, well before the ratification of the Nineteenth Amendment (1920), women had gained the right to vote in most states of the trans-Mississippi West (see Map 19.1).

Then there was the remarkable **Oregon System** that emerged out of the city of Portland during the first two decades of the twentieth century. A formidable coalition of workers and middle-class radicals influenced by Henry George and led by William U'Ren formed the People's Power League. They not only called for direct primaries, initiatives and

≡ **The Octopus** In this 1882 lithograph, the powerful Southern Pacific Railroad is shown as an octopus, with its many tentacles controlling financial interests, farmers, shipping, fruit growers, stage lines, mining, and the wine industry.

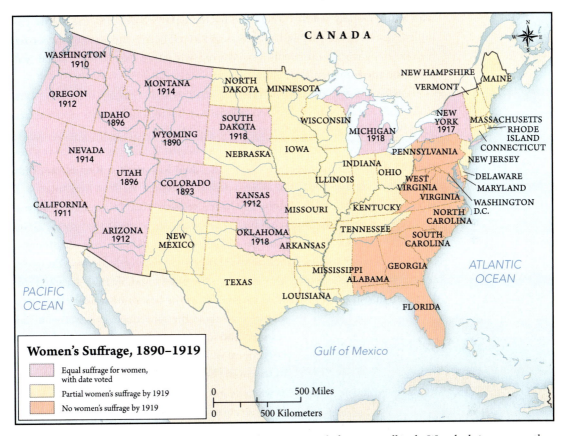

≡ **MAP 19.1** **Women's Suffrage 1890–1919**   As late as 1909, only four states, all in the West, had given women the vote: Wyoming, Utah, Colorado, and Idaho.

referenda, and the popular election of US senators (replacing election by state legislatures) but they also supported women's suffrage and proportional representation based on occupation—including female wage workers and housewives—in a unicameral (one chamber, subject to greater popular control) legislature.

Progressive Reform from the Top

In many ways, the "Oregon system" remains ahead of our time. Other elements of left-wing progressivism would play important roles in building America's version of social democracy during the 1930s, as we will see in Chapter 23. But the political constructions forged during the Progressive Era that would prove most enduring involved both the federal government's role in administering the national economy and the redefinition, at all levels, of what democratic governance was to mean.

In some respects, these changes took place with almost breathtaking speed. Before 1900, demands for federal regulation came mainly from insurgent parties with antimonopoly politics. Then, and for the next two decades, the debate engulfed the two major parties, Democrats and Republicans, and was no longer over *whether* the government should get involved but rather over *how* it should and *where* the power of regulation should reside.

The transition was apparent by 1890, especially with the passage of the Interstate Commerce Act and the Sherman Anti-Trust Act, but the implications were unclear until the first decade of the twentieth century. Then, leaders of the federal executive branch—presidents most prominently—helped define a new framework despite hesitation on the Supreme Court. Theodore Roosevelt, a Republican, who became president in 1901 after an anarchist assassinated William McKinley, was especially important here. On the one hand, Roosevelt had little patience for the arrogance of corporate capital or for the traditionalism of the old governing class. He had strong views both of the "public interest" to which he believed all organizations of labor and capital should submit, and of activist leadership designed to reinvigorate the federal government. On the other hand, he fully accepted the corporation and other large-scale enterprises as the bases of a modern economy and worried about the consequences of both judicial restraint and socialist ideals.

For most of his administration, Roosevelt looked to rein in the heavy-handed tactics of business, such as when he forced a mining company to the table in 1902 during a bitter coal strike. He also hoped to rally public opinion in favor of "reasonable" restraints of trade and find a way to gain administrative leverage over the corporate sector with as little interference as possible from the courts. Throughout his two-term presidency (he won reelection in 1904), Roosevelt was in close contact with the National Civic Foundation, and together they worked to devise such a formula. Indeed, Roosevelt moved steadily, in and out of office, in what we might call a statist direction. While conceding private ownership, he thought of corporations more as public utilities whose operations required strict accountability and federal oversight. He would call this the **New Nationalism**.

Roosevelt's hand-picked successor, Republican William Howard Taft, initially seemed ready to follow Roosevelt's path. But it turned out that he was far more hesitant about the **statism** that Roosevelt

≡ **Theodore Roosevelt and John Muir at Yosemite, 1903**   Roosevelt worked to expand the powers of the presidency. Nowhere was this more so than in the area of conservation. Roosevelt believed natural resources had to be managed efficiently and used wisely.

had come to advocate, about a federal role that appeared nearer to direction than regulation. Following the Supreme Court's *Standard Oil* and *American Tobacco* "rule of reason" decisions in 1911, Taft would lean far more toward corporate, as opposed to federal, administration of the interstate marketplace. Thus, Taft and Roosevelt had a political parting of the ways, and Roosevelt decided to seek another term as president in 1912 as an independent Progressive candidate. In a nod to Roosevelt's combative stance, the Progressive party soon won the nickname "Bull Moose Party."

Woodrow Wilson's New Freedom

The main beneficiary of the Taft/Roosevelt warfare in the Republican Party was Democrat Woodrow Wilson. Born in Virginia, educated at Princeton University, the University of Virginia, and Johns Hopkins University, Wilson went on to serve as president of Princeton University and then as a reform governor of New Jersey. He came to represent what could be called the corporate and cosmopolitan wing of the Democratic Party, which had been controlled since 1896 by William Jennings Bryan and the agrarians of the South and West. Like Roosevelt and Taft, Wilson saw the corporation as a fundamental component of a modern society and sought a middle ground in the expansion of the government's regulatory authority between socialism on the one side and "laissez faire" capitalism on the other. With the Republicans effectively divided and the socialist Eugene V. Debs attracting nearly one million votes, Wilson won the presidency: only the second Democrat (since Grover Cleveland) and first southerner to do so since the War of the Rebellion.

During the 1912 campaign Wilson told the public that while the Republicans offered a "program of regulation," his was one of "liberty." He called his reform program, which included stronger antitrust legislation to protect small businesses as well as tariff reductions, the **New Freedom**. Yet, in truth, Wilson saw the shift in power and authority from the states to the national government as something of a natural evolution, and he tried to walk a line between the agrarian and labor constituents of the Democratic Party (who wanted tough regulation) and the fears of corporate and financial interests who clearly did not.

The results emerged from Congress. The Clayton Anti-Trust Act (1914) prohibited numbers of monopolistic practices while exempting labor from the antitrust prosecutions that had been deployed under the Sherman Anti-Trust Act—it turned out to be a rather hollow exemption as conservative courts continued to issue injunctions and rule against labor unions. The Federal Trade Commission Act authorized the investigation of "unfair methods of competition" and provided for the issuance of "cease and desist" orders. Yet corporations were not required to register with the Commission or submit evidence of their activities, and the Commission's membership was expected to come chiefly from the private sector. In short, Wilson's New Freedom program worked to regulate rather than to break up big business. Here, it seemed, after nearly three decades of thought and experimentation, was a new model for the relationship between the government and the corporate economy—between political and economic power—that would set a basis for the next century.

19.5   Constructing a New Idea of Governance

III   Identify some of the antidemocratic impulses among Progressives.

Ideas about order, expertise, and proper management not only helped frame the ways of business and the role of the regulatory state. They also came to raise serious doubts about the workings of political democracy. These doubts were a half century in the making. Ever since the 1840s and 1850s, sections of the American elite began to pull back from their earlier acceptance of democratic reforms. For the first time, growing numbers of free people who were either poor or in some condition of economic dependency sought political rights that most white men had come to enjoy. Some were people of color, some were women, and a great many were recent immigrants—thousands from Ireland—who were propertyless and Catholic. Defenders of white, male privilege, most in the Whig and then Republican party, sent these efforts down to defeat, defining clearer boundaries of formal political participation and giving notice of the political dilemmas that industrial capitalism might pose.

This political backlash was temporarily reversed by the War of the Rebellion and the emancipation of enslaved people, which made possible an unprecedented expansion of civil and political rights. But as the urban population and the ranks of wage earners continued to swell, as immigration brought over men and women who were not Protestants and did not speak English, as the working class organized in new ways and won support from ethnic communities, as enslaved people moved into the ranks of free laborers, alarms began to ring (see Figure 19.1).

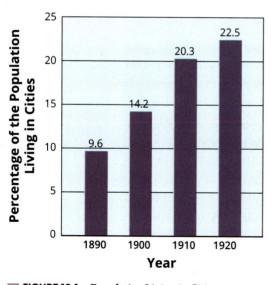

≡ **FIGURE 19.1** **Population Living in Cities, 1890–1920.**

Diluting the Working-Class Vote

Alarmists tended to be of Protestant and Anglo-Saxon background, often residents of industrializing cities, and mostly from the world of commerce and the professions. They worried about a society they knew being overrun by "foreigners," "peasants," "Catholics," and "heathen," able to wield political power and "corrupt" the body politic. "Universal suffrage," one of them insisted, "can only mean the government of ignorance and vice." Their aim was to "purify" the ballot box and secure "educated men" in their proper place as the governing class.

It wasn't that easy to do. Working people had become accustomed to exercising the franchise, and the Fourteenth and Fifteenth Amendments of the Constitution guaranteed the equal protection of the laws while prohibiting disfranchisement on the basis of "race, color, or previous condition of servitude." How then to proceed? A period of experimentation thus ensued.

In the far West, a movement to exclude the Chinese from the United States won enormous support from a cross-section of the public and led to the Chinese Exclusion Act of 1882. In the Southwest, New Mexico and Arizona remained in a prolonged territorial status while the federal government refused to move forward on the citizenship claims that those of Mexican descent had been assured under the 1848 Treaty of Guadalupe Hidalgo following the US-Mexican War. In the states of the formerly rebellious South, the Democrats who toppled Republican regimes began to impose poll taxes together with new registration and ballot box laws designed to discourage poor Black people from voting. And in the urban Northeast, reformers looked to literacy and residency requirements, to less frequent elections and "at-large" voting (all voters can vote on all candidates, a system that disadvantages minority voters and candidates), and to the creation of special municipal boards to be selected only by property owners.

Disfranchisement and Political Modernity

More than anything else, it was the social upheavals of the 1880s and 1890s that gave the momentum for anti-democratic reform a decisive push. The results were most sweeping and hard-fisted in the Deep South where planters and other Democrats from Black-majority districts sought to remove "the ignorant and unpatriotic negro" from "the sphere of politics." Mississippi led the way in 1890 with a constitutional convention that side-stepped the Fifteenth Amendment by legislating, not explicitly against a race, but rather "against the [Black man's] habits and weaknesses." The new constitution required prospective voters to live in the state for two years and the election district for one, to register at least four months before an election, to pay a $2 poll tax cumulative (meaning if not paid one year it would be double the next) , and to be able to read, understand, or give a reasonable

MAPPING AMERICA

Enfranchisement and Disfranchisement, 1867–1904

The enfranchisement of African American men was one of the most visible achievements of Reconstruction. As we saw in Chapter 16, the Reconstruction Acts of March 1867 extended the franchise to African American men in the former Confederate South, and they participated in

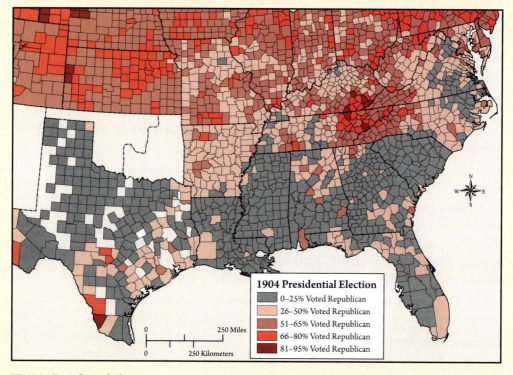

1904 Presidential Election

- 0–25% Voted Republican
- 26–50% Voted Republican
- 51–65% Voted Republican
- 66–80% Voted Republican
- 81–95% Voted Republican

≡ **1904 Presidential Election**

interpretation of the state constitution to the satisfaction of the appointed registrar. It was known as the "Mississippi Plan," and in one way or another—sometimes by constitutional revision, sometimes by statute law—it was the model for many other southern states to follow for the next two decades, reducing the Black electorate to almost nothing (see Table 19.2).

None of the states outside the Deep South enacted such a full package of disfranchising measures, but many, especially in the industrial belt of the North and

elections for new state constitutions that very year. The following year, Black men participated in elections at the state, local, and national levels, dramatically changing the political landscape in the South and ensuring Ulysses S. Grant's election to the presidency and the Republican hold on federal power. The Fifteenth Amendment, ratified in 1870, extended suffrage to Black men who lived outside of the Confederate South. These were defining political moments in American history.

However, beginning with Mississippi in 1890, efforts to disfranchise Black men spread throughout the South. Poll taxes, literacy tests, residency requirements, and other restrictions effectively took away the vote from Black men ("grandfather clauses," exempting descendants of persons eligible to vote before the War, protected the eligibility of white men, who nonetheless faced disfranchisement especially if they were poor and inclined to political insurgency). These strategies proved effective. Black men were quickly purged from the voter rolls. By 1904, only a few small pockets of Republican support survived in the South (see map).

Thinking Geographically

1. In which states had the Republican Party all but disappeared by 1904?
2. Which pockets of the South voted Republican in 1904? What factors might explain this support?
3. Compare the 1904 map with maps showing the results of the 2016 and 2020 presidential elections. What can you infer from the differences in the way the electorate voted in 1904 and in 2016 and 2020?

Midwest, considered or enacted pieces of the package: literacy and residency requirements, poll taxes, and the exclusions of paupers, aliens, and felons. Not all initiatives were explicitly racist; some were enacted to promote political independence and combat fraud. One was voter registration, implemented almost everywhere after the War of the Rebellion, which was meant to prevent ineligible voters from casting ballots. Another was redistricting and at-large elections meant to weaken political machines and empower officials who represented the "entire"

Table 19.2	The Spread of Disfranchisement in the South	
Year	**State**	**Strategies**
1889	Florida	Poll tax
1889	Tennessee	Poll tax
1890	Mississippi	Poll tax, literacy test, understanding clause
1891	Arkansas	Poll tax
1893, 1901	Alabama	Poll tax, literacy test, grandfather clause
1894, 1895	South Carolina	Poll tax, literacy test, understanding clause
1894, 1902	Virginia	Poll tax, literacy test, understanding clause
1897, 1898	Louisiana	Poll tax, literacy test, grandfather clause
1899, 1900	North Carolina	Poll tax, literacy test, grandfather clause
1902	Texas	Poll tax
1908	Georgia	Poll tax, understanding clause, grandfather clause

population rather than subsets within it. Yet another was the embrace of "city managers" (replacing mayors) who presumably were independent from political parties. Still another was the Australian (secret) ballot, first used in 1888, and widely adopted to prevent interference in a voter's deliberations.

By the time of the First World War (1914–1918), and certainly by the 1920s, many of the features of American politics that would prevail across the twentieth century were in place. These included the diminishing significance of partisanship, the bureaucratization of political parties and institutions of government, the increasing importance of nonelected officials in policymaking, and the use of cumbersome registration procedures. In large part as a consequence of the latter, these also included a dramatic decline in popular participation in elections at all levels of government. Black turnout in the South suffered the steepest drop, but white turnout dropped precipitously as well, so that from 1896 to 1916 average southern turnout in presidential elections declined from 64 percent to 24 percent and would continue to fall. In the North and West, the drop was not nearly so steep but substantial nonetheless. In 1896, it averaged about 79 percent, by 1916 around 62 percent, and by 1920 around 49 percent (see Figure 19.2).

Toward the Nineteenth Amendment

The one area in which political participation expanded was women's suffrage. But it was a lengthy, complex, and contradictory process. Part of a century-long struggle waged by women's rights activists, the campaign for the franchise was a rocky one. Surfacing in the late 1840s and 1850s, most famously at the Seneca

Falls, New York, convention of 1848, led by reformers Elizabeth Cady Stanton and Lucretia Mott, suffrage advocates threaded the age of revolution's ideas of natural rights into demands for political as well as civil equality. The Seneca Falls "Declaration of Sentiments" insisted that women "have immediate admission to all the rights and privileges which belong to the citizens of the United States," particularly the "inalienable right to the elective franchise." Styled after the Declaration of Independence, its rejection, often with ridicule, was a bruising one.

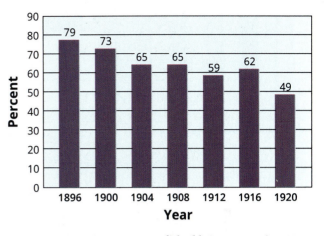

≡ **FIGURE 19.2**   **Participation of Eligible Voters, 1896–1920.**

Yet the door of possibility opened before too long. The War of the Rebellion and its radical trajectory toward emancipation, birthright citizenship, and a Black male franchise pushed at the boundaries of change. Elizabeth Cady Stanton now hoped to "bury the woman and the negro in the citizen," and others in the woman suffrage movement imagined that their prospects for equality would be advanced, too. But they all soon discovered that one-time male allies in the battle to save the Union and free the enslaved were ready to break ranks. For them, the priority was the freedmen and the Republican Party. Even Charles Sumner, who introduced a petition for women's suffrage in the US Senate, decided that it was not "a proper time of the consideration of that question."

For Stanton, Susan B. Anthony, Lucy Stone, and many other suffrage activists, it was a galling betrayal, not only because the Fifteenth Amendment did not include "sex" in its protected categories for the "right to vote," but also because the Fourteenth Amendment, in its section encouraging an African American franchise, explicitly equated voters with "males." Stanton was not alone in wondering why the "colored man" was "enfranchised before the woman," or in sneering that she wouldn't trust "him with all my rights." It was a bad omen.

Indeed, the suffrage movement quickly fractured amid bitterness and recrimination, owing to the depth of the opposition and its own limitations. Composed mainly of white, Protestant women of the educated middle class, the movement had little to say to working women or men, let alone to Black women, even of the urban "better classes," who were establishing reform organizations of their own. When white women suffragists attempted a reunification in 1890, with the founding of the National American Woman Suffrage Association (NAWSA), the arguments of the suffragists seemed a far cry from the Seneca Falls Declaration of Sentiments.

≡ **Suffrage Wagon**   Originally used to deliver milk or baked goods, tradition holds that suffragist Lucy Stone used this wagon at speaking engagements and to distribute copies of *Woman's Journal*, the newspaper she edited. In 1912, nineteen years after Stone's death, women's rights advocates found the wagon in a barn on Stone's property and painted it with slogans.

Instead of claiming the franchise as a natural right, they spoke of the positive effect that women could have on a corrupt political system beset by class and ethnic antagonisms.

Some suffrage advocates in fact spoke of the female franchise as an essential counterweight to the voting power of ignorant and alien men. Carrie Chapman Catt, who eventually became leader of the NAWSA, argued that "there has arisen in America a class of men not intelligent, not patriotic, not moral, nor yet pedigreed . . . who secure passage of many a legislative measure through corrupt means." As Catt saw it, enfranchising native-born women was the surest means to save the "American Republic."

In the South, where opposition to woman suffrage was especially strong, supporters like Rebecca Latimer Felton, Kate Gordon, and Belle Kearney took Catt's perspective even further, framing their enfranchisement as a means of strengthening the forces of white supremacy. "Anglo-Saxon women," Kearney told a NAWSA convention in 1903, were "the medium through which to retain the supremacy of the white race over the African."

For a time, the strategy of emphasizing the cultural attributes that women might bring to the male world of politics did not seem to work. Little headway was made either in referenda or bills in state legislatures. But early in the twentieth century there was a new and militant spark. While notions of moral guardianship did not disappear from the arguments of suffragists, a younger generation began to push the NAWSA toward alliances that dramatically broadened its base. Embodying the best energies of Progressivism, they built local organizations, reached out to working-class women and men, sought the support of trade unions, and took to the streets in well-publicized and often dazzling marches for woman suffrage.

By 1910, women's suffrage was becoming a mass movement—which it had never been before—bringing together a coalition of social reformers who wished to empower workers and Progressives who saw women's rights as an important component of what it meant to be modern. Support came from the American Federation of Labor and Socialist Party as well as from the Progressive "Bull Moose" Party of Theodore Roosevelt. The National Association for the Advancement of Colored People (NAACP) came on board, too, noting that "votes for women mean votes for black women." When, in the midst of conducting a national mobilization of preparedness for World War I, President Woodrow Wilson publicly described women's suffrage as a "war measure," the path to the Nineteenth Amendment of the Constitution was finally cleared: the "right to vote" could no longer be "denied or abridged . . . on account of sex."

How did the Nineteenth Amendment (ratified in 1920) affect relations between white and Black women activists? Ever since the 1890s, educated Black women who set out to fight the ferocious racism of the time saw in women's suffrage a way to turn back the assault on Black civil and political rights. Through organizations like the National Association of Colored Women (NACW), they aligned themselves with both the NAWSA and the WCTU in efforts to promote women's full enfranchisement. By 1914, under the leadership of Mary Church Terrell, the NACW represented 50,000 women in 1,000 clubs. Yet cooperation was limited. For all the outreach that white suffrage activists attempted, they did little to cross the color line that was being drawn more firmly and fiercely than ever before. The construction of a new politics would greatly enlarge the sphere of prospective participants, but its bow before white supremacy was also indicative of a politics meant to shift power further away from the grassroots.

≡ **Suffrage Activists**   African American women used women's clubs as launch pads for political activism. Here delegates to the Banner State Woman's National Baptist Convention gather in 1915.

When the celebrations over the Nineteenth Amendment died down, the fears of its opponents were never realized. Although the size of the electorate had almost doubled, the overall voter turnout rates continued to slide. For the time being, in other words, women's suffrage appeared to reinforce rather than reorient a political culture that had been taking shape for more than three decades. And Black women would have no better opportunities than Black men to make their presence felt in the arenas of formal politics.

Conclusion: Forging a New Society

The Gilded Age witnessed the eruption of a mass crisis in American society, which, as we have seen, led to a number of important popular movements, influenced by antimonopoly, that fought for a more equitable and small-scale society. They included Greenbackers, industrial workers, and Populists. In the aftermath of their defeat, Progressives took the measure of America's fractured society, developed perspectives that owed to these earlier movements but looked to different solutions, and sought to construct something new. They sought to construct a new society based upon a rejection of individualism and unregulated competition, upon the corporation as a new economic form, upon the wisdoms of science and the goal of efficiency, upon ideas of governance that privileged expertise, and upon an active role for government in administering the new corporate economy.

Progressives also regarded themselves as especially well-placed to understand the world and carry out reforms. In many ways they were social engineers who were interested in new methods for bringing about a more stable and prosperous society. Toward that end, many embraced solutions—that would later be recognized as deeply offensive and racist—like eugenics, which sought to reduce the number of what they called the "feeble-minded" and encourage the growth of a population without genetic defects. By the mid-1910s, as global warfare was beginning to press upon the United States, many of the foundations of this new society and this new way of thinking had been forged.

WHAT IF the Ideas of the Oregon System Caught On?

Eras of reform, for the most part, bring new forms of order to what had been a destabilized environment, even when they involve impressive types of experimentation. But they also encouraged some of the reform-minded and their more radical allies—we might call them visionaries—to imagine and perhaps attempt to implement very different ways of doing things. As we saw in this chapter, one of the most interesting examples of this sort of re-envisioning took place in Portland, Oregon, during the first two decades of the twentieth century. There a formidable coalition of workers and middle-class radicals, many influenced by Henry George, took matters into their own hands and formed the People's Power League. They saw themselves as advocates for "the producing and industrial classes," and sought to "defend a citizen's rights against injustice by powerful corporations." Led by a remarkable man named William U'Ren, who had worked as a miner, lawyer, and newspaper editor before reading George's *Progress and Poverty*, they utterly reimagined the structure of popular government. They pioneered numerous progressive political measures, including direct primaries, initiative and referendum, and the popular election of US senators. They also supported women's suffrage.

But even more breathtaking were their proposals for changing how political power was organized and wielded. Reaching back to Pennsylvania's revolutionary-era constitution, they called for a unicameral (one house rather than the usual two, for greater popular control) legislature. And absorbing currents of international political thought, they pushed for proportional representation based not on parties or population but on occupation, including female wage earners and housewives. These were the elements of what came to be known as the "Oregon System." They remain ahead of our own time. But what if the ideas really caught on?

DOCUMENT 19.1: Proposed Constitutional Amendment for Basing Representatives on the Voters' Business Occupation, May 22, 1920

In 1920, the People's Power League proposed an amendment to the state constitution of Oregon that would radically reform legislative representation to be based on occupation rather than the sheer numbers of constituents.

The People's Power League proposes . . . that the voters in every considerable business occupation, women as well as men, must select, nominate and elect their representatives in the legislature. Home-making and house-keeping is a business within the definition of this amendment. By this plan, the voters of each and every occupation equal in number to one hundredth of all the voters of the state may nominate and elect their representatives from their own registered members. The plan embodies the best features of parliamentary methods for control of executive departments, and the legislature will be one house of 100 members and no more.

The following estimate and classification of the representatives under this plan is based upon the census of 1910 . . . [which] will serve to give an idea of the general representation:

Fourteen farmers; fourteen farm housewives; five farm laborers; four tenant workers; three merchants; two manufacturers; seven railroad and other transportation workers; three professional men (capitalists, lawyers, doctors, bankers, priests, and editors); twenty town-dwelling housewives; two women factory workers; three women clerks, stenographers, and school teachers; one for cooks and waiters; one for fishermen; one for actors and other theatrical employees; one for domestic and personal service.

The plan makes the governor and the executive department subordinate to the legislature because government is about 1% law and 99% execution by the officers. . . . The legislature will elect one of its members governor; he can hold office only while he commands the confidence of a majority of the representatives and the people; when he loses the confidence of a majority of the representatives he must either resign or dissolve the legislature and order a new election.

Source: Oregon Voter, June 5, 1920.

DOCUMENT 19.2: William U'Ren's "New Freak"

The proposal of the People's Power League for legislative reapportionment was met in established circles with hostility and derision which account for its ultimate defeat.

Probably no more fantastic governmental structure was ever evolved by the human brain, outside of Russia, than that now submitted formally by W.S. U'Ren, father of the Oregon System. . . . Yet, like every other freak measure it has its inception in actual evils or in imperfections of our present representative form of government. . . . In so far as it seeks to confine voting power to people engaged in occupations (including housewives and personal servants), it implies recognition of the fact that every hobo, leech, lazy rich and parasite loafer should not have a vote. Thus a distinct step in progress is proposed by these reformers. . . . The reformers in their new freak proposal also recognize the fact that the mere granting of the franchise to any and all classes and kinds of people is not an assurance that it will be exercised in a responsible manner. Some inducement to vote is required that will encourage the lethargic citizen to cast his ballot whether he knows what he is voting for or not. So certain features of the voting-by-mail system are introduced. The possibilities of manipulation, fraud, and abuse opened up by permitting mail voting evidently do not daunt the reformers . . . Businessmen as well as farmers often complain that the legislature contains too many lawyers. . . . Yet, experience has shown that in the legislature it is the lawyers who demonstrate more capacity for leadership. . . . It is the lawyers who seem to grasp the problems of all kinds and classes of people better than the members who represent one occupation only. . . . Very likely a legislature composed of non-lawyers, and including two or three lawyers among a hundred members would have to employ a large corps of attorneys to keep itself straight, and even then would scramble the laws of the state into a mess that would give remunerative employment to a generation of lawyers to attempt to straighten out. We have an idea that the lawyers are of greater use and value to the people in the legislature than out of it.

Source: Oregon Voter, June 5, 1920.

Thinking About Contingency

1. What would the state government have looked like if it had been organized under the plan of the People's Power League? Would it or would it not have been workable?
2. Why were opponents so hostile to the plan? Why did they call it the "New Freak"? What did they fear it would bring about?
3. Would the plan have had support among groups and people outside of Oregon? Who would they be?
4. Are there any examples of political organization that show the influence of People's Power League thinking, either today or in the years after it was suggested?

REVIEW QUESTIONS

1. How was the relationship between individuals and the larger social order reimagined in the late nineteenth century and early twentieth century? How did the work of Progressives like Jane Addams and Florence Kelley demonstrate this reimagining?

2. How did Progressives like Walter Rauschenbusch lend moral fervor to the Progressive movement? What was the social gospel?

3. Why did a growing proportion of Americans by the end of the nineteenth century come to see the government as central to resolving the problems of industrial capitalism?

4. How was the industrial workplace reconstructed during this period? Why did the shop floor become a contested space? Why did so many corporations embrace scientific management? What was "pure and simple unionism" that Samuel Gompers was trying to achieve?

5. How did ideas about order, expertise, and proper management contribute to serious doubts about the workings of political democracy? Why were so many Black people disfranchised during this period, while women saw their political participation increase?

KEY TERMS

American Civil Liberties Union (ACLU) (p. 778)

American Federation of Labor (AFL) (p. 799)

Clayton Anti-Trust Act (1914) (p. 798)

corporation (p. 793)

eugenics (p. 788)

Great Merger movement (p. 793)

holding company (p. 794)

Industrial Workers of the World (p. 801)

International Ladies' Garment Workers' Union (ILGWU) (p. 801)

Interstate Commerce Act (1887) (p. 793)

mechanization (p. 796)

muckraking (p. 790)

National Civic Federation (NCF) (p. 798)

New Freedom (p. 805)

New Nationalism (p. 804)

Oregon System (p. 802)

Progressivism (p. 783)

scientific management (p. 796)

settlement houses (p. 785)

settlement house movement (p. 785)

Sherman Anti-Trust Act (1890) (p. 793)

social gospel (p. 785)

specialization (p. 796)

statism (p. 804)

United Mine Workers (UMW) (p. 801)

voluntarism (p. 800)

Woman's Christian Temperance Union (WCTU) (p. 786)

RECOMMENDED READINGS

Victoria B. Brown, *The Education of Jane Addams* (University of Pennsylvania Press, 2004).

Nancy Cohen, *The Reconstruction of American Liberalism, 1865–1914* (University of North Carolina Press, 2001).

Herbert Croly, *The Promise of American Life* (1909).

Julie Greene, *Pure and Simply Politics: The American Federation of Labor and Political Activism, 1881–1917* (Cambridge University Press, 2006).

Robert Johnston, *The Radical Middle Class: Progressive Era Portland, Oregon* (Princeton University Press, 2003).

Thomas Leonard, *Illiberal Reformers: Race, Eugenics, and American Economic in the Progressive Era* (Princeton University Press, 2016).

Michael McGerr, *A Fierce Discontent: The Rise and Fall of the Progressive Movement in America, 1870–1920* (Oxford University Press, 2007).

David Montgomery, *The Fall of the House of Labor: The Workplace, the State, and American Labor Activism, 1865–1925* (Cambridge University Press, 1989).

Daniel Rodgers, *Atlantic Crossings: Social Politics in a Progressive Age* (Harvard University Press, 1998).

Elizabeth Sanders, *Roots of Reform: Farmers, Workers, and the American State, 1877–1917* (University of Chicago, 1999).

Kathryn Sklar, *Florence Kelley and the Nation's Work: The Rise of Women's Political Culture, 1830–1900* (Yale University Press, 1995).

Martin Sklar, *The Corporate Reconstruction of American Capitalism, 1890–1916* (Cambridge University Press, 1988).

20

Empire and Race
1890–1914

Chapter Outline

20.1 Mexican Vistas

Discuss how American involvement in the Mexican economy and politics in the late nineteenth and early twentieth centuries shaped both countries.

20.2 The Caribbean Basin and Hawai'i

Explain the logic of American interests in the Caribbean Basin and the Hawaiian Islands.

20.3 William Seward and the Pacific

Describe the role William Seward played in arguing for the importance of the Pacific for America's destiny.

20.4 Drawing the Color Line at Home

Evaluate how new ideas and relations of race were being constructed in the United States of the late nineteenth and early twentieth centuries.

20.5 A New Empire and a New Colonialism

Assess how American policymakers fashioned a new type of empire and a new colonialism for the United States.

20.6 The Spanish-Cuban-Filipino-American War

Discuss the significance of the Spanish-Cuban-Filipino-American War of 1898.

20.7 The Panama Canal and American Destiny

Describe how the construction of the Panama Canal brought together the new threads of race and empire.

≣ **Displaying Empire** "Indian Defying Civilization" is the title of this photograph of a statue of a mounted Native American warrior waving a defiant fist in front of the Festival Hall at the Louisiana Purchase Exposition (also known as the St. Louis World Fair) in 1904. The 100-year anniversary of the Louisiana Purchase came at a time when the United States envisioned a new imperial place for itself in the world.

In the decade between 1896 and 1906, the Supreme Court of the United States ruled on a series of cases that were argued separately but together suggested how the country was constructing new understandings of race and empire. Best known is *Plessy v. Ferguson,* a case that originated in an 1892 lawsuit brought by a light-skinned man of color—Homer Plessy—against a Louisiana railroad company that forced Black people to ride in segregated cars, as the state's law passed in 1890 had decreed. The Court, dominated by justices from the northern and western states, rejected Plessy's claim that the Louisiana law violated his rights under the Thirteenth and Fourteenth Amendments and proclaimed that the provision of "separate but equal" facilities was not unconstitutional.

Two years later, the Court, with most of the same members, ruled in *Williams v. Mississippi* that Mississippi's constitution of 1890, which imposed poll taxes and literacy requirements as qualifications for voting and required potential jurors in

Timeline

1867	1870	1873	1876	1879	1882	1885	1888	1891

1867 > United States purchases Alaska from Russia

1876–1911 > Porfirio Diaz constructs the *Porfiriato* in Mexico

1890 > Massacre at Wounded Knee; US military suppresses Ghost Dance

criminal cases to be registered voters, did not violate the Constitution's Fourteenth Amendment because it did not specifically disfranchise people of African descent— even though, as a consequence, almost all Black men in the state were then deprived of the elective franchise.

Another three years later, the Court ruled on a series of individual cases that emerged when the United States annexed foreign territories as a result of the Spanish-Cuban-Filipino-American War of 1898. The issue that linked all the cases was whether residents of these territories could claim the same rights as all American citizens. This had been the expectation, beginning with the Northwest Ordinance of 1787, when Florida, Louisiana, Texas, and the Mexican territories of New Mexico and California became part of the United States before the War of the Rebellion. But in 1901, the Court had a different perspective, not only because the Philippines, Guam, Puerto Rico, and Hawai'i were beyond—in some cases well beyond—the North American

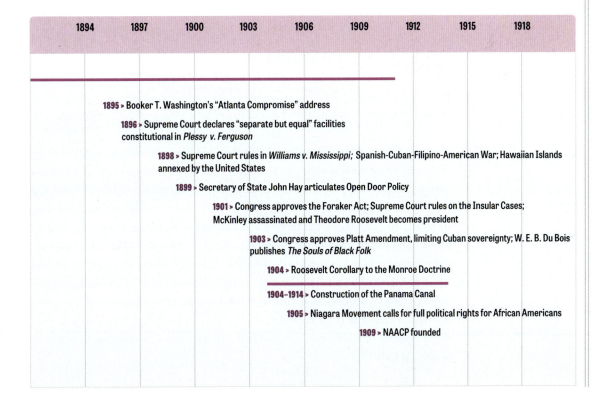

| 1894 | 1897 | 1900 | 1903 | 1906 | 1909 | 1912 | 1915 | 1918 |

1895 ▸ Booker T. Washington's "Atlanta Compromise" address

1896 ▸ Supreme Court declares "separate but equal" facilities constitutional in *Plessy v. Ferguson*

1898 ▸ Supreme Court rules in *Williams v. Mississippi;* Spanish-Cuban-Filipino-American War; Hawaiian Islands annexed by the United States

1899 ▸ Secretary of State John Hay articulates Open Door Policy

1901 ▸ Congress approves the Foraker Act; Supreme Court rules on the Insular Cases; McKinley assassinated and Theodore Roosevelt becomes president

1903 ▸ Congress approves Platt Amendment, limiting Cuban sovereignty; W. E. B. Du Bois publishes *The Souls of Black Folk*

1904 ▸ Roosevelt Corollary to the Monroe Doctrine

1904-1914 ▸ Construction of the Panama Canal

1905 ▸ Niagara Movement calls for full political rights for African Americans

1909 ▸ NAACP founded

continent but also because they were overwhelmingly populated by people of color and of mixed races. As the Court saw it, in what have become known as the "Insular Cases" (because the territories in question were being administered by the War Department's Bureau of Insular Affairs), the constitutional rights and protections that Americans born and naturalized in the United States enjoyed, did not automatically extend to all people who lived in territories under American jurisdiction. Indeed, the Court drew a distinction between what it called "incorporated" and "unincorporated" territories, and only the people in the former qualified for full constitutional rights.

Together, these Supreme Court cases demonstrated that, as a new international imperial power, the United States was prepared to show little regard for the rights of people in territories the nation was colonizing while at the same time accepting, within the framework of the Constitution itself, a second-class status for Americans of African descent that the Court had marked out in the *Dred Scott* case of 1857. Empire and race were inextricably connected as modern America was being forged at the turn of the twentieth century. But was this a throwback to an earlier day or an indication of what the road to modernity brought with it?

20.1 Mexican Vistas

||| Discuss how American involvement in the Mexican economy and politics in the late nineteenth and early twentieth centuries shaped both countries.

The new financial elite that the War of the Rebellion empowered seemed to be busy stabilizing the economy and investing both in America's emerging industries east of the Mississippi and in the development of the trans-Mississippi West, the control of which sparked warfare in the first place. But the vistas of financiers were by no means confined to the territory and economic activities within the nation's borders. Like their antebellum predecessors, they were quick to look for opportunities outside of the United States. And one of the first places investors looked for fields of opportunity after the War of the Rebellion ended in 1865 was the neighboring country of Mexico, with which the United States already had a lengthy, interconnected, and conflict-ridden relationship. In so doing, they would initiate many decades of involvement, not only in the Mexican economy but in Mexican politics as well.

Imperial Eyes on the South

Mexico was itself embroiled in civil warfare between Liberals and Conservatives when, in 1864, France invaded the country, ousted the Liberal regime of Benito Juarez, and imposed Austrian archduke Maximilian as "emperor," chiefly to recover long-standing debts that the Mexican government owed. It was a clear and brazen violation of the Monroe Doctrine, by which the United States warned European powers to keep out of the Western Hemisphere, and the French moves could have sparked American retaliation were it not for the war still raging at home. The Andrew Johnson administration also resisted the opportunity to intervene militarily, though Americans did supply arms and ammunition to Juarez who ultimately prevailed over the French in 1867. But the Juarez Liberals courted more than American military equipment; they also hoped to attract American capital and, since 1865, had been floating millions of dollars of Mexican bonds for foreign purchase.

The Mexicans found interested takers, especially among the financiers and industrialists who had been enriched and empowered during the Civil War. They included men like William E. Dodge, John Jacob Astor, J. P. Morgan, Anson Phelps, and Henry Du Pont, whose vision was robust. "With the Rebellion vanquished, the Union reestablished . . . and Mexico once more a free and vigorous republic, what power would dare stop the western course of Empire?" one banker asked.

As part of the "western course of Empire," some members of the American financial elite dreamed of annexing both northern Mexico and western Canada, creating an even larger continental nation. But for most of them, "empire" was mainly commercial and closely linked to their developmental projects in the trans-Mississippi West. Which is to say that they looked to suppress Indigenous populations, such as the Apaches and the Sonoran Yaqui—still intent on raiding and resisting the advance of capitalist civilization—construct railroads tying central Mexico to the northeastern United States, exploit the mineral and agricultural resources of Mexico, and strengthen their hands in the Caribbean basin and Pacific. For this, as in the West, they needed the cooperation or encouragement of the central Mexican state as well as of provincial officials who often had minds of their own.

For a time, these goals were not easy to pursue. Although Mexican Liberals generally shared the modernizing perspectives of Republicans in the United States, they still smarted from the defeats and humiliations of warfare with the Americans in the 1840s and worried that American investments could compromise the sovereignty of their already troubled country. It was not until Porfirio Diaz claimed power over the Mexican state in 1877 that real headway could be made.

The *Porfiriato*

Porfirio Diaz is a fascinating figure. An army officer and large landowner from the southern part of Mexico who had distinguished himself during the recent war with the French, Diaz had his eyes on the Mexican presidency since the early 1870s. Once in office, he set out to consolidate power and modernize the country that he ruled. Diaz immediately moved to break the grip of provincial bosses, especially in northern Mexico, and simultaneously sought to attract foreign capital for the construction of railroads, mines, plantations, and communication networks. Through a mixture of incentives and coercion, Diaz strengthened the governmental center, and by offering generous concessions he found eager investors. His activity had some of the features of Republican Reconstruction in the South and West, and began a three-decade-long project of state-building and dictatorial rule that would come to be known as the *Porfiriato*.

The timing could not have been better. The very year Diaz took power, Republican Rutherford B. Hayes, himself an investor in Mexico, was inaugurated president after the highly contested election of 1876 and soon sought to cooperate with the Diaz regime. American financiers based in the Northeast who were close to Hayes and supported Diaz quickly reaped the rewards. With the assistance of compliant provincial governors, Diaz provided subsidies and rights-of-way to railroad companies while coming down with a hard fist on Apache raids, peasant unrest, and labor union radicals. Before long, new railroad lines were heading south toward Mexico City from various points on the US-Mexico border, and then linking up with a number of American railroads that traversed the Southwest. By the time the nineteenth century came to a close, Americans not only financed the building of roughly 7,500 miles of track but also owned 80 percent of the stocks and bonds sold by the Mexican railroads. Coming as no surprise, the Mexican Central Railway, the system's main artery, was incorporated in Massachusetts (see Map 20.1).

As in the trans-Mississippi West, the railroads were the entering wedge for other American investments in the Mexican economy, most importantly in the mineral sector. The intervention of the Porfirian state again was crucial. It enacted a new mining code that permitted landholders to own resources lying beneath the soil even though they were not Mexican nationals. Drawing upon their experience in the Rocky Mountains and desert Southwest, American investors—especially the Guggenheims, Rockefellers, Goulds, Dodges, and Phelpses—brought in new technologies and their own engineers to extract the ores, hired Mexicans to do the dangerous work underground, and built rail lines to transport the ores to smelters in the United States. Eventually they built facilities to smelt (a process to extract metals from ores using heat) in Mexico as well.

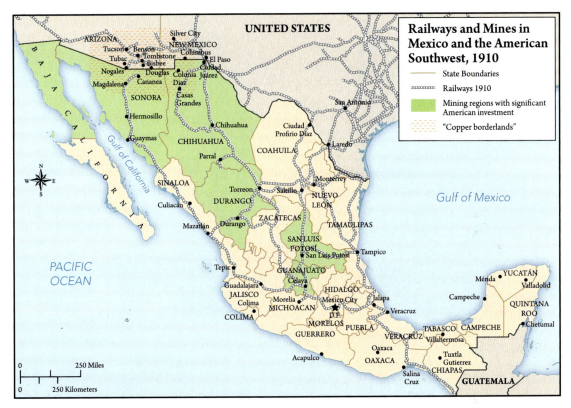

MAP 20.1 Railways and Mining Regions in Mexico and the American Southwest, 1910 By the start of the twentieth century, American investors controlled the silver and copper mines of Mexico and owned 80 percent of the stocks and bonds sold by Mexican railroads.

Silver mining was at the heart of the imperial operation, and Americans came to dominate centers in Chihuahua, Sonora, Durango, San Luis Potosí, and Guanajuato (see again Map 20.1). Little by little, they took controlling interest in silver production and then, as they were already doing in the United States, turned their attention to copper and petroleum. In the process, they created an interconnected industrial borderland that linked mining towns on the US side with those on the Mexican. Once remote and inaccessible, this transnational landscape had, in the words of an American geologist, been "surveyed," "scanned," and "scrutinized," owing to the "desert conquering railway, American enterprise and mining exploration."

An extension of developmental patterns in the trans-Mississippi West came to define other investments in land, agriculture, and corporate organization. Taking advantage of Diaz's efforts to privatize the peasantry's communal landholdings

≡ **Mexican Silver Miners**   This photo from 1890 shows the harsh conditions Mexican mineworkers faced and the basic technologies they employed.

and his willingness to allow them to purchase Mexican property, American investors started a massive land grab and found their way into other areas of the Mexican economy. Mine owners snatched up adjacent lands and turned them into the type of company towns that had already sprung up across the American West (as we saw in Chapter 17). Some of the moneyed Americans established large ranches both for meat and hides and to diversify their portfolios. Bankers, import-export merchants, and manufacturers like Cyrus McCormick of International Harvester channeled their funds into coffee and sugar estates, henequen (used for making rope) plantations, and fields of rubber plants. By 1900, more than one-third of the Mexican land mass was owned by foreigners (mostly Americans) while Diaz's policies at home had rendered over 90 percent of the Mexican peasantry—mostly Indigenous people—landless.

20.2   The Caribbean Basin and Hawai'i

‖‖‖ Explain the logic of American interests in the Caribbean Basin and the Hawaiian Islands.

There were wider implications, too. Just as the trans-Mississippi West served as a staging ground for the extension of America's economic arms into Mexico, so did the various beachheads of American investors in Mexico prepare the way for a new brand of US hegemony in the Western Hemisphere and beyond. American bankers began offering loans to landowners and developers in Central America and the Caribbean and investing in projects that aimed at building a canal across the isthmus of Panama (the narrow strip of land that lies between the Caribbean and the

Pacific Ocean, linking North and South America) in order to move ships from east to west quickly and hence expand American power in the Western Hemisphere. American manufacturers sold advanced machinery and other technologies to creole (people of European descent born in the Western Hemisphere) producers. American merchants, shipping companies, and refiners helped organize the export trade, especially in sugar and other tropical commodities. And the American nation-state, driven by Republican expansionists like James G. Blaine (a leading voice in the party and a former secretary of state), negotiated a series of reciprocity treaties (agreements to ease trading restrictions between the treaty-bound nations) that both strengthened the position of the United States in the hemisphere and challenged the position of Great Britain, the main European rival.

The American Mediterranean

The Spanish colony of Cuba was an important case in point. American involvement with Cuba began as early as the eighteenth century and grew deeper in the early nineteenth as the sugar and slave economy there took off. Northeastern-based mercantile companies established branches in Havana and other ports on the island, provided credit, became involved in slave trading, bought up some of the sugar crop, and acquired a few sugar and coffee plantations. American political interests, mainly in the Democratic Party, pushed for annexation in what seemed an inevitable outcome—John Quincy Adams saw the "laws of political gravitation" at work—until the War of the Rebellion intervened. Little American contact, other than the arrival of defeated Confederates and enslavers looking for a safe haven, occurred immediately thereafter.

But in the late 1870s, when Cuba's first independence movement (known as the Ten Years' War 1868–1878) suffered defeat, new possibilities opened without the need for annexation. American financiers found creole planters desperate for capital to rebuild their sugar plantations and mills. They also began to buy up cash-strapped properties themselves, including the 60,000-acre Constancia plantation in Cienfuegos, thought to be the largest sugar estate in the world. American dollars flowed to other areas of the Cuban economy as well—tobacco, utilities, transportation—while the growing volume of trade made the United States Cuba's most important commercial partner. As US Consul Ramon O. Williams put it in the 1880s, "*De facto*, Cuba is already inside the commercial union of the United States. . . . The island is entirely dependent upon [and related to] the market of the United States."

Similar, though less substantial, projects could be found elsewhere in the Caribbean basin, setting the groundwork for much more formidable corporate undertakings before the end of the century. In Nicaragua, the regime at the time

≡ **Bananas for Export** Workers load bananas into rail cars in Costa Rica, 1904. The intensive monoculture practiced by firms like the United Fruit Company dramatically changed the ecology of Central American landscapes.

combined conservative politics with economic modernization and, like Porfirio Diaz, aimed to reward export producers (mainly coffee) and infrastructure developers with subsidies and legal reforms that made the acquisition of property and the attraction of a labor force more feasible. American investors trained their eyes on the country, initially thinking it the most favorable location for an isthmian canal, and American cultural and economic influence grew accordingly.

In neighboring Costa Rica, American entrepreneur Henry Meiggs was awarded a contract in 1871 to build a railroad from the capital of San Jose to the Caribbean port of Limón. But when the Costa Rican government defaulted on its payments, Meiggs's successor, and relative, managed to extract 800,000 acres of prime land, which was soon producing and exporting bananas. The operation would later be reorganized as the United Fruit Company, which would have a large and heavy-handed presence during the first two-thirds of the twentieth century.

The Hawaiian Islands

The prospect of annexation turned up more significantly not in the Caribbean basin, regarded more and more as the American "Mediterranean," but in distant Hawai'i. It would be a long and turbulent process, resembling the approach of federal officials and social reformers to Native Americans in the Southeast and trans-Mississippi West (discussed in Chapter 17) and with a similar outcome. Just as the Western Hemisphere had been populated by migrants who crossed over from northeast Asia, Hawai'i may have been settled as early as the fourth century CE by Polynesians who had navigated slowly across the Pacific. Their descendants eventually organized four socially complex island kingdoms that battled one another for supremacy. By 1810, the battles were over and the islands were unified under the rule of Kamehameha, a strong leader who established a hereditary dynasty (see Map 20.2).

The problem for Kamehameha and his successors during the first half of the nineteenth century was that European and American merchants and whalers since the late eighteenth century had used Hawai'i as a refueling and provisioning station and had established centers of maritime commerce in Honolulu and Lahaina. By the 1820s, American missionaries had arrived with their version of spirituality and

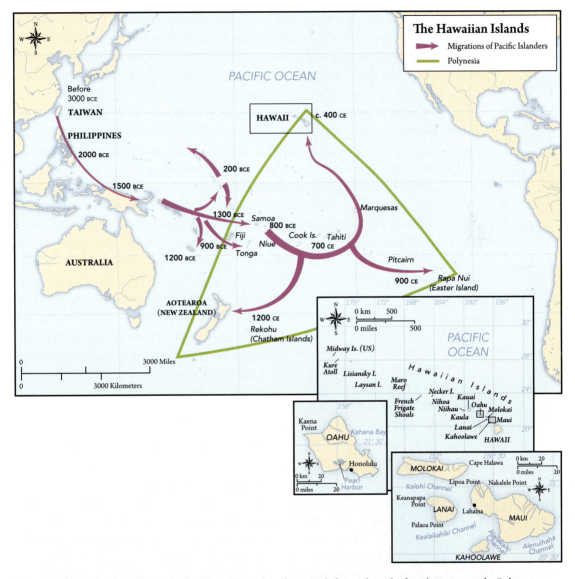

≡ **MAP 20.2   The Hawaiian Islands**   Hawai'i may have been settled as early as the fourth century CE by Polynesians who had navigated across the Pacific. After centuries of conflict among the separate islands, they had been unified since 1810 under a single hereditary monarch as the Kingdom of Hawai'i.

"civilization" for the benefit of the Hawaiian natives. Among the missionaries were the parents of Samuel Chapman Armstrong, who would serve in the Federal Army during the Civil War and then establish the Hampton Normal and Agricultural Institute to educate both African Americans and Native Americans. Would these footholds of economic and cultural activity soon threaten Hawaiian sovereignty?

Rather than attempt to resist the foreign challenge directly, Hawai'i's rulers instead chose—much like the Cherokees in North America—to protect their sovereignty by accommodating the westerners. They converted to Christianity and embraced Euro-American concepts of law, property, and political governance. They hoped that by showing themselves to be "civilized" and "advancing" in western eyes, they would win international acceptance as an independent nation. The Hawaiians organized an elective legislature, began publishing newspapers, privatized property previously controlled by the kingdom, and permitted foreigners to become landowners, as in Mexico and Central America.

It was an enormous undertaking and, for a time, it seemed to work. Great Britain and France jointly recognized Hawaiian sovereignty and the United States signed a Treaty of Friendship, Commerce, and Navigation with Kamehameha III in 1849, which clearly acknowledged the independence of the Hawaiian Kingdom and made provision for commercial reciprocity between the two. Yet, as was true among Native Americans, the cultural and political accommodations of the Hawaiians proved a weak barrier against American imperial designs.

The reforms Hawai'i's rulers enacted allowed economically ambitious Americans, many from missionary backgrounds, to build a foundation of capitalist agriculture, especially for the cultivation of sugar. Slowly in the 1850s and far more rapidly after a reciprocity treaty signed in 1875 gave Hawaiian sugar duty-free (without tax) access to the US market, a plantation economy took off and reshaped the islands. American planters and merchants found common economic interests, and, with African slavery being abolished across the globe, they looked for other sources of contract labor. First, they turned to the Chinese who were already working in the mines and on the railroads in the trans-Mississippi West. Next, they recruited Portuguese laborers, many from the Azores, and then Japanese, Koreans, and Filipinos. By 1890, less the half the population of the islands was native Hawaiian.

The planting economy thrived, but the Americans soon complained about the character of the Hawaiian rulers and the powers Hawaiians could allegedly wield. They pointed to corrupt practices,

≡ **Queen Lili'uokalani**   The last monarch of Kingdom of Hawai'i, shown here in 1891, the year she succeeded her brother, Kalākaua.

venality, wastefulness, and backwardness much as elite reformers in the United States had spoken of urban bosses and political machines and Reconstruction-era governments in the American South. And, as the language and logic of white supremacy came to dominate the perspectives of Euro-American imperialists generally, they doubted that Hawaiians were capable of governing themselves, let alone anybody else.

They did not sit idle with these concerns. By the late 1880s, the Americans began to hatch a plot. Led by businessman Lorrin Thurston and lawyer Sanford Dole, they formed the **Hawaiian League** with a paramilitary arm, much in the manner of southern and western politics, wrote a new constitution that stripped the king (now King Kalākaua) of many powers and shifted them to the legislature now to be chosen by a very limited electorate, and in the summer of 1887 dumped it in Kalākaua's lap, demanding that he submit. It was a deal he couldn't refuse. So Kalākaua reluctantly signed what was known as the "**Bayonet Constitution**." Although they had not taken full control of the government, the Americans had effectively staged a successful coup and were in a position to wrap their imperial arms ever tighter around Hawai'i's political body.

20.3   William Seward and the Pacific

Describe the role William Seward played in arguing for the importance of the Pacific for America's destiny.

Well before the 1887 Hawaiian coup, William H. Seward had imagined Hawai'i's "quiet absorption" into the United States. Best known as a New York governor, US senator, Radical Republican, candidate for the presidency in 1860, and Lincoln's secretary of state, Seward also had a large imperial perspective. He was not interested in establishing sugar plantations or other American-based industries in Hawai'i or anywhere else. Nor was he interested in promoting American settlements overseas. He had also cooled on having Canada and Mexico join the Union.

What did interest Seward was American commercial supremacy in the Pacific, and control over the water-borne highways leading to Asia. "The empire of the seas alone is the real empire," he insisted, and Asia was "the prize … the chief theater of events in the world's great thereafter." So fixed was Seward on the importance of the Pacific to America's future that, despite his antislavery militancy, he wanted California admitted to the Union as quickly as possible "even if she come as a slave state."

≡ **Sitka, Alaska** This 1885 view of an Orthodox Christian church in Sitka shows how the built landscape of Alaska was shaped by several generations of Russian colonists.

Alaska

Seward remained secretary of state after Lincoln's assassination, and he looked hungrily at a number of places stretching from the Caribbean basin west, mainly for the purpose of establishing coaling stations and commercial posts for the Asian trade. Imagining an isthmian canal in the near future, Seward saw Santo Domingo and some of the islands of the French West Indies as strategically important, though he made no diplomatic headway. After visiting the Danish Virgin Islands, Seward signed a treaty for their annexation, but the Senate refused to approve it. He had better luck out in the central Pacific with what are now known as the Midway Islands, which were successfully annexed.

But his greatest achievement, at least by his own lights, was the purchase of Alaska, in 1867, from the Russians for just over $7 million (over $140 million in today's dollars; critics called it Seward's "ice box"). Well aware of commercial activity in this Russian-controlled, though Native-occupied, territory and of Russian interest in pulling back imperially after its disastrous defeat in the Crimean War (1853–1856), Seward saw Alaska as both a means to extend US dominion over North America and as a way station to Japan and China. He sought "possession of the American continent and control over the world."

East Asia

Seward recognized the relation between commercial and political power, and he knew that the threat of military force was necessary to secure American imperial objectives. Yet he also frowned on the use of force as a method of territorial expansion. He didn't permit General Philip Sheridan to cross the border during the Mexican war against the French. Indeed, when Seward looked toward Asia, and especially China, he was intent on respecting the sovereignty of the societies there while cooperating with other Western nations to maintain equal commercial opportunities. The Burlingame Treaty, signed and ratified in 1868, not only acknowledged China's territorial integrity but also abolished the trade in Chinese indentured servants (often referred to as "coolies"), encouraged Chinese immigration to the United States, and guaranteed reciprocal privileges for each of the nation's citizens abroad. All of this, as we saw in Chapter 18, was abrogated by the Chinese Exclusion Act in 1882. Although it would be another three decades before the term came into common usage, Seward plainly envisioned the framework for the Open Door policy discussed later in this chapter.

Seward had not abandoned his interest in the American domestic sphere. His very idea of empire linked domestic and foreign affairs and, in fact, knew no clear borders or boundaries. Commercial supremacy across the globe, he believed, required a strong and stable order at home, built upon flourishing agricultural and industrial economies, and encouraged by a national government ready to support the aspirations of merchants, manufacturers, and farmers. Seward called for a transcontinental railroad as early as the 1840s, advocated a protective tariff, opposed the expansion of enslavement in part because he thought it would make the United States unfit to purse the kind of empire he imagined, and, after Lincoln's death, backed Andrew Johnson's conciliatory approach to the rebellious southern states in the service of national unity. In an important sense, that is, Seward understood the complex imperial tendencies of emerging nation-states, operating as they did both inside and outside their territorial borders, and thus he struggled to extend the reach of the imperial arms that unfolded in so many directions across and beyond the United States in the years after the War of the Rebellion.

20.4   Drawing the Color Line at Home

Evaluate how new ideas and relations of race were being constructed in the United States of the late nineteenth and early twentieth centuries.

Nothing better symbolized the relation between empire at home and abroad than did new ideas about "race." Indeed, nothing better demonstrated how domestic and foreign affairs were inextricably connected. Ideas about racial difference and white supremacy, cast in pseudo-scientific garb, had emerged in the late eighteenth and early nineteenth centuries, fueling the defense of slavery as well as the project of colonization and the discriminatory treatment of African Americans in the Northeast and Midwest. But in the years after the Civil War, these ideas increasingly hardened into a consensus among white people North and South and were deployed to justify both the abandonment of the freedpeople in the former rebellious South and new imperial aspirations in the Western Hemisphere and East Asia.

MAPPING AMERICA

American Expansion from Continental and Oceanic Perspectives

The conventional view of American expansion frames the United States between two oceans. From this perspective, American history begins at the Atlantic coast and ends at the Pacific. But for Secretary of State William H. Seward and other American policymakers of the late nineteenth century, expansion did not end at California. They advocated for American commercial supremacy in

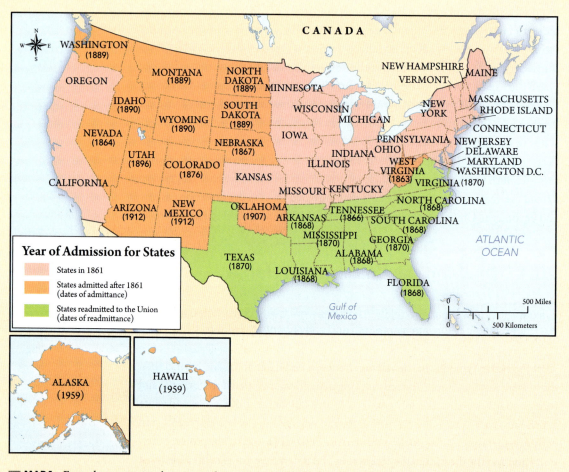

Year of Admission for States

- States in 1861
- States admitted after 1861 (dates of admittance)
- States readmitted to the Union (dates of readmittance)

≡ **MAP 1**   From the conventional continental perspective, the United States steadily expands westward until it reaches the Pacific, with the nation's peoples and states neatly contained within political borders. Alaska and Hawai'i float on the margin, disconnected from the main trajectory of American history.

the Pacific and control over the water-borne highways leading to Asia. They saw Hawai'i and Alaska as both a means to extend US dominion over North America and as way stations to Japan and China.

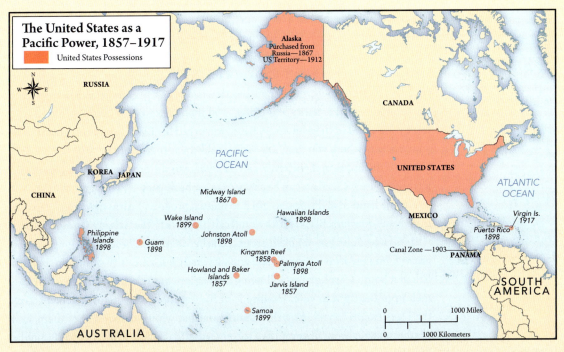

The United States as a Pacific Power, 1857–1917

United States Possessions

Alaska
Purchased from
Russia—1867
US Territory—1912

RUSSIA

CANADA

PACIFIC
OCEAN

KOREA JAPAN

UNITED STATES

CHINA

ATLANTIC
OCEAN

Midway Island
1867

Hawaiian Islands
1898

MEXICO

Virgin Is.
1917

Wake Island
1899

Johnston Atoll
1898

Puerto Rico
1898

Philippine
Islands
1898

Guam
1898

Kingman Reef
1858

Canal Zone —1903

PANAMA

Howland and Baker
Islands
1857

Palmyra Atoll
1898

SOUTH
AMERICA

Jarvis Island
1857

Samoa
1899

0   1000 Miles

0   1000 Kilometers

AUSTRALIA

MAP 2   In oceanic perspective, such as the one endorsed by Seward, the imperial aspirations of nation-states operate both inside and outside their territorial borders. The reach of American imperial ambition extends across the Pacific, with Hawai'i and Alaska forming central nodes in a vast oceanic space.

Thinking Geographically

1. The frontier has powerfully shaped American identity. How does each of the two perspectives show different ways of thinking about the place of the frontier in American history?

2. If you were an official in the State Department in the late nineteenth century, how would these perspectives influence the way you shaped foreign policy?

The World According to Booker T. Washington

No one better reflected the challenges of "race" in the United States around the turn of the twentieth century than did Booker T. Washington. Enslaved in western Virginia as a youth, Washington was educated after emancipation at Samuel Chapman Armstrong's Hampton Normal and Agricultural Institute in Virginia and then headed up the new **Tuskegee Normal and Industrial Institute** (now Tuskegee University) in Alabama. There he won recognition by instructing Black students in teaching methods and the manual arts and by cultivating the support of conservative and philanthropic whites across the country. By 1895, he would be invited to speak before a large and racially mixed audience at Atlanta's Cotton States and International Exposition that September. There he delivered an address that would lend him further notoriety.

Arguing that it had been a mistake for the federal government to give the vote to African American men, that Reconstruction had been a misguided experiment, that agitation for social equality was "folly," and that African Americans would mostly live by the sweat of their brows, Washington urged his Black listeners to "cast down your buckets where you are." That is, he told them to accept the world of the **Jim Crow** South, improve themselves, and contribute to the prosperity of the region. "In all things purely social we can be as separate as the fingers," Washington taught, "yet one as the hand in all things essential to mutual progress." Although praise came in from many quarters, Black critics would call his speech "the **Atlanta Compromise**."

It was a troubling moment all around. Earlier than year, Frederick Douglass, the great champion of civil and political equality, had died, and, as Washington spoke in Atlanta, South Carolina was following Mississippi in excluding African American men from the right to vote. Hundreds of Black people were being lynched across the Deep South for refusing the submission that whites demanded of them, and southern states were passing laws to segregate Black and white people in public life. Allies among the Republicans and Populists were fewer and fewer, and the Democratic Party in the South was increasingly dominated by radical white supremacists. Recognizing the dangers that Black men and women faced, and the apparent futility of fighting back, Washington counseled something of a truce and looked for a solution to what was being called the "Negro problem."

Violence and Race Relations

The "Negro problem" wasn't new to the late nineteenth century. Indeed, it was less a "Negro problem" than a "white problem" with Black people, as Thomas Jefferson had long before revealed. But the "problem" deepened as African Americans pressed for the full freedom they believed had been guaranteed them, and as the first generation of white and Black people born in the post-emancipation era began meeting one another as young adults in the southern states. The results could be explosive because, while the etiquettes and expectations of enslavement were now gone, new ones had yet to take their place: save for the enforced submission of African Americans.

As a result, the Deep South, and especially its rural and small-town districts, pulsed with racial violence during the 1880s and 1890s. Insurgent politics of various sorts led to brutal confrontations that often claimed the lives of militant Black leaders. But it was the gruesome surge in **lynching**—white mob executions, often carried out before hundreds of onlookers—that seemed most characteristic of the unstable social order. Lynchings were most likely to occur in cotton-growing counties where the Black population was large and prone to be on the move. Lynching victims tended to be young Black men relatively new to the areas in which they lived. The tensions and conflicts of the rural economy, rather than rape or other sexual transgressions, often figured in the provocations. Between the early 1880s and the mid-1890s, the number of lynchings increased rapidly. In 1985, the year Booker T. Washington spoke in Atlanta, and for most of the decade, an African American was lynched, on average, every three days (see Map 20.3).

The racial violence was not an exclusively southern affair. Although the overwhelming majority of African

≡ **Lynching** White men and boys in Clinton, Alabama, in 1891 stare placidly at the strung-up body of a Black man. For many white people in the Deep South, lynchings were spectacles; photographs of atrocities were even turned into postcards. This photo appeared in a 1892 pamphlet that the activist Ida B. Wells published to raise awareness of the horrors of lynching.

Americans still lived in the South, the Black population of many northern cities steadily increased in the decades after the Civil War. Race riots, along with politically motivated attacks, erupted in large cities like New York, Chicago, and Philadelphia, as well as in smaller ones like Akron, Ohio, and Springfield, Illinois. In the Pacific Northwest, the violence turned against the Chinese, who as we saw in Chapter 18 had largely been prohibited from immigrating to the United States in 1882. White mobs, composed mostly of workers who feared for their economic prospects, attempted to drive the Chinese out of a number of cities and towns in California, Washington, and Wyoming. Small wonder that the Chinese population of the United States, concentrated as it was in the Far West, dropped by one-third between 1890 and 1910. In California, where most of the Chinese resided, it dropped by as much as one-half.

That accusations of rape and interracial sexual mixing (miscegenation) were central to the discourse of lynching not only in the South but elsewhere in the country suggests what participants in lynch mobs saw at stake. On the one hand, they needed control over the apparatus of the state and local governments in order to avoid prosecution. On the other hand, they rejected state judicial institutions as the appropriate channels for meting out popular justice; they rejected the idea that all individuals should be subject to the authority of the laws and judicial system instead of the direct domination of the "community."

Lynch mobs and other perpetrators of racialized violence sought to reestablish the boundaries they believed were being traversed (either by the state or by alien "racial" groups), to crush the violations they associated with the weakening of their own authority in the face of increasing federal power. And no boundary or violation was more intimate or fundamental than those of patriarchy, gender,

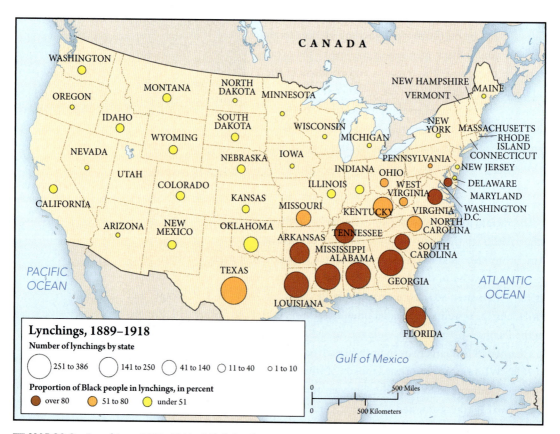

≡ **MAP 20.3 Lynchings, 1889–1918**   While lynching occurred most frequently in the South, atrocities took place in just about every state and territory. In the Southwest and West, Native American, Mexican, and Asian people were the victims as often as Black people.

and sexuality. Just as slavery was constructed around the reproductive capacity of females—the status of enslavement would follow that of the mother—so did the reconfiguration of race at the end of the nineteenth century entail the heightened patrolling of sexual contact. Lynching served as the lethal hand; the regulation of marriage served as the civil.

Separating and Segregating

Although laws against interracial sex and marriage have a history as long as colonial settlement and the emergence of African-descended slavery, they became more comprehensive and widespread after the end of Reconstruction. Supported by pseudo-scientific theories of race that placed Caucasians atop a pyramid of innate differences, miscegenation laws prohibiting interracial marriage were enacted or reenacted in a growing number of states, especially of the South and West, as a means of protecting the biological purity of white people and a way of marking new racial categories. In the states of the South, the laws barred marriage between white and Black people and, in the process, helped define the "one-drop rule" of race, the idea that any level of racial mixing between Black and white categorized the offspring as "Black." In the West, miscegenation laws would encompass Chinese, Hawaiian, Malay, Mongolian, and Native American people, along with Black people (see Map 20.4). Despite the questions they raised about the equal protection clause of the Fourteenth Amendment, the statutes were generally upheld by judges who instead invoked the "laws of nature" and the "police power of the state."

Miscegenation laws were only some of the products of new racial and sociological thinking that emphasized separation, or segregation, as crucial to the management of modern society. Gender and sexuality again emerged as flashpoints for action. Of course, practices of racial separation, especially exclusion, were deeply embedded in the United States and initially emerged in the Northeast and Midwest during the first half of the nineteenth century. Yet the impulses for comprehensive segregation became overpowering toward the end of the nineteenth century, not as a throwback to an earlier day of personal domination, but as an accompaniment to the forces of modernization: the rapid development of cities, industries, and transportation networks that would bring large numbers of people together in new and impersonal ways. Segregation was seen by its advocates as a thoroughly modern way to organize the social worlds of different racial groups, and a welcome alternative to violent encounters or the empowerment of those regarded as "inferior."

Not surprisingly, the first forays into legislated segregation came to two institutions that both typified the South's lurch toward modernity and brought males and females together in close physical proximity: public schools and public

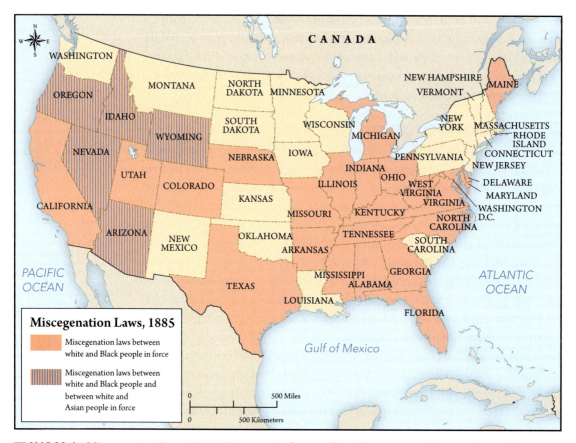

≡ **MAP 20.4   Miscegenation Laws, 1885**   Miscegenation laws regulated the institution of marriage by prohibiting marriages between people of color and white people. Because the categories of race were more diverse in the multicultural West, the sweep of miscegenation laws was broader, but the virulent racism and commitment to white supremacy was nationwide.

transportation (railroads and street cars). Segregation ordinances then spread to virtually all areas of public life—to parks, theaters, waiting rooms, restrooms, and drinking fountains—snowballing in number during the late 1890s and first decade of the twentieth century, once Black men were disfranchised and the US Supreme Court in ***Plessy v. Ferguson*** (1896) ruled that separate accommodations did not violate the Constitution. Arch-segregationists even indulged fantasies of requiring racially divided city blocks and landholding districts.

Racial segregation did not rush forward with the same legal torrent in the Northeast and Midwest that it did in the South, but it was increasingly widespread and hard-fisted. In part, its effects could be seen during the last decades of the nineteenth century in ethnic and racial enclaves that dotted industrializing cities, where "N****r Hill," "New Guinea," and "Little Africa" joined "Little Italy," "Polonia," and "Greektown." But here the lines of separation were hardened less by municipal statutes than by neighborhood protective associations and real estate interests, which played upon concerns about declining property values and the transmission of diseases like tuberculosis. Restrictive covenants backed by threats of personal violence (the Ku Klux Klan would soon be energized in the urban North by these fears) worked as effectively as legislation while contributing to segregation in public schools. Private establishments like restaurants, theaters, and hotels simply refused to serve Black people. By the 1910s under the administration of President Woodrow Wilson, regarded as a southern Progressive, the federal bureaucracy was segregated, too, and many Black employees were fired.

Given the sweep and consequences of segregation and the racial disfranchisement that went along with it, there was remarkably little criticism or resistance. Why? We can point to several reasons. The Republican Party which had once depended on Black votes in the South learned that it could maintain national power without them and therefore abandoned its Black constituents. White Progressives, rather than being troubled by what seemed to be retrograde policies, for the most part welcomed them as enlightened responses to conflict and corruption. And the political insurgents who once courted Black votes—Populists, Socialists, trade unionists—had been defeated or were not prepared to raise alarms; scorning "social equality," they were content to accept the separations and exclusions practiced in their own organizations.

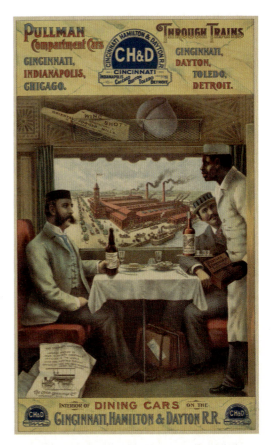

Separate and Unequal   This 1894 advertisement promotes the segregated comfort of Pullman dining cars. The white travelers enjoy a view of a factory humming with industrial activity while being served beer, whiskey, and cigars by a Black porter.

Black Resistance

The only voices to register dissent came from African Americans who struggled to articulate a critique, find an ally, or influence the discussion. The most that those in the South could do was slow the wheels of repressive change. Booker T. Washington himself worked behind the scenes, unsuccessfully, to limit the reach of disfranchisement. Segregation, however, seemed unstoppable. But a glimmer of hope could be seen in the urban North among Black journalists, educators, ministers, and professionals who had come to political maturity with Reconstruction-era

≡ **W. E. B. Du Bois** This portrait was taken in 1907, two years before Du Bois, Ida B. Wells, Mary White Ovington, Mary Church Terrell, and others formed the NAACP.

expectations and were not about to cast down their buckets anywhere. Lead by William Monroe Trotter and W. E. B. Du Bois, they rejected Washington's accommodationist stance and determined to organize for "Negro freedom and growth."

This they did in 1905 when they met on the unsegregated Canadian side of Niagara Falls and drew up a "Declaration of Principles" that was far removed from the Atlanta Compromise in tone and substance. Insisting on full political rights and calling racial discrimination "barbarous," the Declaration refused "to allow the impression … that the Negro American assents to his" status. It was known as the **Niagara Movement** and, four years later, these ringing demands for civil and political equality went into the making of the interracial **National Association for the Advancement of Colored People (NAACP)**, which would help shape Black and civil rights politics for decades to come.

Well before he took part in the Niagara movement, W. E .B. Du Bois, Harvard educated and politically militant, reflected on the development of race in the United States. He asked African Americans, "How does it feel to be a problem?" and wrote powerfully in his book, *Souls of Black Folk*, of the "two-ness—an American, a Negro," that he believed they inevitably experienced. He would become a rival of Booker T. Washington's and a symbol of the Black struggle for freedom and equality.

In much of the southern countryside, formerly enslaved people and their descendants too were charting a way forward and thereby contributing in distinctive ways to the late nineteenth-century making of race. They had long struggled to put their freedom on a safe and independent foundation, seeking land or tenancies that might allow them measures of self-governance. Many had joined with or supported the Union League and Republican Party, had voted and perhaps held office, and may well have aligned with political insurgencies of the 1880s and 1890s (discussed in Chapter 18). Yet, over time, growing numbers of them came to believe that their security and future prospects lay in separating themselves as much as possible from southern whites.

Self-reliance

Such an impulse toward separatism, which had deep roots in Black enslavement, did not signal an acceptance of the segregation and disfranchisement being imposed. Far from it. But they had come to see their survival and development as best served by turning further inward, by pursuing self-reliance even more fully than before. Some searched for new homes in Liberia, on the west coast of Africa. Many more were attracted to **Black Towns** which first appeared in the immediate post-emancipation period and then multiplied from the late 1870s on as the hopes of Reconstruction opportunities faded. Even greater numbers struggled to find small tracts of land that could attract family groups and offer relative safety and security, or clustered on tenant plantations and the edges of market towns spinning webs of community and peoplehood that were toughened by the fierce repression that whites could bring upon them.

In this they were joined by Black teachers, ministers, storekeepers, physicians, and tradesmen, an emerging middle class, who both serviced and aimed to "uplift" the poor working people around them, all pressed together by the tighter racial boundaries that were being drawn yet mindful of the independence and respectability they hoped to display. Gradually they, too, embraced their Blackness, not as a mark of exclusion or inferiority but as a symbol of dignity and pride, of achievement in the face of enormous obstacles and of solidarity in the face of domination. Race, in other words, was being constructed on both sides of a color line now drawn more sharply than ever.

20.5   A New Empire and a New Colonialism

Assess how American policymakers fashioned a new type of empire and a new colonialism for the United States.

Drawing the color line was part of a new vision of the United States and its place in the world. It was part of a new ordering to which social Darwinism lent legitimacy, and a more aggressive sense of "civilization" against "barbarism" that racial thinking and Christian fundamentalism helped to fuel. It was also part of a developing crisis that industrialization was seen to be provoking and a resolution meant to avoid radical change or revolution. By the last decade of the nineteenth century, American policymakers, chiefly associated with the Republican Party, began to clarify a new perspective on empire that had been developing since the end of the Civil War and a new idea of colonialism that was less about territorial occupation and more about economic and political power. In the process, the United States became involved in bloody warfare and had to contemplate what the results would mean for the nation being forged.

Perspectives of Race and Class

In 1902, Nelson A. Miles, the commanding general of the US Army, arrived in the Philippines to survey what remained of a nationalist insurgency there. He seemed well suited to the task. As a young man in the Federal Army, he had earned distinction on several battlefields and was put in charge of an army corps. Soon after major hostilities ceased, Miles was sent to Virginia and then to North Carolina, but before he could settle in to help supervise the reconstruction of the rebellious South, he was dispatched to supervise the reconstruction of the rebellious West.

For the next quarter century, Miles was out in the trans-Mississippi territories fighting Kiowas, Comanches, Sioux, Nez Perce, and Apaches, and subduing both Chief Joseph (in the Far West) and Geronimo (in the Southwest). He then led the brutal suppression of the Native American **Ghost Dance Movement**, which had been inspired by a prophet named Wovoka who envisioned a world soon to come without white people (see Map 20.5). Wovoka preached that followers who performed the Ghost Dance, a ceremony long part of the Native American culture, would see the restoration of their traditional ways of life. The US Cavalry came

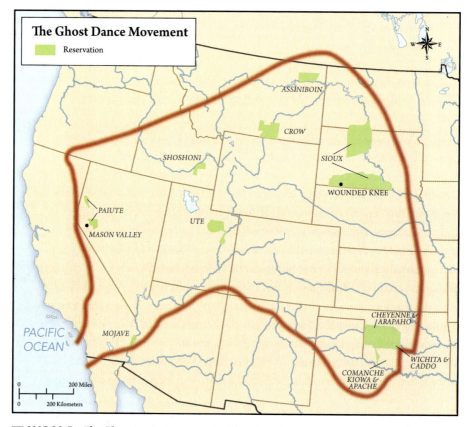

≡ **MAP 20.5   The Ghost Dance Movement**   The Ghost Dance movement represented a wave of spiritual revival across the West. It imagined an end to white colonialism, the reunion of the living and dead, a world of peace, and the restoration of a traditional way of life.

on the scene at the Pine Ridge Reservation in South Dakota and, under Miles's command, massacred nearly three hundred of the prophet's Lakota followers at **Wounded Knee Creek** in late 1890, bringing an effective end to Native American resistance to American internal colonialism. So highly regarded was Miles in official circles, that when the Pullman Strike (discussed in Chapter 18) erupted in 1894 and threatened to disrupt rail traffic across the United States, Miles was put in charge of the federal troops ordered to crush it.

To Nelson Miles there were important similarities among all these episodes. The Pullman Strike, he believed, was like the Confederate and Indigenous rebellions in being yet another battle in the "war of civilization" waged against enemies who would "blow down the beautiful arch of our sovereignty." In its defiance of court injunctions and "allegiance to their dictator Eugene V. Debs," the strike was, in Miles's reckoning, an insurrection against the federal government very much deserving of the military's strong fist. Veteran that Miles was of civil and Indigenous warfare, he requested permission to fire on the striking crowd.

There was great significance to all this. Ever since moving against the slaveholders' rebellion in the 1860s, the American nation-state had been extending its imperial arms across a number of spaces. Mainly through the military, it abolished slavery, subdued Confederate rebels, established national citizenship, enfranchised the freedmen, reorganized governments in the rebellious states, encouraged male-headed households, promoted Christianity, and upheld the rule of contract in the world of the marketplace. Looking west, the nation-state financed railroad development, created large federal territories, extended its sovereignty over Indigenous peoples while punishing those who resisted, and refused to allow territories to become states before they met an assortment of political and cultural criteria.

In the process, the nation-state enabled a new class of finance capitalists to turn their eyes toward Mexico, Central

≡ **Massacre Victim**   Spotted Elk, a Lakota Sioux chief, lies dead in the snow after the 1890 massacre at Wounded Knee, South Dakota.

America, and the Pacific, search for new markets in Asia, and expand the size of the navy. Small wonder that, in 1898, when popular insurrections against Spanish rule created political instabilities in Cuba and the Philippines, the US government took the opportunity to bring "civilization" to the "backward" peoples of color there. It seemed an extension of a civilizing mission more than three decades old, with military personnel serving as the links. Much of the officer corps in the Philippines had been in Native American service in the West, and most of the troops on the ground had been recruited from the western states and territories. The South and especially the West had been proving grounds for new American imperial ambitions overseas.

An Imperial Answer to Domestic Crisis

There were changes as well as continuities. No longer were American policymakers in pursuit of an agro-commercial empire as they had been before the Civil War. Led by William Seward and James G. Blaine, a new type of American empire came to be envisioned. It was an empire organized around access to international markets, reciprocity agreements with foreign states, and sea lanes to Asia. Unlike the objectives of European powers of the time, this American imperial vision would not so much involve the establishment and administration of formal colonies as it would the formation of American zones of influence, principally to the benefit of private investors but also backed by the military arm of the nation-state. And it took shape in an atmosphere of real crises.

What were those crises? Serious domestic unrest was one of them. But so, too, were anticolonial and nationalist rebellions that broke out during the 1890s and first decade of the twentieth century and roiled colonial powers. These rebellious movements either battled for political independence, as in Cuba and the Philippines, or pushed back against the policies and arrogance of European colonizers, as in China and Africa. Almost everywhere they showed the influence of Western political and intellectual ideas, especially in their familiarity with liberal institutions and ideas of modernity. But almost everywhere, too, they were tied to more Indigenous and prophetic traditions—as in the Ghost Dance movement—that sought to sever the cultural arms of the colonizers entirely, or to the aspirations of peasants and the formerly enslaved who imagined a different sort of justice than what liberalism might prescribe.

There was the impact, too, of economic crises. The deep depressions of the 1870s and 1890s, and the social turmoil they produced, left policymakers and industrialists searching for explanations and remedies. Many blamed excessive competition for sapping profits and driving manufacturers in destructive directions. Others blamed labor strikes for disrupting operations and preventing employers from taking charge of their shops. Still others worried about the outflows of gold and the dangers of a devalued currency should greenbacks or free silver triumph. But by the mid-1890s, there was a developing consensus that the problem was "overproduction"—industrialists, using new technologies, were simply producing far more than the American public could consume. The solution required new markets abroad, especially in Latin America and Asia, where the flood of goods could be sold.

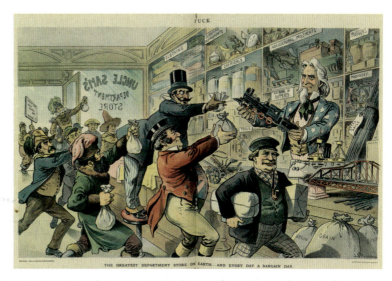

≡ **New Markets for American Products**   This 1899 print shows Uncle Sam standing behind the counter at "Uncle Sam's Department Store," where there is a "Great Sale Now Going On Inside." Customers from Germany, England, France, Russia, Italy, Mexico, Japan, China, Austria, and Turkey anxiously vie to purchase the many commodities proffered by Sam.

The Rise of Consumer Culture

Since the mid-nineteenth century, American retailers, following leads in Britain and France, had been experimenting with new ways of selling manufactured goods, especially to an expanding urban middle class. For one thing, they began establishing retail outlets known as department stores. With family names like Macy's (New York City), Wanamaker's (Philadelphia), and Marshall Field (Chicago), these large stores centralized the sale of many different types of commodities that purchasers had customarily found in specialty shops. They thereby created spatially interconnected marketplaces.

Later in the century, mail-order houses like Montgomery Ward and Sears Roebuck, both out of the Midwest, effectively moved the opportunities for consumption out of the larger cities and into smaller towns and rural districts, where they joined traveling salesmen in introducing goods that local merchants and dry goods stores were unable to stock. Most important, both the department stores and mail-order houses gave rise to advertising agencies that cultivated new awareness of and tastes for foods, clothing, furnishings, and new household technologies. Together they helped create a consumer culture that would take hold by the first decades of the twentieth century and eventually transform national and international economies.

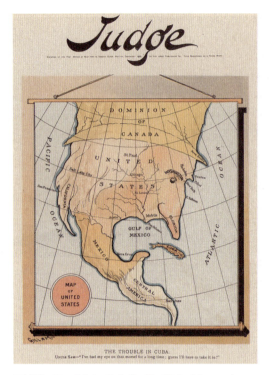

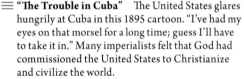

≡ **"The Trouble in Cuba"** The United States glares hungrily at Cuba in this 1895 cartoon. "I've had my eyes on that morsel for a long time; guess I'll have to take it in." Many imperialists felt that God had commissioned the United States to Christianize and civilize the world.

The Open Door

But these transformations remained on the distant horizon in the 1890s, and the problem of overproduction sat front and center. Some investors had been putting their money into railroads, mines, and plantations in Mexico, Central America, and the wider Caribbean basin. By the 1890s, Americans had over $50 million invested in Cuba alone. Others, especially in manufacturing, looked hungrily at Asia, China most prominently, to which textile exports were already growing. The combination of reciprocity treaties, which were especially valuable in Latin America, and access to Pacific markets which Seward had urged, seemed the best way to solve the overproduction crisis within a framework of capitalism. The choice, as naval authority Alfred T. Mahan put it, was between promoting consumption at home through "socialistic" measures or finding markets across the new "frontier" of oceans. In 1899, President McKinley's Secretary of State John Hay, responding to international competition for the China trade, called upon the European powers to respect Chinese territorial integrity and accept equitable commercial opportunity for all foreigners there. It was known as the **Open Door Policy.**

The Open Door had a special urgency because of new challenges the United States began to face in both the western Pacific and the Caribbean. The problem was that the Spanish Empire was tottering in the face of nationalist rebellions. Ever since the 1860s, the authority of Spanish colonizers had been contested in their remaining colonies of Cuba and the Philippines, with demands for political reform, greater autonomy, or outright independence. In Cuba the struggle was initially confined to the less developed eastern end of the island, where disgruntled creole land and slaveholders had joined hands with the enslaved and free people of color to overthrow the Spanish regime. By the late 1880s, they had won some concessions together with the abolition of slavery (1886) but fell short of their main goals.

Insurgencies

In the Philippines, years of peasant unrest were deepened by the discontent of educated Filipinos, often of Chinese descent, who hoped to cast off colonial rule and modernize their society. In the mid-1890s, both the Cuban and Filipino insurgencies reached a new intensity and threatened to overturn the established order. With the aid of exiled activists like Jose Marti, the Cubans reignited their independence movement in 1895 and, this time, mobilized an army 50,000 strong that marched into the western districts where the sugar plantations were located. They imagined a new republic based, at least in theory, on equality between the races. A year later, in 1896, the revolutionaries launched a campaign in the Philippines that would bring together insurgent leaders Andres Bonifacio and Emilio Aguinaldo in a tense alliance.

The United States was most interested in Cuba, owing to a long history of involvement as well as to significant economic investments, but there was no uniformity of opinion about what should be done. The cause of Cuba *libre* had substantial support among the public and in Congress while the Cleveland and McKinley administrations were more cautious, urging the Spanish to end repression against the insurgents and move in a reformist direction. Yet, as the insurgency move into the sugar zones on the shoulders of a multiracial army, fears among Cuban and American businessmen mounted. The US Minister to Spain was not alone in now seeing "a second Santo Domingo" (referring to the Haitian Revolution, a successful eighteenth-century slave rebellion against French colonial rule) in the Cuban insurgency and calling instead for annexation.

20.6   The Spanish-Cuban-Filipino-American War

Discuss the significance of the Spanish-Cuban-Filipino-American War of 1898.

Warfare had been a fact of social and political life in the United States across the nineteenth century. At first, it involved the British Empire making a last-ditch attempt to regain control of North American colonies in the War of 1812. Then there was the massive War of the Rebellion, the most destructive in American history and the second most destructive in the nineteenth-century world (following the Taiping Rebellion in China). All along, warfare erupted between American settlers and Indigenous peoples, substantially aided during the second half of the century by the United States Army: in effect a form of colonial warfare. But the crises in what was left of the Spanish Empire, and especially in Cuba and the Philippines, raised new questions about the scope of American empire, the methods that could be used to expand it, and the consequences for the American republic.

≡ **Fateful Explosion** The front page of William Randolph Hearst's *New York Journal*, February 17, 1898. Yellow (sensationalistic) journalism practiced by Hearst and other newspaper publishers rallied public opinion in support of war.

A Spanish-Cuban-Filipino-American War

President McKinley, who, along with Mark Hanna, represented the corporate wing of the Republican Party, was ready to step into the developing crises and play a crucial role. A strong advocate of reciprocity agreements, the gold standard, and greater presidential authority in foreign affairs, he was less interested in annexation than in expanding the reach of US economic power. Believing by early 1898 that Spain had lost control in Cuba, he sent the Navy's battleship *Maine* to Havana harbor to safeguard order and protect American property (see Map 20.6).

It proved to be a fateful decision. For when the *Maine* was then destroyed in what was likely an accidental explosion, McKinley was ready to implement his goals. Rather than recognize Cuban independence and support the insurgents, as they hoped he would, McKinley asked Congress to declare war against Spain while renouncing any intention "to exercise sovereignty, jurisdiction, or control" over the island. The provision was known as the **Teller Amendment** to the Congressional resolutions.

Then McKinley turned to the Pacific and asked Congress for another resolution, this time to annex the Hawaiian Islands. It was the last phase of a prolonged battle over Hawai'i's future that had set powerful American sugar planters against a skeptical public at home. Now, with war looming and his eyes on Asian markets, McKinley claimed that Hawai'i was necessary to the United States as a military base. "We need Hawai'i just as much and a good deal more than we did California," he declared. "It is manifest destiny." Congress buckled and gave him what he wanted.

What about the Philippines? Unlike Cuba, the United States had few direct economic involvements with the Philippines though, like Hawai'i, they were seen as a potential stepping-stone to the wider Asian trade. The United States had already made the Philippines an objective in the event of hostilities with Spain, and with Assistant Secretary of the Navy Theodore Roosevelt taking the initiative, the US fleet was put on alert. Roosevelt literally ached for war. "I should welcome any war," Roosevelt proclaimed, "for I think the country needs one." So, it seems, did he, having turned himself from a sickly child in an aristocratic family into a tough-talking, game-hunting, virile politician who relished the American West.

McKinley had his reservations about what Roosevelt had done but allowed the orders to stand, and on May 1, 1898, the American fleet under the command of Admiral George Dewey sailed into Manila Bay (see again Map 20.6). Once the shooting started, Manila fell in a matter of hours, Cuba in a matter of months. Not to be denied, Roosevelt resigned his post with the Navy, formed a cavalry regiment, headed off to Cuba, and, on Kettle Hill in July, led his troops into battle. They would claim the victory though at the cost of 200 killed and more than 1,000 wounded. It was, Roosevelt later crowed, "the great day of my life."

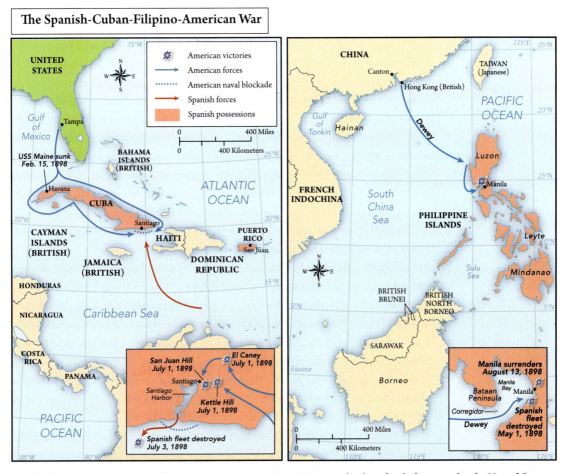

≡ **MAP 20.6**   **The Spanish-Cuban-Filipino-American War**   In a war that lasted only four months, the United States acquired an overseas empire.

Perils of Military Victory

Military victory over the Spanish was very rapid, but it brought perils as well as choices. Insurgents in Cuba and the Philippines hoped that American intervention might clear the road to independence for them. After all, the Teller Amendment rejected annexation and appeared to recognize Cuban sovereignty. In the Philippines, insurgent leader Emilio Aguinaldo, who had been forced into exile by the Spanish for his political activities, returned after Dewey's triumph and imagined some sort of alliance taking shape. But in neither case was the McKinley administration willing to support such independence movements, doubting as it did the capacity of Cubans and Filipinos to govern themselves. As one US Army officer put it, showing how racism knew no territorial boundaries, "Why those people are no more fit for self-government than gunpowder is for hell . . . no more capable of self-government than the savages of Africa."

What would all this mean? McKinley's Secretary of War Elihu Root, himself a prominent corporate lawyer, crafted a set of conditions that an "independent" Cuban government was required to accept. Cuba was prohibited from signing international treaties that might give other foreign nations influence; it had to sell or lease Cuban territory to the United States for coaling and naval stations (the origin of the US base at Guantanamo); and it had to permit the United States to intervene in Cuban affairs "for the preservation of Cuban independence [and] the maintenance of a government adequate for the protection of life, property, and individual liberty." Enacted in 1901 as the **Platt Amendment** to an Army appropriations bill, these conditions, despite strong Cuban objections, were forced into the island's new constitution and regarded as the terms for ending American occupation. It was a bitter pill for Cubans to swallow.

Circumstances were even more complex in the Philippines where, unlike Cuba, the issue of annexation was on the table. While Dewey's fleet destroyed the Spanish fleet, President McKinley sent 5,000 troops to occupy Manila and increased the deployment to 40,000 by the summer. It would be a tough and protracted fight. Emilio Aguinaldo's idea for an alliance with the United States was rebuffed, and so he declared Philippine independence and organized his own government in Malolos, not far from Manila. From early on US troops and political officials spoke of the conflict in racialized terms, referring to Filipinos as "n****rs" and "gugus."

But as much as anything else it was the battle against Native Americans in the trans-Mississippi West that framed the nature of the operation. Major General Adna Chaffee was said to have "brought the Indian Wars with him to the Philippines and wanted to treat the . . . Filipinos the way he had the Apaches in Arizona—by herding them onto reservations." When Aguinaldo's forces turned to guerilla warfare, the Indian analogy seemed to be confirmed and the brutality of the engagements escalated.

Comparing the Filipinos to Native Americans in the West reinforced the views of many policymakers that Filipinos were no more suited to self-rule than the Cubans were. Yet, instead of "herding" Filipinos onto "reservations," McKinley seemed more interested in turning all of the Philippines into a reservation, annexing the islands in order to strengthen access to the China market.

≡ **Counterinsurgency**   American soldiers show off a Gatling gun in Manila in 1899. Frustrated by guerrilla warfare, American soldiers often resorted to brutality, including mass executions, rape, and torture.

Failure of the Anti-Imperialists

Still, the annexation of a distant and multicultural territory was a bold move and provoked significant opposition, as was true in the case of Hawai'i. The opponents were known as **anti-imperialists**, and they staked out political ground high and low. At their most high-minded, they doubted that annexation had any constitutional basis and feared it would transform the United States into a "vulgar empire" founded on "physical force." No republic could survive under such circumstances. But anti-imperialism had a far darker side as well, and even high-mindedness could be tethered to it. Annexing the Philippines, many warned, would open the United States to inferior Asian races, challenge white supremacy, and degrade white American labor. "The racial differences between the Oriental and the Western races are never to be eradicated," it was said, "the two races could never amalgamate."

Theodore Roosevelt disparaged the anti-imperialists as "men of a bygone age," and, condescension aside, he made a deeper point. With few exceptions, those who opposed the annexation of the Philippines were either New England patricians, some with strong antislavery credentials, or Democrats from the South and Midwest, whose vision remained provincial and who embodied the remnants of an agro-commercial economy that was being upended. They cast critical eyes on the modernizing and centralizing trends of the age, and worried about the social and political consequences of the new imperial ambitions.

By contrast, the annexationists were heavily concentrated in the Republican Party and represented the nation's growing metropolitan centers, which rested on foundations of industry and finance, and the hinterlands linked to them. Many, like Roosevelt and Senator Henry Cabot Lodge of Massachusetts, were young, energetic, and identified as "progressive," comfortable with a new role in the world for the United States, and eager to export what they saw as a superior culture and set of institutions.

Does the Constitution Follow the Flag?

Roosevelt, who became president after McKinley was assassinated by a disgruntled office seeker in 1901, built on the principles of the Platt Amendment and offered a framework for the exercise of American power in the Western Hemisphere. Rejecting any hunger for annexation there, he told Congress in 1904 that all the United States desired was "to see the neighboring countries stable, orderly, and prosperous," and that "any country whose people conduct themselves well can count upon our hearty friendship." But there was an explicit threat attached. "Chronic wrongdoing, or an impotence which results in a general loosening of the ties of civilized society," Roosevelt declared in the language of hypermasculinity, "may require intervention by some civilized nation, and in the Western Hemisphere the adherence of the United States to the Monroe Doctrine may force the United States to the exercise of international police power." It became known as the **Roosevelt Corollary** to the Monroe Doctrine, and it would be invoked to justify many US Army occupations in the Caribbean basin over the next several decades (see Map 20.7).

In essence, the Roosevelt Corollary designated the nations of the Western Hemisphere protectorates of the United States. They were permitted self-rule and the rights governments accorded their citizens so long as they could protect themselves from "instabilities." If they couldn't, then the "big stick" of Roosevelt and his successors could be wielded. But what of the Philippines and of Puerto Rice and Guam, which together were ceded by Spain to the United States in 1898? What were they as political entities, and what sort of rights did their populations enjoy? After all, they could have been regarded as federal territories, capable of becoming states and subject to the Constitution.

But few saw this as a possibility on racial, cultural, or logistical grounds. Instead, owing to the **Foraker Act** passed by Congress in 1900 (which established a civilian government in Puerto Rico with an elected legislature and a governor appointed by the US president), and to a series of Supreme Court decisions between 1901 and 1910, collectively known as the **Insular Cases,** a distinctive political status was inscribed into law. The Philippines, Puerto Rico, and Guam would

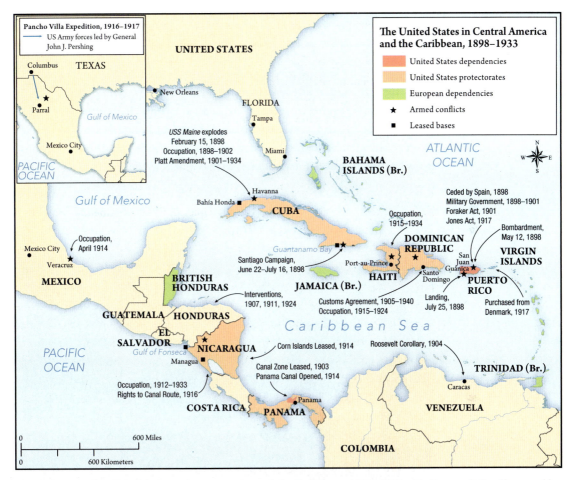

≡ **MAP 20.7   The United States in Latin America and the Caribbean, 1898–1933**   The Roosevelt Corollary would be invoked to justify many US occupations in the Caribbean basin throughout the first half of the twentieth century.

be "unincorporated," left to the authority of Congress, and their peoples would have certain "fundamental" rights but not full rights of citizenship under the Constitution. These territories, in the strange language of the Court, were not "foreign countries" in "an international sense," yet they were "foreign to the United States in a domestic sense," not "incorporated" but "merely appurtenant thereto as a possession." They were "insular" to themselves in governance, while remaining under the sovereign power of the United States. What did this mean? Asked whether, in this new imperial order, the "Constitution would follow the flag," Elihu Root, now Roosevelt's secretary of state, gave what may have been the most direct answer available. "The Constitution indeed follows the flag," he said, "but it doesn't quite catch up."

PERSPECTIVES

America's Civilizing Mission

Drawing the color line was part of a new vision of the United States and its place in the world. It was part of a new ordering to which social Darwinism lent legitimacy, and a more aggressive sense of "civilization" against "barbarism" that racial thinking and Christian fundamentalism helped to fuel. Political cartoons provide an especially valuable source for historians seeking to understand how Americans in the late nineteenth century understood the color line. New technologies made the mass production of cheap newspapers and magazines accessible to a wide readership.

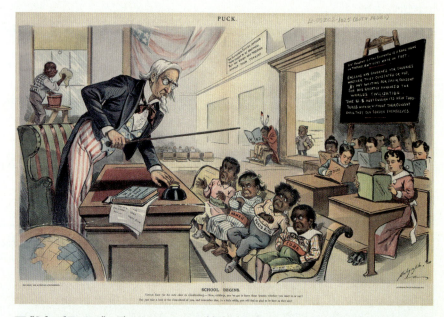

≡ **"School Begins"**   This cartoon was published in the magazine *Puck* in January 1899, as the Senate debated ratification of the peace treaty with Spain, signed the month before. The treaty made the Philippines a US colony and ceded Spanish control of Cuba, Puerto Rico, and Guam. Hawai'i had already been added as a territory in July 1898. A stern-looking Uncle Sam scolds the unruly, brown-skinned students who represent the new possessions. On the side of the classroom, a Black child washes a window; near the door a Native American student attempts to read an upside-down book, and a Chinese student peers in at the threshold.

≡ **"It's Up To Them"** This cartoon was published in *Puck*, in 1901, as brutal guerilla warfare raged across the Philippines. Uncle Sam offers to the Filipinos an armed soldier in one hand, and a schoolteacher in the other. "You can take your choice," he says, "I have plenty of both!"

CONSIDER THIS

The acquisition of overseas territory sparked intense debate. Did empire repudiate the nation's history and ideals, or was empire consistent with the American past, the fulfillment of the nation's role as a responsible world leader? Some, like Mark Twain, the writer who coined the term "Gilded Age," believed imperialism was all about greed: "There is more money in it . . . than there is in any other game that is played," he wrote. Others, such as John Burgess, a prominent political scientist and Theodore Roosevelt's former teacher, felt the United States had a responsibility to take purposeful action: "The civilized states," he maintained, "have a claim upon the uncivilized populations, as well as a duty towards them, and that claim is that they shall become civilized." What perspectives are offered by these cartoons? How do they contribute to the debate?

20.7 The Panama Canal and American Destiny

Describe how the construction of the Panama Canal brought together the new threads of race and empire.

The Spanish-Cuban-Filipino-American War established the United States as an international power and colonizer, as an empire that was not only continental but was now trans-Caribbean and trans-Pacific. The war also raised questions about the boundaries of the American republic and the ways in which a domestically brewing racism would shape the course of the nation's international history. But in many ways, the threads of empire, race, belonging, and progressive modernity, and the fruits of imperial reorganization, came together on a small strip of land in Central America where the United States would build an isthmian canal.

The Panama Canal Zone

Among the territories that fell under the logic of the Supreme Court's rulings in the Insular Cases was the newly acquired Canal Zone running through the republic of Panama. It was the end of a lengthy and bumpy road. American interest in an isthmian crossing dated to at least the California gold rush and intensified as the Pacific trade grew: US shipping would no longer be forced to round the southern tip of South America (Tierra del Fuego) to reach the Pacific if a Central American crossing became available. The sticking point was initially whether Nicaragua or Panama would be a better site. But the die was finally cast when French competitors themselves set out to build a canal across the Isthmus of Panama in 1880.

The undertaking was immense and, as it turned out, after nearly twenty years the French gave up. As they did, Theodore Roosevelt, now president, quickly moved in. Ironically, he first helped Panamanian insurgents win political independence from Colombia, and then, as a reward, gained complete and perpetual control over a strip of land roughly 10 miles wide and 30 miles long in return for $10 million and an annual payment of $250,000.

Completed over a ten-year period, the canal was a colossal feat of engineering and a transformational event in the development of the global economy. This was how many observers viewed it at the time, and how it has mostly been remembered since. But it was also the near-definition of the new American empire. The Zone was a territorial possession of the United States, though like Puerto Rico and the Philippines, "insular" in terms of governance. It was run by a stern American-appointed governor who had no interest in democratic forms and little tolerance for labor unrest. The workforce made up a hierarchy of skill and privilege associated with race and national origins, and segregation and discrimination structured every corner of Zone life.

The managerial and highly skilled positions were filled by white Americans and Europeans. Lesser and unskilled jobs were filled by migrants from the Mediterranean and, especially, by Afro-Caribbeans, most from the sugar plantation island of Barbados. The justice system was tied to the executive branch of the Zone's government. There were no jury trials. And although the Zone was formally set off from the Republic of Panama, tensions spilled over the border between them, and the United States exercised so much influence over politics, finance, and landholding that Panamanian sovereignty was cast into jeopardy.

A Triumph of Progressive Imperialism?

Yet for many Americans of a progressive disposition, or associated with the Progressive movement, the Canal Zone became a source of great interest and admiration. Here, it seemed, was an example of the partnerships they were trying to promote in the United States itself: among an activist state, scientific and managerial expertise, and technological prowess. Little troubled by the political and labor hierarchies that had been constructed, they instead relished the potential wonders of state control. For them, it was possible to imagine an American empire exemplified by the Canal Zone, not as a threat to the republic or a blot on the Constitution, but as an extension of the social experimentation they had been eager to carry out domestically.

Many clearly thrilled at the Canal's completion, ahead of schedule, in mid-August 1914, and they may have followed the great Panama-Pacific International Exposition in San Francisco the next year, meant to celebrate the Canal's opening. But they undoubtedly noticed, too, that the guns of world war had already begun firing, and the rumblings of revolution were already being heard.

Conclusion: The Causes and Consequences of Imperialism

During the late nineteenth and early twentieth centuries, the United States and its economic elites stretched their imperial arms beyond American borders. First in Mexico and Central America, and soon in the Asian Pacific, manufacturers and

≡ **Empire Builder**   In this 1903 cartoon, President Theodore Roosevelt presents Colombia with the fait accompli of his Panama Canal Zone treaty with the new republic of Panama.

financiers looked for new commercial opportunities and sources of investment. Believing that overseas markets offered a resolution to the economic crises of the time and deploying white supremacist policies at home and abroad, the United States then waged warfare against the weakened empire of Spain and nationalist movements in Cuba and the Philippines. In this they were fortified by new constructions of race and race relations, and by the advent of racial segregation in the southern states that federal judges found acceptable despite the Thirteen, Fourteenth, and Fifteenth Amendments to the Constitution, and that meshed comfortably with Progressive views.

But military victories everywhere posed new questions about the nature of the republic Americans were attempting to forge while the annexations of the Philippines and Hawai'i made the United States a colonizer of societies thousands of miles away. For the first time, the United States incorporated territories it had no intention of turning into states, and admitted that the Constitution no longer really followed the flag. The consequences would not be felt only at the time; they would bedevil the country across the twentieth century and continue to haunt us to this very day.

WHAT IF the United States Forced Spain to Grant Independence to Cuba and the Philippines?

It's probably fair to say that, except for a different outcome to the War of the Rebellion, the rush to American empire during the last decades of the nineteenth century would have been very difficult to stop or slow. First unleashed across the trans-Mississippi West, the imperial impulses of the United States were increasingly formidable, determined, and well-financed. The "anti-imperialists" were fighting an uphill battle even if they managed to erect a few hurdles in empire's path, and the defeat of the Democrats in the national election of 1896 pretty much sealed their fate.

Still, there were opportunities to tame empire's excesses or possibly even to put imperial power in the service of admirable ends. What were these? Cuba and the Philippines were not only riven by nationalist insurgencies, effectively independence movements, in the late nineteenth century, but they had leaders who imagined Western-style republics and democracies, sometimes taking as models the United States' own experience of making an (anti-colonial) revolution and creating an independent country. Some, like Emilio Aguinaldo, hoped that American officials would look favorably on their movements, agree to an alliance, and lend them support.

What if the United States recognized the legitimacy of the nationalist movements and used its political and military power, not to conquer and occupy these territories, but with the Monroe Doctrine as a basis, to force the Spanish and other potentially threatening colonial powers, to grant insurgent nationalists their independence and accept their sovereignty? Direct and indirect American power surely would have been more limited and very different sorts of regimes would have emerged in both the Philippines and Cuba. But would the United States have gained important political advantages in its international standing, while relieving itself of the heavy hand necessary to maintain order in overseas territories? Would American democracy have been strengthened at home by allowing a more popular course to take shape abroad? And would the economic rewards of access to markets be maintained?

DOCUMENT 20.1: "Aguinaldo's Case Against the United States," 1899

An essay published in the North American Review *in the name of Filipino rebel leader Emilio Aguinaldo, reprimanding the United States for its behavior in the Philippines.*

> We Filipinos have all along believed that if the American nation at large knew exactly, as we do, what is daily happening in the Philippine Islands, they would rise en masse, and demand that this barbaric war should stop.

You have been deceived all along the line. You have been greatly deceived in the personality of my countrymen. You went to the Philippines under the impression that their inhabitants were ignorant savages, whom Spain had kept in subjection at the bayonet's point. The Filipinos have been described in serious American journals as akin to the hordes of the Khalifa [Islamic caliphate]; and the idea has prevailed that it required only some unknown American Kitchener to march triumphantly from north to south to make the military occupation complete. [A year earlier, in September 1898, General Horatio Kitchener had solidified British control of the Sudan by defeating tribesmen led by caliph Abdullah al-Taashin.] We have been represented by your popular press as if we were Africans or Mohawk Indians. We smile, and deplore the want of ethnological knowledge on the part of our literary friends. We are none of these. We are simply Filipinos.

Now, the moral of all this obviously is: Give us the chance; treat us exactly as you demanded to be treated at the hands of England, when you rebelled against her autocratic methods. . . Now, here is an unique spectacle: the Filipinos fighting for liberty, the American people fighting them to give them liberty. . . .

"Lay down your arms," you say. Did you lay down your arms when you, too, were rebels, and the English under good King George demanded your submission? How in the name of all that is serious do you demand that we shall do what you, being rebels, refused to do? . . .

Source: North American Review, September 1899.

DOCUMENT 20.2: President William McKinley on the Philippines, 1899

At a meeting with a delegation of American Methodist church leaders in 1899, President McKinley explains why he supports annexing the Philippines.

Hold a moment longer! Not quite yet, gentlemen! Before you go I would like to say just a word about the Philippine business. I have been criticized a good deal about the Philippines, but don't deserve it. The truth is I didn't want the Philippines, and when they came to us, as a gift from the gods, I did not know what to do with them. When the Spanish War broke out [Admiral George] Dewey was at Hongkong, and I ordered him to go to Manila and to capture or destroy the Spanish fleet, and he had to; because, if defeated, he had no place to refit on that side of the globe, and if the Dons [Spanish] were victorious they would likely cross the Pacific and ravage our Oregon and California coasts. And so he had to destroy the Spanish fleet, and did it! But that was as far as I thought then.

When I next realized that the Philippines had dropped into our laps I confess I did not know what to do with them. I sought counsel from all sides—Democrats as well as Republicans—but got little help. I thought first we would take only Manila; then Luzon; then other islands perhaps also. I walked the floor of the White House night after night until midnight; and I am not ashamed to tell you, gentlemen, that I went down on my knees and prayed Almighty God for light and guidance more than one night. And one night late it came to me this way—I don't know how it was, but it came: (1) That we could not give them back to Spain—that would be cowardly and dishonorable; (2) that we could not turn them over to France and Germany—our commercial rivals in the Orient—that would be bad business and discreditable; (3) that we could not leave them to themselves—they were unfit for self-government—and they would soon have anarchy and misrule over there worse than Spain's was; and (4) that there was nothing left for us to do but to take them all, and to educate the Filipinos, and uplift and civilize and Christianize them, and by God's grace do the very best we could by them, as our fellow-men for whom Christ also died. And then I went to bed, and went to sleep, and slept soundly, and the next morning I sent for the chief engineer of the War Department (our map-maker), and I told him to put the Philippines on the map of the United States (pointing to a large map on the wall of his office), and there they are, and there they will stay while I am President!

Source: The Christian Advocate, January 22, 1903.

Thinking About Contingency

1. Could the anti-imperialists have broadened their political coalition to prevail in Congress?
2. How would an alternative, anti-imperialist outcome in the Philippines and Cuba have shaped domestic politics?
3. Would this outcome have been possible, given the climate of race and racism already evident in the United States?

REVIEW QUESTIONS

1. How can we account for the interest of American investors in Mexico, and how did their economic and political involvement shape both countries during the Gilded Age?

2. Why were the Hawaiian Islands and the Caribbean Basin of such interest to American investors and policymakers? And how did American political leaders view the Pacific world?

3. In what ways were race relations and ideas of race transformed in the South and in the United States more generally during the late nineteenth and early twentieth centuries?

4. How did newly developing ideas of empire influence the eruption of the Spanish-Cuban-Filipino-American War in 1898, and what sort of challenges did colonialism present to the nation?

5. How did the construction of the Panama Canal follow from the new ideas of empire and race that the United States was constructing?

KEY TERMS

anti-imperialists (p. 855)

Atlanta Compromise (p. 838)

Bayonet Constitution (p. 833)

Black Towns (p. 845)

Foraker Act (p. 856)

Ghost Dance Movement (p. 846)

Hawaiian League (p. 833)

Insular Cases (p. 856)

Jim Crow (p. 838)

lynching (p. 839)

National Association for the Advancement of Colored People (NAACP) (p. 844)

Niagara Movement (p. 844)

Open Door Policy (p. 850)

Platt Amendment (p. 854)

Plessy v. Ferguson (p. 854)

Roosevelt Corollary (p. 856)

Teller Amendment (p. 852)

Tuskegee Normal and Industrial Institute (p. 838)

Wounded Knee Creek (p. 847)

RECOMMENDED READINGS

W. Fitzhugh Brundage, *Lynching in the New South* (University of North Carolina Press, 1993).

Greg Grandin, *Empire's Workshop: Latin America, the United States, and the Rise of the New Imperialism* (Henry Holt, 2007).

Julie Greene, *The Canal Builders: Making America's Empire at the Panama Canal* (Penguin, 2009).

John Mason Hart, *Empire and Revolution: Americans in Mexico Since the Civil War* (University of California Press, 2002).

Paul Kramer, *The Blood of Government: Race, Empire, the United States, and the Philippines* (2006).

Walter LaFeber, *The New Empire: An Interpretation of American Expansion* (Cornell University Press, 1963).

David Levering Lewis, *W.E.B. DuBois: Biography of a Race, 1868–1919* (Henry Holt, 1994).

Leon Litwack, *Trouble in Mind: Black Southerners in the Age of Jim Crow* (Alfred A. Knopf, 1998).

Peggy Pascoe, *What Comes Naturally: Miscegenation Laws and the Making of Race in America* (Oxford University Press, 2009).

C. Vann Woodward, *The Strange Career of Jim Crow* (Oxford University Press, 1955).

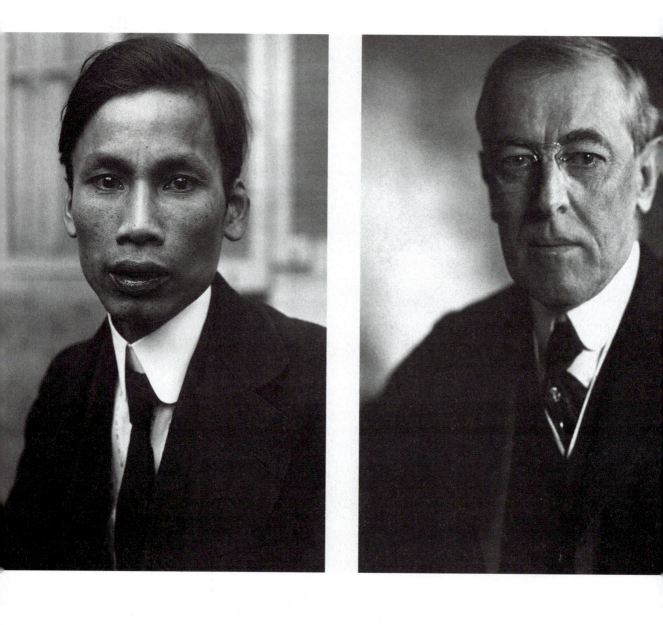

21

War, Revolution, and Reaction
1910–1925

Chapter Outline

≡ **Rival Visions of the Postwar World**   *Left:* Vietnamese leader Ho Chi Minh. As a young man, Minh and other Vietnamese activists unsuccessfully petitioned the delegates to the Versailles peace talks to recognize Vietnamese self-determination and end French colonialism. Minh later led successful military efforts to drive France and then the United States out of Vietnam. *Right:* US President Woodrow Wilson. Wilson participated personally in the Versailles peace talks, championing political self-determination and the creation of an international diplomatic compact, the League of Nations. Wilson did not support the self-determination of colonized peoples, however, and the US Senate rejected the treaty he negotiated.

21.6 Repression and Intolerance

||| Discuss the repressive methods used by the federal government against those who opposed the war effort and the racial and ethnic conflict unleashed as a consequence of this repression.

21.7 Cultural Reaction

||| Assess the cultural changes the war ushered in, including the backlash against the cultural currents of modernity.

21.8 The Second Ku Klux Klan

||| Discuss the rise and impact of the Second Ku Klux Klan.

In early 1919, only a short time after an armistice ending World War I was declared, a Peace Conference assembled near Paris at Versailles, France, the one-time palace of French monarchs. Among those in attendance was a young man, twenty-eight years of age, known at the time as Nguyen Ai Quoc. Educated and from a middle-class family,

Timeline

1910	1911	1912	1913	1914	1915	1916	1917	1918

c.1910 > Great Migration begins

1910–1920 > Mexican Revolution

1914 > Assassination of Archduke Ferdinand; World War I begins

1915 > Founding of the Second Ku Klux Klan near Atlanta, Georgia

1916 > Marcus Garvey establishes the UNIA in the United States

1917 > Congress declares war on Germany and the Central Powers; Bolsheviks seize power in Russian Revolution; Congress passes the Alien Act

1918 > Congress passes Sedition Act; Armistice ends World War I

Nguyen had left his home in the French colony of Indochina (known to the colonized population as the Kingdom of Annam or Vietnam) in 1911, worked as a cook, baker, and dishwasher on a steamship, spent time in England, France, and the United States, and then returned to France before the peace conference began. There he made connections with other Vietnamese expatriates who were interested in gaining independence from French rule.

At the time, Nguyen and many others from colonized lands had learned that President Woodrow Wilson's vision for the postwar world might be of great importance to them. Delivered to the American Congress in January 1918, a year before the Paris Peace Conference, Wilson's Fourteen Points provided a blueprint for a new democratic world order. As part of his Fourteen Points for a just peace, Wilson called for the "adjustment of all colonial claims" based in good measure on the "interests of the populations concerned"—self-determination, as it was interpreted. Wilson traveled

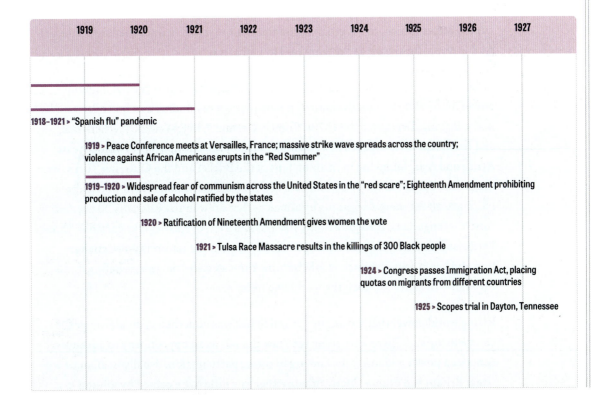

| 1919 | 1920 | 1921 | 1922 | 1923 | 1924 | 1925 | 1926 | 1927 |

1918–1921 ▸ "Spanish flu" pandemic

1919 ▸ Peace Conference meets at Versailles, France; massive strike wave spreads across the country; violence against African Americans erupts in the "Red Summer"

1919–1920 ▸ Widespread fear of communism across the United States in the "red scare"; Eighteenth Amendment prohibiting production and sale of alcohol ratified by the states

1920 ▸ Ratification of Nineteenth Amendment gives women the vote

1921 ▸ Tulsa Race Massacre results in the killings of 300 Black people

1924 ▸ Congress passes Immigration Act, placing quotas on migrants from different countries

1925 ▸ Scopes trial in Dayton, Tennessee

to the Peace Conference and Nguyen hoped for a meeting to secure his support. That would not happen. Instead, Nguyen and a group calling itself "Annam Patriots" sent a letter to Wilson's Secretary of State Robert Lansing with a petition, "Demands of the Annamese People," for reform of the French colonial system based on the principles of freedom that Wilson had enunciated.

Lansing sent a note back to Nguyen acknowledging receipt of the letter and petition and promising to share it with Wilson. But there was no further communication. Before leaving Paris, however, Nguyen met with French socialists and then traveled to the Soviet Union before returning to Indochina, where he then helped found the Vietnamese Communist Party. But Nguyen was as much a nationalist as a communist, and as we will see in Chapter 24, when World War II ended in 1945, he hoped—still embracing American political principles as he understood them—that the United States might aid in the ongoing anticolonial struggle there. Writing a "declaration of independence," Nguyen began it with the words "All men are created equal; they are endowed by their Creator with certain unalienable Rights; among these are Life, Liberty, and the Pursuit of Happiness." Nguyen would lead the resistance to the French and, after they were defeated, would continue the fight, this time against the United States, which, to his great disappointment, stepped in once the French departed. He would be known to the world as Ho Chi Minh.

What had happened? When the United States emerged as a new type of imperial power in the early twentieth century, it joined a host of empires that had been rapidly in the making. Ever since the 1870s, France, Germany, Belgium, the Netherlands, and Japan had been engaged in a scramble for colonies and spheres of influence in Africa and Asia, following in the footsteps of the British and the Ottoman Turks. By the second decade of the twentieth century, the tensions among them were palpable, made all the more dangerous by alliances that drew in the Russians, Slavs, and Austro-Hungarians. It required only the assassination of Austro-Hungarian Archduke Ferdinand and his wife in the summer of 1914 to turn the tensions into conflagration and begin a war—which would become three decades of warfare before it was through—the likes of which the world had never seen.

Rising world power that it was, the United States was nonetheless divided over the course to pursue. There were some who saw the war as an opportunity to advance American power and interests, and urged direct participation, usually in alliance with Great Britain and France. Many others either saw little to be gained by joining in a

European war or forcefully rejected alliances with European imperialists. A small number of pacifists simply rejected warfare. Back in the 1790s, George Washington, in his farewell address as president, warned of "entangling" alliances, and the debates surrounding the Spanish-Cuban-Filipino-American War left bitter tastes in the mouths of many anti-imperialists in the United States. As of 1913, moreover, the presidency was in the hands of Woodrow Wilson, a Democrat whose party had misgivings about adventures overseas. What would the country do and what sort of price would it have to pay? And how would it respond to the possibilities that Ho Chi Minh recognized?

21.1   What Is a "Peace Without Victory"?

||| Evaluate President Wilson's vision for a postwar world.

The United States had to face the consequences of its new international role much sooner than anyone thought likely. The face of Europe was transformed during the nineteenth century, not only owing to episodes of warfare, especially involving France and Germany, but also to the emancipation of peasantries, large-scale population migrations, revolutionary turmoil—some of it nationalist, some of it socialist—between 1830 and 1871, the establishment of new colonies in Africa and Asia, and the unifications of Italy (1861) and Germany (1871). But when the process of change led to a European-based though effectively worldwide conflagration, could the United States follow George Washington's advice and remain neutral? And, if not, how should the country respond and with whom should it ally?

A Wilsonian Vision

Woodrow Wilson stepped into the office of the presidency in March 1913 as a moderate progressive. He was interested in bringing some order and regulation to the corporate economy, and in favoring constituencies of farmers and workers who had long voted Democratic. But unlike the party's agrarian wing that had been led by William Jennings Bryan, Wilson accepted corporate institutions and was mainly concerned with taming their excesses. To that end, as we saw in Chapter 19, he signed the Clayton Anti-Trust Act and the Federal Trade Commission Act (both in 1914), and supported the creation of the Federal Reserve System (1913), a central bank designed to manage the circulation of currency. Although he had counterposed his "New Freedom" to Theodore Roosevelt's "New Nationalism" in the election campaign of 1912, Wilson's domestic policies did not differ very much from Roosevelt's, and over time he came to embrace much of the state regulatory activity that Roosevelt had advocated.

Wilson's move toward statism was chiefly the result of growing American involvement in what would be called the First World War. Only a year and a half into his presidential term, Wilson came face to face with an international crisis of epic proportions. After nearly a century of relative peace, Europe exploded into warfare. The main antagonists were all major imperial powers that had long been stepping on each other's toes: the **Triple Entente** of Britain, France, and Russia on the one side, eventually adding Italy, Romania, and Japan as the Allied Powers, and the **Central Powers** of Germany and Austria-Hungary on the other. But soon, the remainder of Europe from the Mediterranean and the Balkans to the Low Countries was drawn in, together with the Ottoman Empire and Japan. The fighting would eventually spread into Africa and the Middle East, befitting the imperial reach of the adversaries. It was worldwide in its repercussions and turned into a bloodbath on the ground (see Map 21.1).

Wilson was not, at first, inclined to get the United States involved. He wanted the country to embrace neutrality and ran for reelection in 1916 on a platform of remaining on the sidelines. "He Kept Us Out of War" was the campaign slogan of the Democrats, suggesting that the Republicans wished to do otherwise. It seemed to reflect the public's desires. Wilson won reelection, the first Democrat to do so since Andrew Jackson in 1832. But Wilson also saw where things were heading. The Allied Powers and the Central Powers were stalemated along the "Western Front" in Europe—a line stretching south from Belgium across northeastern France—engaged in brutal trench warfare, and American financiers were already lending Britain and France money to keep them in the fight (there was little interest in aiding the Germans, who were generally seen as the aggressors).

Wilson began to envision an outcome to the war brought about, not through American fighting power, but through a new moral and political vision. He called it, in an address to Congress in January 1917, "**peace without victory**." By this, he meant an end to the hostilities that had been raging without the imposition of a harsh and costly peace—no winners or losers. He also wished to see the creation of a new global compact based on mutual disarmament, self-determination, the consent of the governed, the equality of nations, freedom of the seas, and international cooperation to resolve conflicts. In a sense, Wilson imagined that the United States could step in among the exhausted adversaries, mediate an armistice and settlement, and preside over a world of open economic doors, shrinking imperial rivalries, and American moral leadership. It was a remarkable assertion of presidential authority.

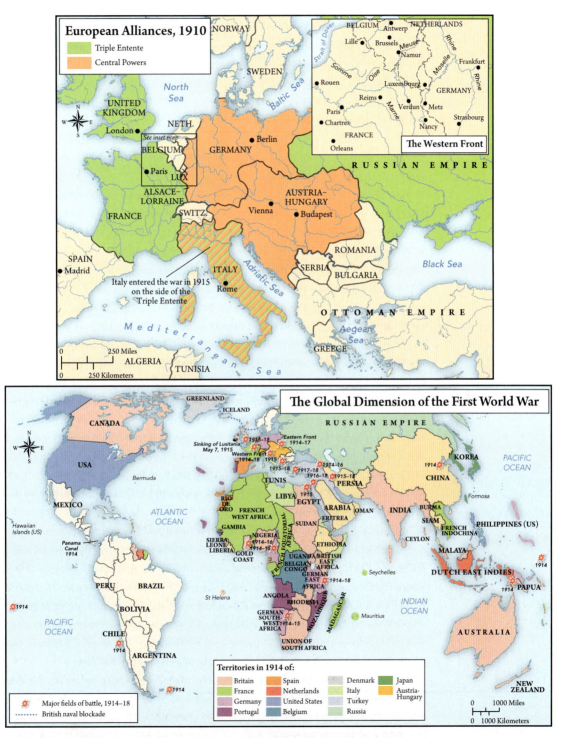

European Alliances, 1910

- Triple Entente
- Central Powers

Italy entered the war in 1915 on the side of the Triple Entente

The Western Front

The Global Dimension of the First World War

Territories in 1914 of:

Britain	Spain	Denmark	Japan
France	Netherlands	Italy	Austria-Hungary
Germany	United States	Turkey	
Portugal	Belgium	Russia	

- ✳ Major fields of battle, 1914–18
- ····· British naval blockade

≡ **MAP 21.1   European Alliances in 1910 and the Global Dimension of World War I**   A system of alliances among European powers created two rigid blocs poised against each other and on hair-trigger alert. When war broke out in July 1914, fighting spilled over into the colonies, where each side sought to weaken the other.

The Mexican Revolution

Europe was not the only foreign policy crisis that the Wilson administration faced. Another had been brewing directly to the south, in the bordering country of Mexico, where a revolution had erupted in 1910. It then quickly moved in very radical directions and tested the limits of Wilson's idealism. Like many revolutions, Mexico's began as something less: as a rebellion against the authoritarian regime of Porfirio Diaz, the military man who had taken power in 1876 and embarked on a heavy-handed program of nation-building (discussed in Chapter 20).

How did the revolution happen? In an effort to modernize the Mexican economy, Diaz had centralized political power, offered incentives to foreign investors (mainly Americans) to exploit resources and construct a rail system, and permitted large landowners to encroach upon the lands of peasant villages, turning communal into private property. For three decades, by manipulating collections of cronies and political clients, Diaz managed to maintain the balances of governance. Then, amid an international economic panic in 1907, the balances began to tilt against him. Peasant unrest spread; railroad workers and miners went on strike; and export booms in oil, copper, and henequen (a succulent plant cultivated for its hard fiber leaves and often used for rope), which had underwritten Diaz's projects, collapsed.

Disgruntled members of the elite and their middle-class allies were the first to rebel. They found a leader in Francisco Madero, from a wealthy family in the Mexican northeast, who was determined to deny Diaz yet another term as president and reform the political system. Although harassed by Diaz, he succeeded more speedily than anyone could have imagined. In the spring of 1911, after mobilizing supporters across northern Mexico, Madero marched into Mexico City while Diaz shipped out from Veracruz. The *Porfiriato*, in power for over three decades, had come to an end.

But Madero had also raised expectations among peasants and workers he was not prepared to satisfy. He was ready for a political revolution but not a social revolution. And before long he had several rebellions on his own hands. They were led, variously, by one of Madero's generals, Victoriano Huerta, who wanted to put the brakes on political change; by Emiliano Zapata in the southern state of Morelos, who led the ranks of dispossessed peasants; by Venustiano Carranza, the governor of Coahuila and a moderate reformer; and by Francisco "Pancho" Villa from the northern state of Chihuahua, who was ready to join hands with Zapata.

As might be expected, the result was bloodshed and more upheaval. Huerta struck first, leading to the overthrow of Madero in 1913 (in the process Huerta had Madero assassinated). Zapata, Carranza, and Villa then began to mobilize against Huerta, carrying the revolution forward and hoping to get some assistance from the United States, mainly in the form of weapons (see Map 21.2).

The Revolution and the United States

Why did the revolutionaries think they could receive assistance from the United States? Wilson had been sitting on the fence in relation to Mexico—"watchful waiting," he called it—but he also refused to recognize the Huerta regime and made no secret of his distaste for Huerta's method of seizing power. What's more, there were significant American interests—financial and other economic investments—in Mexico, and, since he had a group of Texans advising him, Wilson was attuned to their concerns. Thus, when a group of American sailors who had made a refueling stop in the gulf port of Tampico was briefly detained by an official loyal to Huerta, Wilson made his move. Insisting that the "dignity" of the United States

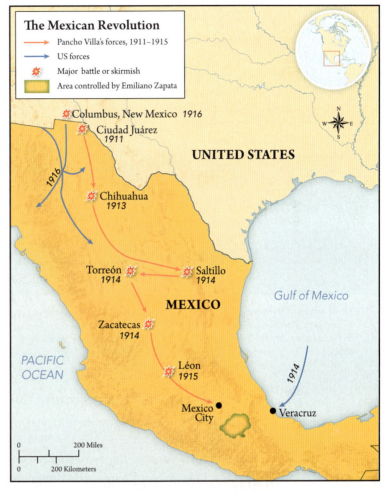

≡ **MAP 21.2   The Mexican Revolution**   By concentrating agricultural lands in the hands of a few, including US mining interests, Díaz's policies impoverished villagers. By 1900, just 1 percent of the population held 85 percent of the land. These tensions exploded into revolution in 1910.

and the rights of its citizens had been "flouted," in the spring of 1914 Wilson ordered the bombardment and marine occupation of nearby Veracruz, Mexico's most important port, with plans for extending the occupation into Tampico and Mexico City. The war in Europe had not begun, and the United States seemed ready to launch an invasion of Mexico.

It was all too familiar. Although Wilson had portrayed the United States as "champions" of "constitutional government in America," he also took pages from the proprietary playbook of Theodore Roosevelt (discussed in Chapter 20).

≡ **US Marines in Veracruz**   US Marines march through the Mexican port city of Veracruz. President Wilson ordered American soldiers to attack and occupy Veracruz after a minor incident between American sailors and a Mexican official.

Comparing the "situation in Mexico" to that of "France at the time of the Revolution," Wilson argued that Mexico now needed "the strong guiding hand of a great nation." Only in this way would the world see "that the Monroe Doctrine [which proclaimed the Western Hemisphere an American sphere of influence] means unselfish friendship for our neighbors." The blow to Huerta was substantial, and when US forces departed Veracruz in November 1914 they left behind a large cache of arms that Huerta's enemies quickly grabbed up.

The Zimmermann Telegram and the Declaration of War

It wasn't long before the American troops were back, this time in 1916 in response to a cross-border raid on the New Mexican town of Columbus led by Pancho Villa. But now the consequences would be greater and connect with the hostilities roiling Europe. The United States was still a neutral party and Germany, bogged down at the front and having its resources drained, decided on a bold plan. On the one hand, the Germans began unrestricted submarine warfare, a new and deadly technology, against the Triple Entente and its supporters (including American shipping). In the most horrific incident a German U-Boat (what German submarines were called) torpedoed and sank a large British passenger ship, the **Lusitania**. More than 1,100 lives were lost, 128 of whom were Americans.

On the other hand, the Germans hoped to tie the United States up in Mexico to blunt the Americans' likely response to the submarine warfare. To that end, German foreign secretary Arthur Zimmermann, with Pancho Villa's raid apparently in mind, raised the possibility of Mexico "reconquering its former territories in Texas, New Mexico, and Arizona" in return for allying with Germany in a war against the United States. The British intercepted the **Zimmermann telegram** and in March 1917 shared this proposal with Wilson. Although the Mexicans, now under Carranza, had rejected the idea, on April 6 Wilson finally asked Congress for a declaration of war against Germany. Now it was an American war, too.

In explaining American war aims both to the American public and to the world, Wilson set out his "**Fourteen Points**," which in many ways echoed his ideas of "peace without victory." They included open peace accords, freedom of navigation on the high seas, the lowering of trade barriers, the securing of national sovereignties, the principle of self-determination in colonial possessions, and "a general association of nations" to defend political independence and territorial integrity. It was a dramatic example of idealism. The Fourteen Points immediately catapulted Wilson into international prominence, perhaps as the leading voice for the shaping of a postwar world.

The Reach of Wilsonian Idealism

In ways Wilson scarcely anticipated, his words and principles riveted the attention of those struggling against European colonialism and pursuing various forms of nationalism. "Ideas—universal ideas—have a knack of rubbing off all geographical distinctions," an Indian nationalist observed in 1918. "It is impossible that the noble truths uttered by President Wilson could be limited in their application. Henceforth, his words are going to be the cry of all small and subject and oppressed nationalities in the world."

Is this what Wilson and the United States intended? He seemed able to "talk the talk," but was he prepared to "walk the walk?" Although Wilson's vision of a postwar world organized around the principle of **self-determination** lifted the hopes of anticolonial movements around the globe, his invasions of revolutionary Mexico suggested what the limits of such a principle might be. Wilson never really considered the potential reach of self-determination, and although he did not specifically exclude colonized peoples of color from its embrace, he thought of self-determination mainly in a European context. As Wilson's Secretary of State Robert Lansing later said, self-determination was not meant to apply to "races, peoples, or communities whose state of barbarism or ignorance deprives them of the capacity to choose intelligently their political affiliations."

The Sinking of the *Lusitania* A German submarine sunk the British passenger ship *Lusitania* in May 1915, killing over 1,000 passengers, some of whom were Americans. The fate of the *Lusitania* provoked outrage in Britain and America as many condemned the German use of submarine warfare.

This is hardly surprising. Wilson was a white southerner, thought Black and non-white people inferior or backward, and viewed Reconstruction as a nightmare. He hailed the film *Birth of a Nation* (1915), one of the first feature films ever made, which presented the Ku Klux Klan as the saviors of the South and nation. Wilson brought racial segregation and exclusion into the federal bureaucracy, and, after the treaty annexing the Philippines was signed in 1898, jumped on the imperial bandwagon. Even in retrospect, he never spoke favorably of the aspirations of Cubans and Filipinos for self-determination in their struggles against Spanish colonizers. At most, self-determination for colonial dependencies could be seen as a gradual process, extended "if they be fit to receive it." It would not, in Wilson's hands, be the entering wedge of a critique of Euro-American imperialism.

21.2   Wartime Mobilizations

Identify the economic and institutional ways in which the United States mobilized to participate in the war.

It was one thing to make the decision to declare war on the Central Powers and formally enter an expanding world war. It was quite another to put the nation on a war footing: to organize industrial production, provide for the distribution supplies, make weaponry and other armaments, and enlist thousands of Americans into the US Armed Forces. What would this require on the part of the federal government and how would such an enlargement of federal power be received by Americans who could easily remember the recent warfare in the Caribbean and the southeast Pacific? And how would the Wilson administration handle dissent and other forms of opposition to the war that might arise?

Building Administrative Structures

Even before the formal declaration of war, Wilson and the Congress had taken steps to put the country in a state of economic and military readiness. First to be created was a Council on National Defense, followed by the Food and Fuel Administration, the United States Railroad Administration, and especially the **War Industries Board**, which coordinated the production, purchasing, and transportation of necessary goods. Each agency represented a partnership between government officials (often cabinet secretaries) and the business sector, a version of the model that organizations like the National Civic Federation (discussed in Chapter 19) pioneered earlier in the century. Indeed, especially prominent among the participants was Bernard Baruch, a wealthy Wall Street trader and financier, who headed up the War Industries Board and encouraged Wilson to centralize authority over war-related activities.

Once American participation in the war began in the spring of 1917, Wilson moved to strengthen the political hand of his administration by establishing the **Committee on Public Information (CPI)**, tasked with shaping public opinion in support of the war effort. It was no small challenge. Skepticism about, if not outright opposition to, American involvement was widespread, and it could be found across a broad political spectrum. There were isolationists among the Republicans, especially in the Midwest and Far West, and among Democrats in the Midwest and South. There were also critics on the left, among Progressives and Socialists, who worried that the war was being waged by rival capitalist powers over the spoils of colonialism. African Americans, for their part, rightly wondered how the United States could be committed to self-determination abroad—making the world "safe for democracy" as Wilson had put it—and to Jim Crow at home.

Mobilizing public support for the war was all the more important because of manpower needs. British and French troops were mired in the trenches and looked desperately to the Americans for the scale of support that would finally tip the military balances to their side. Congress, therefore, enacted a military draft designed both to redefine the loyalties of countless hyphenated Americans and to turn them into an effective fighting force. Eventually, nearly five million men were conscripted, about four million of whom went overseas with the **American Expeditionary Forces**, commanded by General John J. Pershing. Among them were roughly 200,000 African Americans, about the same number who served in the federal army during the Civil War, and they, like their forebears of the 1860s, continued to face the indignity of being assigned to segregated units. It would lodge in many of their memories.

Domestic Dissent and the Russian Revolution

Wars often unsettle societies politically, unleashing grievances as well as aspirations—the War of the Rebellion destroyed slavery, even though Lincoln and his Congress initially vowed to leave it alone—and World War I was no different. Socialist parties had been emerging in Europe since the 1870s and by the early twentieth century had mass bases of support. Socialists and left-wing Progressives in the United States had begun to seek power on the local and national levels, with some success, and many saw opposition to the war as compatible with their misgivings about capitalism and a way to increase their popular support. But perhaps most consequential was a sweeping revolution in Russia, on Europe's eastern edge.

Russia had been ruled by an autocratic Tsar (the word derived from the Latin word *caesar* and was usually understood as equivalent to emperor), Nicholas II,

Selling the War

Soon after America's entry into the war in 1917, the government officially began to shape the public's attitude toward the war effort. The Wilson Administration organized the Committee on Public Information (CPI) and placed George Creel, a Progressive supporter of Wilson and a muckraking journalist, at the head of the agency. As the war went on, the CPI distributed seventy-five million pamphlets and 6,000 press releases. Some 75,000 speakers stumped for their country. Equally

≡ **"Wake Up America: Civilization Calls Every Man, Woman, and Child!"** This 1917 poster encouraged American participation in World War I. Columbia, a feminine symbol of American liberty, is fast asleep as storm clouds gather behind her.

important were images, each one printed by the hundreds of thousands and emblazoned on posters across the country.

To understand the impact of posters, one needs to imagine a time before computers, the Internet, the television, or even the mass use of radio. Although newspapers informed the literate public, posters supplied a primary means of mass communication. Posters appealed to the emotions and motivated action. They portrayed a world without complexity, a world that was two-dimensional.

CONSIDER THIS

Posters were a ubiquitous feature in American cities and towns during this period in American history. They were on the fences of baseball parks, on the sides of public and private buildings, and on the wooden sandwich boards that men and boys wore to advertise some product or event. In the two posters shown here, how did the artists stereotype Germans and women to pique emotions and bend reality? How did they speak to the viewer's deepest needs, desires, or fears? What is the significance of the word "civilization" in the first poster, and "culture" in the second?

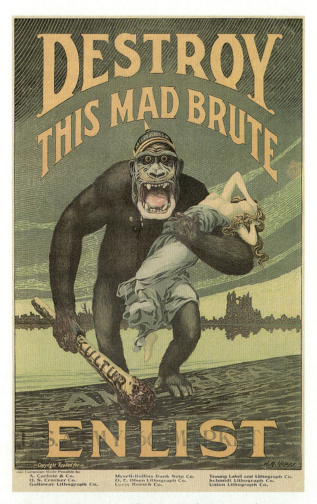

☰ **Propaganda Poster** This propaganda poster employs a different tactic to encourage American men to enlist in the army and defeat Germany. The threat posed by German militarism is represented by a club-wielding gorilla landing on American shores and clutching a vulnerable woman.

who looked across the ethnically mixed Russian lands of Asia with an imperial eye and had nothing but scorn for popular participation in politics. Although he had joined hands with the British and the French, both parliamentary regimes, and had some interest in modernizing Russian society, he was not about to move in a more politically liberal direction.

But the mobilization of Russian men and resources required for the fight against the Central Powers shook Nicholas's regime and, in a sense, he soon faced what Porfirio Diaz had faced in Mexico: a rebellion turned revolution. In March 1917, the Tsar was forced to abdicate in favor of a new provisional government with parliamentary ambitions and reformer Alexander Kerensky at its head. But the tide of radicalization could not be halted. Several months later, in October 1917, the provisional government was itself overturned by a communist revolution—the revolutionaries called themselves **Bolsheviks**—who sought to transform the property basis of Russian society and begin the work of building socialism on a global scale. With Vladimir I. Lenin at the helm, the new Bolshevik regime made a separate peace with the Germans and took what was now known as the Union of Soviet Socialist Republics (USSR) out of the war.

Fearful that domestic dissent might intensify and undercut the American war effort, Congress passed, with Wilson's endorsement, **Espionage (1917) and Sedition (1918) Acts**, which effectively criminalized activities or ideas regarded as interfering with the operations of US Armed Forces or lending sustenance to the country's enemies. Penalties included lengthy prison terms and even execution. In Wilson's view, the acts were necessary to "crush out" such "creatures of passion, disloyalty, and anarchy," and secure the "honor and self-respect of the nation." Members and publications of the Socialist Party, labor organizations like the Industrial Workers of the World (discussed in Chapter 19), and leaders of various racial and ethnic groups—especially Germans—were subject to surveillance and prosecution. More than a few, including Eugene V. Debs (who had been a candidate for the presidency in 1912), either ended up in jail or fled the country. War and civil liberties, it was clear, did not readily mix, and national loyalties could be coerced as well as encouraged.

≡ **Rounding Up Undesirables**   A 1918 cartoon depicts the US government arresting labor organizers, foreigners, and traitors under the Sedition Act. President Wilson sought to use the law, and the lengthy prison terms it imposed, to "crush out" labor unions and supposed traitors.

21.3   War and Peace

|| Understand the role the United States played after entering the war and how the peace process unfolded.

The American declaration of war involved not only expansive and intrusive mobilizations of people and resources but also fighting in what had already become a war of unprecedented casualties. Since 1914 soldiers on both sides had been in trenches across western Europe that barely moved either forward or backward yet also became deathtraps for many thousands who occupied and fought from them. And once the fighting came to a conclusion, what sort of peace would follow? Would a Wilsonian vision of a stable postwar order based on national self-determination come into being, or would the tensions that led to warfare in the first place remain unresolved and threaten the world with more warfare in the future?

Deadly Dynamics

American troops joined a war in which nineteenth-century tactics encountered twentieth-century weaponry. It was contradictory in concept and a lethal military mismatch. The advent of aviation, the modernizing of artillery, the deployment of submarines and armored tanks, and the use of poison gas and other chemical weapons rained death and destruction on the land and at sea. Of the sixty-five million European men mobilized militarily by wartime states, perhaps as many as eleven million died. Another thirty-seven million would be counted as wounded or missing, an astonishing casualty rate of over 50 percent. An entire generation of young European men, of high and low station, perished.

Casualties suffered by American soldiers were not nearly so catastrophic, but they were wrenching nonetheless. Over 100,000 of them met their deaths on the battlefields of Western Europe. But they also turned the military tide against the Central Powers, fortifying the wearied British and French and forcing the Germans to drain their already depleted material resources. An offensive launched by the Triple Entente (now joined by Italy, Romania, and Japan and known as the Allies, or **Allied Powers**) over the summer months of 1918, which would not have been possible without the intervention of the United States, steadily pushed the Germans back toward their own borders. As summer turned to fall, the German military command saw that all hope of victory was lost and a crushing defeat appeared imminent. Calls came for an armistice based on Wilson's Fourteen Points. On November 11, 1918, such an armistice was signed and the bloody fighting seemed to come to an end.

≡ **Over the Top**   American soldiers go "over the top," advancing out of their trenches to attack their enemy. Trench warfare became synonymous with fighting in France as armies fortified themselves in elaborate networks of ditches to evade explosive artillery shells and machine guns.

A Silent Killer: The Influenza Virus

By the time the war was turning in favor of the Allies and against the Central Powers, another killer was on the loose, hatched and spread by war-related mobilization and troop movements. It was not a new weapon or a new military strategy. It was a virus—an H1N1 avian influenza virus—that would sweep across much of the world, cause more sickness and death than the war itself ever did, and may well have helped tip the military balances, too.

What has come to be called the "Spanish Flu" because of misinformation about its origins, first broke out at a military post, Camp Funston, in the state of Kansas—a major training ground for the American Expeditionary Forces bound for Europe—in early March 1918, though it may well have surfaced nearby two months before. Within a week, the influenza virus had reached the East Coast of the United States, where few preventive measures were taken, and by the middle of April 1918, owing to the transport of troops across the Atlantic, the H1N1 flu had reached France and the bloody Western Front. Very quickly, the flu virus surfaced in Britain, Italy, Spain, and parts of Russia, and then by the end of May, it was afflicting military and civilian populations in North Africa, India, Japan, and China. Not surprisingly, the spreading flu badly disrupted military operations in ways that have yet to be fully understood; as best as we know, three-quarters of the French troops, half of the British troops, and nearly a million German troops contracted the virus.

Initially, mortality from the H1N1 flu was not unusually bad; with no antiviral vaccines, no use of intravenous fluids, no antibiotics, and no respirators in the medical repertoire of the time, influenza was always a serious and potentially fatal illness. But that was the "first wave," and as we know from the history of COVID-19, pandemics can move in waves, of different severity, if early responses—especially quarantines—are limited and ineffective. What made the **1918–1921 influenza pandemic** (a disease epidemic that spreads across international borders) so disastrous were the more, and deadlier, waves to come.

Indeed, a second wave of the influenza virus began to spread in the summer of 1918, and, very quickly, was detected on both sides of the Atlantic, owing to the movement of troops in oceanic vessels. Army camps and navy yards in Boston as well as training camps in the West African nation of Sierra Leone showed the first signs of reinfection, and again the disease spread globally. But

≡ **Emergency Responders**   Nurses in St. Louis, Missouri, with stretchers and ambulances, ready to assist victims of the 1918–1919 influenza pandemic. Known then as the "Spanish Flu," the outbreak in fact originated in Kansas and by 1921 killed tens of millions across the globe.

this time the demographics of mortality changed. Ordinarily, those most in danger from influenza are the very young and very old due to the relative weaknesses of their immune systems. During the second wave, however, the flu struck especially hard at people who were generally spared the first time around: those in their 20s and 30s. Between September and December of 1918 there were ten times as many deaths in the United States as there were during this period in 1915.

A third wave of the H1N1 flu began in early 1919 and a fourth started in 1920. Before the pandemic was regarded as over in 1921—the flu variant is still with us and almost resulted in a pandemic in 2014–2015—it had infected at least one-third of the world's human population and claimed the lives of more than 600,000 people in the United States and somewhere between 50 and 100 million people worldwide: many times the number who perished owing directly to war-related deaths and injuries, though it may make sense to include the avian flu as part of the world war casualties. Some in fact believe that the morbidity and mortality related to the flu among troops in Europe may have had an impact on who gained the upper hand in the fighting.

Despite the lack of medical and pharmaceutical interventions that are available to us today, studies of the 1918 influenza pandemic's course in a number of towns and cities in the United States showed that efforts to use social distancing measures, to quarantine, and to isolate those who had contracted the disease or were especially vulnerable to it produced positive results. Fewer people suffered from the flu and fewer people died from its effects. What's more, coordination among public agencies and between public agencies and communities also mitigated the consequences of the influenza pandemic. These are useful perspectives for ourselves and for the future.

Forging Peace at Versailles

But what of the peace? In principle, Wilson's idea of a "peace without victory" suggested a treaty that would not designate clear winners and losers, nor seek to punish acknowledged losers harshly. That Wilson himself went to Versailles, France, in the spring of 1919—the first time a sitting US president ever traveled across the Atlantic—and played a powerful role at the peace conference that took place there further suggested he would be in a good position to turn the principle into reality. As it turns out, Wilson's Fourteen Points were at the center of discussion and debate, and they did help frame the outcome. But the British and, particularly, the French had their own interests in seeing the Germans weakened and disarmed, and they sought ways to ensure that Germany would no longer threaten them militarily. After all, the Germans had invaded France twice since 1870: once in the Franco-Prussian War (1870–1871) and again during World War I.

To that end, the treaty reconfigured German borders in the west and east to shrink German national territory, created a demilitarized zone in the industrial Rhineland, restricted the size of the German military, and imposed significant reparations—payments to the Triple Entente acknowledging responsibility for the war on the German government, eventually equivalent to many billions of dollars. Not quite a "peace without victory," at least insofar as the Germans, who had not formally surrendered, were concerned (see Map 21.3).

Wilsonian notions of "self-determination" did go into the related process of dismantling the empires—Austro-Hungarian and Ottoman—of the Central Powers and redrawing the map of Europe, at least in theory, to recognize the claims of ethnic nationalities. The new countries of Finland, Poland, Yugoslavia, Austria, Hungary, Albania, and the Baltic Republics were created where empires once stood. In other parts of the world, however, the Allies dismantled the Central Powers' empires but did not create independent states; instead, they assigned themselves colonies to administer as "mandates." French and British mandates were also established in the Middle East, including Palestine, and in Africa, where

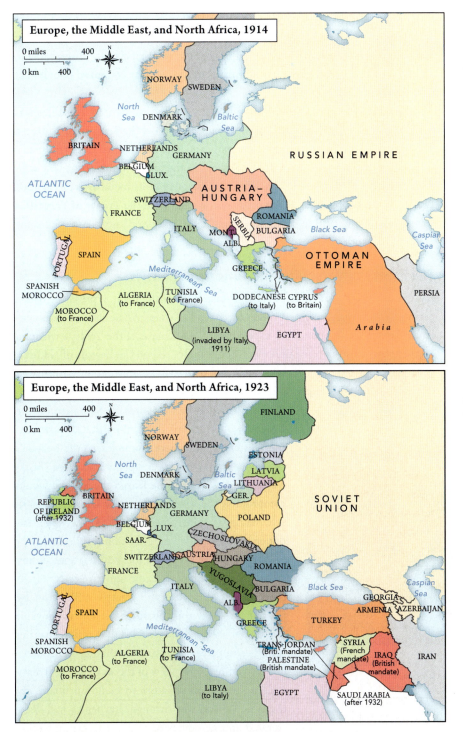

Europe, the Middle East, and North Africa, 1914

Europe, the Middle East, and North Africa, 1923

≡ **MAP 21.3 Europe, the Middle East, and North Africa, 1914 and 1923** Self-determination worked unevenly in Central and Eastern Europe, and it played only a minimal role in the former Ottoman Empire.

the Germans and Ottomans previously had colonial possessions. It was only a partial decolonization, since the British and French empires were extended, but ideas about self-determination, the "adjustment of colonial claims," disarmament, and national integrity helped stir new expectations among colonized people that would affect all colonizers.

Yet perhaps the most significant Wilsonian accomplishment in Versailles was the creation of a "general association of nations," called the **League of Nations**. The League would have a General Assembly and an International Court of Justice to mediate disputes, promote disarmament "to the lowest point consistent with domestic safety," and defend the territorial integrity of its member states against external aggression. It was an idealistic vision and, when the **Treaty of Versailles** was signed in June 1919, Wilson waxed that "at last the world knows America as the savior of the world."

The Treaty of Versailles and American Politics

A great triumph it seemed to be for Wilson and the United States, presiding over a peace after what was imagined as the "war to end all wars." All he had to do was convince the American public and, especially the US Senate, of the Treaty's wisdom. But here the triumph came undone. Attention focused on the League of Nations, and opposition, led by the rival Republicans, proved to be substantial. Some feared that League membership would entangle the United States in international conflicts in which it had no interest. Some feared the League would curtail the United States' power in the Western Hemisphere. Some feared the League's principles would empower smaller and more "backward" nations. And some feared the League would compromise the sovereignty of the United States itself, making it vulnerable to attack. At the very least, opponents demanded modifications to the Treaty.

Wilson was in no mood for modifications of any sort, and he began to campaign tirelessly across the country to secure the treaty's ratification by the Senate. Over the course of twenty-two days in September 1919, he traveled 8,000 miles, making speeches in places large and small, urging his audiences to embrace his view of the war and the Treaty and to press their senators to come on board. By the time Wilson was through, his health had deteriorated and he collapsed with a paralyzing stroke.

≡ **A Skeptical Senate** A confused man representing the US Senate gazes at the peace treaty which President Wilson has deposited on his desk. Wilson went to Europe in person to negotiate the Treaty of Versailles, but the Republican-dominated Senate rejected it.

But even that couldn't get him the votes of two-thirds of the senators (necessary to ratify such a treaty). So the Treaty of Versailles was never ratified by the United States, and the League of Nations would be established without American participation. The United States had unquestionably emerged from World War I as a major, perhaps the major, power on the globe, but its commitment to global peace and security appeared equivocal to say the least.

21.4   Radical Pulses and Transformations

Describe how the war helped unleash radical political forces around the globe and in the United States.

Wars, especially very large ones, tend to have political consequences that could not have been predicted when they first began. This is not only because of the goals and propaganda ordinarily proclaimed but also because warring societies have domestic tensions of their own with which to contend. Because warfare on a large scale requires popular mobilizations, in one way or another it affects the lives of most people involved. And once weaknesses, defeats, and dissent become apparent, openings are created for popular movements, some of them radical in ambition, that had not been available before. World War I was one of those episodes in history when the wheels of change moved forward in explosive directions, and few areas around the globe were not touched by it. In the end, World War I, both because of its catastrophic destructiveness and the political struggles it set in motion, would help frame the remainder of the twentieth century.

Mexico, Russia, and the Globe

The Russian and Mexican Revolutions were the greatest and most far-reaching examples of the radical transformations that occurred during the war decade, and in Mexico the impact and example have been underestimated in the telling of American history. By 1917, as the United States entered World War I, Mexican revolutionaries had not only toppled Diaz and then Huerta but had written up a new constitution committed to social rights, worker empowerment, and agrarian reform: a document far more progressive than the US Constitution even with its Reconstruction Amendments.

The new Mexican constitution guaranteed universal education, an eight-hour workday, a minimum wage, profit-sharing, equal pay for equal work regardless of sex or nationality, assistance for pregnant and nursing women, workmen's compensation, and the right to strike and bargain collectively.

It made ownership of lands, waters, and natural resources conditional on the will of the national government and restricted property ownership to Mexicans and Mexican companies, setting back the influence of foreign investors. Finally, the constitution provided for the division of large estates, the protection of small landholdings, and the return of communal peasant lands that had previously been seized.

The Mexican constitution brimmed with economic nationalism, political liberalism, and social democracy. Reflecting high idealism, it constructed a more inclusive polity than had ever existed either in Mexico or anywhere else in the world. As might be expected, its aspirations were challenging to carry through. Turmoil continued to accompany the process of change. Some of the revolution's great leaders, Pancho Villa and Emiliano Zapata among them, would be felled by assassins. But the stage would also be set for the revolution's last phase, in the 1930s, when the new revolutionary party (PNR—the *Partido Nacional Revolucionario*) headed up by Lazaro Cardenas nationalized all foreign-owned companies, especially in the sectors (oil, mining, railroads, electrical power) where American investments were concentrated. It was a signal historical moment in the Western Hemisphere.

But the pulse of radical change was by no means confined to revolutions in Russia and Mexico; it vibrated across the globe. With the signing of the armistice, Germany was immediately embroiled in a revolution that seemed closely related to the dynamics of the Russian. The imperial government was quickly toppled (the Kaiser abdicated as had the Tsar), the fortunes of the Social Democratic Party were bolstered, a short-lived and brutally repressed communist uprising occurred, and, by the end of the summer of 1919, a German republic was established.

European governments, old and new, eyed the German revolution with concern if not fear, though unrest was also brewing in the colonies. In northern Africa, aggrieved Egyptians and Sudanese sought to throw off their British colonial rulers and laid the groundwork for Egyptian independence in 1922. A Pan-African Conference, representing fifteen countries, met in Paris at the very time of the Versailles conference and looked to promote new forms of self-governance on the African continent. And the student-led May Fourth movement, based in Beijing, advanced popular Chinese nationalism in the face of Japanese encroachments that the Versailles Treaty itself had permitted.

American Pulses

The United States was not immune either. Far from it. A massive strike wave spread across the country in 1919, especially among steel, coal, and railroad workers, who

sought to recover economic ground that wartime inflation and a no-strike pledge had sacrificed. In Seattle,
Washington, 65,000 workers launched a general
strike—when workers across the city joined together
in solidarity—shutting down the city for four days and
conjuring images of the Bolshevik Revolution in Russia.
Women's suffrage activists, in turn, used war-related
political leverage to press President Wilson and the
Congress into passing the **Nineteenth Amendment**,
which determined that the "right of citizens to vote"
would not be "denied or abridged on account of sex." In
short, the amendment granted women suffrage.

Although women had struggled for suffrage since
the 1840s and argued that their direct participation in
electoral politics would enrich American democracy
and put an end to political corruption, they did not, as
we saw in Chapter 19, turn out to vote in proportions
greater than men. It was evidence of a changing political culture that crossed gender lines. But women's
suffrage was indicative of a new social and political
self-confidence, especially among women of the middle class, which had begun to redefine the boundaries
of gender norms.

Women talked in new ways not only about the
rights to which they were entitled but also about
control over their lives and their bodies. Birth con-

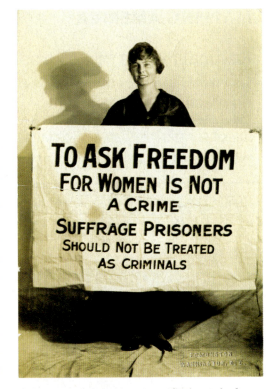

Freedom for Women Lucy Branham, a leader
of the National Woman's Party, poses with a pro-
suffrage banner. Suffrage activists picketed the
White House with similar signs, braving nasty
weather and hostile onlookers to demand the right
to vote.

trol became important to public discussion during the 1910s and, led by
Emma Goldman and Margaret Sanger (with complex intentions as we saw in
Chapter 19), activists established an institutional basis first with clinics and
then with the American Birth Control League, the progenitor of Planned
Parenthood. The Nineteenth Amendment, for its part, laid a foundation for
further rights claims, as the National Woman's Party, organized earlier in the
decade by Alice Paul and Lucy Burns, crafted an Equal Rights Amendment that
would outlaw the denying or abridging of "equality of rights . . . on account of
sex." It was not only ahead of its time, except in Mexico, but remains ahead of
ours (it has yet to be ratified). In important ways, that is, the 1910s gave rise to
modern feminism.

MAPPING AMERICA

Radical Pulses in a Global Context

The Mexican Revolution left between one and two million people dead between 1911 and 1920. China and Africa experienced paroxysms of imperial violence during the same time period. Tens of millions of people fought and died in wars around the world; empires collapsed against a revolutionary tide. These extraordinary events are usually told separately from the history of the United States. But the great upheavals in Mexico, Russia, China, and elsewhere share much in common with the goals of

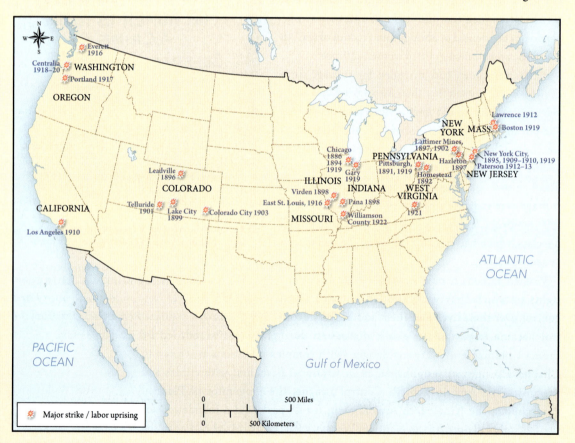

≡ **MAP 1**   At the turn of the twentieth century, the United States stood poised to become the world's great industrial powerhouse, but unresolved, however, was the place that those who labored would occupy within the new industrial order.

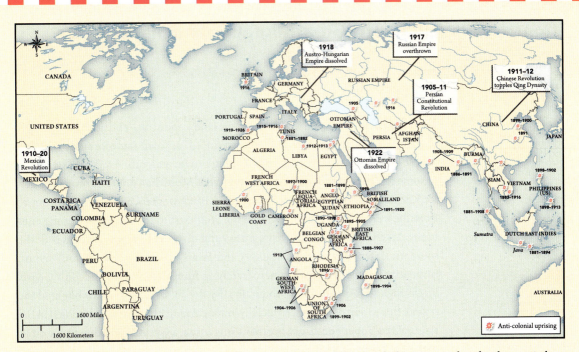

≡ **MAP 2**   The pulse of radical change that vibrated across the United States in the late nineteenth and early twentieth centuries can be seen against a global backdrop. Throughout the world, the inequalities produced by the Gilded Age and modernization provoked fierce discontent. The Russian and Mexican Revolutions were the greatest and most far-reaching examples of the radical transformations that occurred during the period 1910–1920, but they were just two of the many lethal cataclysms that remade the twentieth-century world.

American labor leaders and the aspirations of political activists on the left, both of whom saw their campaigns as part of an epic, worldwide struggle. "The fruits of the toil of millions are boldly stolen to build up colossal fortunes for a few, unprecedented in the history of mankind." These words were not spoken by V. I. Lenin or Emiliano Zapata. They are from the 1892 Omaha Platform of the People's Party.

Thinking Geographically

1. In Map 1, why did some parts of the United States experience more labor strikes than others?

2. In Map 2, what factors account for why some regions of the world experienced more unrest in the period 1890–1920 than others?

21.5 The Great Migration and Black Politics

Explain the significance of the Great Migration in reshaping American politics.

The war decade also began to transform the landscape of race and politics. The signs of change had been apparent since at least the 1870s when some formerly enslaved people talked of leaving the South and organized for emigration to Kansas, Liberia, or some territory in the trans-Mississippi West. More than 6,000 "Exodusters" left for Kansas in 1879 alone. In the meantime, Black workers had been on the move from the worn-out plantation lands of the Southeast to the newly developing ones of the Arkansas-Mississippi Delta, from rural districts to towns and cities of the southern states, and from plantations and farms to lumber and sawmill camps, turpentine camps, and coal mines stretching from the Atlantic and Gulf Coasts up through the Appalachian Mountains. By the 1890s, as Jim Crow blighted the region, there were new signs, especially among young Black men and women in the states of the Upper South, of a northerly migration, a **Great Migration** to the cities of the Northeast and Midwest.

The Scale and Geography of Migration

But the streams of northward migration turned into a flood during the 1910s, tapping communities further to the South. This was because the drumbeats of European war initiated a massive mobilization of industrial production and manpower that for the first time opened the possibilities of meaningful employment for African Americans outside of the South. Encouraged by labor recruiters and railroad companies, thousands sought to escape repression at home and took to the rails, rivers, and roads in search of a better life for themselves and their families. Joining them were thousands more of African descent, mainly from the Caribbean, who fled economic distress, natural disasters, and changes in colonial policies, and headed chiefly to Florida and the Northeast. Between 1915 and 1930, their numbers, together, amounted to more than 1.5 million.

The routes of migration were by no means haphazard. Some spoke of migration "chains" that linked districts in the South with cities in the Northeast and Midwest, and linked family members who began to depart with those left behind by choice or circumstance. Black men and women from the Southeast usually headed to cities like Philadelphia and New York. Those from Georgia, Alabama, Tennessee, and Kentucky usually moved to Pittsburgh, Cleveland, and Detroit. And those from Mississippi, Louisiana, and Arkansas set out for St. Louis, Chicago, and Milwaukee. Networks of kinship quickly took shape so that when Black migrants arrived in a northern city, they had family to look out for them, familiarize them with the new urban environment, and point them to employment opportunities. Some had already moved from the rural to urban South before looking North; most left the rural and small-town South for the large and potentially disorienting northern cities. All of this turned the migration into a social movement in its own right (see Map 21.4).

Cultural and Political Impact

The "Great Migration" proved to be a kaleidoscope of political and cultural intensity, not seen since the War of the Rebellion pulled thousands of enslaved and free people of color into contraband camps and US Army units. In Chicago, Detroit, Cleveland, Pittsburgh, Philadelphia, and especially the Harlem section of New York City, a "New Negro" seemed to be born, shorn of the chains of enslavement and white supremacy, liberated to thrive in a new and charged cultural climate. The results were remarkable in music, literature, and the arts. Regional inventions like jazz and blues, both emerging around the turn of the century in the lower Mississippi Valley, followed along with migrants like Louis Armstrong and

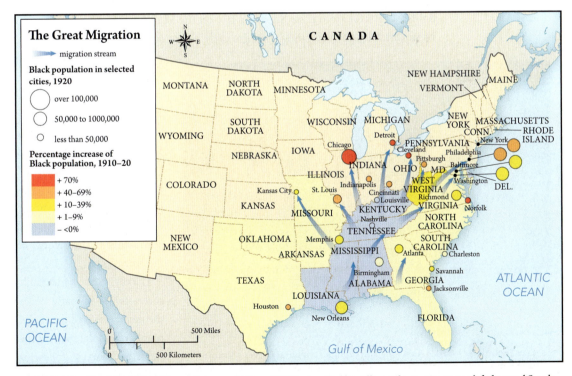

≡ **MAP 21.4   The Great Migration**   Between 1916 and 1920, about half a million African Americans left the rural South for the industrial centers of the North. Their migration remade the racial and cultural landscape of the entire nation.

Bessie Smith into the urban North to become national idioms. Not for nothing is the 1920s referred to as the "**Jazz Age**," when the music electrified white and Black audiences and "race records" (recordings made and marketed exclusively to Black audiences) could find a mass market among African American consumers. Poets like Claude MacKay and Countee Cullen, writers like Richard Wright, Zora Neale Hurston, and Alain Locke, and artists like Romare Bearden and Aaron Douglas redefined their mediums and riveted a prideful new Black public. This creative outpouring celebrating Black culture was often referred to as the **Harlem Renaissance** because much of this activity was centered in the Harlem neighborhood of Manhattan. Talented Black artists and writers flocked to the district, where they broke with tradition and asserted ties to Africa. Langston Hughes drew on African American music in *The Weary Blues* (1926), a groundbreaking collection of poems. He captured the upbeat spirit of the Harlem Renaissance when he asserted, "I am a Negro—and beautiful."

The Great Migration of the 1910s and 1920s also transformed the nation's political landscape, giving rise to new possibilities for Black empowerment and expressions of racial nationalism. And there was no greater embodiment of these possibilities than an African Jamaican named Marcus Garvey. An artisan and political agitator from rural St. Ann's Bay on the island colony, Garvey came to New York City in 1916 along with the early waves of migrants from the South. After a whirlwind tour of the United States, he returned to Harlem, established a branch of an organization called the **Universal Negro Improvement Association (UNIA)**—first established in his native Jamaica), began publishing a newspaper called the *Negro World*, and commenced the work of mobilization.

Garvey was remarkably successful. By the early 1920s, the membership of the UNIA numbered in the many thousands, and Garvey's following in the United States, from the rural and small-town South

≡ **Jazz Trumpeter Louis Armstrong and members of King Oliver's Creole Jazz Band, 1923** Although jazz originated in the southern Mississippi Valley, Black Americans brought the music with them to northern cities during the Great Migration.

to the small-town and urban North, may have exceeded one million. Ultimately encompassing forty-two countries, mainly in the Western Hemisphere and Africa, Garvey's became the largest and most formidable pan-African organization the world has seen.

Although influenced by Booker T. Washington's message of self-help and material improvement (discussed in Chapter 20), Garvey nonetheless rejected the possibility of any meaningful accommodation with whites. Only when Black people could claim an independent and powerful nation of their own, he argued, would they be able to prosper and achieve rights and respect either there or anywhere else. Indeed, Garvey's vision was both nationalist and anticolonial. He called not so much for African repatriation (a "back to Africa" movement as it is generally described) as for the ouster of European colonizers and the establishment of Black self-governance. At a time of brutal repression and grim prospects for African Americans, this project electrified Black audiences and amassed an enormous following even among those who never joined the UNIA. "We may make progress in America, the West Indies, and other foreign countries," Garvey announced, "but there will never be any real lasting progress until the Negro makes of Africa a strong Republic to lend protection to the success we make in foreign lands."

The UNIA therefore took its place on a new spectrum of politics that the Great Migration permitted. Despite the formal segregation and disfranchisement that afflicted African Americans in the southern states, they could now find political breathing room for organization, agitation, voting, and office holding in the North. There would be disputes, some bitter, among them as they debated a way forward, but the new voting blocs that they formed provided the sort of power they had not had since Radical Reconstruction, along with influence that would help transform the American political system.

≡ **Africa, the Land of Opportunity** A stock certificate issued by Black Star Line, a shipping company founded by Marcus Garvey to facilitate pan-African commerce. Garvey called for Black self-governance and independence and believed that Black people would prosper only if they controlled their own institutions.

21.6   Repression and Intolerance

Discuss the repressive methods used by the federal government against those who opposed the war effort and the racial and ethnic conflict unleashed as a consequence of this repression.

The radical transformations produced by the war not only elevated hopes for many people who had been politically marginalized and economically exploited but also provoked backlashes from those who felt threatened by the changes taking place. Wartime is often an enemy of free speech and expression, and governments, even those rhetorically committed to the free exchange of ideas and political association, often persecute dissenters. Already in the 1880s, the rise of socialist and anarchist movements in the United States brought down the fists of repression—think of Haymarket in 1886 and the jailing of Debs in 1894 (discussed in Chapter 18)—as warning shots over the bows of political radicalism, but American entry into World War I intensified the push for political loyalty and the hunt for political opponents. President Wilson might have been looking for a "peace without victory" and the triumph of political "self-determination" abroad, but his administration had little patience for what was regarded as disloyalty at home. Its actions unleashed torrents of political and racial intolerance on the ground.

Political and Racial Repression

The Mexican and especially the Russian Revolution came to worry government officials as militant strikes erupted, an American Communist Party was born (CPUSA, 1919), and threats of violence, accompanied by a series of bombings, appeared to emanate from political radicals, some of whom were foreign born. As a result, President Wilson's Attorney General, A. Mitchell Palmer, assisted by J. Edgar Hoover, who worked in the federal Bureau of Investigation (later the FBI), moved against suspected radicals and used the Sedition Act of 1918 to have many of the foreign born among them deported, some to the new Soviet Union. These are known as the **Palmer Raids**, and although they occurred in 1919 and 1920 (when Palmer's own term came to an end), this **Red Scare** had a chilling effect on political dissent and organizing around the country. Indeed, an investigation of Marcus Garvey and the UNIA that Hoover launched in late 1919 (he was especially suspicious of African Americans and would remain so) eventually led to Garvey's arrest on supposed mail fraud charges, imprisonment, and deportation several years later.

The Red Scare of 1919–1920 was accompanied by what the Black activist and intellectual James Weldon Johnson called the **Red Summer** of 1919, by which he meant that it ran with the blood of Black people. The dislocations of the Great

Migration, the return of African American soldiers who were emboldened by their participation in a "war to save democracy" and reluctant to return to the submissiveness that whites often demanded of them, and the economic readjustments that peacetime entailed saw a spike in ferocious racial violence.

In the southern states, more than eighty lynchings took place, harking back to the bloody 1890s, and in over thirty small towns and large cities across the United States, between May and October, African Americans were targeted by white mobs looking to enforce the racial subordination that they believed was being defied. Charleston, South Carolina, and New Orleans, Louisiana; New London, Connecticut, and Syracuse, New York; Bisbee, Arizona, and East St. Louis, Illinois; New York City and Washington, DC, were among the explosive sites (see Map 21.5).

The violence, as this suggests, observed no geographic boundaries. Chicago's was particularly horrific. A racial incident along a South Side beach in late July that

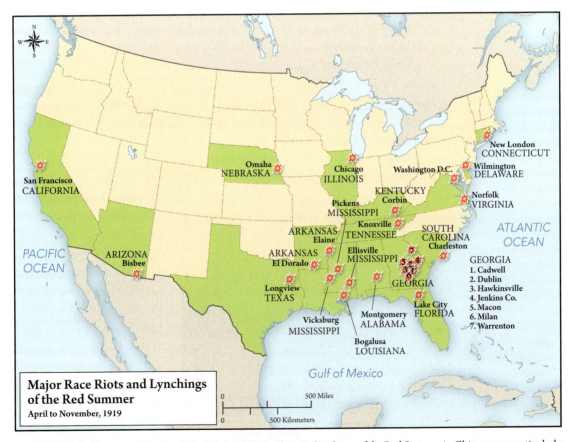

Major Race Riots and Lynchings of the Red Summer
April to November, 1919

≡ **MAP 21.5   Major Race Riots and Lynchings, 1919**   The racial violence of the Red Summer in Chicago was particularly appalling, but every region of the country experienced horrific acts of hostility targeted against Black people.

claimed the life of a Black man exploded into a weeklong riot that left more than thirty people dead, twenty-three of them African American. At the same time, bombs were lobbed at the houses of Black migrants thought to be encroaching on neighborhoods controlled by whites, only the beginning of intense urban conflict over race and residential neighborhoods. But there would be no more bowing. "We are cowards and jackasses if we do not fight a sterner, longer, more unbending battle against the forces of hell in our own land," W. E. B. Du Bois thundered. "We return. We return from fighting. We return fighting."

Even so, the atmosphere of racist hostility continued to hover with brutal effects. And Black people and their communities who sought to live peaceably and comfortably on their own became special targets. Indeed, both their existence and their success in providing for themselves proved to be especially provocative for neighboring whites. Booker T. Washington had advised southern Black people to develop their own communities, educate themselves, and accumulate wealth and property if they wanted to be accepted in American society. But living by Washington's creed, often called "accommodationism," only stirred a vicious backlash from whites.

In early January 1923, rumors of a Black man's assault on a white woman set off a large and ferocious mob near the west Florida town of Rosewood that had come to be overwhelmingly Black in population. Not only did the mob hunt down and murder Black people, but they razed the entire town, effectively expelling Black people from the area.

But Rosewood's murderous destruction was surpassed by the violence that fell upon the Black men, women, and children who had built up and lived in the Greenwood section of Tulsa, Oklahoma. Founded in 1906, Greenwood attracted ambitious Black people who were keen to build a substantial and prosperous community. That they did. By 1920, the population of Greenwood was about 11,000, and the commercial district was so thriving with shops, banks, libraries, and groceries that it was dubbed "Black Wall Street" in recognition of its economic success and middle-class wealth.

≣ **The Wreckage of the Greenwood District in Tulsa, Oklahoma**   The 1921 Tulsa Massacre resulted in dozens of razed city blocks like this one, as well as the deaths of hundreds of Black residents.

White supremacists couldn't abide Black Wall Street. Again, a reported incident of a Black man assaulting a young white woman triggered a rampaging mob that, in the span of two days in 1921 (May 31–June 1), massacred as many as 300 Black people (there is no precise casualty toll), left more than 800 hospitalized, and burned thirty-five square blocks of Greenwood to the ground, destroying all the business and community institutions and leaving half of the population homeless. The **Tulsa Race Massacre**, and massacre it was, is regarded as the worst incident of racial violence in American history and certainly one of the deadliest examples of mob terror inflicted upon any community or group. Still, it would be many decades before the Tulsa Race Massacre made it into the historical record and reminded all Americans, including white Tulsans who knew little to nothing about it, of the bloody stains on America's hands.

Immigration Restriction

Those who feared the radicalism that the war seemed to promote could turn to quieter and more "official" forms of repression. Immigration restriction was one of them. Up through the nineteenth century, the borders of the United States were effectively open to all comers, and the flow of immigrants could reach astonishing numbers as it did both in the 1840s and 1850s and again in the decades between the 1870s and World War I. As we saw in Chapter 17, millions of people from Europe, Asia, and the Caribbean flooded into the country, contributing to American economic might and industrial prowess. Many took the semiskilled and unskilled jobs that were multiplying in steel and munitions plants, chemical and machine tool factories, meatpacking and food processing companies. Even the nativist movement of the 1850s refused to block the tide, focusing instead on limiting the political power of those who arrived. Only the Chinese Exclusion Act of 1882 and the Gentlemen's Agreement of 1907, which prohibited Chinese and Japanese laborers from immigrating, established restrictions.

But those restrictions also set important precedents, turning ideas about racial difference into demonization. Both the Chinese and Japanese were represented as threatening members of the "yellow races" who practiced "heathen" faiths and could pollute the blood of Anglo-Saxons. Receiving support from eugenicists and other pseudoscientists who won popular audiences in the early twentieth century, such racializations were soon extended to Europeans as well, fueling new demands for action during and immediately after World War I. In fact, ideas about racial inferiority were often hitched to those of political subversion. Jews, Italians, and other southern and eastern Europeans, lowered on the scale of civilization by eugenics, were also seen as incubators of anarchism and Bolshevism.

The result was the **Immigration Act of 1924**, which imposed strict quotas on the number of immigrants who could be admitted to the United States from other

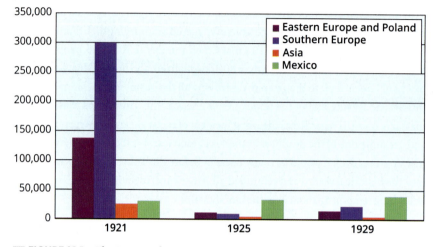

≡ **FIGURE 21.1**   **The Impact of Immigration Restrictions**   The Immigration Act of 1924 targeted specific ethnic groups, diminishing the overall number of immigrants, from 805,000 in 1921 to 280,000 in 1929.

countries (see Figure 21.1). As one might expect, the largest quotas were given to Germany, Britain, and Ireland; some of the smallest were allocated to the countries of southern and eastern Europe, effectively damming the migratory flood of previous decades. Immigration from Africa or the Middle East was, for all intents and purposes, closed off. The adjustments of wartime seem to have played an important role in passage of this legislation. Business interests had once strongly opposed immigration restriction, relishing the cheap labor supply to which they had access. But as they witnessed southern Black people migrating into the North, white women entering the labor force in growing numbers, and Mexicans who were not covered by the act fleeing the revolution at home (it would be the first substantial influx of Mexicans in United States history), their opposition ended. A new regime of border policing had begun.

21.7   Cultural Reaction

‖‖‖ Assess the cultural changes the war ushered in, including the backlash against the cultural currents of modernity.

With border policing came cultural policing. The mobilizations of the war decade weakened the progressive pulses of the 1890s and first decade of the twentieth century and placed new emphasis on conformity as well as political loyalty. The involvement of the United States in World War I encouraged some to think about and act upon ideas of "Americanness" that simultaneously promoted notions of a "melting pot" to absorb people from different ethnic and national backgrounds and suspicions of those who didn't appear to, or want to, assimilate. As a result, the late 1910s and early 1920s saw a number of attacks on the cultures of those who appeared threatening and on the projects of those who represented the spread of a disruptive and alien modernity.

Prohibition

Over the course of the nineteenth century, by far the largest popular movement in the United States was directed toward limiting or ending the sale and consumption of alcoholic beverages: temperance and prohibition. Beginning in the 1830s, and as we saw in Chapter 19, rejuvenated in the 1870s and 1880s, the movement blamed society's ills on the intoxicating influence of alcohol, and associated drink with impoverished families, abusive husbands, and urban corruption. White women, mainly from the middle class, were especially prominent as organizers and agitators, and their targets were working-class saloons and the southern "dives" of "illiterate whites" and "negroes." "Alien illiterates rule our cities today," Frances Willard of the powerful Women's Christian Temperance Union asserted, "the saloon is their palace; the toddy stick their scepter." Like immigration restriction advocates, they linked class status, cultural orientation, and political subversion. "Anglo-Saxon civilization" appeared to be at stake.

Until the twentieth century, temperance and prohibition campaigns looked to state and local governments, which could either pass prohibitory legislation or permit counties and townships to enact what were known as "local-option" laws, deciding for themselves whether they would remain "wet" or go "dry." In this there was considerable success. By World War I perhaps half the population of the country lived in jurisdictions where some form of liquor restriction prevailed. The other half, many in large cities with substantial immigrant, working-class populations, had not been reached by temperance and prohibition—and were often strongly opposed—and temperance statutes themselves varied considerably from state to state and place to place.

By 1913, prohibition campaigners began to eye the federal government for a solution. There were several factors at work in this strategic shift. For one, Progressive reformers had embraced the government, at state and federal levels, as a means of solving the challenges of an increasingly urban and industrial order. For another, rural and small-town districts, where prohibition sentiment was strongest, still had a disproportionate share of power in Congress and state legislatures, at least until the 1920 census returns demanded significant reapportionment. (For the first time the 1920 census would show a majority of the population living in urban places.)

≡ **Drinkers in a New York Bar** New Yorkers gather for a late-night drink in 1919, minutes before a prohibition on alcohol went into effect. Although the Eighteenth Amendment did not come into force until 1920, by that time many Americans lived in areas that had imposed their own restrictions on alcohol consumption.

Now was clearly the time to strike, and strike they did. In December 1917, shortly after the US Congress declared war against Germany, it responded to the pressure applied by prohibition campaigners and passed the **Eighteenth Amendment** to the Constitution, prohibiting "the manufacture, sale, or transportation of intoxicating liquors within . . . the United States and all territory subject to the jurisdiction whereof." A sweeping and remarkable event it was: the first time the Constitution had ever been used to define appropriate cultural practices. The eighteenth was one of four amendments enacted in rapid succession. One (the Sixteenth Amendment) legalized a federal income tax; another (the Seventeenth Amendment) provided for the direct election of US senators. As we have seen, the last of them (the Nineteenth Amendment) established women's suffrage, and the timing was no coincidence. Many women's suffrage advocates also supported prohibition and one of their largest, best-organized foes was the liquor industry. While the Eighteenth Amendment needed to be ratified by the states before it could go into effect, that happened on January 16, 1919, and the country officially "went dry" on January 17, 1920.

Religious Fundamentalism and Evolution

The prohibition campaign was closely tied to evangelical Protestant churches, especially outside of the large industrial cities, and their triumph was emblematic of a new surge of religious fundamentalism across the country. In large part, this represented a cultural response to the great social changes reshaping American society and to the unfolding of modernity, which called many traditional relations and practices into question. Protestant religiosity was powerfully evident in the language of Populism as well as in the agrarian wing of the Democratic Party—remember

William Jennings Bryan's "cross of gold" speech—and, in fundamentalist form, it rejected the claims of science in favor of revealed biblical truth.

First and foremost, fundamentalists (the term derives from a 1915 Baptist text called *The Fundamentals*) believed in the validity of the Scripture, whether as to the virgin birth of Jesus, Christ's resurrection from the dead, the inevitability of his return to earth, or the authenticity of biblical miracles. Especially strong was fundamentalist belief in the creation story of Genesis and human descent from Adam and Eve.

Needless to say, religious fundamentalism ran up against the scientific idea of evolution, which found especially important expression in Charles Darwin's *On the Origin of Species* (1859) and had come to be an intellectual foundation of modernist thought and teaching. Indeed, for growing numbers of evangelical Christians, evolution was the embodiment of a rash of modern "isms," from urbanism and suffragism to socialism and mongrelism (race mixing), that threatened to destroy the world they knew and valued. And they used it as a vehicle to push back against the tide of change. By the mid-1920s, antievolution bills that outlawed the teaching of Darwin in the public schools were making their way through a number of state legislatures, for the most part in the South. One of them was the state legislature of Tennessee, which enacted what was known as the Butler Bill in 1925.

The Butler Bill passed by a wide margin in the Tennessee legislature and might have made but a small dent in the historical record were it not for the notice given it by the **American Civil Liberties Union (ACLU)**. Established in 1920 to protect those harassed by the government for their antiwar activities, the ACLU thought the antievolution bill an ugly attack on the First Amendment's protection of freedom of speech, as well as a violation of the rights of public-school teachers and the constitutional separation of church and state. The organization decided to make a test case and looked for a willing teacher to become the defendant in a lawsuit.

The ACLU found a volunteer in John T. Scopes, a native of Kentucky, who taught general science in the small, east Tennessee town of Dayton. Scopes may never have discussed Darwin in his classes, but he was willing to "admit" that he had in order to get the legal balls rolling. Called the "Darwin bootlegger," suggesting the cultural link between prohibition and antievolution, he was then arrested and put on trial. Still small-town news, so why did this case come to rivet the American public?

What changed everything were the nationally famous attorneys who would participate in the case on opposing sides. Scopes was defended by ACLU member Clarence Darrow, a political radical and labor lawyer who had represented Eugene V. Debs, the Western Federation of Miners, and the American Federation of Labor.

≡ **Anti-Evolution League** A book sale displaying texts from the Anti-Evolution League, a Christian organization that opposed teaching American students about evolution. Fundamentalist Christians objected to teaching anything that contradicted the biblical account of human creation.

He was a religious agnostic and known for his combative style in the courtroom. The plaintiff in the case, the state of Tennessee, managed to retain none other than William Jennings Bryan, several-times presidential candidate of the Democratic Party, hero to much of rural and small-town America, and a devout evangelical. With a population of fewer than 2,000, Dayton was now inundated with journalists and interested spectators who showed up in cars marked "Evolution Special" and "Monkeyland Bound." Indeed, *The State of Tennessee v. John Thomas Scopes* came to be known as the "**Scopes Monkey Trial**," dramatizing the question of whether humans descended from Adam and Eve or the "apes."

The trial lasted eight days, but its most memorable moments came on the seventh. On that day, Darrow decided to put Bryan himself on the stand and cross-examine him. Less interested in the particularities of the case than in attacking the precepts of fundamentalism, Darrow barraged Bryan with questions about the veracity of biblical stories and the relation of science and scripture. After two hours, Bryan was wilting and, in the eyes of many observers, was made the fool. But Bryan remained composed enough to proclaim that "the world shall know that these gentlemen have no other purpose than ridiculing every Christian who believes in the Bible." Darrow, in turn, shot back, that "we have the purpose of preventing bigots and ignoramuses from controlling the education of the United States and you know it."

Owing to the judge's ruling, the jury was not even present for the encounter between Darrow and Bryan and the testimony was expunged from the trial record. No matter. Darrow and the ACLU team didn't want to "win" in Dayton; indeed, they wanted to have Scopes convicted and use the conviction to appeal the decision and the constitutionality of the Butler Law to a higher court. That's what they got. The jury quickly found Scopes guilty; the judge fined him $100.

Like Woodrow Wilson before him, William Jennings Bryan immediately set out on a tour to defend what he had done at the trial, and, like Wilson before him, the trial and the tour exhausted Bryan's health. Within days he was dead. But if Darrow intended to strike a death blow to fundamentalism and the antievolution movement, he was not the winner either. The issue remained contested ground in state legislatures and the courts, and even the popular literature and films, like *Inherit the Wind* (1960), that celebrated the cosmopolitanism of Darrow and the parochialism of Bryan didn't clear the battlefield. Tennessee did not repeal the Butler Law until 1967, and the issue of evolution and creationism in the public schools continues to roil communities and the courts. That is to say, the Scopes trial may well have signaled the beginning rather than the end of a long struggle between science and scripture, state and church, modernity and its critics.

21.8 The Second Ku Klux Klan

III Discuss the rise and impact of the Second Ku Klux Klan.

Many of the currents of cultural and political reaction—anticommunist, antifeminist, prohibitionist, anti-immigrant, and fundamentalist—came together in the largest right-wing organization of the 1910s and 1920s, and perhaps in all of American history, the Ku Klux Klan. In some ways, it was a rebirth. As we saw in Chapter 16, the Klan was first born in the post-emancipation South and gained traction there with the advent of Black suffrage in 1867. Black political organizers and voters, Black churches and schools, and Republican Party leaders were targeted by paramilitary bands that were often reassembled Confederate army units. The damage was considerable to Black and white Republican lives and the party's prospects in the South during the early phases of Radical Reconstruction before the federal government succeeded in driving the Klan into inactivity with threats of arrest and imprisonment. Rifle clubs more directly attached to the Democratic Party stepped into the paramilitary space that the Klan had evacuated and, if anything, did an even more effective job of destroying Black and Republican political power. How could the Klan be born again and then attain such prominence?

Rebirth and Expansion

Although the Klan of the twentieth century harked back to its Reconstruction-era predecessor, it was, in many ways, a different and more far-reaching organization. Refounded in 1915 at Stone Mountain, on the outskirts of Atlanta, Georgia (not incidentally around the time that *Birth of a Nation* premiered in the city),

≡ **The Rebirth of the Klan**   *Left:* A group of hooded Ku Klux Klan members at a meeting in Seattle, Washington, in 1923. Committed to white supremacy, the Klan targeted Black Americans, as well as Jews, Catholics, and immigrants with harassment and violence. *Right:* Women dressed in the hoods and robes of the Ku Klux Klan march down Pennsylvania Avenue in Washington, DC, in 1925. The Klan went to great lengths to portray itself as a patriotic social organization, obscuring its violent, racist activities.

the "second" Ku Klux Klan devoted itself to white supremacy and 100 percent "Americanism." That is to say the Klan set as its enemies all those groups who were regarded as "un-American," as polluting American soil: Jews, Catholics, and immigrants as well as African Americans. For the Klan, true Americans were white, Protestant, and native-born. During the war years, Klan members did the dirty work of the Wilson administration and semiofficial organizations like the American Protective League in harassing draft dodgers, strikers, slackers, and prostitutes, and, on occasion, marching in a patriotic parade.

By the time the war ended, the Klan could claim only a few thousand members. But this changed dramatically during the early 1920s, owing in good part to women's suffrage, the upsurge in political radicalism, and, more than anything else, the advent of prohibition. Portraying itself as a fraternal organization, the Klan hired publicists, adopted business methods, and aligned with the movement to enact and enforce prohibition. Before long, the Klan's membership grew to the many thousands, eventually to several million, and established chapters in all parts of the United States, especially in the Midwest, Mid-Atlantic, and Far West. Many of the members were white men, often of the middle and lower-middle class, who worried about immigration, Black assertiveness, political dissent, and women's independence, and who saw themselves caught between the consolidation of large economic institutions on the one side and restive workers and poor folk on the other. They have been called "reactionary populists." But women joined the Klan, too, less as a rejection of feminism and new political rights than as a way to enforce the family obligations of their dissipated husbands.

Power and Vigilantism

The Klan, in relatively short order, became a major social and political movement. Although the standard gear was now white sheets and hoods, mythologized by Klan members as depictions of Confederate ghosts, which was not the case for the first Ku Klux Klan, the organization paraded brazenly in many cities and towns, including Washington, DC, and could count among its members and supporters mayors, state legislators, congressmen, and even a Supreme Court justice. The Klan held sway politically in Indiana and Oregon, helped lay the path for the Immigration Act of 1924, and cast a long shadow over the political process as far north as Michigan, as far west as California, and as far south as Alabama (see Map 21.6).

Yet, for all its insistence on being a fraternal association, likened to the Masons, the Elks and the Odd Fellows with which it often had connections, the Klan was also given over to vigilantism: night riding, floggings, and cross burnings, violent

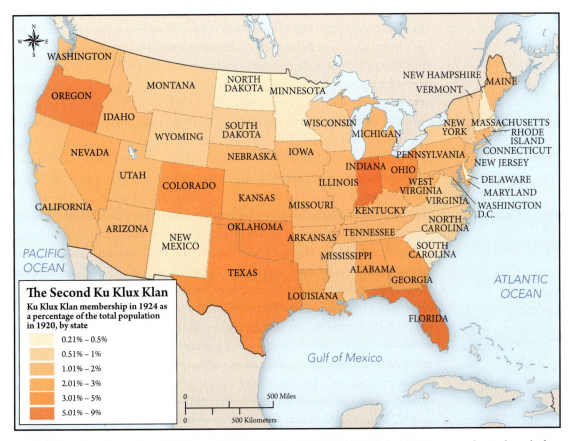

≡ **MAP 21.6   The Second Ku Klux Klan**   The Klan held sway politically in Indiana and Oregon, and cast a long shadow over the political process in states as varied as Michigan, California, and Alabama.

methods used to drive off undesirables, enforce the submission of inferiors, and consecrate the social and political rule of white, Protestant Americanism. They broke strikes, tarred and feathered moonshiners, whipped African Americans, and taunted Catholics; sometimes they engaged in lynchings. Calling themselves "wreckers," "night riders," and "gangs," their vigilante arms not only terrorized ethnic communities but also provoked pitched battles with their opponents. Some Klansmen spoke admiringly of Adolf Hitler in Germany and Benito Mussolini in Italy, emerging fascist leaders who extolled nationalism and racial purification. In many ways, the Klan did bear resemblance to fascist squads, to the Italian Black Shirts and German Brown Shirts, who believed that the road to power was paved with naked aggression and bloodshed, with the destruction of their enemies. It was a frightening and deeply troubling omen for American society.

Conclusion: A Postwar World

The eruption of World War I in 1914 was at once an ending to the Progressive era and a framing of the decades to come. Although President Wilson campaigned for reelection in 1916 on a platform of keeping the country out of the war, he quickly reversed his position and asked Congress for a war declaration and the resources for a wartime mobilization of people and resources. He also advanced a vision of a postwar world in which peace, stability, and popular self-determination would reign and new institutions like the League of Nations would be an international political mechanism. His idealism not only inspired some in the United States; it also inspired colonized people in many parts of the world who imagined Wilson and the United States as allies in their struggles against colonizers.

But Wilsonian idealism was not meant to be so inclusive, and he had a difficult time persuading many Europeans or most Americans of its wisdom. The League of Nations was established but it was toothless. Rather than a smooth road to a peaceful world order, World War I instead gave rise to revolutions in Russia and Mexico, radical movements in China, North Africa, and the United States, and significant demographic changes in the United States—especially the Great Migration—which would transform the racial dynamics and political landscape of the country. World War I and its aftermath also saw a reactionary backlash in politics and culture with new immigration restrictions and intensified hostilities against African Americans, Catholics, and Jews. The Scopes trial in Tennessee saw the contrasting currents meet. They signaled a complex future.

WHAT IF Wilson's Vision of the Postwar World Had Been Realized?

The decade of the 1910s was a time when the world of the nineteenth century seemed to crumble and the future seemed to hang in the balance, when new ideas and possibilities were articulated, and a global idealism could be envisioned. It was a time when the United States first exercised direct leadership in a global context and drew upon some of its most deeply laid principles to imagine a new, and perhaps more peaceful, order of things. The outcome was anything but idealism. Could it have been otherwise?

Historians have long debated this very question. Given the opportunities that World War I brought into being, at enormous cost, and then the dangerous turns that were in evidence during and after the Treaty of Versailles, was there a road to peace and collective security not taken? Without doubt, Wilson's idea of a "peace without victory" and his Fourteen Points imagined just such a world. And he had potential allies across the globe, especially among oppressed and colonized people whose hopes were raised by his rhetoric: in India, China, Vietnam, the Middle East, Africa, and Latin America. A true commitment to global self-determination on the part of the United States might have strengthened the position of progressive forces in many places, including the United States, and may have defanged right-wing movements that were on the rise during the 1920s. German, Italian, and Japanese aggression of the 1930s may then have been more difficult to mount. What were the circumstances that may have enabled such an outcome? And what circumstances stood in the way?

DOCUMENT 21.1: Petition of Vietnamese Nationalists to President Wilson (1919)

During the Peace Conference at Versailles, a group of Vietnamese nationalists led by Ho Chi Minh submitted this petition or set of demands to President Wilson in hopes of making him an ally in their cause.

Since the victory of the Allies, all subject peoples are filled with hope at the prospect that an era of right and justice is opening to them by virtue of the formal and solemn engagements, made before the whole world by the various powers of the agreement in the struggle of civilization against barbarism.

While waiting for the principle of national self-determination to pass from ideal to reality through the effective recognition of the sacred right of all peoples to decide their own destiny, the inhabitants of the ancient Empire of Annam, at the present time French Indochina, present to the noble Governments of the entente in general and in particular to the honorable French Government the following humble claims:

(1) General amnesty for all the native people who have been condemned for political activity;

(2) Reform of Indochinese justice by granting to the native population the same judicial guarantees as the Europeans have, and the total suppression of the special courts which are the

instruments of terrorization and oppression against the most responsible elements of the Vietnamese people;

(3) Freedom of press and speech;

(4) Freedom of association and assembly;

(5) Freedom to emigrate and to travel abroad;

(6) Freedom of education, and creation in every province of technical and professional schools for the native population;

(7) Replacement of the regime of arbitrary decrees by a regime of law;

(8) A permanent delegation of native people elected to attend the French parliament in order to keep the latter informed of their needs;

The Vietnamese people, in presenting these claims, count on the worldwide justice of all the Powers, and rely in particular on the goodwill of the noble French people who hold our destiny in their hands and who, as France is a republic, have taken us under their protection.

For the group of Vietnamese Patriots

Nguyen Ai Quoc

(Ho Chi Minh)

Source: Nguyen Ai Quoc to Robert Lansing, June 18, 1919, Records of the American Commission to Negotiate Peace, docsteach.org

DOCUMENT 21.2: Excerpts from President Wilson's Fourteen Points (1918)

In a speech to Congress on January 8, 1918, President Wilson set out his vision for a peace and the world that would be shaped by it.

It will be our wish and purpose that the processes of peace, when they are begun, shall be absolutely open and that they shall involve and permit henceforth no secret understandings of any kind. The day of conquest and aggrandizement is gone by; so is also the day of secret covenants entered into in the interest of particular governments and likely at some unlooked-for moment to upset the peace of the world. . .

We entered this war because violations of right had occurred which touched us to the quick and made the life of our own people impossible unless they were corrected and the world secure once for all against their recurrence. What we demand in this war, therefore, is nothing peculiar to ourselves. It is that the world be made fit and safe to live in; and particularly that it be made safe for every peace-loving nation which, like our own, wishes to live its own life, determine its own institutions, be assured of justice and fair dealing by the other peoples of the world as against force and selfish aggression. The program of the world's peace, therefore, is our program; and that program, the only possible program, as we see it, is this:

I. Open covenants of peace, openly arrived at, after which there shall be no private international understandings of any kind but diplomacy shall proceed always frankly and in the public view.

II. Absolute freedom of navigation upon the seas, outside territorial waters, alike in peace and in war.

III. The removal, so far as possible, of all economic barriers and the establishment of an equality of trade conditions among all the nations consenting to the peace and associating themselves for its maintenance.

IV. Adequate guarantees given and taken that national armaments will be reduced to the lowest point consistent with domestic safety.

V. A free, open-minded, and absolutely impartial adjustment of all colonial claims, based upon a strict observance of the principle that in determining all such questions of sovereignty the interests of the populations concerned must have equal weight with the equitable claims of the government whose title is to be determined.

VI. The evacuation of all Russian territory and such a settlement of all questions affecting Russia as will secure the best and freest cooperation of the other nations of the world in obtaining for her an unhampered and unembarrassed opportunity for the independent determination of her own political development.

VII. Belgium, the whole world will agree, must be evacuated and restored, without any attempt to limit the sovereignty which she enjoys in common with all other free nations.

VIII. All French territory should be freed and the invaded portions restored, and the wrong done to France by Prussia in 1871 in the matter of Alsace-Lorraine, which has unsettled the peace of the world for nearly fifty years, should be righted, in order that peace may once more be made secure in the interest of all.

IX. A readjustment of the frontiers of Italy should be effected along clearly recognizable lines of nationality.

X. The peoples of Austria-Hungary, whose place among the nations we wish to see safeguarded and assured, should be accorded the freest opportunity to autonomous development.

XI. Rumania, Serbia, and Montenegro should be evacuated; occupied territories restored; Serbia accorded free and secure access to the sea; and the relations of the several Balkan states to one another determined by friendly counsel along historically established lines of allegiance and nationality;

XII. The Turkish portion of the present Ottoman Empire should be assured a secure sovereignty, but the other nationalities which are now under Turkish rule should be assured an undoubted security of life and an absolutely unmolested opportunity of autonomous development.

XIII. An independent Polish state should be erected which should include the territories inhabited by indisputably Polish populations, which should be assured a free and secure access to the sea, and whose political and economic independence and territorial integrity should be guaranteed by international covenant.

XIV. A general association of nations must be formed under specific covenants for the purpose of affording mutual guarantees of political independence and territorial integrity to great and small states alike.

In regard to these essential rectifications of wrong and assertions of right we feel ourselves to be intimate partners of all the governments and peoples associated together against the Imperialists. We cannot be separated in interest or divided in purpose. We stand together until the end.

Source: National Archives.

Thinking About Contingency

1. Did the American response to the nationalist movements in Cuba and the Philippines set the stage for the American response to anticolonial movements after World War I?

2. Could Americans who opposed the League of Nations have been persuaded to support, in some way, anticolonial movements of the post–World War I era?

3. What if Ho Chi Minh and other anticolonial leaders had not looked to the United States as a political example?

4. Would the embrace of at least some anticolonial movements have made it much less likely that the United States would later become involved in the Vietnam War?

REVIEW QUESTIONS

1. What sort of world did Woodrow Wilson envision once World War I ended and what place would the United States occupy in it?

2. In principle, World War I ended with an armistice, but in the Treaty drawn up at Versailles, who were regarded as the winners and who the losers, and what was the price that the losers had to pay?

3. What sort of changes in the political world of Europe and the Middle East did World War I bring about?

4. What were the goals of the revolutionaries in Mexico, and how did their revolution influence the United States?

5. What were the factors that led to the Great Migration, and how did the Great Migration reshape African American communities and American society at large?

6. How did prohibition reflect the conservative reaction of the post–World War I years, and what was its relation to Protestant fundamentalism?

7. What were the goals of the Second Ku Klux Klan, and how influential did it become?

KEY TERMS

1918–1921 influenza pandemic (p. 887)

Allied Powers (p. 885)

American Civil Liberties Union (ACLU) (p. 907)

American Expeditionary Forces (p. 881)

Bolsheviks (p. 884)

Central Powers (p. 874)

Committee on Public Information (CPI) (p. 881)

Eighteenth Amendment (p. 906)

Espionage (1917) and Sedition Acts (1918) (p. 884)

Fourteen Points (p. 879)

Great Migration (p. 896)

Harlem Renaissance (p. 898)

Immigration Act of 1924 (p. 903)

Jazz Age (p. 898)

League of Nations (p. 890)

Lusitania (p. 878)

Nineteenth Amendment (p. 893)

Palmer Raids (p. 900)

"peace without victory" (p. 874)

Red Scare (p. 900)

"Red Summer" (p. 900)

Scopes Monkey Trial (p. 908)

self-determination (p. 879)

Treaty of Versailles (p. 890)

Triple Entente (p. 874)

Tulsa Race Massacre (p. 903)

Universal Negro Improvement Association (UNIA) (p. 898)

War Industries Board (p. 880)

Zimmermann telegram (p. 878)

RECOMMENDED READINGS

Linda Gordon, *The Second Coming of the Ku Klux Klan: The Ku Klux Klan of the 1920s and the American Political Tradition* (Liveright, 2018).

James Grossman, *Land of Hope: Chicago, Black Southerners, and the Great Migration* (Chicago, University of Chicago Press, 1991).

Adam Hochschild, *American Midnight: A Great War, a Violent Peace, and Democracy's Forgotten Crisis* (Mariner, 2022).

Friedrich Katz, *The Secret War in Mexico: The United States, Europe, and the Mexican Revolution* (University of Chicago Press, 1981).

Michael Kazin, *War Against War: The American Fight for Peace, 1914–1918* (Simon and Schuster, 2017).

David Kennedy, *Over Here: The First World War and American Society* (Oxford University Press, 2004).

Erez Manela, *The Wilsonian Moment: Self-Determination and the International Origins of Anticolonial Nationalism* (Oxford University Press, 2009).

Lisa McGirr, *The War on Alcohol: Prohibition and the Rise of the American State* (W.W. Norton, 2019).

Cameron McWhirter, *Red Summer: The Summer of 1919 and the Awakening of Black America* (St. Martin's, 2012).

Isabel Wilkerson, *The Warmth of Other Suns: The Epic Story of America's Great Migration* (Vintage, 2011).

Looking into the Abyss
1920–1934

Chapter Outline

≡ **A Turning Point**   President Franklin Roosevelt delivers a radio address in 1933 about his administration's response to the Great Depression. Known as "Fireside Chats," Roosevelt often used evening radio broadcasts to explain to everyday citizens his plans to revitalize the American economy.

In the depths of what came to be called the "Great Depression" of the 1930s, a twelve-year-old boy living somewhere in Illinois sat down to write a letter to Franklin D. Roosevelt, recently elected president of the United States. Although the boy didn't sign his name, he wished to tell Roosevelt about the suffering of his family. "My father hasn't worked for 5 months," he wrote, and although he went "plenty times" to the relief office, "they won't give us anything." Their rent hadn't been paid for four months and when the landlord came by to collect it, almost on a daily basis, "we won't open the door for him afraid that [we'll] be put out." In fact, the family had been "put out before," and the young boy didn't "want [it] to happen again." The gas, electric, and grocery bills hadn't been paid for months, and his eighteen-year-old brother hadn't gone to school "for two weeks because he got no carfare." His sister, twenty years of age, had not been able to find work, and his father was left to staying at home, "crying all the time," because he couldn't find work either. When the son asked, "Why are you crying?" the father replied, "Why shouldn't I cry when there is nothing in the house."

Timeline

1920	1921	1922	1923	1924	1925	1926	1927	1928

1920 > Republican Warren G. Harding elected president

1920–1921 > Sharp recession following end of World War I, with greatest effect in rural America

1922 > Benito Mussolini's Fascist Party takes power in Italy

1923 > Harding dies in office; succeeded by Vice President Calvin Coolidge

1924 > Calvin Coolidge elected president

1925 > Adolf Hitler publishes *Mein Kampf*; first indications that American economic growth may be slowing

1928 > Herbert Hoover elected president

So the next morning, the boy sat down to write the president, wondering desperately "why they don't help us."

There is no record of President Roosevelt replying to this letter, though it was one of thousands that flooded the White House, from ordinary Americans coast to coast, explaining in vivid and painful language what they had been enduring and asking whether Roosevelt might offer them advice or help. The economic collapse occurred with such speed and reached such depth that even those Americans who were used to struggling to feed and clothe themselves and their families were thrown onto charity that was no longer available. Those Americans who had prospered during the previous decade were often thrown back on resources that had evaporated; some lost everything and were simply bewildered and terrified.

Before long, more than a quarter of the American labor force was unemployed—and these are the "official" figures—while many more saw their paychecks shrink and

| 1929 | 1930 | 1931 | 1932 | 1933 | 1934 | 1935 | 1936 | 1937 |

1929 >
September Beginning of stock market crash

1932 > Franklin D. Roosevelt elected president

1933 >
January Adolf Hitler comes to power in Germany
March Roosevelt inaugurated; begins Hundred Days of New Deal

1934 > Opposition to New Deal mounts on populist left and on the right

opportunities whittled down. Banks closed their doors, savings evaporated, soup lines stretched across the urban landscape. Before long, an "army" of the unemployed descended on Washington, DC. And government—at all levels—was ill-prepared to fill the breach. The Republican Party, which had dominated the federal government, danced to the rhythm of the nation's business interests and imagined the precipitous downturn as a particularly severe episode of market cycles that would soon be righted. Direct interventions in the economy to stimulate production, employment, and demand, they believed, would only make matters worse.

The **Great Depression** was by no means just an American experience. No part of the globe escaped its effects, and some parts spiraled even further downward into economic chaos. Europe, and especially continental Europe, was especially hard hit with the depression coming so quickly on the heels of World War I. Indeed, the Great Depression demonstrated how vast and interconnected the capitalist economy had become. It was a true "world system," exploiting the natural and extractive resources of some areas (Africa, Asia, Latin America) and manufacturing them in others (North America and Europe), financed and distributed by banks and investment houses that knew no borders. But there were no political institutions that had such reach—the League of Nations had already proved useless even as a means of mediating international disputes—and so a "global" economic crisis would have to be resolved on "national" bases. Enormous changes in governance would be the order of the day, and the prospects were potentially chilling. The world seemed to come to a turning point. No one was sure which way it would turn, but for many who felt the ripple effects of warfare, the horizon seemed especially dark.

22.1   How "Roaring" Were the Twenties?

||| Evaluate the nature and limits of the economic boom of the 1920s.

For all of the political and racial turmoil it unleashed, World War I also gave way to a time of economic prosperity and a new consumer culture that brought many Americans within its grasp. There were several causes. In part, it was "pent-up demand," resulting from the material scarcities that wartime imposed. In part, it was the drastic lowering of tax rates on the well-to-do that refilled their coffers. In part, it was technological innovation that brought radios, phonographs, and automobiles into the marketplace. And, in part, it was the emergence of the United States as a creditor nation, now becoming a banker to the world. The images we have of what were called the "roaring twenties" are of lavish parties of F. Scott Fitzgerald's *Great Gatsby*, vibrant youth culture, electrifying jazz bands, pulsating cities filled with recent immigrants from abroad and migrants from the countryside, and a robust stock market heading ever upward. More Americans now lived in urban areas than in rural areas, and more were now employed off the farm than on it. The United States appeared to be a truly urban and industrial society, and a modern one in its tastes and sensibilities.

Drivers of the Economic Boom

After a serious but brief recession at the beginning of the decade, the twenties saw impressive economic growth. Led by the chemical, steel, electrical, and automotive industries, and by the further implementation of scientific management techniques, the mass production of goods became a basic feature of American life. The Gross National Product, a measure of the output of goods and services, grew at an average annual rate of over 4 percent (almost twice what we generally experience today), and the labor force increased more rapidly than the population at large (see Figure 22.1). Although labor unions had been weakened by the Red Scare and the postwar backlash of employers, for a time in the 1920s the real wages of workers increased (meaning their pay rose faster than the cost of living) while their hours on the job decreased. The skilled and semiskilled among them now might have more

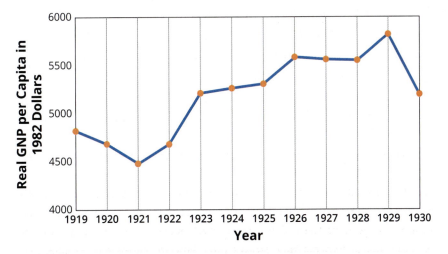

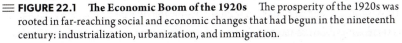

FIGURE 22.1   The Economic Boom of the 1920s   The prosperity of the 1920s was rooted in far-reaching social and economic changes that had begun in the nineteenth century: industrialization, urbanization, and immigration.

time for themselves and their families, and more disposable income for household purchases and recreation.

More and more Americans could shop in department stores, buy radios, and attend new forms of entertainment, none more popular than motion pictures, which made the transition from "silent" films to "talkies" before the end of the decade. Indeed, by the middle of the 1920s, movie theaters were selling 50 million tickets *per week* (the entire population of the United States was only 115 million)! Even automobiles, once regarded as a luxury item, were within reach for many more people, as automakers like Henry Ford implemented assembly lines and looked to mass-produce automobiles that many Americans could afford. By the time the decade was out, about half of all families in the country owned one.

Much of the fuel for the increased consumption came from new sources of credit. To be sure, credit itself was always a part of the exchange economy. Well before the advent of industrialization, farmers and artisans bartered goods and labor or agreed to settle accounts when crops were sold and cash was available; personal debts could run for months or years. Local merchants might establish cash and credit prices for their supplies, and all sorts of people "borrowed" from creditors, sometimes at high rates of interest and sometimes not.

But during the 1910s and especially the 1920s, growing numbers of retailers—many of them new "chain stores" that were spreading across urban America—encouraged customers to make "down payments" on costly appliances like stoves and refrigerators, and pay them off on monthly "installment plans." Automobile companies like Ford and General Motors pioneered in this practice, expanding the market for the cars now rolling off their assembly lines by the thousands. It seemed a solution to the potential crisis of mass production (too many goods, too few buyers): the combination of readily available credit and multimedia advertising—General Motors alone spent millions on advertising in the 1920s—would promote mass consumption, stimulating new desires and drawing workers and ethnic communities into a common commodity culture.

Trouble Under the Radar

But the "roaring" prosperity that this suggested was often more apparent than real. Although several billion dollars' worth of retail goods were being purchased on credit or installment each year, by the mid-1920s, most of the customers, especially for the bigger ticket items, were from middle and upper classes. They were people who had secure, salaried or profit-earning positions and could feel confident in their future economic prospects. Industrial workers, even those with skills, did not quite share in the boom times. While their real wages may have been rising, unemployment and underemployment remained nagging problems and lent caution to their outlooks.

Indeed, the uncertainty of employment most clearly distinguished the experiences of working people from those of the middle class. Almost invariably, workers who were employed faced weeks or months of "seasonal" unemployment: times during the year when the shop or factory closed up because supplies were interrupted or the market slackened. Relatively few of them took advantage of installment buying or acquired the appliances offered up; they preferred to pay cash or, if they used credit, it was for smaller ticket items like phonographs or radios. The wealth that was being generated during the 1920s did boost the living standards of those in the bottom half of urban America, but it went disproportionately to those in the top quarter, and especially in the top tenth. The distribution of wealth during the "roaring twenties" became more, not less, skewed (see Figure 22.2).

If the prosperity of the 1920s was unequally distributed in the cities of the United States, it was nowhere to be seen in the countryside. Farmers had en-

FREEDOM *for the woman who owns a Ford*   To own a Ford car is to be free to venture into new and untried places. It is to answer every challenge of Nature's charms, safely, surely and without fatigue. ¶ Where a narrow lane invites or a steep hill promises a surprise beyond, a Ford will take you there and back, in comfort, trouble-free. ¶ Off and away in this obedient, ever-ready car, women may "recharge the batteries" of tired bodies, newly inspired for the day's work   FORD MOTOR COMPANY, DETROIT, MICHIGAN

≡ **"Freedom for the Woman Who Owns a Ford"**   Automobile companies used new payment options and advertising to lure new customers in the 1920s. Advertisements like this one sought to appeal to a new generation of affluent, independent women who pushed the bounds of male-dominated American society. Ford suggested that the "New Woman" use an automobile to explore the world on her own terms.

joyed high commodity prices during the war years, and the first two decades of the twentieth century in general brought greater incomes and more secure tenures. It was a genuine turnaround from the deteriorating conditions of the 1870s, 1880s, and 1890s that had given rise to the Farmers' Alliance and Populism (see Chapter 18).

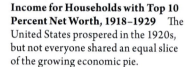

≡ **FIGURE 22.2   Share of National Income for Households with Top 10 Percent Net Worth, 1918–1929**   The United States prospered in the 1920s, but not everyone shared an equal slice of the growing economic pie.

But a steep recession hit in 1920. While urban America quickly sprang back, there was no such recovery in agricultural America. The problems of overproduction reasserted themselves—huge crop surpluses piled up—and, as a result, the prices of major agricultural commodities like corn, wheat, and cotton fell dramatically. Cotton declined from a high of 35 cents a pound to 16 cents a pound; corn dropped from $1.50 to 52 cents a bushel. Farm owners went bankrupt or slid into tenancy, while their children joined the migration to the cities.

Nowhere were the consequences greater than in the South. During the 1920s, the South, easily the most rural region of the United States, was beset by a host of calamities. The collapse of the cotton economy struck blows to white and Black people alike, bringing to an end a period when some African Americans had managed to climb into landownership from the thralls of tenancy and sharecropping, and the wages of laboring folk had crept upward. Hard times and deprivation spread from the cotton fields of the Deep South to the textile mills of the piedmont, and then to the coal mines of Appalachia.

If this wasn't enough, drought in the Southeast, floods in the Mississippi Valley, and the last inroads of the boll weevil (an insect that had been destroying the cotton crop since the turn of the twentieth century) seemed to make the devastation almost biblical in its proportions. Small wonder the Great Migration (discussed in Chapter 21) continued through the 1920s, bringing humble white as well as Black people to the industrial cities of the North. Even so, well over half of the population of the South still lived in the countryside and worked on the land, and, for the country as a whole, despite the pace of urbanization, nearly half the population continued to reside outside of the country's cities and towns and faced challenges not yet known to their urban counterparts.

This is to say that while the economic roar of the "roaring twenties" was for real, it was incomplete and uneven, and rested on shaky foundations. The middle and upper classes seemed well positioned. They saw rising incomes and profits, and could indulge in greater consumption, though their debts had also been growing—sometimes much faster than their savings—and more than a few were risking their assets in the stock market. Urban workers had to tread carefully because regular wages could not be assured, and businesses were quick to trim their payrolls at the first sign of an economic downturn. Many workers and their families could enjoy new forms of recreation and participate more fully in the new consumer economy, but very few managed to save enough to tide them over during a period of hard times. As for farm owners and farm laborers, not to mention the merchants who served them, economic conditions had been going from difficult to dire. It was a worrisome mix, especially because conditions abroad were even more troubling.

22.2 The Great Crash and the Great Depression

Explain how and why the stock market crashed and led to an economic depression.

Never in the course of American history has there been a shock to the economic system quite like the stock market "crash" of 1929 and the economic depression that followed in its wake. The panics of 1819, 1837, 1873, and 1893 were severe and the recessions and depressions they ushered in serious. The downturns of 1907 and 1920 were sudden jolts to the economy and, to some extent,

≡ **Rural Life and City Life** This cartoon, published in *The Chicago Tribune* in 1921, contrasts the relationship between farmers and city dwellers in the 1820s (*left*) and the 1920s (*right*). While the broad shoulders of the farmer of the 1820s can easily support the city gentleman, his counterpart in the 1920s strains to support the urban giant.

signaled underlying economic weaknesses. But none of these led to the losses in wealth, the scale of unemployment, the extent of deprivation, or the duration of distress that was true of the Great Crash and Great Depression. In many ways, they became defining events of the first half of the twentieth century and framed debates over economic policies for the second half.

The Stock Market Crash

Although in telling the story of the great stock market crash, we tend to pinpoint a particular day in October—October 29, "Black Tuesday" is the customary choice—when it happened, the crash in fact took place over the course of about

MAPPING AMERICA

The Mass Culture of the 1920s

By the 1920s, broad changes in American life marked the emergence of a mass, predominantly urban culture that was significantly different from its nineteenth-century predecessor. Automobiles, movies, radios, telephones, magazines, brand names, and chain stores bound Americans together in an interlocking web of shared national experience, as did a new emphasis on consumption.

Women were at the center of many of these broader developments. With her bobbed hair, and slim, boyish figure (achieved by the new fad of dieting) the **flapper** symbolized the personal freedom trumpeted by the emerging mass culture. Hollywood actresses such as Clara Bow, Gloria Swanson, and Mary Pickford were some of best known public figures of the era.

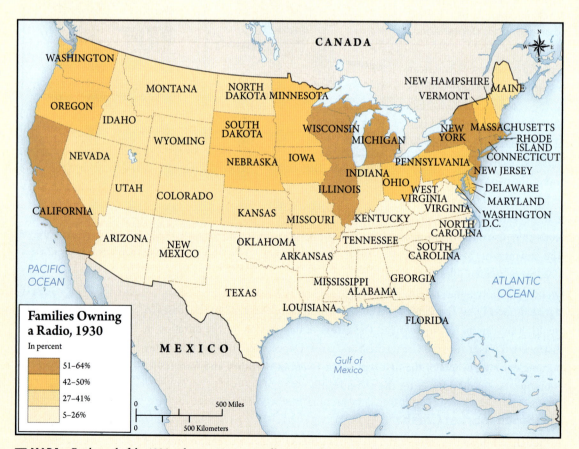

Families Owning a Radio, 1930

In percent

- 51–64%
- 42–50%
- 27–41%
- 5–26%

MAP 1   By the end of the 1920s, close to 50 percent of homes in the United States owned a radio, and the American electronics industry had manufactured nearly 200 million units. In 1921, there were just six radio stations in the entire country. By 1930, there were over six hundred stations broadcasting news and entertainment programs.

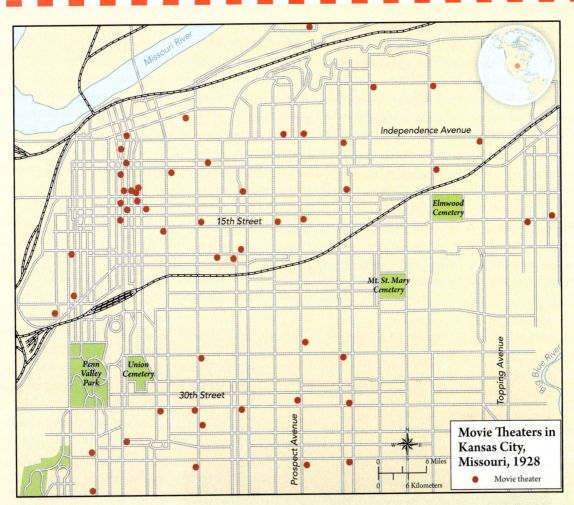

Movie Theaters in Kansas City, Missouri, 1928
● Movie theater

≡ **MAP 2**   During the 1920s, movies developed into a major entertainment medium. Dazzling movie palaces drew huge audiences, particularly after "talking pictures" were introduced in 1927 with the premier of *The Jazz Singer*. By 1930, on average, close to ninety million Americans went to the movies each week, about 70 percent of the population of the entire country. The impact of movies at the local level can be seen in this map of Kansas City, Missouri. In 1928, Kansas City, with a population of about 350,000, had more than fifty downtown theaters.

Thinking Geographically

1. Even more than the automobile, the radio was the most sought-after consumer product of the 1920s. But the distribution of households that owned a radio was uneven. Why do you think some regions of the country had lower ownership rates than others? How does this reflect a growing rural-urban divide?

2. By the end of the 1920s, the film industry had become the fifth largest in the country. About 800 films were produced each year (almost twice as many as the number of films released in 2022). How does this data inform the way you interpret Map 2? Would maps that showed theaters in other US cities in 1928 look similar to Map 2?

two months, from early September to mid-November 1929 when the stock market lost nearly 50 percent of its value (comparable to a drop in the Dow Jones index of about 17,000 points today).

What does this mean? The stock market was based in New York City (as it still is) and was essentially a clearinghouse for the trade in company assets or "shares." When companies wanted to raise money, they might sell shares, meaning pieces of the company, there. The shares would initially be priced roughly according to the value of the company, and then traders would bid on the shares, depending on their view of the company's prospects, pushing the share prices either up or down. If traders were optimistic about a company's likely earnings, they would bid the share price up and everyone who owned shares in the company would benefit by seeing the value of their shares rise. If traders had doubts about the company, they might look to sell their shares and the share price would fall. So long as the overall share price did not deviate too much from the company's value, there was no special problem.

But the stock market was, and is, a speculative institution. Traders (shareholders/investors) try to make money by speculating, or guessing, about whether share prices will go up or down. During the 1920s, because the economy seemed robust, traders were bidding up the prices of many stocks and, at least on paper, boosting the value of their holdings. In the second half of the decade, the speculative fever spread so fast that share prices were often far in excess of what companies might be worth. As long as business was good and likely to get better, this wasn't necessarily problematic; but if traders got nervous or pessimistic, they would start to sell their stocks and prices might then drop quickly and steeply.

There were several warning signs after 1925. Consumer demand seemed to slow and major industries, like automobiles, began to cut their output along with it. Corporate earnings leveled off or began to decline and business inventories grew larger, suggesting that they were unable to sell all of what they were producing. A

≡ **The Trading Floor of the New York Stock Exchange**　Imagining that all was well in the economy and intent on pushing their share prices further upward, investors borrowed money to buy stocks, figuring that there would be no difficulty in paying the loans back.

real estate boom in Florida went bust after a devastating hurricane in 1928. The construction industry was increasingly lackluster. Unemployment grew. But the frenzy on Wall Street accelerated in what President Herbert Hoover, elected in 1928, described as an "orgy of speculation." Imagining that all was well in the economy and intent on pushing their share prices further upward, investors borrowed money to buy stocks, figuring that there would be no difficulty in paying the loans back. Many bought the stocks on "margin," meaning that they only put down a portion of the share price, say 10 percent, and borrowed the rest from stockbrokers.

And then came the reckoning. In March 1929, the market indexes suddenly sank but soon recovered. Another boomlet followed in July and August. But in early September the alarm bells began to ring, and during the last week of October the stock market collapsed. Millions of shares were traded, far more than ever before, and the value of shares evaporated. Billions of dollars were lost and, because of margin buying, banks and brokerage houses had to call in their loans. It was a domino effect of disaster, and although economists and politicians predicted a rapid turnaround, the slide continued. Manufacturers cut production and laid off workers, the currency supply contracted, prices along with wages fell, and the Gross National Product plummeted. Already by the summer of 1930, economic depression, not just recession, seemed to be settling in.

The Republican Response

The Republican Party controlled the national government at the time, as it had, with the exception of the Wilson years, since 1897 (effectively since 1861), and the recently inaugurated president, Herbert Hoover, seemed much readier for such a crisis than his two Republican predecessors. Warren G. Harding's administration was corruption-ridden (1921–1923), with the notorious Teapot Dome scandal, involving bribery to secure oil leases in the West, leaving an especially black mark. Calvin Coolidge (1923–1929), who became president when Harding died in office, was the sort of milk-toast politician that the decade seemed to prefer.

Raised in Iowa and Oregon, Hoover had earned a degree in geology at Stanford University, amassed a fortune in the mining business, and won national and international acclaim as an administrator and humanitarian during World War I for the relief efforts he organized in Belgium and his work in heading the US Food Administration under President Woodrow Wilson. So impressive was Hoover's resume, that Wilson brought him along to the Versailles Peace Conference as an adviser before Hoover went on to help in reconstructing the shattered European economies. Progressive Democrats and Republicans alike lured Hoover to their party (he had remained aloof from them up until that time), and when he chose the Republican Party, he was quickly offered a place in President Harding's cabinet as secretary of commerce, which he occupied during both the Harding and Coolidge administrations.

Hoover had surely learned many lessons about the value of cooperation, efficiency, and centralized management, and he surely had come to recognize that there were tasks in modern society that private interests alone would be unable to carry out. He had, in fact, written a book about the mining industry that called for collective bargaining, an eight-hour workday, and mine-safety precautions. But he was also a great believer in individualism and service (he was brought up a Quaker), and he imagined something of a public-spirited society in which the government could play a coordinating role. Voluntarism, not government interventionism, was his ideal, and sound economics were his means.

Unfortunately, the remedies Hoover initially envisioned were simply not up to the task. He tried to work with business leaders to maintain employment and wages, backed agricultural price supports through a new Federal Farm Board, encouraged the Federal Reserve to prevent a deflationary spiral, and agreed to sign the highly protectionist **Smoot-Hawley Tariff** of 1930, designed to boost the prospects of domestic manufacturers and farmers. He also prodded railroad and utility companies, as well as local governments, to push ahead with infrastructure projects, directing some federal funds toward those ends. "I am convinced we have passed the worst and with continued effort we shall rapidly recover," he told the US Chamber of Commerce in May 1930.

But businesses continued to close up and workers continued to be laid off in greater and greater numbers. The official unemployment rate hit 16 percent in 1931 and was rising; a year later it was near 25 percent. Hoover decided to raise taxes in an attempt to balance the federal budget, hardly a sensible move under the circumstances, and the economic free fall continued. Finally, Hoover shifted course and looked to use the federal government to help stimulate investment, increase the flow of cash, protect home ownership, and provide relief to the millions of needy. Most noteworthy was the **Reconstruction Finance Corporation** (1932), designed to make loans available to hard-strapped banks and other businesses. But time was running out and Hoover had no more cards left to deal.

Bread Line   Unemployed men wait in a bread line in San Francisco, hoping to receive free food. By 1932 a quarter of the American workforce was unemployed and many men who had worked their whole lives were forced to rely on charity to feed their families.

22.3 Challenges of Governance in Europe

||| Discuss how the crises of the 1920s and early 1930s led to authoritarian political solutions in many European countries.

Nations across the Atlantic world, and especially in Europe, had been facing serious economic problems since the end of World War I, both because of war-imposed reparations and because the prewar financial system had been destabilized. While the United States was experiencing an economic boom in the 1920s, elsewhere the decade was characterized by spiraling inflation, growing unemployment, nationalist economic policies, and intensifying social conflict. It seemed, in short, that the dream of peace and stability meant to follow the catastrophe of World War I was turning into a nightmare that could haunt the world again.

The Rise of Fascism

Germany was particularly hard hit. The allies, especially the French, wanted to punish the Germans for bringing on the war and to make sure that Germany would not again be a military threat on the continent. But the reparations payments that Germany was required to make were so large that they shook the foundations of the parliamentary regime established in 1919, known as the **Weimar Republic**, and created turmoil for the next decade and a half.

There was a growing sense there, and in much of the European continent, that the liberalism and internationalism of the nineteenth century were spent forces, that parliamentary governments were weak and politically ineffective, and that democratic methods brought conflict rather than cooperation. Some intellectuals and new political leaders began to speak of the need for a different kind of power and a different sort of purpose. They heralded militarism instead of diplomacy, the superiority of the nation and the cultures tied to it, the mobilization of the "masses" against enemies internal and external, the imposition of order against social unrest, and the organization of society through authoritarian means. The political consequences showed up most consequentially in Italy and Germany.

Italy had been allied with Britain, France, and Russia during World War I and therefore was not subject to reparations or other consequences of defeat. But the country did suffer from economic distress and political unrest, and the parliamentary government seemed unable to resolve a deepening crisis. Socialists had been an important force in Italy since the late nineteenth century, and after the Russian Revolution an Italian Communist Party (PCI) was organized. Once the war ended, the PCI in alliance with a powerful trade union movement engaged in massive strikes in the industrial north of the country and took control of the factories in the city of Turin. It appeared that the revolutionary spirit that had overturned the Tsarist regime in Russia was spreading rapidly beyond Russia's borders.

With Italian elites in near panic, the road was paved for the emergence of a new political leader and political movement. His name was Benito Mussolini and, although once a socialist, he now headed up what he called the **Fascist Party**. Mobilizing disgruntled war veterans, vilifying the socialists and communists, and trading on the fears of big landowners and industrialists, Mussolini and his followers marched on Rome in 1922 and took the reins of power. Initially in broad coalition with three other parties including the Liberals, Mussolini had little but scorn for parliamentary methods and liberal ideology. He and the Fascists celebrated authoritarianism, discipline, and naked aggression. "Fascism," Mussolini crowed, "rejects in democracy the conventional lie of political equality, the spirit of collective irresponsibility and the myth of progress. . . . The present century is the century of authority, a century of the Right, a Fascist century." Using armed Fascist squads, known as Black Shirts, to crush his opponents, Mussolini soon created a one-party state under his direct control and, through it, took on the economic challenges that lay ahead. Some called it a "corporate state." He called himself "Il Duce" or "the leader."

Many of the same political currents were moving through a crisis-ridden Germany, though somewhat later than developments in Italy. In 1923, while Mussolini was already in power, an angry and restless German war veteran named Adolf Hitler organized what he called the **Nazi (National Socialist) Party,** and plotted a coup d'état in the Bavarian city of Munich. The plot was foiled and Hitler went to jail for eight months. There he began work on *Mein Kampf,* his anti-Semitic and anti-communist blueprint for Nazi rule, and mapped his own path to power.

The economic turmoil in Germany during the 1920s and then the onset of the Great Depression showed the weakness of the Weimar

≡ **Mussolini and the Black Shirts**   Benito Mussolini (*center*) poses with members of the fascist paramilitary gang known as the Black Shirts. Mussolini established fascist rule in Italy in a 1922 coup and then used the Black Shirts to violently suppress political dissent.

Republic and strengthened Hitler's hand. His Nazi Party, with its own paramilitary squads known as Brown Shirts, attracted thousands of new members; by the early 1930s the Nazis were edging toward a majority of seats in the Reichstag, the German parliament. In January 1933, the political threshold was crossed. Hitler was appointed the German chancellor (a position equivalent to a president or prime minister) and very quickly, much as Mussolini had done in Italy, turned Germany into a one-party state.

But Germany and Italy were not alone. Other authoritarian regimes took hold in Spain, after a brutal and bloody civil war during the 1930s, and in Greece, Austria, Japan, and Argentina. Much greater centralizations of power came to characterize regimes in Poland, Portugal, Yugoslavia, Bulgaria, Romania, Latvia, Estonia, and Hungary. The lights of political liberalism that still had been flickering in Europe and Asia at the end of World War I were now being steadily extinguished.

Illiberal Pulses in the United States

What would this tilt toward authoritarianism mean for the United States? As in Europe, reactionary politics had increased during the 1920s. There were the Red Scare and Palmer Raids, various forms of antimodernism, and the development of the Ku Klux Klan as a powerful force (see Chapter 21). Increasingly desperate about the economic deterioration all around them, a great many Americans seemed ready for a new departure. Some of the groundwork for a different order, one in which the federal government would play a more dynamic and organizational role, had been laid by the Populists in the 1890s, and then by Progressives in the 1900s and 1910s (see Chapters 18 and 19). Further experimentation had been taking place on the state and local levels. But could greater government authority and direction be compatible with a democracy?

Fears of democratic politics had been growing for a long time. Since the 1850s serious questions had been raised about whether political rights should be extended to a variety of social groups, almost all of whom were heavily represented among the working class: European immigrants, African Americans, and the Chinese. Disfranchisement campaigns abounded in all parts of the country and struck especially hard blows against Black people and poor white people in the South, though registration laws and residency requirements in the North and West served to whittle down the electorates there as well.

Some Progressives not only wished to empower the federal government to take a greater role in the regulation of the economy but also thought that governance was best served when it was in the hands of well-educated experts rather than the representatives of ordinary Americans, who seemed inclined to corrupt practices.

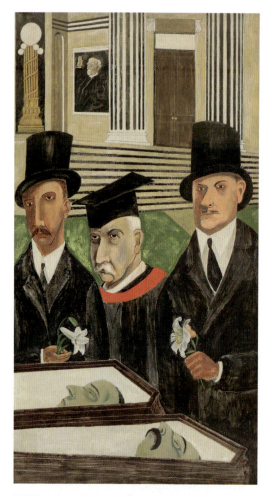

≡ **Martyrs**   A painting by American artist Ben Shahn showing the bodies of Italian anarchists Nicola Sacco and Bartolomeo Vanzetti and the commissioners who upheld their death sentence. For many Americans, their trial and execution symbolized ingrained American hostility toward foreigners.

Prohibition, the culmination of a near-century-long agitation of native-born Protestants, deployed the arms of the federal government to assault the cultural practices of working people across urban America, especially those who resided in immigrant communities and were not Protestant. In the late teens and 1920s, fears of political turmoil, in the United States and Europe, were mainly focused on the political left, on socialists, communists, and anarchists, who were seen as threats to the capitalist system and established order.

The experience of two Italian anarchists, Nicola Sacco and Bartolomeo Vanzetti, demonstrates how these fears could have lethal endings. Recent immigrants at a time of rising hostilities against them and political radicals at a time of crackdowns on dissent and an emerging Red Scare, both Sacco and Vanzetti were so vulnerable that they left the United States to avoid the World War I draft before returning. Then in the spring of 1920, they were arrested shortly after two employees of a shoe factory in Braintree, Massachusetts, were robbed of the company payroll and murdered. Although the evidence presented at their trial a year later was questionable and the judge in the case clearly biased against anarchists like them—he called them "long-haired anarchists" and "Bolsheviki"—the jury found them guilty.

Objections were quickly raised about the trial's procedures and the thinness of the evidence presented. Calls soon came for a retrial, not only from anarchists and other radicals but also from an assortment of luminaries who signed petitions in favor of one: Edna St. Vincent Millay, George Bernard Shaw, and Albert Einstein among them. Indeed, four years after their conviction, another man confessed to participating in the crime as part of a local gang. But it was all for naught. In April 1927, Sacco and Vanzetti were sentenced to death and, despite demonstrations on their behalf throughout the world, they were executed in August. It was another rush to judgment, fueled by war-inspired suspicions of immigrants and hatred of socialists and anarchists.

22.4   Making a "New Deal"

||| Describe how the Roosevelt administration constructed a New Deal and what it was meant to do.

As the crisis of the Great Depression gripped the country with no end in sight and ineffective political means were deployed to tame it, many Americans had a growing sense that the economic and political systems were collapsing and some sort of new departure would be necessary. But what might it entail? More than a few, including prominent intellectuals and journalists, thought a political strongman needed to be installed and a powerful top-down solution imposed. Those on the political left, socialists and communists, argued that capitalism was now in its predicted death throes, and a new social order had to be constructed, one that lent priority to the working class rather than those of wealth. The majority seems to have been losing faith in American institutions and was desperate for concerted action. Could political leaders and movements look to episodes in the past, or would something entirely new have to be devised? The national elections of 1932 presented opportunities for change but also the prospect of continued failure and crisis.

Franklin D. Roosevelt and the Election of 1932

Among those who looked to experiment with new approaches to government intervention was the governor of New York State, Franklin Delano Roosevelt. From an elite family and the cousin of former President Theodore Roosevelt, Franklin Roosevelt had acquired a great deal of experience in the world of politics and governance. Elected to a seat in the New York State Senate, appointed by Woodrow Wilson as an assistant secretary of the navy, nominated as the vice-presidential candidate by the Democrats in 1920, and then elevated to the governorship of New York in 1928, he had become a leading figure in the Democratic Party and was known as something of a reformer. He had campaigned against the corruption of New York City's Tammany Hall and, once the stock market crash deteriorated into economic depression, established a program of public relief in his state. "He believed that government not only could, but should achieve the subordination of private interests to collective interests," one of his advisors said of Roosevelt, and "substitute co-operation for the mad scramble of selfish individualism." He shared, that is, much of the outlook of Progressives, not least that of his relative Theodore.

That Franklin Roosevelt had a strong base of support in New York, the state with the largest population in the country at the time, made him an attractive candidate for the Democratic presidential nomination in 1932. And, despite challenges at the party's Chicago convention—it required two-thirds of the delegates' votes to win, a requirement that has since changed—Roosevelt claimed the prize on the fourth ballot and then broke precedent by flying into the city and accepting the nomination in person. It seemed a harbinger of things to come. The three previous national elections (1920, 1924, and 1928) had brought resounding victories to the Republicans, but this one was, more than anything else, a referendum on the response of Hoover and his party to the Great Depression.

They now took a thumping. Franklin Roosevelt won the presidency in a landslide, receiving nearly 60 percent of the popular vote and the electoral votes of forty-two of forty-eight states (see Map 22.1). The Democrats, in turn, swept the Republicans from national power, winning commanding majorities in both houses of Congress. It was the first time since 1876 that their presidential candidate had won a popular majority, and the first time since 1852 that he had won a majority of the popular and the electoral votes. After many decades of Republican rule—the Wilson administration being the chief exception since the Civil War—the Democrats were now in charge of the federal government. In his speech accepting the Democratic nomination for the presidency, Roosevelt had promised "a new deal for the American people."

What would such a "**New Deal**" be? The Democrats may have been on the verge of becoming a majority party in the country, but they were a bit of a motley crew with potentially deep divisions. On the one hand, in the North and West the Democrats were increasingly urban and progressive. They were constructing a coalition of European immigrants and their children, skilled and semiskilled workers, religious minorities (Catholics and Jews), and growing numbers of African Americans who

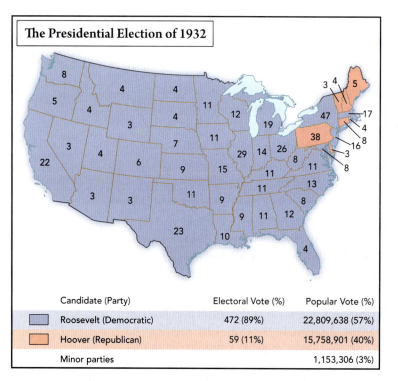

The Presidential Election of 1932

Candidate (Party)	Electoral Vote (%)	Popular Vote (%)
Roosevelt (Democratic)	472 (89%)	22,809,638 (57%)
Hoover (Republican)	59 (11%)	15,758,901 (40%)
Minor parties		1,153,306 (3%)

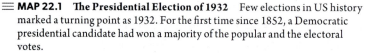

≡ **MAP 22.1** **The Presidential Election of 1932** Few elections in US history marked a turning point as 1932. For the first time since 1852, a Democratic presidential candidate had won a majority of the popular and the electoral votes.

had left the South for northern cities. On the other hand, a long-standing and rock-solid base of the party was in the southern states, and here the Democrats were mostly rural, conservative, native-born, and white. They were large and modest-sized land-owners, merchants, manufacturers in the piedmont, and the urban commercial and professional interests that attended to them. They were also committed defenders of white supremacy.

Although their numbers were declining relative to other parts of the country, southern Democrats enjoyed disproportionate power because Jim Crow–era disfranchisement pretty much destroyed the Republican Party in the South. White Democrats were therefore assured of election and reelection and so, in Congress, they achieved greater seniority than their counterparts in the North and West. This meant that they were in a position to chair the most important congressional committees, and block legislation or shape it to their liking. So, like their slaveholding counterparts of the antebellum period of the nineteenth century, this meant that their expectations and concerns would have to be addressed.

But the crisis facing the Democrats and the country was so serious that it not only promoted unity in Democratic ranks; it also raised the question of whether the president himself should take on "emergency powers." Although electoral means brought Roosevelt and his party into office, want and destitution were widespread, large-scale institutions were shaken to their core, the government seemed helpless, and civil unrest threatened. Even liberal intellectuals like Walter Lippman warned Roosevelt that "the situation requires strong medicine," and "you may have no alternative but to assume dictatorial powers." What would Roosevelt and his party do?

The First Hundred Days

Roosevelt used the occasion of his inaugural address in March 1933 less to enlarge his command of federal power than to calm the emotional waters. He didn't pull punches. He acknowledged the severity of the crisis and promised "action now," focused on getting people back to work. And he offered a steadiness of resolve. "Let me assert my firm belief," Roosevelt famously said, "that the only thing we have to fear is fear itself—nameless, unreasoning, unjustified terror which paralyzes needed effort to turn retreat into advance." Yet Roosevelt also maintained that if Congress faltered in its tasks and the "national emergency" remained "critical," "a temporary departure from that normal balance of public procedure" would be necessary. "I shall not evade the clear course of duty that will then confront me," he insisted. "I shall ask Congress for the one remaining instrument to meet the crisis—broad Executive power to wage a war against the emergency, as great as the power that would be given me if we were in fact invaded by a foreign foe." As Roosevelt

≡ **Executive Power**   President Franklin Roosevelt signs a bill into law. In what came to be known as "The First Hundred Days," Roosevelt signed a flurry of new laws during his first months in office that expanded the power and responsibilities of the executive branch.

suggested, the tasks at hand were so formidable and dangerous that the fate of democratic governance might well be in the balance.

New Deal Remedies

Action came with unprecedented speed and sweep. To begin with, there was legislation designed to stop the economic collapse and shore up faltering institutions. An **Emergency Banking Act** stabilized a financial system in which over 5,000 banks had failed and millions of depositors risked losing their savings. An Unemployment Relief Act, a Federal Emergency Relief Act, and an Emergency Conservation Work Act created public sector employment, including the **Civilian Conservation Corps (CCC)**, at the local, state, and federal levels for those in need of jobs. A Beer-Wine Revenue Act began to turn the tide against prohibition and provided the federal government with needed tax money; prohibition was formally repealed by the Twenty-First Amendment in late 1933, the only constitutional amendment ever to be repealed. An Emergency Farm Credit Act and a Home Owners' Loan Act helped protect farms and homes from immediate foreclosure. And, to loosen the currency supply and help halt deflation, the Roosevelt administration took the United States off the gold standard, which had been at the core of national and international finance since 1900.

There were also two pieces of legislation that attempted to resuscitate the economy by reorganizing the operations of the country's major economic sectors. The **Agricultural Adjustment Act (AAA)** looked to address the problem of overproduction that had bedeviled commercial farmers for more than the previous decade. The idea was to set a target or "parity" price (the prosperous years of 1909–1914 were selected) for agricultural commodities that would raise rural purchasing power, and then to encourage farmers to reduce their crop acreage so that the supplies on the market would decrease and prices for the crops would increase, heading toward "parity." To make sure that farmers followed the plan, the federal government paid them to plow up acreage they had planted or refrain from planting in the first place. In other words, farmers would be paid *not* to grow their crops. It was an idea that had been in circulation since the 1880s— the subtreasury plan of the Farmers' Alliance was a more radical version of it—and it would continue to be a basis of federal farm policy to the present day (see Chapter 18).

Equally significant was the **National Industrial Recovery Act (NIRA)**. This act provided for the federal regulation of hours and wages in various industries and, for the first time, gave industrial workers the right to "organize and bargain

≡ **The Tennessee Valley Authority**   The Roosevelt administration established the Tennessee Valley Authority early in his presidency to promote development and access to electricity in the southern United States. The Fort Loudon Dam in eastern Tennessee used hydroelectric power to electrify home across the southeastern states.

collectively through representatives of their own choosing." In short, it lent legal sanction to labor unions. Further, the act created the **Public Works Administration (PWA)** to undertake the building of roads, bridges, tunnels, airports, and schools, employing thousands to work on vital infrastructure projects. But, perhaps most consequentially, the act authorized the creation under federal supervision of codes, made on an industry-by-industry basis, which would set controls on production, prices, wages, and employment, allowing firms to exert very strong influence over the dynamics of the marketplace and bringing apparent stability to the most important corners of the industrial economy. This is to say that the NIRA made for government-sponsored cartels, just the sort of thing antitrust legislation was meant to prevent.

The Roosevelt administration took an additional step in the direction of planning by establishing the **Tennessee Valley Authority (TVA)**. The TVA promoted economic development, flood control, and rural electrification across an especially impoverished area of the southern states, and thereby tried to more fully integrate the South into modern American society.

All of this, and a host of other pieces of legislation, were enacted in the span of 100 days, a dramatic and widely celebrated achievement, especially as a counterpoint to the relative inaction of the Hoover administration. Roosevelt clearly wasted no time. He hit the ground running and tackled many of the most significant economic problems the country faced. And he began to carve out a framework of centralized planning that simultaneously built upon precedents from the Progressive era—and especially from the mobilizations during World War I—and looked to a new future of government-administered cooperation.

Political Hurdles

But there were potentially troubling features as well. Virtually all of the legislation that was passed during the first 100 days of the New Deal was drafted within the executive branch and sent to Congress, where it was then rushed through with little debate and few if any amendments. In effect, Congress—the legislative branch—allowed the executive to do the legislating and then, for all intents and purposes, rubber-stamped it. What's more, the legislation further shifted power from Congress to the executive by creating many new and formidable federal agencies to carry out the programs. Small wonder that a reporter for the *New York Times* could describe the "atmosphere" in Washington at the time as "strangely reminiscent of Rome in the first weeks after the march of the Black Shirts, or Moscow at the beginning of the Five-Year Plan."

A Republican congressman could even complain that "the power . . . conferred upon the President . . . makes the distinguished dictator Mussolini look like an Egyptian mummy."

But it wasn't only the expansion of executive power that marked the early New Deal legislative process. It was also the strengthening of certain actors in the national economy at the expense of others. The Agricultural Adjustment Act, through the Agricultural Adjustment Administration, privileged farm owners, and especially big farm owners, rather than farm tenants or sharecroppers; the owners would receive the subsidies and, by staffing local committees, they could determine how the funds would be distributed. In many cases, especially in the cotton districts of the South, the federal subsidies were pocketed by landlords who, in turn, reduced their crop acreage by evicting tenants and croppers. It was the beginning of a massive "enclosure" movement that, like English precedents of the seventeenth and eighteenth centuries, drove more and more of the rural laboring population off the land and into towns and cities of the South, North, and West.

≡ **The Blue Eagle**   The Blue Eagle was the symbol of the National Recovery Administration (NRA). The NRA sought to encourage economic recovery by empowering corporations to set wages and prices while supporting collective bargaining and some other protections for workers.

The National Industrial Recovery Act, by means of the National Recovery Administration (NRA), revealed similar privileging and hierarchies. The industrial codes were drawn up by the leaders of the various sectors—coal, steel, automobiles, textiles, rubber tires, oil—and in most cases this meant that the largest firms had the greatest influence. The "big boys in the industry" set the codes and "the little fellows weren't being consulted," smaller businesses quickly complained. Furthermore, while industrialists were eager to impose production and price controls, they were far less interested in upholding the labor regulations as to hours, wages, and collective bargaining that the NIRA had required. With the Blue Eagle of the NRA emblazoned on the offices and products of cooperating firms, a strong measure of corporatism, anticipated during the earlier Progressive Era, seemed to be in evidence.

That Congress moved so quickly to enact the legislation sent down by the Roosevelt administration averted the conditions that Roosevelt warned would require him to embrace "emergency" powers. There was no need to suspend the Constitution, no need to punish the political opposition, no need to infringe civil liberties, no need to use the iron fist of police discipline. Roosevelt himself seemed very much disposed toward liberal constitutionalism. His advisory "Brain Trust" was made up of university professors, and his wife, Eleanor, strongly supported labor, women's, and civil rights. Yet, shortly after assuming the presidency, Roosevelt

Table 22.1 The First Hundred Days: Major Laws and Programs

Law	Date
Emergency Banking Act	March 9
Economy Act	March 15
Civilian Conservation Corps	March 31
Agricultural Adjustment Act	May 12
Farm Mortgage Assistance	May 12
Federal Emergency Relief Act	May 12
Tennessee Valley Authority	May 18
Securities Act of 1933	May 27
Home Owners Loan Corporation	June 13
Public Works Administration	June 16
Railroad Coordination Act	June 16
National Industrial Recovery Act	June 16
Glass-Steagall Banking Act	June 16

invited Hitler to Washington (Hitler declined) and spoke admiringly—as many other American political and business leaders did at the time—of that "Italian gentleman" Mussolini. "I am much interested and deeply impressed by what he has accomplished," Roosevelt explained. There was, quite simply, no telling where the New Deal might go or how strong the embrace of constitutionalism might be.

22.5 The Grip of Depression and Political Disillusion

Examine the reasons why the Great Depression persisted and how it triggered political backlash from the left and right.

When President Roosevelt told the American people in March 1933 that the only thing they had to fear was "fear itself," he was hoping they would join him in positive thinking and adapt their behavior accordingly. But even the speed and sweep of early New Deal measures would not allow for much thinking that was positive. The banking system had been stabilized, and, over the next year, prices began to inch upward and unemployment downward. Yet, in most other respects, the best that could be said was that a floor to the Great Depression may have been found, and this was mainly in the cities. In the countryside, there were few signs of improvement and some indication that things were still getting worse. Was the New Deal heading toward failure?

Continued Despair

Across the country, the picture of daily life as the New Deal unfolded was dispiriting to say the least. Wherever one looked, despair could be seen on the faces of millions of Americans to an extent that appeared to have no precedent. *Fortune* magazine sent poet James Agee and photographer Walker Evans to do a feature on white tenant farmers in Alabama, but the story and photographs sent back were so disturbing that the magazine decided not to publish them; it was not until 1941 that the now-iconic book version, *Let Us Now Praise Famous Men*, was released. Indeed, when Roosevelt's own Secretary of Agriculture, Henry A. Wallace, traveled through the cotton belt of the Deep South, he saw "poverty so abject" that, in his judgment, "the peasantry of Europe" was likely better off by comparison.

Farther west, in Texas, Oklahoma, and other parts of the Great Plains, low commodity prices and deep indebtedness were not the only problems. Severe drought conditions in the early 1930s had steadily stripped the soil of its moisture, ravaged the growing crops, and, when the wind blew, made for dust storms so intense that

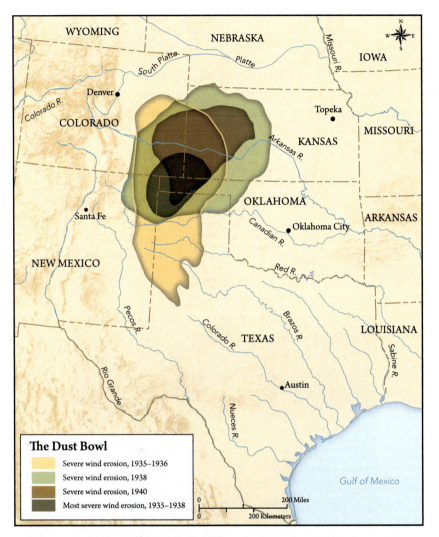

≡ **MAP 22.2 The Dust Bowl**   Millions of tons of soil from the great windstorms that blew west across the Southern Plains landed as far east as the Atlantic Ocean. Its economic and social impact was even wider.

they were known as "black blizzards." Before long, thousands of farm families were displaced, made into refugees in their own land (see Map 22.2). With their few belongings, many then headed North and, especially, West, into the central valleys of California. There they would be derisively called "Okies" wherever they were from, and, if lucky, they might find work alongside Mexican and African American migrants in the fields of big growers who were running near factory-like operations. As Okies, they would also serve as the symbolic victims of the depression's

PERSPECTIVES

Migrant Mother

The Resettlement Administration was among the many programs the Roosevelt administration established to address the poverty of the Great Depression. Designed to move poor families to entirely new areas, often in government-planned communities, the Resettlement Administration also hired photographers to document the lifeways, and the plight, of rural America. The photographers hired by the government produced thousands of pictures.

Ben Shahn spent months traveling through the American South (he was also a painter; his painting of the bodies of Sacco and Vanzetti is shown earlier in this chapter). Arthur Rothstein was only twenty years old when he was hired by the Resettlement Administration as its first photographer. Dorothea Lange snapped the most famous of all the photos produced for the Resettlement

≡ *Migrant Mother*

Administration. Her *Migrant Mother* is unquestionably the most famous image of the Great Depression, and one of the most recognizable photos of the twentieth century.

Migrant Mother (the photo was labeled by Lange as "Destitute pea pickers in California") was taken in early 1936 by Lange, who spent a month photographing migrant farm laborers in southern California. Lange recalled being "drawn by a magnet" to Florence Thompson and her children at a camp in Nipomo. Thompson told Lange that she was thirty-two and had been living on vegetables from the surrounding fields and birds that her children were able to kill. She asked no questions of Lange but did not object to her photograph being taken. The picture was published in local newspapers. It immediately struck a chord.

But Lange took several other photos of Thompson and her children, including those shown here.

≡ **Other photos that Dorothea Lange took of Florence Thompson and her children**

CONSIDER THIS

It is easy to assume that Lange's photos are representations, devoid of argument and message and simply candid images of American life. But ask yourself how Lange captured her subject, how she framed the context, and what emotion or impression she hoped to leave in her viewers. Why do you suppose *Migrant Mother* spoke so powerfully to Americans, and why has it continued to draw us in? Given that Dorothea Lange took many pictures of Florence Thompson, what explains the power of *Migrant Mother*, which became an American icon of hard times, as opposed to the other photographs?

midsection "**Dust Bowl**," memorably captured in John Steinbeck's searing novel, *The Grapes of Wrath* (1939).

The towns and cities of the South and Plains, dependent as they were on the agricultural economy, could hardly escape the prolonged depression, though their industrial and commercial counterparts revealed faint evidence of recovery themselves. Even as deflationary pressures subsided, flat wages and widespread unemployment stifled demand for consumer goods and thus provided no spark to reignite the economy's engines. And it was no longer feasible for people to rely on the practices of family economies—wives and children went out to work when husbands were laid off—if there was little work to be had for anyone. If anything, the depression put new, and in some cases, devastating burdens on family life, undercutting the position and authority of male breadwinners, who could no longer provide, and leaving women and children to redefine their expectations. As one Chicago relief worker put it, "Family relations are becoming strained; fathers feel they have lost their prestige at home; there is much nagging. Children of working age who can earn meager salaries find it hard to turn over all their earnings and deny themselves even the greatest necessities and as a result leave home."

Political Backlash on the Left

The disillusion born of depression could lead to personal resignation, to giving up and scratching by. But it could also lead to anger and resentment ready to boil over. In the Upper Mississippi Valley, farmers took a few pages from the playbook of their Populist predecessors, calling for inflation and a moratorium on farm foreclosures. In some cases, they went further, disrupting property sales, blocking roads, overturning milk vats, and harassing sheriffs and judges who attempted to carry out foreclosures. So threatening did conditions on the ground become that the governor of Iowa put several counties in the state under martial law. "The West," President Roosevelt recognized, "is seething with unrest."

Not only the West. Before the first year of the New Deal was complete, radical voices could be heard in several parts of the country, especially on the northern, western, and southern edges. Perhaps the loudest and most compelling was that of Louisiana's Huey P. Long. Born and raised in Winn Parish, a community with a history of dissent—the parish went Republican, Populist, and Socialist in the decades after the Civil War—Long studied law and entered politics, winning the governorship in 1928 by appealing to the state's humble white folks. Once in office, he built a formidable power base, through means fair and foul, and used it to push through pioneering legislation that modernized Louisiana. Raising taxes on corporate wealth, especially the oil and gas industry (Standard Oil had enormous influence in the state), Long organized public works programs and funded the construction of many roads, bridges, schools, and hospitals. He even made sure that school children had free textbooks. Hated by the rich, Long thus earned the deep loyalty of ordinary Louisianans—even many Black people—and it propelled him to a seat in the US Senate in 1930. Now he could claim the national spotlight, and, in early 1934, thumbing his nose at the Roosevelt administration, Long unfurled his **"Share Our Wealth"** plan.

"Share Our Wealth" was breathtaking in ambition and far ahead of its time. Long called for taxing large personal fortunes and very high annual incomes (in excess of $1 million), and for using the tax revenue to provide a guaranteed annual family income of $2,500, free college tuition and vocational training, old-age pensions, healthcare, veterans' benefits, and a thirty-hour workweek. "If we could only succeed in having the government hold fortunes down to a few million dollars to any one man," Long told a constituent, "then there would be something on which to run the country and for the people." His hope was to redistribute the wealth from the hands of a few and "make every man a king." At the very least, he wanted to build a nationwide movement.

Huey P. Long   As governor of Louisiana, Huey P. Long made a name for himself by raising taxes on corporations and implementing new employment and infrastructure projects. As a senator, he unveiled his ambitious "Share Our Wealth" plan, proposing high taxes on personal fortunes in order to guarantee every family a basic income.

Long was not alone. Out in California in 1934, Francis Townsend, a physician who was troubled by the country's treatment of the elderly and the poor, devised his own plan to stimulate economic growth, employment, and old-age security. How would it work? Townshend proposed that all people over the age of sixty be given a monthly stipend of $200 so long as they retired from the labor force and spent the stipend during the month. A small value-added tax would fund the program and, in the process, he argued, more jobs would be available, more money would go into circulation, younger family members would be relieved of the financial burdens of caring for the elderly, and older folks would be able to look after themselves. Townsend struck a responsive chord among the public and, relatively quickly, Townshend Clubs spread across the United States and attracted over half a million members.

Fellow Californian Upton Sinclair, the writer (most famous for *The Jungle*) and socialist, launched a campaign to **"End Poverty in California"** (**EPIC**) that same year and sought the Democratic nomination for governor. Calling for the state to take control of idle farmlands and factories and turn them into workers' and farm laborers' cooperatives, Sinclair would fund EPIC with taxes on the wealthy and, with the added revenue, also offer pensions to the elderly, widowed, and disabled. The result would be more of a cooperative commonwealth with a social safety net to go along with it. Democratic voters who had helped put Franklin Roosevelt into office two years earlier clearly liked the idea. Sinclair won the party's nomination. But Roosevelt remained silent during the fall election, and Sinclair lost in what turned into a bitter contest.

Thunder on the Right

Bitterness characterized another New Deal critic, Father Charles E. Coughlin of Detroit. Availing himself of radio technology, Coughlin began broadcasting Sunday sermons in 1926 and then, as the depression took hold and deepened, added politics to the mix. Especially concerned about the legions of unemployed autoworkers, Coughlin combined Catholic social justice doctrines with populism and anticommunism. He attacked Herbert Hoover, the Republicans, international bankers, and the gold standard, and demanded the remonetization of silver to increase the money supply. For a time, he endorsed Roosevelt and the New Deal, but the alliance didn't last. By early 1934, Coughlin had the New Deal in his crosshairs, and he looked to build a political movement—called the **National Union for Social Justice**—around inflationary policy, labor rights, and the nationalization of some industries, flavored with anti-Semitic rhetoric. As many as eight million

≡ **Thunder on the Right**   Father Coughlin speaking at a rally in Cleveland in 1936. An early adopter of radio, Coughlin's broadcast sermons became increasingly political during the Great Depression. Coughlin mixed support for unemployed workers with anticommunist and anti-Semitic rhetoric.

Americans may have come on board with the National Union, making Coughlin a force to be reckoned with.

Coughlin's brand of "reactionary" populism together with Upton Sinclair's defeat in the California gubernatorial election suggested that opposition to the New Deal could come from the right wing as well as the left wing. By the summer of 1934, conservative Republicans and Democrats—including onetime presidential candidate Al Smith from Roosevelt's New York—organized the **American Liberty League** to contest New Deal policies that they regarded as socialistic. Not surprisingly, they also attracted some major corporate leaders, including the head of General Motors, who believed that the Roosevelt administration had already gone too far in fighting the depression and reconstructing the American economy. Before much longer, the Liberty Leaguers would be joined by southern Democrats who worried that New Deal policies could threaten white supremacy.

Further to the right was the Ku Klux Klan, whose membership had dropped considerably by the early 1930s but was still active, together with an array of newly established fascist organizations, from the German-American Bund (with about 100,000 members who readily shouted "*heil* Hitler"), to the Silver Shirts, an underground American fascist organization founded by William Dudley Pelley in Asheville, North Carolina, and the Black Legion, a white supremacist organization active in the Midwest in the 1930s. Like the Klan, they would trade in racial purity, anti-Semitism, and paramilitarism; and like the Klan they would celebrate 100 percent Americanism, insisting, in the case of the Bund, that George Washington was the "first fascist" and did not believe that democracy would work. These were American fascism's bare knuckles.

Yet, in many ways more worrisome, were the perspectives of intellectual, political, and business leaders—people in the mainstream—who looked at fascist experimentation, especially in Italy, with interest and admiration, and who were coming to wonder whether liberal democratic institutions were up to the task of the national and global crisis. The president of Columbia University, Nicholas Murray Butler, told incoming freshmen that dictatorships were producing "men of far greater intelligence, far stronger character and far more courage than the system of elections," while a prominent journalist observed that "several of the forces propelling Hitler into power were much the same as those that put Mr. Roosevelt into office—mass despair, impassioned hatred of the *status quo*, and a burning desire to find a savior who might bring luck." In March 1933, as Roosevelt was being inaugurated, *The Nation* magazine, a liberal publication, asked, "Do We Need a Dictator?" and the distinguished philosopher and theologian Reinhold Niebuhr thought "that the liberal culture of modernity is quite unable to give guidance and direction to a confused generation which faces the disintegration of a social system and the task of building a new one."

Franklin Roosevelt held his political cards close to his vest. He is widely regarded as a brilliant politician, not an ideologue, someone who looked for practical solutions and very effectively played competing advisors against one another in their pursuit. He had a charm that even put his enemies at ease, and an affability that could suggest he agreed with a point of view even when he didn't. But he was hardly a blank slate. He brought to the presidency a belief in the virtues of an activist state and a sense that government spending could make a positive difference at times of economic distress. He also saw the need for bold and centralized leadership, and although he sought to make the most of radio in connecting with the electorate (his "**Fireside Chats**" achieved fame) and suggesting where he was headed, he seemed to believe that at times of serious crisis the rules of governance might need to be broken. If liberals could contemplate a suspension of democratic practices and the establishment of a dictatorship to fight the effects of the Great Depression, what was there to stand in the way?

Conclusion: A Great Depression and a New Deal

During much of the decade of the 1920s, it appeared as if the United States had emerged from World War I in a strong political and economic position. The economy boomed, consumer culture spread, and an intellectual/cultural vibrancy bubbled across much of the country. But the prosperity rested on shaky foundations, and when confidence in the economy weakened, the New York Stock Exchange crashed and a deep and unprecedented depression spread everywhere.

The United States was hardly alone and, in Europe, the political consequences became shockingly apparent. There, the war gave way to crisis and deepening doubts about the value of parliamentary regimes. Beginning in Italy and soon spreading elsewhere—especially to war-devastated Germany—democratic rule came under attack, liberal ideas were scorned, and fascism was widely embraced. The United States, too, had a reactionary politics developing in the 1920s and, after the failure of the Hoover administration to tackle the economic crisis, some called for an authoritarian solution.

In 1932, Democrat Franklin Delano Roosevelt was elected to the presidency and his party took control of Congress. He promised a "New Deal" and in his first hundred days had Congress pass a great deal of legislation designed to stop the economic collapse and begin the process of recovery. But the results were only partial, and he faced resistance to his left and to his right, suggesting that a full-blown change in governance might be in the offing.

WHAT IF Roosevelt Had Embraced Emergency Powers?

Franklin Roosevelt's New Deal aimed to stop the economy's free fall and begin a recovery, and while the legislation came rapidly, the impact registered slowly. In truth, power still very much rested in the hands of big corporations and their allies in government at the federal and local levels. After all, the great strikes of the Gilded Age were quashed by governors who summoned police and the National Guard, or by the US attorney general who sent in the army. All large cities in the 1930s had armories, and industrialists deployed private armies, like the Pinkertons, in their defense. And the civil and political rights of various Americans, especially African Americans, were being whittled down by the Supreme Court and destroyed on the ground by white supremacists.

What if Roosevelt, fearful of possible revolution, had, sometime in 1934, chosen to embrace emergency powers, suspended at least parts of the Constitution, revoked the union recognition that corporate leaders generally disliked, and formed a stronger alliance with the corporate sector and southern conservatives in the service of economic revitalization and full employment? And what if, to speed things along, he not only looked to direct attention toward infrastructure projects but also began to put money into rebuilding the US Armed Forces (he had been a secretary of the Navy) and giving the military expanded powers. Some commentators and political leaders were already searching for a "third road" between fascism and communism, perhaps a "temporary dictatorship." What might this have meant for the country and its history? Would it have been accepted by most of the population? And what did his critics offer as alternatives?

DOCUMENT 22.1: Huey P. Long on "Share Our Wealth" (1936)

Despite the sweeping legislation of the New Deal, many Americans remained dissatisfied and wondered who was being favored. Senator Huey Long of Louisiana made this speech on the floor of Congress explaining his "Share Our Wealth" program.

The Share Our Wealth Society proposes to enforce the traditions on which this country was founded, rather than to have them harmed; we aim to carry out the guaranties of our immortal Declaration of Independence and our Constitution of the United States, as interpreted by our forefathers who wrote them and who gave them to us; we will make the works and compacts of the Pilgrim fathers, taken from the Laws of God, from which we were warned never to depart, breathe into our Government again that spirit of liberty, justice, and mercy which they inspired in our founders in the days when they gave life and hope to our country.

It took the genius of labor and the lives of all Americans to produce the wealth of this land. If any man, or 100 men, wind up with all that has been produced by 120,000,000 people, that does not mean that those 100 men produced the wealth of the country; it means that those 100 men stole, directly or indirectly, what 125,000,000 people produced. Let no one tell you that the money masters made this country. They did not such thing. Very few of them ever hewed the forest; very few ever hacked a crosstie; very few ever nailed a board; fewer of them ever laid a brick. Their fortunes came from manipulated finance, control of government, rigging of markets, the spider webs that have grabbed all businesses; they grab the fruits of the land, the conveniences and the luxuries that are intended for 125,000,000 people, and run their heelers to our meetings to set up the cry. "We earned it honestly." The Lord says they did no such thing.

Here is the whole sum and substance of the share-our-wealth movement:

1. Every family to be furnished by the Government a homestead allowance, free of debt, of not less than one-third the average family wealth of the country, which means, at the lowest, that every family shall have the reasonable comforts of life up to a value of from $5,000 to $6,000. No person to have a fortune of more than 100 to 300 times the average family fortune, which means that the limit to fortunes is between $1,500,000 and $5,000,000, with annual capital levy taxes imposed on all above $1,000,000.

2. The yearly income of every family shall be not less than one-third of the average family income, which means that, according to the estimates of the statisticians of the United States Government and Wall Street, no family's annual income would be less than from $2,000 to $2,500. No yearly income shall be allowed to any person larger than from 100 to 300 times the size of the average family income, which means that no person would be allowed to earn in any year more than from $600,000 to $1,800,000, all to be subject to present income-tax laws.

3. To limit or regulate the hours of work to such an extent as to prevent overproduction; the most modern and efficient machinery would be encouraged, so that as much would be produced as possible so as to satisfy all demands of the people, but to also allow the maximum time to the workers for recreation, convenience, education, and luxuries of life.

4. An old-age pension to the persons over 60.

5. To balance agricultural production with what can be consumed according to the laws of God, which includes the preserving and storage of surplus commodities to be paid for and held by the Government for the emergencies when such are needed. This plan of God does not call for destroying any of the things raised to eat or wear, nor does it countenance wholesale destruction of hogs, cattle, or milk.

6. To pay the veterans of our wars what we owe them and to care for their disabled.

7. Education and training for all children to be equal in opportunity in all schools, colleges, universities, and other institutions for training in the professions and vocations of life; to be regulated on the capacity of children to learn, and not on the ability of parents to pay the costs. Training for

life's work to be as much universal and thorough for all walks in life as has been the training in the arts of killing.

8. The raising of revenue and taxes for the support of this program to come from the reduction of swollen fortunes from the top, as well as for the support of public works to give employment whenever there may be any slackening necessary in private enterprise.

Source: "Statement of the Share Our Wealth Movement," May 23, 1935, *Congressional Record*, 74th Congress, 1st Session, Vol. 79, pp. 8040–8043.

DOCUMENT 22.2: Father Charles E. Coughlin, *Principles of the National Union of Social Justice* (1936)

Father Coughlin's explanation of the ambitions and program of his National Union of Social Justice.

Establishing my principles upon this preamble, namely, that we are all creatures of a beneficent God, made to love and serve Him in this world and to enjoy Him forever in the next; and that all this world's wealth of field and forest, of mine and river has been bestowed upon us by a kind Father, therefore, I believe that wealth as we know it originates from the natural resources and from the labor which the sons of God expend upon these resources. It is all ours except for the harsh, cruel and grasping ways of wicked men who first concentrated wealth into the hands of a few, then dominated states and finally commenced to pit state against state in the frightful catastrophes of commercial warfare.

With this as a preamble, then, these following shall be the principles of social justice towards whose realization we must strive.

1. I believe in the right of liberty of conscience and liberty of education, not permitting the state to dictate either my worship to my God or my chosen avocation in life. 2. I believe that every citizen willing to work and capable of working shall receive a just and living annual wage which will enable him to maintain and educate his family according to the standards of American decency. 3. I believe in nationalizing those public necessities which by their very nature are too important to be held in the control of private individuals. By these I mean banking, credit and currency, power, light, oil and natural gas and our God-given natural resources. 4. I believe in private ownership of all other property. 5. I believe in upholding the right to private property yet in controlling it for the public good. 6. I believe in the abolition of the privately owned Federal Reserve Banking system and in the establishment of a Government owned Central Bank. 7. I believe in rescuing from the hands of private owners the right to coin and regulate the value of money, which right must be restored to Congress where it belongs. 10. I believe not only in the right of the laboring man to organize in unions but also in the duty of

the Government which that laboring man supports to facilitate and to protect these organizations against the vested interests of wealth and of intellect. 13. I believe in the broadening of the base of taxation founded upon the ownership of wealth and the capacity to pay. 14. I believe in the simplification of government, and the further lifting of crushing taxation from the slender revenues of the laboring class. 15. I believe that in the event of a war for the defense of our nation and its liberties, there shall be a conscription of wealth as well as a conscription of men. 16. I believe in preferring the sanctity of human rights to the sanctity of property rights. I believe that the chief concern of government shall be for the poor because, as it is witnessed, the rich have ample means of their own to care for themselves.

Source: http://academic.brooklyn.cuny.edu

Thinking About Contingency

1. Given the disastrous consequences of the Great Depression, would most Americans have accepted a dictatorship if it would have alleviated their economic despair?
2. How different was the political culture of the United States from those countries where fascism took root?
3. Do you believe that Franklin Roosevelt would have seized "emergency powers" if necessary?
4. Would ideas like those of Huey Long and Father Coughlin have been strengthened if Roosevelt had moved in a dictatorial direction? What prevented him from doing so?

REVIEW QUESTIONS

1. How widespread was the prosperity in the United States of the 1920s, and who benefitted the most from it?

2. How did the situation in the United States during the 1920s compare with Europe, especially Italy and Germany?

3. What best accounts for the stock market crash of 1929?

4. What did President Hoover attempt to do in order to address the economic crises of the Great Depression?

5. How did Franklin Roosevelt's approach to government policy differ from that of Hoover's?

6. How widespread was political discontent in the early years of the New Deal, and how did it express itself?

KEY TERMS

Agricultural Adjustment Act (AAA) (p. 940)

American Liberty League (p. 950)

Civilian Conservation Corps (CCC) (p. 940)

Dust Bowl (p. 948)

Emergency Banking Act (p. 940)

End Poverty in California (EPIC) (p. 949)

Fascist Party (p. 934)

flapper (p. 928)

Fireside Chats (p. 952)

Great Depression (p. 922)

National Industrial Recovery Act (NIRA) (p. 941)

National Union for Social Justice (p. 950)

Nazi (National Socialist) Party (p. 934)

New Deal (p. 938)

Reconstruction Finance Corporation (p. 932)

Public Works Administration (PWA) (p. 941)

"Share Our Wealth" (p. 949)

Smoot-Hawley Tariff (p. 932)

Tennessee Valley Authority (TVA) (p. 941)

Weimar Republic (p. 933)

RECOMMENDED READINGS

James Agee and Walker Evans, *Let Us Now Praise Famous Men* (Houghton Mifflin, 1941).

Susan P. Benson, *Household Accounts: Working-Class Family Economies in the Interwar United States* (Cornell University Press, 2007).

Alan Brinkley, *Voices of Protest: Huey Long, Father Coughlin, and the Great Depression* (Vintage, 1983).

Lizabeth Cohen, *Making a New Deal: Industrial Workers in Chicago, 1919–1939* (Cambridge University Press, 2008).

Jefferson Cowie, *The Great Exception: The New Deal and the Limits of American Politics* (Princeton University Press, 2017).

John P. Diggins, *Mussolini and Fascism: The View from America* (Princeton University Press, 2016).

Lynn Dumenil, *The Modern Temper: American Culture and Society in the 1920s* (Hill and Wang, 1995).

John Kenneth Galbraith, *The Great Crash, 1929* (Harper Business, 2009).

Ira Katznelson, *Fear Itself: The New Deal and the Origins of Our Time* (Liveright, 2014).

David Kennedy, *Freedom from Fear: The American People in the Great Depression and War, 1929–1945* (Oxford University Press, 2001).

Robert McElvaine, *Down and Out in the Great Depression: Letters from the Forgotten Man* (University of North Carolina Press, 2008).

Michael Topp, *The Sacco and Vanzetti Case: A Brief History with Documents* (Bedford St. Martin, 2004).

23

Birth Pangs of Social Democracy
1933–1940

Chapter Outline

23.1 Pushes from Below

Understand the importance of political pressure from labor and the left in moving the New Deal in a progressive direction.

23.2 Shifting the New Deal to the Left

Describe the legislative measures that moved the New Deal in a politically leftward direction.

23.3 The Triumph of Industrial Unionism

Describe the central role played by the CIO in making possible the establishment of industrial unionism.

23.4 The New Deal Coalition

Appraise the components of the New Deal political coalition.

23.5 African Americans and the New Deal

Explain the growing importance of African Americans in the New Deal and how they influenced the Democratic Party.

23.6 The Big Reach and the Backlash

Discuss the conservative backlash against the New Deal and the limits of the New Deal's reach.

≡ **Documenting American Life from the Ground Up** Between 1940 and 1941, Charles Todd (seated, *center*) and Robert Sonkin recorded the songs and voices of migrant workers in California. They recorded a wide variety of music, including ballads, square dances, and cowboy tunes, as well as traditional tales. Here, Todd poses with a group of Mexican boys and men, ready to record a new song or story.

23.7 Fascist Aggression and International Affairs

||| Explain the rise of fascist aggression in Europe and Asia and the American response.

23.8 A Third Term for Franklin Roosevelt

||| Discuss why FDR sought a precedent-breaking third term.

In 1935, as part of legislation establishing the Works Progress Administration, the New Deal Congress created a Federal Writers' Project (FWP). The idea was to provide work for unemployed writers, artists, editors, archaeologists, and researchers in the interest of the nation's cultural enrichment. Participants included soon-to-be famous Richard Wright, Conrad Aiken, Claude MacKay, Studs Terkel, Zora Neale Hurston, Saul Bellow, and Ralph Ellison, as well as over 6,000 others from the world of arts and

Timeline

1931	1932	1933	1934	1935	1936
1931 > Japan invades Manchuria					
		1933 > Socialist Party holds a Continental Congress			
			1934 > Labor strikes roil industry, agriculture, and transportation		
				1935 > Congress passes the Wagner Act; Congress of Industrial Organizations founded; Italy invades Ethiopia	
					1936 > FDR reelected by large margin; sit-down strikes against General Motors begin

letters. During the next three years, they engaged in a wide range of programs across the country meant to nurture community theaters, explore the histories of towns and rural communities, compile materials of folklore, and support musical productions. Perhaps best known and remembered was the *American Guide* series, books devoted to the history of the country's states and territories, more from the ground up than from the top down.

Even more remarkable were the many interviews FWP employees did with ordinary Americans, over 2,000 of whom were formerly enslaved men and women in the southern states, who reflected on their lives and experiences. The idea, according to the FWP director, was to create a "self-portrait of America," and to this day the fruits of the project are consulted by many Americans attempting to write the country's history and to find records of their ancestors.

1937	1938	1939	1940	1941	1942

1937 ▸ Roosevelt unveils "court packing" plan; a recession hurts economy and New Deal

1938 ▸ *Kristallnacht;* Nazis launch violent campaign against German Jews

1939 ▸ German-Soviet Non-Aggression Pact signed; Germany and Soviet Union attack Poland

1940 ▸ German army occupies France; FDR nominated for third presidential term; FDR defeats Republican Wendell Wilkie in election

The significance of the FWP was perhaps best described by some of its most conservative critics who charged that its intent was to "democratize American culture." So it was. The FWP sought to capture the great panorama of the country's history and cultural life, imagining that the United States was truly forged by the labor, perspectives, beliefs, and struggles of the most ordinary of Americans and that democracy itself should be understood not simply in the ways in which representatives were chosen but also in the ability of citizens to enjoy a full and meaningful life. In this way, the FWP captured what might be called the "social democratic" impulses of the New Deal, especially robust in the years 1935 and 1936.

The idea of "social" democracy was not new to the 1930s. As we saw in previous chapters, it surfaced during the second half of the nineteenth century as capitalism took hold and American industrialization sped forward. Greenbackers, Knights of Labor, Socialists, and Populists began to lay a political and ideological foundation. Left-wing Progressives built upon it in attempting to regulate an increasingly corporate society and debating the government's role in promoting a broadly held notion of the public good.

But it was in the 1930s that American **social democracy** was really born. It was born at a time of great crisis, and one in which democracy itself was being scrutinized at home and rejected abroad in favor of new types of authoritarianism. And, as the FWP recognized, it owed to the struggles of those who had the least power and were among the most vulnerable: white and Black, native-born and immigrant, Catholic, Jewish, and Protestant, workers in industry and agriculture, in places small and large. Together, at this moment, they would leave a lasting imprint on the country's future.

23.1   Pushes from Below

||| Understand the importance of political pressure from labor and the left in moving the New Deal in a progressive direction.

However interested political leaders may be in reform or social change, it is unlikely that they will step out and chart a direction forward on their own. They surely have advisors and constituents to encourage or discourage them, but almost invariably when they come to embrace policies that challenge the power and prerogatives of elites, they have been pushed by popular mobilizations, protests on the ground, often outside the political system and sometimes in defiance of it. Franklin Roosevelt recognized that the model of American governance was in need of change if there was any chance of meeting the challenges of the Great Depression. But although he advocated measures of relief, early New Deal legislation favored large-scale industrialists (as in the NRA codes) and large-scale landowners (as in the distribution of AAA price supports), most of whom worried about labor unrest and how to keep it in check. What gave the New Deal a social democratic character were the struggles that working people engaged in and the demands they raised. Much of the energy came out of the West and the midsection of the country. In the process, they helped to move Roosevelt to the left rather than the right.

A Farm Workers' Strike

In the fall of 1933, the largest agricultural strike in the history of the United States erupted in the San Joaquin Valley of California. Nearly 20,000 cotton pickers walked out of the fields, and they were joined by thousands of other fruit and vegetable pickers along the valley's 400-mile stretch from the edges of Los Angeles north toward the San Francisco Bay area. Many of the strikers were Mexican Americans and Mexican immigrants who followed the harvest along the West Coast, but they were joined by Filipinos, African Americans, and the white "Okies" who had been fleeing the devastating Dust Bowl far to the east. They had long been paid the lowest of wages and offered the barest of shelter, and the growers who employed them responded to the Great Depression by lowering wages further still.

It's not entirely clear what gave the pickers the confidence to take on the growers, some of whom were from the states of the former Confederacy, were firm believers in white supremacy, and had a stranglehold on county and state politics, not to mention the local police. But

≡ **Striking Cotton Pickers** Some of the tens of thousands of striking Mexican and Filipino cotton pickers and other agricultural laborers in the fall of 1933. A sign on a truck encourages the reader not to "scab," a common term for strikebreaking, or taking the job of a striking worker.

it may have been knowledge of New Deal initiatives, like the National Industrial Recovery Act, which seemed to encourage workers to join labor unions. At least many of the pickers thought that Franklin Roosevelt was on their side. And they received further help from organizers with the Cannery and Agricultural Workers Industrial Union (CAWIU) and members of the American Communist Party who hoped to turn their idealism into concrete gains for poor and exploited working people.

The San Joaquin Valley strikes were highly unusual. Ever since the collapse of the Knights of Labor in the 1890s (see Chapter 18), farm workers were among the most vulnerable and least organized laborers in the United States. Many were people of color or recent immigrants who spoke little English. They were constantly on the move, both within the United States and across its borders, and had few if any established political leaders to represent their interests. The irony, in fact, is that Section 7(a) of the NIRA, which protected the right of workers to unionize, did not include them within its legal embrace, a bow to conservative white landowners in the South and West who did have established political leaders to represent their interests.

Spreading Labor and Left-Wing Unrest

Yet, in other respects, the San Joaquin Valley strikes were emblematic of a surge in union organizing and strike activity that followed fast on the first hundred days of the New Deal. Thousands of workers across the country seemed to be responding to John L. Lewis, the president of the United Mine Workers, who told radio audiences that "The President wants you to join a union," which was not true but FDR didn't make any effort to deny it. Union membership skyrocketed, and workers began to stage strikes large and small, some 2,000 strikes in 1934 alone, to secure bargaining rights and recover the losses that had been inflicted on them in recent years.

No single group of workers or sector of the economy predominated in the labor agitation, and some of the strikes were massive: thousands of electrical workers in Toledo, Ohio; hundreds of truck drivers and warehousemen in Minneapolis, Minnesota; over 100,000 workers in San Francisco who, in supporting the struggles of longshoremen there, shut down the entire city for two weeks in a general strike; and over 400,000 textile workers in mills stretching from Maine south to Alabama. More often than not lethal violence broke out between strikers on the one side and armed police and vigilantes defending the interests of their bosses on the other. It was class conflict on a scale not seen since the late nineteenth century.

Labor unrest was part of a wave of organizational activity on the political left. An American Workers' Party, led by A. J. Muste, an African American, was established in 1933 and would play a prominent role in the electrical workers' strike in Toledo. The Socialist Party held a "Continental Congress" that same year and declared independence from "the profit system of business, industry, and finance." The Farmer Labor Party, together with the Progressive Party and Nonpartisan League, would grow in Wisconsin, Minnesota, and the Dakotas. And the Communist Party, which was actively involved in the San Francisco general strike, soon entered its **Popular Front** period, looking to form alliances with progressive forces inside the New Deal and out. Indeed, the Communist Party mobilized thousands of Americans, many young and from immigrant households, to pursue economic democracy and social justice. Communists not only were organizing on the shop floors and supporting labor demands for power and better living standards but also playing an especially important role in defending African Americans in the southern states from racist violence and Jim Crow discrimination. They are best known for providing legal defense for the **Scottsboro Boys**—nine young Black men who had been falsely accused of rape and faced the death penalty—in Alabama in the 1930s, but they stepped in elsewhere to fight lynching and other forms of repression, when other organizations feared to tread.

Energized by popular mobilizations such as these, left-wing New Dealers saw the opportunity to move the administration and the country in a more progressive direction. Many of them were young lawyers, women as well as men, who had imbibed the waters of idealism and may have become involved with the Socialist or Communist parties. Theirs was not a doctrinaire radicalism of a sectarian sort; nor did they care very much about the policy directives of leaders in the Soviet Union, who regarded themselves as the supervisors of Communist parties the world over.

What they did care about was the prospect of creating a more equitable society and of promoting social justice for groups of people—Black, Mexican, Asian, European immigrant—who had long been denied the rights and promises of American life. They often found places in the Justice Department or in the new bureaucratic agencies that early New Deal legislation had established, and the openings they saw had to do with how various policies were carried out. Would the Agricultural Adjustment Act (AAA) mainly benefit big landowners or tenant farmers? Would the National Recovery Administration (NRA) play an active role in encouraging unionism, or would it defer to the interests of large corporations?

PERSPECTIVES

Building an Industrial Society

The pushes from below for economic democracy and social justice that welled up across the United States in the 1930s contrasted with developments in the Soviet Union, where the entire population was mobilized in a series of Five-Year Plans designed to propel the country into an industrial future. "We are advancing full steam ahead along the path of industrialization," Josef Stalin, the leader of the Soviet Union, told his followers, "we are leaving behind age-old backwardness. We are becoming a country of metal."[1] Instead of pushes from below from groups like the cotton pickers of the San Joaquin Valley, Soviet industrial society was directed by a "revolution from above." Two images from the early 1930s capture this juxtaposition.

In 1930, Thomas Hart Benton painted a large mural called *America Today* for the New School for Social Research, a center of progressive thought and education in

≡ **Thomas Hart Benton's** *Steel*

[1]Quoted in Ronald Grigor Suny, *The Soviet Experiment: Russia, the USSR, and the Successor States* (New York: Oxford University Press, 2006), p. 252.

Greenwich Village, New York. *Steel* is one the ten scenes that form Benton's mural. It powerfully promotes the idea that the technological and mechanical foundation of industrial society depended on the sweat of manual labor. The heroic workers in *Steel* dominate the furnace and interact with it in an organic, even symbiotic, way.

We see a different vision of industrial society in this propaganda poster created in 1931 to promote the Five-Year Plan (which was squeezed into four years, 1928–1932). A newly manufactured locomotive hurtles out of a steel factory. The puny people alongside the tracks can only watch as it races full steam ahead toward an industrialized future. On the right, the caption, "Against Religion" reminds the viewer that Soviet industrialization went hand in hand with a dismantling of the country's traditions and beliefs.

≡ **Soviet Propaganda Poster (1931) to Promote the Five-Year Plan**

CONSIDER THIS

Historians interpret the Soviet Union's rapid industrialization in the 1930s as a "revolution," since it sought to transform all aspects of society. Speeches by Stalin and other Soviet leaders often characterized industry as a "battlefield" and workers as "shock troops." Why did those who wished to move the United States in a more progressive direction in the 1930s refrain from using similar language to describe their goals?

23.2   Shifting the New Deal to the Left

||| Describe the legislative measures that moved the New Deal in a politically leftward direction.

It was in this context that the Roosevelt administration clearly shifted the New Deal to the left and, in so doing, placed an indelible imprint on the future development of the United States. Although many of the legislative milestones enacted during the extraordinary year of 1935 had precedents in 1933—historians often distinguish between a "First" and "Second" New Deal—there can be little doubt that the achievements of 1935 made for an utterly new political and cultural playing field and for a new federal role not simply in "administering" American society but in promoting social democracy.

New Federal Initiatives

The **Emergency Relief Appropriations Act** had a dry and cumbersome title, but its impact was something else entirely. For one thing, it refueled the Civilian Conservation Corps and, especially, the Public Works Administration, which constructed bridges (San Francisco-Oakland Bay Bridge), tunnels (the Lincoln Tunnel in New York City), airports (LaGuardia Airport), and naval vessels, not to mention highways, schools, courthouses, and hospitals. These were huge state-sponsored undertakings that would benefit millions. The Act also enabled the creation of the Rural Electrification Administration, which brought electricity to 90 percent of American farms (fewer than 20 percent had electricity beforehand); the Resettlement Administration, which constructed several "greenbelt" suburban towns; and the National Youth Administration, which provided part-time jobs for high school and college students, thereby allowing them to remain in school while contributing to their economically strapped families.

Perhaps the largest and most important agency established by the Emergency Relief Appropriation Act was the **Works Progress Administration (WPA)**, which employed millions of men and women to build infrastructure and promote music, theater, and the arts. Never before had the federal government played a part in encouraging the creative work of writers, actors, artists, or musicians (who had traditionally been dependent on wealthy patrons to earn a living), and through the Federal Music Project and Federal Writers' Project they staged concerts and plays, interviewed thousands of ordinary Americans, including those formerly enslaved, and made possible the completion of books and films that documented, photographically and in words, the struggles of proud poor folk across the nation. The WPA helped make it clear that all sorts of people were important historical actors and had helped to build the United States.

Empowering Ordinary Americans

There was more. In early 1935, the Supreme Court overturned the NRA, arguing that the agency violated accepted ideas of interstate commerce and appropriated lawmaking powers that had been delegated to Congress. It was a major defeat for FDR as well as for labor since Section 7(a) was part of the National Industrial Recovery Act. In stepped

☰ **Art Class Sponsored by the WPA**   The Works Progress Administration (WPA) employed millions of Americans in a variety of public works projects, including promoting the arts. Many of the projects focused on the lives of American people, reflected by the artists portrayed here whose subjects include children at play and groups enjoying a day at the park

New York Senator Robert F. Wagner who then steered the National Labor Relations Act (known as the **Wagner Act** in his honor) through Congress later that year. Even more far-reaching than Section 7(a), the Wagner Act not only guaranteed workers the right to form unions and bargain collectively—and to strike and picket—but it also outlawed a variety of business practices designed to weaken workers' ability to push back, like company-sponsored unions or a blacklist to stigmatize and punish organizers. The Wagner Act legalized a "closed shop" (meaning that if a majority of workers voted to form a union all workers in the shop or factory would have to belong) and established the **National Labor Relations Board (NLRB)** to enforce the provisions of the act if companies sought to sidestep them. The act, as Wagner put it, "seeks to make the worker a free man in the economic as well as in the political field." It was an expansion in the idea of freedom itself.

What of the dramatic inequalities of wealth, which as we saw in Chapter 22, had provoked Huey Long, Frances Townshend, and Father Coughlin to rail against the New Deal and propose redistributionist measures? FDR surprised many of his own supporters in calling for tax reform, and especially for "very high taxes" on large incomes, inheritance, and some corporate dividends. "Our revenue laws," he argued "have operated in many ways to the unfair advantage of the few, and they have done little to prevent an unjust concentration of wealth and economic power." Congress balked on much of the proposed legislation (a fair portion of congressional Democrats were conservative southerners), but the tax rate on multi-million-dollar incomes (there weren't very many of them) was raised to 79 percent, setting a precedent that would frame federal tax policy for the next quarter century. Small wonder that Roosevelt's rich opponents soon branded him "a traitor to his class."

Yet nothing was more consequential in establishing a social democratic framework in the United States than the **Social Security Act**, passed in August 1935 with the energetic aid of Secretary of Labor Frances Perkins. In some ways, the act was a measure of how limited and fragile the social safety net was in American society, certainly compared to what was to be found in much of Europe. Americans who lost their job or could no longer work owing to age or disability had little alternative to fending for themselves or depending on the good graces of their families; most, if they could, worked until their bodies gave out. Poor and needy men, women, and especially children were effectively cast out on their own meager resources and those of their communities. This, of course, was fodder for the grist of New Deal critics like Long, Townsend, and Coughlin.

Despite the efforts of Secretary Perkins, the Social Security Act, when enacted, was a more conservative measure than originally intended. It was financed by payroll taxes on workers as well as employers, did not include health insurance (bowing to pressure from the American Medical Association), and excluded domestic and agricultural workers from its reach (meaning large numbers of women, African Americans, and other racial and ethnic minorities). But the act did set in place unemployment insurance (which encouraged those sixty-five years of age and older to "retire" and leave the labor force), old-age pensions (now known to us as "social security"), and Aid to Dependent Children, a welfare program pressed forward by Perkins and Eleanor Roosevelt.

Together they composed the bases of what we have come to call the modern welfare state. FDR saw the Social Security Act as the "cornerstone of his administration," but it also inscribed central elements of social democracy into the responsibilities of the federal government—responsibilities that would be expected by the overwhelming majority of Americans even when the social democratic impulses faded.

23.3   The Triumph of Industrial Unionism

Describe the central role played by the CIO in making possible the establishment of industrial unionism.

In some respects, social democracy had become easier to legislate than to implement, and nowhere was this truer than among working people. The Wagner Act granted laborers rights they had been fighting for over more than the previous century, but what sort of labor movement would they make? As late as the 1930s, the dominant national labor union was the American Federation of Labor (AFL). Founded in 1886, the AFL was, for the most part, a large collection of "craft" unions (meaning the workers in them were skilled and semiskilled) and therefore was overwhelmingly white, Euro-American, and male. Although interest in organizing the unskilled, regardless of race or gender, had earlier been pursued by the Knights of Labor and then the Industrial Workers of the World (IWW), the AFL resisted such an orientation, which left growing numbers of workers in the burgeoning "mass production industries" (steel, automobiles, electrical, chemical, rubber) unorganized and at the mercy of their employers.

☰ **The Modern Welfare State**   A 1935 poster encouraging American workers to sign up for Social Security. Although the new program did not include all workers (primarily excluding agricultural workers), those who qualified could rely on a pension once they turned sixty-five, allowing them to leave the labor force.

Rise of the CIO

But a revolt was brewing. In the fall of 1935, renegades like John L. Lewis of the United Mine Workers, David Dubinsky of the International Ladies Garment Workers, and Sidney Hillman of the Amalgamated Clothing Workers broke off from the AFL's framework and sought to move in a new direction. To that end, they established the **Congress of Industrial Organizations (CIO)**, dedicated, as its name implied, to organizing all workers in the industrial sector, whether they had craft skills or not. They attracted radical unionists like Walter Reuther of the auto workers, Harry Bridges of the longshoremen, and Michael Quill of the transport workers, and they became a beacon for laboring people who had already been politicized by the IWW, the Communist Party, Irish nationalism, German and American socialism, or Garveyism. That is to say the CIO looked to organize workers of color, African Americans in particular, as well as European immigrants and native-born whites, a major departure from the ways of the AFL.

The results were explosive. CIO unions quickly took on the largest corporations in the steel (U.S. Steel), rubber (Firestone), and auto-making (General Motors) industries, and they used a new tactic to win collective bargaining agreements. It was known as the "**sit-down strike**," which had been pioneered by the IWW in the United States and by factory councils in Italian industrial cities like Turin. What was the idea? Instead of walking off the job and forming picket lines around a factory or work site, as strikers had customarily done, workers "sat down" inside the plants and refused to leave. In effect, the workers were occupying the factories and shutting down production from the inside until their demands were met.

The most consequential of the sit-downs took place in Flint, Michigan, in late 1936 and early 1937. Flint was the home of General Motors (GM) and for all intents and purposes was a company town. Virtually all the city officials, including the police, were on the GM payroll or closely identified with GM interests. But although the sit-down tactic was of dubious legality, and local police quickly attempted to crack down on the strikers, the solidarity of the workers (their union was the United Auto Workers) and the reluctance of Michigan's Democratic governor to send in troops (a far cry from the late nineteenth century when political officials often called them in) made for a stunning victory. GM

☰ **Sit-Down Strikers**   American workers in steel, auto, and other manufacturing industries pioneered a new type of strike in the mid-1930s. Instead of abandoning the factory to picket outside it, they borrowed a tactic from Italian laborers and occupied the factory, where they would sit until their demands were met.

Table 23.1 Union Membership, 1933–1943	
Year	**Number of Members**
1933	2,857,000
1934	3,728,000
1935	3,753,000
1936	4,107,000
1937	5,780,000
1938	8,255,000
1939	8,980,000
1940	8,994,000
1941	10,489,000
1942	10,762,000
1943	13,642,000

agreed to recognize the United Auto Workers (UAW) and the reverberations spread out across the country, mobilizing millions of workers, sparking thousands of strikes, and sending union membership to unprecedented heights.

To be sure, many companies, especially smaller ones, dug in their heels and held out. They didn't believe that they had the resources or profit margins to bargain with unionized workers or they were simply diehard anti-unionists who drew a line in the sand against the social democratic impulses that the New Deal was clearly unleashing. This was especially true among the emerging agri-businesses in California, whose hostility to labor unions was strengthened by their racism. But by the time the decade was out, the expectations of industrial workers and the power of their CIO unions had been transformed. A new structure of labor–management relations had begun to take shape, and organized labor's place at the table of decision-making was being acknowledged.

23.4 The New Deal Coalition

Appraise the components of the New Deal political coalition.

What strengthened labor's hand as it confronted the country's most powerful industrial corporations, and pressed forward a social democratic agenda, were complex alliances with the Democratic Roosevelt administration that reached its apogee in 1936 as FDR ran for a second term. Rather than attempting to publicly appease conservative critics and move toward the center, FDR seemed to embrace the leftward shift of the New Deal. He eagerly campaigned against those he called "economic royalists," the rich and backward looking who wanted to defend their positions at the expense of everyone else. It was a bold plan because there was much the New Deal had still failed to achieve. Although there were encouraging developments, the Great Depression was by no means over and major hurdles remained in the path of further change. Unemployment was still high (see Figure 23.1), the engines of the economy were still turning slowly, wages were only creeping upward, and the Supreme Court continued to lower the boom on FDR's initiatives, the latest being the Agricultural Adjustment Administration in early 1936.

A New Social Alignment

Yet FDR seemed to relish having a leftward breeze at his back. That was the direction in which the public had chosen to move. Despite the disgruntled "royalists," Roosevelt won reelection by landslide proportions against a fairly weak Republican opponent, Alf Landon of Kansas. FDR won more than 60 percent of the popular vote and the electoral votes of all the states except Vermont and Maine. It was a blowout and one that redounded to Roosevelt's benefit not only in Congress but in the states as well, as Democrats increased their majorities and took control of more governorships and state houses. No small matter, as the sit-down strikers in the GM factories of Flint, Michigan learned.

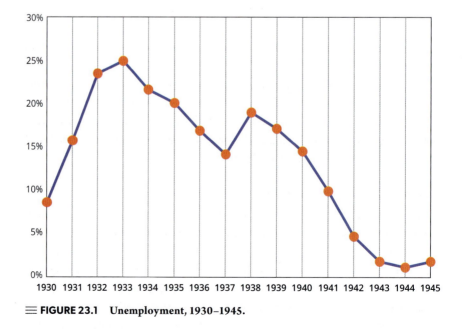

≡ **FIGURE 23.1   Unemployment, 1930–1945.**

Indeed, there is little doubt that FDR's overwhelming reelection in 1936 and the Democratic tidal wave of which it was a part encouraged the steel, auto, and rubber makers, among others, to settle with the CIO unions and avoid more (and probably pointless) conflict. There is also little doubt that the 1936 election solidified a new alignment in American politics and a new coalition in the Democratic Party.

Ever since the Civil War era, and especially since 1896, the Republican Party had ruled the nation and shaped federal policies at home and abroad. Based mainly on the interests of industrialists and financiers as well as their allies among skilled urban workers, native-born Protestants, and Midwestern farmers who produced mostly for the American market, the Republicans favored the manufacturing, banking, and urban sectors of the economy, pressed for higher tariffs, promoted the economic development of the trans-Mississippi West, sought to extend federal authority over all social and ethnic groups within American borders, and supported a variety of imperial projects in the hemisphere and the Pacific.

For their part, the Democrats had been anchored by agricultural interests in the South and West (who raised crops for the international market), merchandising concerns and bankers involved chiefly with foreign trade (who together favored low tariffs), and urban political machines in the large cities that organized the votes of European immigrant groups living in them.

New Deal Democrats maintained the loyalty of southern and western agriculturalists and large numbers of urban dwellers, especially immigrants and Catholics. But they also drew in growing numbers of industrial workers, a variety of ethnic and racial groups, and a cutting edge of industrial firms that were developing new technologies—many propelled forward during World War I—and had come to hold sway on the international market: in the oil, electrical, chemical, auto, and communications industries.

But, of course, the New Deal was not the Democratic Party of old. It was not organized around state rights, local power, agriculture, or inflation; it was organized around centralized federal power, cities and industries, and the circuits of international finance. So how did FDR and the New Deal win the allegiance of political constituencies who had not previously backed these policies?

New Deal Industrialists

It may be surprising that any industrialists would gravitate to the New Deal, given FDR's apparent support for labor rights and the explosive battles that occurred on shop floors during the 1930s, inspired, as many workers believed, by FDR's wishes. But the New Deal also did many things to bolster the interests of big industry (and big agriculture): it enacted the NRA and AAA; it never challenged corporate property ownership; and it could prove attractive to certain kinds of industrial companies.

What were they? They were companies that were becoming or had already become leaders in production and distribution globally (and so were not interested in tariff protection—Democratic low-tariff policies suited them fine), and they were companies in which labor costs were relatively low (meaning they were "capital intensive" and were driven by developing technologies that lowered labor costs) and so were willing and able to concede collective bargaining rights to secure stability. To be sure, all of these companies would have preferred limited federal power and a submissive labor force without union support. But given the circumstances and the dangers of social democracy turning into socialism or communism, they made their peace with the New Deal order and hoped to benefit from it. Smaller industrial companies or those that faced stiffer competition and had proportionally higher labor costs (textiles are a good example) never made their peace; they would be among the leading organizers of opposition to social democracy in general and the New Deal in particular.

Attracting Urban Immigrants

The New Deal exerted other important gravitational pulls. Urban immigrants had tended to vote Democratic when they voted, but by the 1930s the turnout rate among them was relatively low (large numbers had not yet become citizens, if they ever would, and others just chose not to vote) and their horizons were quite local. If immigrants needed work, they looked to their neighborhood party machine bosses who handed out patronage jobs. If they needed economic assistance, they looked to their parish churches or ethnic mutual aid societies. Yet, as the Great Depression deepened, there were few jobs for anyone to hand out and perilously few resources that the churches or aid societies could spare.

Here, the social safety nets that the New Deal were constructing proved enormously important not only in helping poor immigrants survive and subsist, but also in securing their allegiance to the Democratic Party and its social democratic projects, locally and nationally. The Civilian Conservation Corps and the Works Progress Administration provided millions of jobs for the unemployed of different ages. The Home Owners Loan Corporation helped workers pay their mortgages and avoid foreclosure. Section 7(a) and the Wagner Act secured rights and leverage at the workplace. Unemployment insurance and social security offered respectable alternatives to the community and family doles. And the Roosevelt administration, together with urban Democratic political machines, seized the opportunity to defeat prohibition (repealed in 1933), widely understood by many immigrants as an attack on them and their ethnic cultures.

By 1936, immigrants were explaining their support for Roosevelt by saying that "He gave me a job" or "He saved my home." They often imagined FDR as a father figure or intimate friend who cared about them and looked out for their welfare. If the sentiments seemed to be a form of paternalism, they even more powerfully expressed a new set of expectations of the federal government. They would not be quickly or easily forgotten.

23.5   African Americans and the New Deal

Explain the growing importance of African Americans in the New Deal and how they influenced the Democratic Party.

Perhaps the most sweeping transformation in political identification that the New Deal made possible was that of African Americans. Overwhelmingly, most Black men and women of the southern states—enforced by enslavement and then maintained by the refusal of northern and western employers to hire them—suffered under the political repression of Jim Crow. They were disfranchised by poll taxes, literacy requirements, and other onerous voter registration provisions. But during the 1930s, as the political landscape of the nation shifted, they became increasingly important players in the American game of politics. It was new and unexpected.

From Republicans to Democrats

Ever since the time of Radical Reconstruction, African Americans had overwhelmingly supported the Republican Party. It was not hard to understand why. The Republicans were the party of emancipation, national citizenship, civil equality, voting rights, and political participation. They had overseen the defeat of the Confederate rebellion, the abolition of slavery without compensating slaveholders, the enactment of the Thirteenth, Fourteenth, and Fifteenth Amendments to the Constitution, and the mobilization of freedmen politically through organizations like the Union League (see Chapter 16). After Reconstruction ended, when the "lily white" faction among them came to prevail, Republicans still appointed African Americans to patronage positions and jobs in the expanding federal bureaucracy. In a very controversial move, Republican President Theodore Roosevelt even invited Booker T. Washington to dinner at the White House, though he would do little else to combat racism and its humiliating etiquettes.

The Democrats, on the other hand, were the party of secession, redemption, white supremacy, lynching, and Jim Crow. They may have cut "fusion" deals with Black people in a few areas of the South, but they were in no mood to appoint

≡ **Harlem in the Late 1930s**   The Harlem neighborhood of New York was one of the most prominent Black enclaves in northern cities. Along with Bronzeville (Chicago) and the Hill (Pittsburgh), the formation of concentrated urban voting blocs allowed African Americans to wield new influence in local and municipal elections.

Black men to any political positions. Even when the Republicans began to disappoint African Americans by refusing them a fair share of offices and local power, and began to limit their commitment to Black civil and political rights, effectively making Jim Crow national in reach, Black men who could vote (meaning those in the northern and western states) continued to cast their ballots for Republicans. After all, President Woodrow Wilson sent a signal to fellow Democrats in the South by dismissing Black men and women from federal jobs and segregating the bureaucracy for those who managed to remain (see Chapter 20). As late as 1928, African American votes on Chicago's South Side—also known as Bronzeville, where many Black people lived—sent Black Republican Oscar De Priest to Congress, making him the first African American to represent a northern congressional district, and continued to reward white Republican Mayor "Big Bill" Thompson.

But during the 1930s, the political times were changing, and African Americans were ready to reassess their views of the Democratic Party. Although only a few of them had made it onto the voting rolls in the southern states, hundreds of thousands of them had moved north—to the large cities of New York, Philadelphia, Pittsburgh, Cleveland, Detroit, and Chicago—and settled in growing enclaves of Black residents, like Bronzeville, Harlem (NYC), or the Hill (Pittsburgh). Here they could get on the voting rolls, and their numbers made them an increasingly important political bloc in local, state, and national elections.

But why would African Americans throw their support to Democrats, given the odor of white supremacy that had long suffused the party? It was because the Roosevelt administration gradually demonstrated that it both wanted Black votes and was prepared to cultivate them. Unlike any previous nationally elected official, FDR publicly condemned, though didn't urge legislation against, lynching, and his wife, Eleanor Roosevelt, was outspoken in her support for full civil and political rights for African Americans, a reputation that became widely known.

Opening Doors and Extending Resources

New Deal administrative agencies came to include distinguished and highly educated African Americans like Robert C. Weaver, a Harvard PhD who served in the Farm Security Administration; and Mary McLeod Bethune, the leader of the National Association of Colored Women's Clubs, a longtime Republican, who served in the National Youth Administration and directly advised FDR. Other New Dealers pressed to have the concerns of Black tenants and sharecroppers attended to in the distribution of AAA subsidies—they largely failed owing to

≡ **Mary Mcleod Bethune and Eleanor Roosevelt**   Educator and leader of the National Association of Colored Women's Clubs Mary Mcleod Bethune (*left*) and First Lady Eleanor Roosevelt (*right*). A champion of women's organizing and expanded education, Mcleod Bethune also served as an advisor to the Roosevelt administration.

resistance from southern white Democrats—and attempted to prevent evictions when landlords plowed up acreage that had previously been farmed by the tenants and croppers. The New Deal's interest in using the resources of the federal government to fight the Depression and lend aid to working people throughout the United States, even if African Americans were low rungs on the policy totem poles, resonated with their own sense of social justice.

Through organizations like the NAACP, African American leaders would protest Black exclusions from some New Deal programs and pressure the Roosevelt administration to move in the direction of civil rights: to walk the walk and not simply talk the talk. A great many ordinary Black voters remained loyal Republicans for another couple of decades and couldn't help but look at the Democratic Party with suspicious eyes. Yet, by the election of 1936, many African Americans had come to believe that they might have a new avenue of political redress, and those who were able to vote cast their ballots for Franklin Roosevelt and the New Deal. In so doing, they secured his incumbency and established a framework of Democratic politics that would be enduring.

23.6   The Big Reach and the Backlash

Discuss the conservative backlash against the New Deal and the limits of the New Deal's reach.

By the time of his second inauguration in 1937, Franklin Roosevelt was both puffed with power and frustrated at some of the obstacles his New Deal programs still encountered. It should not have been surprising. The wide recognition that emergency action was necessary in the face of the Great Depression gave FDR the opportunity to dramatically expand the reach of the federal government, establish an organizational framework for the country's economic life, and find a welcome place in the lives of millions of Americans who had very little to do with or expect from the federal government beforehand. Yet many of the pieces of New Deal legislation, especially those that appeared to be the marquees, seemed to push at the limits of what the Constitution would allow, and as the New Deal moved to the left, it made a host of enemies who were looking to hedge in the New Deal or take it down. The stage was set for some of the most dramatic political conflicts of the 1930s.

Packing the Court

The biggest obstacles to New Deal programs had been set in place by the Supreme Court of the United States, which had ruled the NRA and AAA unconstitutional and, FDR feared, might do the same with the Wagner Act and Social Security Act as well. Most of the justices were predictably hostile; they had been appointed by previous Republican presidents (Woodrow Wilson, a Democrat, had appointed two, including Louis Brandeis), while Roosevelt had appointed not a one. So he devised a plan to shift the balances on both the Supreme Court and the lower federal courts, where cases were usually first heard.

Complaining of the age of many of the justices and the inefficiencies that resulted because of their caseloads (he would eventually acknowledge that the issue was really one of judicial philosophy), FDR came up with a piece of congressional legislation called the Judicial Procedures Reform Bill that would allow him to appoint a Supreme Court justice or a member of the lower federal courts for every sitting justice or judge over the age of seventy who chose not to retire. The effect would not be a small one. In 1937, when the bill was proposed, six of the nine Supreme Court Justices were over the age of seventy.

It may have appeared that FDR was trampling on the Constitution. In fact, the Constitution doesn't specify the number of Supreme Court justices who can serve at any one time, so no amendment was required. But clearly, he was making a bold move that would enormously expand the power of the presidency. Even many members of his own party, especially from the Midwest and South where there were always misgivings about the centralization of federal power, did not take kindly to it. Nor did a significant portion of the voting public previously devoted to Roosevelt and his New Deal. They all believed that the Judicial Procedures Reform Bill was underhanded if not devious in its inception and smacked of the authoritarianism that had already gained strong footing across Europe, Asia, and Latin America, and always threatened to do so in the Depression-era United States. Quickly, critics referred to the bill as a **court-packing** scheme, and nothing FDR did could save it from a thumping defeat. FDR had, as they say, grossly overplayed his hand, and his reputation would be tarnished accordingly.

The irony is that Roosevelt could have held his cards and still gotten the changes on the Court that he desired. For one thing, as the "court-packing" drama unfolded, the Supreme Court issued rulings suggesting that the Wagner and Social Security Acts would be safe constitutionally (perhaps the justices understood the temper of public opinion). For another thing, during the summer of 1937, FDR had his first Court vacancy to fill and he chose liberal Alabama Democrat (though former member of the Ku Klux Klan) Hugo Black. He would have seven more appointments in the years ahead, and in making them, he would help to transform the constitutional grounding of the Court, giving the green light to a wide range of federal powers that had long been struck down or held in doubt. As FDR later chortled, "We obtained 98 percent of all the objectives intended by the Court plan."

The Right Strikes Back

FDR's victory came at a high price. Although he won a huge victory in the 1936 election, the forces of conservatism, in the Democratic and Republican parties, had been pushing back against the big New Deal programs and the federal spending they required. Roosevelt saw a possible storm brewing, so, despite unemployment still hovering at nearly 15 percent, he spoke during the campaign of balancing the federal budget. By the summer of 1937, he seemed to think that economic signs allowed him to make significant cuts to programs that boosted employment, like public works. The Federal Reserve, showing its own conservatism, had already begun to tighten the supply of money and credit, and business investment appeared to slow along with it. The result was a sharp recession in the fall of 1937: a plunge in the stock market, industrial production, and corporate profits, and a dramatic spike in unemployment to near 20 percent.

Roosevelt and some in his administration complained of what they called a "capital strike," an effort on the part of business and corporate interests to unhinge the economy and the New Deal along with it in the best way they knew how, by halting investments. There was a growing sense, especially among those on the left wing of the New Deal, that a more, not less, activist federal role in the economy was necessary, a sense that was fortified by British economist John Maynard Keynes's *General Theory of Employment, Interest, and Money*, published in 1936. Densely argued, the book nonetheless gained a wide readership and warned that economies could get stuck at high levels of unemployment and low levels of investment. Thus, Keynes called for government spending and other forms of fiscal intervention, even at the cost of large deficits, to encourage greater consumption.

Keynes's ideas would become conventional wisdom among liberal economists and policymakers for the next several decades, but in the late 1930s the prospects for moving in such a direction were narrowing. It was not just the recession (derisively called the "Roosevelt recession") or the attempt to "pack" the Supreme Court. It was also a reinvigorated conservative movement that saw a new opportunity to contest the New Deal's designs. The leaders of it were Democrats from the South, and they had a strong structural base of power in the Congress. That base of power, known as seniority, enabled them to chair congressional committees that vetted legislation before it reached the floor of the House and Senate for votes. They were especially concerned about potential New Deal challenges to the racial hierarchies they saw as foundational to their southern way of life.

But southern Democrats were hardly alone among the conservatives. Republicans from the Midwest and Democrats representing other rural areas of the country joined them, with the support of disgruntled bankers, manufacturers, and agri-businessmen in places like the San Joaquin Valley of California who deeply resented the support they believed the New Deal lent to their farm workers. In 1937, two US Senators—Josiah W. Bailey of North Carolina (a Democrat) and Arthur H. Vandenburg of Michigan (a Republican)—crafted what they called a **Conservative Manifesto**, to register opposition to the course of the New Deal and sketch out an alternative direction in public policy. They called for a number of significant changes: lowering taxes, reducing federal government spending, balancing the budget, supporting the rights of the states, ending sit-down strikes and other labor tactics considered "coercive," and protecting profit and private enterprise. Bailey saw the Manifesto as "a definite rallying ground," designed to unite critics of the New Deal on the right. It would. And it would also serve as a foundation on which conservatives would subsequently build.

23.7   Fascist Aggression and International Affairs

||| Explain the rise of fascist aggression in Europe and Asia and the American response.

Not all of the challenges to the Roosevelt administration and the New Deal came from the domestic front. Increasingly ominous developments were taking place across the globe, suggesting that the economic instabilities of the 1930s were leading in the direction of international political and military hostilities. Italy had invaded Ethiopia (1935). Civil warfare had broken out in Spain (1936). Japan had invaded the Republic of China (1937). And Germany had swept into Austria and parts of Czechoslovakia (1938).

In many regards, what was happening was less a new cycle of warfare than a continuation of the warfare that had erupted in 1914 and was only settled temporarily by an armistice and the Versailles Peace Conference in 1919 (see Chapter 21). The struggles between European and Asian powers, involving empires and further colonial ambitions, had not been put to rest but rather had been redirected and intensified by the consequences of the peace, the Bolshevik Revolution and socialist mobilizations elsewhere, and the effects of the Great Depression. Liberal and leftist regimes faltered in many places (and were brutally crushed in some), and they were replaced by fascist and authoritarian regimes, which combined hard-fisted policies at home with naked aggression abroad, both enhanced by the militarization of their societies and economies. In effect, the globe was engulfed in an ongoing war with tension all around and no end in sight (see Map 23.1).

Japan on the March

The Japanese very clearly stepped onto the world stage as a new imperial power. Ever since the Meiji Restoration of the 1860s, Japan moved to modernize its economy and politics, centralizing political authority and advancing industrialization. The results would soon be seen in the Russo-Japanese War (1905) when the Japanese army surprisingly humbled the Russian army, and in the muscle the Japanese attempted to flex at Versailles, though not with the results they had hoped for. But modernization raised a number of problems, too, most significantly Japan's lack of crucial resources such as oil, rubber, and coal. As a small island nation with a growing population, the Japanese had to look abroad for many necessities, including foodstuffs.

For a time, Japan depended heavily on oil imports from the United States and rubber imports from British colonial possessions in Southeast Asia. That was where

≡ **MAP 23.1**   **Fascist Aggression in Europe, Africa, and Asia, 1933–1941**

oil and rubber were readily available. Yet once the drive for modernization was complicated by economic depression, certainly by the mid-1920s, Japan turned in the direction of further expansion, into Korea, into Taiwan, and into Manchuria, in China's northeast, in 1931. They established imperial outposts throughout. By the 1930s, the growing strength of the Japanese military spilled over into the government itself and formed the basis of a fascist regime that soon marched into China and French-controlled Indochina.

Fascist Italy and Nazi Germany

As we saw in Chapter 22, the Italians in the early 1920s had the first of Europe's fascist states, built on the ashes of communist and socialist movements. Benito Mussolini presided with the aid of paramilitary Black Shirts and an increasingly corporatist economy (meaning that corporate interests received state support for subduing labor). The Italian fascists sought to rejuvenate the economy with large public works and infrastructure projects, not unlike the New Deal, and by engaging in military rearmament. Nationalist to the core, the fascists also traded in racism and anti-Semitism, though not quite as virulently as did their German counterparts. But their march into Ethiopia in 1935, in defiance of the League of Nations, showed the fruits of fascist aggression and militarism, intent as the Italians were on strengthening their position in the horn of Africa and establishing a proving ground for their armies and new air force.

But fascist aggression in Italy was nowhere nearly as threatening as it was in Germany. There, Hitler and the Nazi Party had been in power since 1933 and had been moving to rebuild the country militarily since 1935, in violation of the Versailles peace accords. Expressing his deep hostility to German punishment after World War I and deeply laid German nationalism, Hitler imagined a thousand-year "Reich" (meaning realm or regime) that would spread Germany's Aryan influence

≡ **Nazi Rally**   Fascist Adolf Hitler (*center*) at a rally of his German Nazi Party in 1934. Hitler became Chancellor of Germany in 1933 as part of a governing coalition between the Nazis and conservatives. Once in power he used paramilitary violence and draconian new laws to establish a fascist dictatorship.

and culture across the face of Europe, if not the world. He especially trained his sights on Eastern Europe and the Russian Ukraine, where, he hoped, German settlers in search of land could migrate, offering *Lebensraum* or "breathing space." In these colonized areas agriculture vital to Germany would be developed (the Germans needed food and other resources just like the Japanese did), and undesirables (such as Jews, Romani, and left-wing political radicals) could be sent into exile.

But Hitler also looked to reintegrate those of German birth who lived outside Germany's borders into what he called the "Fatherland." So he marched his army into Austria and then western Czechoslovakia (known as the *Sudetenland*) and claimed them both for the Reich. The French and especially the British did nothing to stand in the way of Hitler's flouting of international borders, and Hitler promptly turned his venom on the Jews within Germany. On the night of November 9, 1938, mobs attacked and desecrated thousands of Jewish-owned stores and synagogues across Germany. On the day after ***Kristallnacht*** (meaning "night of crystal" or "night of broken glass"), 30,000 German Jews were sent to concentration camps. The loss of civil rights and the confiscation of their property was the first step along the path of the Holocaust: the massacre of European Jewry.

Rehearsal for World Warfare?

But perhaps most worrisome of all was a brutal civil war in Spain. Sparked by a right-wing military coup against the leftist Second Spanish Republic in 1936, the **Spanish Civil War** roiled the country for three bloody years. Ominously, it drew in international supporters that anticipated the coming global battle. The republican side received the assistance of the Soviet Union and Mexico, with volunteer brigades also coming from Britain, France, and the United States (the Americans called themselves members of the "Abraham Lincoln Brigade"). The fascist military, known as the *Falangists* and led by General Francisco Franco, received the assistance of the Germans and Italians.

≡ **The Struggle Against Fascism**   *Guernica*, one of the most famous paintings by renowned Spanish artist Pablo Picasso, is named for a Spanish town destroyed by bombing. The air forces of Italy and Germany carried out the attack to aid fellow fascist Francisco Franco as he fought a civil war against mostly left-leaning Spaniards.

The devastating bombing of the Basque town of Guernica by German and Italian air power was captured in its horrific dimensions by the artist Pablo Picasso. It was a symbol of the carnage being inflicted and remains an icon in the struggle against fascism.

The outcome of the civil war proved to be an ominous moment for the future. By the spring of 1939, the *Falangists* won militarily and politically. They would rule Spain, under Franco's leadership, for nearly another four decades, suggesting how powerful and enduring fascism could be on the ground. But they also emboldened the Germans whose ambitions now came to include the whole of Europe. That September, Hitler's armies, the *Wehrmacht*, invaded Poland and set off what we have come to call World War II.

New International Moves

Although FDR and the New Deal had moved in centralized and quasi-authoritarian directions, as was true in Japan, Italy, and Germany, FDR's foreign policy utterly lacked the imperial aggressiveness that was evident in Europe and Asia. Indeed, during the 1930s, the United States reversed a number of aggressive and imperial policies that had been in place since the turn of the twentieth century. In 1933, Roosevelt lent diplomatic recognition to the Soviet Union. Soon thereafter, he withdrew American troops from Haiti and Nicaragua, where they had been an occupying force, and then rolled back the Platt Amendment, which had given the United States the right to intervene in Cuban affairs. Looking out across the Western Hemisphere, FDR called for a **Good Neighbor Policy**, which meant reciprocal trade agreements and noninterference in the domestic politics of Latin American countries. Skepticism abounded in Latin America, given the history of the previous half-century, but it was a far cry from the Roosevelt Corollary to the Monroe Doctrine set down by FDR's cousin and predecessor Theodore (see Chapter 20).

But would there be an American response to fascist aggression overseas? For a time, the Abraham Lincoln Brigade, which attracted young socialists, communists, and republican sympathizers to the fight against the *Falangists* in Spain (more than 3,000 Americans took part and they sustained heavy casualties), was pretty much the extent of it. As in World War I, when Europe was engulfed in warfare, a strong isolationist streak ran across the United States. Led by midwestern Republicans and conservative southern Democrats, the isolationists were intent on keeping the country out of war in either Europe or Asia. Some had earlier opposed the participation of the United States in the League of Nations; some sympathized with the fascists and feared FDR would mobilize against them; the aviation hero Charles

Lindbergh, who made the first solo flight across the Atlantic, was one of them. Most worried that the country could be driven into a destructive war against its own interests, and a few latched onto conspiracy theories that saw arms manufacturers and bankers as the driving forces of intervention.

At all events, congressional isolationists tried to set a high bar. In 1935, they succeeded in passing a Neutrality Act, renewed in the two subsequent years, that prohibited American manufacturers from trading in munitions and other war materials with foreign nations engaged in warfare, and that warned American citizens who boarded ships owned by belligerents that they traveled at their own risk. The United States would not assume responsibility for their safety. Although FDR preferred a more selective embargo, he reluctantly signed the bill. After all, since none of the combatants had officially declared war thus far, the trading ban was effectively moot, and arms dealers continued their business transactions with all sides.

Yet there was more at stake. Roosevelt recognized that the United States was in a fairly weakened condition militarily. The army had fewer than 200,000 troops, the navy fewer than fifty warships, and the army air corps fewer than 1,000 planes. This was the harsh reality in the face of rapid militarization among the fascist nations. Nonetheless, there was still little interest in Congress to increase appropriations for the military. As late as April 1940, FDR's request for a small uptick in the military budget was largely rejected.

But a tipping point was about to be reached. In August 1939, Nazi Germany and the Soviet Union agreed to a limited alliance known as the **German-Soviet Non-Aggression Pact**, and both invaded Poland in September, Germany from the west and the Soviets from the east. The German *Wehrmacht* then moved rapidly through the Low Countries and by the spring of 1940 was storming into France. Paris was in the *Wehrmacht*'s sights, and thousands of British and French troops were trapped in the French coastal town of Dunkirk. They narrowly escaped when a massive flotilla out of south England came to their rescue. On June 14, 1940, the Nazis marched into Paris, menacingly through the Arc de Triomphe, and received the city's surrender. In a matter of months, most of Western Europe had fallen to the Nazis and the British were faced with bombardment and a threatened invasion.

Public opinion in the United States, especially given the aggression of the Nazis, was coming to favor support for the British and the French, and Roosevelt, who still maintained American neutrality, won massive new military spending from the Congress, especially for aircraft and warships. He also managed to have the Neutrality Acts revised so that needed goods could be supplied to Britain and France, though in their own ships, and a Selective Service (conscription) Act passed. Was the country heading toward war?

23.8   A Third Term for Franklin Roosevelt

||| Discuss why FDR sought a precedent-breaking third term.

It was an unfortunate moment for Franklin Roosevelt's term as president to be running out. Ever since the presidency of George Washington, the custom (it was not in the Constitution; only the length of a presidential term was established in Article II, Section 1) was that the chief executive would not serve more than two four-year terms. In fact, nearly one-third of them had served only one term. None had ever even gestured at a third term. And in early 1940 Roosevelt seemed to indicate that he would soon be leaving Washington, DC, for his estate at Hyde Park up the Hudson River in New York State. At least that is what everyone expected to happen.

Running for a Third Term

But the developing war in Europe and Asia appeared to change FDR's thinking. We don't have much of a sense of when he came to consider an unprecedented third term as president or what exactly his logic was. We don't know who advised him in any direction, and it appears that he kept much of his thinking to himself. But when the Democratic Party met in convention in Chicago later that summer, the delegates drafted him for a third term, which meant that he never officially declared his candidacy. His party did that for him. He happily accepted the nomination.

More controversial was Roosevelt's choice for vice president. Instead of asking Texan John Nance Garner, a conservative who had opposed some New Deal initiatives, to stay on, FDR nominated Henry A. Wallace of Iowa. A former Republican turned Democrat, Wallace had been serving as secretary of agriculture and was building a reputation not only as a strong supporter of New Deal programs but as something of a progressive visionary. He was quite the opposite of Garner. Conservative Democrats distrusted Wallace and worried that he opposed Jim Crow in the South. Old-line Democrats were suspicious of his origins as a Republican. Still, Roosevelt was insistent. He said he'd decline the nomination if Wallace was denied a place on the ticket, and Eleanor Roosevelt spoke powerfully in Wallace's favor at the convention. As might be expected, the party yielded and embraced them both.

The Election of 1940

The presidential election campaign revealed fault lines among the Republicans as well. There had long been an isolationist tradition among them, and its leading representative was Ohio's Robert A. Taft, the son of former president William Howard Taft. But the nomination went to a member of the party's more internationalist and interventionist wing (obviously reflecting events overseas), a former corporate

MAPPING AMERICA

The Good Neighbor Policy

In March 1933, in his first inaugural address, Roosevelt announced that US relations with the other American republics would be based on the "policy of the good neighbor, the neighbor who resolutely respects himself and, because he does so, respects the rights of others." The Good Neighbor Policy brought an end to direct US intervention in Latin America and redefined US–Latin American relations in less asymmetrical terms, but United States policy toward the region remained fundamentally

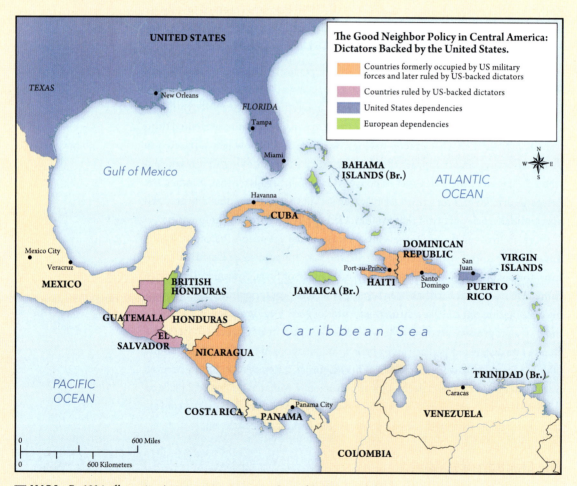

The Good Neighbor Policy in Central America: Dictators Backed by the United States.

- Countries formerly occupied by US military forces and later ruled by US-backed dictators
- Countries ruled by US-backed dictators
- United States dependencies
- European dependencies

MAP 1   By 1934, all ongoing American occupations in Central America and the Caribbean—Haiti, Nicaragua, Cuba, and the Dominican Republic—had come to an end. But in each country, US-trained national guards maintained order, and in all four countries the head of the National Guard, with strong US backing, eventually rose to hold authoritarian power. In the case of Nicaragua, the Somoza family would rule the country until 1979. With American support, dictators also seized control of Guatemala and El Salvador.

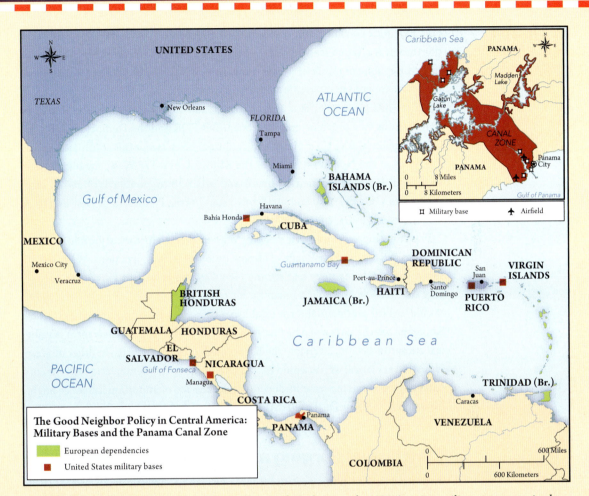

≡ **MAP 2**   Though US occupation forces had withdrawn from the region by 1934, American military power remained undiminished. Permanent bases dotted the Caribbean Basin, and while a treaty was signed between Panama and the United States in 1936 that eliminated Panama's status as an American protectorate, the United States still retained jurisdiction within the Canal Zone.

unchanged. Instead of the Marines, dictatorships now served American interests by preserving order, controlling radical reform movements, and protecting American investments.

Thinking Geographically

1. Mexico is one of the largest countries in Latin America, but it was not ruled by an American-backed dictator. What events in Mexico likely influenced the way the United States shaped its policy toward the rest of Latin America?

2. Roosevelt reputedly said of Anastasio Somoza, the dictator of Nicaragua, that "he's a son of a bitch, but he's our son of a bitch." What did Roosevelt mean?

executive and one-time Democrat from New York named Wendell Wilkie. So on one side there was a Republican turned Democrat (Wallace) and on the other a Democrat turned Republican (Wilkie). It was a measure of how the Great Depression, New Deal, and impending international warfare were realigning politics.

Wilkie had his own appeal and charisma, and 1940 turned into a closer election than the two previous ones had been. But FDR and the Democrats still won handily, maintaining their New Deal coalition. They swept the South along with the states of the Northeast, most of the Midwest, and Far West, suggesting that white southerners remained on board and urban immigrants continued to lend their votes. Only the rural and small-town states of the Plains, upper New England, Michigan, and Indiana went for Wilkie.

Franklin Roosevelt was now stepping onto uncharted historical ground and was about to face a global challenge of almost unfathomable proportions. What would this mean for the country and for the New Deal he had spent two terms putting together? And what would it mean for his critics on both the left and on the right? Would a third presidential term establish a precedent that could be embraced by Roosevelt's successors when he finally had them? Did it suggest a new form of political authoritarianism, a version of what seemed to be taking place in other modern industrial societies? What would be the fate of the social democratic experiments hatched by popular movements during the decade and of important influence on the direction of the New Deal itself? Wartime makes for dangers as well as possibilities.

Conclusion: Forging a Social Democracy

Beginning in 1935, under pressure from industrial and agricultural workers as well as from different groups on the political left, the New Deal moved in a social democratic direction. It not only put the welfare of ordinary Americans front and center but also sought to empower groups in American society who had long been pushed to the sidelines. At the same time, FDR looked to raise taxes on the very wealthy—leveling the playing field a bit—and to reorganize, some called it "packing," the conservative Supreme Court, which had been ruling some of his signature initiatives as unconstitutional. The result was a series of defeats for Roosevelt, including a serious recession in 1937, and the growth of a conservative, anti-New Deal coalition set on reversing his course.

Ominous, too, by the late 1930s were the aggressions of fascist and authoritarian regimes in Europe and Asia that would result in war in 1939. With crises brewing at home and abroad, FDR broke precedent, ran for, and won a third term as president, enabling him to preside over the fate of the New Deal during international warfare. What would be the results for the social democracy that had only recently been born?

WHAT IF the New Deal Continued Its Leftward March?

In 1937, the New Deal seemed to hit the wall in terms of its policy and social democratic initiatives. The combination of the "Roosevelt recession" and the court-packing debacle put FDR on the defensive and, for the first time, gave the initiative to his conservative opponents. There were already indications of this during the 1936 campaign, when Roosevelt, while touting the Social Security and Wagner Acts nonetheless began talking about "balancing the budget."

Even before he became president, FDR had some familiarity with the views of the British economist John Maynard Keynes, who emphasized that depressions could be enduring and that forms of deficit spending on the part of the government could be crucial in restarting significant economic growth. What if FDR had been more attentive to Keynes's ideas and the views of those to his left in the New Deal administration and, instead of cutting back on programs including public works, he used his landslide victory to continue and expand them, really making the federal government an engine of economic growth? Could FDR and the New Deal then have brought the Great Depression to an end instead of watching the country sink once again into economic distress? Would economic strength have changed the country's initial response to fascist aggression abroad and earlier tipped the balances in the direction of military preparedness? Could this have persuaded the fascists—Hitler did not think that the United States would move against him—to temper their ambitions?

DOCUMENT 23.1: "The Conservative Manifesto" by Josiah Bailey (1937)

The "Conservative Manifesto" was drafted in 1937 by a bipartisan group of conservative politicians led by North Carolina congressman Josiah Bailey, who opposed FDR's New Deal policies. The Manifesto included ten points.

1. Immediate revision of taxes on capital gains and undistributed profits in order to free investment funds.
2. Reduced expenditures to achieve a balanced budget, and thus, to still fears deterring business expansion.
3. An end to coercion and violence in relations between capital and labor.
4. Opposition to "unnecessary" government competition with private enterprise.
5. Recognition that private investment and enterprise require a reasonable profit.
6. Safeguarding the collateral upon which credit rests.
7. Reduction of taxes, or if this proved impossible at the moment, firm assurance of no further increases.
8. Maintenance of state rights, home rule, and local self-government, except where proved definitely inadequate.

9. Economical and non-political relief to unemployed with maximum local responsibility.

10. Reliance upon the American form of government and the American system of enterprise.

Source: *New York Times*, December 16, 1937.

DOCUMENT 23.2:   Excerpts from John Maynard Keynes, *The General Theory of Employment, Interest, and Money* (1936)

In The General Theory, *Keynes argues that market forces alone cannot solve the problems of the Great Depression. The solution was direct government action.*

I have called this book *The General Theory of Employment, Interest, and Money*, placing the emphasis on the prefix "general." The object of such a title is to contrast the character of my arguments and conclusions with those of the classical theory of the subject . . . which dominates the economic thought . . . of the governing and academic classes of this generation. I shall argue that the postulates of the classical theory are applicable to a special case only . . . Moreover, the characteristic of the special case assumed by classical theory happen not to be those of the economic society in which we a actually live . . . . If the Treasury were to fill old bottles with banknotes, bury them at suitable depths in disused coal mines . . . and leave it to private enterprise on well-tried principles of laissez-faire to dig the notes up again, there need be no more unemployment and . . . the real income of the community, and its capital wealth also, would probably become a good deal greater than it actually is. It would, indeed, be more sensible to build houses and the like; but if there are political and practical difficulties in the way of this, the above would be better than nothing.

—

Whilst, therefore, the enlargement of the functions of government, involved in the task of adjusting to one another the propensity to consume and the inducement to invest, would seem to a nineteenth-century publicist or to a contemporary American financier to be a terrific encroachment on individualism. I defend it, on the contrary, both as the only practicable means of avoiding the destruction of existing economic forms in their entirety and as the condition of the successful functioning of individual initiative.

For if effective demand is deficient, not only is the public scandal of wasted resources intolerable, but the individual enterpriser who seeks to bring these resources into action is operating with the odds loaded against him. The game of hazard which he plays is furnished with many zeros, so that the players *as a whole* will lose if they have the energy and hope to deal all the cards. Hitherto the increment of the world's wealth has fallen short of the aggregate of positive individual savings; and the difference has been made up by the losses of those whose courage and initiative have not been supplemented by exceptional skill or unusual good fortune. But if effective demand is adequate, average skill and average good fortune will be enough.

The authoritarian state systems of today seem to solve the problem of unemployment at the expense of efficiency and of freedom. It is certain that the world will not much longer tolerate the unemployment which, apart from brief intervals of excitement, is associated and in my opinion, inevitably associated with present-day capitalistic individualism. But it may be possible by a right analysis of the problem to cure the disease whilst preserving efficiency and freedom.

Source: https://www.gutenberg.org/ebooks/15776

Thinking About Contingency

1. What were the major differences in the views of Keynes and the Conservative Manifesto?
2. Although Roosevelt began to move toward the political center, how far was he still from what the Conservative Manifesto envisioned?
3. Whose view of economic policy seems more in line with present-day thinking?
4. What prevented Roosevelt from moving further to the left after 1936?

REVIEW QUESTIONS

1. What is the meaning of "social democracy," and how is it similar to and different from other forms of democracy: political democracy or economic democracy?

2. In 1935, the New Deal successfully implemented the Wagner Act and the Social Security Act. How similar or different were they in their intensions than the New Deal legislation of 1933 and 1934? Do they deserve to be considered part of a "second New Deal?"

3. What was the nature of "industrial unionism?" How did it differ from previous forms of unionism, and what institutional forms did industrial unionism take?

4. How would you describe the New Deal coalition? How different was it than previous Democratic Party coalitions? How was the coalition put together and why might it have endured?

5. African Americans had voted Republican since they gained the franchise in 1867 and continued to do so, where they could still vote, into the 1930s. But during the 1930s, Black people began to shift their political support to the Democratic Party, once the party of white supremacy and still a party in which conservative southern Democrats exercised a great deal of power. Why then would they begin to vote Democratic?

6. During the election campaign of 1936, FDR simultaneously celebrated social democratic initiatives like Social Security and talked of balancing the budget. Does this suggest his own ambivalence about New Deal reform and his ultimate loyalty to capitalism?

7. In 1937, FDR, apparently in an effort to protect New Deal programs like Social Security from being dismantled by the Supreme Court, pushed a scheme to "pack the court." Was this simply a power grab on his part, as his critics alleged, or were there good reasons for his doing this?

8. By the late 1930s, a new conservative movement was beginning to take shape in the United States. Where were its strongest bases of support, and what ideas motivated it beyond hostility to the New Deal and Roosevelt?

9. Until Hitler's invasion of Poland in September 1939, the American public overwhelmingly supported neutrality and opposed involvement in developing hostilities in Europe and Asia. Was this a mistake or a sensible perspective on American priorities?

10. In 1940, Franklin Roosevelt decided to run for a "third term" as president of the United States. Was this a dangerous precedent? Would it empower the presidency in ways well beyond the particular moment of 1940?

KEY TERMS

Congress of Industrial Organizations (CIO) (p. 971)

Conservative Manifesto (p. 982)

court packing (p. 981)

Emergency Relief Appropriations Act (p. 968)

German-Soviet Non-Aggression Pact (p. 988)

Good Neighbor Policy (p. 987)

Kristallnacht (p. 986)

National Labor Relations Board (NLRB) (p. 969)

Popular Front (p. 965)

Scottsboro Boys (p. 965)

sit-down strike (p. 972)

social democracy (p. 962)

Social Security Act (p. 970)

Spanish Civil War (p. 986)

Wagner Act (p. 969)

Works Progress Administration (WPA) (p. 968)

RECOMMENDED READINGS

Alan Brinkley, *The End of Reform: New Deal Liberalism in Recession and War* (Vintage, 1996).

Michael Denning, *The Cultural Front: The Laboring of American Culture in the Twentieth Century* (Verso, 1997).

Laura Kalman, *FDR's Gambit: The Court Packing Fight and the Rise of Legal Liberalism* (Oxford University Press, 2022).

Mark Mazower, *Dark Continent: Europe's Twentieth Century* (Vintage, 2000).

Edward McClelland, *Midnight in Vehicle City: General Motors, Flint, and the Strike That Created the Middle Class* (Beacon, 2022).

Kathryn Olmsted, *Right out of California: The 1930s and the Big Business Roots of Modern Conservatism* (New Press, 2017).

Kim Phillips-Fein, *Invisible Hands: The Businessmen's Crusade Against the New Deal* (Norton, 2010).

Harvard Sitkoff, *A New Deal for Blacks: The Emergence of Civil Rights as a National Issue* (Oxford University Press, 2008).

Ahmed White, *The Last Great Strike: Little Steel, the CIO, and the Struggle for Labor Rights in New Deal America* (University of California Press, 2019).

Flames of Global War, Visions of Global Peace

1940–1945

Chapter Outline

≡ **A Day of Infamy**   The wreckage of Hickam Airfield, December 7, 1941. The surprise attack on Pearl Harbor by the Japanese air force killed over 2,000 Americans (including 121 at Hickam), destroyed or damaged hundreds of planes, sunk numerous ships, and catapulted the United States into World War II.

On an otherwise quiet Memorial Day in 1942, Fred Korematsu, a twenty-three-year-old man of Japanese descent was arrested while walking down a street in his hometown of San Leandro, California, on the outskirts of Oakland. Several weeks earlier, the US military had begun rounding up both Japanese immigrants and Japanese Americans, acting upon instructions that President Franklin Roosevelt had issued in February, known as Executive Order 9066. The United States had declared war on Japan in December 1941 after Japanese war planes attacked the American naval base at Pearl Harbor in the Hawaiian Islands, and Roosevelt wanted all those who might threaten the country's security taken into custody and relocated to internment camps at various places in the West. There they would be kept under armed guard, surrounded by barbed wire, in prison-like conditions. Eventually more than 100,000 men, women, and children of Japanese descent were so "interned," uprooted from their homes and communities and stripped of many of their belongings whether or not they were citizens of the United States.

Korematsu had been born in California to Japanese immigrant parents, spoke little Japanese, and was unable to read it. He had already registered for the military draft

Timeline

1940	1941	1942	1943

1940 ▸ Congress passes Lend-Lease Act providing military support to the British before the United States was officially in the war

1941 ▸ Roosevelt proclaims Four Freedoms as statement of purpose in relation to the European war; the Nazis invade the Soviet Union and the Nazi regime moves toward the Final Solution; the March on Washington movement demands an end to racial discrimination in war industries; Japanese launch a surprise attack on Pearl Harbor; the United States declares war on Japan and Germany

1942 ▸ Roosevelt issues an executive order remanding people of Japanese descent to internment camps; Doolittle raid on Tokyo; Battle of Midway

and then volunteered to serve in the US Navy. None of that mattered because of his Japanese origins, but unlike most others of Japanese ancestry living in the country, Fred Korematsu resisted Roosevelt's policy and the military's coercions and forced relocations it put in place. As a result, he was arrested, tried, sentenced to five years of probation, and sent to a detention center. But a lawyer for the American Civil Liberties Union learned about Korematsu's travails and, together, they brought suit against the constitutionality of the internment order.

The case reached the Supreme Court in 1944 and, in a 6–3 decision, the Court upheld Korematsu's conviction. Writing for the majority, Justice Hugo Black, appointed to the Court by FDR, argued that Korematsu and other Japanese in the West were sent to internment camps not because of "hostility to him and his race" but rather because of "military dangers" and "military urgency." The three justices in the minority, however, were deeply alarmed, saw serious racial discrimination in play, and believed that the ruling was "like a loaded weapon, ready for the hand of any authority that can bring forward a plausible claim of urgent need."

1944	1945	1946	1947

1944 >
June 6 Allied invasion of Normandy, France
November FDR elected to a fourth term as president; Harry Truman becomes vice president

1945 >
April FDR dies; Truman becomes president
May Surrender of Nazi Germany
July Successful test of the atomic bomb
August Atomic bombs dropped on Hiroshima and Nagasaki; Japan surrenders

The justices in the minority were not alone. The *Washington Post* declared the ruling "Legalized Racism," and the *Pittsburgh Courier*, one of the nation's leading African American newspapers, had seen it all before and compared the Court's ruling to the infamous *Dred Scott* decision of 1857. After all, although people of German and Italian descent could also be regarded as "threats" to the country's security, very few, viewed as white, were treated so punitively.

Despite the dissents and protests, the American public at large saw nothing wrong or unconstitutional about what was done to those of Japanese ancestry during the war, and it took another court filing, forty years later (1983) for a federal judge to throw out Korematsu's conviction. Then, in 1988, Congress passed a "Civil Liberties Act" that offered an apology and compensation to those who were detained, and, after another decade, Fred Korematsu, who had become a civil rights activist, was awarded the Medal of Freedom by President Bill Clinton. Yet, to this day, *Korematsu v. United States* has still to be formally overturned by the Supreme Court of the United States.

"The first casualties of war," legal scholars and defenders of civil liberties have often said, "are truth and freedom of expression." And, although wartime does impose some necessary constraints in the service of military success, the burdens of repression often fall most heavily on those with politically dissenting views and of minority racial status. Franklin Roosevelt declared that the war against the fascist powers was being waged to secure the "four freedoms." Those included freedom from fear and freedom of speech as well as freedom from want and freedom of worship. But Roosevelt also issued Executive Order 9066 and mostly worked to squelch protests against racial discrimination during the war effort. These tensions and contradictions suggest that the war being fought on a global scale raised as many questions about forging a future as it did about defending a present.

24.1   War and National Mobilization

Describe how President Roosevelt steered the United States toward involvement in the new world war.

Although it is difficult to pinpoint the moment when the prospects of world warfare became likely or nearly inevitable—Hitler's rise to power, the Japanese invasion of China, the Spanish Civil War—there can be little doubt that the Nazi and Soviet invasions of

Poland in September 1939, the fruits of their Non-Aggression Pact, fully detonated the explosives that had already been lit. Great Britain and France immediately declared war on Germany, and the Wehrmacht began its march across Western Europe, quickly bringing the Netherlands, Belgium, Denmark, Norway, and France under its heel. Before long, the Germans started a devastating aerial bombardment of Britain, prelude to a planned cross–English Channel invasion. As a result, it was more and more difficult for the United States to remain on the sidelines, somehow imagining that isolationism or minimal involvement in the new conflagration could be maintained.

Hitler's Plans and FDR's Views

What did Hitler and the Nazis hope to achieve? Their plan for a new "order" was ever-changing and expanding, as it had been since the mid-1930s. And there is no real evidence for a grand blueprint even when Nazi Germany invaded Poland. But, at the very least, they expected to turn Germany, already an authoritarian state, into the central power in Europe, crush liberal and parliamentary regimes everywhere on the continent, make them clients of Germany, avail themselves of the resources and labor of European countries, and extend their political reach well to the east, to Poland, the Balkans, and the Ukraine. There they could find additional labor, which would be reduced to virtual enslavement, raw materials, and land for German peasant colonists ("breathing space," as they called it). They also intended to establish the supremacy of Aryan culture, which they understood in racial terms, and drive out racial and political undesirables, the Jews, who were regarded as racial *and* political threats, chief among them. As for the United States, it did not really figure in Hitler's immediate plans. "America," he snorted in 1939, "is not dangerous to us."

Franklin Roosevelt saw things differently and increasingly regarded Nazi Germany as a lethal threat to American security and one that would likely need to be confronted. He regretted having signed neutrality legislation, worried that Great Britain would fall to the Nazis without American assistance, and believed that a British defeat would expose the United States to Nazi attack. The United States, Roosevelt insisted, needed to be the "arsenal of democracy" even if it did not formally enter the war.

Still, military preparedness remained a tough sell in Congress. An alliance between southern conservatives and Midwestern isolationists kept any moves in this direction in check. That is, until the spring of 1940. With France about to fall and the Italian fascists formally allied with Germany, Congress came fully around. It not only supported Roosevelt's request for more than $1 billion in defense-related spending, especially for aircraft and naval vessels; it also gave him a half billion more than he asked for. Before long Congress enacted a peacetime military draft and passed a bill appropriating military support for the British, known as **Lend-Lease**. A massive military buildup was underway without war being declared,

PERSPECTIVES

The Four Freedoms, Then and Now

On the night of January 6, 1941, in his State of the Union address, President Roosevelt articulated the core values of a new vision for the country and for humanity: "The first is freedom of speech . . . the second is freedom to worship . . . the third is freedom from want . . . the third is freedom from fear. . . . That is no vision of a distant millennium. It is a definite basis for a kind of world attainable in our own time and generation. That kind of world is the very antithesis of the so-called 'new order' of tyranny which the dictators seek to create." FDR's Four Freedoms' speech prepared Americans for the looming conflict and underscored the country's core beliefs.

After the United States entered the war in December 1941, Roosevelt's advisers knew that they needed powerful, emotional symbols to visualize the American war effort. To do this, they turned to Norman Rockwell, the country's preeminent illustrator and best-loved artist. Rockwell's assignment was to turn Roosevelt's words into images. He did so brilliantly. The four paintings—*Freedom of Speech,*

≡ **Rockwell's *Four Freedoms*** Norman Rockwell gave visual expression to Roosevelt's Four Freedoms, and his paintings were viewed by millions of Americas when the *Saturday Evening Post* published them as cover art early in 1943. Shown here are *Freedom of Speech* and *Freedom of Worship.*

Freedom of Worship, Freedom from Want, and *Freedom from Fear*—ran as covers for *The Saturday Evening Post* from February 20, 1943, to March 13, 1943.

For many Americans in 1943, Rockwell painted America exactly how they wished to see themselves. But the ideals expressed in *Four Freedoms* did not always match reality. African Americans, Asian Americans, Mexican Americans, and other minorities experienced racism and intolerance even as the United States fought against fascism and authoritarianism in Europe and Asia.

In 2018, the artists Hank Willis Thomas and Helen Shur created a series of monumental images that reconceived Rockwell's America. The images reference Rockwell's well-known originals but convey a new narrative about what contemporary freedom looks like in America today.

≡ **Reconceiving Rockwell's America**

CONSIDER THIS

Rockwell's *Four Freedoms* paintings were reproduced and distributed across the nation as posters, reminders to millions of Americans of the cause for which their soldiers were fighting and dying. What is the emotional appeal of *Four Freedoms*? Do Thomas's and Shur's images force you to rethink to whom American freedoms were granted in 1943? In 2023?

yet Roosevelt tied the buildup to principles, what he called "four essential human freedoms" that the policies were meant to defend: freedom of speech, freedom of religion, freedom from want, and freedom from fear. Known as the **Four Freedoms**, it was the first though not the last American statement of purpose in relation to the war.

Developments in East Asia

But the eyes of the Roosevelt administration were not only on developments in Europe; they were also on developments in East Asia, where the Japanese were flexing imperial muscles and making military moves that could be regarded as threatening. China was the focus of attention both because of long-term American interest there (more emotional than economic) and because the Japanese had invaded China in 1937 and engaged in brutal destruction. Perhaps most appalling, after the Japanese marched into the Chinese city of Nanjing, they murdered more than 300,000 men, women, and children, an episode known to this day as the "Rape of Nanjing," in part because, in addition to other atrocities, many thousands of women were sexually assaulted.

Aspiring to be the dominant power in the western Pacific, the Japanese had looked, since the early 1930s, to extend their influence and gain access to essential raw materials. Like the Germans, they sought "breathing space" (to the west rather than to the east) and toward that end took control of the Chinese province of Manchuria, renamed "Manchukuo" by the Japanese, in 1931, quickly settling thousands of Japanese peasants there to produce needed foodstuffs. Dependent on oil, steel, and rubber imports, they also pivoted toward the French, British, and Dutch colonies of Southeast Asia, as well as the Philippines, and began to imagine a Greater East Asia Co-Prosperity Sphere. It was a euphemistic language for Japanese imperialism.

Although the United States had refused to recognize the Japanese puppet state of Manchukuo, no actions were taken in response to Japanese aggression there. After 1937, however, the Roosevelt administration attempted to tighten the reins on the Japanese economy by restricting American exports of scrap metal and high-grade petroleum (used for aircraft), and eventually by freezing Japanese assets in the United States. Now Japanese leaders recognized that they had to take action to free up the supply lines: the question was what action they should take?

The Nazis Turn East

A turning point for all of the global powers came in June 1941. Up until then, the Nazis had focused their might on western Europe and Britain, and seemed poised to move their troops across the English Channel in a large-scale invasion. But suddenly, Hitler abandoned these plans and instead launched a massive—almost four million troops—invasion of the Soviet Union, called Operation Barbarossa. It had not been expected. The Germans and the Soviets had signed a Non-Aggression Pact in 1939, and Josef Stalin, the Soviet leader, mindful of how the hostilities of the 1914–1919 period brought down the Tsarist regime, believed that he had purchased his own form of breathing space along the Soviet Union's western border. Now the Wehrmacht was heading toward Moscow, expecting to destroy the Soviet state and reduce the Soviet Union to a vassal of the Nazi regime (see Map 24.1).

The Nazi about-face raised a host of questions. For the British and their leader, Winston Churchill, the question was whether to establish a formal alliance with Stalin. Churchill was a conservative and vehement anticommunist, but he was also focused on defeating the Nazis and, to that end, saw no option other than extending a hand to the Soviets in hopes of enabling them to turn Hitler's forces back. "I will unsay no word that I have spoken [against communism]," Churchill declared, "but all that fades away before the spectacle which is now unfolding. Any man or state who fights on against Nazism will have our aid."

For the United States, which had recognized the Soviet Union during Roosevelt's first term, the question was whether Stalin could be supplied in the manner of Lend-Lease (it was too early for an alliance, since the United States was not yet in the war). And for the Japanese, the question was whether they should join the Nazis in an attack on the Soviet Union, favored by one faction in the Japanese government called the "northerners," or continue to look southward and move aggressively to

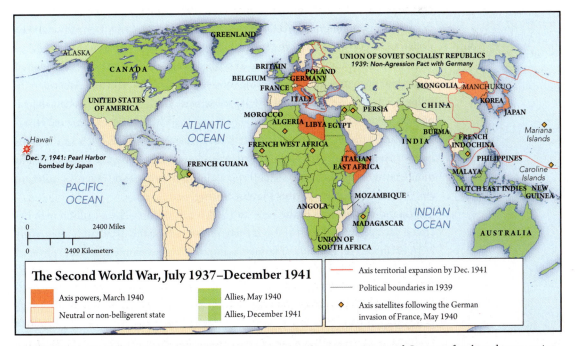

MAP 24.1   World War II, July 1937–December 1941   Until May 1941 Japan and Germany fought and won a series of regional campaigns. But when Japan attacked the United States on December 7, 1941, the conflict acquired a global dimension.

claim the rice paddies, rubber plantations, and oil fields of Indochina, Malaya, and the East Indies, favored by another faction called the "southerners." In July 1941, at a conference with Japanese Emperor Hirohito in attendance, the southerners won out, initiating what was known as the "Southern Operation," and putting Japan and the United States on a new collision course.

Pearl Harbor and American Entry into the War

Why was that? The Japanese had no interest in invading the United States. That would have been pointless and impossible to achieve. But they had to prevent the United States, already a large and formidable power in the Pacific, from intervening against them in Southeast Asia. Thus, they decided to launch a surprise attack on the American fleet stationed in the Hawaiian Islands at Pearl Harbor, hoping to inflict a blow from which the United States would not soon recover, and enable the Japanese to do as they pleased in the South Pacific. It was an audacious move and required sending an aircraft carrier force and flotilla many hundreds of miles from Japan, avoiding detection, and then sending fighter planes from the carrier decks to sink American battleships anchored in Pearl Harbor and destroy American planes on the nearby airfields. In the early morning hours of December 7, 1941, they did just that. The following day, after Roosevelt told a Joint Session of Congress that December 7 "would live in infamy," the United States declared war on Japan and officially gave Roosevelt sweeping war powers. Three days later, Germany and Italy responded by declaring war on the United States. The battle was now fully joined (see Map 24.1).

The Roosevelt administration had by no means been caught unaware. The United States had been on a near-war footing for over a year and a half, and American intelligence had determined that the Japanese were likely to strike, though the expectation was that the strike would be against the Philippines or some other target in the South Pacific (there is no reliable evidence that FDR knew of the Pearl Harbor attack despite the claims of some historians). But now the engines of war mobilization were turned up to full speed, both in terms of military recruitment and training and of war-related manufacturing.

Under the provisions of the Selective Service Acts, forty-three million men between the ages of eighteen and sixty-five registered for the draft, and, after many were exempted on grounds of family responsibility, government service, physical disability, and religious opposition to war, more than ten million were conscripted. When volunteers and women are included, more than sixteen million served in uniform during the course of the war, representing nearly 20 percent of all families in the United States.

At the same time, an economy that had been languishing for years was suddenly operating at full capacity, and the spark and direction, not to mention the resources,

Table 24.1 Military Production in the United States, 1942–1945
297,000 aircraft
193,000 artillery pieces
86,000 tanks
2.4 million military trucks and jeeps
1,200 combat vessels
8,800 total naval vessels
87,000 landing craft
3,300 merchant ships and tankers
14 million shoulder arms
5 million pounds of bombs
40 billion bullets

came by way of the federal government. The New Deal offered some precedent for large-scale government intervention in economic life. Yet what happened during the war far overshadowed what had been done during the 1930s. Indeed, while the private ownership of industry and agriculture remained untouched, the Roosevelt administration took a central role, especially through a War Production Board headed by Sears, Roebuck executive Donald Nelson, in directing production, managing relations between labor and capital, controlling prices, rationing necessary goods, and, of course, footing the bill. War spending grew from about $3.5 billion in 1940 to well over $90 billion in 1944, just under half of it raised by new taxes. There was little resistance, even from conservative critics of the New Deal, because there was no other way and because, despite some coercive measures, Roosevelt created an environment much friendlier to business than to reform.

The results were nothing short of remarkable (see Table 24.1). Roosevelt did not simply want to meet the demands of what was a global war effort; he wanted to exceed them. "It will not be sufficient for us and the other United Nations [as US allies in the fight were called] to produce a slightly superior supply of munitions to that of Germany, Japan, and Italy," FDR insisted in early 1942. "The superiority of the United Nations in munitions and ships must be overwhelming."

The United States would clearly lead the way, given its resources. Manufacturers who had been turning out consumer goods such as clothing and automobiles began to turn out uniforms, tanks, aircraft, warships, and other armaments. New industries were developed when raw materials became inaccessible. When Japanese

MAPPING AMERICA

Wartime Mobilization and the Rise of the Sunbelt

The West and South were transformed by wartime mobilization. Military planners were drawn to the plentiful cheap labor and ample land these regions offered. As the American defense industry ramped up production, people from nonindustrial backgrounds, rural farm workers, and women were drawn into war work. The cities of the South and West, such as Seattle, Los Angeles, Phoenix, Houston, and Dallas, boomed.

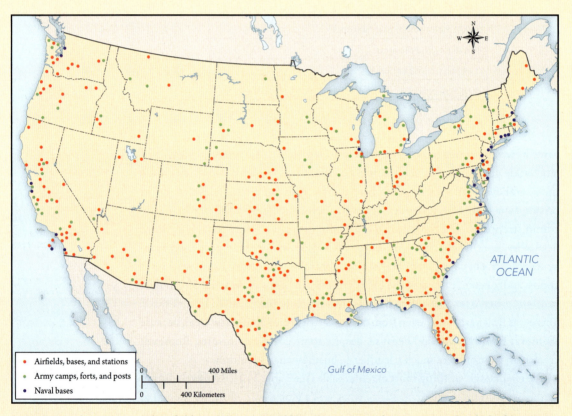

- • Airfields, bases, and stations
- • Army camps, forts, and posts
- • Naval bases

400 Miles

400 Kilometers

ATLANTIC OCEAN

Gulf of Mexico

≡ **MAP 1   Military Bases and Airfields Built During World War II**   By 1945, the West emerged as the leading center of the military-industrial complex. In the South, workers were drawn to the numerous airfields and bases that dotted the region.

≡ **MAP 2   Population Change, 1940–1960**   By the end of the war, nearly two million Americans had moved to California to work in one of its many defense-related industries, and millions more shipped out to the Pacific war from the naval station of San Diego. The shift of the country's population west and south would intensify during the postwar period.

Thinking Geographically

1. How did the construction of hundreds of military installations in the West and South during World War II impact the demographics of these regions? What impact did they have on culture and on politics?

2. Can the great movement of people west and south during and after World War II be thought of as a "migration"? Why or why not?

occupation of much of Southeast Asia cut off supplies of natural rubber, synthetic rubber was devised. Workers who had been unemployed and underemployed were back on the shop floor, generally benefitting from higher wages. Eventually, American industry produced more planes, ships, and tanks than Germany, Italy, and Japan combined. This massive, government-sponsored economic mobilization, not the New Deal, brought the Great Depression to an end.

The war-related economic mobilization also furthered the geographical shifts in the American political economy that had begun during the New Deal. Government spending aided many sectors of the nation's economy, and much of our attention usually goes to steel, automobiles, chemical, and armaments, which often were located in the Northeast and Midwest. But the need for new military bases, training facilities, aircraft plants, and shipyards brought windfalls of government investment to the South and, especially, the Far West. California alone received about 10 percent of all war-time government spending, and the multiplication of these new sites not only ignited the industrialization of regions that had long been devoted to agriculture, mining, processing, and commerce but also led to large-scale migrations. Thousands of men and women relocated, some by virtue of their being in the armed forces, to parts of the Deep South, to Texas, and, perhaps in greatest numbers, to the Pacific coast. Oakland, Los Angeles, San Diego, and Seattle boomed. The foundations of what would later be called the **Sunbelt**, stretching from the Carolinas in the east to southern California in the west, a belt of defense-related industries and research institutions, were being established. They were examples of the war's enormous transformational impact.

24.2   Racialization and Extermination

Understand why certain social and ethnic groups like the Japanese were targeted for persecution during the war and how ideas about race and racial inferiority drove murderous policies such as the Holocaust against Jews.

The war in all theaters, Europe and the Pacific, soon came to stand out not only for the scale of military forces deployed on all sides but also for the exposure of civilian populations to the war's wrath. To be sure, civilians and noncombatants more generally have always been vulnerable when societies went to war. Their capture, punishment, and murder have always been part of the aggression and retribution that warfare brings. Wars among Indigenous peoples and between Indigenous peoples and Euro-Americans surely demonstrated that. But what was quickly being recognized as a "Second World War" brought truly horrific levels of civilian casualties.

More than fifty million men, women, and children who were noncombatants died during this period, more than twice the number of deaths among military personnel. In contrast, during World War I about equal numbers of soldiers and civilians died, roughly eight million each. Increasingly sophisticated weapons technology and the massive use of air power account for some of the great horror; the racialization of the war, on all sides, accounted for much of it as well.

Making of the Holocaust

What does this mean? The first half of the twentieth century, particularly in the broad Atlantic world, saw the linking of racial thought with scientific practice. Ideas about racial difference and hierarchies, which had been taking hold in many places during the nineteenth century, gained further legitimacy from their association with national projects of public health and population growth and from the interest that some scientists lent to them. The eugenics movement, concerned with improving the "stock" of modern societies by encouraging reproduction among social groups thought to be genetically superior ("pro-natalism" as it was known) and discouraging reproduction among those thought to be genetically inferior, leading to calls for sterilization in some cases, thus spread rapidly through Europe and the United States during the early decades of the twentieth century, serving to intensify forms of racism and anti-Semitism.

The bitter fruits of such thinking became especially disastrous in Nazi Germany. The victims were the Jews. Anti-Semitism was by no means a specifically German cultural phenomenon. It was to be found across continental Europe and Russia, in Great Britain, and the United States. The "Protocols of the Elders of Zion," a text alleging a Jewish conspiracy to dominate the world, was first published in Russia in 1903 and then translated and circulated very widely. American auto manufacturer Henry Ford financed the publication of half a million copies. Adolf Hitler himself was deeply influenced by it.

Hitler and the Nazi Reich, that is to say, emerged in an environment where hostility toward the Jews was already rife and, in many areas, fairly deep. But Hitler and the Nazis took anti-Semitism to another level entirely, yoking the racial with the political. The Nazis celebrated the superiority of what they called Aryan civilization, a concept that was simultaneously nationalist, cultural, religious, and racial, and they demonized as enemies those who were not inside their sacred Aryan circle. Those who could not claim German ancestry, were not Protestant, were not white, were often on the move, or who veered to the left politically were eyed with suspicion if not subject to various forms of repression and persecution. Communists, socialists, trade unionists, Slavs, Romani, and gay people all became targets. Many would be killed.

≡ **Anti-Semitic Propaganda**   The postcard promoted an anti-Semitic exhibition that traveled throughout Europe in 1937. The illustration engages in a number of tropes, showing a disheveled man with gold coins (to indicate ill-gotten wealth) and a whip (to symbolize domination). The map of Germany with a hammer and sickle is meant to imply a connection between Judaism and communism.

But the Jews had several strikes against them. They were regarded as racially distinct, loyal to no one but themselves, obsessed with money, and heavily represented among those on the political left, especially the newly powerful Bolshevik Party in the Soviet Union that the Nazis so feared. The picture was a jumble of contradictions. Jews were depicted as inordinately wealthy, able to use their wealth to manipulate the world of politics, unclean, politically radical, and threatening contamination even if their numbers were relatively few. And, in most places, they had few committed allies to defend them. They were, in sum, both despised and vulnerable.

Nazi policy toward the Jews passed through phases. Soon after gaining power, the Nazis moved to push Jews out of the professions and educational institutions, confiscate their property and assets, regulate their behavior and living conditions, ban marriages between Jews and gentiles, and create an environment of general subjugation. Many Jews were herded into new urban "ghettos" or rounded up and sent to labor camps. Others could be shot down in the street, executed for simple acts of disobedience. All had to wear emblems of their inferiority in public—yellow Stars of David sown onto their clothing. But initially the Nazi goal was to expel Jews from the Reich, send them into exile in the East or even to some far-off colony such as Madagascar in the Indian Ocean, ridding Germany of what the Nazis saw as disease and contagion.

Only with the Nazi invasion of the Soviet Union in the summer of 1941 and the further radicalization of the war, did the **Final Solution** of the Jewish "problem" (in other words, their very presence) shift to outright exterminism. From that point forward Jewish men, women, and children were sent by the thousands to death camps—Auschwitz, Birkenau, Treblinka, Belzec, Sobibor, Chelmno, all in Nazi-occupied Poland—not only from Germany but from across the European continent, where they were starved, enslaved, shot, gassed, and incinerated. Owing to its horrific scale of death, this "final," exterminist solution is called the **Holocaust**. By the time the war was over, some six million had been murdered or about two-thirds of all the Jews who lived in Europe as late as 1939 (see Map 24.2).

What did Americans or anyone outside of Germany know of the Holocaust? By the late 1930s, the Roosevelt administration was well aware of Nazi persecution of

The Holocaust

The Holocaust	
■ German Reich	▲ Death camp
□ Country occupied or allied with Germany	■ Concentration camp or internment camp
■ Vichy France	✡ Ghetto
■ Neutral country	

≡ **MAP 24.2   The Holocaust**   Only 2 percent of deportees survived the Nazi death camps. Among the victims were 86 percent of Poland's prewar Jewish population, 75 percent of Dutch Jews, and two-thirds of Romanian Jews. The lack of opposition to German's genocidal campaign helps explain the staggeringly high death toll.

Jews as well as of Jewish efforts to seek safe refuge, but it did relatively little to help. Previous immigration laws, especially the law of 1924, had intentionally set small quotas for immigrants from central and eastern Europe and, despite pressure from some quarters, including from Eleanor Roosevelt, the quotas were not raised and substantial asylum was not offered. News of Nazi death camps then began to seep out by the summer of 1942 (to Britain as well) and was a topic of discussion among American officials by that December.

But aside from strong statements against Nazi atrocities, there was not much action from the Roosevelt administration. In part this was because Roosevelt and the Allies, particularly the British, were focused on defeating the Nazis militarily and refused to deflect attention from this goal. Roosevelt argued that the only way to save Jews was to defeat the Germans. And in part this was because anti-Semitism had its own constituencies of support in the United States and would complicate any efforts to intervene on the Jews' behalf. Ultimately, in January 1944, as evidence of Nazi exterminations continued to mount, Roosevelt created the **War Refugee Board**, which managed to rescue and resettle as many as 200,000 European Jews. But it was far too late for millions of others.

Racism in Asia and at Home

Murderous anti-Semitism was easily the most dreadful and destructive form of racism that afflicted the globe during World War II, but it did not stand alone. Indeed, racism and ethnocentrism were widespread among the Allies as well as the Axis, and they left ugly stains on the United States, especially when it came to the Japanese. Anti-Japanese sentiment grew out of deeper anti-Asian, and especially anti-Chinese, sensibilities that had surfaced in the mid-nineteenth century. Regarded not only as aliens but also as heathens (non-Christians) and "coolies," the Chinese were objects of scorn, derision, and terrorism despite the immense labor they performed in the building of the trans-Mississippi West (see Chapter 17). After 1882 Chinese laborers could no longer immigrate to the United States, and by the early twentieth century, Japanese workers suffered a similar fate. Neither the Chinese nor the Japanese, nor any other Asians except for Filipinos, who were

≡ **Manzanar.** In 1943 photographer Ansel Adams traveled to the Manzanar internment camp in the high desert east of California's Sierra Nevada mountains. His photos highlight the dignity and stability Japanese Americans sought to create despite the suspension of their rights.

under American colonial authority, could be naturalized as citizens of the United States and participate in the country's civil and political life. California, where the Japanese and Chinese lived in greatest numbers, went so far as to deny them the right to buy or own land.

By the time Pearl Harbor was attacked, there was fairly significant prejudice against the Japanese, and the United States exploited it in the process of mobilizing popular sentiment for the war. Generally referred to as "Japs," "Nips" (a play on Nippon, the Japanese term for their own country), apes, and the "yellow peril," the Japanese were deemed racially inferior, prone to violence and mayhem, almost subhuman (or simultaneously superhuman), and treacherous: a race of people who placed little value on life, whether their own or anybody else's. Some American political and military officials called for an outright annihilationist policy against the Japanese, killing as many of them as possible, eliminating them "as a race." A few favored "the extermination of the Japanese in toto." Small wonder that the firebombing of Japanese cities and ultimately the use of an atomic bomb achieved strong levels of public support.

Nothing similar was said about either the Germans or the Italians, and the hands of surveillance and repression touched lightly on the millions of German and Italian ancestry in the United States. Not so with the Japanese, who were thought of as subversives, a veritable "fifth column" waiting to aid the Japanese army whenever it might arrive. As a result, they quickly became targets for mass evacuation and transport to **internment camps** (see Map 24.3). And there was little opposition to this among Democrats or Republicans. Indeed, about two months after Pearl Harbor, in February 1942, President Roosevelt issued Executive Order 9066, under which more than 110,000

MAP 24.3 Japanese American Internment Camps During World War II In February 1942, President Roosevelt issued Executive Order 9066, under which more than 110,000 men, women, and children of Japanese descent were removed from the West Coast states of California, Oregon, and Washington, as well as from parts of Arizona, and sent to one of ten isolated camps.

≡ **Racial Violence**   (*Left*) A Black resident of Detroit is accosted by a white man while police officers look on. During three days of rioting and racial violence in 1943, over thirty Detroit residents were killed, and hundreds wounded, over two-thirds of them Black. (*Right*) In the summer of 1943, American servicemen in Los Angeles engaged in a number of attacks against mostly Mexican American residents. Known as the Zoot Suit riots for the iconic clothing popular with Mexican Americans, nearly a week of violence left hundreds wounded and hundreds more in jail.

men, women, and children of Japanese descent, whether **Issei** (Japanese who were themselves immigrants) or **Nisei** (people of Japanese origins born in the United States and who were citizens under the Fourteenth Amendment) were removed from the West Coast states of California, Oregon, and Washington, as well as from parts of Arizona, and sent to one of ten isolated camps, effectively concentration camps, located in Wyoming, Utah, Arizona, Colorado, Arkansas, Idaho, and the foothills of the California sierras (that camp, Manzanar, was the largest of all the camps). There they were put under armed guard and, in many cases, offered minimal facilities. It was a black mark on American wartime policy though one whose constitutionality would be upheld by the US Supreme Court in 1944 in *Korematsu v. United States* (Fred Korematsu, as we saw, had resisted internment and was appealing his arrest).

The Japanese had their own version of racial supremacy and, as in the United States, it developed in an imperial context. Japan's occupation of Taiwan (1895), Korea (1905), Manchuria (1931), parts of mainland China (1937), and eventually Indochina encouraged widespread discrimination, repression, and violence, including the introduction of sexual slavery among women and girls there, who were euphemistically termed "comfort women." As many as 200,000 females may have been degraded and assaulted in this way. Japanese racial supremacy involved, as well, the representations of the subject peoples as inferiors in a number of respects, together with practices of exploitation and discrimination against those who made their way to Japan itself, some being brought in as contract laborers. The Japanese were determined to maintain as much racial and cultural homogeneity as possible on their home island, even as they hoped to reap the benefits of their imperial reach.

Jim Crow Humiliations and Violence

The American embrace of internment for the Japanese was especially egregious, but it dramatized both the deep traditions of racism in the country as a whole as well as the contradictions of fighting a war against fascism abroad while supporting racism at home. The US military, racially segregated since the Civil War when Black troops first served officially, continued to be segregated despite the protests of African American leaders, while much of American life—in all parts of the country—continued to show the powerful imprint of Jim Crow in relation to politics, housing, education, public accommodations, employment, and social services. Racial tensions simmered on the home front. African Americans courted attack when they crossed into white neighborhoods or exercised rights to which they were legally entitled. Detroit saw three days of rioting in June 1943, which left twenty-five Black people dead, and other cities like Los Angeles; Mobile, Alabama; and Beaumont, Texas, saw racial violence as well.

Draft boards, especially all-white boards, reflected the tense climate and often refused to call African Americans for military service. Most of the African American men and women who did serve during the war (about 1.2 million in all) were assigned to noncombatant roles. Only gradually, as casualties mounted, were African Americans sent into combat, in the air corps as well as in the infantry and navy, where they distinguished themselves. Very few joined the Marines, owing to its previous policy of racial exclusion.

24.3 Openings for Change

Explain why the war provided openings of social change, especially for women and African Americans in the United States.

But if the war encouraged the spread of racism and ethnocentrism, and of brutal violence associated with them, it also opened avenues for change. It was not the first time. Ever since the American Revolution, the engagement of the US government in warfare, with the exception of warfare against Indigenous peoples, often served to disrupt older forms of hierarchy and discrimination, and force a confrontation between the country's stated ideals and its common practices. The War of the Rebellion not only ended slavery but also established birthright citizenship, equal standing before the law, and an end to racial discrimination in voting (at least in theory). World War I helped bring about the enfranchisement of women through the Nineteenth Amendment to the Constitution. Now a world war against fascism with the United States representing itself as the "arsenal of democracy" shook things up even further.

Expanding Struggles for Black Rights

Recognizing that mere support for the fight against fascism would not earn them the equality they had long been denied, African Americans looked to take charge of the political dynamics of war from the outset. The Black-owned *Pittsburgh Courier,* one of the most widely circulated of African American newspapers, went so far as to call explicitly for a "Double Victory," for "victory over our enemies at home and victory over our enemies on the battlefields abroad." The struggle was quickly underway. Building on protest activities of the 1930s that helped desegregate some retail establishments and the CIO, as well as on their growing political clout in northern cities, African American leaders and their organizations, like the NAACP, pressed to end discrimination in the military and the industrial sector. To advance these goals, A. Philip Randolph, president of the Brotherhood of Sleeping Car Porters and influential social democrat, along with the pacifist and socialist Bayard Rustin, planned a mass march on Washington, DC, for July 1, 1941. Expecting 100,000 marchers to participate, they hoped to dramatize the existence of Jim Crow at the heart of the war mobilization and pressure the Roosevelt administration to act.

Worried about the political fallout of this March on Washington movement, President Roosevelt cut a deal with the movement leaders. In return for their calling off the march, Roosevelt issued an executive order banning employment discrimination in defense industries that received federal contracts and establishing the **Fair Employment Practices Committee (FEPC)** to monitor compliance. Traditions of segregation in the military remained tenaciously in place and Roosevelt refused to move against them. But there were new opportunities for African Americans to serve as officers (commanding Black, not white, troops) and to gain flight training when a school for aspiring Black airmen was opened in Tuskegee, Alabama, site of Booker T. Washington's Normal and Industrial Institute. Small steps to be sure, but many African Americans, in the armed services and out, were readying themselves to take much bigger ones.

There was already evidence of activism closer to the ground. Pauli Murray, who grew up in Baltimore and North Carolina before moving to Harlem, found her way forward educationally constantly blocked because of her race and gender. She eventually attended Hunter College in New York (one of the very few in which African Americans could enroll) and Howard University Law School in Washington, DC, a historically Black institution of higher education, but she also decided to take on the humiliating constraints of Jim Crow. First, she first attempted to desegregate a bus

≡ **Tuskegee Airmen**   Black military pilots in Italy listen to a briefing in preparation for a mission. Known as the Tuskegee Airmen for the Alabama college and airfield where they trained, they were the first Black aviators in the US Armed Forces and enjoyed a distinguished reputation during the war.

terminal in Virginia and then helped stage sit-ins and pickets to desegregate restaurants in the nation's capital, tactics that had been honed in the 1930s and later deployed further to the south. In the process, she joined the new **Congress of Racial Equality (CORE)**, which was committed to direct action in the service of racial equality, while many other African Americans flocked to the NAACP, boosting membership to half a million.

Similar forms of activism against Jim Crow were pioneered by Bayard Rustin, a confirmed pacifist and a devotee of Mohandas Gandhi's non-violent resistance that would later be embraced by Martin Luther King, Jr. As early as 1942, Rustin boarded a bus in Louisville, Kentucky, bound for Nashville, Tennessee, and sat in a section open only to whites. Before the bus arrived in Nashville, he was arrested and later released. Five years later, in an effort to test a recent Supreme Court ruling that barred racial discrimination on interstate transportation, he led a bus-based "Journey of Reconciliation" with thirteen other Black and white activists across Virginia and North Carolina. They were all arrested several times, and at one point Rustin was sentenced to three weeks on a North Carolina chain gang. Publicly marginalized both for his political radicalism and his homosexuality, Rustin's courage and insight would nonetheless leave indelible marks on the developing civil rights movement.

There was even more afoot at the time. Swedish economist Gunnar Myrdal, funded by the Carnegie Corporation of New York, published a two-volume study on race relations in the United States in 1944, *An American Dilemma: The Negro Problem and American Democracy*. Myrdal's study not only emphasized white prejudice and oppression but also attributed the travails of African Americans directly to them. *An American Dilemma* would sell thousands of copies and begin to shift the public perspective on the future of race. As the Black writer and poet Langston Hughes now glimpsed, "Pearl Harbor put Jim Crow on the run."

The Women's War

Pauli Murray had come to recognize that Black women suffered their own distinctive forms of discrimination. She cleverly called it "**Jane Crow**," and would devote much of the rest of her life to promoting equality across lines of race and sex. Here, too, she was building upon activism with roots in the nineteenth century, in Black women's and church clubs and in opposition to lynching spearheaded as early as the 1890s by Ida B. Wells (see Chapter 20). It would be a long march; it remains one. But the demands of war mobilization also created new and unforeseen possibilities for a great many women of different racial and ethnic backgrounds.

For one thing, well over a quarter of a million women, including about 6,500 African Americans, joined the US military. Although denied combat roles, they serviced and repaired vital military hardware, tended to wounded soldiers, helped

≡ **Rosie the Riveters**   Dora Miles (*left*) and Dorothy Johnson work together at the Douglas aircraft factory in Long Beach, California. As arms manufacturers expanded to meet the needs of the war, Black Americans and women formed a growing portion of the wartime workforce. The publicity department of the Douglas Aircraft Company boasted that its six plane factories were "an industrial melting pot."

operate airfields, and collected important intelligence, both overseas and at home, in what were known as the Women's Army Corps (WACS) and the naval Women Accepted for Volunteer Emergency Service (WAVES).

More generally, women joined the workforce in the millions, especially in defense-related industries, as production geared up and adult men were inducted into the military. Many women had been employed previously, especially if they were unmarried or African American, but were mainly found in teaching, clerical, and domestic occupations. Now some truly moved to the shop floor, running heavy machinery, constructing planes and tanks, unloading ships. **Rosie the Riveter**, flexing her arm muscle and insisting, "We Can Do It," became a central recruiting tool for women workers as well as a new image of femininity and female accomplishment.

By 1945, women dominated in the overall labor force, composing about 65 percent of it, collected their pay as well as that of their militarily engaged husbands, and negotiated the public world with new senses of freedom and self-assurance. Some, particularly in the white South, saw subversion at play and complained that Eleanor Roosevelt was recruiting their maids to "Eleanor Clubs," intent on breaking the boundaries of Jim Crow. But clearly, the wartime experience would raise new questions about women's "place" and prospects, and about the gender conventions that had long organized the country.

24.4   War in the Pacific

||| Discuss how the war in the Pacific turned against the Japanese.

Still, whatever new openings war mobilizations produced would have amounted to relatively little if the war could not be won militarily and politically. That was no easy task. Once the United States officially entered the war in late 1941, it had a truly global fight on its hands, far larger than anything previously experienced. Theaters of action included thousands of miles in the Pacific, many hundreds of miles in the Atlantic, much of continental Europe, the Mediterranean, and stretches of North Africa (see Map 24.4). The battle against fascism in Europe had, of course, already been joined by the British, French, and Russians, as well as by partisan resistance movements, effectively guerilla bands, often manned by communists and socialists who themselves were tenaciously antifascist, in all areas under fascist occupation. But in the Pacific, the United States battled the Japanese with relatively little Allied help.

The Japanese "Running Wild"

The Japanese leadership recognized that they could not win a long, drawn-out war against the United States. They simply did not have the manpower or resources to do this. What they hoped, instead, was to take advantage of the debilitating blow they struck against the United States at Pearl Harbor and build a military/imperial ring across the western Pacific, stretching from the Aleutian Islands in the north down through Indonesia in the south, where valuable resources and labor could be found and lines of defense constructed. Then they would work out some sort of peace treaty with the United States leaving Japan in the positions of power it had established. The key, as Japanese Admiral Isoroku Yamamoto saw it, was to "run wild" for six months or a year before reaching a settlement.

Run wild the Japanese army and navy did. In very short order, they took Hong Kong, Guam, Wake Island, Thailand, Malaya, the Dutch East Indies, Singapore, and Burma. They took control of parts of New Guinea and the Solomon Islands. They sank two British battleships. By May 1942 they forced an American surrender of the Philippines. And they edged toward Australia before being pushed back. But the Japanese hand was not as strong as it may have seemed. As costly as the Pearl Harbor raid was to the United States, it had no aircraft carriers in port at the time; all escaped the damage inflicted by Japanese planes, and, in this war, it was the aircraft carrier not the battleship that was crucial. The United States could therefore get back on its military feet more quickly than the Japanese had anticipated and begin implementing its own plan of counterattack, called the Orange Plan.

Unveiling the Orange Plan

The first sign of this plan was a daring raid on the Japanese mainland, on Tokyo itself, in April 1942. It was truly audacious. Sixteen medium, B-25, bombers would be loaded onto the deck of an aircraft carrier, the *USS Hornet*, and fly off to drop bombs over Tokyo and other nearby Japanese cities. Then, rather than return to the carrier—the bombers didn't have enough fuel for a return trip—the pilots would bail out over China and hope to be met by friendly forces. Leading the raid was Jimmy Doolittle, who had gained fame as a test pilot in the 1920s and 1930s and

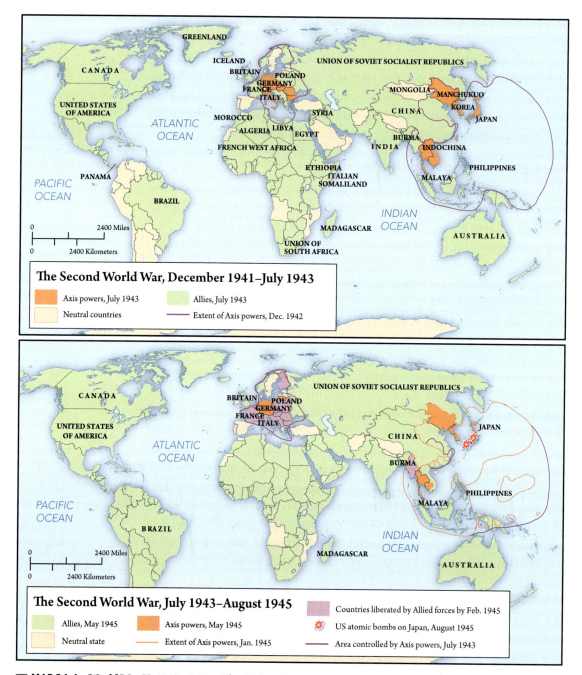

≡ **MAP 24.4 World War II, 1942–1945**   After Midway, Japan was thrown on the defensive. The US Navy and Marines conducted amphibious operations in seizing one Japanese-held island after another. In western Europe, the Allied attack was slow to develop, and a major breakthrough would not be achieved until June 1944.

trained the crews. The intention was to avenge Pearl Harbor and strike a powerful psychological blow against the haughty Japanese.

The *Hornet* steamed past Midway Island north of the Hawaiian Islands, a few hundred miles from Japan, and launched the bombers to carry out their assignments. They all dropped their bombs and, while the damage to Tokyo was not very heavy, the Japanese leadership was stunned by what the Americans could do (not all the pilots returned; three were captured and executed, and one died in prison). Most important, they recognized that they would be vulnerable to further attack unless they secured their Pacific perimeter and took out the American aircraft carriers. As a result, Japanese military planners shifted their immediate focus from the southwest Pacific, where they had a firm and growing hold, to Midway Island, where they hoped to draw out the American carrier fleet, destroy the carriers, and establish a base in range of Hawai'i.

Then came a stroke of good fortune. US intelligence officers intercepted Japanese military messages, learned of the impending attack on Midway, and moved to take on the Japanese fleet. In early June, the battle for Midway raged, and this time the results were very different. Having been previously warned, US forces, led by carrier-based dive-bombers, sank all four Japanese aircraft carriers as well as a heavy cruiser, and managed to destroy more than 200 Japanese fighter planes, killing many of the highly trained Japanese pilots.

One eminent military historian has called the **Battle of Midway** (June 4–7, 1942) "the most stunning and decisive blow in the history of naval warfare." It would prove to be a genuine tipping point in the Pacific Theater. Before Midway, the Japanese had the clear naval edge, with more carriers than the Americans and, with their fighter aircraft, the ability to reach across many miles of ocean. Now it was the United States that had the advantage in carriers and the productive capacity to produce many more ships and planes than the Japanese. There would be long years of intense fighting ahead as American army and naval forces, especially the Marines, looked to capture the many Japanese military outposts strung across the South Pacific before setting their sights on the Philippines and the Japanese mainland. But the United States was now on the offensive, and by the late summer of 1942, with the invasion of Guadalcanal Island in the Solomons, the bloody march was on.

≡ **Shell-Shocked** A US Marine stares blankly after two straight days of battle in the Marshall Islands. The Pacific Theater of the war saw some of the most brutal fighting as American Marines made repeated assaults on Japanese island strongholds.

24.5   War in Europe

||| Describe how the Allies in Europe succeeded in defeating Germany.

The European Theater of war looked very dismal to the United States and its allies between the fall of 1939 and the fall of 1941. Just as the Japanese had moved very quickly and successfully across the South Pacific and Southeast Asia to claim essential supplies and military bases, the Germans had raced into Poland and then turned west and swept through the Low Countries and France. With Italian allies to the south, a fascist regime already in power in Spain, and an invasion of Britain apparently being planned, what lights there were of liberalism and democracy in Europe were rapidly going out. Then the Germans made a surprise move that could have truly ended the European war in their favor, but instead it turned into a stunning setback.

The Soviets Defeat the Nazis

If the Battle of Midway proved to be a tipping point in the Pacific, the Battles of Moscow and then of Stalingrad proved to be tipping points in Europe. The process was much longer. The Nazis invaded the Soviet Union in June 1941, breaking their Non-Aggression Pact and seeking the oil and foodstuffs to be found in the Ukraine and down toward the Caspian Sea. Hitler also reveled in the prospect of destroying "Jewish Bolshevism," an unmistakable sign of the racial radicalization of the Nazi war. Indeed, Hitler not only determined to kill off the Bolsheviks, but he also planned to starve Soviet civilians in an effort to create necessary living space for land-hungry German colonists. He estimated that thirty million Russians would be starved to death in this way.

At first, all went according to Germany's plan. Stalin had not expected the German offensive and his forces were ill-prepared. Nearly four million strong, the Wehrmacht moved rapidly toward Moscow, expecting to finish the job in a matter of months and therefore to avoid the brutal Russian winter that had doomed invasions in the past, most notably Napoleon's in the early nineteenth century. But a combination of Soviet resistance and the vast spaces that the Nazis had to traverse slowed the march. By the time the Germans made it to Moscow, winter was setting in and the offensive stalled; by early 1942, the Germans were in retreat and Stalin was imagining a counteroffensive.

The casualties taken by the Soviets, military and civilian together, were staggering, worsened by Hitler's murderous attack on his enemies and his intention to starve out the Russian population. Stalin soon pleaded with his new Allies, the British and the Americans, to open up a "second front" in the west by staging a cross-English Channel invasion of France and the Netherlands and forcing Hitler to shift many of his troops there. Yet, despite promises from Roosevelt and Churchill, no such invasion was forthcoming, and Stalin fumed that they were ready to sacrifice the Soviet Union to the Nazis or at least wait until casualties on both sides mounted further.

In the meantime, the German army headed south from Moscow toward Stalingrad, hoping to begin a new offensive in the summer of 1942 and open the way to the oil-rich Caucasus. Now, Stalin threw nearly a million troops at the Nazis and so began five months of intense and

The Battle of Stalingrad Soldiers of the Soviet army defend Stalingrad (today Volgograd) from Nazi attack. After nearly six months of brutal urban warfare in the deadly cold, the Nazis retreated, turning the tide of the European Theater against the Germans at the price of nearly two million killed, wounded, or missing.

bloody warfare, some of it hand-to-hand and street-to-street, with, perhaps, the largest number of military personnel engaged that the history of warfare had ever seen. By early February 1943, the decimated and exhausted German armies surrendered, ending the Nazi dream of breathing space to the east and now facing the Allies to the west with enormously diminished military resources. Nearly two million soldiers, on both sides, met their deaths during the Battle of Stalingrad. It was Stalin's Soviet Union and the Russian people, in uniform and out, who turned the tide against the apparently "invincible" Third Reich.

Allied Offensives

But the war was hardly done. The first months of 1943 saw a number of developments that showed the Allied forces very much on the offensive and the Germans and Italians increasingly under siege. American bombers joined British aircraft in the massive bombing of German cities, and by the spring of that year, Berlin, the German capital, was itself being leveled. The idea was not only to inflict devastating damage on German civilians but also to cripple Germany's industrial might. At the same time, German forces were in retreat in North Africa, and in the late summer, the Allies opened a "second front" on the continent, this one on the Italian peninsula.

It was not what Stalin had been demanding. But Churchill persuaded Roosevelt that the Allies should first attack what he called the "soft underbelly of the Axis" before taking on much larger concentrations of German forces in western Europe. Allied forces landed in southern Italy in September, and from there moved north toward Rome while establishing air bases from which American bombers could reach German fortifications in the Balkans. The fascist regime in Italy soon fell, and Mussolini himself was on the run. Within a year and a half, he would be caught by Italian partisans (among the 200,000 who took part in the fight) and executed.

Then, at a meeting in Tehran, Iran, in November 1943, Roosevelt, Churchill, and Stalin (called the "Big Three;" Roosevelt had not met Stalin before this) determined on a cross-channel invasion of France in the late spring of 1944. It was called **Operation Overlord ("D-Day")** and would be commanded by American General Dwight David Eisenhower, a career military officer from the state of Kansas.

D-Day and the Allied Offensives

The operation was very large—over 100,000 Allied troops and more than 10,000 planes would be involved—and also very dangerous. The troops had to cross the English Channel in ships and landing barges, storm the beaches of Normandy, and then assault the well-entrenched German defensive positions, themselves set on the cliffs overlooking the beaches, in the face of withering German fire. The saving grace was that the invading flotilla left the English coast at night, so it would not be detected until the troops were about to come ashore at daylight. Hitler had also underestimated the Allied forces and did not expect the invasion along the Normandy coast; he was looking further to the north in France, Denmark, or even Norway. The invasion, D-Day as it was known, took place on June 6, 1944, and, despite heavy casualties, the Allies pushed forward, dug in, and began bringing in more troops and supplies. Very soon they moved into the French interior. About two months later, on August 25, 1944, the Allies liberated Paris and trained their sights on Germany and the Reich. Allied casualties, although heavy, were nowhere nearly as high as military and political leaders had feared.

Allied troops were now on the ground in Europe pushing west to east and south to north while their bombers continuously pummeled German armies, cities, and industrial sites. Eventually, the German city of Dresden was firebombed; nearly 25,000 German civilians died there. But there was also an Allied push from east to west, and that was the march of Soviet troops. Under Marshal Georgy Zhukov, they pushed the Germans back across the Soviet border in the summer of 1944 and, within a few months, swept through much of eastern Europe, through Romania, Bulgaria, the Baltic states, Hungary, eastern Poland, and Czechoslovakia. At such a pace, it seemed that the Russians, once on the ropes, might reach Berlin and take down the Reich before the British and Americans got there.

24.6 Endings and Beginnings

Compare the different perspectives for the postwar held by world leaders.

The retreat of the German armies, and especially the Allied race toward Berlin from the east as well as the west, raised a host of questions about how the war might end and the peace might begin. The United States, Britain, and the Soviet Union agreed upon the unconditional surrender of the Germans (and

"Into the Jaws of Death" On June 6, Allied forces, primarily British and American, assaulted the Nazi-held beaches of Normandy in northern France—the largest amphibious invasion in history. The outcome was uncertain at first. The first waves of soldiers deposited by the landing craft were mowed down by Germans hiding in concrete bunkers in the cliffs above, and by the end of the first day 2,000 Americans had been killed or wounded. But by gaining a foothold in western Europe, the Allies were able to attack Germany from both east and west, hastening the end of the war.

the Japanese). This time, unlike at the end of World War I, there would be no armistice or peace treaties with conditions attached. But they had different visions of what might be done to the Axis powers and what sort of postwar world might be constructed. Then, too, there were the partisans in France, Italy, Poland, and the Balkans who fought heroically against the fascists, and had their own political agendas, generally of socialist and communist varieties. The tensions and conflicts between them all only grew as the war's end came into sight.

Defining Terms of Surrender

At Tehran in 1943 and then at Yalta, an old Soviet resort town near the Black Sea, in early 1945, Roosevelt, Churchill, and Stalin tried to agree upon terms. Churchill, who presided over Britain and the still far-flung British Empire, was not only interested in preventing Germany from again mounting military hostilities but was also concerned about maintaining British "spheres of influence" in places like Greece and the Middle East. But Churchill, anticommunist that he was, also called for "democratic" governments and "free elections" in Poland and the rest of eastern Europe, potentially challenging Soviet influence there.

For their part, Stalin and the Soviet leadership wanted Germany dramatically reduced, industrially as well as militarily, subject to reparations given the enormous losses that the Soviet economy and people had suffered, and fully de-Nazified. In Stalin's view, Nazis could have no place in a postwar government, and Nazi leaders would be arrested and punished for war crimes. Equally important, he was deeply concerned about the political orientation of eastern Europe as a matter of vital security, and he wanted to make sure that friendly governments would be in place, that the Soviets would have their own "sphere of influence" there. By the time of the **Yalta Conference**, the Soviet army was closing in on Berlin and was therefore in a strong position to have its demands heard if not met.

Roosevelt had his own set of concerns. He recognized the legitimacy of both the British and Soviet claims and shared their interest in occupying and demilitarizing a defeated Germany. But he also wanted the Soviet Union's help in the still ongoing fight against the Japanese, with hopes of defeating them before a full-out invasion of the Japanese mainland was necessary, and their support for Roosevelt's vision of a new international forum called the **United Nations** (previously Roosevelt's term for the Allies) that had been hatched in the fall of 1944 and was imagined as a far more effective organization than the old League of Nations had ever been.

In the end, there were a series of understandings. Germany and Berlin would be divided into four zones—controlled by the United States, Britain, France, and the Soviet Union, respectively—and would be demilitarized,

≡ **Planning the Postwar World** British Prime Minister Winston Churchill (*left*), American President Franklin Roosevelt (*center*), and Soviet Premier Josef Stalin (*right*) were the key leaders of the wartime antifascist alliance. At a conference at Yalta on the Crimean Peninsula in early 1945, the "Big Three" made plans for the final defeat of Germany and the political organization of the postwar world.

de-Nazified, and subject to reparations. The Soviet Union would have sway over the government of Poland, and new borders would be drawn to deprive Germany of about one-quarter of its eastern territory. The Soviet Union would also declare war on Japan within three months of the German surrender and join hands on the United Nations. But these were understandings, and understandings are often subject to misunderstanding.

The Election of 1944 and Roosevelt's Death

To nearly all who surrounded him, Franklin Roosevelt showed the heavy burdens of leading the United States in wartime. The previous November he was elected to a fourth term as president, handily though not overwhelmingly defeating his Republican opponent, the New York governor, Thomas E. Dewey. But Roosevelt had also yielded to moderate and southern Democrats by dropping Henry Wallace as his vice president, who was thought to be far too left-wing, and instead taking on a little known and relatively inexperienced senator from Missouri, a one-time clothing salesman who lacked a college education, named Harry S. Truman. Long-stricken with polio, Roosevelt now looked gaunt and physically depleted, his health rapidly deteriorating. No one knew if he would survive to see the end of the war, let alone preside over the transition to peacetime.

Roosevelt's decision to replace Wallace with Truman was a fateful one. Even before the United States entered the war, there was a growing debate not only over whether the country should get involved but what the country should aspire to if it did get involved. One of the strongest early statements came from Henry Luce, the editor of *Time* magazine, who in February 1941 urged American intervention and sketched out a view of what he called the **American Century**. It was muscular vision of expanding American influence, the end of American isolationism, and the extension of American values and principles across the globe. Luce acknowledged fears that American "constitutional democracy" could not survive the war, and he took the opportunity to express his dissatisfaction with the "socialist doctrines" and "collectivist trends" of the Roosevelt administration and to remind readers of the missed opportunities for world leadership in 1919. Luce spoke of "sharing" with the world's peoples the Bill of Rights, the Declaration of Independence, and the Constitution, but placed special emphasis on the "system of free economic enterprise," insisting that such a system could not prevail in the United States "if it prevails nowhere else." In some ways, Luce's "American Century" was an updated version of the "Open Door."

A little over a year later, in May 1942, then Vice President Henry Wallace answered Henry Luce's clarion call. Wallace shared Luce's sense of the war's great stakes—he called it "a fight between a slave world and a free world"—and of the important idea of "freedom." Yet, whereas Luce imagined an "American Century," Wallace spoke of a **"century of the common man,"** not only in the United States but around the world. "Everywhere the common people are on the march," Wallace observed, and "when freedom-loving people march; when farmers have an opportunity to buy land at reasonable prices and to sell the produce of their land through their own organizations, when workers have the opportunity to form unions and bargain through them collectively, and when children of all the people have the opportunity to attend schools which teach them the truths of the real world in which they live, when these opportunities are open to everyone, then the world moves straight ahead."

Wallace spoke of a "long-drawn-out people's revolution"—moving through America in 1775, France in 1792, Latin America during "the Bolivarian era," Germany in 1848, and Russia in 1917—which enabled them to "learn to think and work together." Now the job was to build a "just, charitable, and enduring" peace that must mean "a better standard of living for the common man, not merely in the United States and England, but also in India, Russia, China, and Latin America—not merely in the United Nations, but also in Germany and Italy, and Japan." And "no nation will have the God-given right to exploit other nations" or to engage in either "military or economic imperialism." In effect, Wallace was calling for a global New Deal and Luce for an end to the New Deal at home and abroad.

Franklin Roosevelt, the embodiment of the New Deal, would not have the opportunity to speak of its postwar fate. One month before the Nazis surrendered in May 1945, Roosevelt suffered a massive and fatal brain hemorrhage. After twelve years in the White House, so long that many Americans knew no other president in their lifetime, FDR was gone. An overpowering moment in modern American political history and culture it was. In many quarters, especially among ordinary folk, white, Black, and brown, the mourning was deep and nearly inconsolable.

Truman, the Atomic Bomb, and Japan's Surrender

Now it was Harry Truman who would preside over the ending of the war with Japan and the transition to some sort of peace. He was not in the best of positions to respond because Roosevelt had kept him out of the loop of war-related decision-making. Thus, Truman had a steep learning curve, and one of the things he immediately learned about was something called the **Manhattan Project**. The project was the result of discoveries in the world of physics earlier in the century that suggested the enormous power of the atom. A number of brilliant European physicists, many in flight from the Nazis, beginning with Albert Einstein, had been at work on nuclear fission experiments—literally splitting the atom and releasing its energy—and, once the war began, they informed the Roosevelt administration

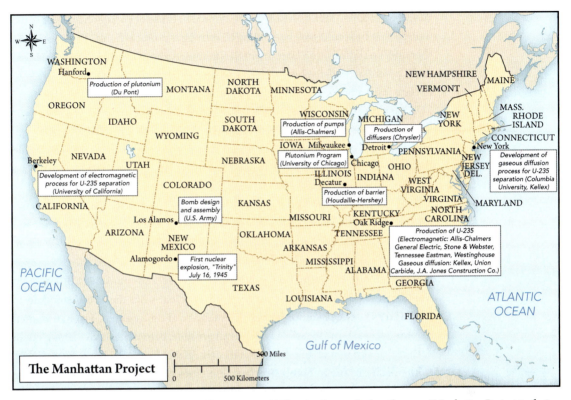

MAP 24.5 The Manhattan Project Beginning in 1942, scientists worked on the secret Manhattan Project to design and build nuclear weapons. The $2 billion project included facilities across the country.

of their belief that an atomic bomb, with enormous destructive potential, could be built. They also worried that the Germans had already begun work toward such a goal, which would have catastrophic consequences had they come up with an atomic bomb first (see Map 24.5).

Einstein and the Hungarian physicist Leo Szilard (both Jews) urged Roosevelt to authorize the research and development of an atomic bomb. Roosevelt agreed and the Manhattan Project was soon proceeding in secrecy, at breakneck speed, in the New Mexican desert town of Los Alamos. The project director was a California physicist named J. Robert Oppenheimer. By July 1945 an atomic weapon was ready to be tested, and on July 16 the test, code named "Trinity," was a success.

Timing is everything in war and politics, and this was surely true when it came to the dawning of a nuclear age. Truman learned of the Trinity test as he was about to sit down for his first, and for the war's last, meeting of the Allied powers, this one in Potsdam, just outside Berlin. By all accounts, he was not only relieved but puffed up by the news, more ready to be tough with Stalin. Truman quickly told Stalin of the new weapon—Stalin already knew about it because of an espionage leak—and figured that he would now be holding the stronger political hand. There were further understandings, and later misunderstandings, about the division of Germany and a potential Soviet sphere of influence in eastern Europe, and Stalin agreed to declare war on Japan and enter the Pacific fight.

What about the bomb and the defeat of Japan? Should Truman just go ahead and drop the bomb? Should he warn the Japanese of the bomb and its likely effects and give them the opportunity to surrender before suffering its destruction? Should the bomb not be dropped and the Japanese mainland be invaded by the United States and Soviet armies?

Truman and his policy advisors had a number of issues with which to contend: how to end the war as quickly as possible, how to limit American casualties, and how to approach the surrender of Japan and its aftermath. There were a few scientists and advisors who worried about the use of the bomb, feared the moral onus that the United States might carry as a result of its use, and counseled a process that would first demonstrate to the Japanese government what the bomb could do to its country and the Japanese people. But such a road was rejected. Truman wanted the war over as soon as feasible and, if at all possible, before the Soviet Union could declare war and mount an offensive of its own, giving it war claims in eastern Asia.

The decision was to bomb two Japanese cities that were simultaneously large civilian and military-related centers: Hiroshima and Nagasaki, not far from each other in Japan's southwest. On August 6, a massive B-29 bomber, the ***Enola Gay***, took off from an American air base in the Mariana Islands, about six hours' flying time from the Japanese mainland, and dropped the first bomb on Hiroshima. Three days later, Nagasaki was hit. In between, the Soviet Union followed its commitment to declare war on Japan.

≡ **Atomic Destruction**   The ruin of the Japanese city of Nagasaki following the second atomic bombing on August 9, 1945. Tens of thousands of residents were killed instantly upon detonation, and tens of thousands more died in the weeks, months, and years to come.

When the awful mushroom clouds cleared, more than 225,000 people lay dead and many thousands more severely injured and suffering radiation poisoning. That was enough. On August 15, the Japanese government surrendered. Their only condition was that Emperor Hirohito be permitted to remain in place. The United States accepted the condition, and the Pacific war, like the Atlantic and Mediterranean one some three months earlier, was now over.

Conclusion: Transforming the American Economy and American Society

Recognizing where the aggressions of the Germans and Japanese were likely headed, the Roosevelt administration began preparing for war in 1940, but the Japanese attack on Pearl Harbor in December 1941 led to a formal declaration and a massive mobilization of men, women, and material for the war effort. It was a process that would begin a major transformation of the American economy and American society that would frame the postwar world. The war, on all sides, was also driven by hardening racism that not only led to the persecution of different ethnic and national groups in the United States but also laid the groundwork for the extermination of much of European Jewry by the Nazi regime.

Once moving almost invincibly in the Pacific and Europe, the Axis powers began to be turned back, the Germans at the Battles of Moscow and Stalingrad in the Soviet Union, and the Japanese at the Battle of Midway out in the South Pacific. But it would require more than another two years, and the first use of the atomic bomb, to bring about their unconditional surrenders. It would also quickly become evident that the wartime allies, especially the United States and the Soviet Union, had very different visions of what a postwar world would look like. Roosevelt's death in early 1945, succeeded as he was by Harry Truman, added further uncertainty to the political mix and raised the question of where the successful war against fascism would lead.

WHAT IF Henry Wallace Had Become President of the United States?

The vice presidency of the United States was once described by Texan John Nance Garner, one of FDR's vice presidents, as "not worth a warm bucket of spit." By this he meant that the office carried no specific powers or responsibilities, except the presidency of the US Senate, which, for the most part involved little more than parliamentary rituals and buried its holder deep beneath the figure of the president. Most of the nation's vice presidents would have agreed with Garner. Except on the rare occasions when something happened to the president, such as death, assassination, or resignation from office, the vice president was irrelevant. Then, according to the constitutional order of succession, the lowly vice president became the commander in chief. Truman only had days to wait, and he would place, in ways we will soon see, a powerful stamp on the postwar future of the United States, and one that was more aligned with the vision of Henry Luce.

But what if Henry Wallace had been kept on as vice president, as most vice presidents generally are when the president seeks reelection? And what if Henry Wallace, who envisioned "a century of the common man," then became president of the United States? What if he had to decide about the use of the atomic bomb, the future of atomic weaponry and energy, and the principles that ought to govern the postwar world, not only in the United States but across the globe? What would that have meant for the American economy and social security net, for its infrastructure, and domestic priorities? What would that have meant for many of the world's people, including those who had been living in the empires of European nations and sought their own independence? And what might that have meant for the relations between the United States and its wartime ally the Soviet Union? Could Wallace's vision of a century in which the interests and aspirations of the "common man" were privileged have truly made for a different country and a different world? The following documents suggest different perspectives on what was at stake in the Pacific and European Wars and on the postwar future of the United States in the world.

DOCUMENT 24.1: Henry Luce, "The American Century," *Life Magazine*, February 17, 1941

Editor of Time *magazine, Henry Luce published this essay in 1941 as a way of encouraging the United States to enter the war already underway.*

In the field of national policy, the fundamental trouble with America has been, and is, that whereas their nation became in the 20th Century the most powerful and the most vital nation in the world, nevertheless Americans were unable to accommodate themselves spiritually and practically to that fact. Hence they have failed to play their part as a world power—a failure which has had disastrous consequences for themselves and for all mankind. And the cure is this: to accept wholeheartedly our duty and our opportunity . . . to exert upon the world the full impact of our influence, for such purposes as we see fit and by such means as we see fit. . . . [T]he 20th Century must be to a significant degree an American Century. . . . Ours cannot come out of a vision of any one man. It must be the product of the imaginations of many men. It must be a sharing with all peoples of our Bill of Rights, our Declaration of Independence, our Constitution, our magnificent industrial products, our technical skills. It must be an internationalism of the people, by the people, and for the people. . . . We must undertake now to be the Good Samaritan of the entire world. It is the manifest duty of our country to undertake to feed all the people of the world who as a result of the worldwide collapse of civilization are hungry and destitute. . . . For every dollar we spend on armaments, we should spend at least a dime in a gigantic effort to feed the world— and all the world should know that we have dedicated ourselves to this task. . . . It is for America and for America alone to determine whether a system of free economic enterprise—an economic order compatible with freedom and progress—shall or shall not prevail in this century. . . . America as the dynamic center of ever-widening spheres of enterprise, America as the training center of the skilled servants of mankind, America as the Good Samaritan . . . and America as the powerhouse of the ideals of Freedom and Justice—out of these elements surely can be fashioned a vision of the 20th Century to which we can and will devote ourselves . . . to create the first great American Century.

Source: Life magazine, February 17, 1941.

DOCUMENT 24.2: Henry Wallace, "Century of the Common Man," May 8, 1942

Henry Wallace sought to respond to Henry Luce's vision of a postwar world in which the United States was dominant with a contrasting vision that focused on the fates of the world's workers and ordinary folk.

This is a fight between a slave world and a free world. Just as the United States in 1862 could not remain half slave and half free, so in 1942 the world must make its decision for a complete victory one way or the other. . . . When the freedom-loving people march; when the farmers have an opportunity to buy land at reasonable prices and to sell the produce of their land through their own organizations, when workers have the opportunity to form unions and bargain through them collectively, and when children of all the people have an opportunity to attend schools which teach them the truths of the real world in which they live—when these opportunities are open to everyone, then the world moves straight ahead. . . . Through the leaders of the Nazi revolution, Satan is now trying to lead the common man of the whole world back into slavery and darkness. For the stark truth is that the violence preached by the Nazis is the devil's own religion of darkness. So also is the doctrine that one race or one class is by heredity superior and that all other races or classes are supposed to be slaves. . . . The march of freedom of the past one hundred and fifty years has been a long-drawn-out people's revolution. In this Great Revolution of the people, there were the American Revolution of 1775, the French Revolution of 1792, the Latin American revolutions of the Bolivarian era, the German Revolution of 1848, and the Russian Revolution of 1917. Each spoke for the common man . . . . Some went to excess. But the significant thing is that the people groped their way to the light. More of them learned to think and work together. The people's revolution aims at peace and not at violence, but if the rights of the common man are attacked, it unleashed the ferocity of a she-bear who has lost a cub. . . . The people, in their millennial and revolutionary march toward manifesting here on earth the dignity that is in every human soul, hold as their credo the Four Freedoms enunciated by President Roosevelt (1941). . . . But when we think about the significance of freedom from want for the average man, then we know that the revolution of the past one hundred and fifty years has not been completed. . . . Some have spoken of the "American Century." I say that the century on which we are entering—the century which will come out of this war—can be and must be the century of the common man. Perhaps it will be America's opportunity to suggest that Freedoms and duties by which the common man must live. Everywhere the common man must learn to build his own industries . . . must learn to increase his productivity so that he and his children can eventually pay to the world community all that they have received. No nation will have the God-given right to exploit other nations. Older nations will have the privilege to help younger nations get started on the path to industrialization, but there must be neither military nor economic imperialism. The methods of the nineteenth century will not work in the people's century which is now about to begin.

Source: Speech given by Henry Wallace to the Free World Association, New York, May 8, 1942. Reprinted in *Century of the Common Man, Two Speeches by Vice President Henry A. Wallace* (New York, 1943).

Thinking About Contingency

1. Why would President Roosevelt accommodate the demands of southern Democrats and other moderates to dump Henry Wallace from the national ticket in 1944?
2. Had Wallace remained vice president and became president on Roosevelt's death, how much power would he have had to redirect American domestic and foreign policy? How did Wallace's vision differ from Henry Luce's?
3. Truman may have been a moderate-conservative southerner, but he also faced pressure from left-of-center New Deal Democrats. How did that shape his own policies and the prospects for a postwar world?
4. Were the seeds of US-Soviet rivalry and hostility already planted before Roosevelt's death?

REVIEW QUESTIONS

1. What were the objectives of the Germans and the Japanese in waging war in Europe and the Pacific?

2. Why did some Americans oppose involvement in the war in Europe even after the Germans invaded Poland and began to bomb England?

3. Is there a relationship between German anti-Semitism and American anti-Japanese sentiment? What were the similarities and differences?

4. In what ways were the lives of American women changed by the war? Would those changes endure, or were they just temporary?

5. How did African Americans attempt to turn the ideology of antifascist warfare to the issues of racism and civil rights?

6. What differences and similarities did the Allies, especially the Soviet Union and the United States, share in their vision of the postwar world?

KEY TERMS

"American Century" (p. 1031)

Battle of Midway (p. 1025)

"century of the common man" (p. 1032)

Congress of Racial Equality (CORE) (p. 1021)

Enola Gay (p. 1034)

Fair Employment Practices Committee (FEPC) (p. 1020)

Final Solution (p. 1014)

Four Freedoms (p. 1006)

Holocaust (p. 1014)

internment camps (p. 1017)

Issei (p. 1018)

"Jane Crow" (p. 1021)

Korematsu v. United States (p. 1018)

Lend-Lease (p. 1003)

Manhattan Project (p. 1032)

Nisei (p. 1018)

Operation Overlord ("D-Day") (p. 1028)

Rosie the Riveter (p. 1022)

Sunbelt (p. 1012)

United Nations (p. 1030)

War Refugee Board (p. 1016)

Yalta Conference (p. 1030)

RECOMMENDED READINGS

Kai Bird and Martin Sherwin, *American Prometheus: The Triumph and Tragedy of J. Robert Oppenheimer* (Vintage, 2006).

John Dower, *War Without Mercy: Race and Power in the Pacific War* (Pantheon, 1986).

Lynn Dumenil, *American Working Women in World War Two* (Bedford St. Martin, 2019).

Saul Friedlander, *Nazi Germany and the Jews, 1939–1945* (2 vols.) (Harper Perennial, 2008).

Lauson F. Inada et al., *Only What We Could Carry: The Japanese-American Internment Experience* (Heyday Books, 2000).

Maggi M. Morehouse, *Fighting in the Jim Crow Army: Black Men and Women Remember World War Two* (Rowman and Littlefield, 2000).

Richard Overy, *Blood and Ruins: The Last Imperial War, 1931–1945* (Viking, 2021).

Cold War America
1945–1957

Nuclear Holocaust   A 1948 painting by Chelsey Bonestell depicts a hypothetical nuclear attack on New York City. The "mushroom cloud" became synonymous with the wonder and terror of the atomic age.

On October 27, 1951, *Collier's* magazine, a popular weekly in the United States devoted to investigative journalism, short stories, and illustrations, published an extraordinary issue on World War III. That's right: World War III! This war had not yet occurred, but *Collier's* assembled a group of distinguished journalists and writers to imagine what might happen if a new world war broke out. It was clear to them that the war would pit the United States against the Soviet Union, and that nuclear weapons, used to force a Japanese surrender in 1945, would be used again (in 1949 the Soviet Union had developed its own atomic bomb).

Collier's had the war start over an incident in Yugoslavia and escalate quickly owing to a Soviet invasion there. The United States, supported by the new United Nations, then declared war on the Soviet Union, and each side began deploying troops in Europe, the Middle East, and Asia. But most frightening was the almost immediate resort to the use of nuclear weapons by both sides. There was little hesitation and less hand

Timeline

1944	1945	1946	1947	1948	1949	1950	1951	1952

1944 ▸ Congress passes GI Bill; International Monetary Fund and World Bank created at Bretton Woods Conference; Supreme Court overturns white primary in *Smith v. Allwright*

1946 ▸ George Kennan's "Long Telegram"

1947 ▸ Winston Churchill makes "Iron Curtain" speech; President Truman announces policy of containing the spread of communism; Congress passes the National Security Act and the Taft-Hartley Act; Marshall Plan for reconstructing war-torn Europe

1948 ▸ Truman elected president over Republican Thomas Dewey

1949 ▸ The Soviet Union explodes its first nuclear weapon; Mao Zedong's communist movement wins control of mainland China

1950 ▸ North Korea invades South Korea and both the United States and the United Nations respond militarily; NSC-68 calls for military superiority over the Soviet Union

1952 ▸ Dwight D. Eisenhower, a Republican, elected as president

wringing. In the process, New York, Washington, DC, Chicago, Philadelphia, Los Angeles, San Francisco, Detroit, and some other cities in the United States, as well as Moscow and a host of other Russian cities and military/industrial centers, were leveled, horrifyingly illustrated by *Collier's*.

But World War III, it seemed, could be won, and in the *Collier's* version the United States, together with the United Nations, came out the winners. Over the course of more than three dreadful years of fighting, the Soviets were pushed back, their leader Josef Stalin deposed, and civil uprisings erupted in the Soviet Union and Eastern Europe. US and UN troops occupied parts of the Soviet Union, destroyed the Soviet stash of nuclear weapons, and watched the Soviet state crumble. In the end, "A New Russia" was born, now with a free press, Christian religion, and democratic institutions. To top it off, there was a massive fashion show for Russian women in Moscow's huge Dynamo Stadium. Capitalism had triumphed; communism had been buried.

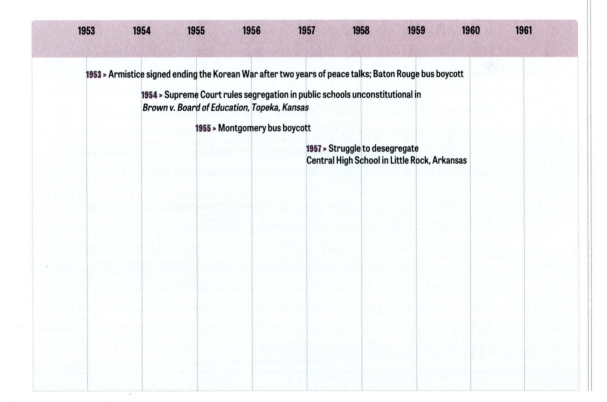

| 1953 | 1954 | 1955 | 1956 | 1957 | 1958 | 1959 | 1960 | 1961 |

1953 ▸ Armistice signed ending the Korean War after two years of peace talks; Baton Rouge bus boycott

1954 ▸ Supreme Court rules segregation in public schools unconstitutional in *Brown v. Board of Education, Topeka, Kansas*

1955 ▸ Montgomery bus boycott

1957 ▸ Struggle to desegregate Central High School in Little Rock, Arkansas

Collier's World War III was remarkable for many things. It assumed that nuclear weapons would be used in any subsequent large, or world, war. It also imagined that, despite immense destruction and loss of life, humanity would not only survive but move on to better things. There could be a winner, it would likely be the United States, and the Soviet Union could be remade in our own image. The writers and artists contributing to the issue understood what nuclear weapons were capable of doing, yet didn't quite understand that the consequences of their use would be long term as well as short term. They did not know that due to radiation survivors would get sick and die, water and soil would be contaminated for decades to come, and the global climate would be destabilized. Equally important, *Collier's* was playing to growing anxieties among the American public over the worsening relations between the United States and the Soviet Union, anxieties that a massive war could easily inflame.

This was the world to which World War II gave rise. It was a world that had never been seen before because now there were nuclear weapons. The adversaries were the United States and its allies, and the Soviet Union and its allies; before too very long, China would join the mix. At one time, they were all wartime allies and each played important roles in the defeat of the Germans and the Japanese. But quickly the dynamics of conflict shifted, and the globe was soon engulfed as a consequence. It was called a **Cold War**—the term was coined by American financier Bernard Baruch, though it was first hinted at by the writer George Orwell—between the major powers, who would come to be called superpowers, because nuclear weapons dramatically raised the stakes of full-scale warfare and discouraged its eruption. Yet the Cold War was generally accompanied by all sorts of hot wars, some directly in relation to it and the contest between capitalism and socialism, and some less so, as in popular struggles against European colonial rule that spread across Africa and Asia.

A Cold War was not destined to occur. More than a few political leaders, policy-makers, and intellectuals imagined something else, as both Henry Luce and Henry Wallace did in their separate ways (see Chapter 24). It occurred because important issues of power were at stake, vastly different perspectives on the development of a postwar world were in play, and the window for meaningful negotiations was seen as steadily closing. But when it did erupt, the Cold War created frameworks of understanding and activity that would shape much of the world for more than the next half century, no place more fully than the United States.

25.1   Making a Cold War

Explain how the Cold War and why it developed between the United States and the Soviet Union.

How did this happen after the Axis powers had been vanquished? The Soviet Union had played a decisive role in defeating Nazi Germany when its armies turned back the attacking Germans and then forced them to surrender. This was the beginning of the end for the Nazi regime. But it was an enormously costly struggle. No country suffered greater casualties during the war than did the Soviet Union, and no country was more determined to see the Germans reduced to a position from which they could never threaten the Soviets, or other Europeans, again. The "big three" leaders of the Allied war effort—Josef Stalin, Franklin Roosevelt, and Winston Churchill—had met at Tehran in 1943 and Yalta in 1945 during the war and appeared to reach agreements about how the conflict would end and a postwar world unfold. There was, however, a great deal at stake and some misunderstandings about what was in fact agreed to and what sort of concessions would be made. Before too long, one-time allies turned into adversaries.

A New Economic Order

The alliance between the United States and the Soviet Union was a fragile and self-interested one to begin with, made possible by the need to defeat the fascist powers. And it was soon clear that there were potentially competing aspirations for the postwar world. The United States emerged from the war as the dominant economic and military power globally. Despite the depression of the 1930s, it had built an economy with enormous productive capacity, and despite the horrors of war, it suffered far fewer casualties than any other major participant. It alone escaped the physical destruction of its territory. There was no invasion, and no cities or military sites, other than Pearl Harbor, were ever attacked. But there was still widespread fear that, with wartime mobilizations over and the troops returning home, the country might well slip back into recession or even depression.

Planning for a postwar world in which the United States would have the broadest economic options and influence began during the war itself. In 1944, representatives from more than forty nations (participants included the famed British economist John Maynard Keynes; the Soviets chose not to attend) met at Bretton Woods, New Hampshire, and began to create new institutions intended to stabilize and promote growth in the world economy. These included the **International Monetary Fund (IMF)** and the International Bank for Reconstruction and Development, generally known as the **World Bank**. Although there were serious disagreements over how these institutions would operate and whose interests would be favored (What would the requirements for aid be? Who could receive aid?), there was broad agreement on the need to rebuild war-torn Europe and Asia and encourage the industrialization of parts of the world, like Latin America, which were still dominated by estate agriculture and impoverished peasantries.

There was agreement, too, on the need to better organize international finance. To that end, the exchange of world currencies would be pegged to the US dollar. The **Bretton Woods Conference**, that is to say, further strengthened the position of the United States, privileging its currency and likely expanding overseas markets for American products. As Assistant Secretary of State Dean Acheson put it at the time, echoing Henry Luce and the much earlier Open Door, "We cannot have full employment and prosperity in the United States without the foreign markets."

Social Democratic Currents

But the global map was still very complicated. Most of Africa and south/southeast Asia remained under the colonial rule of the English, French, Portuguese, and Dutch, and continental Europe was itself the site of political struggles even after the Germans surrendered. There, antifascist resistance movements, which were of the political left, looked to topple the old guard in their home countries and place their imprints on the new postwar order. They were particularly formidable in France, Italy, Greece, and Yugoslavia, and some looked to the Soviet Union as a potential ally. Indeed, the immediate postwar years saw a pronounced shift toward social democracy across Europe—even in Great Britain where Churchill's Conservative Party was swept from office and replaced by the leftist Labour Party—and the construction of what would come to be called "mixed economies" that depended on the financial support and direction of the central state while leaving many markets in place. The result would be new systems of public health care, new social services for families and individuals, new educational opportunities, and new protections for workers and the elderly. In short, there would be new social safety nets, some of which, especially in the Scandinavian countries, were both wide and deep.

≡ **Public Health Care in Britain**   British Minister for Health Aneurin Bevan greets a young hospital patient on the inaugural of the National Health Service (NHS). The implementation of the NHS in 1948 was part of a postwar shift in Britain to a "mixed economy" in which the central government took on a greater role.

Social democratic pressures such as these—for universal health care, worker pensions, free public higher education, veterans' benefits—arose in the United States as well, pushed mainly by the left wing of the labor movement, especially the CIO, and left-leaning New Dealers. Theirs would be the chief political battles of the late 1940s and 1950s. But the outcome would be affected in large part by the developing confrontation with the Soviet Union.

Containment and the Truman Doctrine

It's not clear what would have happened had Roosevelt lived to complete his fourth term in the presidency, just as it is not clear what would have happened in post–Civil War America had Lincoln survived. But by all accounts, Harry Truman and his advisors were increasingly suspicious of Soviet intentions and fairly quick to lay down the gauntlet. Truman had felt empowered at the Potsdam conference in July 1945 owing to the successful test of the atomic bomb and came to believe that Stalin intended to control affairs in Eastern Europe—Poland became the test case, where a government friendly to the Soviet Union was installed—and perhaps move beyond, driven by a dream of communist supremacy.

Truman's view gained support from a "**Long Telegram**" written in early 1946 by George Kennan, a Princeton graduate and lifelong diplomat, who had been posted to the US Embassy in Moscow. Kennan, who was fluent in Russian and regarded as an expert, argued that the Soviet Union would never seek "peaceful coexistence" with the United States. Soviet leaders, he insisted, were fanatically determined to disrupt the Western world and way of life, and were "impervious to the logic of reason." In Kennan's judgment, the Soviets were only "sensitive to the logic of force." Quite simply, they had to be confronted and "contained."

The Long Telegram was widely circulated among American officials and policymakers, and began to shift the tenor of debate away from the goal of achieving diplomatic agreements and toward a tough line. Winston Churchill fortified this perspective several weeks later in a speech at Fulton, Missouri, with Truman in attendance. Declaring that the Soviet Union was determined upon a course of expansion, Churchill also spoke of an "**Iron Curtain** descend[ing] across the [European] continent," from the Baltic to the Adriatic, whose cities and populations now were subject "not only to Soviet influence but to a very high and in some cases increasing measures of control from Moscow."

≡ **Churchill and Truman** Former Prime Minister Winston Churchill (*left*) and President Harry Truman (*right*) at Westminster College in Truman's home state of Missouri. There Churchill delivered a speech decrying the "Iron Curtain" of communism in Eastern Europe, coining a classic phrase of the Cold War.

A year later, in March 1947, as the United States worried about potential Soviet involvement in Greece and Turkey, Truman called for **containment** of the Soviet Union and support for "free people who are resisting subjugation by armed minorities or by outside pressure." It was immediately known as the **Truman Doctrine** and, in one form or another, would shape American foreign policy for decades to come. It may also be regarded as the moment when the Cold War truly began.

Soviet Perspectives

Did Truman and his advisors get it right? Was this what Stalin and the Soviet Union intended to do? Did the "containment" policy make sense, given the risks it entailed? Historians and policymakers have debated these questions for years, and it is doubtful that there can be a definitive resolution. But what can we reasonably say? The Russian Revolution of 1917 established the first communist society in history and brought to power a revolutionary party, the Bolsheviks, that intended to remake Tsarist Russia (an autocratic empire), socialize most private property and the means of production, empower the working class, and serve as a beacon for revolutions around the world aimed at dismantling capitalism and building socialism.

But the Bolsheviks differed among themselves over the steps that needed to be taken. One group, associated with Leon Trotsky, insisted that socialism could never survive alone in the Soviet Union, that it would have to expand across Europe and then around the globe; Bolsheviks therefore should immediately reach out to those engaged in similar political struggles elsewhere and do what they could to support them. Another group, headed by Stalin, focused on the challenges facing the Soviet Union itself, and argued that the country would have to be economically modernized (industrialized and urbanized) and made militarily formidable if it were to survive. They believed that the capitalist powers in Europe and North America were unalterably hostile to them (the United States had already launched one

≡ **"Under the Leadership of the Great Stalin"**   A 1951 propaganda poster exhorts the many nationalities of the Soviet Union to advance toward a communist future under the leadership of Josef Stalin.

invasion during Woodrow Wilson's presidency), and that it made most sense for the Bolsheviks to try to build socialism in one country, theirs, first.

The debate was more than acrimonious. A good deal of blood was spilled. But the group that wanted to build socialism in one country won out, and, when the smoke cleared, Josef Stalin, who had embraced this view, emerged as the leader of the Soviet Union. Stalin was no democrat. He increasingly ruled with an iron hand, and he was quick to get rid of his opponents in the party and country. He also was determined to modernize the industrial and agricultural sectors of the Soviet Union and moved ruthlessly to do so.

Economic modernization is always a painful process, and most of the pain falls on rural people. But European and North American societies modernized over the course of many decades, so some of the consequences were spread out, though Populism in the 1890s suggested how strong the pushback could be (see Chapter 18). Stalin tried to industrialize over a very short period of time, in the late 1920s and 1930s, and the Russian peasantry in particular suffered dreadfully. The human toll was in the millions, and Stalin saw to it that his critics were either eliminated or sent off to prison camps.

But the Soviet Union also avoided being imperiled by the Great Depression. With a socialist socioeconomic framework in place, it was pretty much removed from the international market economy and had managed by the time the war broke out in 1939 to boast heavy industry and a large and well-armed military. Without these, the Nazis would have defeated the Soviet Union quickly and, perhaps, succeeded in bringing the rest of the Atlantic and Mediterranean worlds under their boots.

Although American policymakers and diplomats like George Kennan warned of Soviet plans for "world domination," the likelihood is that, as the war ended, Stalin had more modest goals in mind. The Soviet population had been decimated; perhaps twenty million died between 1939 and 1945. Major Soviet cities, along with their industrial bases, had also been destroyed. Stalin was interested in healing the wounds of war, rebuilding the country, and making sure that the Soviet Union would not be vulnerable to another invasion from the West.

To those ends, he was determined to extract major reparations from Germany in the form of money and industrial resources and ensure that the Soviet Union would have friendly Eastern European states on its border. He may also have hoped that, eventually, the Soviet Union could become a center of political gravity on the global stage and especially for movements and states seeking to build socialist societies. Not surprisingly, Stalin viewed his former allies with some distrust and doubted that they understood his security concerns. Indeed, he worried that the capitalist West might be intent on moving directly against him, perhaps with the help of a de-Nazified Germany.

Stalin's fears gained new substance when the United States joined Great Britain and several Western European countries in forming the **North Atlantic Treaty Organization (NATO)** in 1949, designed to provide for mutual defense against some external foe. Or, as NATO's first general secretary put it, the organization was "to keep the Russians out, the Americans in, and the Germans down." When, several years later, NATO decided to admit West Germany as a member state, the Soviet Union responded by establishing its own collective defense organization, the **Warsaw Pact** (1955), which included Poland, Czechoslovakia, Romania, Bulgaria, Albania, and East Germany. The lines of Cold Warfare were becoming more and more deeply etched (see Map 25.1).

NSC-68 and the Marshall Plan

Some leaders in the United States, like Henry Wallace, had urged that Soviet security concerns be taken seriously and some accommodation with the Soviet Union reached. But their voices were increasingly marginalized or silenced by what turned into a bipartisan effort to mobilize against the spread of communism and establish the United States as the dominant military power in the world. Between 1947 and 1950, Congress created, in large part through the **National Security Act** of 1947, a new Department of Defense, a **Central Intelligence Agency (CIA)**, a National Security Council, an independent Air Force, and a Joint Chiefs of Staff, while authorizing, for the first time in American history, a peacetime military draft.

In the words of a crucial secret document (**NSC-68**) crafted by the **National Security Council (NSC)** in 1950, the United States had to possess "superior overall power" and in "dependable combination with other like-minded nations" be capable not only of defending the Western Hemisphere but also of destroying vital elements of the Soviet Union's military capacity. "Containment" was now interpreted as "calculated and gradual coercion," and, to achieve these goals, the country was urged to embark upon a massive buildup of conventional and nuclear arms. At stake, NSC-68 declared, was the very future of "civilization."

The apocalyptic sound of NSC-68 in part reflected recent developments abroad. In 1949, the Soviet Union exploded its first nuclear weapon while a massive revolution in China, led by Mao Zedong, a one-time nationalist turned communist, swept away the Western-oriented regime of Chiang Kai-shek, and established a communist society in the country with the world's largest population. Mao proclaimed it the People's Republic of China (PRC); for his part, the defeated Chiang Kai-shek, backed by the United States, retreated to the nearby island of Taiwan in the South China Sea. Elsewhere, popular movements had won independence from British rule in India, others were mobilizing in Vietnam and the African

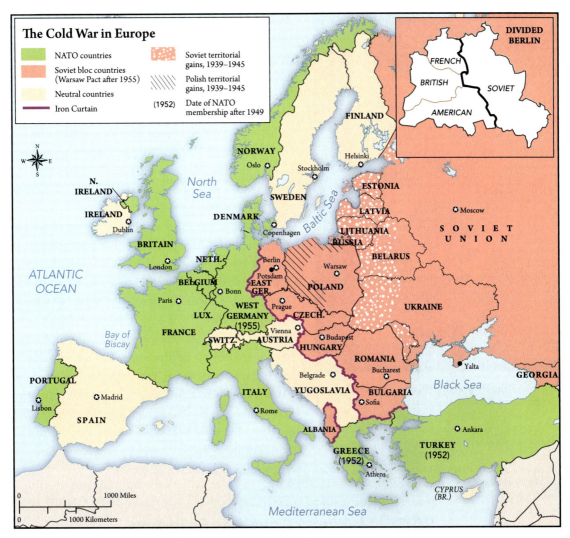

≡ **MAP 25.1   The Cold War in Europe**   By 1950 the Cold War had deeply and intractably divided Europe. Suspicions spawned by disputes at the end of World War II gave rise to what Churchill would call an "iron curtain" falling across Europe.

continent, and movements of the left were taking shape in Cuba and the rest of Latin America.

From the perspective of the Truman administration and many members of the US Congress, these global developments were problematic for American ambitions. Some political leaders were already arguing that communist sympathizers were active in the federal bureaucracy. Many others believed that the United

Promoting the Marshall Plan A poster promoting American aid projects in Europe, commonly known as the Marshall Plan. The flags of countries from Western, Northern, and Southern Europe act as sails pulling the ship of Europe forward. Wary of American influence, Soviet leaders forced Eastern European countries to forgo Marshall Plan aid.

States had to take new initiatives to "contain" or intimidate the communist threat overseas while promoting developments favorable to the expansion of American influence. The Marshall Plan, announced in 1947 by Secretary of State and former general George C. Marshall, though put together largely by his assistants, including George Kennan, called for $16 billion to aid the economies of Western Europe and perhaps Eastern Europe and the Soviet Union as well (substantial aid was provided to Japan and parts of Asia, too, though not under the Marshall Plan).

The catch to the **Marshall Plan** was that all the aid recipients had to accept a set of financial conditions that did not fit well with socialist economic organization, as well as the joint funding of East and West Germany. The Soviet Union rejected these conditions, worried that they would undermine their influence in Eastern Europe and Germany, and forced their Eastern European allies to do the same. Instead, the Soviet Union came up with an alternative aid program for Eastern European economies known as the **Molotov Plan**, after the Soviet foreign minister Vyacheslav Molotov. The Cold War blocs were taking more and more definitive shape, especially in Europe. Could a catastrophic hot war now be prevented?

25.2 Making a Cold War Economy

||| Explain how the American economy was shaped by the Cold War.

For the United States, the postwar period would be characterized by enormous prosperity. For three decades after 1945, the American economy had high rates of growth, low rates of inflation, significant increases in real wages and incomes, and low levels of unemployment. In part, this was the result of important victories by the labor movement, but it was in part due to improving conditions globally, and in part because of government policies. But the larger context was the Cold War, and the demands it seemed to impose as well as the opportunities it appeared to open up.

Labor on the March

When the Germans and Japanese surrendered, few would have predicted an economic boom in the offing. If anything, there was great concern about converting from a wartime to a peacetime economy, finding employment for the millions of men mustered out of the armed services, and avoiding a renewed depression. After all, despite its many interventions and programs, the New Deal had failed to lift the American economy out of the doldrums during the 1930s; only the massive spending required by World War II resulted in full employment. What would happen now that such spending was no longer required?

The battle over the economic future was quickly joined. There was a great deal at stake. War contracts had boosted corporate profits, union membership had grown substantially, and the federal government had imposed controls on prices and rationed goods. Real incomes had risen and there was a "pent-up" demand for commodities that could not be purchased during the war years. But working people were also vulnerable to layoffs and declining paychecks. Women who had entered the labor force in great numbers had to wonder what would happen to them.

The first signs of conflict came in the country's major industries as unionized workers looked to secure their gains and perhaps increase their leverage over corporate decision-making in anticipation of the readjustments ahead. In 1945 and 1946, there were nearly 5,000 strikes involving more than five million workers. These included autoworkers and coal miners, steel workers and meatpackers, electrical workers and railroad workers. Perhaps the most consequential of the strikes occurred at General Motors (GM), where more than 200,000 employees represented by the United Auto Workers (UAW) walked off the job for nearly four months. Led by Walter Reuther, a charismatic former socialist, they not only demanded substantial pay increases but also wanted more significant benefits and a greater say over the pricing of automobiles. They wanted to make sure that consumers would not pay the costs of their own gains. In an important sense, Reuther and the UAW, like much of the CIO generally, hoped to advance social democratic visions that had emerged during the New Deal but had not been realized.

The executives at GM initially rejected the UAW's demands and quest for power. They identified their interests with the national interests—their CEO Charles Wilson would say, "What's good for the country is good for General Motors and vice versa"—and argued that "the freedom of each unit of American business to determine its own destiny" must be preserved. In response, Reuther called upon GM to "open the books" and show how its financial operations worked and why the company would have to pass on any wage increases to consumers through higher prices for cars. GM again refused.

Eventually an agreement was reached which boosted wages and set the basis for what might be called a labor–management—a class—compromise that would be copied by corporations and unions in other industries. It was called the Treaty of Detroit. Through their unions, employees could now count on regular wage increases (COLA, or cost-of-living adjustment clauses were usually included in contracts), and they would receive health insurance and pensions. Yet, in return, they gave up their demands for more control over corporate policy, especially over pricing, and were required to guarantee social peace on the shop floor.

On the one hand, this labor–management compromise greatly increased living standards for unionized employees, now about 40 percent of the workforce, and established new expectations regarding individual and family economic security. Something like a middle-class style of life, with home ownership, car ownership, and vacation time, now seemed possible. On the other hand, the compromise sacrificed democratic initiatives within unions, marginalized shop floor radicals who focused on worker empowerment, and transferred much of the negotiating authority to union bureaucrats. Labor's arguments about the broader public good might then be weakened, and labor organizations might soon be considered just another set of "interest groups," hierarchical in structure and fighting only for their particular concerns. So long as the national economy thrived, the compromise wasn't difficult to maintain, but it was unclear what would happen when and if growth slowed.

≡ **Striking Workers Rally Outside of a General Motors Plant in Detroit, Michigan, in 1945** Over 200,000 General Motors workers went on strike for four months for better pay and more influence over automobile pricing. The workers got their pay increase along with annual cost-of-living adjustments, but in return abandoned their attempt to steer corporate policy.

Whither the New Deal?

In the shorter term, many of the questions raised by CIO unions—about full employment, health insurance, and social welfare—came on the table of political discussion. And the outcomes suggested a great deal about the developing shape of the postwar political economy. During the recent war, New Deal liberals and left-wingers like Senator Robert Wagner of New York, Representative John Dingell of Michigan, and Henry Wallace hoped to expand programs like Social Security to include health coverage and disability insurance and promote a full-employment economy. President Roosevelt himself, in his 1944 State of the Union address, insisted that "individual freedom cannot exist without economic security and independence," and called for "a Second Bill of Rights" that would guarantee all Americans "a useful and remunerative job," "a decent home," "adequate medical care," and "a good education."

President Truman, anticommunist that he was and far more moderate than Henry Wallace, nonetheless embraced many of these goals. The problem was that the political winds were shifting in Congress and the road to achieving the goals grew steeper. Opposition to the New Deal had been building, especially among Republicans and southern Democrats, since the late 1930s, and although wartime mobilization strengthened the hand of the Roosevelt administration and expanded government intervention in the economy, the New Deal's opponents also felt more confident. The midterm elections of 1946 overturned Democratic majorities in both houses of Congress for the first time since 1930, simultaneously increasing the clout of lobbyists like the American Medical Association, which opposed federal health insurance, and the National Association of Manufacturers, which was hostile to unions, and giving conservatives and businessmen the opportunity to trim the sails of the labor movement.

As a result, national health insurance, which Truman supported, went down to defeat and Congress, over Truman's veto, enacted the antilabor **Taft-Hartley Act** of 1947. A throwback to the political dispositions of the 1920s, Taft-Hartley outlawed sympathy strikes, mass picketing, and secondary boycotts, permitted states to pass **right-to-work laws** that would end closed union shops, required union officials to foreswear membership in the Communist Party, and authorized the president to intervene in strikes in the name of national security. A variety of blows were thereby dealt to unionized workers and their organizing projects. In the meantime, a significant unionizing effort in the southern states, known as Operation Dixie, suffered a crushing defeat. Only the **GI Bill**, passed in 1944, which provided war veterans (at least white veterans) with a raft of educational, health, and housing benefits, showed the marks of bipartisanship and kept the social democratic impulse alive.

25.3   A Pivotal Election: 1948

Describe the dynamics of the 1948 presidential election and its consequences for American politics.

In some respects, American politics was coming to an important crossroad, and the election of 1948 showed which way the country would likely move and what the enduring fractures might be. Truman had served out virtually all of Franklin

Roosevelt's fourth term and decided to run for election in his own right. But he had critics within his own party to the left and to the right. As a result, he had to navigate treacherous political waters, especially because FDR's shadow still fell over American politics and some regarded Truman as a poor next act. Given the developing Cold War, the growing opposition to New Deal policies and perspectives, and the many years Democrats had wielded power, Truman appeared to be a vulnerable candidate, all the more so because, in the course of the election campaign, two new political parties fielded presidential candidates and vied for power.

The Political Field of Forces

What did the political landscape look like in 1948? To the left were committed New Dealers and political progressives who wished to extend the social democratic initiatives that had emerged in the 1930s and were dissatisfied with what they saw as Truman's missteps. Joining hands with the left wing of the labor movement, they found a presidential candidate in Henry Wallace, and organized a new **Progressive Party of 1948** (with Teddy Roosevelt's insurgency of 1912 in mind).

To the right were conservative southern Democrats who not only feared the centralized power of the federal government but also objected to initiatives that Truman and the Democratic Party had taken in the direction of civil rights. Truman had established a Committee on Civil Rights, ended segregation in the US military by executive order, and ran for president on a Democratic platform that not only called for the repeal of Taft-Hartley but also supported "equal political participation" and "equal opportunity for employment," in short, a challenge to Jim Crow. Deep South Democrats responded by forming their own party, called the **States' Rights Party ("Dixiecrats")**, and nominated South Carolina governor Strom Thurmond for the presidency. This is to say that in 1948 the Democratic Party had split in three.

The Republicans struggled with their own divisions: on the one side an isolationist wing, led once again by Ohio Senator Robert A. Taft, and, on the other side, an internationalist wing, headed up, again as in 1944, by New York Governor Thomas E. Dewey. And as in 1944, the isolationist wing lost out. Dewey became the party nominee for the presidency and seemed well positioned to end the long Democratic lock on the

☰ **Progressive Party Candidate Henry Wallace**   Shown here addressing a racially diverse crowd at a campaign rally in New Jersey in July 1948. Henry Wallace had occupied several positions in President Roosevelt's administration, including vice president. Situating himself to the left of the New Deal Democrats, Wallace campaigned against racial segregation and sought peaceful coexistence with the Soviet Union.

White House. The Democrats had been there since 1933 and had won four straight national elections, all with FDR at the helm.

An Unexpected Result

How could Dewey lose? The Progressive Party generated a great deal of enthusiasm and constructed a platform that called for a more cooperative approach to the Soviet Union, stronger regulation of big business, a minimum wage, the end to government harassment of leftists, and civil rights for African Americans. But Progressives were soon tarred with the brush of associating with communists and had a tough time when it came to winning votes. For their part, the Dixiecrats supported the maintenance of segregation and the entire apparatus of Jim Crow but won most of their votes in only four states of the former Confederacy: Louisiana, Alabama, Mississippi, and South Carolina.

Surprisingly, Harry Truman ran an extraordinary campaign, crisscrossing the country, denouncing the "do-nothing," and now Republican-controlled, Congress, and trying to coax potential Wallace supporters into his camp. That he had vetoed Taft-Hartley in 1947 helped him with organized labor and that he campaigned in Black urban neighborhoods and put an end to segregation in the military won him the votes of many Black people outside of the South, where they could cast ballots.

Even so, it looked like Dewey would prevail; the Republican *Chicago Daily Tribune* was so sure of this on election night that the paper ran the headline: DEWEY DEFEATS TRUMAN. In fact, it was Truman who prevailed, and more comfortably than might be expected. He won most of the Midwest, West, and South, and, quite remarkably, helped the Democrats reclaim both houses of Congress (see Map 25.2).

What did this mean? It meant that the Democrats would remain in power nationally but that they would have to work and compromise with Republicans who mostly shared their views on the Cold War and accepted many of the New Deal's social welfare measures—the election demonstrated that explicitly fighting the New Deal was a losing strategy—but were committed to limiting the reach of federal initiatives and regulations.

25.4   A Military-Industrial Complex

Recognize the connections between military spending and civilian consumption during the Cold War.

Thus, the reign of the Democrats did not end, as many expected in 1948. Rather, it ended in 1952 when former general and World War II hero Dwight D. Eisenhower accepted the Republican presidential nomination and won the presidency, after both parties had courted him. But the legacies of the New Deal did not end with

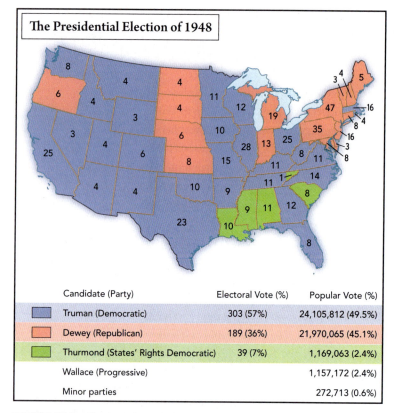

The Presidential Election of 1948

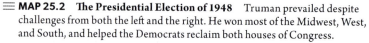

Candidate (Party)	Electoral Vote (%)	Popular Vote (%)
Truman (Democratic)	303 (57%)	24,105,812 (49.5%)
Dewey (Republican)	189 (36%)	21,970,065 (45.1%)
Thurmond (States' Rights Democratic)	39 (7%)	1,169,063 (2.4%)
Wallace (Progressive)		1,157,172 (2.4%)
Minor parties		272,713 (0.6%)

≡ **MAP 25.2   The Presidential Election of 1948**   Truman prevailed despite challenges from both the left and the right. He won most of the Midwest, West, and South, and helped the Democrats reclaim both houses of Congress.

a return of the Republican Party to executive power. Republicans may have campaigned against the policies of the Roosevelt and Truman administrations, but Eisenhower, like Dewey before him, represented the wing of the party that had an internationalist perspective and recognized that the Great Depression and World War II created a new political and economic environment. Missing now were the social democratic elements of the New Deal, those that supported labor and the downtrodden and imagined more rather than less government planning.

A number of federal efforts to stimulate the economy and stave off a return to depression thereby remained in place or were advanced. But they tended to show the marks of a variety of private interest groups rather than the vision of progressives and their liberal allies. They showed the marks of the medical establishment, the automotive industry, the housing industry, the oil and gas industry, and associations of realtors. Congress would not support national health insurance or mass public transit or urban housing development despite the great housing shortage of the immediate postwar years. There would, however, be support for building new interstate highways, eventually 41,000 miles of them, and for encouraging suburban home ownership, doubling the suburban population between 1950 and 1970 (see Map 25.3).

The Cold War Stimulus

There would also be support—massive support—for any sector of the economy that contributed to American militarization and the "fighting" of the Cold War. That support, in the billions of dollars, would go to the research, development,

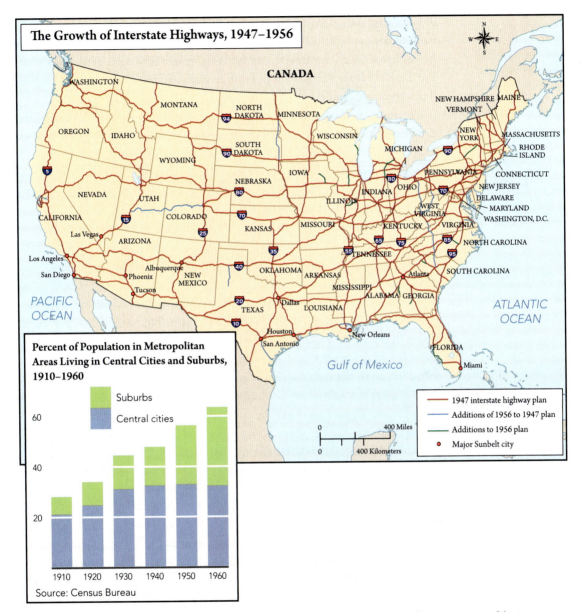

The Growth of Interstate Highways, 1947–1956

CANADA

WASHINGTON
MONTANA
NORTH DAKOTA
MINNESOTA
OREGON
IDAHO
SOUTH DAKOTA
WISCONSIN
MICHIGAN
WYOMING
NEBRASKA
IOWA
NEVADA
UTAH
COLORADO
ILLINOIS
INDIANA   OHIO
PENNSYLVANIA
CALIFORNIA
Las Vegas
ARIZONA
KANSAS
MISSOURI
KENTUCKY
WEST VIRGINIA
VIRGINIA
Los Angeles
San Diego
Albuquerque
Phoenix
NEW MEXICO
OKLAHOMA
ARKANSAS
TENNESSEE
NORTH CAROLINA
Tucson
MISSISSIPPI
ALABAMA   GEORGIA
SOUTH CAROLINA
Atlanta
TEXAS
Dallas
LOUISIANA
Houston
San Antonio
New Orleans
FLORIDA
Miami

NEW HAMPSHIRE   MAINE
VERMONT
NEW YORK
MASSACHUSETTS
RHODE ISLAND
CONNECTICUT
NEW JERSEY
DELAWARE
MARYLAND
WASHINGTON, D.C.

PACIFIC OCEAN
ATLANTIC OCEAN
Gulf of Mexico

1947 interstate highway plan
Additions of 1956 to 1947 plan
Additions to 1956 plan
Major Sunbelt city

0   400 Miles
0   400 Kilometers

Percent of Population in Metropolitan Areas Living in Central Cities and Suburbs, 1910–1960

Suburbs
Central cities

60
40
20

1910 1920 1930 1940 1950 1960
Source: Census Bureau

≡ **MAP 25.3   The Growth of Interstate Highways, 1947–1956**   Across the nation, the construction of the interstate highway system enabled suburban growth, created markets for a new roadside economy, and split cities, obliterating centuries-old patterns of urban development.

and construction of weapons systems, aircraft, warships and submarines, and to new technologies, especially in aerospace and information gathering, that would strengthen the hand of the United States and potentially weaken that of the Soviet Union. There were subsidies and government contracts for private industries, large doses of financial aid for the expansion of higher education, and big outlays for the building of new military bases at home and abroad. Much of the investment found its way to the South, Southwest, and Far West, as well as to parts of the Northeast, and therefore contributed to the population shifts and patterns of suburbanization that were already underway.

Electronics and aviation companies sprouted, not in the downtowns but on the outskirts of Atlanta, Houston, Los Angeles, San Diego, Seattle, and even New York City. Cape Canaveral, the main rocket launching site, was located along the east coast of Florida. The Johnson Space Center and NASA (the National Aeronautics and Space Administration) grew outside Houston. Lockheed was in the Los Angeles suburb of Burbank, General Dynamics in coastal San Diego, Grumman on eastern Long Island, and Boeing very near to Seattle. The "Sunbelt" stretched from Carolina to California and then sustained its expansion with the help of the federal government, first in the "hot" war of the 1940s and then in the "cold" one which followed (see Chapter 24).

For those who worried about how the American economy would fare once war-time mobilizations ended, Cold War spending seemed to be the rabbit that could always be pulled out of the hat, a form of Keynesian economics that leaders across the political spectrum could embrace. "Government planners figure they have found the magic formula for almost endless good times," one conservative journalist observed as early as 1950. "Cold war is the catalyst. Cold war is an automatic pump primer. Turn a spigot, and the public clamors for more arms spending. Turn another and the clamor ceases." That regions of the country with conservative political tendencies directly benefitted from this federal spending helped create a bipartisan consensus on the development of what one later critic would call a "permanent war economy."

New Drivers of Consumption

The boom was real and, it seemed, enduring. Between 1941 and 1969, the average family income in the United States doubled even as the population grew, owing to the **baby boom** of the late 1940s and 1950s, a sign in itself of confidence in the direction of the economy (the birthrate had flattened in the 1930s). Consumer spending increased dramatically not only because of higher incomes but also because of the availability of new forms of credit, especially credit cards. Previously, individual stores and chains had expanded credit; now the credit granting agencies were financial concerns in their own right and national in their reach. Their cards could be used for purchases from many different retailers. Diners Club led the way in 1949, followed by American Express, Bank of America (it became Visa), Hilton Hotels (Carte Blanche), Interbank (later MasterCard), and Chase Manhattan Bank.

By 1957, roughly two-thirds of all American families could report some kind of debt, mostly for installment buying.

The emergence of discount stores, which sought to balance low costs with very high volume, brought further opportunities for mass consumption. Stores like E.J. Korvette, Target, Kresge's, and Wal-Mart opened their doors and quickly moved into the rapidly growing suburbs, anticipating the advent of shopping malls, all fortified by the explosion of advertising through print media, radio, and the new leading edge of communication, television. It appeared to be a virtual economic miracle: military spending fueling civilian consumption in the service of Cold War triumphalism. But where would this lead and would it be worth the price?

Drivers of Consumption   In the 1950s, Americans were encouraged to purchase cars and suburban homes in which to raise their families.

25.5   Making Cold War Culture

||| Evaluate the cultural impact of the Cold War and how it bred conformity.

On one level, it appeared that the Cold War had a unifying and increasingly homogenizing effect on American culture. The population was overwhelmingly white (90 percent) and native-born (93 percent), heading out to the suburbs in droves, buying houses and cars, turning their eyes to other newly available commodities, constructing nuclear families marked by familiar gender hierarchies (the men went off to work, the women remained at home engaged in housekeeping and childrearing), joining churches in record numbers, and aspiring to the comfortable middle class. Not surprisingly, popular media played an important role in creating and celebrating this image. Magazines such as *Life, Look, Good Housekeeping*, and *House Beautiful*, their pages filled with photographs and advertising and their sights set especially on young women, had booming circulations. They equated the good life with the acquisition of material goods, the pursuit of privatization, the

≡ **Patriarchal Households**   Advertisements in the 1950s depicted housewives in their suburban kitchens enjoying the latest appliances. Here, two children ransack their father's briefcase when he comes home from work as their mother prepares dinner.

vitality of patriarchal households, and the embrace of political and social conformity. But was the cultural stability more apparent than real?

The New Age of Television

Nothing proved more important in these regards than did television. First broadcast in 1929 and then fully unveiled during the New York World's Fair of 1939, fewer than 3 percent of all families in the country owned one in 1950, and most of them were well-to-do. After all, a television set then cost about $300, or $3,700 in today's dollars. Ten years later, 90 percent of American families owned a television set. It was still expensive—about $250, or $2,700 in today's dollars—but technologically was more advanced, while steadily rising wages over the decade made it more affordable. It had also become lucrative: more than a billion dollars a year was spent on television advertising. Indeed, all four of the commercial networks at the time (modern cable debuted decades later) depended on advertising dollars for their revenue.

As with the radio that preceded it, television viewers were introduced to a wide array of products for their homes and personal satisfaction; and as with the radio, too, television viewers took in a variety of shows, including comedies and dramas, that were often serialized weekly. But the social range of radio shows, which included important depictions of working-class life, with its hard-scrabble economies and tensions of gender and ethnicity, gave way to programming on television that tended toward westerns and situation comedies, "sitcoms" as they would come to be called, that focused on respectable, middle-class families. With names such as *Father Knows Best, Leave It to Beaver, The Adventures of Ozzie and Harriet,* and *The Donna Reed Show,* the programs achieved great popularity during the 1950s, heralding worlds of comfort, stability, relative harmony, and racial homogeneity. The tensions of family life, between husbands and wives or parents and children or children and their friends, were played out humorously

≡ **Television Culture**   A family in the 1950s gathers around their television to watch a western. By 1959, thirty westerns were airing on prime-time television.

and usually resolved painlessly through deference to proper authority. Women and children might test the boundaries of expected behavior but were quick to retreat in recognition of social expectations. Those who didn't had a tough time finding their way.

In important respects, all of these cultural representations were meant not only to capture the imagined currents of American life but also to contrast what was possible in the United States compared to the Soviet Union and other countries allied with it. Here, in America, was a world of elevated material living conditions, cascading commodities, private spaces, optimism, trust in God, and a robust middle class; there, in the Soviet bloc, was a world of collectivism, material scarcity, overcrowded living quarters, faithlessness, and day-to-day dreariness. Even critics of Cold War culture, who wrote of the staleness, boredom, and sterility of suburban life—Sloan Wilson's novel, *The Man in the Gray Flannel Suit* (1955), subsequently made into a film, was particularly noteworthy—effectively confirmed its centrality to what the United States had become.

Cultural Propaganda and Repression

There was an imperial component to this culture-making process as well. In 1949 and 1950, the newly established CIA secretly formed two organizations designed to spread the image of the United States and American capitalism abroad.

≣ **Cultural Ambassador** Jazz great Louis Armstrong (*center*) and his wife, Lucille (*right*), visit Dusseldorf, Germany, in 1952. Although Armstrong traveled under the auspices of the Congress of Cultural Freedom as an unofficial ambassador for jazz, he was unaware of the CIA connection.

One was Radio Free Europe, which broadcast programs into the Soviet Union and Eastern Europe and sought to disabuse listeners, who needed short-wave radios to tune in, of the "propaganda" to which they were subjected. The other was the Congress of Cultural Freedom, first established in West Berlin and eventually with offices in thirty-five countries, that promoted the display of Western cultural forms: art exhibitions, news services, symphonic and jazz concerts, international conferences. Few of the participants, who included jazz greats like Louis Armstrong and Dizzy Gillespie, knew of the CIA connection, which was not revealed until 1966, so they, too, contributed to the project of "fighting" the Cold War.

As this might suggest, Cold War culture-making and its celebration of conformity relied partly on secrecy and repression. This would leave a deep and lasting stain on the United States. To be sure, antiradicalism and anticommunism had a long history in the country—think of the persecution of anarchists in the 1880s or of domestic radicals after the Russian Revolution (the Red Scare)—and they would energize the heavy hand of the federal government through congressional legislation and the Bureau of Investigation, soon known as the FBI. By the late 1930s, conservative opponents of the New Deal began investigating the influence of communists and socialists, and one of them, Martin Dies, a Democratic congressman from Texas, helped found the **House Un-American Activities Committee (HUAC)**.

Yet the climate of the developing Cold War gave anticommunism new legitimacy, and its crusading ranks came to include Democrats as well as Republicans and many liberals as well as conservatives, resulting in what many termed the

Second Red Scare. Americans for Democratic Action was organized in 1947 by liberal Democrats who had soured on the Soviet Union and the American communists who seemed to support it. In a sense, they enabled the Truman administration to create a Federal Employee Loyalty Program (1947), which made even "sympathetic association" with any group deemed "subversive" grounds for dismissal, and HUAC to launch investigations of trade unionists, writers, artists, teachers, scholars, and filmmakers who were suspected of communist ties. Many not only lost their jobs but were permanently blacklisted, unable to find any work.

One of those repressed by the blacklist was Paul Robeson. An immensely gifted athlete, singer, and actor of African descent with an international following, Robeson had been involved since the 1930s in a variety of progressive causes. He was a vocal supporter of trade unionism, Black civil rights, the war against fascism in Spain, the antilynching movement in the South, the struggle against colonialism in India and elsewhere, and the presidential campaign of Henry Wallace. Robeson also traveled to the Soviet Union, as he did to Spain. When he spoke at a peace conference in Paris in 1949 and said that "We in America do not forget that it was on the backs of the white workers from Europe and on the backs of millions of blacks that the wealth of America was built" and "we shall support peace and friendship among all nations," the alarm bells rang at HUAC. Robeson's acting and singing career came to an end, and his passport was revoked, not to be restored until 1958.

McCarthyism

The Cold War anticommunist crusade reached its apotheosis in the figure of Wisconsin Senator Joseph McCarthy. A small-town Republican who opposed labor and supported business interests, McCarthy hadn't come onto the national radar screen until 1950 when he insisted that he had a list—waving a piece of paper in front of the audience he was addressing—containing the names of over 200 State Department employees who were members of the Communist Party. McCarthy never revealed the names or showed anyone the paper, but the charges gained notoriety because of the Cold War climate in general and the recent events in Asia in particular: most significantly, what was called the "loss" of China to communism.

For the next several years, McCarthy investigated, harassed, and helped to have punished hundreds of Americans, many in high and midlevel political positions. The feeding frenzy of repression he unleashed—it would be called **McCarthyism**—touched the lives of thousands of others. Perhaps 15,000 federal employees lost their jobs, and HUAC was able to provide private employers with data on as many as 60,000 other Americans. Before the worst of it was over, more than thirteen million Americans from all walks of life had to submit to the demands of loyalty programs, and roughly 20 percent of the labor force had to take an oath or gain clearance before they could work.

The McCarthyite "witch hunts" swept through colleges, school districts, journalism, radio and television, and Hollywood, targeting gay men and women as well as those accused of political subversion. Indeed, homosexuality came to be seen as threatening as communism both because of its rejection of mainstream cultural norms and because homosexuals were thought to be particularly vulnerable to bribery and extortion for political ends. This became known as the **lavender scare**.

Especially hard hit by the McCarthyite "witch hunts" was the labor movement. Already on the defensive owing to the Taft-Hartley Act, organized labor, notably the militant CIO, had left-wing activists purged from its ranks. In part, **blacklisting** workers for union activities was a weapon of corporate employers who hoped to challenge labor's reach for power. "Whoever stirs up needless strife in American trade unions," one business publication insisted, "advances the cause of Communism." But labor unions themselves became embroiled in the hunt, seeking legitimacy in the eyes of power holders by moving against radicals in their midst. Many unions thereby lost some of their most energetic leaders, those who saw unions as a progressive force for the country as a whole. The movement wouldn't be the same again and, in many respects, would never recover from the political blows that were landed.

Eventually, McCarthy's tactics and self-absorbed bombast went too far. Even those in public life who embraced the cause of anticommunism came to bridle at the spectacle of untruths and innuendos that McCarthy offered up, worried, perhaps, that they, too, could be next. Little by little, they came to call him out and peel away from his project. And when McCarthy, desperate to retain the attention he had been attracting, set his sights on the US military

≡ **Witch Hunt** US Senator Joseph McCarthy testifying before a Senate committee about the alleged spread of communism in the United States during the early 1950s.

and suspected communists there, the media and the political establishment turned against him. "Have you no sense of decency?" one of those targeted by his interrogation asked.

McCarthy would end up as a broken alcoholic, an apparent disgrace to the nation and institutions he claimed to be defending. But his anticommunist crusade demonstrated how quickly and easily many Americans could be mobilized for political and intellectual repression, a sobering lesson in the perils of fear and demagoguery in the democracy of the United States.

25.6   A Cold War Turns Hot—and Dangerous

Describe how a dangerous "hot" war erupted on the Korean peninsula and how it influenced the Cold War.

McCarthyism and repressive anticommunism emerged in a context of "hot" warfare that "cold" war was meant to avoid. The warfare was not in Europe or the Western Hemisphere nor was it in Southeast Asia. It was on the relatively remote Korean peninsula, no more than a marginal place during World War II, and it suggested how closely "cold" and "hot" warfare were connected: how easily threats and challenges could escalate, how quickly opposing troops could be mobilized, and how the prospect of nuclear war always hung over superpower politics.

Why Korea?

Korea had for decades been a colony of Japan, a source of material resources and labor. But with Japan's defeat, the days of Japanese colonialism seemed at an end and Korean nationalists, of various political stripes, imagined an independent Korean nation. Yet divisions among themselves made a political solution hard to reach and, as a result, the United States and the Soviet Union, having entered, as promised, the Pacific war in August 1945, jointly occupied Korea. The Soviet Union extended its influence north of the 38th parallel and the United States did so south of it. What the Koreans got, on the ground, were two authoritarian regimes. One of them, in "north" Korea, was called the Democratic People's Republic of Korea (DPRK), and the one in "south" Korea was called the Republic of Korea (ROK). Each was intent upon uniting the peninsula under its rule.

The regime in the south, headed up by Syngman Rhee, first hoped to make the move, but the United States declined to give its approval. Then the regime in the north, led by Kim Il Sung, hatched a similar plan, imagining that popular

PERSPECTIVES

Homeward Bound

During the Cold War, Americans turned to the family as a bastion of safety in an insecure world. Suburban homes, especially the ranch-style models built in sprawling housing tracts like Levittown, the prototypical development constructed in the late 1940s on Long Island, New York, provided an affordable bulwark against the dangers of the Cold War. Sometimes equipped with stocked basements or even fallout shelters in case of a nuclear attack, suburban homes seemed secure and stable, filled with happy children, led by a virile father, and supported by a wife and mother who fulfilled her role

≡ **Family in Fallout Shelter** During a nuclear attack, families could find refuge in private bomb shelters. Advertisements for bomb shelters promoted togetherness as the key to survival. In this ad, the father's authority is symbolized by the shovel he clasps like a scepter. Behind him, shelves lined with cans of food and other household items testify to his role as a provider. Next to him sits his submissive wife. Resolute children appear ready to spring into action.

as a homemaker. It was the place, historian Elaine Tyler May says, "where American women and men might be able to ward off their nightmares and live out their dreams."[1]

≡ **The Kitchen Debate**   The 1959 "kitchen debate" between Vice President Richard Nixon (*right*) and Soviet premier Nikita Khrushchev (*left*) at the American National Exhibition in Moscow demonstrated the centrality of the home to both domestic culture and US foreign relations during the Cold War. In the often-heated exchange, Nixon extolled the virtues of the American way of life. For Nixon, like so many other Americans during the Cold War, American superiority rested on the ideal of the suburban home, equipped with modern appliances. "Would it not be better to compete in the relative merits of washing machines than in the strength of rockets?" Nixon asked Khrushchev?[2] Nixon knew that in the sphere of consumer affluence, the United States had the upper hand.

CONSIDER THIS

The surge in suburban housing after World War II was fostered by government policies that underwrote the construction of the vast majority of new developments. Housing starts went from 114,000 in 1944 to an all-time high of 1,692,000 in 1950. What does this say about the federal government's role in promoting an ideal American family? People of color were largely excluded from the new suburban communities built in the postwar period. Were government agencies complicit in fostering residential segregation?

[1]Elaine Tyler May, *Homeward Bound: American Families in the Cold War Era* (New York: Basic Books, 1988), 26.

[2]"When Nixon Took on Khrushchev," *New York Times*, July 25, 1959, p. 3.

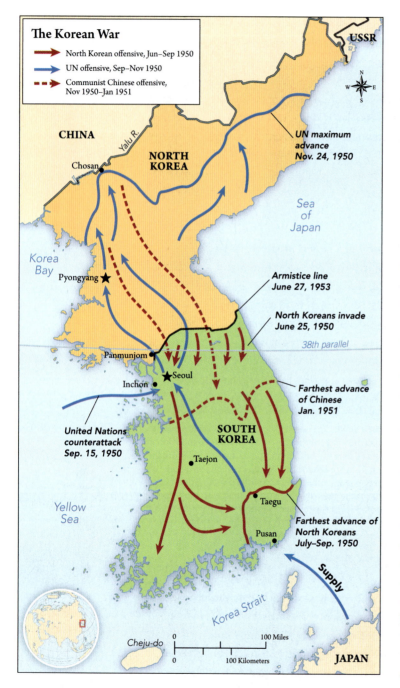

The Korean War

→ North Korean offensive, Jun–Sep 1950
→ UN offensive, Sep–Nov 1950
⇢ Communist Chinese offensive, Nov 1950–Jan 1951

USSR

CHINA

NORTH KOREA

Yalu R.

Chosan

Korea Bay

Pyongyang ★

UN maximum advance Nov. 24, 1950

Sea of Japan

Armistice line June 27, 1953

North Koreans invade June 25, 1950

38th parallel

Panmunjom ●

Inchon

★ Seoul

United Nations counterattack Sep. 15, 1950

Farthest advance of Chinese Jan. 1951

SOUTH KOREA

● Taejon

Yellow Sea

● Taegu

● Pusan

Farthest advance of North Koreans July–Sep. 1950

Supply

Korea Strait

Cheju-do

0 ——— 100 Miles
0 ——— 100 Kilometers

JAPAN

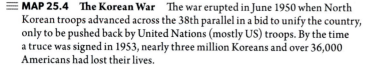

≡ **MAP 25.4 The Korean War** The war erupted in June 1950 when North Korean troops advanced across the 38th parallel in a bid to unify the country, only to be pushed back by United Nations (mostly US) troops. By the time a truce was signed in 1953, nearly three million Koreans and over 36,000 Americans had lost their lives.

dissatisfaction with the Rhee government would redound to his benefit. Unlike the United States, the Soviet Union gave the green light, though did not instigate it. As a result, on June 25, 1950, the military forces of North Korea crossed the 38th parallel and invaded the south. Very quickly the troops from the north occupied the southern capital of Seoul and were moving toward Pusan near the peninsula's southern end. A quick victory seemed likely (see Map 25.4).

Neither the North Koreans nor their Soviet allies expected much of a reaction from the United States. After all, the Korean peninsula seemed to be outside the American "perimeter" of security interests. They miscalculated. The Truman administration responded almost immediately, summoning the United Nations to demand a North Korean withdrawal and mobilizing the United States military for action. Here, the climate of the Cold War was crucial. China had only recently fallen to the communists, Truman was under attack for "losing" it, and an opportunity to stop, or "contain," the spread of communism and the Soviet Union now presented itself.

The UN Security Council passed a resolution denouncing

what the North Koreans had done and pledged to aid the South, militarily if necessary. This was possible because the Soviet Union, a Security Council member, was not in attendance; the Soviets were protesting the UN's simultaneous refusal to admit the People's Republic of China to membership. Truman then might have asked Congress for a declaration of war, as had usually been the case in the past. But declare war against whom? The North Koreans? The Soviet Union? Instead, Truman decided not to go to Congress but to use his executive powers and engage in what he termed a "police action." It was a political tipping point of immense significance. From here on in it would be the American president, not the American Congress, who would determine when the country was at war and what to call it.

A Renegade General

But warfare it surely was with the prospect of escalation constantly threatening. Truman had thousands of troops called up and deployed to South Korea under the command of General Douglas MacArthur, a haughty military man who had a mixed track record in the recently completed World War II. The Japanese had forced him out of the American-controlled Philippines early on in the war. Still brazen, however, MacArthur barreled in, embarking upon a risky invasion at Inchon Bay, just south of the 38th parallel, aided by UN troops moving north from Pusan. Now on the defensive, Kim Il Sung asked the Soviet Union to send troops. This time Stalin balked, and instead urged the Chinese to come to the North's

assistance. At first hesitant, the Chinese warned the United States that if its troops crossed the 38th parallel they would come into the war. MacArthur paid this no heed and did just that. So in November 1950 the Chinese sent a large number of troops into Korea.

Unsettled if not panicked, Truman suggested that he might resort to nuclear weapons if necessary to halt the Chinese offensive. For his part, MacArthur ordered massive bombings of North Korean cities, including the capital of Pyongyang, and also authorized the use of a chemical

☰ **Douglas MacArthur**   General Douglas MacArthur (seated) watches the bombardment of Inchon from bridge of the *USS Mount McKinley* in September 1950. Six months later he was fired by President Truman for insubordination.

weapon called napalm, which burned people as well as buildings. Before too long, MacArthur seemed to be making his own policy, planning not only to take all of Korea but to move into China as well. Aghast at such insubordination and recognizing how MacArthur's ambitions could provoke a much larger war, Truman, in April, sent him into early retirement, though not into obscurity. MacArthur retained many admirers.

Trouble for Ending the War

Yet after nearly a year of hard fighting, in which each side held the clear advantage for a time, the war bogged down and, in July 1951, the United States, the North Koreans, and the Chinese (but not the South Koreans) sat down at a negotiating table. They quickly accepted the idea of a return to the geopolitics of the Korean peninsula on the eve of the war—meaning that North and South would be divided along the 38th parallel and each would be recognized as a sovereign entity, which was why the South Koreans refused to join the talks—but could not settle on a final agreement. What was the problem?

The problem was the status of war prisoners, already numbering in the thousands. Would they simply be exchanged, as the North Koreans and Chinese demanded, "repatriated" in legal terms, or could they choose where they would go, as the United States insisted? It was an issue that spoke to the dynamics of the Cold War and the validation all sides needed. Neither side would budge. Nor was there a cease-fire while the talks went on, and some of the bloodiest and most destructive fighting of the entire war occurred during the "peace talks." By the time the war was over, the United States saw nearly 40,000 of its troops killed and about 100,000 wounded. And nearly half of the casualties were sustained after the peace negotiations began.

By the spring of 1953 it seemed that a thaw might be in the offing. The United States had a new president, Dwight D. Eisenhower, who had been elected in November 1952 and quickly traveled to Korea to see if a resolution could be hastened. In March 1953, Soviet leader Josef Stalin died suddenly, and there was interest among his successors in finding a way to reduce international tensions. The Chinese, too, showed a new flexibility, no longer demanding the immediate repatriation of their prisoners. Only the American negotiators dragged their feet, but ultimately gave in to growing international pressure. On July 27, 1953, an armistice was signed and the war came to a halt.

Legacies of Warfare

The armistice divided the peninsula into northern and southern states and established an internationally patrolled "demilitarized zone" between them. As for the issue of war prisoners, a neutral "repatriations commission" was established to handle the problem. But there would be few steps toward political reunification. The Chinese and the United States kept troops on the ground, and the tensions that provoked war in the first place remained menacingly in place. No peace treaty between the Koreas was ever signed.

The Koreans paid very heavily for the "police action" in which they became embroiled. As many as three million of them on both sides, or about 10 percent of their total population, were either killed, wounded, or reported as missing; another five million became refugees. It would be a long recovery and the deep scars remain to this day, with a modernized South governed through some democratic means, and a highly repressive North ever suffering from food shortages and very low living standards, though intent on developing sophisticated weapons systems. Skirmishes between them regularly erupt and threaten again to spiral into warfare.

For the United States, the Korean War was a troubling reminder that the end of World War II had not brought peace. Rather, it brought a new era of global conflict and destructive nightmares that could easily move in very dangerous directions. Small wonder that *Collier's* magazine published its issue on World War III just over a year after the Korean War had begun. The armistice thus brought a large sigh of relief and some moderation in the harsh climate of anticommunism. McCarthy's fall would begin within months. But, if anything, the militarization of the American economy that had commenced in the late 1940s now moved full speed ahead. A national security state was being constructed and what Eisenhower would later call a "military-industrial complex" was taking full shape. What's more, the "police action" in Korea revealed the new powers that could be claimed by the president and made it clear that vital American interests, possibly requiring military action, stretched across the Pacific and around the globe.

25.7 Nonconformists

Outline the developing cultural resistance to Cold War conformities and how it was expressed in music, literature, and the arts.

An atmosphere of political and cultural conformity surely enveloped the United States during the late 1940s and 1950s. Standards and beliefs about the American economic and political system, America's role in the world, America's allies and enemies, family and sexuality, faith and God appear to have suffused the public, binding most Americans together and turning them against the relative few who chose to dissent. The pledge of allegiance, originally composed by socialist Francis Bellamy in the late nineteenth century, which was officially adopted by Congress

MAPPING AMERICA

The Cold War World

For the United States, the Korean War ushered in a new era of global conflict. It revealed the new powers that could be claimed by the president and made it clear that vital American interests, possibly requiring military action, stretched around the globe. And as decolonization altered the political landscapes of

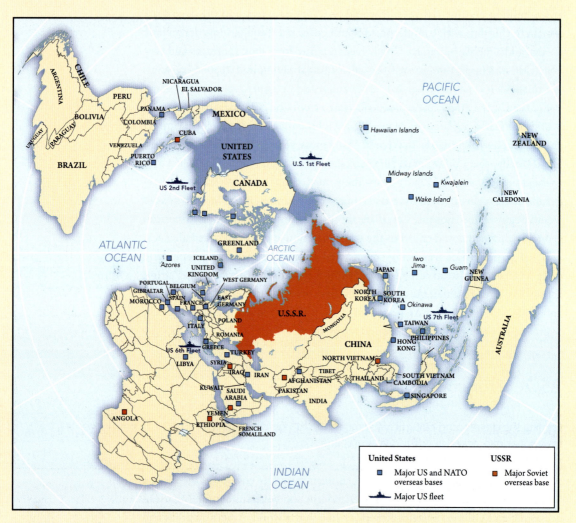

≣ **MAP 1   US and Soviet Military Bases Worldwide, 1959**   The rapid remapping of the globe in the aftermath of World War II solidified lines of confrontation between the United States and the Soviet Union. The United States operated military bases across the globe, from Japan to the Azores, in an effort to contain the Soviet Union.

Asia and Africa after World War II, both the United States and the Soviet Union sought to influence the politics of the newly independent nations that emerged with the collapse of European empires.

Thinking Geographically

US policymakers engaged in the battle against communism worried deeply about Soviet influence in the "Third World"—newly independent countries that emerged in the aftermath of World War II and the disintegration of European colonial empires.

1. Which areas of the world were the focus of the most intense rivalry between the United States and the Soviet Union?

2. What are the legacies today of the fault lines and conflicts of the Cold War?

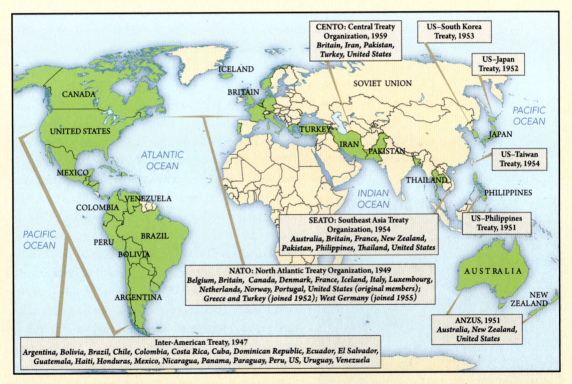

≡ **MAP 2 US Cold War Alliances, 1947–1959** The North Atlantic Treaty Organization (NATO), formed in 1949, was the most important but only one part of a far-flung US system of alliances that encircled the Soviet bloc. To counter communist penetration in former European colonies, US policymakers did not hesitate to make allies of military and other authoritarian regimes.

in 1942, had the words "under God" added to it in 1954. Yet, however much conformity seemed to be the dominant mode of the decade, a number of tempests began to stir as well, all of which fed off previous cultural and political trends and would point the way to larger storms ahead.

The "Beats" and the Folk Revival

Some of the tempests were intellectual. A group of young writers and poets who would be known as the **beat generation** began to craft a critique of mainstream values and sensibilities. First becoming acquainted in uptown New York City around Columbia University in the 1940s, they gravitated to Greenwich Village in lower Manhattan, where the Bohemians of the 1910s and 1920s, to whom they were heirs, had their base. Some then headed out to San Francisco, to the district of North Beach in particular. In various ways they questioned materialism, explored spirituality and Eastern religions, celebrated new gender conventions and sexuality, and experimented with psychedelic drugs. At their center were Allen Ginsberg, William S. Burroughs, and Jack Kerouac, who coined the term "beat generation." Once out in California, they met up with Lawrence Ferlinghetti, who founded the iconic City Lights Books in 1953, Gary Snyder, and some others where the seeds of what would come to be called the counterculture were planted. They also challenged literary censorship—Ginsberg's *Howl and Other Poems* (1956) and Burroughs's *Naked Lunch* (1959) were the subjects of obscenity prosecutions— and paved the way for much greater freedom of expression.

Developing in some relation to the beats was the folk revival movement that grew in New York City in the late 1940s and 1950s. Influenced by acoustic blues musicians as well as country and bluegrass music, folk artists like Pete Seeger and his group The Weavers, influenced by depression-era troubadour Woody Guthrie before them, not only reached into the American musical past but also celebrated the struggles of working men and women along with a range of folk cultures across the nation and around the world. Their songs captivated concert and radio audiences, and created a context in which Peter, Paul, and Mary; the Kingston Trio; Harry Belafonte; Odetta; Bob Dylan; and Joan Baez could take the folk genre in new directions. They would also catch the unwanted attention of HUAC and other suspicious anticommunists who associated them with left-wing causes.

≡ **City Lights Bookstore**   Two women browse in the San Francisco bookstore and hub of the burgeoning countercultural movement. Founder Lawrence Ferlinghetti achieved notoriety for publishing Allen Ginsberg's poem "Howl," which was condemned as obscene.

Birth of Rock and Roll

The 1950s were, then, a time of new cultural creativity and resistance to the more general social norms. And most every area of the arts showed the impact. Abstract expressionism, building on a number of early twentieth-century European styles of painting and sculpture, such as Cubism, Surrealism, and Futurism, took hold during this time as well—again chiefly in New York City—and was advanced by the works of Jackson Pollock, Mark Rothko, and Willem de Kooning, among others. But undoubtedly the most important and influential, and nonconformist, cultural phenomenon of the period was the advent of rock and roll.

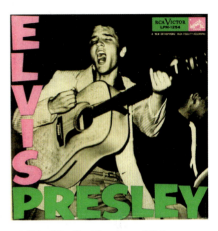

"The King" The cover of Elvis Presley's self-titled 1956 debut album. Borrowing from gospel, country, and blues, as well as pop, Presley's unique style earned him immense fame as the face of rock and roll.

Rock's roots were buried deep in the soil of blues, jazz, gospel, and rhythm and blues music; in short, the music of African Americans, with sprinklings of country and boogie-woogie music. It then burst on the scene with a mix of Black and white artists: Chuck Berry, Bo Diddley, Fats Domino, Bill Haley, Buddy Holly, Jerry Lee Lewis, Little Richard, and most prominent of all, Mississippi's Elvis Presley. Electric, rhythmic, and driven by contagious beats, the music embodied passion, longing, and intense sexual energy. Many guardians of morality were apoplectic as they watched teenagers around the country scream, shout, and sway to the music; take small notice of conventional racial lines; and delight in their own irreverence. Some of the moral guardians sought to have the music banned, and a few organized record burnings. It was to little avail. The cracks in the cultural armor of the 1950s spread and then deepened, setting the stage for further cultural transformations.

25.8 Beginnings of the Civil Rights Movement

||| Evaluate how a civil rights movement began to emerge.

In some ways, the advent of rock and roll, with its crossings of Black and white musical traditions and increasingly integrated musical venues, was indicative of a much larger development that would leave decisive imprint on the remainder of the twentieth century: the struggle for civil rights. To be sure, African Americans battled against slavery and for equality in American society since they first set foot in North America. Their energy and courage, their vision for a true democracy found powerful expression in abolitionism and then in the War of the Rebellion and Reconstruction. But the battle would prove to be a long one. By the late nineteenth and early twentieth centuries, Jim Crow laws and culture not only repressed them in the South but also limited their opportunities in the North and West (see Chapter 20).

Different Directions

A great many African Americans, recognizing the tenacity of white supremacy, embraced the idea of racial empowerment or "emigrationism," believing that the only way they could find a comfortable place in the United States or anywhere else in the world was to have a formidable African state on the world stage. This was the message of Marcus Garvey, and it would continue to have important cultural and political traction among African Americans for the next century. Hundreds of local chapters (they were called "divisions") of the Universal Negro Improvement Association (UNIA) spread across the country, and loyalty to the movement was maintained well after Garvey himself had been deported (see Chapter 21).

But other African Americans demanded that the United States live up to its highest principles for all of its citizens, and they determined to fight on. Many were associated with the NAACP, which also established chapters all over the country, or felt that a simple choice between Black empowerment and civil rights was artificial. Instead, they struggled toward both ends. The 1930s witnessed local mobilizations against segregation in northern cities and school districts, "Don't Buy Where You Can't Work Campaigns," as they were known, and the 1940s saw large-scale efforts to fight discrimination in the military and the rest of American life. The March on Washington movement of 1941 was especially prominent, but there were, as well, smaller-scale actions—as we saw—by Black women and men like Pauli Murray and Bayard Rustin.

The end of World War II brought new hopes and frustrations. African American soldiers returned to the United States after fighting fascism abroad only to be faced with the persistence of Jim Crow at home. They were in no mood to be accommodating. That the Democratic Party included a civil rights plank in its 1948 platform, that Henry Wallace campaigned in the Deep South and was harshly treated by white

☰ **Jim Crow**   A Black male drinking from a "colored" segregated water cooler at an Oklahoma streetcar terminal. Racial segregation policies commonly referred to as "Jim Crow" laws forced Black Americans to use separate (and often inferior) accommodations in public life.

southerners, and that Harry Truman ordered the military desegregated suggested that they might have new allies.

The Making of *Brown v. Board*

The NAACP focused on what might be called a "legal strategy." That meant bringing lawsuits against southern institutions that did not provide facilities that were "equal" even if they were "separate" or that muddied the line between public and private. As a result, the white primary was struck down in 1944 in *Smith v. Allwright*. Southern Democrats had insisted their party was a private "club" and therefore did not come under the jurisdiction of the Fourteenth Amendment, but the Supreme Court now rejected this specious argument. Universities in Texas and Oklahoma were sued because they did not admit Black students or provide separate and equal facilities. The Supreme Court determined, in *McLaurin v. Oklahoma State Regents* (1950) *and Sweatt v. Painter* (1950), that they had to do one or the other.

Along the way, NAACP lawyers, led by the brilliant Thurgood Marshall, set their sights on public schools more generally. In this they hoped not simply to require school districts to offer equal facilities for Black students but to demonstrate that "separate" could never be "equal." Mobilizing the talents of historians and psychologists, as well as activists in five school districts from different parts of the country, they brought suit before the Supreme Court in a case called **Brown v. Board of Education, Topeka, Kansas** (the other districts were in Delaware, Virginia, Washington, DC, and South Carolina) in 1952.

The Court had a new chief justice, Earl Warren, a former California governor and Republican, who had been appointed by President Eisenhower. Sympathetic to the suit, Warren took the time to make sure that the Court would render a unanimous decision. That came in May of 1954. The court ruled that separate facilities could never be equal facilities and therefore that legally segregated schools violated the rights of African Americans under the Thirteenth and Fourteenth Amendments to the Constitution. In effect, the Warren Court, at least in principle, threw out the 1896 Supreme Court decision in *Plessy v. Ferguson* that had pronounced separate but equal constitutionally acceptable.

A Mass Movement Brewing

But African Americans had long recognized that court decisions would do little without activism on the ground. And here, the

≡ **Legal Victory** NAACP lawyers, including Thurgood Marshall (*center*), celebrate the Supreme Court's unanimous verdict in *Brown v. Board of Education*. By ruling that "separate but equal" Jim Crow laws violated the Constitution, the court had dealt a serious blow to legal racial segregation.

1950s saw the beginnings of what would turn into a civil rights "movement." The activists had been involved with local chapters of the NAACP, Black trade unions like the Brotherhood of Sleeping Car Porters, or Garvey's UNIA. Many were also recent war veterans or teachers in segregated educational institutions. As early as 1953, in Baton Rouge, Louisiana, they organized a boycott of city buses that required Black riders to sit in the back and always give their seats to whites who needed them. Led by Baptist minister T. J. Jemison, who grew up in the South but was educated outside of it, the leaders of the **Baton Rouge Bus Boycott** mobilized the entire Black community and in relatively short order brought about major reform.

Their footsteps were followed two years later in Montgomery, Alabama, with another Baptist minister born in the South though educated outside of it, Martin Luther King, as well as important local activists like Rosa Parks and E. D. Nixon leading the way. This time it would take more than a year of bus boycotts, nightly church meetings, and the arrangement of alternative means of transportation. It would also require suffering harassment and intimidation of violent and nonviolent sorts. But the **Montgomery Bus Boycott**, too, won the day and ended segregation on city buses.

Was Jim Crow now being taken apart? Maybe not. The *Brown* decision was of great importance, but it was one thing to declare separate but equal unconstitutional and quite another to desegregate the schools. The Supreme Court had to issue another ruling, in 1955, calling for desegregation with "all deliberate speed," sometimes called "*Brown II.*" Yet white opposition was mobilizing as well. Some in the Deep South and Virginia called for "massive resistance" to *Brown* and desegregation more generally.

A showdown took place in Little Rock, Arkansas, regarded as a relatively moderate state, where a plan to desegregate its Central High School was formulated. Nine black students were chosen to enroll, but white hostility was so great that President Eisenhower had to deputize the Arkansas National Guard and send in federal troops to protect the nine students and allow them to get an education. After a year, and under white pressure, the state government simply closed the school, and growing numbers of white students looked to enroll in private academies to avoid going to school with African American students.

The first signs of a civil rights movement were clearly in evidence: that is to say, a movement involving several strategies, including mass mobilizations, to end Jim Crow in the South and racial discrimination throughout the nation. Ironically, the climate of the Cold War may have aided the development of such a movement because the

Desegregating Central High Black students in Little Rock, Arkansas, arrive at Central High School for class. Resistance to racial integration in schools prompted President Eisenhower to deploy the Arkansas National Guard to protect Black students.

Soviet Union was quick to accuse the US government of hypocrisy, upholding ideas of freedom abroad while permitting the oppression of racial minorities at home.

Bad publicity for sure. But southern Democrats still had a powerful place in the party and in national politics, and white supremacists in the South were intent on defending Jim Crow at all costs. It looked like a long and bloody struggle ahead.

Breaking the Color-Line in the National Pastime

The reach of the civil rights struggle extended beyond the modes of transport and those of education. As a measure of its developing impact, it reached into popular culture, too, no more significantly than in the world of sports. Baseball has complex origins, but it began to take hold in the United States in the middle of the nineteenth century, had professional leagues soon thereafter, and before the century was out, would be called the "national pastime." As might be expected, given the reach of Jim Crow, professional baseball quickly excluded players of African descent who, after a few tries, organized the Negro National League (NNL). With teams in a number of large American cities, the NNL competed before very large crowds of Black spectators and boasted players of great talent, easily the equal of their white counterparts. Before long a Negro American League was added.

≡ **Jackie Robinson** Jackie Robinson became the first Black player in Major League Baseball (MLB) when he joined the Brooklyn Dodgers in 1947. Robinson went on to win the Rookie of the Year Award for the best first-year player, and he eventually entered the Baseball Hall of Fame.

But as World War II drew to a close, there was some interest, especially among sportswriters who knew of the Black talent, in having the color-line broken. Prospects improved when baseball commissioner Kennesaw Mountain Landis, an ardent segregationist, died in 1944 and was replaced by Albert "Happy" Chandler, a former US Senator and governor of Kentucky, who was open to integration despite being a white southerner. As a result, a Major League Committee on Baseball Integration was formed in 1945, and one of its members, Branch Rickey, owner of the Brooklyn Dodgers, soon began negotiating with a young Black star who had been playing for the Kansas City Monarchs of the Negro Leagues named Jackie Robinson. Rickey worried that a Black player would be subjected to harassment by players and fans alike and believed he needed a Black player who "had the guts not to fight back." Robinson was college educated (UCLA) and a war veteran, and when Rickey tested his resolve, Robinson passed. So, after playing briefly with a minor league team, Robinson was in the Dodger lineup at first base in April 1947, integrating the sport.

Rickey knew of the talent in the Negro Leagues and, so, along with Robinson, he signed four other players, including catcher Roy Campanella and pitcher Don Newcombe, all of whom would help the Dodgers win a series of pennants in the 1950s and finally beat the rival New York Yankees in 1955 to become World Series champions. But the Dodgers were not alone. In 1948, the Cleveland Indians signed Larry Doby, and little by little other teams came onboard, though not without opposition and misgivings. Some would resist for more than another decade—the Boston Red Sox would hold out until 1959—demonstrating that racism and racial discrimination was a national, not just a southern, disease.

Conclusion: The Cold War

Not long after the surrenders of Germany and Japan ending World War II, a Cold War descended on the Euro-Atlantic world, and very soon thereafter it encompassed the entire world. It reflected deep ideological and socioeconomic differences between one-time allies, the United States and the Soviet Union, and after the advent of nuclear weaponry, threatened almost unimaginable levels of annihilation. Both the United States and the Soviet Union had ambitious postwar aspirations, and both sought allies in the process: the United States in Western Europe through NATO and the Marshall Plan; the Soviet Union in Eastern Europe through the Warsaw Pact and the Molotov Plan.

In the United States, the developing Cold War left its mark on nearly all areas of life. It led to the development of a national security state and to massive government support for weapons and other means of defense. It encouraged economic stimulus programs designed to prevent a return of the Great Depression and, in so doing, led to a period of widespread prosperity. And it suffused the country's culture, promoting political conformity, a rampant consumerism, and a media committed to noncontroversial offerings even with the new technology of television. Indeed, so focused were American officials on acceptance of capitalism and hostility to communism that they quickly harassed and punished those who appeared to be defiant.

And yet, during the 1950s, signs of political and cultural resistance to the status quo were in evidence. Artists, poets, and musicians began to challenge the cultures of conformity and push against the boundaries that the culture seemed to have established. And in the courts as well as on the ground, a civil rights movement began to take shape, training its sights on Jim Crow in the South and forms of racial discrimination in the North.

WHAT IF the Views of George Kennan Had Been Rejected?

The development of the Cold War proved to be of signal importance not only for the immediate postwar years but for the remainder of the twentieth century as well (as we shall see). And it surely seemed to take shape rapidly. Was there no alternative? Could the decades after World War II have seen something different, and perhaps better?

What if the views of George Kennan in his "Long Telegram" were effectively rejected? What if, as progressive New Dealers were suggesting, the security concerns of the Soviet Union were taken more seriously and, as some atomic scientists were suggesting, atomic weapons were subject to international control or elimination and knowledge of atomic energy was shared? What if the IMF and World Bank, not to mention the Marshall Plan, had fewer conditions attached to their aid, as many international negotiators were suggesting, so that the benefits of economic development could be more widely beneficial?

In such a set of circumstances, which was not out of the realm of possibility, the remilitarization of the Soviet Union and the United States might have been less pronounced and the threat of nuclear warfare greatly diminished. Social policy directed toward health care, mass transit, affordable housing, and urban/suburban development might have been advanced, and the balances of power between labor and capital better stabilized. Anticolonial movements in Asia and Africa might have found it possible to achieve their ends with less violence and struggle and to build their newly independent societies with more resources. The divide between the "developed" and "underdeveloped" areas of the world may have proved easier to shrink and thus world poverty more readily attacked. Tensions and conflicts would surely have arisen, and perhaps the issues of social and economic organization would have been impossible to mediate successfully, at least without global battles of some sort. But the edges and suspicions that the Cold War promoted might have been softened and decreased, increasing the possibility for serious discussions.

DOCUMENT 25.1: George Kennan, "Long Telegram," February 22, 1946

Below are excerpts from the telegram that was sent by George Kennan to President Truman and circulated throughout the administration.

USSR still lives in antagonistic "capitalist encirclement" with which in the long run there can be no peaceful coexistence. [In Stalin's view] everything must be done to advance the relative strength of USSR as factor in international society. Conversely, no opportunity must be missed to reduce strength and influence, collectively as well as individually, of capitalist powers. Soviet efforts, and those of Russia's friends abroad, must be directed toward deepening and exploiting of differences and conflicts between capitalist powers.... At bottom of Kremlin's neurotic view of world affairs is traditional and instinctive Russian sense of insecurity.... For this reason they have always feared foreign penetration, feared direct contact between Western world and their own, feared what would happen if Russians learned truth about world without or if foreigners learned truth about world within. And they have learned to seek security only in patient but deadly struggle for total destruction of rival power.... Internal policy [of USSR] devoted to increasing in every way strength and prestige of Soviet state: intensive military-industrialization; maximum development of armed forces; great displays to impress outsiders; continued secretiveness about internal matters, designed to conceal weaknesses and keep opponents in the dark.... Toward colonial areas and backward or dependent peoples, Soviet policy, even on official plane, will be directed toward weakening of power and influence and contacts of advanced Western nations, on theory ... there will be created a vacuum which will favor Communist-Soviet penetration.... In summary, we have here a political force committed fanatically to the belief that with US there can be no permanent modus vivendi that it is desirable and necessary that the internal harmony of our society be disrupted, our traditional way of life destroyed, the international authority of our state be broken, if Soviet power is to be secure.... [T]he vast fund of objective fact about human society is not, as with us, the measure against which outlook is constantly being tested and re-formed.... We must see that our public is educated to realities of Russian situation. I cannot over-emphasize the importance of this. Press cannot do this alone. It must be done mainly by Government.... Much depends on health and vigor of our own society. World communism is like malignant parasite which feeds only on diseased tissue. This is point at which domestic and foreign policies meet.... I would like to record my conviction that problem is within our power to solve—and that without recourse to any military conflict.

Source: The Foreign Relations of the United States, 1946, Vol. VI, Eastern Europe, the Soviet Union (Washington, DC: US Department of State, Office of the Historian, 1969).

DOCUMENT 25.2: The 1948 Progressive Party Platform

This excerpt comes from the platform of the Progressive Party, ratified at its national convention for the election of 1948.

The American people want peace. But old parties, obedient to the dictates of monopoly and the military, prepare for war in the name of peace. They refuse to negotiate a settlement of differences with the Soviet Union. They reject the United States as an instrument for promoting world peace and reconstruction. They use the Marshall Plan to rebuild Nazi Germany as a war base and to subjugate the economies of other European countries to American big business. They finance and arm corrupt, fascist governments in China, Greece, Turkey, and elsewhere, through the

Truman Doctrine, wasting billions in American resources and squandering America's heritage as the enemy of despotism. They encircle the globe with military bases which other peoples cannot but view as threats to their freedom and security. They protect the war-making industrial and financial barons of Nazi Germany and imperial Japan and restore them to power. They stockpile atomic bombs. . . . They impose a peacetime draft and move toward Universal Military Training. They fill policy-making positions in government with generals and Wall Street bankers. Peace cannot be won—but profits can—by spending ever-increasing billions of the people's money in war preparations. . . . They move to outlaw the Communist Party as a decisive step in their assault on the democratic rights of labor, of national, racial, and political minorities, and of all those who oppose their drive to war. . . . They support the House Committee on Un-American Activities in its vilification and persecution of citizens in total disregard of the Bill of Rights. . . . They concoct a spurious "loyalty" program to create an atmosphere of fear and hysteria in government and industry. . . . The Progressive Party holds that basic to the organization of world peace is a return to the purpose of Franklin Roosevelt to seek areas of international agreement rather than disagreement. It was his conviction that within the framework of the United Nations different social and economic systems can and must live together. If peace is to be achieved capitalist United States and communist Russia must establish good relations and work together. . . . The Progressive Party demands negotiation and discussion with the Soviet Union to find areas of agreement to win the peace. . . . We demand the repudiation of the Truman Doctrine and an end to military and economic intervention in support of reactionary and fascist regimes in China, Greece, Turkey, the Middle East, and Latin America. . . . We demand repeal of the provisions of the National Security Act which are mobilizing the nation for war, preparing a labor draft, and organizing a monopoly-militarist dictatorship. . . . The Progressive Party will work through the United Nations for a world disarmament agreement to outlaw the atomic bomb, bacteriological warfare, and all other instruments of mass destruction.

Source: The Platform of the Progressive Party adopted at the Founding Convention, Philadelphia, July 23–25, 1948.

Thinking About Contingency

1. How can we account for the different perspectives of George Kennan and the Progressive Party?
2. Why was Kennan's "Long Telegram" so convincing to many political leaders and policymakers in the United States?
3. Can an effective rebuttal to the "Long Telegram" be mounted, and what would it say? Does the Progressive Party platform offer a rebuttal?

REVIEW QUESTIONS

1. Why were Harry Truman and Josef Stalin so concerned about the political future of Eastern Europe? What did each hope to gain in the post-war diplomatic jockeying?

2. What was the relationship between the developing Cold War and efforts to promote growth in the American economy? Which sectors of the American economy benefitted most and why?

3. What did the National Security Act attempt to do? What institutions did it create, and how enduring did they turn out to be?

4. How much of a "threat" did American leftists pose to the stability of the American political system? Did the architects of harassment and repression have a case to be made, and did they succeed in their objectives?

5. Why did the Cold War turn hot on the Korean peninsula in the early 1950s? What were the issues? What was settled and what was not?

6. What were the most important mediums for the promotion of Cold War culture? How many Americans did they effectively reach?

7. Given the climate of repression in the 1950s United States, how were artists, activists, and musicians able to gain a footing?

8. How did the first signs of a Civil Rights movement emerge in the 1950s?

KEY TERMS

baby boom (p.1060)

Baton Rouge Bus Boycott (p. 1080)

beat generation (p. 1076)

blacklisting (p. 1066)

Bretton Woods Conference (p. 1046)

Brown v. Board of Education, Topeka, Kansas (p. 1079)

Central Intelligence Agency (CIA) (p. 1050)

Cold War (p. 1044)

containment (p. 1048)

GI Bill (p. 1055)

House Un-American Activities Committee (HUAC) (p. 1064)

International Monetary Fund (IMF) (p. 1045)

Iron Curtain (p. 1047)

lavender scare (p. 1066)

Long Telegram (p. 1047)

Marshall Plan (p. 1052)

McCarthyism (p. 1065)

Molotov Plan (p. 1052)

Montgomery Bus Boycott (p. 1080)

National Security Act (p. 1050)

National Security Council (NSC) (p. 1050)

North Atlantic Treaty Organization (NATO) (p. 1050)

NSC-68 (p. 1050)

Progressive Party of 1948 (p. 1056)

right-to-work laws (p. 1055)

Second Red Scare (p. 1065)

States' Rights Party ("Dixiecrats") (p. 1056)

Taft-Hartley Act (p. 1055)

Truman Doctrine (p. 1048)

Warsaw Pact (p. 1050)

World Bank (p. 1045)

RECOMMENDED READINGS

A. J. Baime, *Dewey Defeats Truman: The 1948 Election and the Battle for America's Soul* (Mariner Books, 2020).

Lizabeth Cohen, *A Consumers' Republic: The Politics of Mass Consumption in Postwar America* (Vintage, 2013).

Bruce Cummings, *The Korean War: A History* (Modern Library, 2011).

Mary Dudziak, *Cold War Civil Rights* (Princeton University Press, 2011).

Elaine Tyler May, *Homeward Bound: American Families in the Cold War Era* (Basic Books, 2017).

Seymour Melman, *The Permanent War Economy: American Capitalism in Decline* (Simon and Schuster, 1974).

Louis Menand, *The Free World: Art and Culture in the Cold War* (Farrar, Straus and Giroux, 2021).

David Oshinsky, *A Conspiracy So Immense: The World of Joe McCarthy* (Free Press, 2019).

Jo Ann Robinson, *The Montgomery Bus Boycott and the Women Who Started It* (University of Tennessee Press, 1987).

Frances S. Saunders, *The Cultural Cold War: The CIA and the World of Arts and Letters* (New Press, 2013).

Odd Arne Westad, *The Cold War: A World History* (Basic Books, 2017).

26

Rebellion on the Left, Resurgence on the Right
1957–1968

Chapter Outline

≡ **Flower Power**   An antiwar protestor offers a flower to a military police officer at the Pentagon in October 1967.

26.8 The Year 1968

‖ Explain the national and international significance of 1968.

26.9 The Backlash

‖ Describe the emergence of George Wallace as a political force and why the country began turning toward the right in the late 1960s.

On October 21, 1967, roughly 100,000 men, women, and even some children came to Washington, DC, to register their opposition to the involvement of the US military in the civil war in Vietnam. They were organized by the National Mobilization Committee to End the War in Vietnam, and they first arrived at the great National Mall stretching between the US Capitol and the Washington Monument to hear speeches by writers and political figures from the United States and abroad denouncing the war and calling for peace.

Timeline

1957	1958	1959	1960	1961	1962

1957 › Soviet Union successfully launches first satellite known as "Sputnik"

1960 › Black students stage sit-down at Woolworth's Department Store in Greensboro, North Carolina; SNCC is founded; John F. Kennedy is elected president over Richard Nixon in one of the closest elections in American history

1961 › Freedom Rides organized to desegregate interstate transportation; Bay of Pigs invasion organized by the CIA fails; Soviet Union constructs wall between East and West Berlin

1962 › Cuban Missile Crisis brings world close to nuclear war

Afterward, the protestors marched across the Potomac River and headed toward the Pentagon, which houses the Department of Defense and serves as a symbol for the American military. As the protestors neared the Pentagon, they could see that it was ringed by federal marshals, military police, and thousands of US troops armed with rifles and riot gear to fend them off. Minor clashes soon took place and, perhaps, 700 of the protestors were arrested before the protest came to an end.

Many in the media heaped scorn on what the protestors had done and called the large protest a failure. But, in truth, it was the beginning of what would become a mass anti-war movement that began to turn the tide of American public opinion against the war while drawing the projects of modern liberalism into question. Eventually the antiwar movement would help pressure the US government to withdraw all its troops from Vietnam—after more than 50,000 of them had been killed and many more wounded—and bring the war to an ignominious end.

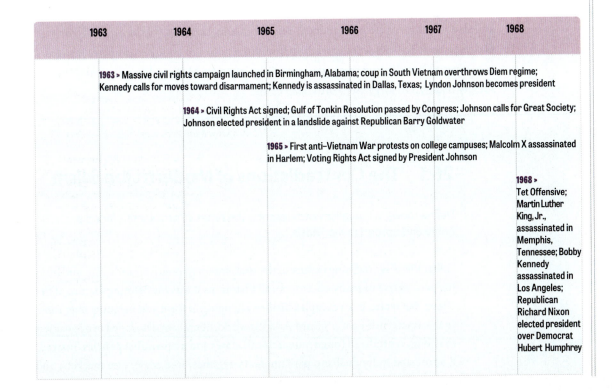

| 1963 | 1964 | 1965 | 1966 | 1967 | 1968 |

1963 › Massive civil rights campaign launched in Birmingham, Alabama; coup in South Vietnam overthrows Diem regime; Kennedy calls for moves toward disarmament; Kennedy is assassinated in Dallas, Texas; Lyndon Johnson becomes president

1964 › Civil Rights Act signed; Gulf of Tonkin Resolution passed by Congress; Johnson calls for Great Society; Johnson elected president in a landslide against Republican Barry Goldwater

1965 › First anti–Vietnam War protests on college campuses; Malcolm X assassinated in Harlem; Voting Rights Act signed by President Johnson

1968 › Tet Offensive; Martin Luther King, Jr., assassinated in Memphis, Tennessee; Bobby Kennedy assassinated in Los Angeles; Republican Richard Nixon elected president over Democrat Hubert Humphrey

Since the end of World War II, modern American liberalism sought to forge a prosperous society by combining social welfare measures at home with a fierce anticommunism both at home and abroad. It resulted in the 1950 "Treaty of Detroit" extending the prospects of a middle-class life to unionized workers, educational and home-owning benefits to (mostly white) war veterans, and inducements to the massive suburbanization that swept the country in the 1950s and 1960s, together with a national security apparatus meant to stimulate the economy and ward off the threats of socialism and communism. But as the Korean War demonstrated, the containment of communism could draw the country into hot, rather than cold, warfare as a large number of political leaders from both parties believed that when one country—especially in the "Third World"—fell into the grips of communism, others would follow, something like falling dominoes.

Modern liberalism therefore depended in part on preventing this from happening, and after the French abandoned their colony in Vietnam, the United States stepped in, beginning a long and bloody involvement. By the mid-1960s, the administration of President Lyndon B. Johnson, which had been calling for waging wars on poverty and racism at home, began to shift focus to waging war on communists in Vietnam. Johnson and his advisors imagined that both wars could be waged simultaneously, and that the costs could be managed. Yet before long there was turmoil on all fronts and popular rebellions were spreading from inner cities to college campuses while a conservative backlash was energizing middle America. Modern liberalism and the society it aimed to forge went into deep crisis.

26.1 The Contradictions of Modern Liberalism

||| Define modern liberalism and describe the types of problems it faced at home and abroad in the 1960s.

"Liberalism" is a defining feature of the contemporary political landscape, and from the perspective of many observers and historians it was *the* defining feature of the 1960s. But it also has a complex history, changing in form and meaning over time. In the nineteenth-century Euro-Atlantic world, liberalism developed in opposition to strong, centralized (often monarchical) states and mercantilist policies. Instead, it advocated individualism, parliamentary regimes, free trade, free markets, and low taxes. But the "liberalism" with which we are currently familiar was a product of late nineteenth- and early twentieth-century Progressivism and then of the New Deal (see Chapters 19 and 23). For these liberals, it made most sense to think of the world as consisting of social groups rather than individuals. They came to believe that prosperity and social well-being would best be promoted by a partnership between the public and private sectors, and that "experts" were best suited to the tasks of organizing institutions and making social policy. By 1960, it seemed clear that this modern liberalism and its economic growth model had achieved a wide consensus in American public life, embraced by many Republicans as well as Democrats. But liberalism would hit formidable shoals over the next decade and face new opposition.

Perils of the New Frontier

President Eisenhower, a Republican who entered office in 1953, exemplified the nature of the liberal consensus. Although he ran for the presidency pledging a rollback in federal power, he maintained and even enlarged much of it, especially to stimulate economic growth. During Eisenhower's presidency, the reach of social security was expanded, a Department of Health, Education, and Welfare was established, and massive federal spending created an interstate highway system that linked the country together as never before. When Eisenhower prepared to step down after two terms, the Republicans nominated Richard Nixon, his vice president, as their presidential candidate who seemed ready to carry on as Eisenhower had done.

The Democrats turned to a young senator, forty-three years of age, from Massachusetts named John F. Kennedy. Kennedy had rather limited political experience, but he had served heroically in the Pacific theater during World War II, came from a very wealthy and politically prominent family, and seemed to exude the youth and idealism of a new generation. Indeed, he talked endlessly about the new generation he hoped to lead and marked out the challenges the generation would face, mainly in fighting communism abroad. He warned that the United States was falling behind the Soviet Union in scientific research and achievement (the Soviets had launched the first satellite into space, "Sputnik," in 1957 to the consternation of the American public because it suggested that they could deliver nuclear warheads by intercontinental missile), that a developing "missile gap" was putting American security in jeopardy, and that the country was perched on a "New Frontier" of science and space, peace and war, and poverty and plenty.

The presidential election of 1960 remains one of the closest in American history. Only 125,000 popular votes separated the two candidates (one-quarter of 1 percent of all votes cast), and there is some reason to believe that voting irregularities in Illinois and Texas, meaning fraud, turned the tide in Kennedy's favor (see Map 26.1). Summoning

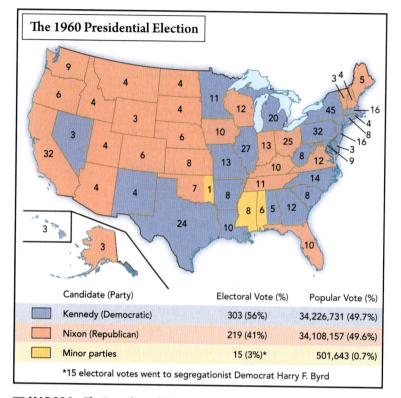

The 1960 Presidential Election

Candidate (Party)	Electoral Vote (%)	Popular Vote (%)
Kennedy (Democratic)	303 (56%)	34,226,731 (49.7%)
Nixon (Republican)	219 (41%)	34,108,157 (49.6%)
Minor parties	15 (3%)*	501,643 (0.7%)

*15 electoral votes went to segregationist Democrat Harry F. Byrd

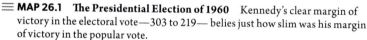

MAP 26.1 **The Presidential Election of 1960** Kennedy's clear margin of victory in the electoral vote—303 to 219— belies just how slim was his margin of victory in the popular vote.

Americans to embrace a new sense of purpose—"Ask not what your country can do for you, ask what you can do for your country"—Kennedy then set out to steer the liberal ship. But within weeks the ship hit turbulent waters.

The waters were off the shore of Cuba and symbolized the revolutionary changes that were sweeping Latin America, as well as Africa and Asia. Long under the repressive hands of American investors and the island elites who supported them, a movement led by Fidel Castro came to power in Cuba in 1959. Like movements that had already spread through Central and South America since the 1940s, Castro's was of the political left, seeking to readjust the balances of power in favor of peasants and workers who had been ground down and exploited. Before too long, Castro nationalized foreign property, enacted land reform, and sent his opponents from the middle and upper classes packing. He also accepted economic aid from the Soviet Union, though Castro's revolutionary model was far closer to Mexico's earlier in the twentieth century.

Ever since Theodore Roosevelt's "corollary" to the Monroe Doctrine, which threatened American police action if Latin American governments could not maintain order and stability, the United States had intervened on many occasions in the countries of the Caribbean basin. During the first half of the twentieth century alone, American troops had been sent into Panama, Honduras, Nicaragua, Haiti, El Salvador, and the Dominican Republic, sometimes for lengthy stays.

But in 1954 a different sort of intervention occurred, one that seemed to take a page from the filibusterers of the nineteenth century. The CIA, the secret agency created by the National Security Act of 1947, organized and helped carry out the overthrow of the leftist government of Jacobo Arbenz Guzman in Guatemala, where the American-owned United Fruit Company had massive holdings, and, even before Kennedy assumed the presidency, the agency was at work on a plan to assassinate Castro and topple his regime.

Kennedy learned of the CIA plan in early April 1961 and gave the go-ahead. The plan involved a paramilitary invasion by Cuban exiles, shipping out of Guatemala and landing at what was known as the "Bay of Pigs" (*Playa Giron*), with the aid of CIA-backed air power. The invasion failed miserably. Very quickly the invaders were rounded up and imprisoned, Castro had a huge military and public relations victory, and the Kennedy administration had egg on its face. Kennedy felt burned by the CIA and began an investigation into its Latin American activities; he would never again trust CIA advice. Meantime Castro's alliance with the Soviet Union deepened, economically and militarily. In the process, in an effort to deter another invasion, the Soviet Union, under the leadership of Nikita Khrushchev, began a secret operation of its own, this one to send arms and troops into Cuba, including missiles with nuclear warheads capable of reaching American cities.

The Cuban Missile Crisis

What was going on here? Cold War tensions were high in 1961 and 1962 not only because of the **Bay of Pigs Invasion** but also because a variety of conflicts were surfacing in Laos and Vietnam in Southeast Asia, and in Africa, the Mediterranean, and Eastern Europe, all of which threatened head-on confrontations between the United States and the Soviet Union. Worried about Soviet control over East Germany and Berlin, Premier Nikita Khrushchev decided to build a wall in Berlin to staunch the flow of Germans to the west, especially those with skills and educations. For his part, Kennedy ordered the US military to install nuclear missiles at American bases in Turkey and Italy, in easy range of Moscow and Leningrad, and called for increased defense spending, more men drafted into the military, and the construction of "fallout shelters" in case of nuclear war.

Truth was that for all of Kennedy's talk of a "missile gap," it was the Soviets who were far behind in the stock of nuclear weapons as well as in the number of missiles capable of delivering them. Thus, Khrushchev's arming of Cuba was an effort not just to prevent another US attempt to overthrow Castro but also to give the Soviet Union a stronger military hand. The problem was that the "secret" operation did not remain secret for very long. An American spy plane flying over Cuba took photographs of the Soviet military buildup, and in October 1962 Kennedy demanded that the missiles be removed (see Map 26.2).

The air suddenly crackled with a crisis the likes of which had not been seen since the end of World War II, even in Korea. Fearing an imminent American attack, Khrushchev warned of retaliation; Kennedy in turn warned that a missile attack

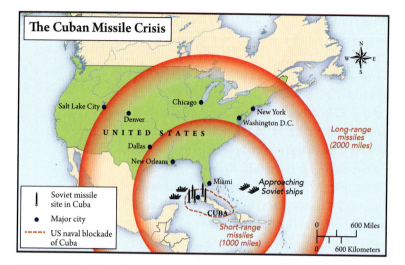

≡ **MAP 26.2** **The Cuban Missile Crisis** The Cuban Missile Crisis of October 1962 transformed abstract talk of nuclear disaster into palpable, gut-wrenching fear. For two weeks annihilation seemed an imminent prospect.

≡ **Cold Warrior** President John F. Kennedy in front of an American missile. Kennedy believed the United States would be endangered if it did not keep pace with the Soviet Union in the production of long-range missiles.

from Cuba would be regarded as a Soviet attack on the United States and bring a massive American nuclear response. It looked as though World War III was about to begin and some of Kennedy's advisors, including his brother Robert Kennedy, the Attorney General, were hawkish, seeing the opportunity to wipe out the missiles and the Castro regime in one blow.

Already suspicious of military opinion after the Bay of Pigs disaster, Kennedy chose a less risky course. Instead of launching an attack, he established what he called a "quarantine," or a blockade, of the island, to prevent any Soviet ship from getting through until the missiles were taken out. Angered as he was at Kennedy's move, Khrushchev knew that the Soviet Union could not win if the conflict escalated, and so, through secret channels, a deal began to take shape. The Soviets would withdraw their missiles in return for an American pledge not to invade Cuba, and, as a sidelight, Kennedy would remove American missiles from Turkey, as near to the Soviet Union as the Soviet missiles in Cuba were to the United States.

The crisis was defused and a massive sigh of relief could be heard around the globe. Sobered by what had nearly happened, Kennedy began to seek an international treaty banning the testing of nuclear weapons and perhaps a path toward what Khrushchev himself had termed "peaceful coexistence" between the superpowers. But it was equally clear that Cold War liberalism invited great dangers and no longer clear that either the United States or the Soviet Union could control the global politics of the Cold War era.

26.2   The Civil Rights "Movement" Takes Off

Explain how civil rights activism became a "movement" and how it shaped public policy.

The Kennedy administration faced challenges closer to home as well, and none were more significant than an expanding civil rights movement in the South. Struggles against the repression and discrimination of Jim Crow had been taking shape for decades, and a variety of strategies—the courts, the churches, boycotts—had been used to weaken segregation and obtain civil and political equality for African Americans. But the struggles were not well coordinated nor did they involve mass mobilizations. The NAACP led the campaign through the courts, though made only limited efforts to rally activity at the grassroots. Bus boycotts in Baton Rouge and Montgomery as well as a school desegregation initiative in Little Rock were hatched locally even if they had learned about what was going on elsewhere. By the late 1950s and early 1960s, however, things began to change.

Building Blocks

The Montgomery Bus Boycott not only struck a major blow against Jim Crow. It also gave rise to a new organization known as the **Southern Christian Leadership Conference (SCLC)**. Initially proposed by civil rights activist Bayard Rustin, the SCLC would be led by Rev. Martin Luther King, Jr., include Black ministers from other southern states—Ralph Abernathy of Montgomery, Fred Shuttlesworth from Birmingham, Joseph Lowery from Mobile among them—and coordinate the battles against segregation on the ground.

By 1960, there was a growing sense that the tide of change might be moving against Jim Crow, and it spurred further activism and organization. In February of that year, four Black students from nearby North Carolina Agricultural and Technical University, a historically Black college or university (HBCU), walked into the Woolworth's Department store in Greensboro, sat down at the lunch counter from which African Americans were excluded, and asked to be served. That is, they staged a "sit-in." Perhaps they knew of Pauli Murray's sit-in in New York years before (see Chapter 24). Either way, it was a courageous move. Defying the boundaries of Jim Crow often brought swift and lethal retaliation from southern whites, and in this instance the servers were white women. The students surely knew of the risks, especially after fourteen-year-old Emmett Till, who lived in Chicago but was visiting family in Mississippi, was lynched in the summer of 1955 after rumors spread that he disrespected a white woman.

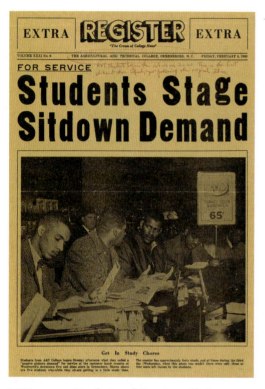

Desegregating the Lunch Counter   The front page of the student newspaper for Greensboro, North Carolina's Agricultural and Technical College informs its readers of a "sit-in" protest at the local Woolworth's department store lunch counter. After six months of protest, Woolworth's relented and desegregated its lunch counters in the summer of 1960.

Hostile white people did come into Woolworth's and physically harassed the students but so did sympathetic white and Black students who lent them support. Before too long, Woolworth's, a national department store chain, changed its policy and sit-ins were spreading across the South and even into the North—by the end of the year thousands took part—aimed at desegregating lunch counters and other public facilities. A movement wave seemed to be building.

Yet there was more. Two months after the Greensboro sit-in, in April 1960, Ella Baker, a staff member of SCLC, organized a meeting of Black students at Shaw University, another HBCU, in Atlanta. Baker had a long history as a civil rights activist, and the students were interested in mobilizing African Americans at the grassroots. To that end, they formed the **Student Non-Violent Coordinating Committee (SNCC)**. Although its resources were limited, SNCC became a magnet for young Black students and intellectuals committed to change, and it initially joined hands with organizations like the SCLC, the Congress of Racial Equality (CORE), and the Fellowship for Reconciliation (FOR) to further their goals.

Freedom Rides

One of first activities that SNCC and its allies took up was an extraordinary set of **Freedom Rides** in 1961. What were these? Segregation infected all areas of southern public life, including the means of transportation despite the results of the Montgomery and Baton Rouge bus boycotts: streetcars, buses, and trains were all marked by Jim Crow regulations. Even when buses moving across state lines entered these states, they were expected to respect segregation laws on the vehicles and in the bus terminals. Black activists saw the opening, in part because Bayard Rustin had already led the way in the 1940s (see Chapter 24). Interstate commerce was regulated by the federal, not the state, governments, so if they attempted to desegregate the bus system, the federal government and courts would have to get involved.

That is just what they did. Recognizing that they courted great dangers, activists recruited among white as well as Black college students, trained them in nonviolent techniques, and then got on buses and headed south from Newark, New Jersey; Washington, DC; Nashville, Tennessee; and St. Louis, Missouri. At first, they encountered few problems. But once they reached Alabama and Mississippi that changed dramatically. The buses were pelted with rocks, sprayed with bullets, and sometimes were firebombed. When the Freedom Riders got off the buses and tried to desegregate the bus terminals, they were mercilessly beaten by local whites and arrested by the local police (see Map 26.3).

It was, to say the least, a terrifying ordeal. But the riders kept coming. Before the year was out, more than sixty Freedom Rides involving over 450 riders, most of whom were under thirty, male, and Black, took place; over 300 of the riders were arrested at some point. Many of the riders then went on to sit-in at restaurants, lunch counters, and hotels, extending the logic of the rides. One of the riders was John Lewis, a twenty-one-year-old son of Alabama sharecroppers. SNCC and the Freedom Rides were just the beginning. He would emerge as an important movement leader before winning election to a seat in the US Congress that he held until his death in 2020.

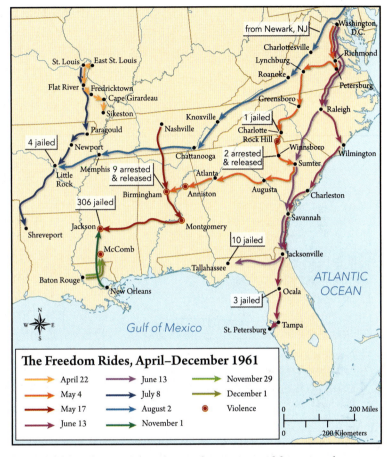

≡ **MAP 26.3   The Freedom Rides**   As buses penetrated deeper into the segregated South, they encountered increasing violence, and when Freedom Riders disembarked, they were beaten by local whites and arrested by the police.

Challenges for the Kennedy Administration

The Kennedy administration had limited interest in civil rights. They saw it as a distraction from the issues of the Cold War and made few gestures in its direction, save for a strategic phone call Kennedy placed to Coretta Scott King (the wife of Martin Luther King, Jr.) during the fall election campaign of 1960 when Martin Luther King, Jr., had been jailed. It won Kennedy large numbers of traditionally Republican Black votes in the North, and maybe the election. Kennedy worried that violent confrontations, such as those the Freedom Riders provoked, would damage the image of the United States during the Cold War; the Soviet Union relished the self-righteous

≡ **Freedom Riders**   Freedom Riders David Dennis and Julia Aaron are escorted by a Mississippi National Guardsman in May 1961. Freedom Riders took on the dangerous task of integrating interstate buses in the Deep South. Many of the buses were attacked, and about two-thirds of the riders were arrested.

hypocrisy of the Americans when it came to racial equality. And he feared that taking a sympathetic stand on civil rights issues would offend southern Democrats who, for the most part, strongly supported Jim Crow.

But now Kennedy was stuck. He fumed about the Freedom Riders' brazen tactics and initially called for a "cooling off" period, meaning a halt to the rides to let matters settle. None of the riders were amused. "We have been cooling off for 350 years," James Farmer, the head of CORE countered, "and if we cooled off any more we'd be in a deep freeze." Attorney General Robert Kennedy was also in no mood to act, reluctant to have the Justice Department "take sides" in the matter. But the Interstate Commerce Commission (ICC) and the Supreme Court had previously ruled against segregation on buses traveling across state lines (thanks partly to Rustin), and Robert Kennedy saw no alternative to petitioning the ICC to step in. Several months later the ICC issued another ruling and found in favor of the Freedom Riders. The buses and the bus terminals would now be desegregated. They had won.

26.3   A Mass Civil Rights Movement

||| Describe the new civil rights strategies in Birmingham and the March on Washington.

Yet how much had they won? The Freedom Rides, like the bus boycotts before them, took on important symbols of Jim Crow racism. But even in bringing about changes in the laws, much of southern life remained as segregated as it had been and federal officials had to figure out how they would enforce laws that were now on the books. After all, the pace of desegregation in the public schools was painfully slow despite the authority of the Supreme Court in *Brown*. What's more, Alabama had elected a new governor named George C. Wallace, who, in his inaugural address in January 1963, stridently supported "segregation now, segregation tomorrow, segregation forever." White Citizens' Councils and the Ku Klux Klan were intimidating any southerner who failed to embrace white supremacy, and especially civil rights activists—"troublemakers" and "outside agitators," as they were called—whether from the South or the North.

Project "C"

With this in mind, King and the SCLC came up with a bold new strategy. Instead of selecting particular targets of Jim Crow, they would select an entire city and move against Jim Crow racism across its public spaces. They would conduct marches, boycotts, and sit-ins hoping to capture the attention of the American public and the federal government and transform the entire town. They called the plan "Project C" for "confrontation."

They did not choose an easy target. Indeed, they chose as tough a town as there was: Birmingham, Alabama. In the north-central part of the state, Birmingham—unlike most of the Deep South—was an industrial and mining center, and known as the most segregated city to be found anywhere in the United States. To make matters worse, Jim Crow in Birmingham was fortified by a no-holds-barred public safety commissioner named Eugene "Bull" Connor. But King and the SCLC hoped that by pursuing a campaign of nonviolence and forcing mass arrests, they could even wear down Bull Connor.

The Birmingham campaign nearly failed. Demonstrators began their protests in early April 1963 but, despite their courage and tenacity, they didn't seem to be getting anywhere. Hundreds were arrested and jailed, including Martin Luther King, Jr., but the white authorities in Birmingham didn't flinch and the federal government didn't move. Then the movement organizers decided on a new and even more dangerous tactic: they would mobilize hundreds of school children, at the elementary and high school levels, to march in the streets in support of the campaign. Connor would have none of it and unleashed dogs and high-power water hoses on the Black children. Many of them were flattened, injured, and arrested. The jails filled with determined and peaceful Black kids, and newspapers around the country and the world printed photographs of the melee. Nightly news programs ran video footage.

The Kennedy administration, already tangling with Alabama and Mississippi over the desegregation of their state universities, now decided to act. In a nationally televised speech from the Oval Office of the White House on June 22, 1963, President Kennedy forcefully explained, "we are confronted primarily with a

≡ **Violence in Birmingham** A Birmingham, Alabama, police officer attacks protestors with a baton in one hand and a snarling dog in the other. The notorious Birmingham sheriff Eugene Connor responded to civil rights protests with fire hoses, police dogs, beatings, and mass arrests.

moral issue [and a moral crisis]." "The heart of the question," he said, "is whether all Americans are to be afforded equal rights and equal opportunities, whether we are going to treat our fellow Americans as we want to be treated." "We preach freedom around the world," Kennedy maintained, "but are we to say to the world, and much more importantly for each other, that this is the land of the free except for the Negroes; that we have no second-class citizens except the Negroes; that we have . . . no master race except with respect to the Negroes?" Kennedy concluded by pledging to send civil rights legislation to Congress aimed at ending racial segregation throughout the country.

The March on Washington

Two months later, over a quarter of a million people came to Washington, DC, to march in support of "jobs and freedom." As they assembled in front of the Lincoln Memorial, lining the reflecting pools as far as the eye could see on the centennial of the Emancipation Proclamation, Martin Luther King, Jr., famously walked to the podium. In one of the most memorable speeches of the era, he called on Americans to be true to their founding principles and help realize the promises of emancipation and Reconstruction. He also spoke movingly of his "dream" that "one day the sons of former slaves and the sons of former slave-owners will be able to sit down together at the table of brotherhood."

Although we celebrate King's demand for racial equality, the march was also meant to demand an end to discrimination at the workplace and a commitment to economic opportunity for African Americans who had long been mired in poverty and social injustice. In an important sense, the march not only exemplified the powerful effect the civil rights movement was having on the United States; it also illuminated the challenges and conflicts that remained to be tackled.

King advocated nonviolence and civil disobedience, influenced as he was by a reading of the Bible and the example of Mohandas Gandhi, who led a movement for independence in India in the late 1940s before being assassinated. Like his predecessors in the NAACP, King imagined an interracial movement that would be driven by the moral imperatives of the Judeo-Christian tradition and the political principles of the Declaration of Independence and Bill of Rights, a movement that would secure the achievements of emancipation and the Reconstruction amendments—Thirteenth, Fourteenth, and Fifteenth. In many ways it was a fundamentally liberal dream.

But there was pushback even within the movement itself. Young Black men and women who gravitated to SNCC came to resent the attention King received after they had done much of the local organizing. Some called him "De Lawd," expressing their frustration with the top-down approach they associated with King and the SCLC. They also came to question King's inter-racialism—increasingly insisting that theirs was a movement of African Americans in which whites had little place—and his emphasis on nonviolence, deeply aware as they were of their own vulnerabilities and need for means of self-defense.

Equally significant, as the demand for "jobs" as well as "freedom" suggested, African Americans in the North and West, not directly subject to Jim Crow, still suffered from poor housing, poor education, and limited employment opportunities, not to mention a deepening hopelessness among the young. It wouldn't be long before they made their presence felt, with explosive force, and pushed at the boundaries of liberalism itself.

≡ **The March on Washington** Over 200,000 people attended the March on Washington for Jobs and Freedom in August 1963. Organized to highlight the unequal conditions in which Black Americans across the country lived and worked, the march is best remembered as the occasion for Martin Luther King, Jr.'s "I Have a Dream" speech.

26.4 The Birth of the Great Society

Understand the significance of the Kennedy assassination and how Lyndon Johnson's Great Society arose in its aftermath.

When John F. Kennedy was inaugurated president, he announced that the "torch had been passed to a new generation" of leadership "tempered by war [and] disciplined by a hard and bitter peace." That "torch" was, he believed, the torch of freedom and human rights to be carried against the challenges of communism, with men like him at the front. What he had not recognized or understood was that the new generation also included African Americans who were already reminding Kennedy and the entire country that the torch had to light a path of freedom and human rights within the United States, had to be meaningful to Black citizens as well as white, to the poor as well as to the wealthy and comfortable. In a sense, they were carrying a torch that had been lit by New Deal social democrats, and their mass movement for civil rights opened up a remarkable moment of opportunity to build a great society.

The Assassination of John F. Kennedy

President Kennedy would never live to see that moment, and it may well be that he would not have been able to seize it and carry it through if he had. Indeed, he never was able to craft and press civil rights legislation through the US Congress that he had insisted was the country's moral responsibility. In part, it was the obstructionism of southern Democrats who felt determined to stare down racial liberalism. But there was tragedy as well. On November 22, 1963, five months to the day after he addressed the American public on the moral necessity of civil rights, Kennedy was assassinated in Dallas, Texas, as he rode through the streets in a motorcade.

Kennedy was visiting Dallas to shore up support among Texas Democrats in anticipation of his reelection campaign in 1964. And it's still not entirely clear what was afoot. Officially, an investigation known as the *Warren Commission Report*, named after sitting Supreme Court Justice Earl Warren, who headed it, determined that Kennedy was shot by a lone gunman, Lee Harvey Oswald, who used a high-powered rifle as he perched in the Texas School Book Depository several floors above the city streets. But from that day on there have been many other theories as to what transpired and who was involved. Some have suggested a plot hatched by the CIA (given Kennedy's attitude toward the agency after the Bay of Pigs); some suggested a plot hatched by members of organized crime (because as Attorney General, Robert Kennedy had them in his sights, and Lee Harvey Oswald was himself shot down before trial by a local Dallas strip-club owner with mob connections); and some suggested a plot by ultra-right-wing businessmen who detested Kennedy's liberalism and his interest in halting the spread of nuclear weapons. It is doubtful that we will ever know for sure, though the main conclusions of the *Warren Commission Report* have been widely accepted.

Yet, whatever led to Kennedy's assassination, it brought into the presidency Lyndon Baines Johnson, the sitting vice president from the state of Texas. Johnson had long been a power in the US Congress and by the 1950s had become majority leader in the Senate. So influential was he with fellow Democrats that in 1960 he sought the nomination for the presidency without campaigning or entering any of the few primaries. Along the way, he developed an especially nasty relationship with the Kennedys, and although he was put on the ticket in 1960 with an eye toward the electoral votes of Texas, he was galled to serve as vice president in Kennedy's shadow.

LBJ Takes Charge

Now Johnson stepped out of the shadow and into the public light. Although liberal Democrats worried that Johnson's Texas conservatism might undermine Kennedy's push for civil rights legislation, Johnson very quickly revealed that his commitment to Kennedy's agenda was robust. He began to steer a civil rights bill through Congress far more effectively than the Kennedy administration had been able to do. Drawing on his impressive skills as Senate majority leader, Johnson built a coalition of Democrats from the North and West along with sympathetic Republicans to skirt the opposition of southern Democrats he was ready to stare down. By July, the bill was on his desk to sign, a landmark piece of legislation—the **Civil Rights Act of 1964**—which outlawed discrimination on account of "race, color, religion, sex, or national origin" in public accommodations, schools, and workplaces and created the **Equal Employment Opportunity Commission (EEOC)** to investigate claims of noncompliance.

But Johnson intended to go further still. In his first State of the Union address in January 1964, he declared an "unconditional **War on Poverty** in America," and later that spring spoke of moving toward a "**Great Society**" in which "men are more concerned with the quality of their goals than the quantity of their goods." It seemed to be another, and even more expansive, example of the social democratic impulse that had grown out of the mobilizations and New Deal of the 1930s. Johnson imagined new investments in cities and transportation networks, new

≡ **LBJ with Civil Rights Leaders**   President Lyndon B. Johnson (*center*) meets with civil rights leaders, including Dr. Martin Luther King, Jr. (*left*), in January 1964. Some worried that the Texan Johnson would not continue Kennedy's push for civil rights legislation, but Johnson ultimately signed a new Civil Rights Act in 1964.

initiatives to protect the environment, new access to health care for the elderly and the poor, and new improvements in public education to accompany the fight against poverty and racial discrimination.

Pressure from Below

In many respects, this was a platform on which he would run for the presidency in 1964, but it was also a response to growing pressure from a number of quarters. Two years earlier, socialist Michael Harrington published *The Other America*. It was a book that alerted a complacent public—it became a bestseller and President Kennedy read it and was moved by it—to the fact that nearly one-quarter of all Americans, white as well as Black, lived in conditions of poverty: not only in cities but in rural areas like Appalachia and the Deep South. That same year, a new organization of left-wing college students called **Students for a Democratic Society (SDS)** produced a founding manifesto, called the "Port Huron Statement," that not only criticized American racism, imperialism, its military-industrial complex, and welfare state but also called for nuclear disarmament, global economic reform, "participatory democracy," and the devotion of resources to human needs rather than economic profits.

As Johnson was lining up votes for his civil rights bill, SNCC activists, for their part, were well along in planning **Freedom Summer**, a project aimed at securing political rights that African Americans had long been denied. But it was a dangerous undertaking. SNCC set their sights on Mississippi, a largely rural state where the Ku Klux Klan and the White Citizens' Council wielded great power, and sought to mobilize Black men and women, many of them desperately poor, to register to vote. It didn't take long before they saw what they were up against. In June, three SNCC activists—James Chaney, Andrew Goodman, and Michael Schwerner—were kidnapped and murdered by the local Klan, their bodies only discovered two months later in a shallow grave. The threat of violence and death thus hung over SNCC members throughout the summer, and although few Black Mississippians were able to register, Freedom Summer attracted important national attention. It also brought to light the heroic grassroots work of activists like Bob Moses, a brilliant man of African descent who left a teaching job in New York City to organize in Mississippi.

The struggle against racial poverty and discrimination was not only to be found in the South. In the North, where more than four million African Americans had migrated between 1915 and 1965, racial unrest was bubbling close to the surface of many cities. Suburbanization of the 1950s and early 1960s had eroded urban tax bases, undercutting social services. Housing discrimination left most Black families in what were called "ghettos," effectively residential zones that were overwhelmingly Black, where jobs were in short supply and public schools poorly funded and inadequate. And Black residents there were left to the harsh justice of all-white police forces. The ghettoes of Rochester and Harlem exploded that summer, initiating several years of veritable insurrections that spread from Newark and New York City in the east to Watts, California, in the west. At the Democratic Convention that nominated Lyndon Johnson for the presidency in Atlantic City (NJ) in August 1964, the **Mississippi Freedom Democratic Party,**

Fannie Lou Hamer   Hamer led Black Mississippians in the Mississippi Freedom Democratic Party to the 1964 Democratic National Convention and demanded a seat. Although nearly half of Mississippi's population was Black, officeholders in the state, as well as the official delegation to the Democratic Convention, were white.

led by the extraordinary Fannie Lou Hamer (from a family of sharecroppers), demanded to be seated at the convention instead of the all-white state delegation.

The Election of 1964

Johnson had the fortune of running against a controversial Republican candidate for president, Barry Goldwater, a senator from Arizona. Unlike Eisenhower and Nixon before him, Goldwater was a new conservative deeply critical of federal power, even in the area of civil rights, business regulations, foreign aid, and liberal ambitions. He believed in individual freedom from government authority, state rights, vehement anticommunism, American military superiority, and a drastic reduction of federal spending. In short, he not only challenged the legacy of the New Deal and the emerging idea of a Great Society but he also rejected the politics of the internationalist wing of the Republican Party. "Extremism in the defense of liberty is no vice," Goldwater told the Republican nominating convention in the summer of 1964, "and moderation in the pursuit of justice is no virtue."

Johnson ran a campaign that invoked the legacy of John F. Kennedy and painted Goldwater as an extremist and warmonger who might be willing to launch a nuclear attack. It worked better than anyone could have imagined. When Election Day arrived in November 1964, Johnson received over 60 percent of the popular vote and the electoral votes of every state except Arizona and five states of the Deep South.

Johnson's victory was of landslide proportions and seemed to give him a mandate for his ambitious Great Society agenda.

Enacting the Great Society

Johnson and his congressional allies moved on a number of fronts to implement that vision. They created a Job Corps to help provide employment for urban youth, a Head Start program for preschoolers, an Upward Bound program for those looking forward to college, Medicare and Medicaid programs for the elderly and poor (limited forms of national health care), and community action agencies that were to promote "maximum feasible participation" by poor folk in overseeing the implementation of these many initiatives.

Mindful, too, of the courageous struggles of African Americans in the Deep South for the electoral franchise and the ability to wield political power at all levels, Johnson called for and signed a **Voting Rights Act of 1965**, which outlawed methods traditionally used to disfranchise Black voters, such as literacy requirements and poll taxes, and subjected southern states with histories of racial discrimination to federal oversight of their electoral practices.

A heady roster of achievements it was, and in a political atmosphere in which liberal and civil rights perspectives seemed to reign supreme, the Congress passed and Johnson readily signed—at the foot of the Statue of Liberty no less—the **Immigration and Nationality Act of 1965 (Hart-Celler Act)**. The legislation overhauled the quota-based system enacted in 1924, which had discriminated against potential immigrants from Asia and southern and eastern Europe, and instead simply capped the total number of annual visas available to each country. At the same time, the legislation opened the door not only to highly skilled immigrants but also to those who already had family members living in the United States, regardless of their country of origin. Before too long, the volume and demographic character of immigration began to shift: many more immigrants began arriving and the proportion of those from Asia and Latin America increased dramatically (see Figure 26.1).

≡ **Marching for Voting Rights**   A Black protestor wearing face paint declaring "VOTE." The 1965 Voting Rights Act was designed to ban a number of common tactics that southern states in particular used to disfranchise eligible Black voters.

But the liberal achievements of the Johnson administration came with built-in problems that were not apparent at first. Lyndon Johnson not only advanced Kennedy's legacy on civil rights and antipoverty; he also implemented Kennedy's modified Keynesian economic policies, which meant significant tax cuts for individuals and corporations to promote economic growth. The top tax brackets were dropped from 90 percent to 70 percent, and corporate taxes were slashed even more substantially. It was an alternative to direct federal spending and to the redistributionist projects that social democrats embraced but liberals rejected. And for a short time, the cuts seemed to work, providing a boost to the American economy in the early 1960s (there had been a recession in the late 1950s) and bringing in substantial revenues. Yet by the time Great Society programs were unveiled, Johnson and the Congress offered relatively meager funding, enough to get the programs off the ground but not enough to sustain them in a meaningful way. The Great Society, that is, was constrained by the limits of liberalism and liberal policy.

Perhaps even more important, Johnson's sweeping domestic initiatives soon had to vie with new challenges overseas. For just as Johnson was declaring an unconditional War on Poverty, he and his administration were becoming mired in another war, thousands of miles across the Pacific, in the bitterly divided country of Vietnam.

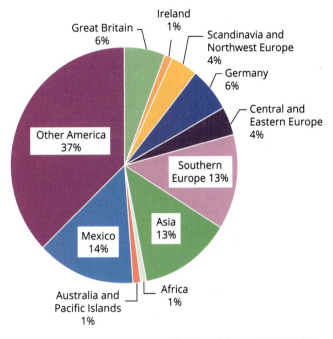

≡ **FIGURE 26.1 Immigration to the United States, 1966–1969**
The 1965 immigration law reversed the quota system that had restricted immigration for nearly fifty years. It enabled a new wave of immigrants from Asia and Latin America to enter the country legally.

26.5 The Quagmire of Vietnam

❙❙❙ Discuss how the United States became involved in the Vietnam War.

Although the Cold War meant that the United States and the Soviet Union would avoid direct hostilities, it did not mean that serious military conflicts subsided. The Korean War showed how quickly brutal warfare could erupt, and American efforts to overthrow the Castro regime in Cuba demonstrated how the pursuit of political influence and military superiority could risk the nuclear Armageddon that Cold Warfare was meant to prevent. Indeed, the hot wars of the 1950s and 1960s often

MAPPING AMERICA

The Impact of the Voting Rights Act of 1965

The Fifteenth Amendment guaranteed all male citizens, including former slaves, the right to vote. The Nineteenth Amendment extended suffrage to women. But beginning in the 1890s, poll taxes, literacy requirements, and other measures throughout the South resulted in the disfranchisement of most of the Black population. By 1960, only one in twenty Black people of voting age were registered to vote.

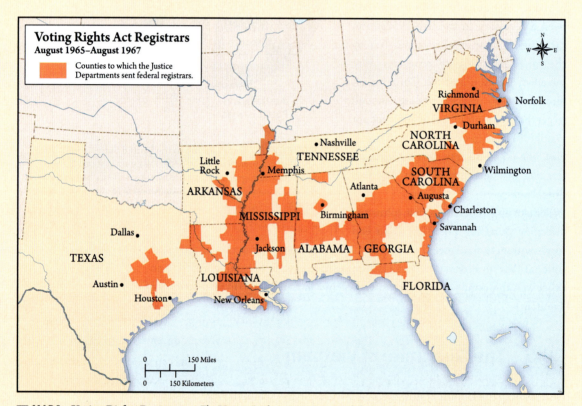

MAP 1   Voting Rights Registrars   The Voting Rights Act empowered the Attorney General to assign federal registrars to enroll voters. Soon after its passage in August 1965, Attorney General Nicholas Katzenbach deployed federal registrars in nine southern states to register new voters.

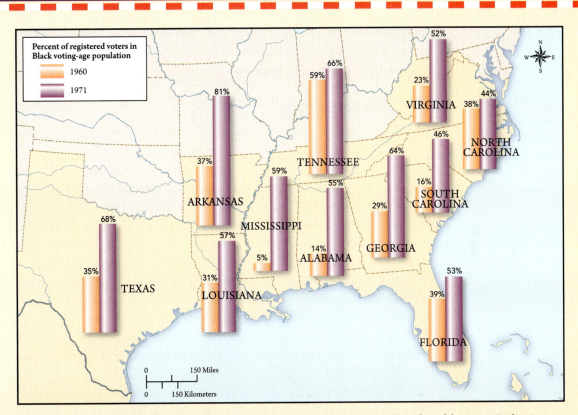

≡ **MAP 2**   **Percentage of Registered Voters in Black Voting-Age Population**   The effect of the Voting Rights Act was not immediate. While only a handful of cities impeded the implementation of the law, many rural areas put up stiff resistance. But by 1971, 62 percent of the Black voting population of the South had been registered. In Mississippi, the number of registered Black voters soared from 28,500 in 1964 to 251,000 in 1968. Similar increases were recorded in other southern states.

Thinking Geographically

The Voting Rights Act of 1965 was one of the hallmark achievements of the Great Society. It mitigated voting disparities among Black and white people, in the process transforming American politics.

1. What factors would account for why federal registrars were sent to some counties of the South and not others? Why do you think Alabama and Mississippi had much higher increases in the percentage of registered Black voters than Tennessee, Florida, or North Carolina?

2. The Supreme Court struck down a key section of the Voting Rights Act in 2013. Is the Voting Rights Act a relic of the past? Is the right to vote being challenged today?

involved anticolonial struggles in Africa and Asia that assumed political importance for the superpowers. For the United States, none was more consequential or
disastrous than the war being waged in Vietnam.

The French Forced Out

How did the United States become embroiled in a war in Vietnam? It's a long story
but the simple answer is: the tragic logic of "containment." Vietnam had been part of
the French colony of Indochina, which also included what would become Laos and
Cambodia, and since the 1940s had been convulsed by guerilla warfare. Vietnamese
who sought an end to French rule began to build a nationalist movement aimed at
independence. They were led by Ho Chi Minh, a native-born Vietnamese, who managed to travel widely and become highly educated. In the 1910s and 1920s, Ho spent
time in the United States, Britain, and France, where he joined a group of Vietnamese
exiles and, as we saw in Chapter 21, tried to persuade the Allies at Versailles—taking
a cue from Woodrow Wilson's ideals about self-determination—to end French colonial rule. Ho also gravitated toward socialism and visited both the Soviet Union and
China. By the time he returned to Vietnam in the 1940s, he was determined to lead
the fight against the French and hoped that the United States might assist him, since
he was deeply influenced by the Declaration of Independence.

The US government had no such intention. They saw the French as important
allies and French colonialism in Southeast Asia as a hedge against the spread of
communism there (especially after China came under communist rule in 1949).
Although no troops were sent, the United States did provide significant financial support to the French military effort. But it was to little avail. Ho Chi Minh's
movement, known as the Viet Minh, outmaneuvered the French and in a decisive
battle at **Dien Bien Phu** in the north of Vietnam in 1954—Eisenhower considered
sending military assistance to the besieged French army, including the possible use
of nuclear weapons—forced the French to surrender.

For the Eisenhower administration, what had happened in Vietnam seemed to
be an example of what he called the "falling domino principle." He meant that if
you allowed one place to fall to socialism or communism, other places would soon
follow. "You knock over the first one," Eisenhower warned, "and what will happen
to the last one is the certainty that it will go over very quickly." Now what? A peace
conference met in Geneva and carved out an agreement that, something in the
manner of Korea before it, divided Vietnam in two at the 17th parallel—the north
under the control of the Viet Minh and the south under the control of a government identified with France and the United States—with the proviso that unifica-
tion elections would be held in 1956 (see Map 26.4).

The United States Steps In

France, China, and the Viet Minh signed on; the United States did not. When 1956 came around, the regime in the south, now under the rule of a former colonial official, and a Catholic, named Ngo Dinh Diem (and with the support of the United States), refused to hold the elections fearing that the Viet Minh would win. Instead, Diem clamped down on opposition in the country-side, in the army, and among the majority Buddhists within the south. Before long, Diem had a growing rebellion on his hands increasingly organized by what was called the National Liberation Front (NLF), or the Viet Cong, in alliance with the northern Viet Minh.

This was the situation when John F. Kennedy became pres-ident, and he sent his Secretary of Defense Robert McNamara and Army General Maxwell Taylor to South Vietnam for an assessment. Kennedy received an optimistic report about the

≡ **MAP 26.4** **The Partition of Vietnam, 1954**

prospects of turning back the NLF with adequate American aid, but Kennedy was reluctant to escalate US involvement. He did send several hundred "advisors" to train South Vietnamese troops and gave the green light to an army coup that toppled the Diem regime. But he made no further moves before his death, and there is some evidence, though not especially convincing, that he intended to scale back American involvement.

Lyndon Johnson, like Woodrow Wilson decades earlier, campaigned for the presidency in 1964 by telling the American public that he would keep them out of war. "We are not about to send American boys nine or ten thousand miles from home to do what Asian boys ought to be doing for themselves," he insisted that October. But Johnson already had significant leverage to do otherwise. In August, just two months before, after an incident involving US and North Vietnamese vessels (the United States and South Vietnam were conducting operations) in the Gulf of Tonkin, along the coast of North Vietnam, Congress, with only two dissenting votes, gave him the power to use whatever military means of response he deemed necessary. It was known as the **Gulf of Tonkin Resolution** and was tantamount to a declaration of war, though as in the Korean "police action," Congress effectively ceded war-making authority to the president.

Johnson sat tight during the weeks leading up to the election, but with his victory secured he began a process of rapid escalation. In early 1965, after an NLF attack on US airbases in the South, Johnson ordered the bombing of North Vietnam and the deployment of the first combat troops. By the end of the year, there were nearly 200,000 American troops on the ground in South Vietnam, and their numbers would grow steadily to as many as 550,000 by the end of the decade. With Johnson at the helm, US troops became the main fighting force in South Vietnam and the American military commenced a struggle in the jungles and rice paddies of Southeast Asia the type of which it had never seen before.

Johnson's Logic of Intervention

Why was Johnson so determined to do this? At his most idealistic, Johnson could see American involvement in Vietnam as an international extension of the Great Society he pursued at home. Here was, by his reckoning, a backward rural society engulfed in poverty. Vietnam,

≡ **Quagmire** US soldiers carry the body of a fallen comrade to an evacuation helicopter. When this photo was taken in late 1965, there were already nearly 200,000 US soldiers in Vietnam. That number would almost triple over the next four years.

like many similar areas of the world, needed to be modernized—Johnson's advisors such as economist W.W. Rostow especially pushed this line—and only the United States could help carry this through. But, like his predecessors in the presidency, Johnson also feared another path of development if the Americans did not intervene, one sponsored by the communists. The United States, he firmly believed, had to make a stand in Vietnam both to prevent its fall to the communists and to send a signal to communist insurgents elsewhere that the United States was prepared to use its military might to defeat them. As an assistant to McNamara put it in a memo describing US aims: "70%—To avoid a humiliating US defeat (to our reputation as a guarantor). 20%—To keep the SVN (South Vietnam and adjacent territory) from Chinese hands. 10%—To permit the people of SVN to enjoy a better, freer way of life."

On paper, the United States should have had little reason to worry about a "humiliating defeat." The United States had five times the population of Vietnam (175 million to 35 million) along with a military and economic resource base that was second to none in the world. Massive airpower, massive ground power, sophisticated technology, and nuclear weaponry. The problem was that these advantages could be counterbalanced by the war the North Vietnamese and Viet Cong intended to fight. It was a guerilla war, fought on terrain of their choosing, with troops who blended into locally supportive populations, over matters of decisive political importance to them. They were defending their homes and seeking a better future. The Americans and the South Vietnamese military stood strong in the few cities of South Vietnam, but the surrounding countryside was, for the most part, controlled by the Viet Cong. The task for the United States therefore was to "pacify" the countryside: meaning to kill as many Viet Cong as possible—the "body count" became the most important statistic—and to control more and more rural villages.

Such a strategy came at increasing cost. If the "body count" was key, then the Viet Cong had to be hunted down and engaged in battle. But this also meant that American troops began to suffer significant casualties (which newspapers and the evening television news increasingly brought home in grim detail) and that the process of "pacification" put American troops on a lethal collision course with South Vietnamese villagers. Vietnamese men, women, and children were harassed and killed, their villages were destroyed, and they were subject to air attacks with firebombs and napalm. Not much chance of winning their "hearts and minds," as planners had hoped to do. Eventually some Vietnamese civilians would be massacred by US troops, as they were at **My Lai** in March 1968.

Although General William C. Westmoreland, Johnson's commander in Vietnam, insisted that victory was in sight, the truth was that the United States and its South Vietnamese allies were losing (see Map 26.5). The Viet Cong kept

≡ **MAP 26.5** **The Vietnam War**   As the war in Vietnam unfolded, the worst fears of the Johnson administration were realized. Despite sending in ever more troops, and ordering more bombing of North Vietnam, enemy resistance did not weaken.

expanding their control over the rural districts, the bombings in the South and the North—intended to demoralize the Viet Minh and Viet Cong and force them to give up—weren't working as planned, and sections of the American public began to have doubts about what was going on.

26.6   An Antiwar Movement

Explain why the Vietnam War generated growing opposition in the United States.

When American involvement in what was a civil war in Vietnam commenced, there was little pushback from the public. And the Gulf of Tonkin Resolution received only two opposition votes in the US Senate despite the dubious nature of the incident itself, not to mention the military commitment it allowed and the tremendous empowerment of the president it enabled. But once American troops were on the ground in large numbers and the death and destruction the United States inflicted on the Vietnamese became increasingly evident, rumblings of dissent began to be heard. This is to say that the Johnson administration was soon confronting a "war at home."

Spread of Protest

As early as March 1965, students and faculty at the University of Michigan held a "teach-in" on the Vietnam War and the broader issues of American foreign policy that led to it. Soon thereafter more than 20,000 opponents of the war held their first "march on Washington" while organizing smaller demonstrations in New York and San Francisco. Mobilizations that had originally aided the civil rights movement in the American South now aided a growing movement against the Vietnam War.

College students were especially concerned since the men among them were subject to the military draft and possibly destined to fight in the jungles of Vietnam. Students for a Democratic Society (SDS), which emerged in 1962 with a critique of American foreign policy, saw its membership increase very rapidly. It would be joined by a host of older pacifist organizations like the Fellowship for Reconciliation and the War Resisters' League, and religious groups, both from the traditional peace churches like the Quakers and Mennonites as well as mainstream reform denominations.

Increasingly vocal and impressive as it was, this antiwar movement lacked a coherent center or set of demands. Some antiwar activists called for the immediate withdrawal of all American troops. Some wanted a cease-fire and negotiations between the warring parties or at least a halt to American bombing of the North and South. Some intended to display their opposition in public ways through demonstrations while others began to engage in acts of civil disobedience: refusing military induction when called, burning their draft cards, blocking access to military installations. And some actively supported the goals of the NLF. Robert McNamara's son, so alienated by his father's war-making role, hung an NLF flag on the wall of his college dormitory.

But even if the antiwar movement had not mapped out a clear strategy, it made its presence felt. By the spring of 1966, more than a third of the American public had turned against the war aims of the Johnson administration and favored the withdrawal of American troops, up from just 20 percent the previous year. What's more, the antiwar movement was fortified by a more general youth rebellion of the mid-1960s with its roots in the beats, folk revival, and rock and roll of the 1950s.

Questioning the values of American consumerism and the repressive atmosphere as to politics, sexuality, and lifestyle, young men and women of the middle and upper class (mostly white) attempted to chart out a different course toward personal freedom and fulfillment. They shunned the garb of the uptight business world, experimented with sex and drugs (a birth control pill had been approved for contraceptive use in 1960), and attempted to create spaces free of inhibitions. Theirs became known as the "counterculture," an apparent rejection of the norms of bourgeois society; many of them were called **hippies** (the term came from the beat-influenced "hipster," suggesting social and cultural rebels). Their relationship to the antiwar movement and the political movements of civil rights and SDS was complex and often contradictory, but together they made for an atmosphere of general rebelliousness that would forever define the "Sixties."

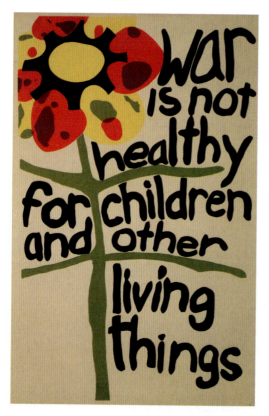

≡ **Antiwar Poster** Another Mother for Peace (AMP) is a grassroots organization founded in 1967 in opposition to the US war in Vietnam. "War Is Not Healthy" was created by Los Angeles artist Lorraine Schneider in 1967 and adopted by AMP as its logo. It immediately became one of the most recognizable images of the antiwar movement.

Contradictions of Warfare

Yet, as the antiwar movement became a force and framed much of the discussion of America's role in the world, it left a tense legacy, and one that antiwar activists were increasingly mindful of. On the one hand, antiwar protests and acts of civil disobedience against the war did strike at the war-making capacity of the United States. Nearly 200,000 men of draft age were granted exemptions as conscientious objectors—moral opposition to war that had traditionally been granted only to religious groups like Quakers. Perhaps as many as 50,000 left the United States for Canada and Europe to avoid the draft, and thousands of others received deferments for attending college and some graduate schools or for teaching in public schools. More than a few used the resources at their disposal to get medical exemptions of various sorts.

On the other hand, the concerted opposition to the war that was disproportionately to be found among those of the middle and upper classes left the burden of enlistment and casualties on the shoulders of the working class and the poor. Indeed, roughly eight of ten men who served in the American military during the Vietnam War were from the working class or the ranks of the poor, and although most of them were white, growing numbers of poor and working-class African American men found themselves in the military—and usually in Vietnam—too. Some African Americans had enlisted as an escape from the grim circumstances of inner cities and unemployment, and in an effort to gain an education and generous benefits (the military was now desegregated and offered real opportunities for promotion). Others were drafted and had few resources to find a way out. For the next few years, Black troops would sustain disproportionately high casualties in a war thousands of miles from their homes.

26.7   Escalation of African American Rebellion

Understand the reasons for the explosion of Black rebellion in the cities of the North and West.

The escalation of American involvement in the Vietnam War and the military's growing reliance on Black troops raised a number of difficult issues for civil rights leaders. It was increasingly apparent that the United States, whatever its rhetoric, was attempting to quash the aspirations of the Vietnamese, themselves regarded as people of color, for self-determination. Activist Paul Robeson had already worried that "Negro sharecroppers from Mississippi" would be sent "to shoot down brown-skinned peasants in Vietnam—to serve the interests of those who oppose Negro liberation at home and colonial freedom abroad." At the same time, the war was being waged by President Johnson, who had supported civil rights and voting rights legislation and had called for a War on Poverty. Could civil rights leaders afford to oppose Johnson? And how would they address issues of inequality and discrimination that were truly national in scope?

PERSPECTIVES

Civil Rights and the Vietnam War

From the outset of the Vietnam War, the burden of the conflict was borne disproportionately by the working class and the poor. Eligible African American men were drafted at much higher rates than white males, many of whom were able to obtain deferments or avoid service by joining the Army Reserve or the National Guard. Though African Americans were just 10 percent of the total population of the United States, they formed 20 percent of the combat troops in the field. This disparity was noted as early as 1965 when the Student Nonviolent Coordinating Committee (SNCC) issued a statement declaring that Black people should not "fight in Vietnam for the white man's freedom, until all the Negro people are free in Mississippi."[1] Two years later, African American boxer Muhammad Ali was sentenced to jail and stripped of his titles when he refused induction. As the civil rights movement broadened, other groups saw their own struggles reflected in the aspirations of the Vietnamese.

Harlem Peace March   Men, women, and children march down a street in Harlem, New York, in the Harlem Peace March of April 15, 1967. The rally, organized by Martin Luther King, Jr., included over 125,000 people. The protesters carry signs that express solidarity with "Vietnamese freedom fighters" and point to the great disparity in Black casualty rates and the earnings of Black men compared to whites.

[1]https://content.wisconsinhistory.org/digital/collection/p15932coll2/id/34414

≡ *Viet Nam/Aztlan*
Viet Nam/Aztlan (1973) by Mexican American artist Malaquías Montoya shows the links between the antiwar and civil rights movements. Its design equates Vietnam with Aztlán, the mythic Chicano homeland located in the southwestern United States. The poster expresses the view that Chicanos, like the Vietnamese, are a "conquered and occupied people." In the middle, a Vietnamese soldier and a Chicano man merge together. At the bottom, beneath yellow and brown clenched fists, the Spanish command *Fuera* is rendered in bold, dark letters: "get out."

CONSIDER THIS

Eleven days before the Harlem Peace March, Martin Luther King, Jr., spoke at Riverside Church in New York and stated, "It would be very inconsistent for me to teach and preach nonviolence in this situation and then applaud violence when thousands of thousands of people, both adults and children, are being maimed and mutilated and many killed in this way."[2] How does King link civil rights to the war in Vietnam? How do the Harlem Peace March protesters reveal the connections between racism and US foreign policy? How does Malaquías Montoya connect national identity with historical memory?

[2]http://www.beaboutpeace.com/archives/2011/01/martin_luther_k.html

≡ **Redlining**   Urban zoning restrictions imposed by city governments and banks restricted the opportunities for Black Americans to rent or buy homes to certain areas of the city. Over the course of decades these practices lowered home values and tax bases in Black parts of cities, undercutting Black families' ability to build wealth and limiting their access to social services. The red zones in this 1937 map of Philadelphia—areas with a predominate Black population—were used by the Home Owners' Loan Corporation to identify neighborhoods where investment and lending were discouraged.

From South to North

After the passage of the Voting Rights Act in 1965, attention began to shift from the South to the North and from the issues of civil and political equality to those of housing, education, and economic opportunity. Northern cities and states did not have a legal framework of segregation and disfranchisement, but through collusion between real estate interests, insurance companies, and representatives of white communities they were able to deny African Americans access to decent housing and good public schools. **Redlining**, a process which marked urban areas as risky sites for loans and investments because of their racial character, played an important role in confining African Americans to certain parts of a city, preventing them from purchasing or renting homes elsewhere, and eroding the tax base where they lived that could be used for education and other social services.

Martin Luther King, Jr., and the SCLC thus set their sights on Chicago in 1965 and 1966 in an effort to break the hold of these discriminatory practices. They held demonstrations, rallies, and nonviolent protests. But they failed badly and were shocked by what they saw. Mayor Richard Daley, who was not sympathetic to King, went through the motions to take the wind out of the demonstrations though otherwise did very little. Some local African American leaders had their own concerns about King and the SCLC intervening despite an active and welcoming "freedom movement" on the ground.

Yet most troubling was the white backlash. At one point, when King led protesters into the all-white neighborhood of Cicero, they were greeted with bitter verbal harassment and flying bottles and bricks, one of which hit King. "I have seen many demonstrations in the south," King ruefully reflected, "but I have never seen anything so hostile and so hateful as I've seen here today."

King's perspective on the struggle was therefore in transition and showed the marks of the structural obstacles to Black advancement that he was coming to grasp as well as the deepening political and intellectual challenges to his ideas about the movement. Some of the challenges were anticipated by SNCC in the South, questioning nonviolence and moving more clearly in the direction of Black empowerment. But it was the turbulence in the urban North that began to reframe the goals of the civil rights movement. No one was more significant to the reframing than a brilliant and charismatic activist named Malcolm X.

Malcolm X and the Nation of Islam

Malcolm X was born Malcolm Little to a family of Garveyites in Omaha, Nebraska, in 1925. He had a rough childhood. His father was murdered, probably by white vigilantes, and his mother was hospitalized after a nervous breakdown. Malcolm was taken in by his half-sister. Turning to petty crime as a teenager, Malcolm ended up in prison, where he began to read voraciously and eventually converted to the **Nation of Islam**, an organization of Black Muslims many of whom, like their leader Elijah Muhammad, had been influenced by Marcus Garvey. Assigned a number of ministries after his release from prison, Malcolm (who took the surname X, dropping Little, which he and other Black Muslims regarded as a "slave" name) arrived in Harlem in the mid-1950s and developed a growing reputation as a recruiter and speaker.

Malcolm X rejected the thinking on civil rights and Black prospects associated with Martin Luther King, Jr., and the main currents of the movement. He saw the goal of integration as a delusion, mistrusted the motives of the federal government, and questioned the tactic of nonviolent civil disobedience. For Malcolm, white racism was deep and intractable. African Americans, he believed, had to rely upon themselves and their communities, reject alliances with whites, and embrace armed self-defense for their own protection. The Nation of Islam imagined the creation of a Black state. Leaders like King, he insisted, were taking Black people down the wrong path; they were "chumps" and "stooges," manipulated by white liberals and the federal government.

≡ **Malcolm X**   Malcolm X enjoyed popularity as a speaker and organizer after converting to Islam. Unlike King, Malcolm X believed that integration would not be helpful for Black Americans, that they must instead rely on themselves and their own institutions and communities if they hoped to prosper.

In important ways, Malcolm X tapped into ideas and perspectives that many poor Black people already held. Slavery and Jim Crow had taught them that power rested in white hands, few white people understood their needs and aspirations, and they were mostly ground down economically and left to their own devices anyway. Small wonder that Malcolm X spoke to large and enthusiastic crowds in Harlem, indeed in the very neighborhoods where Marcus Garvey and the UNIA served as magnets a half century before. Like Garvey, he spoke a language of Black nationalism and Pan-Africanism (see Chapter 21).

Convergences and Black Power

The differences between Malcolm X and Martin Luther King, Jr., seemed fundamental and almost impossible to bridge. But by the mid-1960s both leaders were moving toward one another. King increasingly saw racism as embedded in the entire political economy of the United States and came to view the Vietnam War as an example of American imperialism against people of color overseas. Malcolm X began to see the world in newer ways, too. Increasing tensions with Elijah Muhammad resulted in his leaving the Nation of Islam in early 1964, and a pilgrimage to Mecca soon thereafter convinced him that there were some white people who were truly welcoming and could be trusted. King and Malcolm in fact met briefly in 1964 a short time before Malcolm X was gunned down by hitmen employed by the Nation of Islam in February 1965, yet another assassination of a prominent leader.

It was a devastating blow to African Americans who hoped for dignity and social justice, but Malcolm's ideas would have wide influence. Before long, movement activists like Stokely Carmichael (later Kwame Ture) talked of "**Black Power**," a slogan that was imprecise but nonetheless captured both the sense of Black political alienation in the United States and the notion of empowerment as a model for future struggles. In various forms, Black Power already had traction around the globe—in the Caribbean, South Africa, and elsewhere on the African continent—and it would inspire a cultural transformation that could be seen in music, art, literature, and language.

By 1968, Martin Luther King, Jr., publicly broke with the Johnson administration over the Vietnam War. "What do the peasants think as we ally ourselves with the landlords . . . or test out our latest weapons on them, just as the Germans tested out new medicines and new tortures in the concentration camps? Where are the roots of the independent Vietnam we claim to be building?" he asked. "Somehow this madness must cease. I speak as a child of God and a brother to the

≡ **Black Power** American track and field Olympic medalists Tommie Smith and John Carlos raise their fists in a "Black Power" salute at the 1968 medal ceremonies in Mexico City. "Black Power" captured both the feeling of political alienation from the United States as well a commitment to international solidarity.

suffering poor of Vietnam. . . I speak for the poor of America who are paying a double price of smashed hopes at home, and death and corruption in Vietnam. I speak as a citizen of the world . . . and as one who loves America. . . . The initiative in this war is ours."

26.8 The Year 1968

||| Explain the national and international significance of 1968.

Historians often speak of decades as framing the course of events—the 1950s or the 1960s—even though the chronological boundaries of change can be imprecise. They also can point to particular years that seemed to be especially significant or amount to important turning points. Think of 1776, 1848, 1896, or 1929. We can argue about whether any one year can be singled out, but in the second half of the twentieth century a good case can be made, in the United States and in many other parts of the world, for 1968. During that single year, many of the tensions besetting American society exploded, and it first became clear that a new political course was about to be charted.

The Tet Offensive and the Fall of LBJ

The year 1968 was dreadful from start to finish. It opened in late January with a shocking development in Vietnam, a massive attack by the Viet Cong and the North Vietnamese on major cities and provincial capitals in South Vietnam, an American air base at Tan Son Nhut, and the US Embassy in Saigon. It came to be called the "**Tet Offensive**" because it took place during the Tet Lunar New Year celebration. Its objective was to strike a telling blow against the United States and its South Vietnamese allies and perhaps to spark more popular uprisings in South Vietnam's cities. Although the offensive was eventually crushed—at great cost to all sides—it brought home to American policymakers what some had already been thinking: that the war could not be won. Secretary of Defense McNamara, one of the war's architects and cheerleaders, now advised Johnson to halt the bombing of the North and seek a negotiated withdrawal.

President Johnson didn't seem interested in McNamara's advice and soon showed him the door. But it was also apparent that Johnson's own political future was in jeopardy. Among other things, 1968 was a presidential election year and virtually everyone expected that Johnson would seek another term. This, after all, is what sitting presidents normally did. But by the beginning of 1968, Johnson faced a challenge for the nomination within the Democratic Party. It came from

Eugene McCarthy, a little-known senator from Minnesota, who began to campaign on a peace platform. "I am concerned," McCarthy said in announcing his candidacy, "that the Administration seems to have set no limit to the price it is willing to pay for a military victory." No one gave him much of a chance, but after the debacle of the Tet Offensive, public opinion began to shift further against the war and when New Hampshire held its primary in early March, McCarthy nearly defeated Johnson (he lost 49 percent to 42 percent).

It was a stunning turn of events, and within days another challenger entered the field—Robert F. Kennedy. Kennedy (Bobby as he was usually known) was John F. Kennedy's brother, his attorney general, and in 1966 had become a US senator from New York. Kennedy's politics were complex, but over the course of the 1960s he seemed to be moving in an increasingly liberal direction. He embraced the civil rights movement, which as attorney general he had greeted with ambivalence, and was moved by struggles against poverty and social injustice. He had also become a critic of the war in Vietnam. Although he declined to become a candidate for the presidency in the fall of 1967 when approached by antiwar Democrats, now that Johnson's blood was in the water Kennedy played a shark.

Johnson clearly had a fight on his hands, and few in politics were tougher fighters than Johnson. Yet on March 31, in a nationally televised address from the White House Oval Office, Johnson announced a halt to the bombing of North Vietnam and a willingness to sit down with the North Vietnamese "to discuss the means of bringing this ugly war to an end." He seemed to have heard the rumble from within his party and determined to fashion himself as something of a peace candidate.

Then the other shoe dropped. Johnson concluded his speech by saying that he would "not seek, and will not accept the nomination of my party for another term as your president." Even Johnson's close advisors were unaware of this decision, and they shared the shock all around. Within a month, Johnson's vice president, Hubert H. Humphrey, himself a former senator from Minnesota, threw his hat into the ring for the nomination and in so doing threw the 1968 election into further turmoil.

≡ **An Anguished President, July 1968** President Johnson listens to a tape sent home by his son-in-law Charles Robb, a marine in Vietnam. Although American forces beat back the Tet Offensive, it had become clear that the Vietnam War would not be won.

The Assassination of Martin Luther King, Jr.

While the Democrats became embroiled in conflict over the Vietnam War and their standard-bearer in the coming election, an event of immense tragedy occurred in Memphis,

Tennessee. Martin Luther King, Jr., who had shifted the civil rights movement to the North, had begun to listen to his Black Power critics; he had come out against the war and traveled to Memphis to support a bitter strike of sanitation workers seeking improved working conditions and recognition of their union. The trip suggested his understanding about the relation of racism and economic inequality, and his interest in the struggles of organized labor. On the night of April 3, King spoke to a large rally. "Like anybody, I would like to live a long life," he said with a prophetic air, "longevity has its place. But I'm not concerned about that now. I've seen the Promised Land. I may not get there with you. But I want you to know tonight that we, as a people, will get to the Promised Land." The next day, April 4, as he stood with aides on the balcony of the Lorraine Motel in downtown Memphis, a white supremacist named James Earl Ray shot him down.

Martin Luther King, Jr., had long courted death. He had been arrested countless times; his home had been bombed; he had been assaulted with knives and bricks and bottles. But his assassination was a shock nationally and internationally. He had come to symbolize, in the United States and around the globe, the struggle for peace, equality, and social justice. That night riots broke out in many American cities, perhaps the worst of them in Washington, DC. Troops of the US Army and Marines as well as the National Guard were mobilized. In Indianapolis, campaigning for the upcoming Indiana primary, Bobby Kennedy responded to the news by stepping before a large crowd and, with anguish, telling them of Martin Luther King, Jr.'s death. Kennedy recognized what it meant to the many African Americans who listened to him, but there was nothing patronizing about his words. After quoting the ancient Greek tragedian Aeschylus, he said quietly, "What we need in the United States is not division; what we need in the United States is not hatred; what we need in the United States is not violence and lawlessness, but is love, and wisdom, and compassion toward one another, and a feeling of justice toward those who still suffer within our country, whether they be white or whether they be black."

The Assassination of Robert Kennedy

King's death left an important political vacuum. It also seemed emblematic of where American politics was heading. Conflict, bitterness, and disarray seemed to abound, and the means of violence were becoming central to their resolution. As attention returned to the presidential campaign, Humphrey pretty much sat out the primaries as Kennedy and McCarthy pursued them with

☰ **"What we need in the United States is not hatred."**   Senator Robert Kennedy breaks the news of Martin Luther King, Jr.'s assassination to an Indianapolis crowd. Although aides encouraged Kennedy to cancel the speech, Kennedy insisted on going ahead, pleading Americans to show "love, and wisdom, and compassion" toward each other.

great intensity, effectively pitting antiwar Democrats against one another. Who would be in a position to challenge Humphrey, the Democratic insider (most delegates at this point were still chosen by party officials and conventions in the states), for the nomination when the national convention met in Chicago that August?

As May turned into June, the battle reached its pinnacle and both insurgent candidates competed for the votes of Californians. McCarthy, who had just won the Oregon primary, had a large following among college students and young, middle-class, white liberal Democrats. Kennedy had wider appeal, not only to young liberals but also to African Americans, Latinos, and the traditionally Democratic white working class. The California primary was held on June 5, and when it became clear that Kennedy was the winner, he spoke to his supporters at the Ambassador Hotel in Los Angeles about going "on to Chicago and winning there." But as he moved through the hotel's kitchen, Kennedy was shot and killed by a Palestinian immigrant named Sirhan Sirhan, who bitterly opposed Kennedy's support of Israel.

Convulsive Politics at Home and Abroad

The assassination of Robert Kennedy marked another assassination in the space of two months, and the second assassination of a Kennedy in five years. The fabric of American politics seemed to be unraveling. Some believed that Kennedy was headed toward winning the Democratic nomination had he lived. Perhaps. But after his assassination, the clear favorite was Humphrey, who had lined up the party establishment. The antiwar movement was in no mood to throw in the towel, however. Instead, SDS joined with the National Mobilization Committee to End the Vietnam War and other antiwar groups to organize a massive protest at the Democrats' national convention in Chicago. They opposed Humphrey, who was tainted by Johnson's war and had not come out against it, and they wanted an antiwar plank in the party's platform. A good many of them were fed up with mainstream politics entirely.

The Chicago convention had two scenes of action: one inside the convention hall where Humphrey won

☰ **Vietnam War Demonstrators** Opponents of the Vietnam War gather around the Logan monument in Grant Park, near the site of the 1968 Democratic National Convention in Chicago, demanding that the party, and its presumptive nominee Hubert H. Humphrey, denounce the war. Many demonstrators viewed Humphrey as untrustworthy if not the enemy.

the nomination and the antiwar plank was defeated despite loud protests from many delegates; and one in the streets of Chicago where Mayor Richard Daley unleashed a brutal police force on the demonstrators. Indeed, investigators later termed what went on a "police riot," replete with teargassing, beatings, arrests, and other assaults. A prominent delegate from Connecticut, Senator Abraham Ribicoff, stepped to the podium in the convention arena and denounced "the Gestapo tactics on the streets of Chicago" while Daley, in attendance at the time, gestured back scornfully.

The antiwar movement and convention demonstrations were examples of a global surge of political unrest that marked the year of 1968. Protests against the Vietnam War spread across Britain and continental Europe, through nations that were allies of the United States. They were part of a broader tide of political activism, especially among the young, that swept across France and Northern Ireland, Czechoslovakia and Poland, Brazil and Argentina, Senegal and Pakistan, Mexico and Spain. In May 1968, France was convulsed by protests that linked the universities and factories, saw general strikes, and nearly brought the government down. In Mexico, a massive student movement roiled the country, especially around Mexico City, through the summer and into the fall during which hundreds of activists were massacred and thousands arrested by the police. And in Northern Ireland, the Irish Republican Army (IRA), itself influenced by the American civil rights movement, began to fight against British occupation and anti-Catholic discrimination.

Protests had convulsed university campuses in the United States as well: at Howard University, Bowie State College (MD), Orangeburg State (SC), the University of California, and most notably Columbia University, where SDS and the Student Afro-American Society occupied the administration office because of the university's involvement with war-related research and efforts to build in poor, Black adjacent neighborhoods. To many observers, it appeared that American society was becoming unhinged.

26.9   The Backlash

Describe the emergence of George Wallace as a political force and why the country began turning toward the right in the late 1960s.

The violence in the streets of Chicago, in the inner cities from New York to Los Angeles, and on college campuses may have disheartened many liberals and those to their left, but it also provoked a growing backlash in other quarters. Liberalism and a counterculture may seem to have defined the decade of the 1960s, but under the radar a backlash was developing which would influence the American political system in ways that appeared unimaginable after conservative Republican Barry Goldwater was shellacked in the election of 1964. Yet 1968 would demonstrate that Goldwater and the conservative forces he represented were anything but a small flicker in the dominant current of liberalism. They were, in fact, the harbingers of a larger shift to the political right.

The Rise of George Wallace and the Rebirth of Richard Nixon

What was happening? Quite simply, the social and political perspectives of Great Society liberals and antiwar activists had much less appeal than reports by the media would have suggested. White voters in rural and suburban America, together with white ethnics in the cities, pushed back. They began to bridle at what they saw as the flaunting of traditional values. They remained supportive of the war effort in Vietnam, complained of unruly students and hostile African Americans, and expressed a desire for "law and order." One figure on the political landscape who attempted to harness this discontent was George C. Wallace.

Wallace had been the governor of Alabama who gained notoriety for his defense of segregation and opposition to the integration of the state's universities. But as early as 1964 he tested the national waters for his views, not so much about Jim Crow as about the overreach of the federal government, the threat of communism at home and abroad, the cultural elitism of East Coast intellectuals, and the apparently brazen disregard for the law in many American cities. Making a run for the Democratic nomination that year, Wallace managed to win a significant share of the primary vote in Wisconsin, Maryland, and Indiana, a sign that he might have traction outside the South.

Four years later, Wallace decided to run as the presidential candidate of the right-wing **American Independent Party**, denouncing the "Eastern establishment," hippies, demonstrators, and welfare mothers, calling for a military victory in Vietnam, and styling himself as the candidate of "law and order." "You elect me president," he told one crowd, "and if a group of anarchists lay down in front of my automobile, it's gonna be the last one they ever gonna want to lay down in front of."

≡ **Backlash**   White supporters at a rally for George Wallace of the right-wing American Independent Party. Wallace became famous for his support of segregation, and he increased his appeal by condemning federal overreach, communism, and East Coast elites.

No one took better notice of the public temper that Wallace tapped into than Richard Nixon. Nixon had lost the presidential election in 1960, and when he was later defeated for the governorship of California, it appeared as though his political career was at an end. "You won't have Nixon to kick around anymore," he angrily told a press conference at that time. But by 1968, Nixon had climbed back into contention for the Republican nomination, and despite challenges from New York Governor Nelson Rockefeller and California Governor Ronald Reagan, he won it. Nixon presented himself as the voice of the "great majority of Americans" who were "the non-shouters, the non-demonstrators, those who give steel to the backbone of America." They were the **silent majority**.

The "silent majority," as Nixon recognized, was overwhelmingly white, and he looked to marshal their voting power by appealing to "law and order" and trying to win the support of whites in the South who had long voted Democratic but were angered by the movement for civil rights. One of Nixon's advisors called it the **Southern Strategy**. He also pledged to bring the Vietnam War to an "honorable" end, even though he said nothing about how he would do it.

The election of 1968, like that of 1960, proved to be extraordinarily close, but the outcome was very different. Reading the tea leaves of Democratic sentiment on the war, Hubert Humphrey finally began to distance himself from the Johnson administration and call for a bombing halt. Johnson himself, looking to tip the balances in Humphrey's favor, ordered a halt to the bombing of North Vietnam and suggested a possible peace deal. It became known as the "October surprise."

But it was not enough. Richard Nixon squeaked out a narrow victory, and the Republican Party reclaimed the presidency. Equally significant, George Wallace won nearly ten million popular votes (about 14 percent of the total) and the electoral votes of Arkansas, Louisiana, Mississippi, Alabama, and Georgia. Amid the rebellions of the left, in the United States and around the world, the country now seemed to be veering to the right (see Map 26.6).

Conclusion: The Contradictions and Limits of Modern Liberalism

The near decade between 1957 and 1968 began with a robust and seemingly unopposed modern liberalism. A young Democrat, John F. Kennedy, won the presidency and called for the making of a "New Frontier." A civil rights movement struck major blows against the Jim Crow system in the South, leading Congress to enact Civil Rights and Voting Rights bills. And although Kennedy was assassinated, new president Lyndon Johnson called for both a "War on Poverty" and a "Great Society."

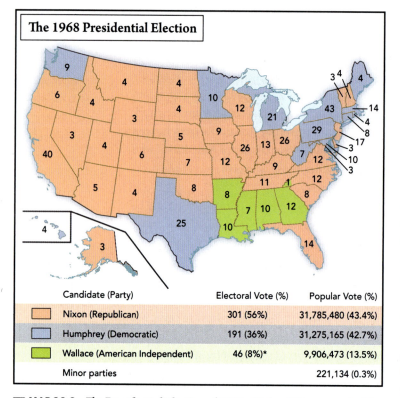

The 1968 Presidential Election

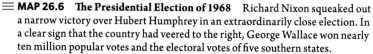

Candidate (Party)	Electoral Vote (%)	Popular Vote (%)
Nixon (Republican)	301 (56%)	31,785,480 (43.4%)
Humphrey (Democratic)	191 (36%)	31,275,165 (42.7%)
Wallace (American Independent)	46 (8%)*	9,906,473 (13.5%)
Minor parties		221,134 (0.3%)

≡ **MAP 26.6   The Presidential Election of 1968**   Richard Nixon squeaked out a narrow victory over Hubert Humphrey in an extraordinarily close election. In a clear sign that the country had veered to the right, George Wallace won nearly ten million popular votes and the electoral votes of five southern states.

But the contradictions and limits of modern liberalism were also becoming apparent. Committed to anticommunism, the United States became involved in a bloody and destructive civil war in Vietnam which alienated a large section of the American public. Poverty and discrimination fueled race riots, really Black rebellions, in many of the country's large cities. The civil rights movement fractured, owing to the rise of Black Power and its defeats in northern cities like Chicago. And the liberal perspective that economic growth was fundamental to social change and social peace came into question. By 1968, there was a combustible mix which exploded in Vietnam and in the streets of the United States. Before the year was out, American politics, reliably liberal since the 1930s, took a right turn backed by white people who came to fear the substance and direction of change.

WHAT IF Martin Luther King, Jr., and Robert F. Kennedy Had Not Been Assassinated?

One of the things that scholars have learned in recent decades is to doubt the overall influence of great men and women in historical outcomes. We have come to look at the work and impact of local activists, the ideas sprouted closer to the ground, and the courage that ordinary people are able to show in their quest for change.

But leaders do play very significant roles in capturing the tenor of opinion, the direction of history, and the aspirations of those at the grassroots. They help organize and articulate what their followers feel and need. And when something happens to them, especially to those who are especially good in their roles, their movements suffer major, sometimes disastrous, blows.

During 1968, two important leaders were assassinated: Martin Luther King, Jr., and Bobby Kennedy. King had helped to build a mass movement for change, had a very large following among whites as well as African Americans, and showed an impressive capacity to learn from his mistakes and move in new directions. He was also one of the great orators of the twentieth century. Bobby Kennedy was not a movement builder and, over the years, had a mixed record of liberalism. But by 1968 he alone among national Democratic political figures had embraced antiwar and social justice perspectives and retained the support of ethnic whites together with people of color.

What would have happened had King and Kennedy lived? Could King have played an effective role in linking the moral claims of civil rights with the systemic critiques of Black Power? Could Kennedy have helped to show white working- and lower middle-class voters the way forward in progressive politics that would have required strong coalitions with African Americans? Could they have helped tie antiwar sensibilities with a vision for domestic economic prosperity and opportunity? What might the future have looked like with their voices and energies still active? It is worth contemplating, especially as we move through the next decades of US history.

DOCUMENT 26.1: Martin Luther King, Jr., "I've Been to the Mountaintop," April 3, 1968

Martin Luther King, Jr., traveled to Memphis in early April 1968 to support a strike of sanitation workers, who were overwhelmingly Black. It was part of his concerns about economic as well as racial inequality. This is part of the speech he gave the night before he was assassinated.

Something is happening in our world. The masses of people are rising up. And wherever they are assembled today, whether they are in Johannesburg, South Africa; Nairobi, Kenya; Accra, Ghana; New York City; Atlanta, Georgia; Jackson, Mississippi; or Memphis, Tennessee—the cry is the same: "We want to be free." . . . We have been forced to the point where we are going to have to grapple with the problems that men have been trying to grapple with through history. . . . Men, for years now, having been talking about war and peace. But now, no longer can they just talk about it. It is no longer a choice between violence and nonviolence in the world; it's nonviolence or non-existence. . . . We've got to stay together and maintain unity. . . . When the slaves get together, that's the beginning of getting out of slavery. . . . The issue is injustice. The issue is the refusal of Memphis to be fair and honest in its dealings with its public servants, who happen to be sanitation workers. . . . Now we're going to march again, and we've got to march again, in order to put the issue where it is supposed to be—and force everyone to see that there are thirteen hundred of God's children here suffering, sometimes going hungry. . . . Now the other thing we have to do is this: always anchor our external direct action with the power of economic withdrawal. Now, we are poor people. . . . [But] never stop and forget that collectively—that means all of us together—collectively we are richer than all the nations of the world, with the exception of nine . . . . That's power right there, if we know how to pool it. We don't have to argue with anybody. We don't have to curse and go around acting bad with our words. We don't need any bricks and bottles. We don't need any Molotov cocktails. We just need to go around to these stores, and to these massive industries in our country, and say, "God sent us by here, to say that you're not treating his children right. And we've come here to ask you to make the first item on your agenda fair treatment where God's children are concerned." . . . But not only that, we've got to strengthen black institutions. I call upon you to take your money out of the banks downtown and deposit your money in Tri-State Bank. We want a "bank-in" movement in Memphis. . . . You have six or seven black insurance companies here in the city of Memphis. Take your insurance there. We have to have an "insurance-in." . . . We begin the process of building a greater economic base. And at the same time we are putting pressure where it really hurts. . . . We've got to give ourselves to this struggle until the end. . . . We've got to see it through. . . . [The question before you tonight is not], "If I stop to help the sanitation worker, what will happen to my job?" Not "if I stop to help the sanitation workers what will happen to all of the hours I usually spend in my office every day and every week as a pastor?" The question is not, "If I stop to help this man in need, what will happen to me?" The question is, "If I do not stop to help the sanitation workers, what will happen to them?" That's the question.

Source: https://www.afscme.org/about/history/mlk/mountaintop

DOCUMENT 26.2: Robert F. Kennedy, Statement on Assassination of Martin Luther King, Jr., Indianapolis, Indiana (April 4, 1968)

On the night of April 4, 1968, Bobby Kennedy was campaigning in Indiana for the Democratic presidential nomination when he learned of Martin Luther King, Jr.'s assassination. Having suffered the assassination of his brother and president, John F. Kennedy, he addressed a crowd of mostly Black men, women, and children, informing them of what had happened and asking that they embrace the nonviolent lessons that King had taught:

I have bad news for you, for all of our fellow citizens, and people who love peace all over the world, and that is that Martin Luther King was shot and killed tonight.

Martin Luther King dedicated his life to love and to justice for his fellow human beings, and he died because of that effort.

In this difficult day, in this difficult time for the United States, it is perhaps well to ask what kind of a nation we are and what direction we want to move in. For those of you who are black—considering the evidence there evidently is that there were white people who were responsible—you can be filled with bitterness, with hatred, and a desire for revenge. We can move in that direction as a country, in great polarization—black people amongst black, white people amongst white, filled with hatred toward one another.

Or we can make an effort, as Martin Luther King did, to understand and to comprehend, and to replace that violence, that stain of bloodshed that has spread across our land, with an effort to understand with compassion and love.

For those of you who are black and are tempted to be filled with hatred and distrust at the injustice of such an act, against all white people, I can only say that I feel in my own heart the same kind of feeling. I had a member of my family killed, but he was killed by a white man. But we have to make an effort in the United States, we have to make an effort to understand, to go beyond these rather difficult times.

My favorite poet was Aeschylus. He wrote: "In our sleep, pain which cannot forget falls drop by drop upon the heart until, in our own despair, against our will, comes wisdom through the awful grace of God."

What we need in the United States is not division; what we need in the United States is not hatred; what we need in the United States is not violence or lawlessness; but love and wisdom, and compassion toward one another, and a feeling of justice toward those who still suffer within our country, whether they be white or they be black.

So I shall ask you tonight to return home, to say a prayer for the family of Martin Luther King, that's true, but more importantly to say a prayer for our own country, which all of us love—a prayer for understanding and that compassion of which I spoke.

We can do well in this country. We will have difficult times; we've had difficult times in the past; we will have difficult times in the future. It is not the end of violence; it is not the end of lawlessness; it is not the end of disorder.

But the vast majority of white people and the vast majority of black people in this country want to live together, want to improve the quality of our life, and want justice for all human beings who abide in our land.

Let us dedicate ourselves to what the Greeks wrote so many years ago: to tame the savageness of man and make gentle the life of this world.

Let us dedicate ourselves to that, and say a prayer for our country and for our people.

Source: https://www.jfklibrary.org/learn/about-jfk/the-kennedy-family/robert-f-kennedy/robert-f-kennedy-speeches/statement-on-assassination-of-martin-luther-king-jr-indianapolis-indiana-april-4-1968

Thinking About Contingency

1. What are the main themes of Martin Luther King, Jr.'s speech, and are there similarities with Robert F. Kennedy's speech? What are King and Kennedy most concerned about?
2. Why would King support the cause of Memphis sanitation workers? Was their strike a civil rights issue?
3. In what direction might the civil rights movement have gone if King had not been assassinated?
4. If he had not been assassinated, how might Kennedy, as the Democratic presidential nominee, have appealed to white working-class voters as well as to African Americans? In his speech in Indianapolis, how did Kennedy ask Americans to think about the assassination of Martin Luther King, Jr.?

REVIEW QUESTIONS

1. Why did President Kennedy support the CIA operation against Fidel Castro at the Bay of Pigs, and how did he react when it failed?

2. In what ways did civil rights activism of the 1950s become a movement by the 1960s? What were the components of a movement?

3. How were the Freedom Rides and Project C part of the civil rights movement? How can we mark the civil rights movement's successes, and what were its failures?

4. How did President Johnson manage to support civil rights legislation and a War on Poverty, on the one hand, and send thousands of American troops to fight against communism in the jungles of Vietnam, on the other?

5. Were there any connections between the civil rights movement and the anti–Vietnam War movement?

6. Republican Barry Goldwater, a right-wing conservative, was badly beaten in the election of 1964, but did his candidacy have longer-term results?

7. Why did 1968 prove to be such a pivotal year in the United States and around the globe? Did the events of that year set history on a different path or not?

KEY TERMS

American Independent Party (p. 1130)

Bay of Pigs Invasion (p. 1095)

Black Power (p. 1124)

Civil Rights Act of 1964 (p. 1105)

Dien Bien Phu (p. 1112)

Equal Employment Opportunity Commission (EEOC) (p. 1105)

Freedom Rides (p. 1098)

Freedom Summer (p. 1106)

Great Society (p. 1105)

Gulf of Tonkin Resolution (p. 1114)

hippies (p. 1118)

Immigration and Nationality Act of 1965 (Hart-Celler Act) (p. 1108)

Mississippi Freedom Democratic Party (p. 1107)

My Lai (p. 1115)

Nation of Islam (p. 1123)

redlining (p. 1122)

silent majority (p. 1131)

Southern Christian Leadership Conference (SCLC) (p. 1097)

Southern Strategy (p. 1131)

Students for a Democratic Society (SDS) (p. 1106)

Student Non-Violent Coordinating Committee (SNCC) (p. 1098)

Tet Offensive (p. 1125)

Voting Rights Act of 1965 (p. 1108)

War on Poverty (p. 1105)

RECOMMENDED READINGS

Kevin Boyle, *The Shattering: America in the 1960s* (W.W. Norton, 2021).

Dan Carter, *The Politics of Rage: George Wallace, the Origins of the New Conservatism, and the Transformation of American Politics* (Louisiana State University Press, 2000).

Elizabeth Hinton, *From the War on Poverty to the War on Crime: The Making of Mass Incarceration in America* (Harvard University Press, 2017).

Thomas C. Holt, *The Movement: African-American Struggles for Civil Rights* (Oxford University Press, 2021).

Mark Kurlansky, *1968: The Year That Rocked the World* (Random House, 2005).

Frederick Logevall, *Embers of War: The Fall of an Empire and the Making of America's Vietnam* (Random House, 2014).

Richard Rothstein, *The Color of Law: A Forgotten History of How Our Government Segregated America* (Liveright, 2018).

Thomas Sugrue, *The Origins of the Urban Crisis: Race and Inequality in Postwar Detroit* (Princeton University Press, 2014).

27

Destabilizations
1969–1979

Chapter Outline

≡ **A Blighted Landscape**   A boy considers the automobile wreckage and other waste discarded along the shore of the Bronx River in New York, 1970. Americans increasingly worried about the future of the natural environment throughout the 1970s and demanded that American rivers and streams be protected from pollution.

On the night of July 15, 1979, President Jimmy Carter, a Democrat from Georgia who was elected in 1976, spoke to the American people from the Oval Office of the White House "about a fundamental threat to American democracy." He was not referring to "political or civil liberties" or to "the outward strength of America." The threat was rather "a crisis of confidence." From Carter's perspective, he could see "growing doubt about the meaning of our own lives and in the loss of a unity of purpose for our nation," both of which threatened the "social fabric of the country." Carter went on to deride the tendency to "worship self-indulgence and consumption," to define our identities "not by what one does, but by what one owns." He also saw "a growing disrespect for the government and for churches and for schools, the news media and other institutions."

Carter insisted that this crisis did not happen overnight. It came "upon us gradually" as a result of "shocks and tragedy that was a product of changes over the last generation": the assassinations of political leaders, the agony of Vietnam, the Watergate scandal, the precipitous rise in the price of oil, and the failure of the government

Timeline

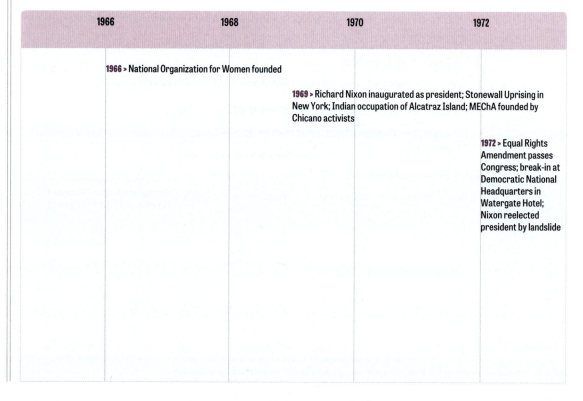

1966	1968	1970	1972

1966 > National Organization for Women founded

1969 > Richard Nixon inaugurated as president; Stonewall Uprising in New York; Indian occupation of Alcatraz Island; MEChA founded by Chicano activists

1972 > Equal Rights Amendment passes Congress; break-in at Democratic National Headquarters in Watergate Hotel; Nixon reelected president by landslide

to adequately address the country's problems. Now, from Carter's perspective, the United States had reached a "turning point," and he advised the country to choose the "path of common purpose and the restoration of American values." He also pledged, in particular, to face up to the energy crisis that had erupted over the previous decade and cut American "dependence on foreign oil" through a number of initiatives, including the development of "alternative sources of fuel."

Carter's was not a message of optimism—it came to be called the "malaise speech," even though he never used the term—but one that reflected changes that appeared to put the country on its heels and sow doubt and dissatisfaction among millions of Americans. The postwar policies and framework of power designed to maintain prosperity through economic growth, secure the country's leadership in the world, and create social stability at home through an activist federal government seemed to be coming undone. The social movements of the 1960s, civil rights and antiwar in particular, called into question the liberal commitment to equality at home and the price

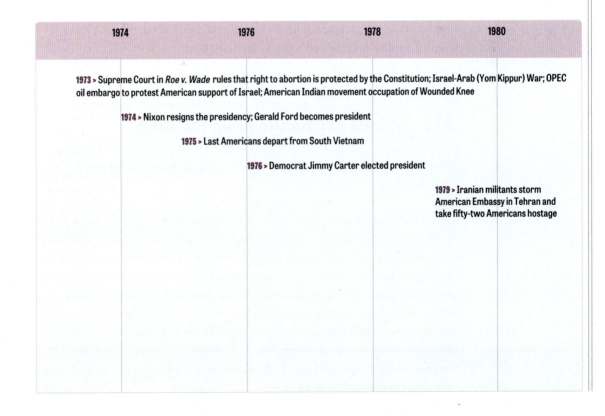

| 1974 | 1976 | 1978 | 1980 |

1973 > Supreme Court in *Roe v. Wade* rules that right to abortion is protected by the Constitution; Israel-Arab (Yom Kippur) War; OPEC oil embargo to protest American support of Israel; American Indian movement occupation of Wounded Knee

1974 > Nixon resigns the presidency; Gerald Ford becomes president

1975 > Last Americans depart from South Vietnam

1976 > Democrat Jimmy Carter elected president

1979 > Iranian militants storm American Embassy in Tehran and take fifty-two Americans hostage

of intervening against communism abroad. Urban rebellions demonstrated the limits of economic growth in an apparently "affluent society" and the impact of discrimination in housing, employment, and education for a large segment of America's minority populations. And the efforts made by the federal government to redress these imbalances in economic and social life through public policies generated a backlash from white Americans who had benefitted from government initiatives in the past but now saw racial minorities making gains at their own expense.

By the end of the 1960s, these challenges had created deep divisions in American society over cultural and political issues (the war, racial discrimination, middle-class values, the role of the government) that raised questions about whether the postwar ambitions of forging an "American century" would survive. There were, as President Carter would emphasize, no quick solutions. But over the course of the 1970s, those ambitions would be destabilized by economic readjustments, new business offensives, foreign policy debacles, resistance to government remedies for social ills, and a crisis in the office of the presidency itself that undercut popular belief in the integrity of American political institutions. By the time the decade drew to a close, a new economic and political framework of power and policy was under construction and new assumptions about how power and policy worked were developing, marking out a major transition for the country and much of the world.

27.1 Winds of Change Keep Blowing

Discuss the ongoing struggles for civil rights among women and other social groups.

The challenges that civil rights activists brought against the structure of power in the United States not only reshaped laws, practices, and policies around issues of race and racial discrimination. They also energized other Americans who had long experienced discriminatory treatment and began to demand the rights that the Constitution seemed to guarantee. In the process they provoked confrontations in areas of the country, such as the Southwest, that had been relatively quiet. And they questioned how power was deployed in the most personal and intimate relations—about gender and sexuality. In so doing, they forced a reckoning that the country had tried to avoid and offered an expansive perspective on a reformed nation that they hoped to forge.

A New Feminism

Women's rights had been on and off the political agenda since the 1840s when supporters of women's civil and political equality met at Seneca Falls (1848) and then pressed again for the elective franchise during Radical Reconstruction. After many setbacks, that struggle achieved a major victory with the Nineteenth Amendment in 1920 (see Chapter 21). It also contributed to the emergence of the "New Woman" of the 1920s and to the introduction, in 1923 by Alice Paul and the National Women's Party, of an Equal Rights Amendment to the Constitution: "Men and women shall have equal rights in the United States and every place subject to its jurisdiction."

The Equal Rights Amendment made little headway at the time, and the New Woman faltered during the hardships of the 1930s. Although women entered the workforce and the military in massive numbers during World War II, the 1950s appeared to mark a return to traditional understandings of gender relations as popular culture celebrated women's roles as mothers and homemakers. Yet appearances could be deceiving. As was true among African Americans, the great sacrifices women made during the war and the new opportunities of life that employment and military service offered to them could not be suppressed so easily. Discontent started to bubble closer and closer to the surface.

Already in the early 1950s, Simone de Beauvoir, a French intellectual, published a book that would begin to shake up thinking on this issue. The book was called *The Second Sex* (1953), and it argued that womanhood was a social construction rather than a

≡ **Lobbying for Women's Rights**   Activist Betty Friedan meets with reporters at the New York State Assembly in 1967. Friedan's 1963 book *The Feminine Mystique* argued that American women should try to find meaning and purpose outside the home.

biological assignment, and that women's legal and social subordination over the ages owed to a culture that was firmly centered on men and male power. The book was not an easy read; well over 700 pages in length, it mixed philosophy, psychology, history, and literary criticism. But *The Second Sex* briefly became a bestseller in the United States, and the perspectives it offered found a receptive audience, especially among educated women of the middle and upper-middle class.

Not long after, another book, this one written by an American named Betty Friedan, had an even greater impact. A writer and journalist who had been involved in labor union work and political organizing, Friedan had turned her attention to women's lives. In 1963, she published *The Feminine Mystique*. As much an exposé as a critique, *The Feminine Mystique* presented a devastating picture of (mostly suburban) housewives, who, she argued, were trapped by domesticity, depressed and dissatisfied, and isolated from real life. The solution, as Friedan saw it, was not for women to struggle for change within the household, but rather to strike out on their own and find meaningful work.

The Feminine Mystique was part of an escalating challenge to the imbalances of power, within families and society at large, that limited women's opportunities and left them in a position of legal and cultural subordination. Friedan struck a chord for many middle-class women, who imagined more for themselves than housekeeping, motherhood, and volunteer work, especially as growing numbers became college educated. But there was far more to it. Friedan soon joined hands with women who had been active in politics and bridled at the federal government's failure to enforce laws against gender discrimination that had been inscribed in the 1964 Civil Rights Act. In 1966, Friedan and twenty-seven other women, including African American activists Pauli Murray and Shirley Chisholm, established the **National Organization for Women (NOW)** to fight for women's equality.

Discontent was bubbling up from other political quarters, too. Women like Casey Hayden and Mary King, who had been deeply involved with the civil rights movement and SNCC, chafed at their second-class treatment by men who regarded themselves as the leaders and women as assistants or helpers. Although the sexism within civil rights and other New Left organizations could be exaggerated, it stung more and more young female activists and led them to reflect on gender inequality and what would be required to topple it. Indeed, in a more general climate of youth radicalism, they came to question not just unequal pay or limited employment prospects but an entire range of discriminations and indignities, whether within families (housekeeping and child-rearing), in social life, in sexual relations, and in public spaces.

In 1970, Robin Morgan, who had led a protest against the Miss America Pageant two years earlier for its depiction of women as little more than sexual objects, published a collection of essays entitled *Sisterhood Is Powerful*. It simultaneously advanced a critique of male domination and called for a new radical feminism to take political form. As Carol Hanisch put it that same year, "One of the first things we discover is that personal problems are political problems. There are no personal solutions at this time. There is only collective action for a collective solution." "The personal is political" became the rallying cry of for a variety of individual and group actions ranging from consciousness-raising sessions to protests. Whether called "second-wave feminism" or the "women's liberation movement," these efforts represented a collective struggle for equality and freedom from oppression and male supremacy.

By the early 1970s, the momentum of feminism was pushing on a number of fronts. In the arenas of formal politics, owing in good part to the work of NOW, the Equal Rights Amendment was reintroduced and by the spring of 1972 was overwhelmingly approved by both Houses of Congress and sent on to the states for ratification (three-quarters of the state legislatures needed to sign on), this after fifty years of failed efforts.

Emphasizing the importance of women's power over their own bodies, feminists also moved into the areas of sexuality and reproduction to demand the legalization of abortion. Here, they had the help of NOW as well as some support in state legislatures that allowed abortions when the health of the mother or condition of the fetus was in question. But with the organization of the **National Abortion Rights League (NARAL)** in 1969, feminists insisted that abortion was a basic constitutional right and began to look to the courts for redress.

The moment came in 1972, when the Supreme Court heard a case challenging a Texas state law that made abortions illegal except in the circumstance of rape. The case originated in a suit brought several years earlier by a plaintiff named Norma McCorvey—who had unsuccessfully sought an abortion—against the Dallas County Attorney Henry Wade. Given the sensitivity of the matter, McCorvey was officially designated as Jane Roe to disguise her identity. The following year, 1973, by a vote of 7–2, the Court struck down the Texas law in a ruling known as ***Roe v. Wade***, arguing that it infringed on a "right to privacy." "We recognize," Justice Potter Stewart wrote in concurrence, "the right of the individual, married or single, to be free from unwanted government intrusion into matters so fundamentally affecting a person as the right of a woman to decide whether or not to terminate her pregnancy." It was a sea change in public understandings of women's rights and women's power.

But the ramifications of feminism and women's power went further still. Since the nineteenth century, feminism and women's rights were made to appeal chiefly to white, middle-class women, many of whom had gained an education and were

≡ **Women's Liberation**   Members of the National
Women's Liberation Party protest the 1968 Miss America
Beauty Pageant. Women's Liberation activists argued that
beauty pageants encouraged the idea that women should
be beautiful objects, rather than people in their own right.
Here, two activists make the point that the Miss America
Pageant was no different than a cattle auction.

active in a variety of social reform movements
even if they lacked the right to vote. Working-
class women, who faced many different challenges than their middle-class counterparts,
were largely ignored, and Black women hardly
made it onto the feminist radar screen, reflec-
tions of how class and race figured in American
social and political life.

But in the context of the civil rights movement, the feminist impulses of the late 1960s
and 1970s spread in new directions. Radical
feminism and socialist feminism looked to join
women's rights to issues of class and economic
inequalities, and to interrogate matters of sexual orientation in new ways, together offering
novel forms of solidarity. Black feminists also
took hold of the issues of women's rights and
emphasized the double burdens of race *and*
gender discrimination. Political activists like
Angela Davis together with poets and writers like bell hooks, Audre Lorde, and
Alice Walker laid important intellectual groundwork, not only demanding that the
struggles of Black women be recognized but also demonstrating how Black feminism pushed the feminist project in far more expansive directions and revealed
how race was embedded in the very structure of American society. It was later to
be called "intersectionality" and "critical race theory."

Gay Liberation

Feminism and women's liberation not only challenged hierarchies of power based
on gender but also advanced new possibilities for sexual expression. Fortified by
more effective means of birth control, especially the birth control pill, approved by
the FDA for use in 1960, and then by the legalization of abortion, women and men
could reject the customary association of sexual intimacy with reproduction and
experiment with forms of sexuality that had previously been frowned upon. The
1960s thus brought about a "sexual revolution," particularly among young people.

New ideas about sexuality made for important openings in American culture
more generally. Gay men and women, who had long been relegated to a social underground by popular disapproval as well as by state and municipal laws against
sodomy and obscenity, now saw the chance to find a stable place in public life and
to fight against discrimination in education and the workplace. As early as 1950,

the Mattachine Society, a gay rights organization, was founded in Los Angeles, followed soon thereafter by a lesbian counterpart, the Daughters of Bilitis. Like civil rights and feminist activists, gay rights advocates brought suit in courts and occasionally sponsored picket lines around government buildings to protest gay exclusions from federal employment and military service—the US Armed Forces did not permit openly gay men or women to join.

Even more consequential at this point was the emergence of urban districts—in New York City, San Francisco, Los Angeles, and Chicago—where large numbers of gay men and women lived and could socialize with one another: and where men and women looking for vibrant same-sex environments could seek refuge from repressive and potentially dangerous locations elsewhere. Bookstores, community centers, bars and clubs, bathhouses, and theaters multiplied, offering services, educations, and forms of sociability and sexual pleasure. All of which made for an unexpected and explosive turning point in 1969, beginning with the **Stonewall Uprising** in New York City.

In late June of that year, the New York Police Department decided to raid a gay bar in the Greenwich Village neighborhood named the Stonewall Inn. Raids of bars like Stonewall were not uncommon, as local authorities tried to harass both owners and customers. But this time, the patrons and neighborhood residents fought back when police roughly dragged people out of the bar, provoking a riot that destroyed the Inn, forced the police to retreat, and drew thousands into the streets for three days of protest. "Gay Power" was scrawled on buildings and sidewalks all over the neighborhood, reflecting both anger and a new sense of collective determination. "It was just kind of like everything over the years had come to a head on that one particular night in the one particular place," a participant observed. "Everyone in the crowd felt that we were never going to go back."

Within weeks, gay men and women in New York City, seeking to maintain the momentum

≡ **Gay Power** In the wake of the Stonewall Uprising, New Yorkers formed the Gay Liberation Front (GLF), one of thousands of new homosexual support and advocacy groups founded in the 1970s. Organizations like the GLF helped more gay Americans "come out of the closet" and live openly as homosexual men or women.

of Stonewall, established the **Gay Liberation Front (GLF).** The organization, which evoked the style of other left groups of the time, was dedicated to demanding justice for homosexuals and challenging the sanctity of the heterosexual nuclear family and traditional gender roles, of pushing at the boundaries of conventional sexuality. The ripple effect was notable. By the mid-1970s, gay and lesbian organizations had multiplied, not only in the largest cities along the coasts but also in smaller ones in the interior and in college and university towns where an atmosphere of tolerance and free thinking was better developed. As the decade of the 1970s drew to a close, these organizations could be counted in the thousands, enabling more and more men and women to "come out of the closet" and try to find an accepted place in family and public life. To be sure, a great deal of resistance remained and many hurdles had to be jumped, but the vital groundwork for a broader embrace of sexual differences had been laid.

Struggles in the Southwest

For Americans who understood race simply in terms of Black and white, the Southwest had long confounded the picture. Conquered from Mexico between 1836 and 1846, the subsequent states of Texas, New Mexico, Arizona, and California had large populations of Native and Hispanic descent and borderlands that were easily traversed. Although Mexican Americans were officially citizens under the Fourteenth Amendment (Native Americans were finally granted citizenship in 1924) and, after 1930, were denoted as "white" in the federal census, they suffered discriminatory treatment in work, housing, education, and recreation. They also rubbed shoulders with growing numbers of Mexicans who crossed the border to join family members, find work, or both.

The migration of Mexicans into the United States had become significant during the 1910s as revolution scorched the Mexican countryside (see Chapter 21). It was not unlike previous patterns of immigration. Migrants came to the United States to find work, sent money back to their families at home, and usually planned to return to Mexico at some point. But the proximity of the two nations and the great demand for Mexican labor in the agricultural fields and mines of the Southwest intensified the movement. Mexican immigrants were exempted from the quotas set by the Immigration Act of 1924, and when the manpower mobilizations during World War II exacerbated labor shortages, the United States and Mexico signed a guest worker agreement, known as the **Bracero program**, that offered contract laborers a temporary legal status.

The Bracero program was a flashpoint of conflict on both sides of the border, but especially in the United States. Although agricultural and mining interests in the Southwest benefitted from the influx of Mexican workers, labor unions in the United States complained about the program's effects on the wages and employment opportunities of Americans. What's more, the Bracero program also encouraged undocumented immigrants to cross the border—sometimes swimming across the Rio Grande and other rivers, leading them to be derisively called "wetbacks"—in hopes of finding jobs as well. Thus, in the mid-1950s, the US government both ended the Bracero program and began a crackdown on undocumented immigration known as Operation Wetback. The US-Mexican border, which had long been porous and only minimally regulated, was now to be policed and better secured. This was the beginning of a lengthy and bitter border struggle for people of Mexican descent.

Yet those who had crossed the border and lived even temporarily in the United States faced challenges of their own. They suffered discrimination and segregation in education and housing, and many who worked in the fields, either under the Bracero program or in an undocumented status, were burdened by very low pay, inadequate housing, brutal working conditions, and little protection against extreme exploitation. Indeed, it appeared as though employers had the strong upper hand given the vulnerabilities of Mexican migrants and the long-standing difficulties of organizing agricultural workers.

But as was true among other groups who had been subject to exploitation and discrimination, things began to change by the mid-1960s. Two American-born activists of Mexican descent, Dolores Huerta and Cesar Chavez, founded the **United Farm Workers of America (UFW)**, started to organize field workers, and quickly joined a strike against grape growers in Delano, California (1965). Both Huerta and Chavez had supported Latino civil rights struggles before turning to union building, and Chavez, who had worked in the fields and served in the US Navy, had been influenced (like Martin Luther King) by Mohandas Gandhi's ideas about nonviolent resistance. In 1966, Chavez led a 250-mile march of farm workers from Delano to Sacramento, California, to put their demands for better conditions before the state legislature. Two years later, in 1968, he went on a twenty-five-day hunger strike for justice to dramatize the plight of migrant laborers.

" Across the San Joaquin Valley, across California, across the entire Southwest of the United States, wherever there are Mexican people, wherever there are farm workers, our movement is spreading like flames across a dry plain. Our Pilgrimage is the match that will light our cause for all farm workers to see what is happening here, so that they may do as we have done. The time has come for the liberation of the poor farm worker. History is on our side. MAY THE STRIKE GO ON! VIVA LA CAUSA!"

Cesar Chavez

☰ **Cesar Chavez** Chavez cofounded and led the United Farm Workers (UFW), a labor union for agricultural workers. Taking lessons from the civil rights movement, Chavez used nonviolent protest tactics such as marches and hunger strikes to bring attention to the plight of farm workers in the Southwest.

Democratic presidential candidate Robert F. Kennedy expressed his support for the farm workers, and before too long other major political figures came on board as well.

The struggle would be difficult nonetheless. California's agricultural companies, mostly large-scale corporate enterprises, had millions of dollars to spend attacking the UFW together with the support of the state's new governor, Ronald Reagan, who called the farm workers "barbarians." But Chavez and the UFW had learned a great deal from earlier civil rights activism, and not only organized strikes but also appealed to the American public to support their fight for dignity by boycotting California-grown grapes and other food crops, lettuce in particular, until the employers came to the negotiating table. Boycotts, especially on a national level, are very tough to carry out, but the boycott movement caught on and achieved enough traction to shift the balances of power. By the early 1970s, strikes were spreading across the fields of California and some other states with large agricultural economies, notably Texas, and the effects of the grape and lettuce boycotts were being felt by the growers. Grudgingly, the growers yielded, and agreed to recognize the UFW as the farm workers' representative.

The organizing of the UFW was part of a larger movement for social change that caught fire across the Southwest during the 1960s and early 1970s. Activists embraced an identity they called "**Chicano**" (at one time a derogatory term for those of Mexican descent) and a perspective of themselves as the Indigenous people of a territory they called Aztlan, which had been stolen by the United States in the wake of the US-Mexican War (1846–1848). They advanced a "Plan Espiritual de Aztlan," which emphasized a version of Chicano nationalism (community building and control), and spoke of themselves as a "Bronze People with a Bronze culture." Nowhere was the mobilization more energized or radical than on college campuses, where Mexican Americans began to arrive in growing numbers during the 1960s.

In 1969, in connection with the Plan Espiritual, activists formed the **Movimiento Estudiantil Chicano De Aztlan (MEChA)**, which called for the development of Chicano studies programs and the rejection of a more moderate assimilationism that had long been the goal of Mexican American leaders. With echoes of the Black Power movement, MEChA emphasized the "brownhood of our Aztec and Maya heritage" and spoke of political and economic self-determination. By the early 1970s, MEChA could claim chapters across the Southwest and on other campuses with Chicano students (see Map 27.1).

Red Power

Other than African Americans, no group in American society had suffered the consequences of settler colonialism and the establishment of the American republic

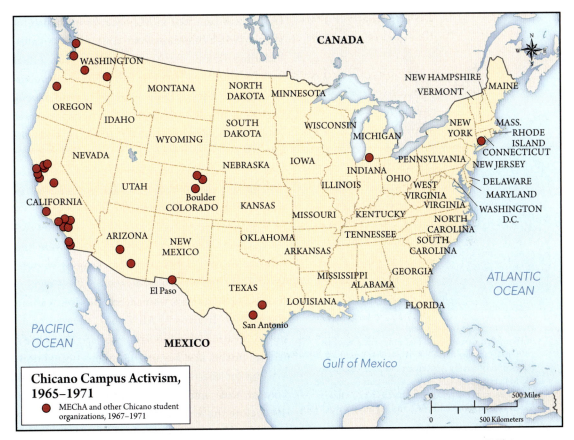

≡ **MAP 27.1   Chicano Campus Activism, 1965–1971**   With echoes of the Black Power movement, MEChA emphasized the "brownhood of our Aztec and Maya heritage" and spoke of political and economic self-determination. MEChA now includes 400 chapters across the United States.

more than the Indigenous inhabitants of the North American continent. Slaughtered by pathogens and warfare, offered no constitutional rights or standing, expelled from their lands, and, in the face of western development, confined to reservations, Indigenous peoples struggled to maintain their cultures, avoid impoverishment, and defend their besieged communities with little to show for what they had endured. Although full citizenship was finally granted by the US Congress in 1924—they alone lacked birthright citizenship under the Fourteenth Amendment—and they received some economic and cultural aid from the New Deal during the 1930s, many found themselves in urban slums, with few job prospects, poor schooling, and police harassment by the 1960s owing to federal efforts to move them off reservations.

But just as the civil rights and antiwar movements energized a variety of social groups that had long faced discrimination, an **American Indian Movement**

≡ **Occupying Wounded Knee**   The occupation of Wounded Knee, South Dakota—the site of an 1890 massacre by the US Army—was one of a series of protests by American Indian movement (AIM) activists in the 1970s. Other sites occupied by protesting Native American activists included Alcatraz Island in California and Plymouth Rock in Massachusetts.

(AIM) was launched in Minneapolis in the fateful year of 1968 by a group of one-time prison inmates, including Dennis Banks. From there they joined with Indian groups in a variety of urban centers composing what they called a **Red Power movement** determined to call public attention to their current plight and advocate not only for economic and educational programs but also for treaty rights that had long been rescinded, land claims that had long been rejected, and the preservation of Indigenous cultures that were rapidly being erased.

As might be expected, the American Indian and Red Power movements took their cues from the projects of civil rights activists, engaging in public protest and civil disobedience. In 1969, eighty-nine Indigenous men, women, and children, calling themselves "Indians of All Tribes," steered boats out to Alcatraz Island in San Francisco Bay, once a federal prison, and began a 19-month occupation. Calling for the return of Alcatraz to Indigenous control, their numbers eventually grew to about 400 before the federal government, cutting off water and power and sending in troops, finally forced them off the island.

But this was only the first in a series of protests that erupted over the next few years, all dramatizing the ways in which the federal government had deprived Indians of their lands, subsistence, cultural heritage, treaty rights, and any secure basis for maintaining their tribal communities. In 1970, while the Alcatraz protest was still going on, AIM activists occupied Plymouth Rock, Massachusetts, and called for a National Day of Mourning to coincide with the American Thanksgiving, hoping to "work towards a more humane America, a more Indian America, where men and nature once again are important, and where Indian values of honor, truth, and brotherhood prevail." Two years later a Trail of Broken Treaties caravan arrived in Washington, DC, and proceeded to occupy the Bureau of Indian Affairs for six days, demanding the restoration of treaty rights and the return of Indigenous lands.

Perhaps most dramatic was a seventy-one-day occupation of Wounded Knee, on the Pine Ridge Reservation in South Dakota, led by Oglala Lakota members of the AIM. Gunfire erupted, casualties were sustained by AIM activists and federal agents, and AIM leaders Dennis Banks and Russell Means were arrested (the charges against them were eventually dropped). The occupation in 1973 laid the basis for a lawsuit that ultimately reached the Supreme Court and resulted in the acknowledgment of government illegality and wrongdoing. Although AIM was disbanded in 1978, in good part because harassment had led to the imprisonment of many of its leaders, the struggle for Indigenous justice and historical recognition remains robust to this day.

27.2   Tremors in National Politics

Compare Nixon's policies on the Vietnam War and his conflicts with the antiwar movement.

The emergence of radical feminism, gay rights, Chicano nationalism, and the American Indian movement took place in an environment of potential shifts in national political power. And not in directions that would likely benefit them. Since the 1930s, the Democratic Party had, with the exception of Dwight Eisenhower's two terms during the 1950s, largely controlled politics at the federal and state levels. They had built an unwieldy coalition of ethnic, Black, and working-class voters in the North and West along with conservative whites in the South. But the election of Richard Nixon to the presidency in 1968 and the unexpected appeal of George Wallace that year also suggested that the winds of change might be blowing from the right as well as the left. Together they made for an enormous political storm.

Nixon as President

Richard Nixon campaigned for the presidency promising to end the Vietnam War, calling for "law and order" in the country, and pursuing a "southern strategy" designed to bring white voters into the Republican Party. He also seemed to represent an alternative to the establishment, eastern wing of the Republican Party, hailing as he did from California, where Republican conservatism was especially strong. But when Nixon became president, Congress was still controlled by Democrats, and moderates were still a force among Republicans.

   In some respects, Nixon's policies were less a radical break from the past than a modification of what liberal Democrats had constructed. Indeed, they suggested that liberal sensibilities about an activist state and the importance

PERSPECTIVES

Real Indians

Beginning with the first encounters with Indigenous peoples, European explorers tended to generalize about "Indians." In similar fashion, many Americans today expect all Indians to look, dress, and speak like the horseback-riding, buffalo-hunting Indians they see on television or in the movies, and Indians who do not fit these images are often regarded as somehow "less Indian." As Colin Calloway reminds us, "some people feel that Indians cannot be Indians if they drive pickup trucks instead of ride horses, live in condos instead of tepees, or wear business suits instead of buckskins."[1] Such ideas freeze Indigenous peoples in an unchanging past.

≡ **"The Crying Indian"**   In 1971, the antilitter organization Keep America Beautiful ran a marketing campaign to promote a cleaner America. The television commercial featured a man dressed in traditional Native American garb who paddles in a birch bark canoe through an increasingly polluted landscape. At the end of the commercial, as cars whiz by on a crowded interstate, a passenger hurls garbage at the man's feet. In a stern voice, the narrator comments: "Some people have a deep, abiding respect for the natural beauty that was once this country. And some people don't." The camera zooms in on the man's face to reveal a single tear falling slowly down his cheek. The commercial aired repeatedly throughout the 1970s, and images of "The Crying Indian" were plastered on billboards and featured in print media. But the success of the Keep America Beautiful commercial should not belie the fact that it was based on the stereotype of the "disappearing Indian." In the commercial, the man paddled his canoe out of the distant past, appearing as a visual relic of an Indigenous people that had long since vanished. The "Crying Indian" was an anachronism who did not belong in modern society (he was not even a real Native American: the actor was an Italian American).

[1]Colin G. Calloway, *First Peoples: A Documentary Survey of American Indian History* (Boston: Bedford/St. Martin's, 2004), 495.

≡ **"Have You Ever Seen a Real Indian?"** In 2001, the American Indian Tribal College Fund launched a campaign to combat persistent stereotyping about Native Americans. The ad featured Dr. Lori Arviso Alvord, the first Navajo woman to be board certified for surgery and former associate dean at Dartmouth Medical School. Other ads in the campaign featured Rick West, founding director of the National Museum of the American Indian, and director and screenwriter Dean Bear Claw.

CONSIDER THIS

Most negative stereotypes about Native Americans stem from decades of oppression. But even positive stereotypes hold people to different standards that tend to dehumanize them. The image of "The Crying Indian" who lives in harmony with nature may appear positive, but how is it also negative? How did the Indian College Fund campaign counter stereotypes like "The Crying Indian"?

of social safety nets had established something of a consensus across partisan lines. The Nixon administration looked to promote public transit (among other things the Amtrak rail system was created); provide a guaranteed annual income of $1,600 to poor American families (an alternative to welfare); support health care reform (opposed to a single-payer approach that had surfaced in Congress); tolerate gestures in the direction of open housing and **affirmative action**; and endorse the Equal Rights Amendment (as had been done by both parties since the 1940s). When inflation began to threaten the economy, the Nixon administration imposed wage and price controls and soon took the country off the gold standard that had been in place since 1900. With the country's heightened concern over the threats of environmental pollution to water, forests, and wildlife following the 1962 publication of Rachel Carson's *Silent Spring*, Nixon (though not himself an ardent environmentalist) addressed Congress on the topic of the environment and proposed the establishment of a new federal agency that would consolidate many of the environmental responsibilities of the federal government. The goal of the **Environmental Protection Agency (EPA)** was to be able to address environmental problems more efficiently; Congress approved the new agency in 1970, and between 1970 and 1974, Nixon and Congress approved a variety of bills to safeguard the environment, including the Clean Air Act, the Endangered Species Act, and the Safe Drinking Water Act.

But Nixon also embraced what he called the "New Federalism," an idea that power and resources should devolve from the federal government to the states and localities where programs would then be administered (Congress was hostile to this and little happened). And he did move to undercut Great Society programs such as the Office of Economic Opportunity and the Job Corps, and to hamstring the Housing and Urban Development (HUD) agency, which was attempting to address the urban crisis. In a sense, the Nixon administration accepted the political world that the New Deal had built and the Great Society enlarged—spending on Social Security, Medicare, and Medicaid increased under his watch—while limiting Great Society initiatives that had been designed to assist people of color and the poor. It was a policy package meant to appeal to white voters who had previously been Democrats but believed that initiatives in the direction of African Americans had gone "too far." Nixon's selection of conservative Maryland governor Spiro Agnew, who ridiculed liberals and protesters as "nattering nabobs of negativism," as his vice president and his attempt to appoint two Supreme Court justices (Clement Haynesworth and G. Harrold Carswell) with records as segregationists (they were not confirmed), were clearly nods to white southerners and resentful whites more generally.

The War in Vietnam and at Home

Recognizing public frustrations over the Vietnam War, Nixon campaigned for the presidency in 1968 insisting that he would end the war and had a "secret plan" to do it (he didn't). But the antiwar movement in the United States, which had been swaying public opinion for several years, ramped up the pressure in 1969, holding massive demonstrations across the country and in Washington, DC. Although Nixon had little patience for the demonstrators, he knew that he had to act or go the way of the previous administration.

Bombs Away President Nixon began withdrawing US troops from Vietnam while increasing American bombing raids. Bombing soon extended beyond Vietnam as Nixon targeted Laos and Cambodia for attack as well, violating international law. The tons of bombs dropped on these countries dwarfed numbers from previous conflicts.

Nixon's approach, developed in part by his National Security Advisor Henry Kissinger, was what they called "peace with honor." This meant extricating the United States from the war without it looking like an American defeat. To do this, Nixon and Kissinger determined on a course of "Vietnamization": withdrawing many of the American troops, turning more of the fighting over to South Vietnamese soldiers, increasing financial support for the South Vietnamese government, and launching the massive bombardment of North Vietnam as well as of neighboring Cambodia and Laos to knock out what the administration insisted were North Vietnamese supply lines to the south. The bombing of Cambodia and Laos violated international law and thus was conducted secretly, but it was designed to force the North Vietnamese government to negotiate a truce on terms the Nixon administration could accept.

If Nixon and Kissinger thought that dropping thousands of bombs on North Vietnam, Cambodia, and Laos would demoralize the North Vietnamese leadership, they were badly mistaken. The North Vietnamese had been fighting against Euro-American powers, first the French and then the United States, since the end of World War II and had shown enormous determination even in the face of great losses. They knew the government of South Vietnam was weak and the United States was looking for an end to an unwinnable war. Secret negotiations between the two sides did begin in late 1969, but they quickly bogged down owing to the toughness of the North (they wanted an opportunity to control all of Vietnam and pushed for elections they expected to win) and the resistance of the South to any concessions that might give the North the upper hand.

From the first, Nixon regarded antiwar activists as his enemies: he saw them as part of a large wave of disruptive radicalism, including Black militants and left-wing college students, that threatened his administration and angered his political base. As a result, he authorized the expansion of a federal **Counter Intelligence Program (COINTELPRO)** and directed it to infiltrate a raft of organizations on the left, while local police created their own squads to harass and intimidate radicals and protestors within their jurisdictions. The FBI also became involved, and undercover agents secreted their way into political meetings, often to encourage violence and internal conflict. The **Black Panthers**, who mixed community activism with revolutionary rhetoric denouncing American imperialism (a manifestation of the antiwar movement), became special targets: nearly thirty, including Chicago leader Fred Hampton, were murdered and many hundreds were arrested. It was an indication of Nixon's willingness to embrace political repression and the clandestine networks through which his administration readily worked.

Even so, antiwar protests intensified as bombs rained down on Southeast Asia, and they were no longer erupting only in major cities and on elite college campuses. The spring of 1970 witnessed such a large wave of protest that many colleges had to close down for the semester. In May, the demonstrations turned lethal: first at Kent State University in Ohio where Ohio National Guardsmen shot and killed four unarmed students, and then at historically Black, Jackson State University in Mississippi, where two students died and more than ten others were injured.

≡ **Four Dead in Ohio** President Nixon's bombing campaigns helped spark renewed antiwar protest. A 1970 protest at Kent State University in Ohio culminated in violence when Ohio National Guard troops opened fire on the demonstrators, killing four and injuring nine more. Mary Ann Vecchio screams as she kneels over the body of Kent State University student Jeffrey Miller. This photo, taken by John Filo, won the Pulitzer Prize.

China and the Soviet Union

Nixon's debacle in Vietnam followed a long-standing bipartisan effort to contain the expansion of communism and socialism even when a military victory proved unattainable. After all, Nixon had made a reputation in national politics as a Cold Warrior and vehement anticommunist. That certainly seemed evident when socialist Salvador Allende was democratically elected as president in Chile in 1970, and Nixon first imposed economic sanctions and then supported (through the CIA) a Chilean military coup on September 11, 1973, that overthrew Allende and claimed his life. General Augusto Pinochet, who directed the coup, stepped in and not only reversed Allende's socialist policies with the help of University of Chicago–educated economists but also assumed dictatorial powers, initiating a regime of brutal repression against Allende's supporters.

But when it came to superpower politics, Nixon made a remarkable shift. Ever since the communists won their revolution and established the People's Republic of China (PRC) under the leadership of Mao Zedong in 1949, Nixon had supported their diplomatic isolation. The United States only recognized the pro-Western regime in Taiwan (which had been defeated and driven off the mainland by Mao) and opposed admitting the PRC to membership in the United Nations. During the 1950s, as senator and vice president, he happily attacked Democrats for "losing" China to the communists.

Yet, much as anticommunist politicians tried to paint the PRC and the Soviet Union as a unified communist bloc, it had become increasingly clear by the mid-1960s that they were more rivals than allies, with their own objectives and conflicting ambitions. Understanding this, Nixon saw an opportunity to shake up the global stage and reorient American policies. With Kissinger as a go-between, Nixon laid plans for a historic visit. He would travel to the PRC in late February 1972 and meet both Mao Zedong and second-in-command Zhou Enlai, hoping to normalize relations with China that had been closed down for almost a quarter century. It was, Nixon rightly crowed, a "week that changed the world."

Soviet leaders were shocked by Nixon's move and feared a US-China alliance in the making, to their detriment. But Nixon had another card to play. In May, he became the first American president to travel to Moscow (FDR had once visited

≡ **Nixon and Mao** President Nixon greets Chairman Mao Zedong of the People's Republic of China. Although Nixon had supported the diplomatic isolation of China for over twenty years, he reversed course, shaking up the global stage and reorienting US foreign policy.

elsewhere in the Soviet Union) where he met with Soviet Premier Leonid Brezhnev. Their "summit" ranged across a number of issues, including East-West trade, and ended with them signing two arms control treaties—the **Strategic Arms Limitation Treaty (SALT)**, which limited offensive nuclear weapons, and the **Anti-Ballistic Missile Treaty (ABM),** which limited defensive anti-ballistic missile systems. They also issued a declaration for future cooperation in the direction of disarmament. These were two remarkable moments in a dangerous Cold War.

27.3   Watergate

Discuss the making of the Watergate scandal and the outcome that led Nixon to resign the presidency.

Although the American economy was showing signs of shakiness and the Vietnam War was still dragging on, Nixon's foreign policy successes in the Soviet Union and especially in China would seem to have bolstered his confidence as he looked to reelection in 1972. His ability to mix continuity on certain forms of federal power, including the reinforcement of social safety nets, with actions that would appeal to disgruntled white ethnic voters, suggested the makings of a longer-term strategy for himself and the Republican Party. At the same time, Nixon's easy resort to political repression against those he imagined as his enemies hinted at a dark and possibly paranoid underside, one made all the more worrisome given the power that the presidency and the executive branch of government had accumulated since the 1930s. The result would be catastrophic for him and the country, a political moment that would cast a very long and dark shadow.

Election of 1972

For Democrats, the war in Vietnam held center stage during the presidential election campaign of 1972. Smarting from their defeat in 1968 and the divisions the war created among them, Democrats moved to make the nomination process more open, tied to state primaries rather than dealings behind closed doors. The result was the emergence of George McGovern, a senator from the state of South Dakota, who energized the party's antiwar wing while alienating long-time party bosses accustomed to choosing the standard-bearer themselves. McGovern demanded an immediate end to the war and sought to appeal to progressive Democrats.

McGovern's main rivals were Edmund Muskie, a senator from Maine who had run for vice president on Hubert Humphrey's ticket in 1968, and George Wallace, who decided to seek the Democratic nomination by courting white ethnic resentments but was seriously wounded in an assassination attempt in May (yet another incident of political violence); he had to drop out of the race after winning primaries in Florida, Michigan, and Maryland. When the Democratic convention, which now included a far greater diversity of delegates than ever before, threw its support to McGovern, some of the old established leaders, especially from organized labor and big cities like Chicago, who scorned the antiwar movement, effectively decided to sit out the election.

Branded as a radical out of touch with the American mainstream by some Democrats as well as Republicans, McGovern was therefore in a weakened position to begin with. Matters only became worse when his running mate, Senator Thomas Eagleton of Missouri, was forced off the ticket when news surfaced that he had suffered from depression and been treated with electroshock therapy (McGovern then chose Sargent Shriver, who had run the Peace Corps and was a member of the Kennedy family, to replace Eagleton). By the time election day arrived, Nixon had a commanding lead and won a landslide victory, with over 60 percent of the popular vote and the electoral vote of forty-nine states (all except for Massachusetts and the District of Columbia): this despite the ratification of the Twenty-Sixth Amendment (1971) to the Constitution, which lowered the voting age from twenty-one to eighteen. Apparently, the youth vote was more conservative than many observers assumed.

But there was an unsettling episode along the way. The Republican Party and many of Nixon's aides had established, very early on, the **Committee to Re-Elect the President (CREEP)**, which ran a "dirty tricks" campaign to undercut the Democrats. It reflected Nixon's worries about his leadership and support and his paranoia about potential opponents, especially Edward Kennedy, the Massachusetts senator whose brothers John and Robert had both been assassinated. CREEP circulated false letters and charges, traded in rumors, tried to blame the Wallace assassination attempt on the McGovern campaign, and constructed an "enemies list" of prominent politicians, journalists, and celebrities who were targeted for harassment.

In mid-June 1972 men hired by CREEP burglarized the offices of the Democratic National Committee (DNC) in Washington, DC's **Watergate Hotel**. They were searching for damaging information in the DNC's files, not unlike other operations that CREEP had already conducted. But this time they were caught by a security guard and arrested. Nixon immediately denied any knowledge or involvement—his press secretary called it a "third-rate burglary"—but he pressured the CIA to block a pending FBI investigation of the incident. Not much more was made of the break-in during the campaign, and Nixon imagined that the situation was destined to be forgotten.

The Cover-Up

Nixon probably did not order the break-in at the Watergate Hotel, but his attempt to cover it up was his big mistake and the beginning of his end in office. Owing in good part to the reporting of Bob Woodward and Carl Bernstein, who worked for the *Washington Post*, more and more information about CREEP's activities began to filter out. Some of the most important leads came by way of an FBI insider who kept his identity secret: he was simply known as "Deep Throat" (his real name, Mark Felt, was only revealed in 2005). Before too long Congress began an investigation that increasingly implicated close aides in Nixon's administration and encouraged others to come forward to testify and possibly reduce their own legal liabilities.

Nixon attempted to cut his losses and keep the investigation away from the White House by firing some of his advisors and invoking "executive privilege": the power that the president has under the Constitution to resist demands from other branches of the federal government, especially Congress. But the courts called him to account, particularly after one administrative official admitted to Congress that Nixon taped conversations in the Oval Office. Once the Supreme Court ordered Nixon to hand over all the tapes, which showed clear evidence of him orchestrating a cover-up, defying Congress, and obstructing justice, the pressure mounted. The House of Representatives had begun to consider the question of impeachment in early 1974, and in late July its Judiciary Committee passed three articles of impeachment (effectively presidential indictments) for obstruction of justice, abuse of power, and contempt of Congress. The full House would soon vote on these and, if passed, the Senate would decide whether to remove Nixon from office.

Nixon's Resignation

The erosion of Nixon's position as president raised the issue of succession, but that had already become complicated. Spiro T. Agnew, Nixon's vice president, had gotten into legal trouble, not for anything related to Watergate, but for taking bribes and evading taxes while he was governor of Maryland. In the fall of 1973, as Watergate was becoming increasingly perilous to Nixon, Agnew was forced to resign. Nixon then appointed Gerald Ford, the House minority leader from Michigan, as his new vice president.

With articles of impeachment passed by the House Judiciary Committee and the White House tapes plainly demonstrating the validity of the charges—he explicitly told his aides to "stonewall" and "cover up" the investigations—it was apparent to Republican leaders that Nixon's fate was sealed. Led by Senator Barry Goldwater (AZ), they went to the White House in early August and told Nixon that there was nothing more they could do, that he would be impeached by the House and then convicted by the Senate. The next day, August 8, Richard Nixon resigned the presidency and Gerald Ford took the oath of office. Never before had a US president resigned or left office under circumstances of wrongdoing.

Ford attempted to turn the political page. With somber tones he told the country, as Nixon departed, "our long national nightmare is over." But maybe not. One month later, unexpectedly and to the shock of many Americans, Ford issued Nixon a blanket pardon for all federal crimes he committed or may have committed. This meant that Nixon could not be prosecuted for laws he likely broke as president when, it seemed, the Constitution protected him from indictment. It surely looked as though a deal had been cut, and whether or not this was the case (the matter is disputed to this day), the "national nightmare" of Watergate and the abuse of power that it exposed would remain deeply imprinted on the American political consciousness.

The End of a Presidency   Tourists outside the White House learn of President Nixon's imminent resignation. Nixon remains the only president to have ever abdicated the office. Had he remained, he likely would have become the second president (after Andrew Johnson) to face impeachment proceedings.

27.4   Swirls of Trouble

Explain the reasons for the growing backlash against civil rights and feminism.

The Watergate scandals and investigations hung over the country for most of 1973 and 1974, but other developments were erupting at the time which, much as Watergate, would mark destabilizations of the postwar political world. They suggested that the moves made in the direction of civil rights and gender equality would generate strong opposition as well as strong support, heralding conservative sensibilities at the grassroots and in unexpected places. They also suggested that the economic conditions—robust growth aided by federal policies—making for prosperity and an expanding middle class may have run their course and would cast many Americans onto unsettling seas.

Busing and Its Discontents

Ever since the Supreme Court declared school segregation unconstitutional in 1954, school districts struggled over the issue of implementation (see Chapter 25). It was one thing to decide that laws mandating segregated schools had to be over- turned; it was quite another to construct plans for integration or to take on the challenges of racial segregation when they were products, as in the northern and western United States, not of laws (de jure) but of residential patterns and other fac- ets of day-to-day life (de facto). Segregation and racial discrimination, that is, knew no regional boundaries but might need to be fought with a variety of weapons.

The challenges of desegregation were all the more daunting because many white parents wished to keep their children out of desegregated schools. Some enrolled their children in private schools; many more moved out of urban districts subject to desegregation orders and found homes in the overwhelmingly white suburbs (known as "white flight"). But in large metropolitan districts, whether in the south- ern states or elsewhere, integration had to take account of school district lines that had been drawn explicitly to maintain racial separation. And one of the solutions was to bus children across those lines to effectively create school integration where none had previously existed.

Children had ridden buses to school in the United States for decades, and ini- tially federal courts offered support for busing plans. In *Milliken v. Bradley* (1971), one such court supported an NAACP lawsuit to use state-mandated busing to de- segregate school districts in Detroit and many of the surrounding areas. That same year, the Supreme Court, in *Swann v. Charlotte-Mecklenburg Board of Education*, seemed to uphold the use of busing as a tool for integration.

Yet, although the Nixon administration initially agreed to sustain school deseg- regation, Nixon soon denounced what he called "forced busing." He was plainly responding to growing opposition to busing, especially among ethnic whites (some Black parents objected to busing as well), who opposed racial integration and mobilized behind the idea of neighborhood schools and community control of education. Nixon was also wary of how the busing issue energized the George Wallace campaign during the 1972 election. But Nixon's critique of busing gave a green light to those who would push back.

Some of the strongest opposition to busing occurred in Boston, Massachusetts, a city with a liberal reputation but one that had long been tarnished by racial division and discriminatory districting. There a busing plan overseen by a federal district judge created a firestorm of protest, especially in the predominately Irish American neighborhoods of South Boston (known as "Southie"). Led by Louise Day Hicks, who helped establish the antibusing organization Restore Our Alienated Rights (ROAR), busing opponents conducted marches and sit-ins (strange homage to the civil rights movement) while engaging in acts of violence against the buses, those viewed as busing supporters, and the integrated schools themselves.

≡ **Antibusing March** White protestors in South Boston march to protest racial integration in public schools. The shamrocks on the protester's sign reference the Irish heritage of many South Boston residents and highlight the racial and ethnic divisions in the city.

The federal judge stayed the course, and busing continued. But white flight swept through Boston as it had in other affected cities, and there were soon signs that the federal judiciary was moving in different directions too. During his first term, Nixon had the opportunity to make four appointments to the Supreme Court. And although the segregationists failed confirmation, he was able to name other conservatives as the new justices: Warren Burger, Harry Blackmun, Lewis Powell, and William Rehnquist, two of whom (Powell and Rehnquist) had records of opposition to civil rights. Thus, when *Milliken v. Bradley* came to the Court on appeal in 1974, the justices struck down the busing plan by a 5–4 vote. It was an early indication of resistance to federal power in the area of racial equality, and support for local efforts to preserve "communities."

Backlash Against Feminism

While the feminist critique of women's subordination in the household and confinement to motherhood energized a growing number of educated, mostly middle-class women, it also struck a raw nerve among many other women who accepted traditional gender roles and found measures of protection and comfort within them. Some were Catholic or influenced by a rising tide of evangelical Protestantism; some lived in communities that looked upon expanding liberal politics with disfavor and felt threatened by new attitudes about sexuality and abortion, not to mention about the implications of the Equal Rights Amendment.

These women found a powerful voice in Phyllis Schlafly. Growing up in a prosperous Catholic family in St. Louis and receiving a graduate degree from Harvard, Schlafly became involved in conservative politics in the early 1960s—strongly supporting Barry Goldwater in 1964—and then emerged as a lightning rod for the backlash against feminism in the early 1970s. In 1972, Schlafly founded **STOP ERA** (STOP stood for "Stop Taking Our Privileges,") a lobbying organization devoted to defending the "traditional family" and defeating the ERA, which had already been passed by Congress and ratified by many of the states. Through her grassroots organizing, especially among Christian conservatives in the South, Schlafly was one of the first to make the conservative "family values" sentiment a polarizing issue.

It seemed like an uphill fight, but Schlafly took the battle to the states and localities and, in the process, catalyzed a reaction that was clearly brewing under the surface. Schlafly represented the STOP ERA movement as standing up for "family values" and against the elimination of gender distinctions that, she insisted, the ERA embodied. She warned that women would lose important benefits, be thrown on their own resources, and be subject to the military draft as men were. She argued that feminism belittled housewives and the lives they chose to lead, made middle-aged women vulnerable to enhance the prospects of the young and career-oriented, and questioned the authority they had gained in the home and over child-rearing. In effect, Schlafly warned that feminism and the ERA would shift power away from women rather than bring it to them.

The STOP ERA campaign began after the ERA had been passed by Congress and sent to the states for ratification. Some states almost immediately ratified it, and momentum was building for achieving the requisite thirty-eight (three-fourths of the fifty states) needed for ratification. But Schlafly and STOP first slowed the momentum and then helped turn it around. Although a few more states ratified the ERA, five (Idaho, Nebraska, Tennessee, Kentucky, and South Dakota) would vote to revoke their ratifications, and as the decade of the 1970s came to an end, the ERA had failed ratification and faced very dim prospects of getting over the bar of thirty-eight states (see Map 27.2).

Schlafly, along with organizations like Happiness of Women, did a remarkable job of both derailing a movement that appeared on the verge of a significant political and constitutional victory and finding a language to challenge feminism and the liberal/radical values it appeared to represent. In this way, antifeminism—like antibusing—were not only responses to social movements for change in American society; they were also building blocks of a new conservative politics that would soon be rearing its head on the national stage.

≡ **MAP 27.2 Ratifying the Equal Rights Amendment** Stiff opposition in the South and parts of the West crippled the Equal Rights Amendment (ERA). The deadline to ratify the ERA passed in 1982, but efforts to revive it continue.

27.5 Economic Instability and the Neoliberal Turn

|| Describe the developing economic crises of the 1970s and the rise of a neoliberal approach to governance.

The crisis atmosphere of the 1970s was not only produced by backlashes against civil rights and feminism or by Watergate. It was also produced, and deepened, by a changing and weakening American economy. New competition in the international marketplace and the effort to pay for both the Vietnam War and social programs at home without raising taxes combined to undercut economic growth, increase inflation, and raise unemployment. Corporate employers looked, as well, for the opportunity to recover many of the gains that organized labor had won for working people over the years, especially in the industrial sector, provoking bitter strikes. On top of it all, Americans' dependence on fossil fuels—especially oil—for their energy needs was revealed in painful ways, as Middle Eastern oil producers flexed their muscles, creating shortages and major price hikes. It appeared to many as though a lengthy era of prosperity was coming to an end and an uncertain future was hovering over the country. And it appeared as though a new political orientation in policymaking circles, and new arguments about where power should lie, was beginning to be forged.

A New Economic Playing Field

The economic destabilizations of the 1970s were, in part, the unanticipated product of policies the United States had devised. When World War II ended, American business and political leaders worried that the country might slip back into the economic doldrums of the 1930s. After all, trading partners across the Atlantic and, potentially, the Pacific had been devastated by the war while the American economy itself had to shift from a wartime to a peacetime footing. To limit such a risk, the United States sent billions of dollars in economic assistance through the Marshall Plan to war-torn Western Europe as well as various forms of aid to Japan during the American occupation (see Chapter 25).

It all worked extremely well. That was now the problem. By the early 1970s, European and Asian economies were thriving and increasingly able to compete with the United States. European and Korean-made steel, Japanese-made cars, German-made ships, and Taiwanese-made electronics began to arrive in the American market, their appeal boosted by rising inflation that increased the prices of domestically made goods. In 1971, the country posted an unfavorable

☰ **Japanese Cars**   Low-cost Datsun models produced by Japanese car manufacturer Nissan await transportation for sale at an American port sometime in the 1970s. Although American foreign aid had been critical in assisting war-torn countries like Germany and Japan recover from World War II, American manufacturers now had to compete with quality imports from these countries.

balance of trade—meaning that the value of foreign imports exceeded that of American exports—for the first time since the late nineteenth century. It was a sign that American economic power, although still formidable, was not quite what it used to be.

American industrialists responded in a number of ways. To begin with, they attempted to maintain or increase profit margins by cutting labor costs. They could do this by replacing workers with new machinery, accelerating the pace of work (known as "speed-up") so that the same number of workers would produce more goods, or reducing benefits like health care. Some corporations moved to do all of this. But there was a price to be paid. Workers in the heavily unionized mass-production industries, like automobiles, steel, and coal mining, pushed back and went out on strike in near record numbers. Sometimes they even defied their own union bosses and engaged in what were known as "wildcat" strikes. At other times they might try to displace those bosses with more militant and dem-ocratically inclined leaders. Mineworker and steelworker unions were especially roiled by these tensions.

More effective in the long run was relocation. Rather than struggle with or-ganized workers, industrialists and other large employers could move their op-erations to sections of the country, such as the Sunbelt, where labor costs and taxes were low, unions were weak or marginalized, and local governments were staunchly pro-business. A foundation had already been established during World War II, when a booming—and federally financed—defense sector began devel-oping in Texas, Arizona, and southern California at the expense of places like Bridgeport, Connecticut, Chicago, and Detroit. Industrialists also began to look across American borders, to Canada, Mexico, the Dominican Republic, and Hong Kong, for the assembly of automobiles, the production of textiles, and the man-ufacture of electrical appliances, especially televisions, radios, and stereophonic equipment.

Together, these initiatives advanced the deindustrialization of the Northeast and Midwest, and as American manufacturers shed workers and closed plants, these areas formed a growing **Rust Belt**. This, in turn, weakened the labor unions that had helped increase incomes and living standards for the American working class. Over two and a half decades after World War II, the United States had achieved a global economic supremacy built around robust manufacturing, a strong dollar, significant levels of unionization, and federal investment. Now, the industrial sector was in decline, the service sector (where wages were sub-stantially lower) was on the rise, the value of the dollar was fluctuating against foreign currencies, and unions were being hobbled by aggressive employers. As **globalization**, or the free flow of goods, ideas, and information throughout the world, increased, the United States was faced with different economic challenges. A new playing field of power was emerging, which did not bode well for the future of most Americans, while a new perspective on markets and the role of the state was emerging along with it.

Neoliberalism and the Carter Administration

The Keynesian economic orientation that took hold during the New Deal and dominated economic policy through the 1960s always had its critics. Conservative politicians and economists during the 1930s complained of the federal government's overreach, what they regarded as "socialistic" programs, and heavy-handed taxation and regulation. But their ideas only began to gain traction during the 1960s and especially during the economic troubles of the 1970s. Although they were unable to account for the new phenomenon of **stagflation** (economic slowdown and high rates of inflation—recessions and depressions usually brought deflation, or price declines), they began to blame the very prosperity that postwar economic growth had achieved (see Table 27.1). Led by thinkers like Milton Friedman of the University of Chicago and by publications like *Fortune* magazine and *Business Week*, they looked to disrupt the Keynesian mindset and push the country in a different policy direction: to find a new form of economic liberalism, like the liberalism of the nineteenth century, that was more attentive to promoting the freedom and power of markets. The new liberalism would eventually be known as "neoliberalism."

Table 27.1 Stagflation, 1970–1980			
Year	**Inflation % Change**	**Annual Unemployment Rate %**	**Combined %**
1970	5.9	4.9	10.8
1971	4.3	5.9	10.2
1972	3.3	5.6	8.9
1973	6.2	4.9	11.1
1974	11.0	5.6	16.6
1975	9.1	8.5	17.6
1976	5.8	7.7	13.5
1977	6.5	7.1	13.6
1978	7.7	6.1	13.8
1979	11.3	5.8	17.1
1980	13.5	7.1	20.6

Why did they believe that the economy was in trouble? Chief among their complaints were the higher wages that workers had won. "The greatest problem facing the Western world in the early 1970s," *Fortune* intoned, "is cost-push inflation powered by excessive wage increases." So long as unions remained strong, employers would not be able to exert the necessary "discipline" to hold wages and benefits in check, cast doubt on the virtues of full employment, bring down inflation, and raise profits. This is to say that in the new economic thinking of the early 1970s, inflation was made to replace unemployment as the most serious threat facing the United States.

Some of the fruits of this thinking would be seen, not so much in the administration of Gerald Ford, who became president when Nixon resigned, but in the subsequent administration of Democrat Jimmy Carter, who defeated Ford in a close election in 1976. Carter was new to the national political stage. He was from rural Georgia and in the peanut farming business, graduated from the Naval Academy at Annapolis where he had studied nuclear engineering, and had been elected Georgia's governor in 1970 on a campaign against racial discrimination. Although a longshot, he managed to win the Democratic Party's presidential nomination, suggesting that, after McGovern's disastrous defeat in 1972, a white southern moderate who would speak of new "limits" to federal initiatives and keep traditional Democratic "interests" like labor unions at arm's length could win.

Carter was the first Democrat to hold the presidency since the 1930s who focused on reducing inflation and cutting federal expenditures. Although he took rising unemployment seriously (it was at just over 7 percent), Carter and his advisors saw rising inflation as a more serious problem (it was 6.5 percent when he took office and peaked at over 11 percent two years later). He therefore hoped to keep the lid on both wages and prices, cut the size of the federal budget, and deregulate the banking, airlines, trucking, and communications industries to promote competition. Liberal Democrats were unsettled, while conservatives generally expressed their support. But the economic crisis that Carter faced, worsened by gasoline shortages and price spikes, seemed resistant even to these measures.

So, in the summer of 1979, President Carter addressed the nation. He did not offer new policies or programs. Instead, he spoke of a "crisis of confidence" across the land, a deadening of national "spirit" and "will," a loss of "unity of purpose," an excessive materialism that, he believed, made it difficult for Americans to surmount the problems that were bedeviling them. It sounded like a sermon befitting Carter's southern Baptist roots, and for a short time it seemed to strike a resonant chord. But what is known as the "malaise" speech (although, as we saw earlier in this chapter, he never used that word in it) and Carter himself were soon overtaken by events he could not control.

MAPPING AMERICA

Rust Belt and White Flight

The changing and weakening American economy of the 1970s brought about shifts in how people worked and where they lived. By the time the decade drew to a close, a new economic and political framework of power and policy was under construction, marking out a major transition for the country. The efforts made by the federal government to redress imbalances in economic and social life through public policies generated a backlash from white Americans who had benefitted from government initiatives in the past but now saw racial minorities making gains at their own expense. These two maps chart these developments at national and local levels.

Thinking Geographically

The economic and demographic landscape of the United States was transformed in the 1970s. By the end of the decade, fewer than 25 percent of workers belonged to a union. At the same time, the populations of Florida, Texas, California, and other Sunbelt states soared.

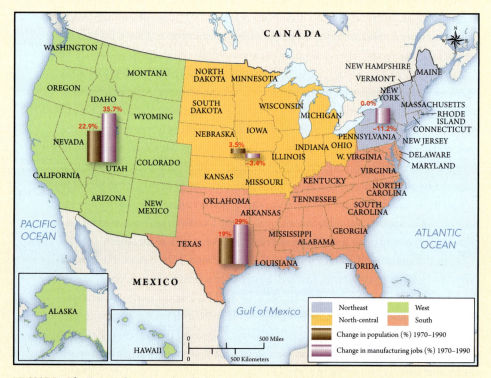

≡ **MAP 1**   **The Rust Belt**   Economic decline transformed America's regions as more and more people abandoned the cold and expensive northern states for the low taxes and booming economies of the Sunbelt. By 1980 the Northeast and Midwest had shed thousands of manufacturing jobs.

1. How do these maps show the effects of deindustrialization at both national and local levels? Do the maps show a connection between deindustrialization and white flight?

2. What impact do you think the population shifts shown on these maps had on national politics? On local politics?

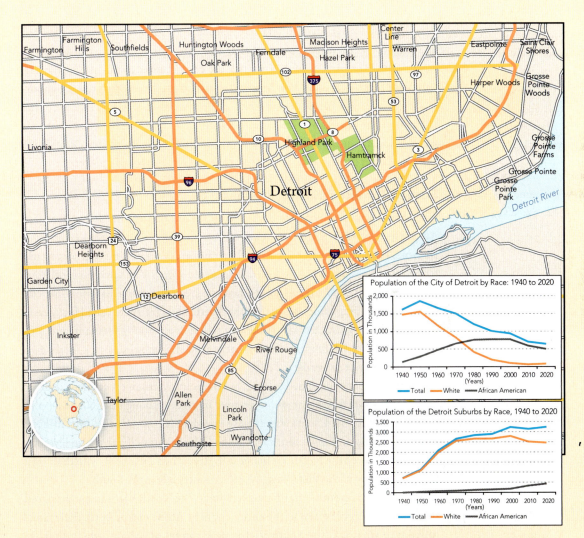

≡ **MAP 2   White Flight: Detroit, Michigan**   The destabilizations of the 1960s and 1970s brought about white flight in all major American cities, but no city experienced white flight as dramatically as Detroit. The population of "Motor City" was just under two million in 1950. It was the nation's fourth largest city with a thriving manufacturing sector—nearly half of the world's cars and trucks were produced in its metropolitan area. It was also overwhelmingly white. But beginning in the 1950s, the postwar baby boom, government policies that encouraged home ownership, highway construction, and the fear of racial integration contributed to an immense white flight to the suburbs. In 1980, the white population of Detroit was just 15% of what it had been in 1950. During the same period the white population of Detroit's suburbs grew by 80%, to 2,700,000.

27.6 Storms Abroad

Describe how international events contributed to the crises of the 1970s.

When Jimmy Carter gave his "malaise" speech, the United States was embroiled in a major crisis overseas, and one that had a number of immediate consequences for Americans in all parts of the country. The crisis erupted in the Middle Eastern nation of Iran, a long-time American ally, but it also reflected the growing importance of the Middle East for the reach of US power abroad as well as for the configurations of power at home. The crisis came on top of a decade of destabilizations, which included the ending of the Vietnam War, and, before it was done, would help sink the Carter presidency and usher in a new era of conservative power.

Ending America's Longest War

Congress never formally declared war against the North Vietnamese, but if we date American involvement from the Gulf of Tonkin Resolution in 1964 (American advisors were already on the ground there for several years), the war was nearly ten years old in early 1973, when American and North Vietnamese negotiators, Henry Kissinger and Le Duc Tho, reached an agreement after a massive American December bombing campaign against the North. The agreement called for a cease-fire, the withdrawal of the last American troops from South Vietnam, and ultimately the "peaceful" reunification of Vietnam itself. Signed in Paris, it was known as the **Paris Peace Accords**.

American troops continued to leave, but the South Vietnamese regime dug in its heels and the North Vietnamese responded in kind. Although the Nixon administration had promised South Vietnamese President Nguyen Van Thieu continued American support, antiwar sentiment in the United States effectively tied Nixon's hands and allowed the North Vietnamese to strengthen their hold, with their own troops and those of the Viet Cong, over the countryside in the South.

By early 1975, months after Nixon left office, the North Vietnamese prepared to complete their conquest of the entire country. At the end of April, their tanks rolled into what was the South Vietnamese capital of Saigon, which they renamed Ho Chi Minh City, for their great leader (who had died in 1969), while President Thieu fled. On April 30, the last Americans were evacuated, under fire and by helicopter, from the US Embassy. Over a decade in duration, the war in Vietnam was the longest, by far, to that point, in American history. And although "peace with honor" was the goal, the war in fact ended in defeat for the United States.

Israel, the Arab States, and Oil

The face of the modern Middle East was produced, first, by World War I, when the Ottoman Empire was destroyed and the lands of Palestine and Greater Persia were carved up under European auspices, and then by the creation of the state of Israel in 1948 after a bitter war with Palestinian inhabitants and surrounding Arab countries. A magnet for European Jews who survived the Holocaust, Israel was recognized by the Truman administration the next year and admitted to membership in the United Nations. But tensions continued to simmer among the Palestinians, many of whom had been displaced and now resided in Jordan, and their Arab allies who refused to recognize the legitimacy of the Israeli state.

The tensions percolated during the 1950s and 1960s and then exploded into war in June 1967, pitting Israel against a coalition of Egypt, Syria, and Jordan. The war lasted a mere six days—it became known as the **Six-Day War**—as Israeli air and ground power not only hobbled the Arab coalition militarily but succeeded in occupying the Sinai Peninsula to the west, the West Bank of the Jordan River and the Old City of Jerusalem to the east, and the Golan Heights to the north, greatly expanding the territorial reach of Israel. Many, many more Palestinians fled their homes in Israel, most to nearby Jordan, and the Israelis now emerged, not simply as a contested nation-state but also as an occupying power.

The relations between Israel and the United States had deepened in the two decades following Israeli independence. In part this owed to the moral onus of the Holocaust and in part to the political influence of American Jews, some of whom saw Israelis as reclaiming the biblical Promised Land. But most important was the place of Israel in Cold War power politics. Israel, that is, was regarded by American policymakers, whether Democrat or Republican, as a vital hedge against possible Soviet expansion into the Middle East and the rich and vital oilfields that were to be found there.

The United States tried to walk a fine line in the Middle East, supporting Israel with economic and military aid (no country in the world, by the early 1970s, received more than the Israelis did) while cultivating the friendship of oil-producing states like Saudi Arabia, Kuwait, Iran, and Iraq, none of which recognized Israel, where American and European oil companies had major investments and whence American consumers got nearly half of their oil for gasoline, heating, and many other needs (see Map 27.3). The situation became all the more complicated when, in 1959, these Arab states along with Venezuela, established the **Organization of Petroleum Exporting Countries (OPEC)** to exert more control over the production and pricing of oil.

The diplomatic balance was maintained into the early 1970s, and the price of oil and gasoline remained remarkably low in the United States, enabling American

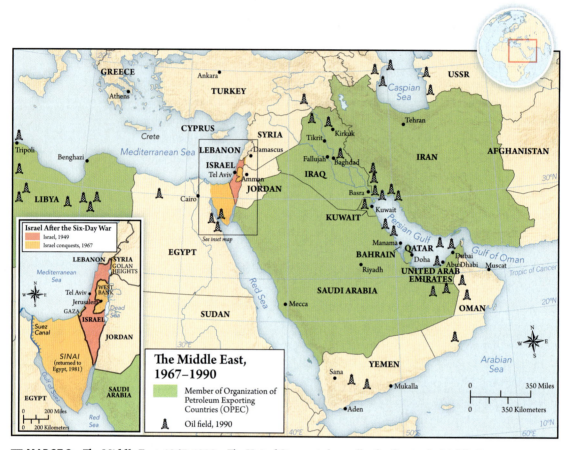

≡ **MAP 27.3 The Middle East, 1967–1990** The United States tried to walk a fine line in the Middle East, supporting Israel with economic and military aid while cultivating the friendship of oil-producing states like Saudi Arabia, Kuwait, Iran, and Iraq.

consumers to drive their gas-guzzling automobiles (car manufacturers had no incentive to promote fuel efficiency with gas costing less than 40 cents a gallon!) with little concern. Then the balances shifted dramatically. In October 1973, as Jews in Israel and elsewhere observed the holy day of Yom Kippur, Egypt and Syria launched surprise attacks through the Sinai and Golan Heights. This time, the Israelis were unprepared and a lengthier struggle ensued. Troops from neighboring Arab states as well as military aid from both the Soviet Union (to Egypt and Syria) and the United States (to Israel) poured in. The crisis, it seemed, threatened to go global and bring the superpowers nose to nose.

The Israelis managed to push the Syrians out of the Golan Heights and the Egyptians back across the Sinai. By the end of October, a cease-fire had been called and the war came to an end, with Israel still in control of Sinai, the West Bank, and Golan, and with the Egyptian and Syrian militaries in tatters. But OPEC would have the final word. Angered by American support for the Israelis, OPEC raised oil prices, reduced oil production, and imposed an oil embargo—the United States would not receive oil shipments—that lasted until March of the next year. Suddenly, American complacency about the price of gasoline came to a wrenching end. The price of a gallon of gas increased by about 60 percent, and shortages nationwide forced consumers to wait in long lines at the gas pumps or find other means of transportation. A stumbling economy was further destabilized and sank into recession.

A bright spot, however, appeared on the horizon in 1978. The Carter administration had devoted a great deal of attention to the Middle East in hopes of working out a peace between Israel and its Arab neighbors for the long term. To that end, with Egypt's President Anwar Sadat first on board, President Carter convened an unprecedented meeting at his presidential retreat in Camp David, Maryland, between Sadat and the newly elected, and conservative, Israeli Prime Minister Menachem Begin. After a tense two weeks that September, Sadat and Begin reached an agreement, known as the **Camp David Accords**, that would provide a framework for the protection of Israeli security interests and Israel's withdrawal from the now-occupied West Bank of the Jordan River to make possible the creation of a Palestinian state. As a measure of the world's response to this extraordinary diplomatic agreement, both Sadat and Begin received the Nobel Peace Prize that year. But the optimism soon faded, and it would be another fifteen years before a new effort, this time more international, could be made to bring peace to the Middle East. For his courageous initiative, Egypt's president Sadat was assassinated in 1981 by Islamic jihadists who believed he had betrayed them.

Islamic Revolution and American Hostages

Some Americans, and President Carter himself, began to recognize that the United States faced a serious **energy crisis**, that conservation and energy efficiency needed to be promoted, and alternatives to oil and other fossil fuels needed to be developed. And nothing dramatized the problem more than an explosive series of events in Iran.

Along with Saudi Arabia, Iran seemed to be one of the strongest Arab allies of the United States in the Middle East. Not only was Iran a major oil producer, but it also shared a long border with the Soviet Union and thereby was regarded as an important piece of Cold War political real estate. It was so important that when a democratically elected regime came to power under the leadership of Mohammed Mosaddegh in 1953 and determined to nationalize the oil fields in Iran, the CIA supported a coup d'état that overthrew him and put a member of the royal family, Mohammad Reza Pahlavi, back at the helm as Shah (Persian for "king").

The Shah was a good ally for the United States. He was staunchly hostile to the Soviet Union and to leftists at home, was intent on modernizing (and Westernizing) Iran, and was happy to keep the oil flowing into international markets. But the Shah also ruled with an iron hand and despite the signs of economic growth, poverty was widespread in the countryside. An opposition movement driven by Islamic students began to pressure the Iranian regime. The students' leader, who had been forced into exile, was an Islamic cleric and fundamentalist named Ayatollah Ruhollah Khomeini. And their goal was to establish not a "modern" Iranian state but a conservative Islamic republic.

Their opening came in early 1979 when, in the face of mounting demonstrations, the Shah and his family fled and Khomeini returned from exile to assume leadership of Iran and craft a new, Islamic constitution. Although some American policymakers imagined that Khomeini might be a moderate politically, they quickly found that he blamed the United States for Iran's problems and cast the United States as the country's enemy. Yet another piece in shifting power relations in the Middle East and another challenge to energy demands.

But matters worsened. The Shah had not only fled Iran; he was sick with cancer and sought treatment in the United States, which had long supported him. This, for Khomeini and his many youthful followers, was the last straw. They demanded that the United States send the Shah back to Iran for

☰ **Americans Held Hostage**   Following the Islamic Revolution in 1979, revolutionaries captured the American embassy in Tehran and held fifty-two diplomats and staff captive. At the end of his term, Carter's administration negotiated to free the hostages, though they did not return to the United States until Ronald Reagan had been sworn in as the fortieth president.

trial, and when the United States refused, a large group of Islamist radicals broke into the US Embassy in Tehran and took fifty-two Americans who worked there hostage. President Carter, who eventually made an unsuccessful attempt to rescue the hostages, looked powerless, and Americans looked on angrily and fearfully as gas prices continued to rise. It seemed a sorry though fitting end to a decade of de-stabilizations. It would be another year before the hostages were released.

Conclusion: Winds of Change

The winds of change that had been blowing across the 1960s continued well into the 1970s as previously marginalized social groups began pressing for rights they had long been denied. The women's movement succeeded in getting the Equal Rights Amendment through Congress and out to the states, and struggles for gay, Chicano, and Native American rights were energized. But the backlash that already was in evidence in the late 1960s exploded as well, leading especially to popular conservative movements against civil rights and feminism. Busing and the ERA would come into the political crosshairs and be weakened or defeated.

The instabilities of domestic politics reached into the executive branch of the federal government, as the Watergate scandal took down the presidency of Richard Nixon and tarnished the reputation of the office in the eyes of many Americans. It seemed an example of larger American woes as the robust postwar economy was increasingly beset by stagflation, the price of oil and gas skyrocketed owing to tensions in the Middle East, and, as the decade came to a close, fifty-two Americans working in the US embassy in Iran were violently taken hostage by militant Islamist students. Jimmy Carter's "malaise" speech didn't do him much good politically, but it seemed to capture the American mood.

WHAT IF the Watergate Break-In Had Not Been Detected?

The Watergate scandal that brought down the Nixon presidency and alerted the country to the dangers of executive power began because burglars hired by the Committee to Re-Elect the President inadvertently left some tape on one of the doors they had broken into, alerting a security guard who had them arrested. But, what if the burglars, who were "professionals," had done the job properly, collected what they needed, and left the premises undetected? The break-in would have been recognized, but it would have been difficult to connect the dots, and after the 1972 election, there would have been little incentive or support to do so.

In all likelihood, Nixon would have escaped any scrutiny. At most, the scandal would have blown over and Nixon would have remained in office. What then? Knowledge of his administration's "dirty tricks" and repressive policies, which were revealed during the Watergate hearings and subsequent investigations, may have been left out of the public spotlight, while Nixon's foreign policy successes would have framed his presidency. Congressional efforts to rein in the power of the executive branch of government may not even have gotten off the ground, and the Republican Party may have been in a stronger political position in 1976 than turned out to be the case. But the Republicans, if they kept power, would have faced many of the challenges that wreaked havoc on the Carter administration. What would this have meant for foreign and domestic developments?

DOCUMENT 27.1: Philip Kurland, "What Watergate Revealed About Presidential Power in America," 1974

The following is an excerpt from a talk delivered by conservative law professor Philip Kurland to MBA students in 1974, several months before Nixon resigned.

The Watergate affair is different. It is different because the immediate criminal acts are but symptoms of a deeper and more fundamental ailment. It is different because it is not concerned with underlings, but with personages who once held the governance of the nation in their soiled hands. It is different because the essence of the wrongdoing is not to be found in the greed for money. It is different because it raises important constitutional questions, not least of which is, as President Nixon constantly reminds us, the question of the proper status of the presidency itself in our constitutional democracy ... Even so, the immediate events of Watergate are not so threatening to our democracy as the more fundamental ailment of which Watergate is only a symptom. The power of arrogance, the cancer that could kill our republic, was fully impregnated by the Kennedy administration, grew under the Johnson administration, and only achieved its culmination under Nixon.

Watergate, however, has brought the specter of totalitarianism to the attention of the American public. Now, as hardly ever before, we are cognizant of the crisis that we face. For the first time in many years, Congress is seeking to assert itself. The question is whether or not it is too late to restore the constitutional balance that our Founding Fathers created.

Since Roosevelt's tenure, all meaningful government power has been vested in the national government. The only governmental powers that states now exercise are those allowed to them by the national government. State government is politically as well as economically bankrupt. And, within the national government, power has, since Roosevelt's day, been concentrated in the executive branch. This is not a result of the Nixon incumbency.

Today we are suffering not only from a corruption of the constitution through perversion of the institutions of government, but a corruption of the constitution because the men we have chosen for high office are unworthy. A US president who tells us that he is "not a crook" thereby affords little reassurance of his qualifications for office, even if we could still credit him with a capacity for the whole truth. It is not enough that the US president is "not a crook." . . . We live in an age when it is no longer the love of money that is the root of all evil; for our time, it is the love of power that is the root of all evil.

Source: Chicago Booth Review, March 9, 1974.

DOCUMENT 27.2: Assessment of Watergate's Impact

In 2018, two researchers assessed the impact of political reforms that came in the wake of Watergate.

While contemporary coverage of former President Richard Nixon focuses on the Watergate burglary and cover-up that ultimately led to his resignation, the Nixon administration was rife with unethical and undemocratic conduct. Secret and potentially illegal use of military force, illegal campaign contributions, domestic spying, outright bribery,[1] and the misuse of the machinery of government to attack political opponents[1] were just a few of the widespread abuses discovered by the Watergate investigators and subsequent congressional inquiries. Unsurprisingly, an administration led by a dishonest and unethical chief executive—with little respect for the rule of law—was prone to abusing its power.

The breadth of Nixon's abuses was matched by the subsequent response. Although the post-Watergate period is widely understood as an era of reform, over time, the full extent of the changes has faded from view. The 1970s saw a wholesale remaking of America's campaign finance system, including the creation of the Federal Election Commission (FEC) and the introduction of comprehensive limits on how much money political campaigns can raise and spend. There were also historic new protections against abuses of executive power, including the Privacy Act—which restricted government use of personal data—and the Foreign Intelligence Surveillance Act (FISA), which created a process to limit the power of intelligence agencies to spy on American citizens. The era also saw changes to congressional budget procedures, an effort to limit foreign military interventions overseas, civil service and ethics reforms, and much more.

Broadly, these reforms sought to provide for a more ethical, transparent government; combat the corrupting influence of money in politics; protect people against governmental abuses of power; and place limits on extraordinary exercises of presidential power. The following sections provide a brief overview of the extensive reforms put in place in response to Nixon's abuses of power, some having been enacted while he was still in office. While the descriptions of these reforms are not intended to be exhaustive, they provide a sense of the breadth of the response and provide an example for current policymakers.

Source: Sam Berger and Alex Tausanovitch, "The Lessons from Watergate," July 30, 2018, Center for American Progress.

Thinking About Contingency

1. Had Nixon escaped accountability and remained in office for his full term, how might that have influenced his Republican Party and the tenor of American politics more generally?
2. Had the Watergate burglars not been apprehended in June 1972, would the "dirty tricks" of the Nixon administration eventually have been exposed?
3. If the media environment in the early 1970s was the same as that which we are used to today, would Nixon have escaped certain impeachment and resignation even if the burglars had been caught?

REVIEW QUESTIONS

1. How did the social movements of the 1960s call into question the liberal commitment to equality at home and the price of intervening against communism abroad?

2. How were the goals of the women's liberation movement, the American Indian movement, and the Gay Liberation Front similar? How were they different? Why did Cesar Chavez and Dolores Huerta organize farm workers in California? Are there any connections between these movements and the Progressives of the early twentieth century?

3. What strategies did civil rights activists use to attack de facto segregation? Why did the residents of South Boston vehemently oppose busing? How did conservative politicians like Richard Nixon use coded language to appeal to white working-class voters?

4. What were some of the outcomes of the conservative backlash against civil rights? Why did the Equal Rights Amendment fail?

5. What is the enduring legacy of the Watergate scandal?

6. How did the international events of the 1970s contribute to a sense of instability?

7. What did Jimmy Carter say in his "malaise speech?" How did it sow doubt and dissatisfaction among voters?

KEY TERMS

affirmative action (p. 1156)

American Indian movement (AIM) (p. 1151)

Anti-Ballistic Missile Treaty (ABM) (p. 1160)

Black Panthers (p. 1158)

Bracero program (p. 1148)

Camp David Accords (p. 1177)

Chicano (p. 1150)

Counter Intelligence Program (COINTELPRO) (p. 1158)

Committee to Re-Elect the President (CREEP) (p. 1161)

energy crisis (p. 1177)

Environmental Protection Agency (EPA) (p. 1156)

Gay Liberation Front (GLF) (p. 1148)

globalization (p. 1169)

Movimiento Estudiantil Chicano de Aztlan (MEChA) (p. 1150)

National Abortion Rights League (NARAL) (p. 1145)

National Organization for Women (NOW) (p. 1144)

Organization of Petroleum Exporting Countries (OPEC) (p. 1175)

Paris Peace Accords (p. 1174)

Red Power movement (p. 1152)

Roe v. Wade (p. 1145)

Rust Belt (p. 1169)

Six-Day War (p. 1175)

stagflation (p. 1170)

Stonewall Uprising (p. 1147)

STOP ERA (p. 1166)

Strategic Arms Limitation Treaty (SALT) (p. 1160)

United Farm Workers of America (UFWA) (p. 1149)

Watergate Hotel (p. 1161)

RECOMMENDED READINGS

Dennis Banks and Richard Erdoes, *Ojibwa Warrior: Dennis Banks and the Rise of the American Indian Movement* (University of Oklahoma Press, 2004).

Jefferson Cowie, *Stayin' Alive: The 1970s and the Last Days of the Working Class* (The New Press, 2012).

Donald Critchlow, *Phyllis Schlafly and the Grassroots Conservatism* (Princeton University Press, 2005).

Lillian Faderman, *The Gay Revolution: Story of the Struggle* (Simon and Schuster, 2016).

Neil Foley, *Mexicans in the Making of America* (Harvard University Press, 2014).

Ronald Formisano, *Boston Against Busing: Race, Class, and Ethnicity in the 1960s and 1970s* (University of North Carolina Press, 1991).

Garrett Graff, *Watergate: A New History* (Avid Reader, 2022).

Bruce Schulman, *The Seventies: The Great Shift in American Culture, Society, and Politics* (Da Capo Press, 2002).

Salim Yaqub, *Imperfect Strangers: Americans, Arabs, and U.S.-Middle Eastern Relations in the 1970s* (Cornell University Press, 2016).

28

A New Conservatism and Its Discontents
1980–1989

Chapter Outline

28.1 Political Shifts

Describe the conservative ascendancy of the 1980s and what it revealed about the geographical shift in power in the United States and the Republican Party.

28.2 Economic Shifts

Describe how the conservative ascendancy hastened the shift in power in the American economy and the geography of the economic landscape.

28.3 Cultural Shifts

Explain the strengthening of social conservatism and the eruption of "culture wars" in many areas of American life in the 1980s.

28.4 A New Cold War

Analyze the dynamics of the new Cold War and identify the forms of resistance that emerged.

28.5 Domestic Warfare

Detail the impact of the "war on drugs" in the 1970s and 1980s on the social fabric of the United States.

28.6 The Collapse of the Cold War Order

Identify the process by which the Cold War came to an end during the last years of the 1980s.

≡ **The Fall of the Berlin Wall**   A West German man smashes the Berlin Wall with a pickaxe. The concrete wall that split West Berlin from East Berlin was a defining image of the Cold War.

The press conference on November 9, 1989, was unexpected, and its meaning was not entirely clear. An official of the East German government announced that the restrictions on travel that had long confined East Germans would be lifted immediately, though passports and visas would still be required and the imposing **Berlin Wall**—8 feet high in two thick rows replete with watchtowers, electronic sensors, and a "no man's land"—would remain intact. But within hours, thousands of East and West Germans swarmed to the Wall and met in a joyous celebration. Border guards, even at the notorious Checkpoint Charlie, didn't bother to look at anyone's credentials; some took photographs, hoping to record a truly historic moment. Within a week, the Wall itself began to be dismantled by the hands of German people seeking at once to destroy a dark symbol of their past and usher in a new and brighter future.

There were many questions still to be addressed. Would the divided Germany be reunified? Would East Germany be integrated into the Western European economy?

Timeline

1979	1980	1981	1982	1983	1984	1985

1979 ▸ Iran hostage crisis

1980 ▸ Ronald Reagan elected president

1981 ▸ Reagan survives assassination attempt; Professional Air Traffic Controller's Union strike; beginning of the AIDS crisis

1981–1982 ▸ Federal Reserve Board interest rate increase leads to severe recession

1982 ▸ A million demonstrators gather in Central Park demanding nuclear disarmament

1983 ▸ Reagan announces "Star Wars" anti-ballistic missile program; United States invades Grenada

1984 ▸ Geraldine Ferraro (Democrat) is first woman nominated for vice president; Reagan wins reelection

1985 ▸ Mikhail Gorbachev becomes premier of the Soviet Union

And how would the balances of power established by the Cold War be readjusted? In November 1989, the only certainty was that the "fall of the Berlin Wall" encapsulated an enormous shift in power not only for Europe, the Soviet Union, and the United States but for the entire globe.

The ending of the Cold War was the most dramatic example of political, economic, and cultural shifts that grew out of the destabilizations of the 1970s and would touch many areas of American life. By the 1980s these shifts defined the direction of American society and the experiences of those who lived in the United States.

During this decade, conservatism was ascendant. Manufacturing continued to decline, and the service and financial sectors became increasingly important. The long-term consensus around government activism was undermined. The Democratic Party that had been shaped by the New Deal and then by the Great Society was thrown into crisis. And the momentum of political movements demanding rights and a more

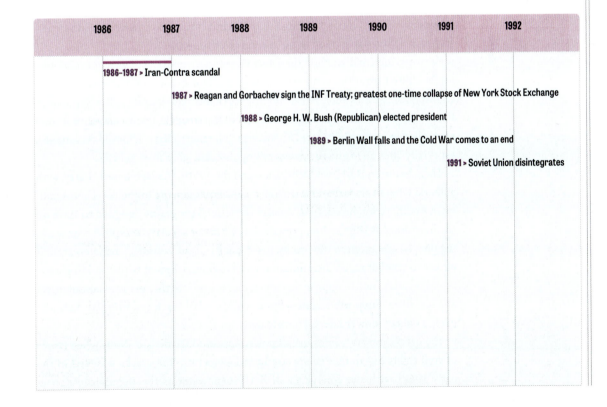

| 1986 | 1987 | 1988 | 1989 | 1990 | 1991 | 1992 |

1986–1987 › Iran-Contra scandal

1987 › Reagan and Gorbachev sign the INF Treaty; greatest one-time collapse of New York Stock Exchange

1988 › George H. W. Bush (Republican) elected president

1989 › Berlin Wall falls and the Cold War comes to an end

1991 › Soviet Union disintegrates

equitable society was reversed. Perhaps most surprising of all, as the events in Germany suggest, the Soviet Union began to unravel and the Cold War that had shaped the political world came to a sudden and stunning end. We continue to live with the results.

28.1   Political Shifts

Describe the conservative ascendancy of the 1980s and what it revealed about the geographical shift in power in the United States and the Republican Party.

American history is marked by several large-scale shifts in the locations and sources of power. A brief review of these shifts provides context for understanding the conservative ascendancy of the 1980s.

Between the ratification of the Constitution and the Civil War, the southern states had disproportionate political power and the slave-plantation economy was the foundation of the country's greatest wealth and economic growth. The Democratic Party, created during the 1830s and controlled chiefly by southern enslavers, held the upper hand in the federal government.

Between the Civil War and the Great Depression, political power and economic might shifted from the southern states to the Northeast and Midwest, from the countryside to cities and towns, and from agriculture to industry. The Republican Party, established during the 1850s as part of the struggle against slavery but soon controlled by industrialists and financiers in Northern cities, achieved dominance, especially after 1896 and the defeat of Populist and labor insurgencies.

Then, between the Great Depression and the 1970s, the Democratic Party, with a liberal wing in the urban North and a conservative wing in the rural and small-town South, reorganized: first, around the federal programs designed to stave off the hardships of Depression, provide new forms of security and power for working people, and reignite the productive capacity of the country; and later, around efforts to combat racial discrimination and impoverishment while building a national security state to oppose the Soviet Union and halt the spread of communism and socialism. Supported by a coalition that included Black and white workers, the party's hold on power seemed formidable.

The cracks in this framework of power appeared in the late 1940s when issues of civil rights began to alienate southern Democrats. The cracks widened in the early 1960s with the emergence of Barry Goldwater as the Republican Party's presidential candidate and by the late 1960s with growing urban unrest, Black militancy, and the debacle of the Vietnam War. Republican Richard Nixon won two terms as president, though the Watergate scandal may have obscured the faltering of the Democrats. By 1980, it became clear that a new framework of political power and a new perspective on public policies was taking hold.

Ronald Reagan and the Election of 1980

Ronald Reagan was an unlikely torchbearer of a new political order. Born in 1911 to an Illinois family of modest means, he was a liberal Democrat and supporter of FDR and the New Deal before moving to California. There he gained minor fame as a movie actor and served as president of the Screen Actors' Guild, an entertainment industry union. But the Cold War turned him into a vehement anticommunist and pushed him farther to the right. He came to the attention of conservatives in 1964 when he backed Barry Goldwater and gave a televised speech warning about the creeping power of the Democratic-controlled federal government in raising taxes, regulating businesses, and enacting civil rights legislation.

Very quickly Reagan became a conservative favorite for the governorship of California, which he won in 1966. Once in office, he railed against student protesters at the University of California, Black rebellion in the cities, and a culture of "permissiveness" across the country. Reviled by the political left, Reagan earned the admiration of conservatives throughout the United States. After two terms in the California statehouse, he nearly won the 1976 Republican presidential nomination over the incumbent President Gerald Ford. By 1980 the tide had turned fully in his favor; he became the Republican presidential nominee—with Texan George H. W. Bush as his vice-presidential running mate—on a platform opposing abortion and the ERA, supporting major tax cuts, and calling for a military buildup to fend off an imagined Soviet weapons superiority.

Reagan's nomination signaled the ascendancy of a new force in the Republican Party. For almost a century after the Civil War, Republican leadership and power came chiefly from a broad corridor stretching from New England through the Middle West. Nearly all Republican presidents during this period came from Ohio and Illinois. Since the 1940s, the party itself was divided between an internationalist wing in the Northeast that had made its peace with much of the New Deal (Dwight Eisenhower and Nelson Rockefeller were examples) and an isolationist wing in the Midwest that wished to roll back New Deal activism and the power it had given to labor (Robert Taft was the leader).

But Goldwater's 1964 campaign showed a change that proved enduring: the rise of the Sunbelt wing of the party, whose conservatism was fueled by opposition to taxes and civil rights and by the support of Christian fundamentalists and

MAPPING AMERICA

Power Shifts

Between the Civil War and the Great Depression, political power and economic might shifted from the southern states to the Northeast and Midwest, from the countryside to cities and towns, and from agriculture to industry. The Republican Party achieved dominance, especially after 1896 and the defeat of Populist and labor insurgencies.

Then, between the Great Depression and the 1970s, the Democratic Party, with a liberal wing in the urban North and a conservative wing in the rural and small-town South, held sway. Supported by a coalition that included Black and white workers, the party's hold on power seemed formidable.

The cracks in this framework of power appeared in the late 1940s when issues of civil rights began to alienate southern Democrats. The cracks widened in the early 1960s with the emergence of Barry Goldwater as the Republican Party's presidential candidate, and by the late 1960s with growing urban unrest, Black militancy, and the debacle of the

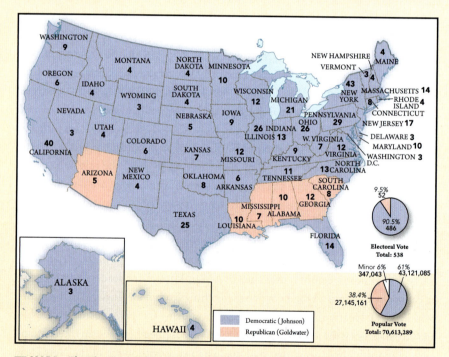

≡ **MAP 1   The Election of 1964**   Lyndon B. Johnson's landslide victory in 1964—he received 60 percent of the popular vote and he won the electoral vote in all but six states—included many of the elements of the liberal New Deal coalition first forged by Franklin Delano Roosevelt in 1932. Though Republican candidate Barry Goldwater was shellacked in the election, the victories he won in the South were a sign of a developing backlash. Goldwater and the conservative forces he represented were the harbingers of a larger shift to the political right.

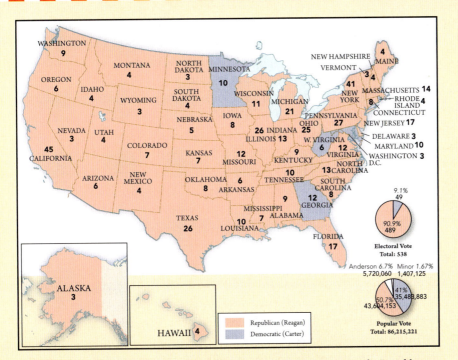

≡ **MAP 2 The Election of 1980** Ronald Reagan's nomination in 1980 as the Republican candidate for president signaled the ascendancy of a new force in the Republican Party. For almost a century after the Civil War, Republican leadership and power came chiefly from a broad corridor stretching from New England through the Middle West. But Goldwater's 1964 campaign showed a change that proved enduring: the rise of the Sunbelt wing of the party, whose conservatism was fueled by opposition to taxes and civil rights and by the support of Christian fundamentalists and far-right-wing anticommunists. Reagan's trouncing of Jimmy Carter in the 1980 election thus signaled a major shift in power. A new conservatism now framed the life of the country.

Vietnam War, the cracks had widened into a fissure. The 1980 presidential election made it clear that a new framework of political power and a new perspective on public policies had taken hold.

Thinking Geographically

Landslides mark fundamental shifts in power.

1. Compare the two maps. Are there any states that voted Democratic in 1964 that did not vote Republican in 1980?

2. Compare either of these maps to maps that show the results of the 2016 or 2020 election. What are the main differences between the 1964 and 1980 maps and the 2016/2020 maps? What do these differences say about the political climate today compared to 1980? To 1964?

far-right-wing anticommunists. Richard Nixon was from California and, with the exception of Gerald Ford, who hailed from Michigan and who became president after Nixon's resignation, no Republican presidential candidate would come from outside the Sunbelt until Donald Trump in 2016.

Initially, few thought that actor and former governor Ronald Reagan could defeat President Carter. The country had long been wedded to liberal-leaning economic policy perspectives and had rejected Goldwater's conservatism, which bore resemblance to Reagan's. But Carter himself was hobbled by economic stagflation, the Iran hostage crisis, which he failed to resolve, and a liberal revolt in his own party that sought to nominate Massachusetts Senator Edward (Ted) Kennedy, brother of the slain John F. Kennedy and Robert F. Kennedy. Public discontent seemed palpable; Carter's approval rating had dropped to about 30 percent.

Reagan kicked off his campaign in Philadelphia, Mississippi, where three civil rights workers had been murdered in 1964. There he took a state rights stance to please conservatives who were hostile to Black rights and empowerment. Although opinion polls suggested a close race, Reagan finished his one televised debate with Carter, only a week before the election, by asking viewers if they felt better off in 1980 than they did in 1976. The answer came in a near landslide for Reagan, who swept the popular vote by 10 percentage points and won the electoral votes of all but six states and the District of Columbia. Adding insult to Carter's injury, the Americans being held hostage in Iran for more than a year were finally released on January 20, 1981, moments after Ronald Reagan was inaugurated as president.

The Conservative Agenda

Conservative Republicans were thrilled by Reagan's victory, which seemed to give him a mandate to govern. They hoped to retract the reach of the federal government, weaken policies that provided social safety nets, especially for African Americans, and move away from "détente" toward a more confrontational stance with the Soviet Union. Conservatives also sought to mobilize against abortion rights and uphold the practice of public-school prayer that the courts had ruled as an unconstitutional violation of the separation of church and state.

While Reagan shared these objectives, his top priorities were cutting federal taxes, reducing federal spending for nonmilitary purposes, and accelerating the shift toward deregulation that had begun under Carter. Although Reagan's economic views and those of his advisors were shaped by the neoliberalism of the 1970s, they moved further toward supply-side economics.

Supply-side economics, whose leading advocate was an economist named Arthur Laffer, was designed to address the concerns of Republicans and Democrats alike that tax cuts would reduce federal revenues and either increase deficits (many conservative Republicans wanted a balanced budget) or undermine government spending on entitlement programs (favored by Democrats). The logic of the supply-siders seems counterintuitive even while politically appealing. Cutting taxes would supposedly give people more money to save and invest, promoting increased economic growth. Increased economic growth would then generate more tax revenue even at lower rates of taxation. Laffer went so far as to predict that tax cuts would bring in more tax revenue than had previously been the case.

Several members of Congress as well as economists and financial journalists were dubious about this—George H. W. Bush had called these ideas "voodoo economics" during his primary run against Reagan—but Reagan's sweeping election victory together with a failed assassination attempt on him in March 1981 (he was seriously wounded by a gunshot from a disturbed man named John Hinckley) gave him the necessary political clout a few months later to get a massive tax cut through Congress with the help of southern Democrats. Reagan's tax package reduced the tax rate on the highest income earners from 71 to 28 percent, on capital gains (increases in the value of capital assets like stock investments and real estate holdings) from 28 to 20 percent, and on corporations from 46 to 35 percent. Middle-income earners received some tax relief as well. But the tax cuts were windfalls for the wealthy, particularly for the top 1 percent of income earners, and a major blow to federal revenue. Contrary to supply-side theory, federal deficits and the overall federal debt grew dramatically, tripling over the course of the 1980s.

Reagan's goal of cutting federal spending met more formidable barriers. A substantial portion of the annual federal budget was **nondiscretionary spending**: allocated to programs that either kept the government solvent (payments on the federal debt) or that enjoyed enormous popular support (Social Security and Medicare), together amounting to nearly 60 percent. **Discretionary spending** on infrastructure projects, education, and antipoverty programs did come into the Reagan administration's crosshairs but only made up about 20 percent of the budget, so reductions in these would have limited impact on the federal revenue picture.

Reagan and his allies had much more success in scaling back government regulations on businesses and the environment and in curbing the power of organized labor. They moved to weaken the oversight of the Environmental Protection Agency (EPA), the Occupational Safety and

≡ **On the Picket Line**   Striking air-traffic controllers picket near Dallas–Fort Worth Airport in 1981.

Health Administration (OSHA), the Food and Drug Administration (FDA), the Securities and Exchange Commission (SEC), and savings and loan associations (S&L). They made deep cuts in urban spending and reduced government support for job-training programs. And when the Professional Air Traffic Controllers Organization (PATCO) went out on strike in the summer of 1981, Reagan fired almost 11,000 of them (ironically PATCO had endorsed Reagan during the 1980 election campaign) and broke the union.

As a result, corporations had less to answer for when they polluted the air and water, workers had fewer protections at their workplaces, food and drug producers had more leeway in what they sold to the public, **insider trading** (when investors knew in advance about mergers, stock offerings, and acquisitions that would change the value of stocks) on Wall Street was effectively encouraged, and savings banks got involved in risky mortgage and lending activities. Union busting and other antilabor actions taken by employers were rarely challenged while unionized workers were increasingly reluctant to strike, undermining their leverage and discouraging their membership. In 1979, union membership in the United States had reached a high point of about 21 million, or nearly 22 percent of the labor force; by 1990, it had dropped to less than 17 million, or 16 percent of the labor force. The decline would continue nearly to the present day.

When it came to military spending, however, Reagan was anything but miserly. He had campaigned for the presidency warning that the United States had fallen behind the Soviet Union in armaments, and he would go on to describe the Soviet Union as "an evil empire." He significantly increased the military budget and authorized the development of high-tech bombers and antimissile systems designed to protect the country from a possible Soviet attack, even though scientists doubted that some of this technology would work. After its defeat in Vietnam, the American military was now back in the good graces of the government and the public. But filling military and defense-related coffers only worsened the federal budget deficit and, with it, any chance of restoring social service expenditures.

28.2 Economic Shifts

Describe how the conservative ascendancy hastened the shift in power in the American economy and the geography of the economic landscape.

Increases in government spending on defense, which favored the Sunbelt, exemplified one of the important economic shifts during the 1980s. So, too, did the continuing decline of the American Rust Belt, as deindustrialization became an economic fact of life (as discussed in Chapter 27). Manufacturers who blamed their profit woes on powerful labor unions relocated to more friendly business environments: perhaps in the Sunbelt; perhaps in Mexico or in Asia. Between 1975 and 1994, investments made by American corporations outside the United States more than doubled. Economic dynamism began to shift to the growing service sector (which includes retail, health care, travel, and restaurants) as well as to emerging financial and high-tech companies that benefitted from new government policies, deregulation, lower labor costs, and limited traditions of unionization. Celebrations of entrepreneurship, the marketplace, and even greed led many observers to describe a new "Gilded Age." Not surprisingly, inequalities of wealth surged, reversing a trend that had taken shape during the 1930s and the immediate postwar decades (see Figure 28.1). But first the economy had to endure a very serious recession.

The Recession of 1981–1982

The post–World War II American economy brought wide, though uneven, prosperity between 1946 and the early 1970s. The share of national wealth owned by the very richest Americans declined between the late 1920s and the late 1970s, while the share of wealth and incomes of those with modest means increased,

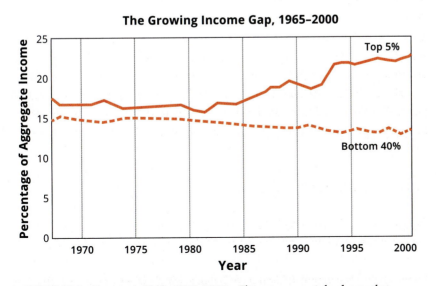

The Growing Income Gap, 1965–2000

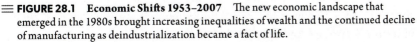

≡ **FIGURE 28.1 Economic Shifts 1953–2007** The new economic landscape that emerged in the 1980s brought increasing inequalities of wealth and the continued decline of manufacturing as deindustrialization became a fact of life.

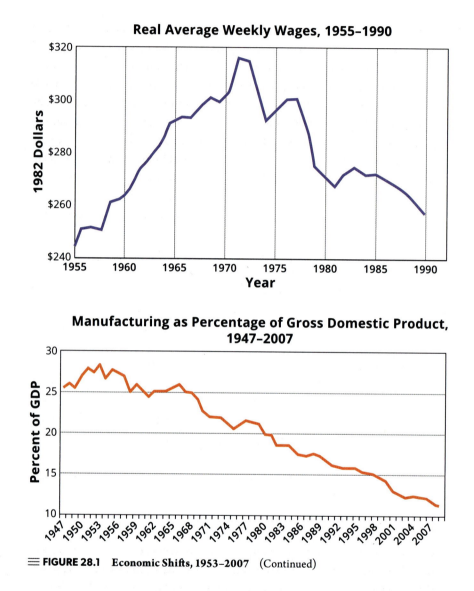

Real Average Weekly Wages, 1955–1990

Manufacturing as Percentage of Gross Domestic Product, 1947–2007

≡ **FIGURE 28.1** **Economic Shifts, 1953–2007** (Continued)

owing in good part to federal programs, the strength of labor unions, and relatively low rates of inflation through the 1960s. But during the 1970s, rising international competition and dramatic increases in the price of oil began to hit the economy, and especially the manufacturing sector, very hard. They produced an unprecedented combination of declining production, growing unemployment, and spiraling inflation—or stagflation (see Chapter 27).

The Reagan administration, through the workings of the Federal Reserve (the Fed), sought to combat the economic problems by focusing on inflation. The Fed raised interest rates sharply to slow economic activity and cut the price of goods and services, triggering a deep recession—a decline in the Gross Domestic Product (GDP)—beginning in 1981. The inflation rate did drop, and quickly, from a high of 13.2 percent to 4.8 percent before the end of the year. But unemployment also spiked, topping out at 10.8 percent, a level not seen since the Great Depression of the 1930s. Unemployment would remain at over 8 percent for the next two and a half years. Plant closings, which had begun in 1979, became more widespread, particularly in the Rust Belt, and the consequences of the recession were especially severe because of Reagan administration policies that reduced spending for unemployment insurance and for programs that had provided assistance to the poor. More businesses closed in 1982 (24,000) than in any year since 1933. And the poverty rate, an indicator of gripping hardship, increased from 11.7 percent to 15 percent, its highest level since the 1950s (see again Figure 28.1).

Reagan's policies during the recession sparked outrage among liberals and labor leaders, and, for a time, seemed to put him in hot political water. But the effects of these policies, although not immediately apparent, proved to be consequential. Two-thirds of the manufacturing jobs lost in the recession would never be regained, hastening the deindustrialization of the country and deepening the woes of the Rust Belt. At the same time, owing to high interest rates and lowering inflation, the financial sector became increasingly formidable. The recession, that is, not only imperiled the livelihood of many American workers; it also rearranged the economic landscape and helped to forge a new American economy.

The New Economic Landscape

The economic landscape that emerged from the recession of 1981–1982 was marked by rapid economic growth in the Sunbelt, new prominence and power in the financial, insurance, and real estate sectors, and the remarkable expansion of the technology sector (especially information technology). And although the neoliberal mantra of free and minimally regulated markets heralded these developments, they in fact owed to federal government assistance.

Growth in the Sunbelt built upon an established foundation of military bases and aerospace industries that the Reagan military buildup and space-related projects reenergized. The National Aeronautics and Space Administration (NASA) had facilities stretching from the Atlantic coast of Florida (Cape Canaveral), through northern Alabama (Huntsville Space and Rocket Center) and the

≡ **Greed Is Good**   In the 1987 film *Wall Street*, Gordon Gekko (played by Michael Douglas) exemplified the "greed is good" ethos of Reagan-era finance.

Gulf Coast of Texas (Houston's Johnson Space Center) and into central California (Edwards Air Force Base) and Pasadena (the Jet Propulsion Lab at Cal Tech). The Space Shuttle program, which had its first launch in 1981, increased the flow of federal dollars that had been drying up since the last crewed flight to the moon in the early 1970s.

To the West, Southern California was a special beneficiary of federal defense and aerospace spending, providing good-paying jobs for thousands of engineers, contractors, technicians, and white-collar employees, and strengthening the Republican and conservative hold on the region. And in Seattle, the Boeing Corporation profited from federal government contracts in the defense, aerospace, and commercial airline industries.

Supply-siders had argued that large tax cuts would not only put more money in the pockets of consumers but also encourage investment in production. In reality, much of the wealth that Reagan tax cuts bolstered went to pay exorbitant salaries and bonuses to executives, particularly in the finance, insurance, and real estate sectors. Finance companies and private equity firms developed high-return/high-risk assets or used their cash to acquire undervalued companies or oversee mergers between them. They might then downsize the operations and workforces to increase profit margins and dividends for shareholders. Sometimes the end game of such acquisitions and mergers was bankruptcy, reorganization, and resale, lining the pockets of financiers and their investors at the expense of laid-off workers and their communities.

Banking deregulation similarly expanded the field of lending and investment for large and small institutions alike, some of which had customarily focused on local and regional clienteles. By issuing mortgages to prospective homeowners and then reselling those mortgages to financial companies that "bundled" them ("third-party lenders" as they came to be known), banks could fill their vaults with more cash and issue more mortgages, thereby increasing real estate values and multiplying the number of home buyers who might be overextended. Thus, what the new economic landscape produced were massive fortunes based on extremely shaky and potentially volatile foundations that linked the Sunbelt to financial institutions in the Northeast and Midwest.

Government spending for research and development also supported an emerging **information economy** that simultaneously served the Reagan military build-up and advanced the creation of new communications, electronics, and computer technologies. The ground was laid during World War II and the 1950s for the first digital computers and integrated circuits (small silicon "chips"), but the pace of change accelerated during the late 1970s and early 1980s. Bill Gates and Paul Allen founded Microsoft in 1975 while Steve Jobs and Steve Wozniak founded Apple around the same time. All of them had grown up on the West Coast, dropped out of college, and set up shop in their parents' garages. And all set their sights on building computers for home use. By the end of the 1980s, around 20 million personal computers were being sold annually. **Silicon Valley**, south of San Francisco, attracted many of the new high-tech and computer software companies, taking its place alongside Austin, Texas, and suburban Boston as one of the hubs of this new economy (see Figure 28.2).

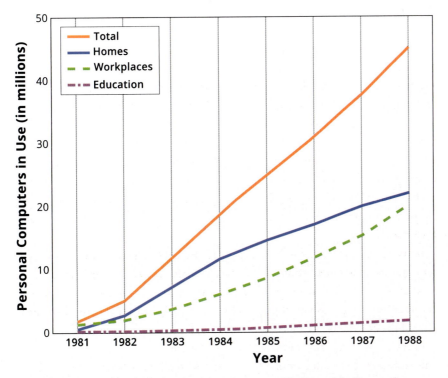

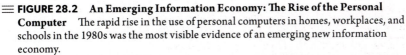 **FIGURE 28.2** **An Emerging Information Economy: The Rise of the Personal Computer** The rapid rise in the use of personal computers in homes, workplaces, and schools in the 1980s was the most visible evidence of an emerging new information economy.

28.3   Cultural Shifts

||| Explain the strengthening of social conservatism and the eruption of "culture wars" in many areas of American life in the 1980s.

Many Sunbelt conservatives had cultural as well as economic aspirations and perspectives that found a sympathetic advocate in President Reagan. Like Reagan, these conservatives were attracted to anticommunism not only because they feared for the fate of individual freedoms but also because they associated communism with irreligion and godlessness. The student activism of the 1960s and the "counterculture," which celebrated women's liberation, sexual experimentation, and new ideas about sexuality and gender roles, troubled them, too. The conservative ascendancy of the 1980s therefore gave them the opportunity to push for cultural change, initiating a **culture war** that influenced nearly every aspect of American society and sowed divisions that resonate to the present day.

The Rise of the Religious Right

Religious fervor has ebbed and flowed over the course of American history. During the 1740s and again in the 1830s, "Great Awakenings" disrupted familiar hierarchies and energized reform movements. Anti-Catholicism shaped politics from the Revolution well into the twentieth century, giving Nativism a long and destructive life. The Social Gospel movement influenced Progressivism, while Christian fundamentalism fortified legal prohibition in the 1920s (see Chapters 19 and 21). Formal church membership has historically been very high in the United States.

Yet, from the late 1970s through the 1980s, the United States witnessed the emergence of a new force in cultural and political life. Known as the **religious right** and distinguished by its Protestant evangelical orientation and social conservatism, it formed a significant component of the conservative ascendancy. The foundation was established during the 1950s and 1960s with the opening of large evangelist churches, some having thousands of members, and with the growth of "televangelism" as media-conscious ministers recognized the power of television to promote both message and influence. Pat Robertson established the Christian Broadcast Network, while Jim and Tammy Faye Bakker launched the Trinity Broadcasting Network. Along with other evangelists, they preached to a viewership of nearly twenty million by 1980. Then, in 1979, Jerry Falwell, who gained notoriety with his "Old Time Gospel Hour" telecast, joined with conservative activist Paul Weyrich to create the **Moral Majority.** Their goal was to carry Protestant social conservatism more directly into American politics. "Get 'em baptized, get 'em saved, and get 'em registered to vote," Falwell roared.

The Moral Majority and the religious right were fueled by such issues as anticommunism, civil rights, sexuality, and the relations of church and state. The legalization of abortion, the rise of feminism, and the courts' refusal to extend tax-exempt status to Christian schools that engaged in racial discrimination sounded alarm bells for those who valued the "traditional" family, saw homosexuality as a threat if not a sin, and regarded the United States as a Christian nation. Many had joined evangelical churches in the 1950s and 1960s and, especially after *Roe v. Wade* and congressional passage of the ERA, mobilized in support of conservative candidates for office, whether local or national. Seats on school boards, which often determined curricula and textbooks, were no less important than seats in Congress or state legislatures.

≡ **Conservative Allies** Reverend Jerry Falwell and President Ronald Reagan together at a Baptist fundamentalist conference. Although Reagan had little track record as a social conservative, he actively courted the support of the religious right and its leaders like Falwell.

The religious right was especially powerful in the Sunbelt, from the Shenandoah Valley of Virginia to southern and central California. Indeed, California was especially receptive to the religious right owing to large migrations of white Protestants from the South and the Plains and to the importance of the defense industry, which fueled Cold War sensibilities, not to mention apocalyptic visions, even among engineers and technicians.

President Reagan was not initially inclined to social conservatism. As California governor, he had signed an abortion rights bill, and he didn't have much of a reputation as a "family" man. He had divorced his first wife, remarried, and didn't pay much attention to his children. But Reagan quickly recognized that the religious right could make for powerful political allies. He spoke before the newly established Religious Roundtable in 1980, expressed support for the Christian schools that had lost their tax-exempt status because of their racist admission policies, and appointed religious conservatives to his administration, including a surgeon general, Dr. C. Everett Koop, who vehemently opposed abortion.

Conservative Challenges on Campus

Conservatives had long viewed American college campuses as breeding grounds for liberals and the left. Antiwar activism in the 1960s and early 1970s seemed to produce graduates who were hostile to warfare, imperialism, and capitalism. They had been taught, according to conservatives, by leftist professors protected in their positions by academic tenure (disparaged by one critic as "tenured radicals"). The emergence of Black studies, women's studies, and ethnic studies programs in the 1970s, often in response to student demands, seemed, from a conservative perspective, a mockery of the traditional curriculum, while the use of affirmative action to diversify the college student body seemed an affront to well-qualified white students.

Conservative faculty and intellectuals attacked trends in the academy, especially in the humanities, that marginalized the traditional canon and appeared to embrace moral relativism. Allan Bloom, who taught at the University of Chicago, wrote a particularly biting critique in the conservative *National Review* that took aim at "liberal education" for its rejection of academic standards, promotion of instantaneous gratification and sexual hedonism, and casual regard for the lineages of Western thought, much of which he blamed on the weakening of the middle-class family. Published several years later as *The Closing of the American Mind*, Bloom's critique formed part of a wider conservative backlash.

Conservative students took up the challenge as well. They started their own campus newspapers with funding from conservative donors, ridiculed liberal ideas and values, and protested initiatives that gave advantage to applicants on racial or ethnic grounds. The *Dartmouth Review*, which began publishing in 1980, gained notoriety not only for its conservatism but also for its thinly veiled racism and targeting of gay men and women. Although their impact on campus life and politics proved to be limited—the most notable campus protests of the decade were against apartheid in South Africa—many of these young conservative editors would carry their ideas and work into public political life. Prominent alumnae included author and provocateur Dinesh D'Souza, Fox talk-show host Laura Ingraham, entrepreneur Peter Thiel, and US Senator Ted Cruz.

AIDS and the Crisis of Public Health

Several months after Ronald Reagan was inaugurated, doctors in New York City, San Francisco, and Los Angeles began noticing an unusual and deadly disease that was afflicting young, previously healthy, gay men. The patients had contracted rare infections, and many of them eventually developed an aggressive cancer known as Kaposi's sarcoma that ravaged their bodies before they died. By the end of the summer of 1981, there was talk of a "gay cancer" and meetings took place in gay communities. Within a year, the Centers for Disease Control in Atlanta attributed what had turned into an epidemic among gay men to depleted immune systems, and named the disease Acquired Immune Deficiency Syndrome or AIDS. Medical researchers soon learned that AIDS was produced by a virus that they would call the human immunodeficiency virus or HIV.

Because the virus appeared to be transmitted chiefly through sexual contact, it provoked a response fueled by the emerging culture wars. Since the Stonewall riot of 1969, a gay rights movement had emerged, especially in cities with large gay and lesbian populations, and opened the closet into which most had sequestered. Gay bookstores, bars, and other gathering places that enabled gay men to associate with each other without fear of police harassment became available, part of a larger phenomenon of sexual liberation that was evident among heterosexuals as well and that offended social conservatives.

Conservative gays were more likely to remain closeted, but the AIDS virus was no respecter of political affiliation. Terry Dolan, founder of the National Conservative Political Action Committee, and Roy Cohn, lawyer and chief counsel for Senator Joseph McCarthy (and a confidant of Donald Trump), both succumbed to the disease; so, too, did conservative critic Allan Bloom. Yet, for many social conservatives, who viewed homosexuality as sinful, the AIDS epidemic was God's punishment for violating his commands. Catholic pundit and Republican advisor Patrick Buchanan, soon to be Reagan White House communications director, scoffed at "the poor homosexuals" who had "declared war on nature, and now nature is exacting an awful retribution." William Buckley, Jr., editor of the *National Review*, went so far as to demand that "everyone detected with AIDS" be "tattooed in the upper forearm . . . and on the buttocks," a measure reminiscent of the Nazi persecution of Jews.

Repugnant as such sentiments are, it was the lack of response from the Reagan administration that cost lives. His administration refused to lend support to local officials who hoped to take on the epidemic, and cut the budget of the federal Public Health Service that was determined to make AIDS research and prevention a priority. Outside of Washington, DC, the response was no more encouraging. Although Mayor Dianne Feinstein of San Francisco did back public health measures, Mayor Edward Koch of New York City, a virus epicenter, barely took action until later in the 1980s, in part because of rumors about his own sexuality.

AIDS-related deaths increased exponentially (Figure 28.3), from 900 in 1982, to near 5,000 in 1984, to almost 12,000 in 1986, and to more than 18,000 in 1988. In all, during the 1980s, AIDS claimed the lives of more than 100,000 Americans (including intravenous drug users), and mortality would continue to rise over the next twenty years, peaking in 1995. Only the mobilization of committed AIDS activists succeeded in shifting public opinion and, through new organizations like **AIDS Coalition to Unleash Power (ACT-UP)**, managed to boost funding for research and education. By the late 1990s an effective antiviral treatment had been discovered. But AIDS had already spread, becoming the fourth leading cause of death around the globe. It also exposed the weaknesses and inadequacies of the American public health care system, owing to structural deficiencies and susceptibility to cultural pressures.

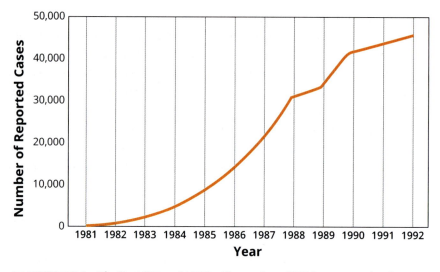

≡ **FIGURE 28.3** **The Rapid Rise of AIDS** The number of AIDS cases soared in the 1980s, and mortality would continue to rise well into the 1990s.

Struggles over the Courts

Conservative efforts to shift the culture in a rightward direction turned the federal courts into more of a political battleground than they had been since the 1930s. According to the Constitution, presidents have the power, with the consent of the Senate, to appoint federal judges, whether to the Supreme Court or to the lower federal courts (circuit courts and courts of appeal). Traditionally, and with some exceptions, the Senate has supported presidential court appointments even if they were members of the opposition party. Reagan, who promised during his campaign to appoint justices favored by conservatives, would have four opportunities to choose new Supreme Court Justices.

The first three appointments were to replace retiring justices already on the conservative side, and in 1981 Reagan broke precedent in selecting the first woman ever to be nominated. Sandra Day O'Connor was an Arizona Republican who had served as the state's attorney general, a state senator, and a state court judge. Although she was hostile to affirmative action and labor rights, so far as anyone could see she was not an opponent of abortion rights. But while social conservatives expressed disappointment, O'Connor was unanimously confirmed.

When conservative Chief Justice Warren Burger announced his retirement, Reagan made two moves more appealing to the Republican Party's conservative wing. He elevated Associate Justice William Rehnquist to the position of Chief Justice and, to fill Rehnquist's slot, nominated Antonin Scalia. Rehnquist was one of the most conservative members on the Court. He not only opposed

Roe v. Wade but favored state rights over federal powers and, as a young clerk, opposed the school desegregation decision in *Brown*. Scalia was a fiery conservative who had briefly served on the US Court of Appeals. With an **originalist** perspective, Scalia believed the court should decide cases based on the "original intent" of the Constitution's framers. He was an opponent of abortion rights, which, he insisted, had no constitutional basis. Scalia won unanimous confirmation and Rehnquist won the support of two-thirds of the Senators, including some Democrats.

It was Reagan's next nomination that roiled the confirmation process. When Nixon-appointed Associate Justice Lewis Powell decided to step down, Reagan nominated Robert Bork to replace him. Bork was a well-regarded law school professor, a one-time solicitor general (he would argue the federal government's cases before the Supreme Court), and a member of the federal Court of Appeals in the District of Columbia. Yet he was also a hardcore conservative, a confirmed originalist, and a skeptic about the federal government's power to enforce civil or abortion rights. Social conservatives were gleeful, imagining this as the opportunity to, as one Christian publication put it, "ensure future decades will bring morality, godliness, and justice back into focus."

Liberals, feminists, and civil rights activists mobilized against Bork. Democrats remembered the role Bork had played in enabling Richard Nixon's "Saturday Night Massacre" during the Watergate crisis, firing the special prosecutor when no one else would. The opposition in the Senate was led by Ted Kennedy of Massachusetts, who charged during the confirmation hearings that "Robert Bork's America is a land in which women would be forced into back-alley abortions, blacks would sit at segregated lunch counters, rogue police could break down citizens' doors in midnight raids, school children could not be taught about evolution, writers and artists could be censored at the whim of the Government, and the doors of the Federal courts would be shut on the fingers of citizens for whom the judiciary is the protector of individual rights at the heart of our democracy." Bork did not help himself by responding to questions at his confirmation hearings with an arrogant tone; but the political die was unmistakably cast. Bork's nomination was rejected by 58–42, and nominations for the Supreme Court have been politically and culturally divisive ever since.

Desperate to fill the seat, Reagan nominated Anthony Kennedy, a federal judge and mainline conservative, who won quick confirmation. Yet if it appeared that the conservative cultural ascendancy had reached a stumbling point, a larger picture of the federal judiciary would show otherwise. During his presidency, Reagan was able to appoint half the judges on the federal benches—383 in sum, the most of any previous president—almost all of whom were well-to-do, white men with conservative dispositions; only seven of these appointments were African American and only twenty-eight were women. Many would serve for years to come and leave deep conservative imprints.

PERSPECTIVES

Family Values

The conservative ascendancy of the 1980s gave the religious right the opportunity to push for cultural change, initiating a culture war that influenced nearly every aspect of American society. Many of the battles of the culture wars were centered on the family. Televangelists Pat Robertson, Jerry Falwell, and others on the religious right sounded alarm bells for those who valued the "traditional" family, saw homosexuality as a threat if not a sin, and regarded the United States as a Christian nation. In Falwell's view, young people "have learned to disrespect the family as God has established it." Only by returning to "biblical basics" could America be saved.[1]

Family Values, 1974 Coal miner Wayne Gipson, his wife, and four children say a prayer before dinner in their home near Chattanooga, Tennessee. Their simple meal consists of stew, crackers, and iced tea. The original caption that accompanies the photo indicates that the family was planning on going to Disney World over the Christmas holiday.

[1]Jerry Falwell, *Listen, America!* (Garden City, NY: Doubleday, 1990), 17.

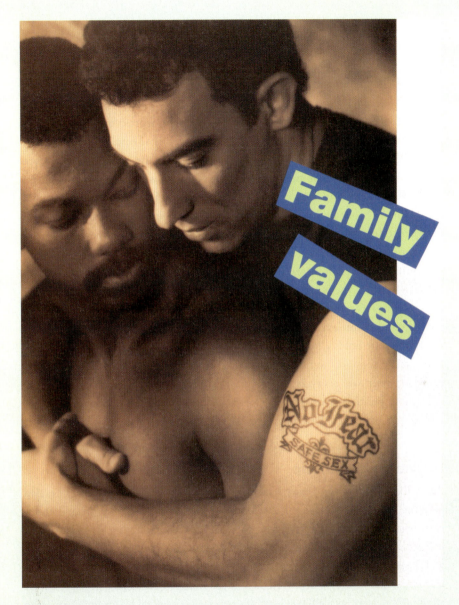

Family Values, 1992
This photograph, part of a series sponsored by the San Francisco AIDS Foundation, shows a Black man and a white man in an embrace. The white man sports a tattoo that reads: "No Fear/ Safe Sex."

CONSIDER THIS

The increasing visibility of gay relationships, coupled with growing numbers of working women and escalating rates of divorce and teenage pregnancies, made many on the religious right feel that the traditional American family was in decline in the 1980s. How does the first photo portray the kind of family that Americans on the religious right could feel good about? Why did the photographer of the second image apply the label "Family Values"? What meaning did they wish to convey?

28.4   A New Cold War

||| Analyze the dynamics of the new Cold War and identify the forms of resistance that emerged.

During the 1970s, American foreign policy had been defined by two important trends. One was détente; the other was the **Vietnam Syndrome**, the public aversion to getting into armed intervention overseas after the country's experience with the Vietnam War. Somewhat under the radar, however, a new phenomenon was developing among both conservative critics of détente and Democrats who had become disenchanted with their party's antiwar politics and apparent pacifism in international affairs. They were known as "hawks." Together they insisted on the continued threats posed by the Soviet Union—the Soviets were expansionist, determined to attain military superiority, and not to be trusted on arms control treaties—and on the obligation of the United States to intervene abroad in support of "democracy," that is to say against communist or socialist movements and governments. Some even drew a distinction between **authoritarian regimes** (in which the state holds all the power over the social order—something the United States could support) and **totalitarian regimes** such as the Soviet Union, which exercise power over every aspect of citizens' lives. These critics, who included intellectuals, politicians, and policymakers, came to be called **neoconservatives**, and Reagan embraced their mantra of "peace through strength."

Nuclear Brinkmanship

Accordingly, Reagan not only authorized increased military spending; he also gave the go-ahead to programs that would augment the American arsenal of nuclear weapons and escalate the arms race with the Soviet Union. These included the MX, an intercontinental ballistic missile (ICBM) with multiple warheads, and the mobile, precision Pershing and Tomahawk "cruise" missiles, with nuclear warheads, that would be deployed in Western Europe to fend off a possible Soviet attack. There were, as well, two aircraft previously cancelled by Jimmy Carter: the supersonic B-1 bomber, capable of delivering nuclear weapons to distant targets, and the "Stealth" B-2 bomber that could not be detected by radar.

Reagan's military advisers also developed new strategies for fighting, and winning, a nuclear war. Secretary of Defense Caspar Weinberger issued a "Defense Guidance" in 1982 which imagined a "protracted" nuclear war with the Soviet Union, while some members of the Reagan administration were cavalier about America's ability to survive an all-out nuclear exchange (like *Collier's* magazine in

1951!). One official predicted that the United States could recover from one within four years, suggesting that Americans should "dig a hole, cover it with a couple of doors and then throw three feet of dirt on top." "The human race is very resilient," Reagan's Arms Control and Disarmament negotiator opined.

Reagan took special interest in the idea of an anti-ballistic missile defense that could ward off a surprise Soviet attack. To that end, he proposed a **Strategic Defense Initiative (SDI)** shortly after he had described the Soviet Union as an "evil empire" to a meeting of evangelicals. The technology would, in Reagan's telling, involve lasers, particle beams, and other computer-reliant sensors that, he believed, would be so effective as to make nuclear warfare "obsolete." Skeptics dubbed the plan "Star Wars," referencing the 1977 film megahit, and scientists widely disparaged the feasibility of the project (SDI would eventually be cancelled in 1993 but not before millions were spent on research).

Whatever the viability of SDI, Soviet leaders were alarmed. Not only was this a violation of previous arms control treaties, but, from the Soviet perspective, it could encourage the United States to launch a preemptive (or first) nuclear strike. Cold War tensions reached a level of intensity and danger not seen since the Cuban Missile Crisis of 1962, and likely contributed to the shooting down by Soviet fighter pilots of a Korean Airlines passenger jet that had inadvertently strayed over Soviet territory. The Soviets apparently thought the flight was engaged in espionage. Nearly 300 passengers—including 61 Americans—lost their lives, and Reagan, joining the horrified reaction in many parts of the world, described the incident as "an act of barbarism."

Rolling Back Socialism in the Caribbean Basin

Whatever the rhetoric, the Reagan administration did not actually seek a military confrontation with the Soviet Union. But the effort to challenge Soviet expansionism and reverse the Vietnam Syndrome for the sake of rolling back socialism in the Third World focused attention on Central America and the Caribbean. There, Reagan believed that US intervention in civil wars would involve little risk and probably achieve success, unlike in Vietnam (see Map 28.1).

The administration's sights were first set on El Salvador, where a dictatorship supported by the military and the landed elite was fighting a leftist guerilla movement. El Salvador's dictatorship had a reputation for brutally repressing the opposition. They murdered the prominent Archbishop Oscar Romero and four Catholic American women, three of whom were nuns, along with massacring hundreds of civilians. The Carter administration had lent the dictatorship some support, but Reagan greatly increased it. From the perspective of Reagan and his advisors, this was a fight, bearing some resemblance to the situation in South Vietnam in the

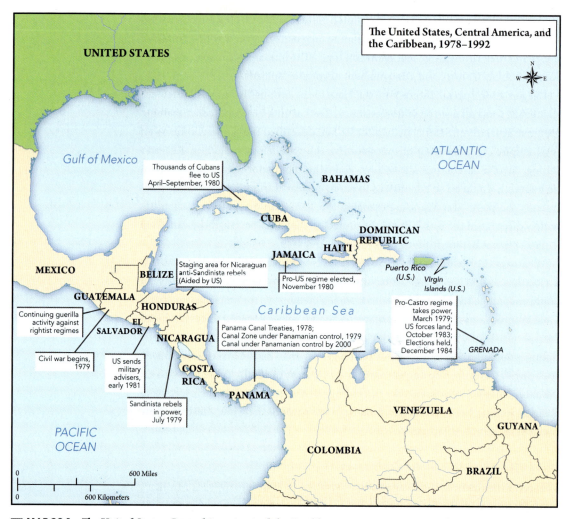

The United States, Central America, and the Caribbean, 1978–1992

UNITED STATES

Gulf of Mexico

ATLANTIC OCEAN

Thousands of Cubans flee to US April–September, 1980

BAHAMAS

CUBA

DOMINICAN REPUBLIC

HAITI

JAMAICA

Puerto Rico (U.S.)

Virgin Islands (U.S.)

MEXICO

BELIZE

Staging area for Nicaraguan anti-Sandinista rebels (Aided by US)

Pro-US regime elected, November 1980

GUATEMALA

HONDURAS

Caribbean Sea

Pro-Castro regime takes power, March 1979; US forces land, October 1983; Elections held, December 1984

GRENADA

Continuing guerilla activity against rightist regimes

EL SALVADOR

NICARAGUA

Panama Canal Treaties, 1978; Canal Zone under Panamanian control, 1979 Canal under Panamanian control by 2000

Civil war begins, 1979

US sends military advisers, early 1981

COSTA RICA

Sandinista rebels in power, July 1979

PANAMA

VENEZUELA

GUYANA

PACIFIC OCEAN

COLOMBIA

BRAZIL

0   600 Miles

0   600 Kilometers

≡ **MAP 28.1** **The United States, Central America, and the Caribbean, 1978–1992** During his two terms in office, Ronald Reagan used US power to suppress left-wing radicalism. Known as the "Reagan Doctrine," this policy was designed to prevent the development of another Cuba.

1960s, that, as one put it, "you can win." Eventually, the Reagan administration sent nearly $1 billion in financial support as well as military personnel to train the dictatorship's troops. Fearing a domestic conservative backlash from a left-wing victory in El Salvador, some hawkish Democrats supported these initiatives, too.

More consequential to the Reagan administration was Nicaragua. There, in 1979, a socialist movement—known as the **Sandinistas**, named after Nicaraguan revolutionary hero Augusto Sandino—had overthrown the regime of longtime dictator Anastasio Somoza. Although the Sandinistas and their leaders received aid from Cuba, they had substantial popular support in this overwhelmingly rural country, including from the Catholic Church, which had mostly shed conservatism and embraced **liberation theology**, widespread across Latin America, that urged social concern for the poor and liberation for the oppressed. To consolidate their power, the Sandinistas quickly embarked on a program of land reform.

For Reagan and his neoconservative advisors, the Sandinistas were a direct threat to the national security of the United States owing to their socialist policies and ideology. And they moved to undermine the Sandinista regime chiefly by supporting counter-revolutionary soldiers, known as the **Contras**, from the Somoza dictatorship. Reagan waxed nearly poetic about what the Contras meant to him: "God bless them," he would say, because, sharing their convictions, he was "a contra too." More specifically, the administration began to funnel millions of dollars to arm and train the Contras. When Congress placed restrictions on what could be done (the Reagan administration was, after all, seeking to overthrow an internationally recognized government), the administration rechanneled aide covertly through the CIA. There would be a nasty reckoning.

In neither El Salvador nor Nicaragua were American troops deployed. In this, the Reagan administration seemed to heed the lessons of Vietnam. Their objective, in both countries, was to defeat leftist insurgencies or overthrow socialist governments without putting American lives at risk, as had been the case in Vietnam. But things proved different on the Caribbean island of Grenada, where a socialist movement had taken power in 1979 in a bloodless coup. The new government allied with Cuba and the Soviet Union, and further worried the Reagan administration when, with Cuban assistance, it built a new airport boasting a runway that could accommodate Soviet military aircraft.

When a struggle occurred within the Grenadian leftist government in September 1983, Reagan decided to make his move. Using the presence of several hundred American medical students in Grenada as a pretext, the Reagan administration, in late October, launched an invasion to evacuate the students and simultaneously undermine the regime. Several thousand Marine and Army troops, joined by a few hundred from friendly Caribbean nations, were landed on the island. The press was kept at bay so that neither fighting nor casualties would be reported—the return of the students to the United States did get extensive media attention—and in three days the leftist government had been deposed and a new interim government had been installed, promising elections in a year. With little information about what had transpired in Grenada, save for the coverage of the evacuated students, the American public seemed to support the invasion. The US military handed out thousands of medals to its troops and to Pentagon officials; more important, Reagan had sent a clear signal to socialist movements elsewhere that the United

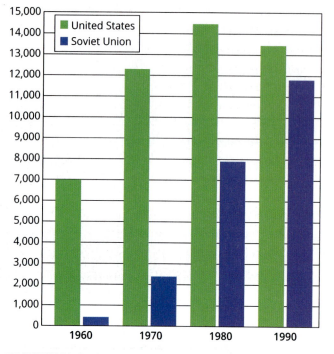

States was not reluctant to intervene militarily against them, perhaps putting the "Vietnam Syndrome" to rest.

Resistance to the Nuclear Arms Race

Concerns over the Reagan administration's policies in Central America would grow over the course of the 1980s, but more consequential resistance mobilized against the accelerating nuclear arms race between the United States and the USSR (see Figure 28.4). Popular support for nuclear disarmament has a history as old as that of nuclear weaponry. Worries about the consequences of the development of the atomic bomb troubled scientists, including Albert Einstein, during and immediately after World War II. A peace movement, directed chiefly against nuclear weapons, emerged in Japan during the early 1950s, and the Campaign for Nuclear Disarmament (CND) as well as the Women's Strike for Peace demonstrated against nuclear weapons in the late 1950s and early 1960s.

But the disarmament movements of the early 1980s were far larger and more international than anything that had come before. The expansion of nuclear arsenals, as well as the planning for a survivable and winnable tactical or all-out nuclear war, provoked fear and outrage in many parts of the world. The European Nuclear Disarmament (END) campaign, directed against the deployment of both American cruise missiles and comparable Soviet SS-20s, was particularly robust, with demonstrations involving hundreds of thousands of protesters. END also reached out to anti-Soviet dissidents in Eastern Europe toward the goal of a truly pan-European disarmament movement.

Anti–nuclear weapons protests took place in the United States, too. The largest, in New York City, drew nearly one million people in June 1982. In the United States, the movement focused on the achievement of a **nuclear freeze**: a halt to the production and deployment of all nuclear weapons as a first step toward a wider superpower disarmament. Over two million Americans signed petitions that were delivered to the US and the Soviet missions at the United Nations in 1982. Nuclear freeze resolutions were passed by city councils, county governments, and state legislatures in many parts of the country and nuclear freeze referenda won popular majorities on Election Day in 1982 in nine states and thirty-four localities. There never was or would be a larger referendum on a single issue in American history.

A few months later, in May 1983, the House of Representatives passed a nuclear freeze resolution by 278–149, but the Senate rejected it. And although Reagan dismissed the nuclear freeze campaign as a "very dangerous fraud" which "ignore[d] the facts of history and the aggressive impulses of an evil empire," he and his administration took notice, recognizing the threat to their nuclear buildup and potentially to Reagan's reelection in 1984. Before too long, the nuclear disarmament movement would bear unexpected fruits.

≡ **Marching Against Nuclear Weapons**
Thousands of protesters carrying signs march on New York's East Side in a parade against the use of nuclear weapons. The parade moved to Central Park, where a large disarmament rally was held on the Great Lawn.

28.5   **Domestic Warfare**

Detail the impact of the "war on drugs" in the 1970s and 1980s on the social fabric of the United States.

The intensification of the Cold War during the 1980s had a domestic counterpart that reflected the cultural, political, and economic shifts already underway. Since the late 1960s, there had been mounting concern in the public and among political officials about urban unrest, crime, and the negative consequences of countercultural life styles. In many ways, the conservative ascendancy of the 1980s was enabled by calls for "law and order" and for concerted government efforts to fight crime and the growing use of drugs. Elected officials at the national and local level used the language of warfare to describe the problems and measures deemed necessary to defeat them. And although white Republicans appeared to be most vocal about the threats and most determined to intervene forcefully, the new domestic warfare became a bipartisan project, eventually gaining support from Blacks as well as whites. The results involved the transformation of policing and the advent of mass incarceration. They also demonstrated that the conservative perspective on the nature of and solution to social problems was achieving increased traction.

The War on Drugs

Although the production and consumption of alcohol had been flashpoints of American politics from the founding of the Republic to the repeal of the prohibition Amendment (see Chapter 21), narcotics and other addictive drugs had a much quieter history. The use of opium was widespread and unregulated during most of the nineteenth century, while heroin and cocaine could be purchased over the counter and used for medicinal purposes into the twentieth. Coca-Cola, which originally included coca leaves in its recipe, was devised in the late nineteenth century as both a "temperance drink" and a tonic for a number of maladies (some still recommend it for indigestion and hangovers). Federal regulation began in 1914 (drug regulations had been enacted by a few states beforehand), and it was pursued mainly through taxation. A Federal Bureau of Narcotics was created in 1930 within the Treasury Department.

But it was the increased use of recreational drugs such as marijuana, the addiction to heroin among many American troops in Vietnam, and the social conflicts of the decade that set the stage for new initiatives. In 1970, Congress passed a Comprehensive Drug Abuse Prevention and Control Act, aimed mainly at the pharmaceutical industry, and in 1971 President Richard Nixon designated drug abuse "public enemy number one" and declared "war" on it. Soon thereafter, the Nixon administration oversaw the establishment of the **Drug Enforcement Administration (DEA)**, which moved against the trafficking of controlled substances, and supported sentencing reform and the granting of no-knock warrants: meaning that drug enforcement agents could simply barge into suspected sites of drug use and distribution.

Nixon's **war on drugs** was designed in good part to weaken his perceived political enemies. As Nixon aide John Ehrlichman later put it, "You want to know what this is really about? The Nixon White House had two enemies: the antiwar left and black people. We knew we couldn't make it illegal to be against the war or blacks, but by getting the public to associate the hippies with marijuana and blacks with heroin, and then by criminalizing both heavily, we could arrest their leaders, raid their homes, break up their meetings, and vilify them night after night on the evening news."

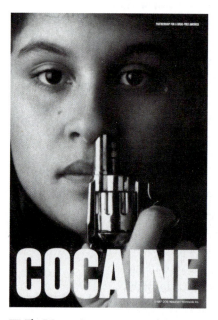

≡ **The War on Drugs** An antidrug poster dramatizing cocaine's potential for self-harm. The election of Ronald Reagan moved the drug war into high gear.

The election of Ronald Reagan moved the drug war into high gear. Federal funds for drug enforcement increased more than ten-fold—from $8 million to $95 million—in a few short years, steep penalties and **mandatory sentencing laws** were enacted, and a major anti–drug abuse campaign—"Just Say No!"—was spearheaded by First Lady Nancy Reagan. For his part, Vice President George H. W. Bush sought to involve the CIA, which he once headed, as well as the US military to check international drug trafficking.

But it was the appearance of "crack" cocaine in the mid-1980s, an especially potent and addictive drug, that grabbed public attention because it seemed to be circulating in poor Black sections of inner cities and contributing to a host of serious social and public health problems. Observers pointed to increases in violent crime, the explosion of gangs and gang warfare, and the birth of "crack babies" whose mothers were addicts, burdening hospitals and welfare systems. Los Angeles Police Chief Daryl Gates notoriously stated that drug users "should be taken out and shot," but the bandwagon of panic and retribution soon came to include the Supreme Court, congressional Democrats and Republicans, a large portion of the Congressional Black Caucus, and a great many Black community leaders who worried about what was happening in their streets. The Supreme Court extended police and prosecutors more leeway in obtaining evidence, including "probable cause" as a basis for search warrants. Congressional legislation giving judges more discretion in setting bail, ending parole in federal prisons, and establishing mandatory minimum drug sentences, especially harsh for crack-related offenses, passed with large bipartisan majorities. And some state legislatures embraced particularly draconian measures to stem the tide, including a zero tolerance approach to drug abuse and trafficking. With drug-abuse coverage saturating the media, many Americans grew alarmed. By the late 1980s, according to one poll, two-thirds regarded drug abuse as the nation's number-one problem.

The Militarization of the Police

Declaring a "war" on drugs suggested the necessity of a military response. Historically, the police and the US Armed Forces had little directly to do with one another. Professional police forces took shape in large American cities in the mid-nineteenth century, replacing informal night watch patrols, and were tasked with keeping order on city streets. For a time, they were unarmed and even lacked uniforms, but they quickly became part of the patronage system of local political bosses and were widely accused of corrupt practices, of being "on the take." The police were also deployed to break up labor strikes, arrest labor leaders and others deemed "radicals," and disrupt political demonstrations. In the southern and southwestern states, where there were few large cities and many people lived in rural areas, policing initially took the form of slave patrols and later mounted units, like the Texas Rangers, who played major roles in the repression of African Americans, Mexican Americans, and other immigrant groups. Indeed, it was the enslavement of African Americans that gave policing a national basis through the Fugitive Slave Acts (1793, 1850) and the federalization of slave catchers and posses.

The role of the US military in policing was complex. Although its focus was on national defense, much of its activity was set on containing and suppressing domestic dissent and on crushing rebellious Confederates in the South and Indigenous peoples in the West. Still, the maintenance of domestic order was, for the most part, left to county and municipal police or to the National Guard, under the control of state governors.

The urban rebellions of the 1960s, however, convinced public officials that a new approach that would enable the police to take on the jobs of containing criminal and disorderly activity was needed. Among the first moves was the creation of **Special Weapons and Tactics (SWAT)** teams which carried military-grade weapons (submachine guns, assault rifles, grenades) and received training for deployment in riots, hostage taking, drug, and terror-related incidents. By the mid-1980s, at the height of the drug war, almost every city in the country with more than 100,000 residents had a SWAT team, while smaller cities looked to establish them.

In 1986 President Reagan signed National Security Directive 221, which declared illegal drugs a threat to the nation's security. In so doing, he blurred the line between police and the military. Federal funds flowed to localities for the purpose of drug enforcement, and in 1987 Congress alerted police forces to the availability of surplus military equipment. By the late 1980s, there was talk of setting up detention centers for drug offenders or sending them into exile. Even so, politicians from both parties complained that the federal drug war was "lackadaisical" or ineffective.

The militarization of the police, which not only involved the use of armored vehicles and assault weaponry but also racial profiling and the depiction of inner cities as "battlefields," would have consequences for the country well after alarm over drug abuse began to die down. African Americans and other people of color were increasingly regarded as the "enemy" and likely to be involved in illegal or illicit activity; the suppression of crime, from the perspective of police and public officials, demanded their harassment and the use of deadly force against those who resisted in any way. And, for a time, there was little concern from urban dwellers who believed that they gained greater public safety in return. Before long, new federal units, with military-grade weapons, would be involved in urban and border policing.

The Advent of Mass Incarceration

The war on drugs and the militarization of the police contributed to the dramatic rise of incarceration rates in the United States. Today the country has the dubious distinction of holding more people in prison—whether state, local, or federal—and incarcerating adults at a higher rate than any other country in the world. By the early 2000s, about 2.3 million men, women, and minors were in jails and penitentiaries, and the networks of policing, surveillance, prosecution, parole, and construction are so extensive that the United States can now be referred to as having a carceral state. Taking into account those who are on parole and probation, the number mired in the prison system increases to about seven million (see Map 28.2).

The impact of this massive increase in incarceration has fallen most heavily on the poor, and especially on poor people of color. One in three young Black boys and one in six Latino boys can expect to suffer incarceration at some point in their lives; this is true for only one in seventeen white boys. But the incarceration net is not only gendered male; the fastest growing prison population today is composed of women and, particularly, women of color.

The great increase in the size of the prison population began in the late 1970s but accelerated rapidly during the 1980s. When President Reagan took office in 1981, there were 327,000 Americans incarcerated. Four years later the number had nearly doubled to 627,000. The war on drugs and drug-related policing were certainly responsible for some of this, but so, too, was a larger shift in public opinion. The shift was dramatic. During the 1960s, a prison reform movement raised questions about the use of incarceration and its influence in deterring crime; it also emphasized the importance of rehabilitation as a way to lower rates of recidivism. The death penalty was briefly ruled unconstitutional by the Supreme Court (1972–1976).

By the 1980s, interest in reform and rehabilitation had evaporated. Concerns about violent crime and victims' rights, which the conservative ascendancy reinforced, changed the climate of public opinion and contributed to an expanding perspective that only punishment, coupled with lengthy prison terms and the reestablishment of the death penalty, could restore order and safety. Liberal Democrats, who had once been attracted to prison reform, now enthusiastically shifted gears. By the late 1980s, those with an interest in building a carceral state were multiplying and politically formidable. Prison construction outpaced school construction. Privatization of penitentiaries began to be considered and was soon adopted. Many communities saw economic benefits, including jobs and services, from having penitentiaries in their midst. And powerful corporations realized profits from supplying the infrastructures that prisons demanded. By the mid-1990s, the momentum of mass incarceration seemed unstoppable.

Mass Incarceration in the United States

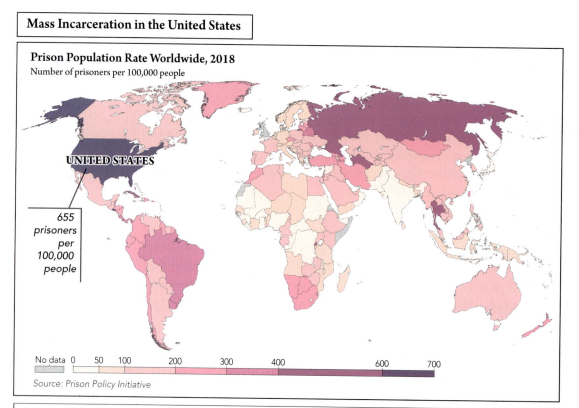

Prison Population Rate Worldwide, 2018
Number of prisoners per 100,000 people

UNITED STATES

655 prisoners per 100,000 people

No data 0   50   100   200   300   400   600   700

Source: Prison Policy Initiative

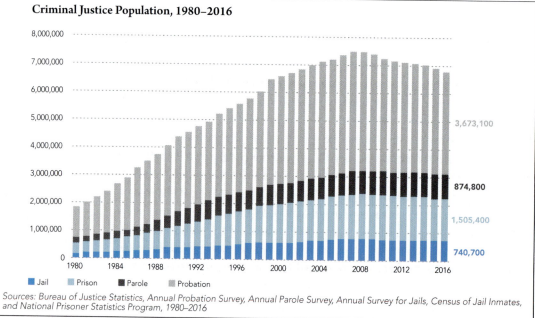

Criminal Justice Population, 1980–2016

8,000,000

7,000,000

6,000,000

5,000,000

4,000,000

3,000,000

2,000,000

1,000,000

0

1980   1984   1988   1992   1996   2000   2004   2008   2012   2016

3,673,100

874,800

1,505,400

740,700

■ Jail   ■ Prison   ■ Parole   ■ Probation

Sources: Bureau of Justice Statistics, Annual Probation Survey, Annual Parole Survey, Annual Survey for Jails, Census of Jail Inmates, and National Prisoner Statistics Program, 1980–2016

≡ **MAP 28.2   Mass Incarceration in the United States**   Beginning in the 1980s, the US prison population skyrocketed. The United States locks up people at a higher rate than any country in the world.

28.6   The Collapse of the Cold War Order

Identify the process by which the Cold War came to an end during the last years of the 1980s.

At the beginning of the 1980s, it appeared that the Cold War had been reignited and the world set again on a path toward nuclear warfare. The United States and the Soviet Union renewed their arms races. The Soviet Union sent troops into Afghanistan to suppress a mostly Islamic insurgency against a regime it favored. The United States intervened in the affairs of El Salvador, Nicaragua, and Grenada, and it also lent financial support to the anti-Soviet Afghan rebels.

But by the end of the decade, a remarkable and unexpected shift took place. The Soviet Union and the United States commenced arms-control agreements. The Soviet Union began reform initiatives within its borders while loosening its grip on allied communist governments in Eastern Europe. The United States suffered setbacks in foreign affairs, most notably a scandal connected with support for the Nicaraguan contras. And popular rebellions spread across Eastern Europe, effectively dismantling the political edifice built by the Soviet Union after World War II. By the early 1990s the Soviet Union was gone, newly elected governments took power from the Baltic to the Balkans, and the Cold War that had shaped the globe for the previous half century appeared to be over.

Morasses at Home and Abroad

Despite the steep recession early in his first term, Ronald Reagan won reelection in an even greater landslide in 1984 than he had in 1980. His Democratic opponent, Walter Mondale of Minnesota, who had been Jimmy Carter's vice president, failed to formulate a persuasive attack on Reagan, though he attempted to stir enthusiasm by selecting New York's Geraldine Ferraro as his running mate. It was the first time a woman had ever found a place on a major party presidential ticket. Reagan won 59 percent of the popular vote and the electoral votes of every state but Minnesota and the District of Columbia. But if Reagan's popularity was at its zenith, he did not have a clear agenda for his second term, and his administration was quickly mired in scandals and diplomatic setbacks.

Some of the scandals grew out of Reagan administration financial deregulations, which encouraged insider trading and speculative investments by banks and S&Ls. High-profile financiers were prosecuted and jailed, and bank failures spread across the country. As if reflecting these developments, the stock market suffered the largest drop in its history on a Monday in October 1987, losing 23 percent of its value, and setting off a domino effect worldwide. Scandals erupted on the religious right as well when a number of televangelists admitted to having affairs or paying

≡ **Deadly Attack**   The aftermath of a suicide truck bombing of the US Marines barracks in Beirut, Lebanon. The blast—the single deadliest attack on US forces abroad since World War II—claimed the lives of 241 American service members.

prostitutes for sex, and then begged their congregants for forgiveness. Their hypocrisy struck a blow to their followers and eventually resulted in the collapse of Jerry Falwell's Moral Majority, though not of the social conservative currents in the country.

But the most serious, and politically damaging, scandal involved the Reagan administration's efforts to prop up the Nicaraguan Contras. And it was one of a series of intertwined foreign policy debacles. Iran and Iraq had begun an immensely destructive war in 1980, and Reagan chose to support the Iraqis and their dictatorial leader Saddam Hussein, regarded as vital to US interests, mainly because of Iraq's oil fields. In nearby Lebanon, civil warfare involving Sunni and Shi'ite Muslims as well as minority Druse Christians had exploded in the 1970s, and in 1982, given Lebanon's strategic proximity to Israel and Syria, the Reagan administration sent in US troops as part of an international peacekeeping force. Before they were withdrawn in 1984, nearly 250 American Marines were killed by a suicide bomber and a number of Americans were taken hostage.

Although Reagan vowed never to negotiate with "terrorists" for the release of the hostages in Lebanon, members of his administration began a truly byzantine effort to get the hostages back while continuing to provide funding for the Contras despite congressional prohibitions. How did this happen? Reagan administration officials started to sell weapons to the Iranians, who they initially opposed in their war with Iraq, so that the Iranians might pressure their Lebanese allies to release the American hostages. The money from the weapons sales would then be funneled secretly, by way of Israel and the CIA, to the Contras in Nicaragua. Accordingly, the arms were sent to Iran, although the Lebanese refused to release all the hostages. The money from the arms sales financed the purchase of weapons for the Contras, which were delivered clandestinely by air. It all went well until 1986 when one of the planes was shot down in Nicaragua.

Although Reagan initially denied that the United States had "traded arms or anything else for hostages," investigations by journalists and then by Congress blew that story apart. The **Iran-Contra scandal** led to the indictment and conviction of eleven Reagan administration officials, including the head of the National Security Council and the secretary of defense. Had Reagan not been so popular until then, he could easily have been impeached for defying Congress and lying about it. In the end, those who were convicted for their involvement in Iran-Contra soon had those convictions overturned on appeal, and the others charged were later pardoned by Reagan's Republican successor, George H. W. Bush. But the damage in the court of public opinion was devastating, and Reagan's approval rating sank.

The Peculiar End to the Cold War

Perhaps the most important figure in the complex world politics of the 1980s was a new Soviet leader named Mikhail Gorbachev. He had come up through the ranks of the Communist Party and, while a committed socialist, was increasingly critical of how the Soviet state controlled the domestic economy and the political life of the

≡ **Nuclear Diplomacy**   President Reagan and Soviet Premier Mikhail Gorbachev meet in Iceland to discuss limits on nuclear weapons. Convinced that ending the nuclear arms race was essential for his country, Gorbachev met several times with Reagan to discuss the topic, and the two eventually agreed to a treaty eliminating certain nuclear missiles.

country. What he saw was a rigid bureaucracy, an unproductive economy, and an aging leadership. He also recognized that the Cold War arms race was siphoning money to the military that could be better used to improve the material lives of Soviet citizens.

In March 1985, after the death of two older Soviet leaders in rapid succession, Gorbachev became general secretary of the Communist Party and, by extension, premier of the Soviet Union. He quickly set out on a reform agenda. One initiative, called *glasnost* (or opening), was meant to relax restrictions on the exchange of ideas, encourage more political debate, and make the Soviet state more transparent. The other reform initiative, called *perestroika*, aimed at economic liberalization by loosening centralized direction and permitting the establishment of some privately run businesses.

It was, however, in foreign affairs that Gorbachev truly shook the ground. He pulled all Soviet troops out of Afghanistan and some out of Eastern Europe. He vowed no longer to interfere in the affairs of other socialist nations, particularly those in the Eastern bloc. And he proclaimed a unilateral moratorium on nuclear testing in the Soviet Union. But his main goal was to negotiate an end to the nuclear arms race along with dramatic reductions in nuclear weapon arsenals. Doing so, Gorbachev believed, was critical to the future of his country.

In effect, Gorbachev called Reagan out. And Reagan, despite the wariness of some of his advisors, took up the challenge. The two initially met in Geneva in November

1985, and although no agreement was crafted, Reagan and Gorbachev agreed to meet again. Over the course of the next three years, the leaders would meet several times. Remarkably, given Reagan's earlier depiction of the Soviet Union as an "evil empire" capable of "barbarism," he and Gorbachev came to like and even to trust one another. Little by little, Reagan's own worries about the existence of nuclear stockpiles came into line with Gorbachev's determination to move down the path of nuclear disarmament. They ultimately signed a treaty eliminating all intermediate-range nuclear weapons and discussed at one point a 50 percent reduction in both their nuclear arsenals. Gorbachev went so far as to suggest the elimination of all nuclear weapons by 1996, an idea that Reagan also claimed to consider.

This was as far as things would go in nuclear diplomacy before Reagan's second term was finished in 1989. But the impact of Gorbachev's acceptance of self-determination in Eastern Europe was more dramatic still. Rumblings of discontent had been heard there since the late 1960s when Soviet tanks crushed a reform movement in Czechoslovakia. By the early 1980s, the Solidarity labor movement in Poland began to pressure the Soviet-backed regime, and when Gorbachev made it clear that Soviet tanks would no longer roll their way, reformers across Eastern Europe rose to oust their Cold War governments and conduct new elections. With the exception of Romania all this happened without bloodshed, nowhere more dramatically than in Germany.

A divided Germany had been the symbol of the Cold War, with the Wall in Berlin revealing the intensity of superpower rivalry. Yet demonstrations would soon erupt in East Berlin, and despite its reputation for repression, the Soviet-backed government made no move to suppress them. Indeed, the restrictions on movement that had long kept the Germanys separated were repealed in November 1989, and crowds of East and West Berliners not only joined one another; almost immediately, they began to rip the Wall apart, tossing pieces of stone and concrete into the air and onto the ground, marking the apparent ending of a world order—a dramatic power shift—that had been in place and framed the meaning and conduct of American and global politics for nearly half a century.

Scholars and other observers have debated the ending of the Cold War. Was this turn of events the result of early Reagan-era toughness that forced the Soviet Union to the negotiating table, in part because the arms race imposed undue burdens on the Soviet people? Or was it Gorbachev's reformism that made arms reduction negotiations, as well as the reformist uprisings, possible? There is no easy resolution to this debate; different interpretations reflect perspectives that span the political spectrum. But it is hard not to see a confluence of important events creating a political space that was previously unavailable. And it is especially important to recognize that popular mobilizations around nuclear disarmament and then around political reform in Eastern Europe were crucial to the outcome. The forces for change came from below as well as from above. Whether there would be a hopeful new beginning or political instability remained to be seen.

Conclusion: The New Conservatism

The decade of the 1980s saw a number of very significant shifts in power, both in the United States and around the world. A new conservativism, once thought moribund, began to frame the discussion of political and economic life, and came to power in the federal government really for the first time since the 1920s. From the perch of the presidency, Ronald Reagan spoke a language of optimism while declaring that the federal government was the problem rather than the solution to the challenges that beset the country. He steered through large tax cuts and continued a process of deregulation, begun under the Carter administration, that bolstered the financial sector and contributed to a widening inequality of wealth. Reagan also broke a strike of the Professional Air Traffic Controllers—sending a warning to the labor movement of his intentions to favor business at their expense—spoke in degrading terms of those on welfare and launched a war on drugs that laid the path toward mass incarceration. The American economy, too, saw an important shift in power, already begun in the 1970s, away from the old manufacturing belt from the Northeast through the Midwest and out to the Sunbelt and to countries like Mexico and China, where employers and corporations found a more profitable environment and the service and financial sectors were booming.

The shift to a new conservatism could also be felt in religious and cultural life, with the rise of the Moral Majority and the growth of evangelical Christianity, and with a pushback against the rights movements of the 1960s and 1970s. Conservative newspapers began to appear on college campuses, launching the careers of a great many young activists, and the Reagan administration was able to shift the federal courts, including the Supreme Court, in a more conservative direction. It was a trend that was replicated in Great Britain, as Margaret Thatcher took power, but also discouraged many political and public health officials from responding to the AIDS epidemic of the mid-1980s, associated as it was with homosexuality.

Perhaps the greatest shift in power came in the Soviet Union where Mikhail Gorbachev first initiated unprecedented economic and political reforms, pushed the Reagan administration to accept a more robust approach to nuclear arms control, and then allowed Soviet allies in Eastern Europe to break away and reorganize their societies and governments. Before it was through, the Cold War, which had threatened the planet since the end of World War II, seemingly came to an end, and the Soviet Union itself began to unravel. But it was unclear what sort of world would then be forged.

WHAT IF Drug Abuse Was Viewed as a Public Health Crisis?

In November 2016, the Surgeon General of the United States, Dr. Vivek Murthy, issued an important report in response to the raging opioid epidemic that had been afflicting the United States for more than a decade. Murthy insisted that we, as a society, change our thinking about drug abuse. Rather than looking at drug abuse as a product of "moral failure" or simply as a form of criminality, it should be viewed as a manifestation of complex social and biological determinants, and, ultimately, as a problem of public health. By this he meant that drug abuse should be approached with scientific research and treated by the use of prevention and recovery programs.

Murthy was not the first to call for a reorientation of public understandings and policies in relation to drug abuse and addiction. A variety of scientists and public health officials in the 1970s and 1980s urged similar approaches to the use of recreational drugs, like marijuana, as well as to more addictive drugs like heroin and crack cocaine. Following the lead of a number of European countries—the Netherlands, Portugal, and Great Britain—they urged the decriminalization of certain drugs, the establishment of needle exchange programs, and the use of methadone to wean addicts off heroin. The reports from Europe suggested that these programs could be successful and certainly worked far better than the resort to toughening drug laws and focusing on drug trafficking. But such programs that were established in the 1980s, mostly on the state and local level, received little support and were quickly shut down in favor of more punitive practices. Those that gained more recognition, such as "Just Say No" and D.A.R.E. (Drug Abuse and Resistance Education), proved to be ineffective.

But what if a public health approach had gained more traction? What if developments in Europe could have become more central to the discussion in the United States? Could a public health approach to drugs have shifted ideas about crime and criminality and have limited the militarization of urban police forces? And could such an approach have served to turn attention to recovery and rehabilitation rather than to incarceration? Given the public concern in recent years over opioid abuse, might issues of race have been influential, since most opioid abusers are white and many crack cocaine abusers were Black? Was this why it was easy to resort to criminality as a solution rather than public health?

DOCUMENT 28.1: Nancy Reagan, "Just Say No" (1982)

Nancy Reagan embraced the war on drugs as fervently as her husband. In 1982 she launched her "Just Say No" campaign.

As a mother, I've always thought of September as a special month, a time when we bundled our children off to school, to the warmth of an environment in which they could fulfill the promise and hope in those restless minds. But so much has happened over these last years, so much to shake the foundations of all that we know and all that we believe in. Today there's a drug and alcohol abuse epidemic in this country, and no one is safe from it—not you, not me, and certainly not our children, because this epidemic has their names written on it. Many of you may be thinking: "Well, drugs don't concern me." But it does concern you. It concerns us all because of the way it tears at our lives and because it's aimed at destroying the brightness and life of the sons and daughters of the United States.

For 5 years I've been traveling across the country—learning and listening. And one of the most hopeful signs I've seen is the building of an essential, new awareness of how terrible and threatening drug abuse is to our society. This was one of the main purposes when I started, so of course it makes me happy that that's been accomplished. But each time I meet with someone new or receive another letter from a troubled person on drugs, I yearn to find a way to help share the message that cries out from them. As a parent, I'm especially concerned about what drugs are doing to young mothers and their newborn children. Listen to this news account from a hospital in Florida of a child born to a mother with a cocaine habit: "Nearby, a baby named Paul lies motionless in an incubator, feeding tubes riddling his tiny body. He needs a respirator to breathe and a daily spinal tap to relieve fluid buildup on his brain. Only 1 month old, he's already suffered 2 strokes."

Drugs take away the dream from every child's heart and replace it with a nightmare, and it's time we in America stand up and replace those dreams. Each of us has to put our principles and consciences on the line, whether in social settings or in the workplace, to set forth solid standards and stick to them. There's no moral middle ground. Indifference is not an option. We want you to help us create an outspoken intolerance for drug use. For the sake of our children, I implore each of you to be unyielding and inflexible in your opposition to drugs.

Our young people are helping us lead the way. Not long ago, in Oakland, California, I was asked by a group of children what to do if they were offered drugs, and I answered, "Just say no." Soon after that, those children in Oakland formed a Just Say No club, and now there are over 10,000 such clubs all over the country. Our job is never easy because drug criminals are ingenious. They work every day to plot a new and better way to steal our children's lives, just as they've done by developing this new drug, crack. For every door that we close, they open a new door to death. They prosper on our unwillingness to act. So, we must be smarter and stronger and tougher than they are.

So, to my young friends out there: Life can be great, but not when you can't see it. So, open your eyes to life: to see it in the vivid colors that God gave us as a precious gift to His children, to enjoy life to the fullest, and to make it count. Say yes to your life. And when it comes to drugs and alcohol just say no.

Source: https://www.reaganfoundation.org/

DOCUMENT 28.2: Marsha Rosenbaum, "Just Say What? An Alternative View on Solving America's Drug Problem" (National Council on Crime and Delinquency, 1989)

Dr. Marsha Rosenbaum is the former director of the San Francisco office of the Drug Policy Alliance.

Our society must make a greater investment in drug education which does not simply attempt to scare young people into the conventional, prohibitionist view of drugs but includes education designed to impart a more factual understanding of drugs and drug-related problems.

The "Just Say No" curriculum can be inherently dangerous. When children are told that all illegal drugs (including marijuana) are extremely dangerous and addictive, and subsequently learn through experimentation that this is false, the rest of the message is discredited. A more honest drug education strategy would stress the dangers of all drugs, including those that are legal, and the value of abstinence. It would state that some, but not all drugs are highly addictive, and that many people do control their recreational use of illegal drugs. This may sound like dangerous heresy, but young people are going to find this out for themselves anyway. If we are honest we will not lose the confidence and trust of our youth. If we have been honest about a drug's effects, we can talk about the dangers of drug abuse without sounding like the "party line."

Given that illegal drug abuse has a deleterious physiological effect, it should be defined primarily as a health-related problem that should reside in the public health domain. In so doing, we might obtain better epidemiological data to estimate the true extent of the problem and re-allocate our resources from criminal justice to treatment, prevention, and education.

In reality, we do not know the exact extent of illegal drug abuse in this country. We base our estimates on three sources, the High School Senior Survey, the Household Survey, and the Drug Abuse Warning Network, each of which has limited value. If we approach illegal drug abuse as we do other "illness" patterns, and mount a full epidemiologic study (as is done with smallpox), we would be better informed on how best to respond to the problem.

By *not* putting the "drug problem" in the public health domain, we may be contributing to the failure of United States drug policy. A public health approach to illegal drugs would enable us to devote more of our limited resources to treatment of the problem. Since 1970, a larger proportion of tax dollars has been spent on interdiction, eradication and law enforcement than on treatment, prevention and education . . . This trend needs to be reversed.

Funds targeted for law enforcement and other social agencies could be partially used to support treatment programs that have some chance of diverting drug abusers away from self-destructive and socially harmful lives of addiction and crime. Many of these programs would be transitional treatment programs intended to detoxify individuals and prepare them for a drug free, productive, and satisfying life. And, they would be targeted to drug abusers who are unable to pay for treatment services.

The drug abuse of the underclass is not in and of itself the problem. Drug abuse is a *symptom* of a much deeper problem faced by tens of millions of individuals with blocked opportunities and severely limited life options.

Until we bring these alienated and excluded Americans into the mainstream, no significant progress can be accomplished in reducing drug abuse. People must have a *reason* to restrict use or abstain from drugs. The more one has to lose, the more one tends to control the use of substances that may put those possessions (material and other) in jeopardy; the less one has to lose, the less likely one is to control one's drug use. People with meaningful jobs, intact families, and social responsibilities try to preserve these by maintaining control and not abusing drugs.

To bring the millions of excluded and alienated Americans back into the mainstream, something approaching the 1960s "War on Poverty" is needed.

By *not* putting the "drug problem" in the public health domain, we may be contributing to the failure of United States drug policy. A public health approach to illegal drugs would enable us to devote more of our limited resources to treatment of the problem. Since 1970, a larger proportion of tax dollars has been spent on interdiction, eradication and law enforcement than on treatment, prevention and education. This trend needs to be reversed.

Source: https://www.ojp.gov/ncjrs/virtual-library/abstracts/just-say-what-alternative-view-solving-americas-drug-problem

Thinking About Contingency

1. Why wasn't drug abuse regarded as a public health problem by most politicians and policymakers in the 1980s?
2. Why would Nancy Reagan, given her influence, want to focus on "just saying no?"
3. What would it have taken for drug abuse to have been recognized as a public health problem?
4. How do you think race figured into the formulation of the drug problem?
5. How is the heroin and crack cocaine crisis of the 1980s similar to the opioid crisis today?

REVIEW QUESTIONS

1. How did demographic and economic shifts contribute to the conservative ascendancy in the 1980s?

2. What were the important economic policies of the Reagan administration, and how did they affect the economic landscape of the nation?

3. How different was the geographical makeup of the Republican Party in the 1980s from the party in the 1950s?

4. What were the cultural objectives that conservatives pursued during the 1980s, and how successful were they at achieving them?

5. The Cold War and related international tensions had domestic counterparts in the "wars" on drugs and crime. Were these related developments?

6. Cold War tensions escalated in the early 1980s, but after 1986 they began to ease and the Cold War soon came to an end. What were the most important factors in bringing this about?

KEY TERMS

AIDS Coalition to Unleash Power (ACT-UP) (p. 1203)

authoritarian regime (p. 1208)

Berlin Wall (p. 1186)

Contras (p. 1211)

culture war (p. 1200)

discretionary spending (p. 1193)

Drug Enforcement Administration (DEA) (p. 1214)

glasnost (p. 1221)

information economy (p. 1199)

insider trading (p. 1194)

Iran-Contra scandal (p. 1220)

liberation theology (p. 1211)

mandatory sentencing laws (p. 1215)

Moral Majority (p. 1200)

neoconservative (p. 1208)

nondiscretionary spending (p. 1193)

nuclear freeze (p. 1212)

originalist (p. 1205)

perestroika (p. 1221)

religious right (p. 1200)

Sandinistas (p. 1210)

Silicon Valley (p. 1199)

Special Weapons and Tactics (SWAT) (p. 1216)

Strategic Defense Initiative (SDI) (p. 1209)

supply-side economics (p. 1192)

totalitarian regime (p. 1208)

Vietnam Syndrome (p. 1208)

war on drugs (p. 1214)

RECOMMENDED READINGS

Radley Balko, *The Rise of the Warrior Cop: The Militarization of America's Police Forces* (PublicAffairs, 2014).

Donald T. Critchlow, *The Conservative Ascendancy: How the Republican Right Rose to Power in Modern America* (University of Kansas Press, 2011).

David Farber, ed., *The War on Drugs: A History* (NYU Press, 2021).

Joshua Freeman, *American Empire, 1945–2000* (Viking, 2012).

Marie Gottschalk, *The Prison and the Gallows: The Politics of Mass Incarceration in America* (Cambridge University Press, 2006).

Andrei Grachev, *Gorbachev's Gamble: Soviet Foreign Policy and the End of the Cold War* (Polity Press, 2008).

Michael B. Katz, *The Price of Citizenship: Redefining the American Welfare State* (Henry Holt and Company, 2001).

Kevin Kruse and Julian Zelizer, *Fault Lines: A History of the United States Since 1974* (W.W. Norton, 2019).

Doug Rossinow, *The Reagan Era: A History of the 1980s* (Columbia University Press, 2015).

Kirkpatrick Sale, *Power Shift: The Rise of the Southern Rim and Its Challenge to the Eastern Establishment* (Random House, 1975).

Ross A. Slotten, *Plague Years: A Doctor's Journey Through the AIDS Crisis* (University of Chicago Press, 2020).

Lawrence E. Walsh, *Firewall: The Iran-Contra Conspiracy and Cover-Up* (W.W. Norton, 1997).

29

New World Disorder
1989–2004

Chapter Outline

29.1 A Complex Peace Dividend

Compare and contrast how the post–Cold War "peace dividend" shaped the lives of different groups of Americans.

29.2 Political Warfare

Explain how a period of political warfare was unleashed in the United States that would involve Republicans and Democrats as well as groups of extremists.

29.3 Global Volatility

Explain how the end of the Cold War contributed to the unraveling of centralized states and new and deadly conflicts around the world.

29.4 The Road to 9/11

Discuss America's response to the terror attacks of September 11, 2001.

≡ **Not the End of History**   Although hopes were high that the fall of the Berlin Wall might mark a new and more peaceful era, that new order never arrived. Despite the end of the Cold War, American armed forces continued to engage in conflicts throughout the world. Here a US soldier guards a position in Mogadishu, the capital of Somalia, in 1993.

In the summer of 1989, political scientist Francis Fukuyama published "The End of History?" In his article, Fukuyama reflected on the ending of the Cold War and its meaning for the world. His claims were audacious. Fukuyama was not, of course, suggesting that history had come to an end. How could that be so long as human beings walked the earth? Rather, he argued that, with the dissolution of the Soviet Union and the ending of the superpower conflict that had defined the globe since 1945, humankind had reached an end to a long process of ideological evolution. Western liberal values and democracy, he insisted, had not only triumphed, but they were to be universalized among nations and societies. They therefore represented "the final form of human government."

Although Fukuyama's ideas quickly drew serious criticism—as one might expect—they also seemed to capture a widespread sense that the ending of the Cold War had closed the door on an entire era of history and opened the door to something new and possibly better. After all, the Cold War had divided the world into rival camps and political economies; fostered revolutions and "hot"

Timeline

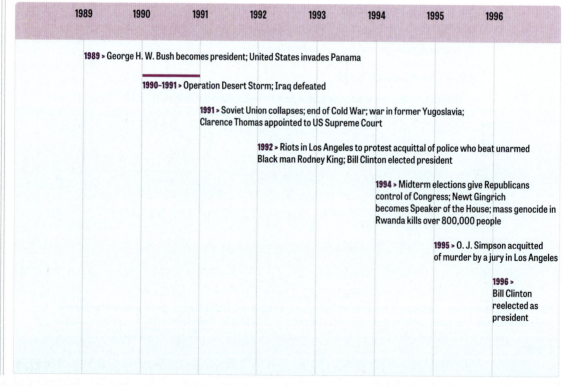

1989	1990	1991	1992	1993	1994	1995	1996

1989 > George H. W. Bush becomes president; United States invades Panama

1990–1991 > Operation Desert Storm; Iraq defeated

1991 > Soviet Union collapses; end of Cold War; war in former Yugoslavia; Clarence Thomas appointed to US Supreme Court

1992 > Riots in Los Angeles to protest acquittal of police who beat unarmed Black man Rodney King; Bill Clinton elected president

1994 > Midterm elections give Republicans control of Congress; Newt Gingrich becomes Speaker of the House; mass genocide in Rwanda kills over 800,000 people

1995 > O. J. Simpson acquitted of murder by a jury in Los Angeles

1996 > Bill Clinton reelected as president

wars in Latin America, Africa, the Middle East, and Asia; and held humanity hostage to weapons of unfathomable destruction. Recognizing the enormous resources that had been devoted to military spending for nearly half a century, American and European leaders began to speak of a "peace dividend," in which the energies and resources spent on weaponry would be redirected to more constructive social purposes.

The visions could be grander still. Even before the Soviet Union collapsed, its leader, Mikhail Gorbachev, spoke to the United Nations General Assembly in December 1988 of a **new world order** waiting to emerge. Gorbachev described a world in which cooperation between nations would replace conflict, the United Nations would be strengthened, rival economic blocs would dissolve, nuclear disarmament would prevail, the use of force would be discredited, wealthier nations would aid developing countries, and environmental protection would assume international importance. With fewer specifics, American President George H. W. Bush embraced the concept as well. A "new world

1997	1998	1999	2000	2001	2002	2003	2004

1998 > Bill Clinton is impeached by the House of Representatives; he is later acquitted

2000 > The Supreme Court awards George W. Bush the presidency in a contested election

2001 > Al Qaeda attacks the United States on September 11; US-led coalition forces invade Afghanistan

2003 > US-led coalition forces invade Iraq

order," he imagined, involved "new ways of working with other nations, peaceful settlements of disputes, solidarity against aggression, reduced and controlled arsenals, and just treatment of people."

A hopeful vision, and yet history demonstrates that the passing of one era and the emergence of a new one is often accompanied by unrest, dislocation, disorientation, and violence. And although the Cold War era was indeed marked by truly existential crises of survival, it had also framed global politics and organized political identities for decades. What would happen when that framework ceased to exist? The emerging new order seemed to leave one country—the United States—as the sole superpower, with no real rivals on the planet. It also seemed to designate one social system—capitalism—as the only viable political and economic structure. But might the "new world order," with its utopian prospects, disguise the potential new *disorder* that the end of the Cold War could usher in? When President Bush invoked the "new world order" in 1991, he had only recently sent American troops into Panama to topple the government of Manuel Noriega, who was wanted for drug-trafficking (bringing condemnation from the United Nations) and had just engaged in a quick but brutal war against the Iraqi regime of Saddam Hussein. Perhaps Francis Fukuyama was right about only one thing: the end of the Cold War defined a turning point of great significance for the entire world.

29.1   A Complex Peace Dividend

Compare and contrast how the post–Cold War "peace dividend" shaped the lives of different groups of Americans.

After a brief but serious recession in the early 1990s, the American economy experienced an economic boom for the remainder of the decade. Although it did not match the quarter century following World War II in overall performance, the economic expansion proved to be the lengthiest on modern record and touched the lives of most Americans regardless of their racial or ethnic backgrounds. Unemployment fell to levels not seen since 1973 (below 5 percent), and family incomes widely rose. Before the decade was out, median household income reached an all-time high (over $42,000) and, quite remarkably, the federal government had a budget surplus following years of massive deficits.

This seemed to be the peace dividend many had hoped for now that the Cold War had come to an end. But the closer one looked the more complex—and deceptive—that dividend turned out to be. Many of the trends of the previous decade not only continued but, in some cases, accelerated. Inequality in incomes and wealth, increasingly evident during the 1980s, soared during the 1990s while the real wages (measured against inflation) of middle and working-class Americans remained stagnant or even declined. Home ownership increased and consumption became more robust, but people worked longer hours and took on increasing levels of debt. While optimists imagined that a new era of prosperity had arrived, pessimists warned that the prosperity rested on an unstable foundation (see Figure 29.1).

FIGURE 29.1 A Complex Peace Dividend The peace dividend generated wealth for many Americans, but at the same time, the disparities between the rich and the poor accelerated.

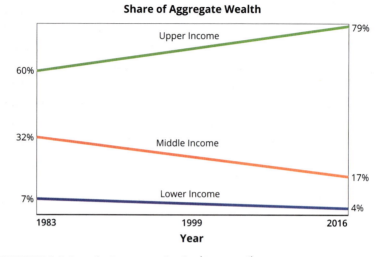

Share of Aggregate Wealth

FIGURE 29.1 **A Complex Peace Dividend**   (Continued)

A New World of Finance and Technology

The great driver of the 1990s economic boom was the stock market, a phenomenon not seen since the 1920s. Between 1990 and 2000, the major share price indexes grew by unprecedented amounts, lining the pockets of investors and corporations (see again Figure 29.1). The Dow Jones average, which measures the stock values of the country's largest companies, nearly quadrupled. The NASDAQ (National Association of Securities Dealers Automated Quotations), which measures the values of technology stocks, increased more than seven-fold. Ordinarily, stock prices reflect the profitability of companies, but during the 1990s, stock values far exceeded rates of corporate profits or increases in productivity.

There were several reasons for this. Corporations began purchasing huge blocks of stock either to carry out mergers and acquisitions (buying up other companies or merging with them) or to boost their own share prices (Chapter 28). When there are more buyers than sellers, the stock price rises. Since many CEOs and other executives received company stock as part of their compensation packages, increasing share prices further enriched them. Equally important, the decade witnessed the dot-com boom: the creation of the Internet, the proliferation of telecommunication and software companies, and the growth of online-only retailers like Amazon (established by Jeff Bezos in 1994 as a bookseller) and search engines like Google (established in 1998). Investors saw unrivalled possibilities to strike it rich and bought stocks in the technology sector hoping to ride the wave. But share prices were often dramatically overvalued (which meant that they greatly exceeded the value of the company), putting investors and employees alike at potential risk.

The stock market boom was encouraged by government policies that kept interest rates low, which stimulated stock and other corporate investments, and repealed restrictions on the activities in which commercial, as opposed to investment, banks could engage. Ever since the New Deal, commercial banks, which mainly serviced individual depositors, were prohibited from partaking in stock or real estate speculation (Chapter 22). But in the late 1990s, Congress removed those restrictions and gave commercial banks new investment opportunities using the money of depositors who rarely benefitted from, or were even aware of, what was happening to the funds in their checking and savings accounts. The biggest banks increasingly invested in real estate, insurance, and securities markets that offered high risks as well as high potential rewards. Not surprisingly, the number of hedge funds grew significantly during the decade, as did the use of sophisticated computer programs to carry out their complex tasks, another indication of the power of the American financial sector that was launched during the 1980s.

The boom in the technology and telecommunications industries gave enormous energy and sophistication, not to mention reach, to developments that had begun during the 1980s. Cable television, which first emerged in the late 1940s to give rural and underserved communities access to broadcast networks, quickly grew to provide programming that the big three networks (CBS, NBC, ABC) lacked or refused. Home Box Office (HBO) brought unedited or uninterrupted films into viewers' homes; Entertainment and Sports Programming Network (ESPN) gave fans of numerous sports a much wider range of options; and Music Television (MTV) made music videos a central part of youth culture and transformed the music industry. By the 1990s nearly a majority of households with televisions had become cable subscribers, even though cable was "pay" TV. By the turn of the new century, that proportion had risen to 60 percent.

Equally important was the emergence of cable news, especially the Cable News Network (CNN), founded in 1980. Instead of waiting for the 6 p.m. or 11 p.m. news broadcast on public access stations, viewers could now tune in at any time to find out what was happening at home and abroad, with more expansive coverage of politics, business, sports, and entertainment. The possibilities were only slowly realized during the 1980s but became transformational during

≡ **Technology Titan**   Computing entrepreneur Bill Gates poses in Times Square in 2001 with the latest generation of the Windows operating system.

≡ **Broadcasting the War**   A CNN camera crew in action during the First Gulf War, 1991.

the 1990s as cable viewers literally got front-row seats to developing news stories in real time. Although the Vietnam War received TV coverage, the reporting featured the work of broadcast journalists who filed their stories after battles or other events. In contrast, the First Gulf War of 1990–1991 was broadcast live from beginning to end. While CNN offered traditional news coverage with limited editorializing, its popularity gave rise during the 1990s to more politically oriented news and information outlets such as MSNBC and Fox News, both launched in 1996. The cultural and political impact would be enormous.

Perhaps most consequential for ordinary Americans was the advent of cell phone technology. The idea for mobile telephones had percolated since the 1940s, but the first, and very large, mobile phone was manufactured and offered for sale by Motorola in 1983 at a price of nearly $4,000. The Motorola phone was remarkably popular given the cost, though it relied on a system that was not secured and vulnerable to eavesdropping. This changed in the early 1990s with the arrival of digital, 2G cellular networks and smaller hand-held devices. While dial-up conversations were the main function of these phones, the first SMS text message was sent in Finland in 1993 and IBM devised an early version of a smartphone that same year. Daily life and communication would never be the same.

Race on View

The explosion of telecommunication networks and new media outlets had an enormous impact on how Americans would see each other and the world. This was especially true when it came to race. MTV began by focusing on white audiences and the music of white performers, but under pressure the channel expanded its repertoire of videos. Michael Jackson was the first of the Black recording artists MTV promoted—notably his smash 1982 album *Thriller*—opening the door to others in the mid- to late 1980s. By the early 1990s, hip-hop and rap music, which emerged from poor Black and Latino communities like New York's Harlem and the South Bronx in the late 1970s, won a massive following among young people across lines of race and ethnicity. Controversial because of lyrics which seemed to celebrate hostility to the police, "gangstas," and misogyny, hip-hop and rap also served as a critique of racial inequalities and poverty as well as expressions of artistry and imagination. When the music went mainstream during the early 1990s,

it elevated new Black performers who defied categories of racial acceptance to positions of cultural
authority and wealth.

These cultural productions reflected the increasing complexity of race in the post–civil
rights era. Two episodes that received massive
media attention embodied these complexities. One was the 1991 nomination of Clarence
Thomas to a position on the Supreme Court
by Republican president George H. W. Bush.
Thurgood Marshall, a towering figure of civil rights jurisprudence and the only (and first)
African American justice, was retiring due to
ill health. The forty-three-year-old Thomas had

≡ **Hip-Hop Royalty**   Public Enemy in the early 1990s.

served on the US Court of Appeals in the District of Columbia for just over a year,
but he was Black and conservative, and so might satisfy Black people who wanted to maintain a seat on the Court while rewarding conservatives still bruised by
Robert Bork's rejection a few years before (see Chapter 28). Although a beneficiary of such policies, Thomas was known to be deeply hostile both to civil rights
legislation and affirmative action programs. Civil rights advocates—Black and
white—made their opposition to Thomas's nomination clear: "we're going to Bork
him," one activist threatened. But Thomas had come from a humble background
and, following the advice of his conservative supporters, refused to express any of
his views on controversial subjects like *Roe v. Wade* or civil rights law during his
confirmation hearings.

Moderate Democratic Senator Joe Biden of Delaware chaired the Senate
Judiciary Committee and seemed intent on steering the process toward confirmation when sexual harassment allegations against Thomas surfaced. The accus-
er was Anita Hill, a Black law professor at the University of Oklahoma, who had
worked with Thomas at the federal Equal Employment Opportunity Commission
(EEOC) before Thomas became a judge. Biden had heard about the charges but
declined to take them seriously; now he had to give Hill the chance to testify.

Hill's testimony was explosive and damning. She described incidents that
ranged from unwanted sexual attention to Thomas's explicit talk of pornographic
films. Thomas flatly denied the allegations, provocatively calling them a "high tech
lynching for uppity blacks." And although Hill's stories seemed credible, Biden
and the other white male senators sitting in judgment questioned her character
rather than Thomas's. Thomas was confirmed in the end, by a narrow 52–48 vote,
and continues as a bedrock of conservatism on the Supreme Court more than

thirty years later. But Anita Hill's appearance both highlighted political divisions among Black people—different viewpoints of the working class and an expanding professional and middle class—and dramatized the issue of sexual harassment in the workplace that millions of women of all races endured despite Title VII of the 1964 Civil Rights Act. Although not fully apparent at the time, the long-term effects would be significant.

The complexities of race and class played out with special drama two years later in what turned into one of the most watched and discussed criminal trials in American history. Standing accused was O. J. Simpson, a Black celebrity known best as a football star and actor. In June 1994, Simpson's ex-wife, Nicole Brown Simpson, who was white, and her friend Ronald Goldman, also white, were found stabbed to death outside Nicole Simpson's home in Los Angeles. Although O. J. Simpson was quickly questioned and released, when a warrant went out for his arrest, Simpson fled, initiating a car chase broadcast live on national television. Some viewers thought he might take his own life; many believed Simpson's behavior indicated his guilt. Ultimately the chase came to an end, and Simpson turned himself in. The subsequent trial, which began in November 1994, lasted nearly a year.

Simpson had tremendous public visibility and the resources to assemble a top-flight legal defense team. His lawyers included Robert Kardashian (husband of Kris and father of Kim, Kourtney, and Khloé of later fame) and Johnnie Cochrane, a Black lawyer who practiced in Los Angeles and had served as a county district attorney. Los Angeles prosecutors thought they had a strong case, but Simpson's lawyers, especially Cochrane, were able to raise doubts in the minds of the jurors, who were majority female and Black, about the reliability of the evidence and the racist motives of the police. Most memorably, Simpson theatrically demonstrated that the gloves he was supposed to have worn to commit the murders were too small for his hands. "If it doesn't fit," Cochrane said during his closing argument, "you must acquit!"

The jury did acquit Simpson. But most interesting was the public reaction, which followed closely along racial lines and showed the clashing perspectives at the heart of American cultural and political life. The overwhelming majority of Black people, women as well as men, working class as well as middle class, believed

≡ **"If it doesn't fit, you must acquit!"**   O. J. Simpson, on trial for the murders of his ex-wife and her friend, demonstrates to jurors—and a nationwide live audience—that a glove found at the crime scene was too small for his hands.

the jury verdict was correct; the majority of white and Latino people believed that Simpson was guilty and the verdict was "racially motivated." They all had considerable opportunities to form their own opinions because the trial was televised from beginning to end and, with twenty-four-hour news programming like CNN, journalists and legal experts could share their views of the trial for hours. When the verdict finally was announced on the morning of October 3, 1995, more than 150 million viewers—almost 60 percent of the entire country—tuned in.

The Simpson trial was not the first experience that Los Angeles had with race and the new media ecosystem. In March 1991 a Black man named Rodney King was pulled over by the Los Angeles County police after a car chase. Suspected of drunk driving and ordered out of the car, King was then brutally beaten by at least four of the officers while more than a dozen looked on. Ordinarily, nothing would have come of this incident of racially motivated police brutality—three of the officers were white, one was Latino—but a witness named George Holliday recorded the episode. Holliday, who was white, contacted the police to see if they would be interested in his recording. When the officers rebuffed him, he brought his video to a local television station, which broadcast it that same night. The video soon went viral across the country. The four policemen were then charged with assault and excessive use of force, but their trial was moved out of Los Angeles to a neighboring county where a jury of ten white people and no Black people was seated.

Despite the compelling video evidence, in late April 1992 the jury shockingly acquitted the police officers, two of whom were later convicted in a civil lawsuit. King, himself, later won a settlement against the city. But enraged by the blatant racism, Black Los Angeles erupted. Rioting spread over the course of six days, mostly in the poor Black South-Central district, fed by other frictions between Black people and Korean Americans in the city. Before it was over, more than sixty people had been killed, more than 2,000 injured, more than 12,000 arrested, and more than $1 billion in property had been damaged or destroyed. Covered almost continuously on television, the riots—which touched off violence in a number of other cities—not only exposed the deep racial tensions and hostilities between Black residents and the police. They also revealed the economic inequalities that left poor city-dwellers powerless, vulnerable, and angry, as well as the simmering tensions between the Black community and newer immigrant communities, like the Koreans. It was all an unsettling reminder of who the peace dividend was reaching and who was left out.

The racial disparities and contradictions were then brought home more peacefully but no less powerfully in the fall of 1995 when nearly 900,000 African Americans, mostly men, assembled on the National Mall in Washington, DC, for a "Million Man March." Organized by Louis Farrakhan, the controversial leader

PERSPECTIVES

Race and Sex at the Turn of the Millennium

The increasing complexity of race and sex in the post–civil rights era came into focus during the nomination hearings for Clarence Thomas to the Supreme Court in 1991. The nationally televised questioning and testimony by both Thomas and Anita Hill sparked a debate on the seemingly conflicting issues of women's rights and Black rights. Some African Americans, even women, joined attacks on Hill, seeing her accusations against a prominent Black man as disloyalty to the race. Thomas cast himself as a victim of racism despite the fact that Hill, too, is Black, calling the hearing "a high-tech lynching for uppity blacks who in any way deign to think for themselves." Others accused then-Senator Joseph Biden, chair of the Senate Judiciary Committee, of allowing Thomas and his defenders to degrade Hill's character and destroy her credibility. The committee was also criticized for agreeing to only examine Thomas's behavior in the workplace. Consequently, witnesses who

Anita Hill Testifying Before the Senate Judiciary Committee   Hill endured harsh questioning from members of the Judiciary Committee; at least one senator accused her of lying under oath.

were prepared to come forward with evidence of sexual harassment by Thomas outside of work never testified. In the end, Thomas was confirmed by a narrow margin, but Anita Hill became a symbol and catalyst for the #MeToo movement decades before it had a name.

☰ **Clarence Thomas with Joseph Biden and Strom Thurmond** Thomas enjoys a laugh with Committee Chairman Joseph Biden and Senator Strom Thurmond of South Carolina. Thomas's 52–48 confirmation victory was the slimmest in over a century.

CONSIDER THIS

The Clarence Thomas hearings spawned an intense debate in the Black community about Anita Hill's responsibility to women and her right to publicly criticize Thomas. They also dramatized the issue of sexual harassment in the workplace that millions of women endure. How are issues of Black rights and women's rights connected and contradictory at the same time? Can you think of other periods in US history where African American rights and women's rights have clashed?

of the Nation of Islam, speakers nonetheless included a wide array of Black leaders, from Jesse Jackson, Rosa Parks, and poet Maya Angelou to pop-star Stevie Wonder. Together they not only emphasized the need to build Black political power but also counseled Black men and husbands to commit themselves to the health and well-being of their children, families, and communities: to turn inward as well as outward in promoting the destiny of the race.

A Changing of the Guard

Among the politicians who saw the possibilities of the "Internet highway" was Al Gore, a Tennessee senator from a powerful political family and in 1993 the new vice president of the United States. He had been elected the previous November on a ticket with Bill Clinton, the governor of Arkansas, who became the first Democrat to win the presidency since 1976. Both men seemed to be departures from previous national candidates. They were of the baby-boomer generation, influenced by the cultural and political changes of the 1960s (Clinton admitted to smoking marijuana though insisted that he didn't "inhale"). Both also hailed from the South—it was unusual to have two southerners on the ticket—and seemed ready to take on the challenges of a post–Cold War America.

But it was unclear where they fit on the political spectrum. Clinton got involved with the Democratic Leadership Council (DLC) during the 1980s in an effort to move the party toward the political center and win back white voters who had supported Ronald Reagan. Yet he also needed to maintain the allegiance of party liberals. It was a difficult line to toe. As organized labor lost its power because of deindustrialization and Republican attacks, the Democratic Party had come to depend on Black voters who suffered most in the new economy and wealthy whites who were socially liberal though more moderate on economic policy.

Clinton was helped in the election by a recession during the fourth year of Bush's presidency as well as by popular exhaustion with the lengthy reign of Reagan and Bush. He was helped, too, by the entry into the presidential race of Ross Perot, a billionaire businessman from Texas, who insisted that the economy was "broken" and effectively campaigned as an independent candidate against Bush. Clinton tried to speak to the concerns of "middle-class" voters who were, he told them, paying more and getting less from the government, who "worked hard and played by the rules" but nonetheless lost out to the rich and the "special interests." Like Perot, Clinton argued that the economy was in bad repair and needed to be fixed. "It's the economy, stupid!," one of his campaign advisors regularly chanted.

The strategy worked. Although Clinton won only a plurality of the popular vote (43 percent), he won an overwhelming majority of the electoral votes by reclaiming a number of southern states that had been going Republican. Perot failed to win any electoral votes, but he won nearly 20 percent of the popular vote, more than any third-party or independent presidential candidate since the election of 1856. It was an achievement that signaled both voter dissatisfaction with the two main political parties and a willingness to move in new directions.

The Clinton administration quickly took on an issue that had bedeviled Democrats and the country as a whole since the New Deal: health care. The United States was the only advanced nation in the world to lack a system of government-sponsored universal health in-

≡ **A New Direction**   Bill and Hillary Clinton with Al and Tipper Gore at a 1992 campaign event. Both hailed from Sunbelt states (Arkansas and Tennessee, respectively) and won back southern states that had begun to go reliably Republican.

surance. Earlier efforts to move in that direction by Harry Truman, Lyndon Johnson, and Richard Nixon had collapsed. As a result, as many as fifty million Americans either were inadequately covered or lacked health insurance entirely, and the US health care system cost more on a per capita basis than any other in the world. Clinton learned that there might be a public groundswell for some sort of health care reform, and although he wished to avoid looking like a "tax and spend liberal," he saw this as an important and potentially winning issue. And he had an idea of how the political shoals might be navigated.

Clinton organized a task force headed by his wife, Hillary Rodham Clinton, a formidable lawyer with particular interest in child advocacy though with relatively little direct experience in politics. The task force could have tried to build upon the systems of Medicare and Medicaid, focusing on more of a publicly funded (or "single-payer") approach, which would have appealed to the progressive wing of the Democratic Party. Instead, the task force chose to rely on the private sector, with responsibility left chiefly to employers, a structure of "managed competition" that would keep premiums charged by health insurance companies in check. Initially, this apparently moderate approach won support from both parties, as well as from larger corporations that wanted to bring order to the system. But smaller businesses objected to the plan's mandate requiring employers to provide health coverage, and further doubts were raised owing to the secrecy of the task force's proceedings and the complexity of the 1,300-page proposal itself. Health insurance and pharmaceutical companies, together with some physicians' groups, began to mount resistance to the plan, and Republicans soon joined them. They warned of an expanded government bureaucracy, restrictions on patient choice, and possible health care "rationing." While seeking to steer clear of a government-run health care system, the Clinton administration plan was tarred with that brush anyway and couldn't recover. The initiative went down to defeat without even coming to the floor of Congress. It was a sign of where things were headed.

29.2   Political Warfare

Explain how a period of political warfare was unleashed in the United States that would involve Republicans and Democrats as well as groups of extremists.

The failure of the health care initiative not only was a disappointment to the Clinton administration; it was also a signal to Republican opponents that he was vulnerable to attack. From the time he decided to run for president, Bill Clinton rankled many conservatives because he seemed to symbolize the culture wars they lost in the 1960s. Even though Clinton appeared interested in moving the Democratic Party to the right and thus acknowledging the influence of the Reagan presidency, he was cast as a radical and an enemy who had to be taken down. Despite their long reign in power, or perhaps because of it, Republicans were now prepared to declare war on Clinton and the Democratic Party and to fight with new weapons.

Newt Gingrich and the Contract for America

The leader in the Republican battle against Clinton and his administration—including his wife, Hillary—was Georgia congressman Newt Gingrich. Gingrich had earned a doctorate in history and was teaching at a small Georgia college when he decided to run for Congress in the 1970s. Georgia was still a bastion of the Democratic Party, as Jimmy Carter's rise to the presidency showed, but it had been trending conservative in a backlash to civil rights protests and school desegregation. "White flight" from cities like Atlanta to metropolitan suburbs was one of the manifestations and gave Republicans new electoral traction.

After three losses, Gingrich finally won a seat in 1978 and he soon began organizing young conservatives who had been elected to the House of Representatives as part of the Reagan ascendancy. Gingrich was not only conservative in his politics, but he also believed that the best way to secure conservative power was by demonizing the Democrats, portraying them as "radicals," "liars," "hypocrites," and "traitors," and mounting an aggressive campaign against them. He and other conservatives were helped in this by new forms of media that circulated their messages widely. They first availed themselves of a new cable network, C-SPAN (Cable-Satellite Public Affairs Network) to broadcast their speeches from the floor of the House of Representatives. They also benefitted from the explosion of "talk radio" programming, which was overwhelmingly conservative, to

≡ **A "Contract with America"** House Minority Whip Newt Gingrich of Georgia addresses a rally of Republican candidates on Capitol Hill in the run-up to the 1994 midterm elections.

advance their views and criticize their opponents. None of the talk radio broadcasters ("shock jocks" as they came to be called) was more consequential than Rush Limbaugh, a college dropout, who reached an audience of more than twenty million. He lambasted "commie-libs," "feminazis," and "environmentalist wackos" and soon set his sights on the Clinton White House.

Gingrich and his Republican allies in Congress looked to the midterm elections in 1994 in hopes of taking control of both the House and the Senate. Although the party in power usually suffers legislative defeats in the midterms, this would not be an easy task. The Democrats had held congressional majorities since the early 1950s, save for six years in the 1980s (1981–1987) when Republicans took charge in the Senate. The plan, formulated by Gingrich and Texas Republican colleague Dick Armey, was to rally all Republican candidates and incumbents around a set of policy initiatives called the **Contract with America**, which they promised to support if they prevailed in the election. The Contract called for a constitutional amendment requiring a balanced federal budget, term limits for elected officials, a congressional line-item veto, tax cuts, Social Security reform, anticrime legislation, and welfare reform. These initiatives were designed to shrink the size of the federal government, limit social spending programs, strengthen the private sector, and increase the vulnerabilities of minority populations. In effect, although congressional elections generally revolve around state and local issues, the Contract with America gave the 1994 midterms a national stage. The strategy paid off. The Republicans gained fifty-four seats in the House and nine in the Senate, and now commanded both chambers. They also won a slew of governorships even in states like New York that normally went Democratic. To top it off, Gingrich was rewarded by being elected Speaker of the House of Representatives, a position of significant power.

The Paramilitary Right

On the morning of April 19, 1995, a few months after the 1994 midterms, a vehicle packed with explosives detonated in front of the Alfred P. Murrah Federal Building, a US government complex, in Oklahoma City, Oklahoma. The blast could be heard more than 50 miles away and the destruction was immense. Much of the formidable Murrah Federal Building was leveled, leaving a hole 30 feet wide and 8 feet deep, and structures within a four-block radius were badly damaged. Most tragically, the explosion took the lives of 168 people, including 19 children, inside and wounded more than another 500. It was, to that point, the deadliest act of terrorism in American history.

Fairly quickly a suspect in the bombing named Timothy McVeigh was arrested. Although he claimed to be acting on his own, McVeigh was in fact part of a larger "white power" and antigovernment movement that had been growing since the late 1970s but experienced rapid expansion during the early 1990s. Like many other movement adherents, McVeigh was a military veteran who fell under the influence of right-wing extremists and racists while in the service. Once out of uniform, McVeigh moved around a great deal, briefly joined the Ku Klux Klan in Arizona, and then became involved with the notorious Michigan Militia and, especially, one of its members who was already interested in blowing up the Murrah Building.

The **white power movement** emerged out of disenchantments with the Vietnam War, a sense among some white veterans that they had been betrayed by the military and political leadership, suffered trauma for no reason, and sacrificed for no recognized cause. The Watergate scandals, the civil rights and feminist movements, and the economic woes of the late 1970s and early 1980s bred further anger at the disruption

≡ **Homegrown Terror** The aftermath of a devastating truck bomb in Oklahoma City, Oklahoma, on April 19, 1995. The attack was carried out by a far-right extremist named Timothy McVeigh.

of familiar race and gender relations as well as hostility to the federal government itself (see Chapters 27 and 28). Bringing together neo-Nazis, Klansmen, and members of the Christian Identity movement, which predicted a racial apocalypse, white power activists were soon plotting to overthrow the government and eliminate other enemies. Many had been influenced by *The Turner Diaries*, a novel published in 1978, that narrated a violent revolution and race war in the United States resulting in the overthrow of a Jewish-controlled federal government and the extermination of Jewish people, Black people, other people of color, politicians, and liberals. McVeigh was carrying the novel with him as he drove to and from Oklahoma City.

The end of the Cold War turned the white power and antigovernment movement in an ideological direction that vilified global internationalism, with anti-Semitic overtones, and the new world order it appeared to herald. Young "skinheads," mostly from cities, were increasingly attracted to the movement's violent orientation, as counterparts in England and Germany had been. Federal suppression of white separatists involved in illegal weapons trafficking in Ruby Ridge, Idaho (1992), and of a religious cult (the Branch Davidians) in Waco, Texas (1993), further inflamed hostility to the government and spawned a militia movement that soon had more than 50,000 members—and perhaps as many as five million sympathizers and supporters—in all fifty states. Militias embraced the racism of the white power movement and a wider hatred for various forms of government "tyranny." Taxation, immigration, land rights, local sovereignty, and, of course, gun rights were hot-button issues; many militia members were neo-Confederates and advocates of white "homelands" policies, which would confine different racial and ethnic groups to specific territories around the country, something like Indian reservations.

Timothy McVeigh was tried, convicted, and sentenced to death for his part in the Oklahoma City bombing. Two others were tried as accomplices and sentenced to prison terms. But the episode was a culmination and a catalyst: a brutal example of right-wing paramilitarism and a magnet for further activity and recruitment, much of it now taking place on the Internet. Newt Gingrich and his Republican colleagues had no connection with either the white power or militia movements, yet it was no accident that they shared a similar timeline of development. Trading on fears of crime, multiculturalism, and government overreach, especially as to gun rights, Gingrich's was the electoral side of the new forms of political warfare being waged.

Outflanking the Republicans

Several days after the bombing of the Murrah Building, President Clinton traveled to Oklahoma City and, before a large audience of mourners, gave an eloquent eulogy that summoned public sympathy for the lives lost and cast racial and political hatreds as a threat to everything America was supposed to embody. "When there is talk of hatred," Clinton advised, "let us stand up and talk against it." The president struck a resonant chord; a large majority of Americans appreciated what he said and did. And, in many ways, the eulogy was the beginning of a reset to Clinton's presidency. It also seems to have temporarily dampened the surge in right-wing extremism.

To be sure, Clinton knew he was in political trouble. He recognized the midterms as a referendum on his presidency and feared that he could well join Jimmy Carter as a one-term president when national elections were held the next year. If he couldn't get a health care plan enacted when Democrats controlled both houses of Congress, how could he get anything done with Republicans in charge? Taking the advice of a conservative-leaning consultant named Dick Morris, he therefore decided on a new course. For all intents and purposes, Clinton would beat the Republicans at their own game.

This did not require all that much of a political shift. A savvy politician, Clinton always believed that politics was the art of the possible, that it required a keen sense of where the wind was blowing and a willingness to compromise. Although health care seemed to be a strongly liberal issue, Clinton simultaneously threw his support in the direction of more conservative priorities: budgetary caution, free trade, and anticrime legislation. In so doing, he acknowledged corporate economic interests on the one side and public concerns about drug-related crime on the other.

While he often spoke of the woes of the middle class and depended on the support of African Americans—the great Black novelist Toni Morrison remarkably called him "our first Black president"—Clinton stocked his cabinet with "deficit hawks"

☰ **Militarized Police**   The 1994 Crime Bill was part of President Clinton's attempt to make Democrats appear tough on crime. While Clinton claimed the bill helped decrease violent crime, it also institutionalized mass incarceration as a core part of American public policy. In this photo, a SWAT team in Los Angeles raids the house of a suspected criminal.

who had strong connections to the worlds of finance and big corporations. They quickly persuaded him to focus on reducing budget deficits—which meant limiting the scale of government programs that benefitted the elderly, the poor, and people of color—and enhancing the international position of big businesses. Clinton therefore abandoned talk of a middle-class tax cut and helped steer the **North American Free Trade Agreement (NAFTA)**, which Bush had negotiated, through Congress. The treaty lowered trade barriers between the United States, Canada, and Mexico, not only opening markets for exporters but also enabling companies to close up shop in the United States and move their operations to Mexico where labor costs were far lower and regulations less burdensome. Many Democrats objected to the treaty because it threatened good-paying and unionized jobs in the United States, but Clinton chose to join hands with centrist Democrats and Republicans to get the treaty ratified. Viewed by Clinton as a policy success, NAFTA would come back to haunt the Democratic Party later on.

Recognizing that Republicans, and especially Newt Gingrich, had long portrayed Democrats as "soft" on crime, Clinton also embraced a "get tough" approach that he had rolled out during the 1992 campaign when he took on a Black rapper, Sister Souljah, for her racially charged lyrics. Although banning the manufacture of semiautomatic assault weapons and targeting violence against women, the Violent Crime Control and Law Enforcement Act of 1994 (known as the 1994 Crime Bill) dramatically increased funding for police hiring (100,000 new officers) and prison construction, made gang membership a federal offense, eliminated inmates' access to higher education, expanded use of the federal death penalty, and made provision for "three strikes" laws, mandating life imprisonment for repeat offenders. Clinton won the support of the National Organization of Police Officers and would attribute declining rates of violent crime over the course of the 1990s to the bill's effects. Yet, at the same time, rates of imprisonment at state and federal levels spiked, and would continue to grow, as mass incarceration, already evident in the 1980s, became a foundational component of public policy and the American social order (see Chapter 28).

If anything, Clinton's desire to save his presidency after the midterm debacle led him further to the right. He signed the **Defense of Marriage Act**, a conservative measure meant to demonize gay marriage and define legal marriage as a "union between one man and one woman" (it passed overwhelmingly in Congress), backslid on his promise to end the ban on gay people in the military (deciding instead on a weak, "**Don't Ask, Don't Tell**" policy which still left gay recruits subject to exclusion), and called into question the scope and methods of affirmative action. Proclaiming in his 1996 State of the Union address that "the era of big government is over," Clinton then took on welfare reform, another albatross that the Republicans hung on the necks of Democrats. He had earlier promised, as a seeming nod to Reagan, to "end welfare as we know it" and, after negotiating with Newt Gingrich, signed the **Personal Responsibility and Work Opportunity Act (PRWOA)** in August 1996. As the name suggests, PRWOA reflected a bipartisan view that poverty had cyclical cultural causes and dependency on the federal government had to be broken. The act replaced the prevailing system of welfare, Aid to Families with Dependent Children (AFDC), which had its origins in the New Deal and Great Society (Chapter 26). Clinton's reforms gave more latitude to the states for implementation, limited the time that recipients could get benefits, required them to get jobs within two years of receiving welfare (there was funding for job training), and reduced eligibility for food stamps. Although economic growth during the late

1990s made it appear that welfare reform was working as the numbers on welfare rolls declined, reform left a great many families more vulnerable when the country's economic fortunes changed.

Conundrums of Immigration

Among those who lost welfare benefits owing to PRWOA were legal immigrants in the United States. Their numbers had been growing rapidly in the country since the mid-1960s when Congress passed, in 1965, the Immigration and Nationality Act (see Chapter 26). That act pried open the gates that had been closed since 1924 by the National Origins Act, which had set strict quotas, especially for potential migrants from southern and Eastern Europe, while maintaining the ban on Asians. The sources of immigration thereby began to shift away from Europe and toward Asia, Africa, and Latin America (including the Caribbean basin), accelerated by the ending of the Vietnam War and warfare in El Salvador and Nicaragua. Legal immigration grew from about 4.5 million in the 1970s to more than 9 million in the 1990s, accounting for a substantial share of the country's overall population growth (see Figure 29.2).

About half of the immigrants during these years came from Latin America. So substantial was this migration that by the turn of the twenty-first century, people of Hispanic descent surpassed the number of those of African descent living in the United States. They were joined by immigrants from across Asia: Vietnamese, Laotians, Cambodians, and Filipinos from the southeast; Indians, Pakistanis,

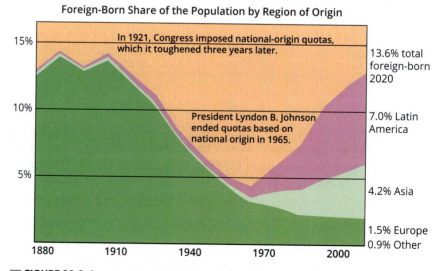

Foreign-Born Share of the Population by Region of Origin

≡ **FIGURE 29.2 Immigration, 1880–2017**   About forty-five million foreign-born Americans reside in the United States, close to 14 percent of the total population. In 1965, about 5 percent of the US population was foreign-born.

Bangladeshis, and Iranians from farther to the west; and Chinese, including Taiwanese, and Koreans from the east. They spoke many different languages, practiced different faiths (Buddhist, Hindu, Muslim, Catholic), and came from different social backgrounds. Some were poor and from rural areas; some were well-educated with professional skills and, perhaps, monetary resources.

For the most part, wherever they came from, immigrants headed to large metropolitan centers like Los Angeles, San Francisco, Chicago, Houston, Miami, Washington, DC, and New York. Enclaves known as Koreatown, Little Tokyo, Cambodia Town, and Little Havana soon sprouted, promoting a middle class of shopkeepers and a jealous regard of their communities. Ethnic tensions and conflicts could easily erupt, as the riots sparked by the arrest of Rodney King in Los Angeles demonstrated. The United States had a new and potentially volatile racial and ethnic mix.

California and the Southwest became cauldrons of multiculturalism and political struggles over immigration and its economic consequences. Conservative Republicans increasingly found traction by warning that immigrants took jobs from native-born Americans and posed threats to American values and culture. Some pushed for laws making English the "official language" in states like Texas, Florida, Arizona, and California, or outright banning bilingualism. But the focus was less on legal immigrants than on undocumented immigrants, derisively called "illegal aliens," and the supposed challenges they posed to state and local governments and the locales in which they lived, even if temporarily.

Efforts to fashion some type of federal immigration reform began to take shape in the 1980s but proved difficult to enact owing to the divisions reform created in both parties, especially the Republican Party. Republicans who were most strongly pro-business recognized their supporters' dependence on hiring undocumented workers and were reluctant to limit or cut off the migrant flow. Others felt the pressure from worried whites and long-settled immigrant groups looked to turn off the spigot. As a result, Congress could not put together a comprehensive immigration reform package. The best that they could do was pass a bill that offered legal status to some undocumented workers, bolstered the border patrol, and penalized employers who hired the undocumented, though the penalties proved impossible to enforce.

≡ **Immigrant Workers** Immigrants in Los Angeles wait to pick up work as day laborers. Immigrants faced a variety of measures meant to make them feel unwelcome, including efforts to ban bilingualism or to refer to them as "illegal aliens."

MAPPING AMERICA

Demographic Change, 1960–2000

The US Census Bureau uses the Diversity Index (DI) to measure the probability that two people chosen at random will be from different racial and ethnic groups.

The DI takes the percentage of each group in each county's population and calculates the chance that any two people are from different groups. The index ranges from 0 (no diversity) to 100 (highest diversity). The DI shows that diversity surged between 1960 and 2000.

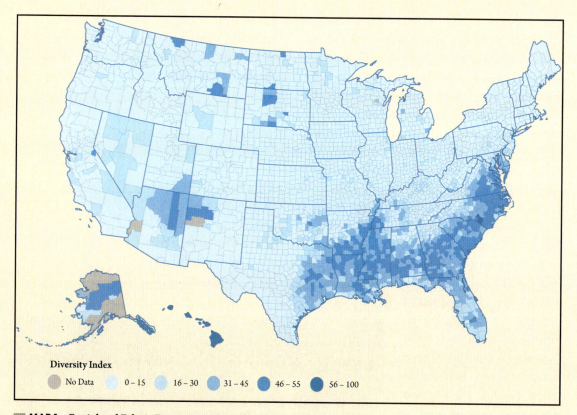

Diversity Index

No Data   0 – 15   16 – 30   31 – 45   46 – 55   56 – 100

≡ **MAP 1   Racial and Ethnic Diversity, 1960**   The DI index was 20 in 1960. Diversity was highest in the South and parts of the West.

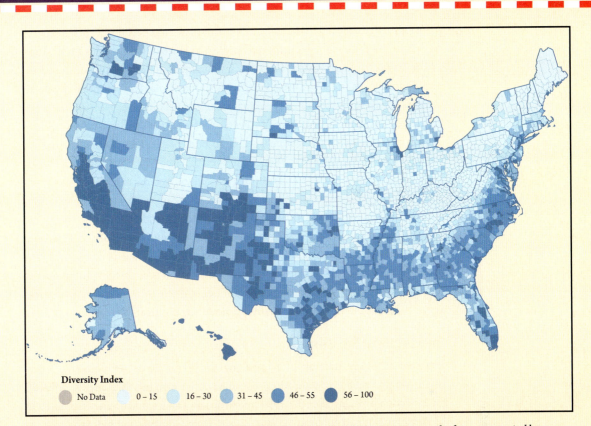

Diversity Index

No Data   0 – 15   16 – 30   31 – 45   46 – 55   56 – 100

≡ **MAP 2   Racial and Ethnic Diversity, 2000**   The DI Index rose to 49 in 2000. During the forty-year period between 1960 and 2000, the Southwest experienced the biggest increase in diversity.

Thinking Geographically

E Pluribus Unum—"out of many, one"—is the traditional motto of the United States. Is it, in fact, true?

1. In Map 1, the South has the highest level of diversity. What about southern society in 1960 puts its DI score into a more nuanced perspective?

2. Thinking about American society today, is the DI the best way to measure diversity? Can you suggest other ways to measure diversity?

3. In 2020 the DI score was 61. Demographers estimate that in 2060 the DI score will be over 70. Which regions of the country do you expect will experience the biggest increase in diversity between 2020 and 2060, as measured by the DI?

The initiative then fell to the states. California saw an especially heated and nasty contest in 1994. Republicans put a referendum on the ballot, known as Proposition 187 or "Save Our State," that would deny undocumented immigrants social and educational services and make them vulnerable to arrest and deportation. Republican Governor Pete Wilson, who was seeking reelection despite a very low approval rating, seized the issue in an attempt to reverse his fortunes. Vilifying "illegal aliens," Wilson ran incendiary ads that pictured thousands of Mexicans flowing across the border virtually unchecked. "They keep coming," the voice-over warned. "Two million illegal immigrants to California. The federal government won't stop them at the border, yet requires us to pay billions to take care of them." Although opinion on Proposition 187 was initially split, when the November election arrived, the referendum prevailed by nearly 60 percent of the vote and Pete Wilson came from behind to win another term as governor. Opponents quickly sued and succeeded in having Proposition 187 overturned in the federal courts as unconstitutional. But the public sentiment it embodied would influence the federal welfare reform package of 1996 and mark another front in the mounting political warfare.

Impeaching Bill Clinton

President Clinton's strategy of outflanking the Republicans on domestic policy issues—it was called "triangulation"—seemed to be working. Although written off for reelection by many after the 1994 midterms, he easily won another term in 1996 by defeating both Republican Senator Robert Dole (Kansas) and independent candidate Ross Perot. But the Republicans were by no means ready to back down, especially because they retained control of both Houses of Congress. Well before the 1996 election, they had launched investigations of Clinton for financial improprieties in an Arkansas real estate deal during the 1980s and for sexual harassment while he was governor of that state. Although neither of the investigations resulted in charges of criminal wrongdoing, they showed how careless Clinton was in his financial affairs and how flagrantly he may have abused his power in his personal affairs. They also showed that his enemies were ready to go to great lengths to undermine his presidency.

Clinton didn't help himself out. In early 1998, word leaked about a sexual relationship he had with a young White House intern, only a few years older than his daughter Chelsea, named Monica Lewinsky. Suddenly on the spot, Clinton not only lied to his family, lawyers, and closest aides but also lied under oath about Lewinsky when he was subject to a deposition in another case: a sexual harassment suit brought by a woman, Paula Jones, who had worked for him in Arkansas. Eventually, Clinton acknowledged the relationship and apologized to the nation, though not to Lewinsky, for what he had done. The Republican independent counsel leading the investigations, Kenneth Starr, recommended impeachment proceedings and released a lengthy report which contained explicit details about the Clinton–Lewinsky relationship.

Clinton had clearly behaved in a brazen and inappropriate way and had misled the American public about what had happened. But did this rise to the level of an impeachable offense, which the Constitution describes as "treason, bribery, or other high crimes and misdemeanors"? House Republicans apparently thought so. They brought articles of impeachment against Clinton for perjury (lying under oath) and obstruction of justice. When the vote to impeach came before the House on December 19, 1998, all but a handful of Republicans and only five Democrats voted in support. Bill Clinton became only the second sitting president in American history (Andrew Johnson was the other) to suffer impeachment. The case then went to the Senate, which, under the Constitution, would sit in judgment.

Many Democrats, including those who were leaders in the women's movement and had denounced the treatment of Anita Hill, came to Clinton's defense, at least on the question of impeachment. And there was, in fact, little chance he would be convicted and removed from office by the Senate, since conviction required a two-thirds vote of the members, and Republicans had nowhere near the requisite number of votes. Indeed, they could muster no more than fifty votes for conviction, with a few Republicans joining all of the Democrats in voting to acquit.

Bill Clinton remained in office for the rest of his term. Remarkably, despite the tawdriness of the episode, the damage was minimal. If anything, the public seemed to think that congressional Republicans had greatly overstepped; Clinton's conduct may have stained his personal reputation, but his job approval rating grew to over 70 percent. The Republicans had mounted the most serious offensive the Constitution allowed them, and they lost in Congress as well as the court of public opinion. What remained to be seen was whether it was simply a battle or the entire war.

29.3   **Global Volatility**

Explain how the end of the Cold War contributed to the unraveling of centralized states and new and deadly conflicts around the world.

With the end of the Cold War, the American public turned its attention away from events around the globe to focus on what was happening at home. After all, according to American and Soviet leaders alike, the emergent new world order would replace decades of militarized conflict and the threat of nuclear warfare with an era of international peace and cooperation. Yet, however dangerous, the Cold War had established a framework of global politics in which opposing sides were easy to recognize and the main actors were established states and their allies. What would happen when this framework of power began to disintegrate? Was there anything to replace it that was conducive to peace and cooperation? In fact, the end of the

Cold War brought new imbalances of power to the world stage and, as a result, new conflicts and actors appeared that proved very difficult to manage through customary diplomatic means. Before the end of the decade, the world may have become an even more dangerous place than it had been before 1989.

Unraveling

Ever since the seventeenth century, the political trajectory of the Euro-American world had been in the direction of state-building and consolidation. The local power of estate owners, lords, princes, and small kingdoms was increasingly undermined first by absolute monarchs and then by developing nation-states. So enduring was this trend that by the twentieth century, the nation-state seemed the political norm against which other political units were measured and legitimized. The state edifice would stand even if the rulers came and went.

In this respect, the end of the Cold War brought about a remarkable reversal, first apparent in the Soviet Union. The Soviet Union emerged in 1922 as a consequence of the Bolshevik Revolution. It was a union of fifteen separate republics (thus the Union of Soviet Socialist Republics—USSR) stretching from the Baltic to the Black Sea and to the Pacific, with Russia, by far the largest of them, at its center. The task for Soviet leaders was to maintain the allegiance of these republics through a combination of rewards and possible penalties. And, between 1922 and the mid-1980s it worked, despite some ripples. But when Mikhail Gorbachev set out on a program of political and economic reform, the balances tipped away from the center and stimulated movements for self-governance and independence. One by one, the Soviet republics broke away from the Soviet Union and established governments of their own choosing. Rather than stepping in to prevent this from happening, Gorbachev did nothing. By 1991, the Soviet Union had disintegrated, the Communist Party had been banned, fourteen independent republics came into being, and a Russian federation took shape (see Map 29.1). History can shift into reverse.

The centrifugal energies that were unleashed in the Soviet Union soon became evident in the countries of Eastern Europe that had surrounded the Soviet Union to the west and composed the Warsaw Pact of Soviet satellites (Chapter 25). The loyalties of these countries had long been regarded as crucial to the security of the Soviet Union, and on several occasions—especially in Hungary in 1956 and Czechoslovakia in 1968—the Soviets intervened militarily to crush reformist unrest. This time it was different. Under Gorbachev, there was no intervention and, one after another, the members of the Warsaw Pact rejected their alliance with the Soviet Union and began to topple the communist governments that had ruled over them: Poland, Czechoslovakia, Hungary, Yugoslavia, Albania, Bulgaria, East Germany, and Romania (Map 29.1). Astonishingly, all of this happened, save for

Romania, without bloodshed; in Romania, the four-decade-old government of
Nicolae Ceausescu was not only overthrown, but Ceausescu and his wife, Elena,
were tried and executed. More unraveling ensued.

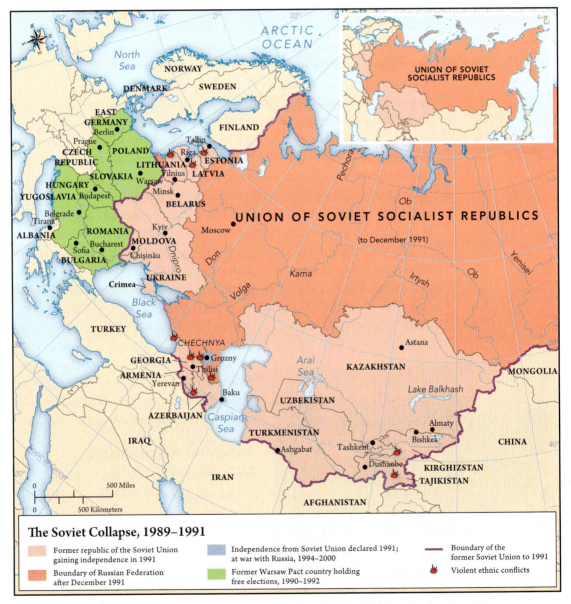

The Soviet Collapse, 1989–1991

▨	Former republic of the Soviet Union gaining independence in 1991
▨	Boundary of Russian Federation after December 1991
▨	Independence from Soviet Union declared 1991; at war with Russia, 1994–2000
▨	Former Warsaw Pact country holding free elections, 1990–1992
——	Boundary of the former Soviet Union to 1991
✸	Violent ethnic conflicts

MAP 29.1   The Soviet Collapse, 1989–1991   Between 1989 and 1991, the Soviet Empire collapsed, starting in
Eastern Europe and culminating in the dissolution of the Soviet Union. To Russia's west, Ukraine, Belarus, Estonia,
Latvia, and Lithuania gained independence, and in the Caucasus, the republics of Armenia, Georgia, and Azerbaijan
secured their freedom. In what had been Soviet Central Asia, a half-dozen predominantly Muslim republics emerged.

The speed and relative peacefulness of this process of dissolution was all the more remarkable given the tensions and animosities to be found in each of the Warsaw Pact countries. During World War II, many of the people in them sided with the Nazis and aided in the extermination of Jews and those regarded as political undesirables. Others opposed the Nazis and joined the resistance to fight against them. Soviet occupation during the war and political control thereafter kept these divisions in check, but what would happen once independence from the Soviet Union was proclaimed? Equally problematic were deep ethnic and religious differences that had long shaped the culture and politics of Eastern Europe, particularly in the Balkan nation of Yugoslavia, where East met West most convulsively.

Czechoslovakia very quickly split in two, the product of a "Velvet Revolution" that overthrew communist power: the Czech Republic with its capital of Prague to the west, and the Slovak Republic with its capital of Bratislava to the east. Yugoslavia, a confederation of six republics that had achieved political stability under communist leader Josip Tito, was another story. There the end of the Cold War unleashed bitter and bloody fighting that turned the republics and their ethnic and religious groups against each other. Part of the problem was the legacy of World War II; much of the problem was the rise of Serbian and Croatian nationalism and deep hostility against Muslims, who were most numerous in the republic of Bosnia. War broke out in 1991 and, after the slaughter of civilians and the massacre of Muslims in Srebrenica, continued first, until the US-brokered Dayton (OH) Accords in 1995, and then again until 1999 when the United States, the United Nations, and NATO forcefully stepped in. Today, in place of Yugoslavia, one can find a collection of smaller state entities: Croatia, Bosnia and Herzegovina, Slovenia, Montenegro, Macedonia, and Kosovo, and ongoing tensions in many of them (see again Map 29.1).

Turmoil in Africa and the Middle East

Ethno-religious strife and civil warfare were by no means confined to Eastern Europe. They erupted forcefully on the African continent and in the Middle East as well. Located on the horn of east Africa, the republic of Somalia, which had gained independence in 1961, descended into civil war in 1991 shortly after the overthrow of a lengthy dictatorship. Somalia's colonial past, which involved the British, the

≡ **Mourning the Victims of Genocide**   A Bosnian Muslim mourns at a funeral for some of the men and boys killed in the Srebrenica massacre. In 2004 an international court unanimously ruled that the killing of over 8,000 male residents of Srebrenica was an act of genocide.

Italians, and the French and made for different institutional structures and linguistic traditions, created a context for conflict; a sudden political vacuum that made it difficult to reestablish a central government encouraged rival clans and warlords to vie for power. Violence and the threat of mass starvation led to the intervention of UN peacekeepers and, briefly, US troops, but warfare persisted and, by the end of the decade, Somalia had broken up into a number of regional power centers.

Events in Rwanda proved equally explosive and far more deadly. Independent since 1962 after decades of German and Belgian colonial rule, Rwanda was divided between two ethnic groups: the majority Hutu and the minority Tutsi. Struggles that solidified Hutu power sent many Tutsis into neighboring states as refugees, but in 1990 they struck back and invaded Rwanda. Amid bitter fighting, the Hutu government began to persecute and execute Tutsis who remained behind and, in the spring of 1994, after the Hutu leader's plane was shot down and blamed on the Tutsis (it remains unclear who was responsible) a genocidal massacre of Tutsis commenced. Within the span of only three months, more than 800,000 Tutsis were slaughtered. But the Tutsi military soon gained the upper hand and, for their part, wreaked vengeance on Hutus held responsible for the genocide, killing as many as 100,000 of them. It was a bloodbath of epically tragic proportions that seeped into and destabilized surrounding countries, too, before a coalition government in Rwanda turned things in a more peaceful direction.

In South Africa, the strife was not between rival ethnic and religious groups but between the minority white, Afrikaner (of Dutch descent) government and the majority African population which had endured a brutal **apartheid** regime imposed in 1948 but with roots in the late nineteenth century. The Black struggle was organized chiefly by the African National Congress (ANC), which had been inspired by Garveyites (Chapter 25) and American civil rights activists. But the ANC was bitterly opposed by the white government, which inflicted devastating repression and jailed ANC leaders, including Nelson Mandela, in 1960. Then, during the 1980s the ANC went on the offensive both in South Africa and internationally, mobilizing many Western nations, the US and British governments only reluctantly, to impose economic sanctions on the apartheid regime and spurring mass antiapartheid movements in Europe and the United States, with college students playing important roles. In 1990, buoyed by this support, the ANC was able to negotiate

≡ **President Nelson Mandela** Newly elected South African president Nelson Mandela with members of the Congressional Black Caucus in October 1994.

Mandela's release and then an end to the apartheid system. With majority rule now in place, Mandela was elected South Africa's president in 1994. It was a huge, and welcome, turn of events.

Conflict roiled the Middle East as it did Africa. To a large extent, this was a continuation of the long-term Arab-Israeli contest that had erupted into warfare in 1967 and 1973, led to Israeli occupation of the Golan Heights, the Gaza Strip, and much of the West Bank of the Jordan River, and stirred deep discontent among Palestinians: they had no homeland, were denied basic rights, and suffered impoverishment wherever they lived (Chapter 27). In 1987, the twentieth anniversary of the Six-Day War, Palestinians in Gaza and the West Bank launched a rebellion—an **Intifada** or "shaking up"—that put these issues on the table and drew international attention. By the early 1990s, a peace agreement had been worked out between the Israelis and the Palestinian Liberation Organization (PLO) that provided for the withdrawal of Israeli forces from Gaza and a part of the West Bank and seemed to lay the groundwork for a Palestinian state. But the agreement proved to be short-lived, and the Intifada exposed a deepening rift between the PLO and a more radical Palestinian organization called Hamas, driven by a new Islamic fundamentalism that emerged during the Intifada itself.

Growing strains among Islamic peoples were further evidenced by a brutal war between Iraq and Iran beginning in 1980. The Iraqi state, which was controlled by Sunni Muslims and headed by autocrat Saddam Hussein, worried about the new Shi'ite regime in Iran and its potential export of the 1979 revolution that had brought the Ayatollah Khomeini to power (Iraq was home to many Shi'ites as well). The Iraqis launched a preemptive strike which quickly bogged down into trench warfare, replete with chemical weapons, before the Iranians made a counterattack. Stalemate ensued with mounting casualties on both sides until a truce was worked out in 1988. But across the Middle East and eastward into Afghanistan and Pakistan, it was clear that Islamic states and non-state organizations had emerged as important forces on the global stage. One of them, established in 1988 as both the Iran-Iraq and the Soviet-Afghan wars ended, was called Al Qaeda, Arabic for the "foundation," and led by a Saudi Arabian named Osama Bin Laden.

29.4   The Road to 9/11

||| Discuss America's response to the terror attacks of September 11, 2001.

The end of the Cold War seemed to demand a reorientation of American foreign policy. Ever since the late 1940s, American political leaders had forged a bipartisan consensus around the containment of the Soviet Union together with opposition

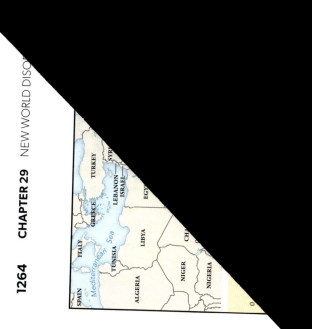

to the spread of communist and socialist move

the world. Although periods of détente opened t

peaceful coexistence, renewed Cold Warfare co

the early 1980s with the ascendancy of Ronald

Union was no more and the socialist world dep

porter, how would a new foreign policy be forge

tives? Should the American military be dramati

international bases closed up? Should NATO be

ty turned over to the European Union alone? Sh

es be reconsidered? The new world order had left

position globally but at the same time in need of

The First Gulf War

Before serious discussion about the road ahea_ __ ___ _ _

boiled over in the Middle East. In the summer of 1990, the Iraqi government of
Saddam Hussein launched an invasion and occupation of Kuwait, on its border
to the south. Kuwait was not a beacon of freedom and democracy; it had an authoritarian political order. But Kuwait was also a major global supplier of oil, and
its conquest would enable Iraq to control a very large portion of the international
oil market while putting oil giant and American ally Saudi Arabia, a neighbor of
Kuwait's, at risk of Iraqi attack.

Whatever foreign policies might change as a result of the end of the Cold War,
the importance of oil to American national security was never questioned. The
Bush administration immediately insisted that the Iraqis be confronted and forced
to retreat. Reluctant to act unilaterally and by executive fiat, Bush succeeded in
assembling a large international coalition, including Russia and some other Arab
states, and winning narrow congressional support for military action (Map 29.2).
Thousands of American troops were sent to Saudi Arabia to be readied for action.
When Hussein then refused to bow to the pressure of a UN Security Council
demand that he withdraw his forces from Kuwait, a massive US-led air and land
operation—known as **Operation Desert Storm (First Gulf War)**—was launched,
and broadcast in real time by CNN and other global networks.

Desert Storm lived up to its name. Within days the Iraqi army was expelled from
Kuwait and coalition forces moved rapidly into southern Iraq. Coalition ground
troops and computer-directed air strikes devastated the Iraqi army while the Iraqi
capital of Bagdad suffered massive bombardment by cruise missiles as well as
manned aircraft. After six weeks, Hussein sought a cease-fire that left him in power
but apparently badly weakened. Indeed, Bush and the coalition imagined that popular uprisings in Iraq would soon topple the Hussein regime without requiring an

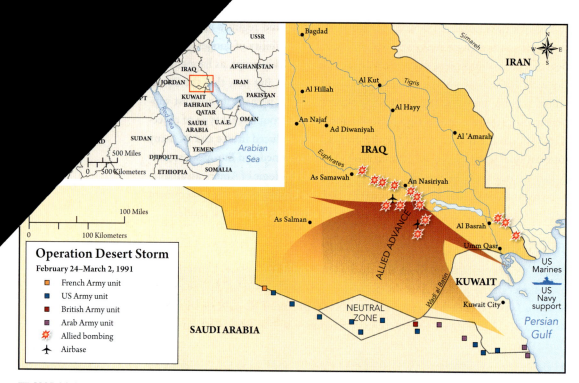

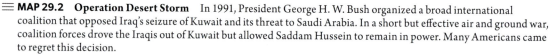

≡ **MAP 29.2   Operation Desert Storm**   In 1991, President George H. W. Bush organized a broad international coalition that opposed Iraq's seizure of Kuwait and its threat to Saudi Arabia. In a short but effective air and ground war, coalition forces drove the Iraqis out of Kuwait but allowed Saddam Hussein to remain in power. Many Americans came to regret this decision.

occupation of the country. Very quickly, the troops who fought in Desert Storm left Iraq, having sustained few casualties, and Bush pointed to the war as an example of the type of collective security that a post–Cold War world might make possible. But the Iraqi uprisings never materialized and, from his base in Afghanistan, Al Qaeda's Osama Bin Laden fumed at the American military's deployment in his native Saudi Arabia.

What Is Our Mission?

President Bush may have regarded Operation Desert Storm—the First Gulf War—as an example of conflict resolution in the post–Cold War world, but it also suggested that the United States would need to remain combat ready. As a result, ideas about downsizing the military and reining in the sprawling network of US bases around the world were never seriously entertained. The United States, it appeared, would fully embrace its position as the lone superpower and maintain the necessary military might. If anything, the Gulf War suggested that the use of high-tech weaponry, including drones, could well change the nature of warfare itself and encourage development of new and sophisticated means of destruction that might also keep many ground troops out of harm's way.

It was, of course, one thing to mobilize a response to an American security threat but quite another to navigate the currents of a rapidly changing world in which the main US adversary was no longer on the scene. Did the United States have a serious rival? Would China fill that role, even though the two countries were more and more involved with each other? The Russians and the members of the old Warsaw Pact seemed eager to embrace some form of capitalism as well as representative institutions based on popular elections. For its part, NATO was hoping to bring some of the countries of Eastern Europe into the fold, though not the Russians, who took a dim view of such a move, and thereby boost European security (see Map 29.3).

The Clinton administration had no real answers to these geopolitical questions, though President Clinton did take the opportunity to court the new Russian leader, Boris Yeltsin. The problem became acute when humanitarian crises arose owing

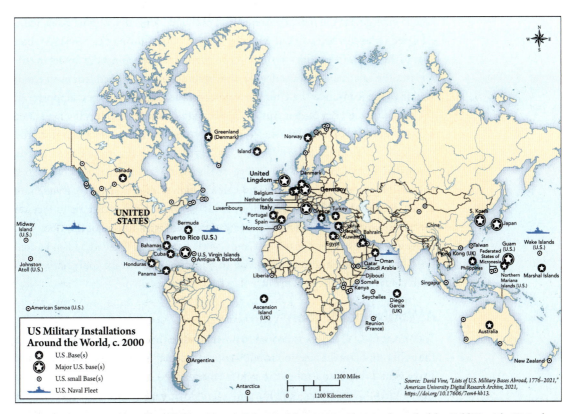

≡ **MAP 29.3   US Military Installations Around the World, c. 2000**   Despite the end of the Cold War, The United States kept its military budget at high levels and considered the entire globe as its sphere of influence.

to conflicts that did not involve American allies or areas of direct national interest: in Somalia, the Balkans, and Rwanda. Should the United States intervene to prevent genocide or provide aid to refugees and suffering civilians? Clinton's perspective seemed haphazard. Troops were sent to Somalia to assist in distributing food and other supplies, but they got caught in the crosshairs of fighting and suffered casualties (the downing of two Blackhawk helicopters and the death of nearly twenty American soldiers). When ethno-religious war broke out in the former Yugoslavia, the United States remained on the sidelines until the Srebrenica massacre; then the United States helped broker a truce, supplied peacekeepers, and participated in NATO-led airstrikes to halt anti-Muslim violence in Kosovo. The genocide in Rwanda cried out for some sort of response, but here the Clinton administration simply refused to act, raising questions about the relative value placed on the lives of Europeans and Africans.

The growing international threat of the period came not from established states but rather from non-state actors, often motivated by religious fundamentalism, who used terror tactics meant to punish enemies and disturb the status quo. Al Qaeda emerged as the most consequential of them. Ironically, Osama Bin Laden, Al Qaeda's leader, had worked with the United States during the Soviet-Afghan War of the 1980s in an effort to support the Afghan rebels against the Soviet invaders. But the relationship soured when the United States stationed troops in Saudi Arabia in the lead-up to the Gulf War and continued to be the major supporter of the state of Israel. Bin Laden and Al Qaeda were committed to leading a *jihad* or holy war against the infidels in the West, and by the early 1990s effectively declared war against the United States. In 1993, an Egyptian radical with ties to Al Qaeda detonated a truck bomb in the garage of the World Trade Center in New York City, killing six people and inflicting half a billion dollars in damage. By the late 1990s, the number of Al Qaeda–directed attacks multiplied and came to include the bombing of American embassies in Kenya and Tanzania and of the *USS Cole*, an American destroyer docked in Yemen. Well aware of Al Qaeda and Bin Laden, the Clinton administration made plans to hunt him down and cripple his organization, but never carried them out.

A Worrisome Election

The threat of Al Qaeda was not well known among the American public. Indeed, the public mood as the election of 2000 approached suggested that the Democratic Party would retain control of the White House. The economy was booming, the stock market was roaring, inflation and unemployment were low, the government was running a budget surplus, and the country was neither at war nor deeply entangled in conflicts abroad. Polling showed that nearly seven Americans in ten were satisfied with how things were going. The political warfare that Republicans had been waging against Clinton appeared to have flopped.

The Democrats chose the sitting Vice President Al Gore as their candidate for the presidency. Bill Clinton's impeachment seemed to have left little mark on either Clinton or Gore; indeed, Clinton would leave office with remarkable popularity. Rather than mount a campaign that smacked of the Contract for America, which now seemed relegated to the political dustbin, the Republicans nominated George W. Bush, the son of President George H. W. Bush and the governor of Texas, who was regarded as an affable lightweight. Bush promised a "compassionate conservatism," lower taxes, and an interest in bipartisanship, a far cry from the take-no-prisoners approach of Newt Gingrich, who had been forced out of the speakership due to ethics violations.

But the election turned out to be exceedingly close. Gore distanced himself from Clinton and ran a weak campaign; Bush came across during the election debates as more competent than many assumed. On Election Day, there was a mixed result. Gore won the popular vote by about half a million ballots, but the Electoral College tally was so tight that the election's outcome would rest on the returns in the state of Florida, where a handful of votes separated the candidates. At first, it seemed that Gore would prevail; then it appeared that Bush was the winner. Finally, it was apparent that Election Day would not produce a winner and a recount, the first in American history, would be necessary. The recount dragged on with each side bringing its case to court, either to stop the recount (the Bush side, which was still ahead by a few hundred votes) or continue the recount (the Gore side, which was gaining ground little by little). The legal struggle ultimately reached the Supreme Court, which had a majority of Republican-appointed judges. On December 12, 2000, more than a month after Election Day, the justices determined in a 5–4 vote that the recount should be halted and Bush declared president (see Map 29.4). Never before had the high court intervened in a national election. The Court could in fact have refused to take the case and let the recount continue. The damage to the country's political institutions would be considerable.

Terror from the Skies

The Bush administration, like the Clinton administration before it, focused on domestic policy issues. Bush quickly pushed an education reform initiative called the **No Child Left Behind Act**, which required school districts to administer standardized tests evaluated by the federal government. He also pushed through a massive tax cut which, like those enacted by the Reagan administration, proved to be a windfall for the wealthy. Little attention was turned to the international arena, though intelligence reports were very worrisome. They began warning of possible Al Qaeda

The Presidential Election of 2000

Candidate (Party)	Electoral Vote (%)	Popular Vote (%)
Bush (Republican)	271 (50.5%)	50,455,156 (47.9%)
Gore (Democratic)	266 (49.5%)	50,992,335 (48.4%)
Other candidates		3,949,150 (3.7%)

≡ **MAP 29.4 The 2000 Presidential Election**   For the first time in American history, the results of the presidential election were recounted—and then by the Supreme Court. It was the first time that the high court intervened in a national election.

attacks *within* the United States in a series of briefings between May and August 2001: a strike was "imminent," something "very, very, very big," and "Bin Laden determined to strike in U.S." None of this was heeded by Bush or top national security officials in Washington.

Catastrophe struck on September 11, 2001. Early that day, nineteen Saudi and other Middle Eastern operatives affiliated with Al Qaeda, who were in the United States, succeeded in boarding four airliners despite the presence of metal detectors. They hijacked the planes, using box cutters as weapons, and flew them on suicide missions for which they had trained secretly at different sites around the country. Two of the planes hit the World Trade Center in lower Manhattan, one hit the Pentagon, and a fourth, heading either toward the Capitol or the White House, crashed into a field in rural Pennsylvania after passengers attempted to seize control. The Twin Towers of the World Trade Center were consumed in flames and soon collapsed in massive rubble; the Pentagon, one of the world's largest buildings, was badly damaged. In all, nearly 3,000 people died, many more were injured, and the country was on high alert for further terrorist acts.

Before the day was over, American intelligence officials strongly suspected the work of **Al Qaeda**. That night, President Bush vowed vengeance not only against the "terrorists who committed these acts" but also against "those who harbor them." What would this mean? If another country had attacked the United States, Congress could declare war against it. But Al Qaeda wasn't a country or any type of state. What could be done? Bush chose to make a different type of war declaration. He declared that the United States would now be engaged in a **War on Terror**, and not against Al Qaeda alone. It would be a "war against all those who seek to support terror and a war against those governments that support or shelter them." And the war would not end until "every terrorist group of global reach" was defeated. It was a sweeping and audacious project. Yet how would such a war be fought, and when could such a war really be over?

States of War and Surveillance

As Pearl Harbor demonstrated decades earlier, nothing unifies a country more quickly than a deadly attack against it. Given the deep partisan divisions of the time, the unity that immediately surfaced was both remarkable and potentially dangerous. President Bush's declaration of war against terrorism had few critics and many enablers. This permitted him and Congress to move with almost lightning speed in a couple of directions. First, there was an effort to increase security within the United States so that attackers such as the terrorists of September 11 would have much more difficulty getting into the United States and communicating with one another. Congress passed the **USA Patriot Act**, which dramatically expanded the government's ability to put American citizens and others residing in the United States under surveillance: permitting domestic wiretapping, the tracking of Internet and financial activity, and the easier procurement of search warrants. Congress also established a cabinet-level **Department of Homeland Security**, which included a **Transportation Safety Administration (TSA)**, both designed to tighten border security and passenger control at American airports. Before long, a massive counter-terrorism apparatus was in place employing nearly a million people. Unbeknownst to Congress, the Bush administration also initiated a secret program of domestic surveillance and then, by executive order, established military tribunals to try suspected

≡ **Out of a Clear Blue Sky** The Twin Towers in New York City, shortly after the second of two commercial airplanes hijacked by terrorists crashed through the north tower.

≡ **Prison Camp at Guantanamo Bay, Cuba** Detainees (in orange jumpsuits, kneeling) being processed at Camp X-Ray, a detention facility for suspected terrorists at Guantanamo Bay, Cuba, in January 2002.

terrorists and a detention center at the US Naval base at **Guantanamo Bay**, Cuba, where, it was believed, American laws and rights would offer no protections to the accused—based on a perspective that the Insular Cases associated with the Spanish-Cuban-Filipino-American War had established.

The Bush administration moved, as well, to bring the 9/11 terrorists to justice and destroy Al Qaeda. Understanding that the Afghan government, under the command of Islamic fundamentalists known as the **Taliban**, allowed Osama Bin Laden and the Al Qaeda leadership to operate there, Bush demanded that the Afghans surrender the Al Qaeda leaders and close down their training bases. When the Taliban refused, Bush ordered a multipronged—air, ground, and Special Forces—attack which toppled the Taliban regime and captured many suspected terrorists, though failed to find Bin Laden. But the situation in Afghanistan was now extremely unstable, so American troops remained to protect a newly installed government, prevent the Taliban from regaining power, and continue the hunt for Bin Laden. It was the beginning of a very long, bloody, and tempestuous occupation: the longest in all of American history.

Perhaps most unsettling, the Bush administration turned its attention to Iraq. There was no evidence that the Iraqis had anything to do with the 9/11 attacks and, by all accounts, Saddam Hussein was hostile to Al Qaeda. Yet ever since the end of the First Gulf War of 1990–1991, some neoconservatives in the foreign policy establishment hoped to finish the job that George H. W. Bush had begun and remove Hussein from power. With Bill Clinton in the White House, they had limited leverage; with Bush in the White House, they were in new positions of power, none more consequential than new Vice President Dick Cheney and Secretary of Defense Donald Rumsfeld. The 9/11 terror attacks gave them the opportunity, as Rumsfeld put it, to "go-massive—sweep it all up—things related and not."

Regime change in Iraq—overthrowing Hussein and having him replaced with a more favorably disposed government—would give the United States an expanded base of power in the Middle East, both to intimidate prospective terrorists and reorder the region in a way more compatible with supposed American interests. The argument made for military action was not that the Iraqis provided a haven for Al Qaeda but rather that the Iraqis were building **weapons of mass destruction (WMDs)**—chemical and biological weapons—in order to promote terrorism. Bush and Cheney went even further to claim that there were ties between Hussein and Al Qaeda, though no such evidence was ever presented.

The argument about WMDs was dubious, and it turned out to be patently false. But given the temper of the political moment, few political figures or media outlets pushed back against what was clearly a call for preemptive warfare. Congress buckled and in a bipartisan action gave Bush authorization to use military force.

That he did. In March 2003, Bush launched **Operation Iraqi Freedom (Second Gulf War)** with a strategy of "shock and awe." Nearly 150,000 American troops were sent into action, and air strikes decimated the Iraqi army, devastated Bagdad, and forced Hussein into hiding. In a few weeks—not unlike the First Gulf War—George Bush could declare "mission accomplished" and tout the liberation of Iraq. His advisers imagined a ground-swell of support for the United States and a rapid transition to democracy.

They miscalculated badly. In some ways, the overthrow of Saddam Hussein revealed what the breakup of Yugoslavia had shown a decade earlier: that strongmen had held together complex regimes with rival ethnic and religious groups who would turn brutally against each other once the strongmen were deposed. Iraq was riven by conflicts between Sunni and Shi'ite Muslims, and between Iraqi Muslims and Kurds who occupied a semiautonomous region in the northeast of the country. The American occupation forces quickly disbanded Hussein's army, which encouraged the troops and their officers, who were now out of work, to become involved in what was soon civil warfare. Hundreds of Iraqis were rounded up by the Americans and imprisoned—often tortured—at Abu Ghraib prison in Bagdad (once a dungeon for Hussein's political enemies) and at other "dark" locations around the world, including Guantanamo. Before George W. Bush's two terms were up in 2008, there were

☰ **"Mission Accomplished?"** US President George W. Bush, on board the aircraft carrier *USS Abraham Lincoln* with a "Mission Accomplished" banner behind him, claims on May 1, 2003, that major combat action in Iraq had been a success. In reality, US combat troops would be mired in Iraq for many more years.

160,000 American troops in Iraq, 30,000 in Afghanistan, and thousands of suspected terrorists held without charge or trial, many tortured, at institutions of detention under American control. What began with Bush's father hailing a "new world order" had descended into new and deadly "disorder," and what had been proclaimed as the "end of history" and the triumph of liberal democratic values had morphed into domestic surveillance, endless wars, and charges of war crimes.

Conclusion: Not the End of History

The end of the decades-long Cold War brought a widespread sense of optimism, not only in the United States but also in much of the world. The superpower rivalries that threatened near-planetary destruction had apparently come to an end. The need for Cold War–related military spending had dramatically eased, and the belief that there would be a "peace dividend" for many Americans began to be embraced. Attention could now turn to domestic issues, and a new leadership born for the first time in the post–World War II era had been elected with its antennas tuned to a robust and hi-tech-driven way forward. Economically, the 1990s would almost rival the 1950s as a time of prosperity.

But the optimism did not last for very long. Racial tensions that had always simmered burst forth in destructive riots, deepening concerns about crime and welfare, and surges of mass incarceration. National politics was soon roiled by a Republican Party, increasingly beholden to the hard right, that waged partisan warfare on the Clinton administration, undermined a health care initiative, pushed the Democrats to the right as well, and ultimately resulted in Clinton's impeachment. And it became increasingly clear that, while stoking existential anxiety, the Cold War had established a structure of global politics that was now in disarray. Warfare broke out in the Balkans, east and central Africa, and the Middle East, and the First Gulf War showed that the price of peace would be very high. Non-state actors, some deploying the methods of terrorism, registered new power in the world, culminating in the massive attack on September 11, 2001, that not only claimed the lives of almost 3,000 women and men on American soil but also led to an apparently unending "War on Terror," growing domestic surveillance in the name of antiterrorism, and the stationing of thousands of American troops in Iraq and Afghanistan. An imagined "new world order" had descended into deadly "disorder," and the apparent triumph of liberal democratic values had given way to government surveillance, unending wars, and war crimes of global proportion.

WHAT IF the 9/11 Plot Had Been Foiled?

The terrorist attacks of September 11, 2001, are so indelibly imprinted on the national and international consciousness that it is difficult to imagine a world in which that disaster did not occur. But as the 9/11 Commission (established by President Bush) reported in 2004, there were many warning signs over many months that went unheeded, even though the Bush administration received daily intelligence briefings. There were, indeed, many opportunities for intelligence and government officials to act and possibly foil the plot. After all, other terrorist plots before and after 9/11 were recognized and foiled; we haven't had anything like 9/11 since that event.

What if the 9/11 plot had been foiled? How different might our country and world be? Needless to say, thousands of people who lost their lives would have survived and many thousands of others who were injured or suffered serious health problems because of their proximity to the devastation would have gone on to live better lives. Beyond this, however, the alternative picture is less clear than we might imagine. If the 9/11 plot had been foiled, either Al Qaeda would have continued to plan murderous attacks against the United States or the Bush administration, having uncovered the plot and discovered the perpetrators, might have determined to punish Al Qaeda, as the Clinton administration had planned to, much in the way that happened: demanding that the Taliban give the Al Qaeda leadership up and launching a military attack when the Taliban balked. Given the powerful leaders in the Bush administration who were hoping to accomplish a political reordering of the Middle East beginning with Iraq and Saddam Hussein, some version of Operation Iraqi Freedom could easily have been authorized; WMDs were invented as it was. At all events, even if the 9/11 attack did not take place, the United States could well have ended up in Afghanistan and Iraq, bogged down in civil warfare with few means of easy escape. In some ways, 9/11 may have deflected our attention from underlying developments that were moving in the same direction whether or not a massive terrorist attack served as the trigger.

DOCUMENT 29.1:   Excerpt from the *9/11 Commission Report* (2004)

The National Commission on Terrorist Attacks Upon the United States (also known as the 9/11 Commission) was an independent, bipartisan commission that prepared a full and complete account of the circumstances surrounding the September 11, 2001, terrorist attacks. The Commission released its final report in 2004.

Public Statement

Release of 9/11 Commission Report

The Hon. Thomas H. Kean and the Hon. Lee H. Hamilton, July 22, 2004

Good morning. Today, we present this Report and these recommendations to the President of the United States, the United States Congress, and the American people. This report represents the unanimous conclusion of the National Commission on Terrorist Attacks upon the United States.

On September 11, 2001, 19 men armed with knives, box-cutters, mace and pepper spray penetrated the defenses of the most powerful nation in the world. They inflicted unbearable trauma on our people, and turned the international order upside down.

We ask each of you to remember how you felt that day—the grief, the enormous sense of loss. We also came together that day as a nation—young and old, rich and poor, Republicans and Democrats. We all had a deep sense of hurt. We also had a deep sense of purpose. We knew what we had to do, as a nation, to respond. And we did.

But on that September day we were unprepared. We did not grasp the magnitude of a threat that had been gathering over time. As we detail in our report, this was a failure of policy, management, capability, and—above all—a failure of imagination.

Findings

We recognize that we have the benefit of hindsight. And, since the plotters were flexible and resourceful, we cannot know whether any single step or series of steps would have defeated them. What we can say with confidence is that none of the measures adopted by the US government before 9/11 disturbed or even delayed the progress of the al Qaeda plot.

There were several unexploited opportunities.

- Our government did not watchlist future hijackers Hazmi and Mihdhar before they arrived in the United States, or take adequate steps to find them once they were here.
- Our government did not link the arrest of Zacarias Moussaoui, described as interested in flight training for the purpose of using an airplane in a terrorist act, to the heightened indications of attack.
- Our government did not discover false statements on visa applications, or recognize passports manipulated in a fraudulent manner.
- Our government did not expand no-fly lists to include names from terrorist watchlists, or require airline passengers to be more thoroughly screened.

These examples make up part of a broader national security picture, where the government failed to protect the American people. The United States government was simply not active enough in combating the terrorist threat before 9/11.

- Our diplomacy and foreign policy failed to extricate bin Laden from his Afghan sanctuary.
- Our military forces and covert action capabilities did not have the options on the table to defeat al Qaeda or kill or capture bin Laden and his chief lieutenants.
- Our intelligence and law-enforcement agencies did not manage or share information, or effectively follow leads, to keep pace with a nimble enemy.
- Our border, immigration, and aviation security agencies were not integrated into the counterterrorism effort; and
- Much of our response on the day of 9/11 was improvised and ineffective, even as extraordinary individual acts of heroism saved countless lives.

Our failure took place over many years and Administrations. There is no single individual who is responsible for this failure. Yet individuals and institutions are not absolved of responsibility. Any person in a senior position within our government during this time bears some element of responsibility for the government's actions.

It is not our purpose to assign blame. As we said at the outset, we look back so that we can look forward. Our goal is to prevent future attacks.

Every expert with whom we spoke told us that an attack of even greater magnitude is now possible—and even probable. We do not have the luxury of time. We must prepare and we must act.

The al Qaeda network and its affiliates are sophisticated, patient, disciplined, and lethal. Usama Bin Ladin built an infrastructure and organization that was able to attract, train and use recruits against ever more ambitious targets. He rallied new zealots with each demonstration of al Qaeda's capability. His message and hate-filled ideology have instructed and inspired untold recruits and imitators. He and al Qaeda:

- despise America and its policies;
- exploit political grievances and hopelessness within the Arab and Islamic world;
- indoctrinate the disaffected and pervert one of the world's great religions; and
- seek creative methods to kill Americans in limitless numbers, including the use of chemical, biological and nuclear weapons.

Put simply, the United States is presented with one of the great security challenges in our history. We have struck blows against the terrorists since 9/11. We have prevented attacks on the homeland. We believe we are safer today than we were on 9/11—but we are not safe.

Because al Qaeda represents an ideology—not a finite group of people—we should not expect the danger to recede for years to come. No matter whom we kill or capture—including Usama Bin Ladin—there will still be those who plot against us. Bin Ladin has inspired affiliates and imitators. The societies they prey on are vulnerable; the terrorist ideology is potent; and the means for inflicting harm are readily available. We cannot let our guard down.

Source: https://9-11commission.gov/report/

Thinking About Contingency

1. Why would the Bush administration ignore the warnings about Al Qaeda throughout the summer of 2001?
2. Do you think the 9/11 attack gave the neoconservative hawks in the Bush administration a stronger argument about solidifying American dominance in the Middle East?
3. Can you imagine how the disruption of the 9/11 plot would have led to a better outcome domestically and globally, and what would that have looked like?

REVIEW QUESTIONS

1. Why were the benefits of the post–Cold War "peace dividend" shared unequally among different groups in American society?

2. How did the boom in the technology and tele-communications industries transform culture and politics in the 1990s?

3. How did hip-hop and rap serve as a critique of racial inequalities and poverty?

4. How did the Clarence Thomas hearings and the O. J. Simpson murder trial underscore the complexities of race and sex at the turn of the millennium?

5. What are the damaging legacies of the 2000 presidential election?

6. What was the immediate impact of 9/11 on American politics and foreign policy?

7. What were the long-term consequences of the "War on Terror"?

8. How did the nation's sense of urgency after 9/11 propel changes in actions both at home and abroad?

9. What was the US case for invading Iraq? How did events belie the Bush administration's claim of "mission accomplished"?

KEY TERMS

Al Qaeda (p. 1268)

apartheid (p. 1261)

Contract with America (p. 1247)

Defense of Marriage Act (p. 1251)

Department of Homeland Security (p. 1269)

"Don't Ask, Don't Tell" (p. 1251)

Guantanamo Bay (p. 1270)

Intifada (p. 1262)

new world order (p. 1233)

No Child Left Behind Act (p. 1267)

North American Free Trade Agreement (NAFTA) (p. 1250)

Operation Desert Storm (First Gulf War) (p. 1263)

Operation Iraqi Freedom (Second Gulf War) (p. 1271)

Personal Responsibility and Work Opportunity Act (PRWOA) (p. 1251)

Taliban (p. 1270)

Transportation Safety Administration (TSA) (p. 1269)

USA Patriot Act (p. 1269)

War on Terror (p. 1268)

weapons of mass destruction (WMDs) (p. 1270)

white power movement (p. 1248)

RECOMMENDED READINGS

Michelle Alexander, *The New Jim Crow: Mass Incarceration in an Age of Color Blindness* (New Press, 2010).

Barbara Demick, *Logavina Street: Life and Death in a Sarajevo Neighborhood* (Spiegel and Grau, 2012).

Nicole Hemmer, *Partisans: The Conservative Revolutionaries Who Remade American Politics in the 1990s* (Basic Books, 2022).

Kevin Kruse and Julian Zelizer, *Fault Lines: A History of the United States Since 1974* (W.W. Norton, 2020).

Patrick Maney, *Bill Clinton: New Gilded Age President* (University of Kansas Press, 2016).

Jane Mayer, *The Dark Side: The Inside Story of How the War on Terror Turned into a War on American Ideals* (Anchor Books, 2008).

Anthony Summers and Robyn Swan, *The Eleventh Day: The Full Story of 9/11* (Ballantine Books, 2012).

Jeffrey Toobin, *The Run of His Life: The People Versus O.J. Simpson* (Random House, 2015).

Julian Zelizer, *Burning Down the House: Newt Gingrich, the Fall of a Speaker, and the Rise of the New Republican Party* (Penguin Books, 2020).

Destinies

2005–The Present

Chapter Outline

≡ **Marching for Justice** Protestors in New York march to demand justice for Jacob Blake, a twenty-nine-year-old Black man killed by police in Kenosha, Wisconsin. While Americans have denounced police brutality and murder throughout their history, in the decade since the 2012 killing of Trayvon Martin, protestors and activists have consistently highlighted how such violence is targeted at people of color, and specifically Black men.

Almost every modern president, Democrat or Republican, who addressed the public at a time of crisis has declared both that the country would make it through and that, despite the challenges and travails of the moment, America's "best days" still lay ahead. America is back! America is moving forward again! Never bet against America!

These are examples of what some have called a "providential" idea of destiny, a notion that God or a higher power has marked the United States for a special journey of greatness that would not be derailed by secular events. That idea was proclaimed at the nation's founding, echoing an earlier concept of a "city on a hill," which President

Timeline

2005	2007	2009	2011	2013

2005 > Hurricane Katrina devastates New Orleans

2008 > Financial crash leads to Great Recession; Barack Obama elected president

2009 > Tea Party movement organized

2010 > Affordable Care Act signed into law by Obama; Supreme Court rules in *Citizens United v. Federal Election Commission* against government restrictions on political contributions

2012 > Barack Obama reelected president

2013 > Supreme Court in *Shelby County v. Holder* rules important section of Voting Rights Act of 1965 unconstitutional; Black Lives Matter organized

Ronald Reagan particularly relished even when he took it out of context. To be sure, millions of the world's people over the past three centuries have flocked to North America and the United States to seek better lives, political safety, economic opportunities, and a host of freedoms unavailable to them in their countries of origin. For many of them, America has been a "beacon" in a world of distress and deprivation.

But America's destiny and distinctiveness have come in for rude shocks, particularly over the past half century. The nation's heritage of slavery and racism has been revealed in significant and painful ways, and much as we would like to think that

2015	2017	2019	2021	2023

2015 › Supreme Court in *Obergefell v. Hodges* rules that same-sex marriage is protected under the Constitution; Paris Climate Agreement signed with the support of 191 nations, including the United States; China passes Japan to become world's second biggest economy

2016 › Hillary Clinton becomes first woman nominated for president by a major political party; Donald Trump elected president

2017 › Trump accused of encouraging Russian interference in 2016 election and Special Counsel investigation begun

2019 › Special Counsel investigation report concludes that Russians interfered in 2016 election with Trump's encouragement; Donald Trump impeached by House of Representatives for abuse of power and obstruction of Congress; first COVID-19 infections reported in Wuhan, China

2020 › COVID-19 pandemic erupts in the United States; Kamala Harris becomes first woman and person of Indian and African descent to be nominated for the vice presidency; Joe Biden elected president; Trump refuses to concede and insists that the election was "stolen" from him; COVID-19 vaccines developed and begin to be distributed

2021 › Violent mob of Trump supporters storms US Capitol to disrupt certification of 2020 presidential election; Trump impeached a second time; Joe Biden inaugurated as president; Kamala Harris becomes first woman and person of Indian and African descent to be sworn in as vice president

2022 › Russia invades Ukraine

2023 › Former President Donald Trump indicted on federal charges for mishandling classified documents

progress is at the core of the modern American experience, we now know very well that it can unfold slowly or even give way to retreat. The nation's apparent military invincibility has been tested in ways not previously imagined, and wars have been lost in Vietnam or have resulted in lengthy deadlocks before they were abandoned (as in Iraq and Afghanistan). The nation's self-satisfaction as the wealthiest and most economically dynamic in history has been shaken by gross inequalities and flattened incomes for the middle and working class; parents recognize that their children and grandchildren might not achieve the standards of living that they have. The nation's long-standing sense of getting hold of the reins of nature and bending them to its will has now backfired, so that we can speak of a truly existential crisis for Americans, human beings elsewhere, and possibly many forms of life on the planet. And the nation's belief in its global strength, its position as the superpower, and its imperial might have been challenged on several fronts, perhaps most consequentially by China, a once dominant power that has reemerged on the world stage. History, if anything, is not linear, and the paths to the future are not ordained. They branch in many potentially different directions.

30.1   Climate Change

Discuss the meaning of climate change and summarize the political conflicts over addressing it.

In the early morning hours of Monday, August 29, 2005, a massive hurricane made landfall along the Gulf Coast of Louisiana. It began forming near the Bahamas five days earlier and entered the Caribbean two days later carrying the name given it by the World Meteorological Organization—Katrina. By Sunday evening, August 28, the storm had reached Category 5, the most severe, which meant that its winds gusted at over 160 miles per hour. The National Weather Service issued a dire warning that the storm would likely result in "human suffering incredible by modern standards," and public officials took note. Louisiana's governor declared a "state of emergency," calling on the federal government for assistance, and the mayor of New Orleans together with officials in the surrounding parishes ordered mandatory evacuations. Well over one million people fled the city, roughly 75 percent of the metropolitan population; some of those who remained took shelter in the Superdome, the city's huge, covered sports arena.

Just before Katrina hit the Louisiana coast, its winds weakened in velocity—it was designated a Category 3, with sustained winds of 126 miles per hour—and veered a bit east so that the hurricane's "eye" missed New Orleans by about 20 miles. In fact, at its peak Katrina's winds battering New Orleans probably didn't exceed 80 miles per hour. Some breathed a sigh of relief, thinking that New Orleans had "dodged the bullet." What they failed to notice was that the storm surge, a massive rise in the tides owing to Katrina's rain and winds, had breached the levee system and began flooding the city, much of which had been built on land below sea level. Before long, more than three-quarters of New Orleans and almost all of neighboring St. Bernard Parish were underwater. The devastation was widespread. By some estimates, between 1,300 and 1,800 people lost their lives, mostly by drowning. About 50,000 people crowded into the New Orleans Convention Center and the Superdome, where conditions were abysmal. The National Oceanic and Atmospheric Administration (NOAA) estimated that Katrina inflicted some $125 billion in total damages, and the population of New Orleans dropped 50 percent after the hurricane. Although many residents returned, the population is still below what it was before disaster struck.

Katrina was not the most formidable hurricane of the 2005 season. That distinction went to Hurricane Wilma, which not only reached Category 5 at landfall in Mexico in October but also was the most intense storm ever recorded in the Atlantic basin and the second most intense ever recorded in all of the Western Hemisphere. Before the year was out, 2005 had set the record for the most hurricanes (fifteen) and named tropical storms (twenty-eight) since the weather service began keeping records in the mid-nineteenth century.

Hurricanes, even large and destructive ones, have always been facts of life in the Caribbean basin and along the coasts of the United States and Mexico. But Katrina and the 2005 hurricane season were indicative of worrisome trends over the previous three decades. Hurricanes and other tropical storms have become more numerous and more intense, while the storm "season" has also lengthened. The season once stretched from mid-June to mid-October; it now stretches from late May until the end of November. And all of this is part of a crisis that has confronted the entire planet. The crisis is climate change, and it threatens to disrupt the lives of humans, along with most other life on our planet, beyond repair.

Over Earth's several-billion-year history, its climate has changed many times. There have been ice ages, when much of the surface was covered with glaciers, and there have been extended periods of warming, when the glaciers receded and new forms of plant life and other vegetation spread to once-barren regions. At times, climate change was the result of devastating events such as the impact of asteroids (one finished off the dinosaurs) or of volcanic explosions, which made for sun-blocking clouds that lingered for many years. But the challenge of climate change we now face is human-made, ironically the result of what we have called "progress" over the past two centuries.

Industrial Revolutions

The industrial revolutions of the nineteenth and twentieth centuries, which brought new forms of production, distribution, and transportation, required new and unprecedented sources of energy. Humans had long depended on natural resources like wood and peat to keep them warm and cook their food, and on water power to carry them down rivers and streams and to propel their early machines. They also depended on animal power to pull carts and plows. The industrial revolutions were made possible by the use of "fossil fuels"—coal, oil, and natural gas—which are the remains of plants and animals that have decomposed over long periods of time. Burning these fuels could yield enormous energy. Yet, when these fuels are burned or extracted for use, they release gasses such as carbon dioxide and methane that remain in the atmosphere and trap heat. These "greenhouse gasses" thus create the sort of warming effect that greenhouses do for plants. Because heat is trapped, the temperature of both the atmosphere and the oceans rises (see Figure 30.1).

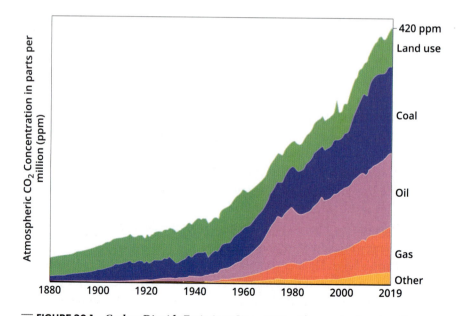

≡ **FIGURE 30.1** **Carbon Dioxide Emissions Since 1880**   The ongoing burning of fossil fuels, which releases large amounts of carbon dioxide into the atmosphere, results in an appreciable buildup of atmospheric carbon dioxide over time, strengthening the greenhouse effect.

Climate Change

Global temperatures began a steep ascent in the late 1970s and have continued to break records. The ten warmest years we know of have occurred since 2005, and meteorologists are certain that this trend will continue, with potentially catastrophic consequences. As temperatures warm on the earth's surface, ice packs and glaciers in the Northern and Southern Hemispheres melt, causing ocean levels to rise and potentially inundate coastal lands and cities. Warming temperatures evaporate more of the ocean waters into the atmosphere, producing heavier precipitation and changing weather patterns more generally. Some regions become increasingly prone to downpours and flooding, while others bake under drought conditions. Warming waters jeopardize most aquatic life as well, with devastating consequences to the fishing industry and global food supply. Ocean reefs are dying off, while fish populations diminish and migrate. Wetlands and marshes, too, are vulnerable to the effects. In Louisiana it was the steady erosion of coastal wetlands, worsened by oil drilling and related canal building, that exposed New Orleans to Katrina's devastating storm surge (see Map 30.1).

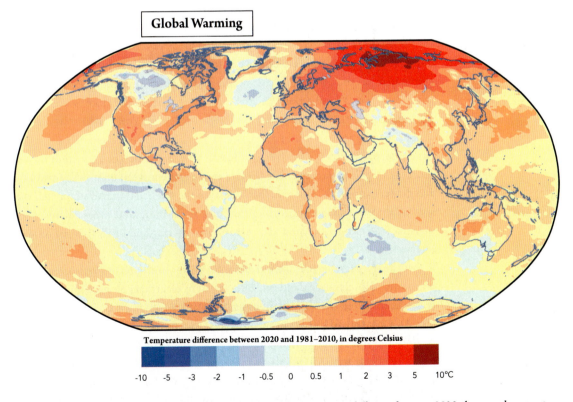

≡ **MAP 30.1   Global Warming**   The widespread and notable temperature difference between 2020, the second warmest year on record, and the thirty-year baseline between 1981 and 2010 suggests that the pace of climate change is accelerating.

≡ **Climate Change, the Economy, and Social Protest**   A participant in the
2014 People's Climate March in New York City (*left*) advocates for an economy
based on clean energy, while delegates from coal-rich West Virginia show their
appreciation for then-candidate Donald Trump's support of the coal industry at
the 2016 Republican National Nominating Convention (*right*).

Scientists began to warn of climate change during the 1980s, predicting worrisome temperature rises by the mid-twenty-first century. They were not alone. Fossil fuel companies like Shell and Exxon conducted their own investigations, and although they came up with similar predictions, they kept them under wraps because of the negative implications for their businesses. Congress began to hold hearings as early as 1988, and by the mid-1990s an international agreement was signed that looked to the reduction of carbon emissions.

As climate change came to public consciousness, some Americans recognized the impending threat to the planet and called for a coordinated response. On the one hand, greenhouse gas emissions had to be dramatically reduced or effectively eliminated; on the other hand, renewable and nonpolluting energy technologies (such as solar and wind power) had to be developed to take the place of fossil fuels. And there are citizens, politicians, and business leaders concerned about how a shift in energy production and consumption would affect an economy that was still largely dependent on the fossil-fuel industry. They are reluctant to commit the resources to tackling human-made climate change, and instead urge a very cautious and gradual approach. Some, in fact, question the science that had supported the idea of climate change, suggesting that global warming and other related phenomena were either exaggerated or naturally occurring and likely to resist human interventions.

Despite the growing use of wind and solar power, and such innovations as vehicles powered by electricity and gas (hybrids) or by electricity alone, climate change is accelerating and the window of opportunity for reversing it is closing very rapidly. As a measure of this concern, delegates from nearly 200 nations met in Paris in 2015 and reached an agreement to pursue policies that would limit the rise in global temperatures. All but six of those nations in attendance ratified the treaty in 2016. In the United States, ratification of the Paris Accords was opposed—unsuccessfully—by many Republicans, owing to the potential costs and international supervision. And there has since been something of a seesaw regarding American participation. When Republican Donald Trump was elected president in 2016 and took office in 2017, he quickly withdrew the United States from the Paris agreement, much to the dismay of those who saw it as an important step on the path to controlling climate change. Four years later, after Democrat Joseph Biden won the presidency, he quickly issued an executive order rejoining the accord.

The perils of climate change have inspired a grassroots movement, mostly associated with the Democratic Party, to support a "Green New Deal": a massive government-backed effort to fight climate change, end reliance on fossil fuels, develop energy technologies for many areas of life that would no longer strain the environment, and create well-paying jobs in a growing "clean energy" sector. But the Green New Deal is strongly opposed by many Republicans and other conservatives who fear the expanded power of the federal government, the consequences for the fossil fuel industry, and the higher taxes that may be needed to support the projects. The fight has been bitter, and its outcome will shape the future of the United States and the world. No issue is more consequential for the destiny of America and its people.

30.2   Race and Social Justice

Explain the meaning of systemic racism and describe the social justice struggles against it.

Of the New Orleans residents who did not flee the city as Katrina barreled in—either by choice or circumstance—the overwhelming majority were Black. Of those who sheltered, under rapidly deteriorating conditions in the Superdome, the overwhelming majority were Black. And of those who perished by drowning, exposure, or acute health issues, the overwhelming majority were Black. To be sure, New Orleans, in 2005, was a Black-majority city, but the media footage and stories about Katrina also showed what it meant to be Black in the city: to be disproportionately subject to suffering, displacement, illness, inadequate housing, and dire poverty. The federal census in 2010 showed that, while the Black population still outnumbered the white, it had declined by about 125,000, or 37 percent, since 2000: most all of the decline a result of Katrina.

≡ **Dazed and Confused**   Residents wade through a flooded street two days after Hurricane Katrina struck New Orleans. The city's largely Black population was abandoned, without state or federal assistance, for days; more than 1,000 people died as a result of the storm.

PERSPECTIVES

The Anthropocene

The role of human beings in the Earth's history is reflected in the **Anthropocene**, an unofficial name that has been proposed by some scientists for the geological epoch we are now in. "Anthropo" (human) reflects the fact that, by many measures, humans are the most influential species on the planet. Human activities in industrial-capitalist societies like the United States have radically altered weather patterns and ecosystems around the world. As scientists Charles Langmuir and Wallace Broecker argue, human beings have fundamentally changed the character of Earth as a planet: "For the first time a single species dominates the entire surface, sits at the top of all terrestrial and oceanic food chains, and has taken over much of the biosphere for its own purposes."[1] Human-induced climate change is the most visible manifestation of the Anthropocene.

Climate change has amplified the destructiveness of wildfires that burn large swaths of Western forests each year. The 2018 Camp Fire in northern California was the deadliest and most destructive wildfire in the state's history. Named after Camp Creek Road in Butte County, California, eighty-five people were killed; damage from the wildfire exceeded $16 billion.

≡ **Paradise, California**   A scorched vehicle lies amid the remains of an incinerated house in November 2018.

[1]Charles Langmuir and Wallace Broecker, *How to Build a Habitable Planet* (Princeton, NJ: Princeton University Press, 2012), 597.

Climate change also proceeds in less dramatic ways. Steadily rising sea levels imperil coastal communities across the United States. This image provides an aerial view of the Yupik village of Newtok in western Alaska, May 25, 2019. The village, with a population of 380, is sinking as the permafrost beneath it thaws. Erosion has already wiped out nearly a mile of Newtok's land, and it is estimated that the entire village will be underwater by 2025. The residents are in the process of moving to Mertarvik, a new village site about nine miles away. Newtok is the first community in Alaska that has already begun relocation as a result of climate change, initiating a process that many other Alaskan villages may soon have to undergo.

≡ **Newtok, Alaska** The village is forecast to be entirely underwater by 2025.

CONSIDER THIS

In 2018, fossil fuels represented 80 percent of all energy use worldwide. Despite the increase in clean energy like wind power and solar power, fossil fuels underpin most of modern American industry and agriculture. How should American society respond to the sustainability challenges of the Anthropocene? Are there connections between climate change and social issues?

"The Arc of the Moral Universe Is Long"

"The arc of the moral universe is long," Martin Luther King once said, quoting the abolitionist Theodore Parker, "but it bends toward justice." This sense of hopefulness in the face of a steep climb, raised by the civil rights movement of the 1950s and 1960s, seemed to dissipate during the 1980s and 1990s. Owing to federal legislation and initiatives in some of the states, a well-educated Black middle class had been growing and new political leaders began to emerge, claiming seats of power and influence from the municipal to the national levels. Thurgood Marshall, the eminent civil rights lawyer, earned a seat on the US Supreme Court in 1967. In 1992, Carol Mosely Braun of Illinois became the first Black woman elected to the US Senate. Civil rights activist John Lewis won a congressional seat from Georgia in 1986. In 1990, Virginia's Douglas Wilder became the first Black man elected governor of a former Confederate—indeed of any—state. Black men and women have served as mayors of New York, Cleveland, Los Angeles, Detroit, Newark, Philadelphia, Washington, DC, Charlotte (NC), Memphis (TN) and a host of other cities.

Yet, for most Black Americans, the post–civil rights era has been hard, dreary, and dispiriting. Deindustrialization claimed the decent-paying jobs created in the wake of the Great Migration (Chapter 27). White flight undercut the tax base in many cities and the social and educational services for the Black people who remained there. Housing discrimination and a tradition of "red-lining" continued to imperil Black living standards (Chapter 26). The urban rebellions of the 1960s ratcheted up policing while the drug wars of the 1970s and 1980s expanded racial profiling and helped account for the mass incarceration of Black men, and increasingly Black women, that still afflicts us. When the fiftieth anniversary of the *Brown v. Board of Education* decision was commemorated in 2004, little was said of the progress that had been made and more was lamented about the burdens of racism and segregation that continued to weigh on Black communities.

Then something remarkable happened. In 2007, Barack Obama, a man of African descent, a first-term US senator from Illinois, and a one-time state senator and community organizer, announced his candidacy for president in the 2008 national election. He spoke eloquently in a language of change and hope, and he attracted an enthusiastic following not only among people of color but among many liberal white people—especially young ones. Despite his obvious appeal, few observers gave him much of a chance—especially since his major opponent for the Democratic nomination was the well-known Hillary Rodham Clinton, and a Black candidate had never come close to winning such a campaign. In the summer of 2008, Obama became the first African American to be nominated by a major political party (the Democratic) for the presidency, and in November he swept to victory over his Republican opponent, Senator John McCain, by decisive margins in both the popular and electoral votes (see Map 30.2).

There was palpable excitement in the United States and around the world. No other major power had ever elected a person of color as its leader, and, in the immediate aftermath of the election, some observers imagined that Obama's election marked our transition to a "postracial" society, a society where people would be judged, not by the color of their skin but by the content of their character, as King had put it in August 1963. Overseas, many who had viewed the United States with very critical eyes (if not alarm) responded with admiration, if not joy. Only months after his inauguration, the Nobel Prize committee, based in Sweden, awarded Obama its coveted Peace Prize for his "extraordinary efforts to strengthen international diplomacy and cooperation between people."

The Presidential Election of 2008

Candidate (Party)		Electoral Vote (%)	Popular Vote (%)
	Obama (Democratic)	365 (67.8%)	69,500,000 (52.9%)
	McCain (Republican)	173 (32.2%)	59,900,000 (45.6%)
	Minor parties	0 (0%)	2,013,371 (1.5%)

≡ **MAP 30.2   The Election of 2008**   Victories in key states in the Midwest and Northeast propelled Obama to victory.

The Great Recession of 2008

But the idea of President Barack Obama as the symbol of a "postracial" United States crumbled quickly. He inherited the worst economic crisis since the Great Depression, which made his promises of "hope" and "change" seem increasingly remote. After robust economic growth during the 1990s and into the 2000s, fueled by unregulated speculation and manipulation of the housing market, a financial panic struck. Some of the largest American banks, having piled their

≡ **Running on a Message of Hope and Change**
Presidential candidate Barack Obama drew enthusiastic, diverse, and multigenerational crowds during his 2008 presidential campaign.

resources into **subprime mortgages** (those well below the market rate that could balloon over time), found themselves nearly bankrupt when the housing market faltered in 2008. Trillions of dollars were lost as the stock market tanked. Many homeowners were forced to default on their mortgage payments, and the global financial system tottered because much of it was organized around US currency and banking institutions. Businesses laid off hundreds of thousands of people, and by October 2009, the unemployment rate peaked at an astonishing 10 percent. Black and Latino people were especially hard-hit by job loss (see Figure 30.2). Not a few feared that a Great Depression would befall us.

When he took office in 2009, President Obama drew upon the advice of many former members of the Clinton administration and was convinced that he had to "bail out" the financial sector, continuing a policy that the Bush administration had begun in the weeks before the election. Billions of dollars were directed to banks argued by some to be "too big to fail" in order to stabilize their balance sheets and enable capital and credit to flow once again. But rather than stirring anger from the left, the bailouts stimulated political mobilizations on the right, most dramatically captured by the rise of the "Tea Party" movement (referencing the Revolutionary period's insurgent event). While the Tea Partyers were economic conservatives who complained of high taxes, government spending, and federal overreach, many were also right-wing populists who not only protested against the elites in public life but also saw themselves as pitted against growing minority populations of color that Obama appeared to symbolize. When Obama then moved from bailing

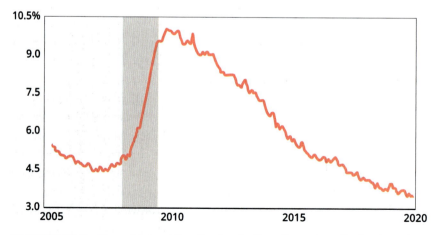

☰ **FIGURE 30.2   Unemployment Rate During the Great Recession**   By October 2009, the unemployment rate peaked at 10 percent. Black and Latino people were especially hard-hit.

out the banks to reforming the health care system so that more Americans could be covered, the Tea Partyers gained further traction, denouncing Obama's plan as "socialism" replete with "death panels" tasked with parceling out medical treatment to those they favored and leaving others to die. The **Affordable Care Act (ACA)**, which would provide insurance for many millions of people who previously lacked or were denied health insurance, was derisively labeled "Obamacare" by Tea Party adherents.

Opponents of the Affordable Care Act   Supporters of the Tea Party movement, like these protesters in Albany, New York, in 2009, falsely believed that the Affordable Care Act (which they derisively labeled "Obamacare") would lead to the rationing of health care through "death panels." Here, an elderly woman holds a sign reading "Obama Lies Granny Dies."

The Growth of the Tea Party Movement

The **Tea Party movement** became an influential part of the Republican Party by exploiting a fear held by many white Americans: becoming a racial minority in a land where they had always been a privileged majority. Social scientists predicted that by the middle of the twenty-first century, people of color (Black, Latino, and Asian people, in particular) would together form a majority and white people would fall into minority status. Tea Partyers depicted people of color as favored clients of the Democrats and saw immigrants (especially from Mexico, Central America, and South Asia) as threats to "replace" them. And no one embodied this changing demography more clearly than Barack Obama.

Even before Obama's election, rumors circulated in Republican circles about his origins and faith. Because his father was from Kenya and his mother was a white anthropologist who did field work in Indonesia, some claimed that he was born outside the United States and therefore was ineligible to be president under Article Two of the Constitution. Others insisted that he was a Muslim and therefore a threatening figure in the post-9/11 era. Before long, New York real estate magnate Donald Trump began to peddle the theory that Obama was foreign-born and demanded that Obama's birth certificate be produced. Trump and others who shared his view came to be called "birthers," and Trump eventually parlayed the publicity into his run for the presidency in 2016, after Obama's two terms in office expired (he was reelected in 2012).

Obama was not born abroad nor was he a Muslim. He was born in Hawaii and was of the Protestant faith. But the birther idea gained real support in the Republican Party and showed how close to the surface unease with Obama (a Black president) was and how deep the racial anxieties of many Americans ran. Never before in American history had a candidate for president or an elected president been charged with ineligibility. The sentiment harked back to the days of Reconstruction when white southerners railed against the enfranchisement of Black men, regarded their political participation as illegitimate, and used violent means to deprive Black people of the vote and political office.

Donald Trump understood the sources of his appeal. When he opened his campaign for the presidency, he took aim at Mexican immigrants: "They're bringing drugs, they're bringing crime, they're rapists . . ." he declared, conjuring a time when white people were the face of America and America was the economic dynamo of the world. He would "make America great again." Not by accident, Trump touted "America First," the slogan of both the 1920s Ku Klux Klan and the opponents of the war against fascism in the 1940s. Despite his inexperience, racist language, and sexual predation (he was almost derailed when evidence of his attitudes and behavior was revealed), Trump won the 2016 election, beating the Democratic nominee, Hillary Clinton, who hoped to be the first woman ever elected to the presidency. Once in office, Trump attempted to build a wall along the southern border of the United States and Mexico, discourage undocumented immigration by separating parents and children once they arrived, ban Muslims from many countries from entering the United States, vilify Black-run cities in the United States and countries around the world, and repeal President Obama's important initiatives—most notably health care.

Trump's election was seen by white supremacists and other right-wing nationalists as a major opening. They regarded Trump as a political ally who shared their objectives, and over the course of his presidency, they were never dissuaded

≡ **White Supremacists and Right-Wing Nationalists**   White nationalists, neo-Nazis, and other supporters of white supremacist movements gathered in Charlottesville, Virginia, for a "Unite the Right" rally on August 12, 2017.

by him. When neo-Nazis marched on Charlottesville, Virginia, in 2017 chanting "Jews will not replace us" and left a counter-protester dead, Trump said that there were "very fine people on both sides." When some members of his own party expressed white supremacist views, he remained silent. When meeting with a group of US senators, he referred to Haiti and African nations as "s—thole countries" and argued that immigration from Norway would be much preferable. When a number of women of color, three of whom were born in the United States, won election to Congress in 2018, Trump tweeted derisively, "Why don't they go back and help fix the totally broken and crime-infested places from where they came." In effect, he validated the worst dispositions of his followers.

Black Lives Matter

Despite an increasingly hostile climate, Black activists began to mobilize. Many were motivated by the police killings of unarmed Black men and women for which the killers were not held to account. And when a jury acquitted an armed neighborhood watch captain after he fatally shot a Black 17-year-old named Trayvon Martin in 2012 (Obama remarked that Martin could have been "my son" and "could have been me thirty-five years ago"), the following year an organization called **Black Lives Matter (BLM)** was formed by three Black women: Alicia Garza, Patrisse Cullors, and Opal Tometi. BLM developed a national (and eventually international) network of support and set their sights on protesting the police murder and profiling of people of color and on making Americans aware of the **systemic racism** permeating American institutions. As Black men and women continued to die in police custody, the BLM movement gained momentum. On May 25, 2020, after a Black man named George Floyd was brutally asphyxiated by Minneapolis police in full view of onlookers (one of whom filmed the murder), the streets of Minneapolis

≡ **Black Lives Matter**   Murals and flowers in a spontaneous tribute to George Floyd at the site of his May 25, 2020, murder by a police officer in Minneapolis (*left*). While Minneapolis and other cities were rocked in the days after his murder by destructive riots, the summer of 2020 was marked by peaceful Black Lives Matter protests attended by hundreds of thousands of people, like this one in New York City (*right*).

and many other communities around the country exploded in rage. Despite the quarantines imposed by the COVID-19 pandemic, hundreds of thousands of peaceful protesters also took to the streets around the country and worldwide calling for an end to police brutality.

Antiracist protests not only engulfed the United States but raised awareness of the ways in which slavery and racism have been deeply etched into the fabric of American life. Universities and corporations began to investigate their own historical ties to slavery and the slave trade. Confederate monuments that long stood across the southern states and as far west as California were taken down. The Confederate flag was increasingly regarded as a symbol of white supremacy and treason. Even military bases changed their names if they had commemorated one-time Confederates and slaveholders. In 2020 California senator Kamala Harris, a woman of both Black and South Asian heritage, sought the Democratic nomination for president and then was chosen by nominee Joe Biden to be his vice president. She became the first woman and person of color to hold that office.

Yet the country's deep political divisions continue to be carved by race and by understandings of white supremacy. For all the progress that has been made over the past half century, Black people earn far less money on average than do white people, have accumulated far less wealth, live disproportionately in communities with poor schools, are far more likely to be incarcerated, are far less likely to have access to adequate health care, and remain greatly underrepresented among business and other institutional leaders. The destiny of American society during the rest of the twenty-first century will be shaped by how these historic inequalities are addressed.

30.3 Economic Inequality and Public Health

||| Explain how economic inequality may compromise access to health care.

Hurricane Katrina's impact on New Orleans revealed not only the effects of climate change and racial discrimination but also the depths of economic inequalities and their consequences in many parts of the United States. Renowned as a tourist destination for its vibrant and unique culture, many observers noted somberly that Katrina exposed New Orleans as more like a city in the developing world than a jewel of the United States. Beset by great inequalities of wealth and grinding poverty, many residents of New Orleans lived in dilapidated housing, had no savings, were disproportionately unemployed or employed in minimum wage service sector jobs, and lacked the resources and means of transportation that would have allowed them to flee the city in advance of the storm.

The inequalities of wealth that have shaped our society are not only about race and racism. They are also about class and an ever-widening divide between the very wealthy and most middle- and working-class families. **Social stratification** has, of course, always existed in the United States, and at certain times and places economic inequalities were considerable. But public policies, especially during the twentieth century, were designed to keep them from becoming extreme. During the Progressive era, Congress enacted a **graduated income tax** for the first time and made some efforts to limit corporate power (see Chapter 19). During the New Deal, the Roosevelt administration supported the right of collective bargaining for labor unions, raised taxes on individuals and corporations, and regulated the banking sector (see Chapter 22). During the 1960s, Great Society programs set their sights on poor urban Black communities and poor rural white ones (see Chapter 26).

Beginning in the 1970s, however, important changes took place. The United States, which was the world's economic superpower since the end of World War II, faced growing competition, especially from other industrial nations, including Japan, and saw corporate profit rates decline. Business leaders launched an offensive against organized labor to strengthen themselves and then started to shift their operations to parts of the country that did not have traditions of unionization (such as the Sunbelt) or to foreign countries where labor costs were extremely low. Corporate and individual taxes were cut in the 1980s while government-sponsored deregulation unleashed the financial sector and new forms of speculative investment. Deindustrialization dramatically weakened the manufacturing sector where high-paying union jobs had taken hold and the initiative in job creation moved to the service sector, where wages were low and union organization minimal. An emerging "information" and "hi-tech" economy in the 1990s only accentuated the trends: well-paying jobs were claimed by the well-educated, and those who lacked college degrees faced declining employment opportunities that could support middle- or secure working-class standards of living (Figure 30.3). Automation and the spiraling costs of higher education—especially as state legislatures offered less and less support to their public universities—only made matters worse. Wages went flat for most Americans while the corporate and financial sectors thrived, at least at the top levels. Already by the turn of the twenty-first century, the top 1 percent of income earners received nearly 40 percent of the annual income in the United States.

Economic recessions, particularly since the 1970s, have tended to boost the fortunes of the wealthy and cast middle- and working-class Americans into more precarious circumstances. Economic recoveries have increasingly been "jobless," meaning that when growth resumes the employment picture is not much

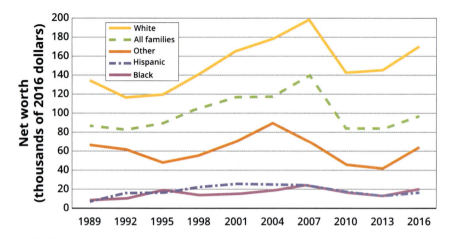

≡ **FIGURE 30.3** **Economic Inequality** As this graph shows, race and racism have shaped the inequalities of wealth in American society. But these inequalities are also about class and an ever-widening divide between the very wealthy and most middle- and working-class families. In 2018, the top 1 percent of income earners received nearly 40 percent of the annual income in the United States.

improved. The Great Crash and Recession of 2008 further accelerated the process. Since public policy favored corporations and finance, including the automobile industry, they recovered quickly; homeowners who were defaulting on their mortgages and workers who had been laid off had a much tougher time. Many middle- and working-class families saw their wealth and savings evaporate as they were forced to sell their homes at a loss, and it would be years before unemployment rates reached pre–Great Recession levels. Those able to return to the workforce received wages that remained stagnant. The distribution of income and wealth in the United States is currently more skewed than in any other industrialized nation.

Public Health

The consequences of extreme economic inequality for American society can be seen in various areas of life—in savings rates, debt loads, education levels, home-ownership, and those truly living paycheck to paycheck—but perhaps nowhere more dramatically or tragically than in health care and public health more generally. The United States has the dubious distinction among industrialized nations of lacking a universal health care system and, as a result, having the highest per capita health care costs (Figure 30.4). Although the Affordable Care Act has significantly increased the number of Americans who have at least some type of health insurance (though coverages and costs vary a great deal), around 25 million Americans, many of them children, remain uninsured with limited access to medical care other

Health Consumption Expenditure per Capita, US Dollars, PPP Adjusted, 2019

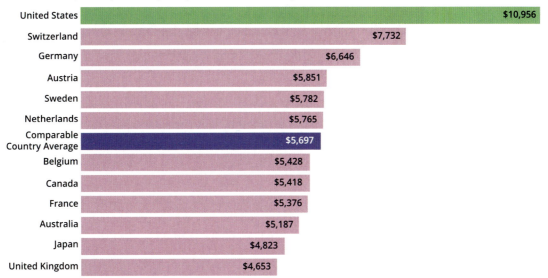

Notes: U.S. value obtained from National Health Expenditure data. Health consumption does not include investments in structures equipment or research.

≡ **FIGURE 30.4   Per Capita Health Care Costs Worldwide**   On average, other wealthy countries spend about half as much per person on health care than the United States.

than in overcrowded hospital emergency rooms. Among the uninsured, Black and Latino individuals and families are disproportionally represented.

Over the past decade, both economic inequality and health care have become potent political issues, with deepening divides between Democrats and Republicans. The Democratic Party has looked favorably at expanding access to health care, though they are split over the best way to remedy the problem. Some are content with private health insurance but wish to regulate it so that costs stay in check and people with "preexisting" health conditions—meaning some chronic illness like diabetes, cancer, rheumatoid arthritis, or heart disease—are not excluded. Other Democrats believe that, at the very least, a public option— meaning government-supplied health insurance—should be available or that a government-sponsored universal health care system, like Medicare, should be enacted: Medicare for All, it is often called. For their part, Republicans generally oppose health care reform and seem wedded to the private insurance system without any mandates that prevailed until 2010 when the Affordable Care Act was signed into law. Not surprisingly, ever since, Republicans have tried to repeal the Affordable Care Act (unsuccessfully so far), complaining of too much government oversight and too many constraints on health care providers.

The health care industry, from hospitals to medical groups to insurance companies to pharmaceutical companies, is extremely powerful and, so far, has obstructed the establishment of a public, universal health care system.

Both health care reform and economic inequality have become hot-button political issues and, especially since 2016, have roiled national politics. That election year Senator Bernie Sanders, a democratic socialist from Vermont, campaigned for the Democratic presidential nomination railing against corporate power and calling for universal health care; he lost by only a narrow margin to Hillary Clinton. Four years later, the issues had become so salient that almost all Democratic presidential candidates in 2020—hoping to defeat incumbent Donald Trump—embraced some form of expanded health care with, at minimum, a public option while calling for government policies to take on climate change, racism, a deteriorating national infrastructure, and the very skewed distribution of wealth. All of these initiatives, they proposed, would be financed by tax increases on corporations and the very rich.

The COVID-19 Pandemic

As the 2020 presidential campaign moved into high gear, a global pandemic caused by the novel coronavirus surfaced in China and rapidly spread around the world. COVID-19 was extremely contagious and potentially deadly, particularly for seniors and anyone with preexisting health issues. The initial response by many governments (including that of the United States) was slow, as if hoping the threat was not serious. But by mid-March, that hope proved to be false. Infection rates soared, hospitalizations became overwhelming in many places, and COVID-related deaths began to spike. Although the Trump administration was reluctant to mandate quarantines, mask wearing, and social distancing, public officials in many parts of the country took the lead. Businesses were ordered closed, schools moved to remote learning, offices were evacuated, travel was restricted, and public events were cancelled. The economy in the United States and elsewhere came to a near standstill, and job losses eclipsed even the unemployment caused by the 2008 recession.

COVID-19's impact and the suffering it inflicted knew no social boundaries. The virus did not discriminate by race or class. Rich and poor contracted the disease. Rich and poor were hospitalized and put on ventilators. Rich and poor died in great numbers, isolated by quarantine measures from family. But it was also clear that certain communities were more adversely affected than others. Areas where people of color lived in substantial numbers, where poorer people lived in close quarters with one another, where disproportionate numbers of undocumented immigrants resided, and with fewer and under-resourced medical facilities took the brunt of the pandemic. There infection rates were the highest. There hospitals lacked adequate space for the very ill. There the most effective treatments and equipment were in short supply. And there the deaths mounted most rapidly. Those lacking health insurance, citizenship, or regular access to physicians and other health providers often tried to ride the virus out at home, with unfortunate results: family members and friends were more subject to infection, and by the time they were forced to seek medical attention it was too late.

Thanks to the innovative work of medical researchers, effective COVID-19 vaccines were developed within a year and made available to the American public. By the summer of 2021, Americans began to resume many of their pre-pandemic activities. Most European countries were heading in that direction as well, though Latin America, Africa, and South Asia continued to suffer from the virus, with limited access to vaccines. The distinctions between what is often called the "global north" and the "global south," or between wealthier and poorer nations on different sides of the equator, have become starkly visible: further warnings to the planet for the decades ahead.

Like Hurricane Katrina, COVID-19 also exposed a stark and unsettling picture of American society. It showed a health care system that was inadequate to the challenges of a globalized environment. It demonstrated how inequalities of race and class made the difference between sickness and health, death and life. It revealed how decentralized decision-making created confusion and vulnerability, and how leadership was often wanting when most needed. It evinced the deep suspicions that many Americans held about medical professionals and educated elites more generally, which often had a basis in routine mistreatment and condescension. And it showed that in our current information economy, some were able to weather the storm, remain at their work, and continue to receive incomes while many others were let go, left to their own resources, and confronted with basic issues of survival. Some COVID-19-type

≡ **Health Crisis**   In the dense and diverse borough of Queens, New York, members of the public wait for hours outside a local hospital to be tested for COVID-19 on March 24, 2020.

pandemic will surely occur again, and the American destiny—like the world's—will depend on the lessons we have learned from the experience with COVID-19 and how the society will choose to respond.

30.4   Gender and Sexual Orientation

Identify the factors that have enabled the LGBTQ+ community to make real social and political gains in the last two decades and the obstacles that still remain.

Although Hurricane Katrina confronted the American public with the social disparities and exclusions of which many were unaware or preferred to ignore, the past two decades have witnessed some remarkable—and successful—struggles to diminish them. Among the most powerful have been the struggles for equal rights and recognitions around the question of sexual orientation and gender identity. As we saw in Chapter 27, a gay rights movement emerged in the 1960s and 1970s which dramatized the hostilities and discriminations that homosexual men and women endured. The AIDS crisis of the 1980s further showed how reticent political and medical officials could be when it came to lethal diseases that disproportionately afflicted gay communities. It took years and thousands of deaths before President Reagan acknowledged AIDS and the need to mount a counterattack (see Chapter 28).

But the AIDS epidemic not only spurred organized activism; it also reminded Americans that gay men and women were their friends, coworkers, and family members; that they knew them, loved them, and shared social space with them; that they were citizens and rights bearers like anybody else; and that different sexual orientations should not be considered threatening. These recognitions, which came from personal familiarity, would prove crucial to the struggle, for in the 1990s and early 2000s some large issues were still to be resolved. Two of the most important were the rights of gay men and women to serve in the military (they had been officially banned since 1982) and to marry in civil unions. Such rights were not incidental. Military service was not only a badge of honor but also a potential vehicle of mobility and economic security. Civil marriage not only recognized the union of same-sex couples and families but also enabled them to enjoy the rights of heterosexual married couples as to medical care, inheritance, income sharing, and child-raising.

The Right of Sexual Orientation

Resistance to change came from many quarters, political and religious opposition chief among them. Even Democratic presidents like Bill Clinton and Barack Obama were reluctant to embrace what many supporters argued were basic civil and human rights. And in the early 1990s the American public was in many cases strongly opposed. But little by little that opposition eroded and progress was made. In 2011 the military ban against openly gay men and women was repealed, and many counties and then states increasingly permitted same-sex civil marriage. Then, in 2015, a closely divided Supreme Court decided, in **Obergefell v. Hodges**, that same-sex marriage was a constitutional right protected by the Fourteenth Amendment, thereby overruling those states and localities that had refused to

acknowledge it. This was a crucial moment in the civil rights history of the United States and an opening for deeper discussions of sexuality, including the rights of those who identify as transgender.

The notion of sexual orientation existing on a spectrum, rather than in a simple binary of heterosexuality and homosexuality, has been one of the great cultural achievements of the movement. Owing to the activism of a range of groups, we have come to recognize the complexity of sexuality and now regularly refer to LGBTQ+ (lesbian, gay, bisex-

≡ **Celebrating Marriage Equality**   Gay Americans and supporters celebrate the 2015 *Obergefell* decision in Washington, DC. Gay Americans' legal right to marriage was the result of decades of activism by activists who often faced extreme hostility to the idea that homosexual and heterosexual Americans should enjoy the same rights.

ual, transgender, queer/questioning, and other) rights, interests, and challenges, and we can speak of "cisgender" when an individual's gender identity matches their gender assignment at birth. The very idea of "queer," which refers to those who identify as not heterosexual, not cisgender, or both, is an indication of how the instabilities of sexual orientation may be accepted. In more and more areas of life, **transgender ("trans")** (when gender expression and birth gender assignment don't match) is recognized (reinforced by the 2020 Supreme Court decision in *Bostock v. Clayton County*) as an identity with full rights and opportunities.

Still, a consensus has by no means been achieved. Those who are part of the LGBTQ+ community have been confronted with discrimination and brutal violence. Local school boards and other organizations—notably churches and religious affiliates—in a variety of locations have refused to yield in their belief that only heterosexuality is "normal" and acceptable or to address the needs of

LGBTQ+ individuals. Many battles will continue to be fought, with outcomes that will define the boundaries of belonging in the United States. Indeed, the political right is increasingly targeting those who are transgender, especially those in need of help in "transitioning," as well as those who otherwise reject traditional gender categories. Historical change is very bumpy with unexpected lurches forward, detours off the path of progress, and painful setbacks that can quickly become U-turns.

#MeToo Movement

Gender issues stirred controversy and brought change elsewhere. The campaign for women's rights suffered a major setback in the 1970s when the Equal Rights Amendment (ERA), first passed by Congress and ratified by many of the states, was defeated by a mobilization in the remaining states against the ERA and feminism more generally. Among the consequences were that women had more difficulty attaining equal pay and power in the workplace and in combatting sexual harassment and assault at home, work, school, and everyday life. But an important change came in 2016 when presidential candidate Donald Trump was accused of sexual misconduct and assault by a number of women and was recorded expressing sexually predatory sentiments; and in 2017 when a powerful movie producer named Harvey Weinstein was accused—and then convicted—of sexual harassment, assault, and rape by several well-known actresses.

These accusations energized what is called the **#MeToo movement** (the phrase was first used in 2006 by activist Tarana Burke), aimed at confronting sexual misconduct of many sorts—from sexually aggressive language and images to sexual assaults—identifying the perpetrators whether well-known or obscure, cultivating public awareness and empathy, punishing the guilty parties, and encouraging actions at various levels to end the abuses and attacks. Journalistic exposes have received major

≡ **The #MeToo Movement**   Tarana Burke (*center*), founder of the #MeToo movement, joins a march against sexual harassment and assault in Hollywood, California, in November 2017.

attention and prestigious awards, and many Americans have been forced to examine the impact of attitudes and behaviors they previously considered innocuous. Major figures (mostly male) in political and cultural life have been forced to resign their posts or have faced prosecution; others have found themselves shunned or deprived of their one-time public status. Two Supreme Court nominees, Clarence Thomas in 1991 and more recently Brett Kavanaugh in 2018, were only narrowly confirmed by the Senate after credible allegations of harassment and assault were made against them, and they fared less favorably in the court of public opinion.

Schools, universities, and corporations have developed programs to make students and employees more aware of the nature of sexual misconduct and have often adopted a zero-tolerance policy toward those who engage in sexual harassment or assault. Although there has been some unboundedness to #MeToo and confusion about where lines should be drawn—some tend to regard all forms of misconduct, however egregious or minor, as fundamentally the same—there has also been the sort of reckoning that has never taken place before. Whether this will be a step on the path to greater gender equality or promote the type of backlash that may revitalize older gender hierarchies remains to be seen.

30.5   **Democracy Under Siege**

III   Characterize the main threats to political democracy in the United States.

The aftermath of Hurricane Katrina provoked some white New Orleanians to imagine a different future for the city. "The hurricane drove poor people and criminals out of the city, and we hope they don't come back," one local realtor scoffed. "The party's finally over for these people . . . and now they're going to have to find someplace else to live." He was not alone. There was a sense among some members of the city elite that the balances of political power could now be readjusted in what had long been a Black-majority city with a formidable leadership of color. The political stakes could be high. New Orleans was a bastion of Democratic support in an otherwise heavily Republican state, and the results had been evident in state politics. In 2005, all branches of the Louisiana state government—the governor and both houses of the legislature—were in Democratic hands.

The United States has long been recognized as having a deeply rooted democratic political tradition, stretching back into the early republic, that distinguished it from other industrializing countries at the time. This is often the basis for claims of American exceptionalism. And there can be little doubt that the course of

American politics has largely been defined by representative institutions, electorally based transfers of power, and a wide elective franchise, at least as concerns white men. But the political arc has not been a smooth one, and it has often bent toward injustice. During the first half of the nineteenth century, most states gave white adult men the right to vote, whether or not they owned property, yet in some cases simultaneously took that right away from free men of color who had it. During the 1850s, as antislavery developed a mass movement, efforts were made in some places (especially the Northeast and Mid-Atlantic), to undermine the political rights and power of European immigrants, most notably ones of Catholic faith. During Reconstruction, Congress granted the franchise to adult Black men in both the South and the North (a massive extension of voting rights) but at the same time refused to grant the franchise to any women, white or Black (see Chapter 16). At the end of the nineteenth century, Southern states deprived Black men of the voting rights that they had since Reconstruction and Northern states enacted registration laws that made voting more difficult for European immigrants (see Chapter 19). Congress had already passed a Chinese Exclusion Act (1882) and made it clear that neither the Chinese nor Native Americans could enjoy the rights of American citizenship, but as we saw in Chapter 21, in 1919 they saw fit to finally enfranchise women (by the Nineteenth Amendment, ratified in 1920).

The civil rights movement used the Reconstruction laws and amendments as a springboard to argue for a democracy that was not restricted on account of race, and in 1965 a Voting Rights Act passed Congress which prohibited the use of discriminatory methods—like poll taxes and literacy tests—that had effectively denied Black men and women the right to vote and seek public office (see Chapter 26). The act envisioned a much more inclusive democracy than what had prevailed, and it lent power to Black people in cities like New Orleans where they had been denied it for more than sixty years. Soon the voting age was reduced from twenty-one to eighteen (1971), the voting rights of adults who were not proficient in English or had disabilities gained protection (1975, 1982), and Congress enacted a law (1993) making voter registration easier (called the "Motor Voter" law).

Yet what seemed to be defining moments would not endure. During Reconstruction and the Gilded Age, Black men generally supported

≡ **Early Voting**   Voters line up to cast their votes before Election Day in 2022. Early voting, along with mail-in ballot options and automatic voter registration, is part of the renewed efforts to ensure everyone with the right to vote has the opportunity to participate in American democracy. But they remain highly contested, especially by Republicans.

the Republican Party owing to its role in defeating southern enslavers and securing emancipation and the rights of citizenship. That political allegiance began to shift during the New Deal—at least in those areas of the North and West where Black people could vote. When the Voting Rights Act ended Jim Crow disfranchisement in the South, Black voters generally became loyal Democrats, since the party was taking stands in favor of civil and political rights and against forms of racial discrimination, and the Republicans increasingly tried to limit what the federal government could do in these regards.

The Threat of Big Money in Politics

But the past thirty years have seen new threats to political democracy in the United States. One is the increasing influence of big money on the platforms and candidates of both main political parties. The sources of the money may differ between Democrats and Republicans (while the financial sector is likely to donate generously to both parties, fossil fuel interests are more likely to donate to Republican candidates, and the education sector is more likely to contribute to Democratic candidates), but the dependence has grown unchecked, and campaign finance reform efforts have been limited or have allowed for loopholes. For its part, the Supreme Court made campaign finance reform even more difficult when it ruled in 2010 in **Citizens United v. Federal Election Commission** that the First Amendment's free speech clause prohibited the government from limiting the amount of money that corporations or individuals might contribute to political campaigns. This decision unmistakably enhanced the power of special interests and lobbyists at the expense of ordinary voters.

As for voting rights, there have been mixed results. On the one hand, many states have increased voter access by establishing early voting and, in some cases, mail-in ballots; on the other hand, after the presidential election of 2000, which was finally settled by the Supreme Court, there was a growing recognition on the part of political operatives (most of them Republicans) that small shifts in turnout could swing elections. And since Black people and other minority groups tended to vote Democratic (the political leanings of Asian American and Pacific Islander voters have been more complicated), some politicians began to complain of "corruption" at the polls (meaning that voters who were not eligible to vote cast ballots) and some states (many of them in the South) began to explore new requirements for voter registration, especially the use of forms of identification that would prove more difficult for poor and Black voters. These efforts were supported by the Supreme Court in 2013 when it ruled in **Shelby County v. Holder** that federal oversight of elections in states and localities having histories of voter suppression as mandated by the Voting Rights Act was unconstitutional.

The election of Donald Trump and greater Republican control over state legislatures and governorships advanced the process. Claiming that he would have won the popular as well as the electoral vote (he lost the popular vote in 2016 by about three million votes) if the ballots of several million "illegal immigrants" had not been counted, Trump stirred suspicions of immigrants, especially Latinos, and encouraged Republicans to denounce corruption and call for greater election "integrity" despite the fact that studies of voter irregularities have shown that very few fraudulent ballots are ever cast. The charges were further ramped up in 2020, when President Trump warned of fraud and denounced efforts to enable eligible voters to participate amid the COVID-19 pandemic by extending early voting and making mail-in voting more accessible.

When, after Democrat Joe Biden was officially declared the winner, Trump then insisted that the election had been "stolen," pointing especially to the results in districts with large numbers of Black and other minority voters, and refused to concede defeat as all losing presidential candidates had previously done, the legitimacy of the electoral process was drawn into question. Most Republican officials and the overwhelming majority of Republican voters backed Trump's views, and on January 6, 2021, when Congress was scheduled to officially certify the election of Biden, many Republican senators and representatives refused to do so, and a large mob of Trump supporters descended on the US Capitol with the intent—following Trump's advice—of stopping the formal certification. Rioters battered down doors and windows, attempted to get into the House and Senate chambers and House and Senate offices (with some success), and called for Vice President Mike Pence, who presided, to be hanged. Pence escaped unharmed, as did other House and Senate members, but the Capitol was ransacked and several people—including police—were killed or wounded. For many observers, January 6 was deemed an "insurrection" or attempted "coup d'etat."

The Threats Posed by a President's Abuse of Office

The 2020 election topped off a Trump presidency that was marred by attempts to subvert American political democracy. During the 2016 campaign, Trump called on the Russians to help him defeat his Democratic opponent, Hillary Clinton, and there is evidence that Russian operatives did intervene—hacking into emails and helping to make them public—to his benefit. A subsequent investigation suggested both that the Russians interfered in the election and Trump was likely guilty of obstruction of justice in attempting to mislead the investigators, though no penalty was imposed. In 2019, Trump pressured the president of Ukraine to investigate Joe Biden and his family in hopes of weakening a likely election opponent, and when this was revealed the now-Democratic controlled House of Representatives passed articles of impeachment against Trump (he was acquitted in the Republican-controlled Senate). After the January 6 insurrection, the House impeached Trump for an unprecedented second time, though he and his allies continued to question the legitimacy of Biden's presidency while state legislatures with Republican majorities have adopted additional voter restrictions.

Insurrection Insurrectionists supporting President Trump attack the US Capitol on January 6, 2021, in a failed effort to prevent the certification of the 2020 presidential election. While insurrectionists portrayed themselves as concerned citizens, many were members of paramilitary or extremist groups that actively sought violence.

Political Trajectories Around the Globe

The twentieth century was marked by attempts of political regimes around the world to subvert democratic political rights through disfranchisement, coercion, vote manipulation, or outright violence. Such efforts were often directed at racial minorities, immigrants, and the poor. In addition, many Americans have had good reason to be skeptical of the intentions of politicians and the political process. The outsized importance of money in politics has resulted in a deep cynicism regardless of party affiliation. Indeed, over the past half century there has been a growing number of voters who call themselves Independents rather than Democrats or Republicans, a phenomenon that may be obscured by talk of deep "partisan divides."

The fate of democracy in the United States is a more urgent subject of discussion than at any point in our history, with the possible exception of the Civil War era. In the immediate post–Cold War period, it was possible for some to speak of an "end of history," especially an end to a variety of authoritarian regimes, and in turn an expansion of liberal democracy. Now, it appears that the political trajectory of many societies around the globe is away from liberal democracy and toward authoritarianism: a trajectory that could easily be advanced by the disruptions of climate change.

There are further questions that have been asked since the 1990s. How can a democracy be sustained in the midst of extreme inequalities of wealth and new technologies that have unprecedented surveillance capacities (sometimes called "surveillance capitalism")? Do voting and representation, even when unhindered, have much meaning when a very small portion of the population has extraordinary economic power along with the capacity to harvest enormous quantities of information about us? The answers to these questions will be crucial to the destiny of the United States.

30.6 The Reemergence of China as a Global Power

Discuss the significance of China's remarkable political and economic rise for the future of the United States.

The devastation wrought by Hurricane Katrina was not only an event of consequence for New Orleans, the Gulf Coast, and American society. It was also an event of consequence internationally because Katrina revealed the massive impact of climate change and exposed the poverty and crisis mismanagement that afflicted the United States. "The images about Katrina seen around the world communicated considerable chaos and suffering," American diplomat Richard Haass conceded. "The dominant overseas reaction has been sympathy mixed with shock and horror of what was seen by many as evidence of racism and a reminder of the extreme poverty in which many Americans live. The world's only superpower appeared to be anything but." A "grand failure" was the predominant international verdict.

This seemed a far cry from the international position the United States occupied just a decade earlier. Then the United States appeared to have defeated its major rivals and emerged as the dominant global power; the "world's only superpower," as Haass put it. Although political volatility engulfed much of the globe and non-state actors increasingly left a violent imprint, no one doubted that the United States was the world's economic, political, and military powerhouse. The Soviet Union had unraveled and was making a very bumpy transition to some form of capitalism. The European Union had incorporated much of the former Eastern Bloc. The Japanese "miracle" of the 1960s–1980s had begun to sputter. A peace between Israel and the Palestinians, known as the Oslo Accords, had been brokered in 1993, and a treaty between warring factions in Northern Ireland, known as "the Good Friday Agreement," had been signed in 1998, both with the help of the Clinton administration. One year later, in 1999, nearly a decade of bloody fighting across the former Yugoslavia came to an end. And the rising Asian power, the People's Republic of China, appeared to be an American ally with a growing but still second-tier industrial economy.

The 9/11 terrorist attack on the United States didn't so much shatter American global power as reveal the vulnerabilities and weaknesses that the disorders of the 1990s had obscured. While ostensibly triumphant, American political and diplomatic leaders struggled to find a new framework for the country's foreign policy. Diplomatic relevance suddenly seemed more decentered now that the United States and the Soviet Union no longer served as magnetic poles. What had seemed like American triumphs were now shrouded in ambiguity. The Oslo Accords had in fact been hammered out in secret talks between Israel and the Palestinian Liberation Organization (PLO) 1993–1995 before the United States became directly involved. The brutal war that devastated the Balkans in the 1990s generated no clear response from the United States, and the peace was ultimately a NATO-supervised affair. The ghastly Rwandan genocide of 1994 drew no American response. The warning signs coming from non-state actors, sometimes called terrorists, such as Al Qaeda, were largely ignored despite bombings they perpetrated during the 1990s that targeted American embassies and military assets abroad as well the 1993 attack at the World Trade Center at home.

Neoconservatives in the United States lambasted the drifting nature of post–Cold War foreign policy and demanded greater assertiveness of American power, especially in the oil-rich Middle East. They got their opportunity in 2001 when Republican George W. Bush became president and the attacks of 9/11 occurred. Not surprisingly, they pushed for a wide-ranging response—Bush called it a "war on terror"—and set their sights not only on Afghanistan, where the Al-Qaeda leadership was based, but also on Iraq, which had nothing to do with 9/11. The neocons called for "regime change," the overthrow of the Iraqi strongman Saddam Hussein, and the installation of a government more in line with American objectives (see Chapter 29). And they thought it would be easily done, imagining a wellspring of popular Iraqi support for the American "liberators." But there were rude awakenings: Iraq and Afghanistan descended into political and military chaos, and Al Qaeda's leader, Osama Bin Laden, evaded capture until 2011. American troops would be on the ground for years, new Islamic insurgents such as the Islamic State of Iraq and Syria (ISIS) would arise and terrorize large swaths of the region in the name of a new "califate" (a single Islamic government), and when the United States ultimately withdrew its forces in 2021 many of the original targets were still in place, some more emboldened.

The wars in Iraq and Afghanistan had unexpected political repercussions in the United States. Initially, both the American attack on Afghanistan and the invasion of Iraq won substantial bipartisan support. Congressional Democrats as well as Republicans voted to give President Bush military authorization to act as he saw fit. But when it became apparent that the evidence used to support the Iraqi invasion

≣ **Mutual Admirers**   Donald Trump and Vladimir Putin meet in Helsinki for a summit in July 2018. At a press conference, Trump stated that he believed Putin's claims that Russia did not interfere in the 2016 US elections, despite strong evidence to the contrary. In a statement, Republican Senator John McCain said that "No prior president has ever abased himself more abjectly before a tyrant."

(weapons of mass destruction housed there) had been invented, liberal Democrats turned into war critics, and demands for an end to the Iraq war and a larger reassessment of the war in Afghanistan helped Barack Obama win the Democratic presidential nomination in 2008 (his main opponent, Hillary Clinton, had voted in support of the war) and then the presidency. Over time, however, the mounting costs and casualties had an impact on the Republican Party as well. Donald Trump, who campaigned for the presidency in 2016 as a nationalist under the slogan "Make America Great Again," called for a more general pullback of the country's military presence around the world. And he clearly struck a resonant chord.

Russia came to embrace a new nationalism even earlier, and the leader was former KGB (the Russian security agency) operative Vladimir Putin. During the 1980s and 1990s, Putin rose in the political ranks and in 1999 became Russia's president. Determined to maintain the global recognition that the Soviet Union had enjoyed, he simultaneously aligned himself with some of the newly wealthy Russian "oligarchs," cracked down on political opponents, and in 2014 flexed Russian muscles in Ukraine, illegally annexing the district of Crimea, and in 2015 in a civil war in Syria, in effective opposition to the United States. Putin's actions frayed relations with the Obama administration and Democrats more generally. As a result, he clearly sought to aid Trump's campaign in 2016 and undermine Clinton's. Despite, or perhaps because of, his attempts to interfere in the American political process, he received favored treatment from President Trump who expressed admiration for Putin's authoritarian dispositions and advanced his own version of nationalism.

The emergence of Putin, who has remained in office for over two decades, is symptomatic of an authoritarian and right-wing nationalist turn in many parts of the twenty-first century world. Right-wing "populists" as they are often called, because they seek to mobilize popular support for nationalist and "antielitist" policies, have taken power in parts of Eastern Europe, Latin America, and Asia, and have shown considerable strength in Western Europe and the United States. Most everywhere, they trade on hostilities to immigrants and other minorities, whether racial or cultural, and speak a language of "peoplehood" that is exclusive rather than inclusive, marking out enemies and threatening them with repression.

The Rise of China

Some of these tendencies can be seen in the country that has experienced the most remarkable rise of the post–Cold War world: China. Once the dominant empire in the Eurasian world during the Ming dynasty (1368–1644) and more than a century under the Qing dynasty (1644–1912), Chinese power began to crumble during the nineteenth century in the face of Euro-Atlantic challenges. The Opium Wars (1839–1842, 1856–1860) enabled the British to gain territorial footholds and trading rights in Hong Kong and China's densely populated southeast. The Open Door policy and the Chinese Exclusion Act of the late nineteenth century added the United States to the mix. The massive Taiping Rebellion (1850–1864) shook the already weakened Qing rulers, and by the end of the nineteenth century the imperial-minded Japanese were positioned in Manchuria, Taiwan, and on China's northeast border. The Qing dynasty finally collapsed as a result of a nationalist revolution in 1911, which, in turn, fueled, first, an anticolonial movement in the aftermath of World War I, known as the May Fourth movement, and then Mao Zedong's long road to power, completed in 1949 with the birth of the People's Republic.

For the next thirty years, Mao and the Chinese Communist Party (PCP) worked to build socialism in what was an overwhelmingly rural and peasant-based society and effectively closed itself off to the West, though having developed atomic weaponry and intervened to support the North in the Korean War, China was regarded as a military power (see Chapter 25). With the death of Mao (1976) following an opening to the United States that was embraced by President Nixon and Secretary of State Kissinger, the new Chinese leadership hoped to move the country toward industrial modernization and wider economic transformation. With reformer Deng Xiaoping at the helm, they encouraged the development of market institutions, the breakup of rural communes, the creation of special economic zones for international trade, and the establishment of diplomatic relations with countries outside the communist and socialist world. They also loosened state control over political and cultural expression, promoting exchanges of students, intellectuals, and entrepreneurs with capitalist countries like the United States.

As Mikhail Gorbachev discovered in the Soviet Union, the challenge was to navigate economic and political liberalization without surrendering the socialist project and the integrity of the state (see Chapter 28). The Chinese saw what was happening there, and when a democracy movement organized by students surfaced in 1989, the government responded with a brutal crackdown on protesters, including a massacre of hundreds of them at Tiananmen Square in Beijing. Some thought this might be a tipping point in China, especially given the momentous international events of that year. But rather than undermining the power and authority of the Chinese state and Communist Party, Tiananmen Square led in the opposite direction. Chinese leaders moved to tighten the reins of political liberalization while using the authority of the central state to promote economic development and international financial networks. "Socialism with Chinese characteristics" they termed it. As a result, the democracy movement was suppressed and China became a magnet for international investment and the repository of billions of dollars in international currencies, none more significant than American dollars. Foreign-owned and "joint venture" enterprises proliferated, giving shape to something of a hybrid economic system: a few large state-owned operations in the strategic industrial and financial sectors together with a great many private enterprises that still had close ties to local government officials.

Some called the system "market socialism." Others called it "state capitalism." Either way, the impact was enormous and, in many ways, unprecedented. Beginning in the 1990s, Chinese investment rates took off and economic growth rates exploded. The export sector was especially robust. As early as 2000, China exported $37 billion of hi-tech products to the United States, most produced by foreign companies and joint ventures, and over the next two decades the Chinese began to invest very large amounts of capital in overseas projects, especially in Africa, the Middle East, and Latin America. By the 2010s, China was the world's largest importer of oil and the most important trading partner for many nations across the globe. By 2015, China stood as the world's second largest economy behind the United States, and it is likely that China will surpass the United States before 2030.

Within China, there was an urban boom with some new cities built nearly overnight and older ones like Shanghai utterly transformed. There was also growing investment in and reform of the educational system, modification of the land system in the countryside, and a greater orientation to the production and circulation of consumer goods. Newly wealthy classes emerged, and a massive infrastructure of roads, railways, and airports has been constructed to integrate what is the fourth largest (by physical size) country in the world now boasting the second largest population (behind India) at 1.4 billion, more than four times that of the United States.

But these changes also came with new problems and challenges. The rapid industrialization of China has depended heavily on fossil-fuel energy sources like coal and oil, resulting in extremely high levels of pollution. The efforts to integrate the many regions of the country have led to the repression of ethnic minorities such as the Uyghurs and Tibetans on China's northwestern border and to the suppression of democratic political movements in Hong Kong, transferred back from British to Chinese control in 1997. The efforts to promote very high rates of economic growth have resulted in large-scale inequalities of wealth, both between cities and the countryside and between internal migrants and more settled populations. The attempt to maintain some loyalty to socialist—and Maoist—ideals amid the expansion of markets in goods and labor has led the central government and the still-reigning Communist Party to devise symbols and political languages that can hover over the process. Xi Jinping, the most powerful leader to have emerged since the passing of Mao Zedong, has been careful to link his vision of the "China Dream" with a "rejuvenation" of Maoist ideas. He has also linked it to greater military prowess, especially in the Pacific. The outbreak of COVID-19 in 2019–2020 showed both the strong reach of the Chinese state's power and the still opaque face it turns to the world.

As we might expect, China's recent rise, and especially its growing economic and military power, has unnerved many American policymakers, whether Democrat or Republican. They have worried about American trade imbalances owing to the importation of low-priced Chinese goods and about China's vast currency resources—dollars in particular—that could potentially destabilize the international financial system and give China great influence over the American economy. More and more of them view China as the chief rival of the United States, and one that already threatens American "interests" and America's ability to remain the world's superpower.

Vladimir Putin's determination to invade and annex the neighboring country of Ukraine beginning in March 2022 has further destabilized the structure of global power while deepening tensions between China and the United States. Looking to recover from the economic and political setbacks inflicted by COVID-19, the Chinese have simultaneously allied with Russia (and thus against the United States and the European Union, though to what extent we do not yet know) and turned a militarist face toward the western Pacific. And no place better captures the tensions and dangers than the island state of Taiwan, long claimed as a territory by the People's Republic and long defended by the United States. If a military conflict erupts in the Pacific, Taiwan will likely be ground zero. International tensions are probably at their highest point since the early 1980s.

MAPPING AMERICA

China Then and Now

The rise of China in the last fifty years is remarkable. But it also marks a return to the global position China enjoyed throughout most of its history. For centuries, China was the world's wealthiest society. Up until about 1800 China dominated world markets. It was a major exporter of luxury goods that the rest of the world craved—silk, tea, porcelain, and spices. A European traveler in sixteenth-century Beijing observed that "all these things were to be had in such abundance that I feel there are not enough words in the dictionary to name them all."[2] But after 1800, China's economic power declined sharply following the expansion of European industrializing empires. By 1900, its share of manufacturing had declined to just 8 percent of the world's total output.

Cartograms are maps that size territories based on the information being depicted. The two cartograms below show the world's regions in proportion to their share of global wealth.

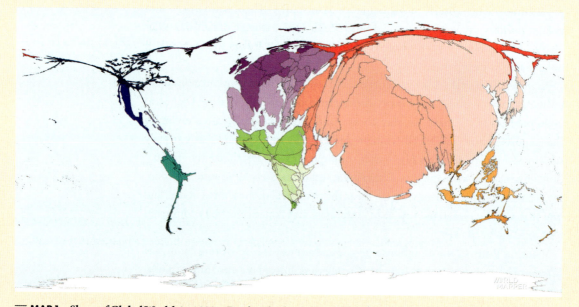

≡ **MAP 1**   **Share of Global Wealth in 1500**   Five hundred years ago, China (and to a lesser extent, India) was the world's leading economic power. It is represented in the cartogram as an enormous light-pink blob. In contrast, the territory that would become the United States is a tiny sliver.

[2]Rebecca D. Catz, ed., *The Travels of Mendes Pinto* (Chicago: University of Chicago Press, 1989), 600.

≡ **MAP 2   Share of Global Wealth in 2018**   After centuries of economic insignificance, by the early twenty-first century China had returned to its leading position. This cartogram depicts world wealth in 2018. Large blobs indicate the powerful economies of the United States, Japan, and Western Europe, but they are overshadowed by China's swelling might.

Thinking Geographically

The reemergence of China on the global stage after two centuries of decline demonstrates that history can move in unexpected directions.

1. If you were able to travel back in time to 1500 CE, would you have been able to predict that European, and later, American economic power would eclipse China's a few hundred years later? In 1900, when China's economy was at its nadir, would you have been able to predict its ascent to preeminence a hundred years later?

2. In looking at the 2018 cartogram, does it appear that other regions besides China, Japan, the United States, and Western Europe could contend for economic supremacy in the second half of the twenty-first century?

3. How do you think the world will appear in 2050? Will climate change affect the way the cartogram looks?

The reemergence of China on the global stage after two centuries of decline demonstrates that history can move in unexpected directions, that history's arc is not linear and can be misshapen, that progress can be followed by retreat as well as defeat, that the self-satisfaction and haughtiness that victories can bring may eventually devolve into painful reckonings and humiliations. The United States looks out on a challenge-laden twenty-first century with significant choices about what type of society and what sort of actor in the world it will be. And as was true in the early republic, the gaze is to the west and the Pacific, where it was then believed that American destiny would reside. The destinies that now may be imagined and pursued are many and varied; and what is achieved will reveal that historical destinies are not ordained, however high-minded they may be. Historical destinies have always been and will always be struggled for by the people who live them.

Conclusion: The Arc of History

Historians work at interpreting and making meaning of the past. We are much more cautious about suggesting what the past means for the future. But it is also clear that as we look ahead and contemplate the destinies of the United States, especially over the next half century, there are a number of clear challenges. And the impact of Hurricane Katrina helps us imagine how those challenges may be connected.

Perhaps more than anything else, Katrina symbolized both the consequences of climate change and how those consequences threaten not only the United States but the entire planet. In important ways, Katrina also offered stark views of how our deep history of racism exposed African Americans and other people of color to the most devastating effects of the storm *and* to the greatest problems of repairing their lives and communities. By extension, Katrina showed us how racism is part and parcel of an even wider crisis of economic inequality. Only a small number of individuals and their families own the overwhelming majority of this country's wealth and, as a result, wield a very disproportionate share of power.

The devastation poor people of color endured in New Orleans because of Katrina and their very limited ability to participate in discussions of how to rebuild the city—and who would benefit—showed how hopes stirred by the civil rights movement about having a more robust democracy have faltered. And the political world of Katrina's aftermath is indicative of much wider attacks on democratic politics, and especially on the access that people of color, whether native-born or immigrant, will have. Fears of the changing demographics in the United States, which will make white people the numerical minority by midcentury, are important drivers of this backlash, as is the lengthy decline of the country's once formidable industrial sector. The January 6, 2021, insurrectionary attempt to prevent the transfer of presidential power from Donald Trump to Joe Biden revealed that we could move more quickly than most recognized from democracy to authoritarianism.

As has been true of other unanticipated crises, such as COVID-19, Katrina offered distressing perspectives on the shortcomings of our current health care system and the issues of public health more generally. What responsibilities and obligations do we, as a society, have for supporting the well-being of the people who live within our borders, whether or not they are citizens? How can we stand on a world stage, with new rivals such as China flexing their power, if we have more and more difficulty managing the problems that erupt in our own country?

It is, however, important to remember other, and inspiring, histories. The high principles of the Declaration of Independence, the Reconstruction Amendments, the New Deal, and the Great Society, even if observed in the breach by founders and many of those who have succeeded them, have also served as beacons for many men and women here and around the world. Although we seem to be sliding into a social and political—in fact existential—set of crises, many remain committed to the ideals of equality, democracy, economic opportunity, diversity, fairness, and inclusion. Over the past seventy-five years, there have been achievements for women, people of color, people with different sexual orientations and gender identities, people with disabilities, and people who have been mired in poverty that would have been unimaginable before and often felt truly stunning when they were happening. Some of these gains have been contested and pushed back; others have gained further traction. Together they demonstrate that forging a nation is an ongoing process, marked by victories and defeats, possibilities and disappointments. But as Frederick Douglass put it so eloquently, recognizing that people are the history makers, "if there is no struggle, there is no progress."

WHAT IF the January 6, 2021, Insurrection Had Succeeded?

January 6, 2021, has been etched into American historical memory much like September 11, 2001 (9/11), a day of shocking political violence that transformed the country. Hundreds of armed demonstrators descended on the US Capitol as Congress was about to make Joe Biden's election to the presidency official. They did so in an effort to bring a halt to the transition in power that had never before been disrupted, even on the eve of the War of the Rebellion. They clearly hoped to intimidate members of Congress and force Vice President Mike Pence, who presided, to refuse his assigned role of simply counting the official electoral votes. Instead, they wanted him to claim that there was voting fraud and award the presidency to incumbent President Donald Trump. As it turned out, Pence spurned the insurrectionists'—and Trump's—demands, even as insurrectionists threatened to hang him. And, when the insurrection was suppressed, he proceeded with the count and the transition as planned. Joe Biden, not Donald Trump, became president of the United States.

But what if the insurrection had succeeded? It is not at all far-fetched. Vice President Pence is often celebrated for his ultimate adherence to the Constitution, but in the weeks after the November 2020 election, he stood with Trump in questioning the election's outcome and didn't stray even when Trump insisted that the election was "stolen." Pence had been a Trump loyalist throughout their term in office, and Trump had reason to believe that Pence would do his bidding. Pence himself consulted legal authorities to determine what his constitutional role could be and seemed to waver until the very end. What if Pence had buckled and stopped the congressional proceedings? And what if Trump then called out the National Guard and the Army to secure the Capitol for him—effectively dissolving Congress? Would that have been the end of American democracy?

DOCUMENT 30.1: Views of Americans on the January 6 Insurrection

This paper was published in 2023 by the Brookings Institution in Washington, DC.

Today marks two years since Americans turned on their televisions to watch something that many thought was impossible—a violent mob attacking the Capitol of the United States with the intention of disrupting the Electoral College vote count. Those days were followed by the creation of a House Select Committee and ten drama filled hearings that began on June 9, 2022 and ended December 19, 2022.

Many expected that the hearings would change public opinion, but on the second anniversary of the January 6 violent invasion of the US Capitol, sentiment remains mostly divided along party lines and has barely budged since the first anniversary of this event. Americans remain split on

Table 30.1	How Much Responsibility Does Donald Trump Bear for January 6?			
	A Lot	**Some**	**Not Much**	**None**
January 2022	43	18	16	20
June 2022	41	18	14	25
December 2022	45	19	13	21

the issue of whether former president Donald Trump committed crimes related to this event and whether he should be charged, and the dramatic testimony delivered at the public hearings of the Select Committee changed few minds.

During the past year, Quinnipiac University conducted a series of polls probing sentiment about January 6. Concerning the former president's responsibility for events at the Capitol, here are the results from the beginning, middle, and end of 2022 [see Table 30.1].

Opinion about the seriousness of the January 6 events was also stable. In January 2022, 50% of Americans thought that these events represented an attack on democracy that should never be forgotten, compared to 44% who believed that the country was making too much of these events and that it was time to move on. In December, Americans remained divided on this issue, 54% to 41%.

In July, the NPR/PBS/Marist survey posed the question differently but got similar results. Presented with three different assessments of January 6, 50% of respondents said that it was an insurrection that threatened democracy, 19% regarded it as constitutionally protected political protest, and 25% deemed it unfortunate but believed that it was time to move on.

Public opinion about the seriousness of Donald Trump's actions related to January 6 showed a similar pattern of division and stability. In June 2022, according to Quinnipiac, 46% of Americans believed that Trump had committed a crime, but 47% disagreed. In July, after several more explosive public hearings, 48% thought that he had committed a crime, compared to 44% who didn't. By December, sentiment remained unchanged, 47% to 43%.

Source: Brookings Institution, January 6, 2023.

DOCUMENT 30.2: The January 6 Insurrection and American Relations with China

This is the perspective of Robert Daly, who heads the Kissinger Institute on China and the United States. He wrote this article the day after the January 6 insurrection.

Viewed broadly, the first forty years of U.S.–China relations were a discussion—or argument—about China's trajectory: where it had been, what it was becoming, what its people and government thought and desired. China was the unknown and the American-led world order was the constant.

The Trump administration and the events of January 6 have balanced that discussion in a perilous way; in the eyes of Americans, Chinese, and the rest of the world, the United States, like China, is now a variable with a dangerously uncertain range of possible values.

If the Biden administration is to build the coalitions needed to compete with China, it must address global doubts about the United States through a program of restoration at home and sophisticated public diplomacy worldwide. Diplomacy, and public diplomacy in particular, must receive the same priority as the Defense Department if the United States is to recover some part of its former status.

Due to the legacy of President Trump and January 6, President Biden's public diplomats will not be able to rely on China's bellicosity and brutality to do their work for them. America's performance over the past four years has given Beijing the ammunition it needs to counter such attacks. America's claims to continued global influence must be founded not on warnings about China's many misdeeds, but on demonstrations of American consistency and competence. Under President Biden, the United States must tell a new, true, and compelling American story. Our diplomats must be given the resources to begin this work immediately.

Source: wilsoncenter.org.

Thinking About Contingency

1. What do you think that members of Congress would have done if Vice President Pence refused to certify the electoral vote and declare Biden the president? Would Republican members have supported Pence and repressed any effort of Democrats to contest Pence's actions?
2. Would the National Guard and US Army have obeyed Trump's orders and allowed Trump to stay in office?
3. How would Russia and China and other countries around the world have reacted if the insurrection had succeeded? Would international criticism have forced Trump to step down?
4. How would the American public have responded, and what would it have taken to keep Trump in office?

REVIEW QUESTIONS

1. What is climate change? What are the political conflicts associated with climate change? What are the connections between climate change and inequality?

2. How does systemic racism affect all levels of American society? What have been the social justice struggles against systemic racism?

3. How does economic inequality compromise access to health care?

4. What factors have enabled the LGBTQ+ community to make social and political gains in the last two decades? What obstacles still remain?

5. What are the main threats to political democracy in the United States? How are these threats paralleled by developments in other countries? What impact would the insurrection of January 6, 2021, have had on democratic institutions if it had succeeded?

6. What accounts for China's remarkable political and economic rise? What does this bode for the future of the United States?

KEY TERMS

Affordable Care Act (ACA Obamacare) (p. 1293)

Anthropocene (p. 1288)

Black Lives Matter (BLM) (p. 1295)

Citizens United v. Federal Election Commission (p. 1307)

graduated income tax (p. 1297)

#MeToo movement (p. 1304)

Obergefell v. Hodges (p. 1303)

Shelby County v. Holder (p. 1307)

social stratification (p. 1297)

subprime mortgage (p. 1292)

systemic racism (p. 1295)

Tea Party movement (p. 1293)

transgender ("trans") (p. 1303)

RECOMMENDED READINGS

Ruth Ben-Ghiat, *Strongmen: Mussolini to the Present* (W.W. Norton, 2021).

Andy Horowitz, *Katrina: A History, 1915–2015* (Harvard University Press, 2020).

Klaus Mulhahn, *Making China Modern: From the Great Qing to Xi Jinping* (Harvard University Press, 2019).

Pippa Norris and Ronald Inglehart, *Cultural Backlash: Trump, Brexit, and Authoritarian Populism* (Cambridge University Press, 2019).

Barack Obama, *A Promised Land* (Random House, 2020).

Mathew Reimer and Leighton Brown, *We Are Everywhere: Protest, Power, and Pride in the History of Queer Liberation* (Ten Speed Press, 2019).

Richard Rothstein, *The Color of Law: A Forgotten History of How Our Government Segregated America* (Liveright Press, 2017).

Shoshana Zuboff, *Surveillance Capitalism: The Fight for a Human Future at the New Frontier of Power* (Public Affairs, 2019).

Appendix A
Historical Documents

The Declaration of Independence (1776)

When in the course of human events, it becomes necessary for one people to dissolve the political bands which have connected them with another, and to assume, among the powers of the earth, the separate and equal station to which the Laws of Nature and of Nature's God entitle them, a decent respect to the opinions of mankind requires that they should declare the causes which impel them to the separation.

We hold these truths to be self-evident, that all men are created equal, that they are endowed by their Creator with certain unalienable Rights, that among these are life, liberty and the pursuit of happiness. That to secure these rights, governments are instituted among men, deriving their just powers from the consent of the governed; that whenever any form of government becomes destructive of these ends, it is the right of the people to alter or to abolish it, and to institute new Government, laying its foundation on such principles and organizing its powers in such form, as to them shall seem most likely to effect their safety and happiness. Prudence, indeed, will dictate that Governments long established should not be changed for light and transient causes; and, accordingly, all experience hath shown, that mankind are more disposed to suffer, while evils are sufferable, than to right themselves by abolishing the forms to which they are accustomed. But when a long train of abuses and usurpations, pursuing invariably the same object evinces a design to reduce them under absolute despotism, it is their right, it is their duty, to throw off such government, and to provide new guards for their future security. Such has been the patient sufferance of these colonies; and such is now the necessity which constrains them to alter their former systems of government. The history of the present King of Great Britain is a history of repeated injuries and usurpations, all having in direct object the establishment of an absolute tyranny over these States. To prove this, let facts be submitted to a candid world:

He has refused his assent to laws, the most wholesome and necessary for the public good.

He has forbidden his governors to pass laws of immediate and pressing importance, unless suspended in their operation till his assent should be obtained; and, when so suspended, he has utterly neglected to attend to them.

He has refused to pass other laws for the accommodation of large districts of people, unless those people would relinquish the right of representation in the legislature, a right inestimable to them and formidable to tyrants only.

He has called together legislative bodies at places unusual, uncomfortable, and distant from the depository of their public records, for the sole purpose of fatiguing them into compliance with his measures.

He has dissolved representative houses repeatedly, for opposing with manly firmness his invasions on the rights of the people.

He has refused for a long time, after such dissolutions, to cause others to be elected; whereby the legislative powers, incapable of annihilation, have returned to the People at large for their exercise; the State remaining in the mean time exposed to all the dangers of invasion from without, and convulsions within.

He has endeavored to prevent the population of these States; for that purpose obstructing the laws for naturalization of foreigners; refusing to pass others to encourage their migrations hither, and raising the conditions of new appropriations of lands.

He has obstructed the administration of justice, by refusing his assent to laws for establishing judiciary powers.

He has made judges dependent on his will alone, for the tenure of their offices, and the amount and payment of their salaries.

He has erected a multitude of new offices, and sent hither swarms of officers to harass our people, and eat out their substance.

He has kept among us, in times of peace, standing armies without the consent of our legislatures.

He has affected to render the Military independent of, and superior to, the civil power.

He has combined with others to subject us to a jurisdiction foreign to our constitution and unacknowledged by our laws; giving his assent to their acts of pretended legislation:

For quartering large bodies of armed troops among us;

For protecting them, by a mock trial, from punishment for any murders which they should commit on the inhabitants of these States;

For cutting off our trade with all parts of the world;

For imposing taxes on us without our Consent;

For depriving us, in many cases, of the benefits of Trial by Jury;

For transporting us beyond Seas to be tried for pretended offences;

For abolishing the free System of English Laws in a neighbouring Province, establishing therein an Arbitrary government, and enlarging its Boundaries so as to render it at once an example and fit instrument for introducing the same absolute rule into these colonies;

For taking away our charters, abolishing our most valuable laws, and altering fundamentally the forms of our governments;

For suspending our own legislatures, and declaring themselves invested with power to legislate for us in all cases whatsoever.

He has abdicated government here, by declaring us out of his protection and waging war against us.

He has plundered our seas, ravaged our coasts, burnt our towns, and destroyed the lives of our people.

He is at this time transporting large armies of foreign mercenaries to complete the works of death, desolation and tyranny, already begun with circumstances of cruelty and perfidy scarcely paralleled in the most barbarous ages, and totally unworthy the head of a civilized nation.

He has constrained our fellow citizens taken captive on the high seas to bear arms against their country, to become the executioners of their friends and brethren, or to fall themselves by their hands.

He has excited domestic insurrections amongst us, and has endeavored to bring on the inhabitants of our frontiers, the merciless Indian savages, whose known rule of warfare, is an undistinguished destruction of all ages, sexes and conditions.

In every stage of these oppressions we have petitioned for redress in the most humble terms; our repeated petitions have been answered only by repeated injury. A prince whose character is thus marked by every act which may define a tyrant, is unfit to be the ruler of a free people.

Nor have we been wanting in attentions to our British brethren. We have warned them from time to time of attempts by their legislature to extend an unwarrantable jurisdiction over us. We have reminded them of the circumstances of our emigration and settlement here. We have appealed to their native justice and magnanimity, and we have conjured them by the ties of our common kindred to disavow these usurpations, which, would inevitably interrupt our connections and correspondence. They, too, have been deaf to the voice of justice and of consanguinity. We must, therefore, acquiesce in the necessity, which denounces our separation, and hold them, as we hold the rest of mankind, enemies in war, in peace friends.

We, therefore, the representatives of the United States of America, in general Congress, assembled, appealing to the Supreme Judge of the world for the rectitude of our intentions, do, in the name, and by the authority of the good people of these colonies, solemnly publish and declare, that these united colonies are, and of right ought to be free and independent states; that they are absolved from all allegiance to the British Crown, and that all political connection between them and the state of Great Britain, is and ought to be totally dissolved; and that, as free and independent states, they have full power to levy war, conclude peace, contract alliances, establish commerce, and to do all other acts and things which independent states may of right do. And for the support of this declaration, with a firm reliance on the protection of Divine Providence, we mutually pledge to each other our lives, our fortunes and our sacred honor.

The Constitution of the United States of America (Ratified 1788)

We the People of the United States, in Order to form a more perfect Union, establish Justice, insure domestic Tranquility, provide for the common defence, promote the general Welfare, and secure the Blessings of Liberty to ourselves and our Posterity, do ordain and establish this Constitution for the United States of America.

Article I

SECTION 1

All legislative Powers herein granted shall be vested in a Congress of the United States, which shall consist of a Senate and House of Representatives.

SECTION 2

The House of Representatives shall be composed of Members chosen every second Year by the People of the several States, and the Electors in each State shall have the Qualifications requisite for Electors of the most numerous Branch of the State Legislature.

No Person shall be a Representative who shall not have attained to the Age of twenty five Years, and been seven Years a Citizen of the United States, and who shall not, when elected, be an Inhabitant of that State in which he shall be chosen.

Representatives and direct Taxes shall be apportioned among the several States which may be included within this Union, according to their respective Numbers, which shall be determined by adding to the whole Number of free Persons, including those bound to Service for a Term of Years, and excluding Indians not taxed, three fifths of all other Persons. The actual Enumeration shall be made within three Years after the first Meeting of the Congress of the United States, and within every subsequent Term of ten Years, in such Manner as they shall by Law direct. The Number of Representatives shall not exceed one for every thirty Thousand, but each State shall have at Least one Representative; and until such enumeration shall be made, the State of New Hampshire shall be entitled to choose three, Massachusetts eight, Rhode-Island and Providence Plantations one, Connecticut five, New York six, New Jersey four, Pennsylvania eight, Delaware one, Maryland six, Virginia ten, North Carolina five, South Carolina five, and Georgia three.

When vacancies happen in the Representation from any State, the Executive Authority thereof shall issue Writs of Election to fill such Vacancies.

The House of Representatives shall choose their Speaker and other Officers; and shall have the sole Power of Impeachment.

SECTION 3

The Senate of the United States shall be composed of two Senators from each State, chosen by the Legislature thereof for six Years; and each Senator shall have one Vote.

Immediately after they shall be assembled in Consequence of the first Election, they shall be divided as equally as may be into three Classes. The Seats of the Senators of the first Class shall be vacated at the Expiration of the second Year, of the second Class at the Expiration of the fourth Year, and of the third Class at the Expiration of the sixth Year, so that one third may be chosen every second Year; and if Vacancies happen by Resignation, or otherwise, during the Recess of the Legislature of any State, the Executive thereof may make temporary Appointments until the next Meeting of the Legislature, which shall then fill such Vacancies.

No Person shall be a Senator who shall not have attained to the Age of thirty Years, and been nine Years a Citizen of the United States, and who shall not, when elected, be an Inhabitant of that State for which he shall be chosen.

The Vice President of the United States shall be President of the Senate, but shall have no Vote, unless they be equally divided.

The Senate shall choose their other Officers, and also a President pro tempore, in the Absence of the Vice President, or when he shall exercise the Office of President of the United States.

The Senate shall have the sole Power to try all Impeachments. When sitting for that Purpose, they shall be on Oath or Affirmation. When the President of the United States is tried, the Chief Justice shall preside: And no Person shall be convicted without the Concurrence of two thirds of the Members present.

Judgment in Cases of Impeachment shall not extend further than to removal from Office, and disqualification to hold and enjoy any Office of honor, Trust or Profit under the United States: but the Party convicted shall nevertheless be liable and subject to Indictment, Trial, Judgment and Punishment, according to Law.

SECTION 4

The Times, Places and Manner of holding Elections for Senators and Representatives, shall be prescribed in each State by the Legislature thereof; but the Congress may at any time by Law make or alter such Regulations, except as to the Places of chusing Senators.

The Congress shall assemble at least once in every Year, and such Meeting shall be on the first Monday in December, unless they shall by Law appoint a different Day.

SECTION 5

Each House shall be the Judge of the Elections, Returns and Qualifications of its own Members, and a Majority of each shall constitute a Quorum to do Business; but a smaller Number may adjourn from day to day, and may be authorized to compel the Attendance of absent Members, in such Manner, and under such Penalties as each House may provide.

Each House may determine the Rules of its Proceedings, punish its Members for disorderly Behaviour, and, with the Concurrence of two thirds, expel a Member.

Each House shall keep a Journal of its Proceedings, and from time to time publish the same, excepting such Parts as may in their Judgment require Secrecy; and the Yeas and Nays of the Members of either House on any question shall, at the Desire of one fifth of those Present, be entered on the Journal.

Neither House, during the Session of Congress, shall, without the Consent of the other, adjourn for more than three days, nor to any other Place than that in which the two Houses shall be sitting.

SECTION 6

The Senators and Representatives shall receive a Compensation for their Services, to be ascertained by Law, and paid out of the Treasury of the United States. They shall in all Cases, except Treason, Felony and Breach of the Peace, be privileged from Arrest during their Attendance at the Session of their respective Houses, and in going to and returning from the same; and for any Speech or Debate in either House, they shall not be questioned in any other Place.

No Senator or Representative shall, during the Time for which he was elected, be appointed to any civil Office under the Authority of the United States, which shall have been created, or the Emoluments whereof shall have been increased during such time; and no Person holding any Office under the United States, shall be a Member of either House during his Continuance in Office.

SECTION 7

All Bills for raising Revenue shall originate in the House of Representatives; but the Senate may propose or concur with Amendments as on other Bills.

Every Bill which shall have passed the House of Representatives and the Senate, shall, before it become a Law, be presented to the President of the United States: If he approve he shall sign it, but if not he shall return it, with his Objections to that

House in which it shall have originated, who shall enter the Objections at large on their Journal, and proceed to reconsider it. If after such Reconsideration two thirds of that House shall agree to pass the Bill, it shall be sent, together with the Objections, to the other House, by which it shall likewise be reconsidered, and if approved by two thirds of that House, it shall become a Law. But in all such Cases the Votes of both Houses shall be determined by yeas and Nays, and the Names of the Persons voting for and against the Bill shall be entered on the Journal of each House respectively. If any Bill shall not be returned by the President within ten Days (Sundays excepted) after it shall have been presented to him, the Same shall be a Law, in like Manner as if he had signed it, unless the Congress by their Adjournment prevent its Return, in which Case it shall not be a Law.

Every Order, Resolution, or Vote to which the Concurrence of the Senate and House of Representatives may be necessary (except on a question of Adjournment) shall be presented to the President of the United States; and before the Same shall take Effect, shall be approved by him, or being disapproved by him, shall be re-passed by two thirds of the Senate and House of Representatives, according to the Rules and Limitations prescribed in the Case of a Bill.

SECTION 8

The Congress shall have Power

To lay and collect Taxes, Duties, Imposts and Excises, to pay the Debts and provide for the common Defence and general Welfare of the United States; but all Duties, Imposts and Excises shall be uniform throughout the United States;

To borrow Money on the credit of the United States;

To regulate Commerce with foreign Nations, and among the several States, and with the Indian Tribes;

To establish an uniform Rule of Naturalization, and uniform Laws on the subject of Bankruptcies throughout the United States;

To coin Money, regulate the Value thereof, and of foreign Coin, and fix the Standard of Weights and Measures;

To provide for the Punishment of counterfeiting the Securities and current Coin of the United States;

To establish Post Offices and post Roads;

To promote the Progress of Science and useful Arts, by securing for limited Times to Authors and Inventors the exclusive Right to their respective Writings and Discoveries;

To constitute Tribunals inferior to the supreme Court;

To define and punish Piracies and Felonies committed on the high Seas, and Offences against the Law of Nations;

To declare War, grant Letters of Marque and Reprisal, and make Rules concerning Captures on Land and Water;

To raise and support Armies, but no Appropriation of Money to that Use shall be for a longer Term than two Years;

To provide and maintain a Navy;

To make Rules for the Government and Regulation of the land and naval Forces;

To provide for calling forth the Militia to execute the Laws of the Union, suppress Insurrections and repel Invasions;

To provide for organizing, arming, and disciplining the Militia, and for governing such Part of them as may be employed in the Service of the United States, reserving to the States respectively, the Appointment of the Officers, and the Authority of training the Militia according to the discipline prescribed by Congress;

To exercise exclusive Legislation in all Cases whatsoever, over such District (not exceeding ten Miles square) as may, by Cession of particular States, and the Acceptance of Congress, become the Seat of the Government of the United States, and to exercise like Authority over all Places purchased by the Consent of the Legislature of the State in which the Same shall be, for the Erection of Forts, Magazines, Arsenals, dock-Yards, and other needful Buildings;—And

To make all Laws which shall be necessary and proper for carrying into Execution the foregoing Powers, and all other Powers vested by this Constitution in the Government of the United States, or in any Department or Officer thereof.

SECTION 9

The Migration or Importation of such Persons as any of the States now existing shall think proper to admit, shall not be prohibited by the Congress prior to the Year one thousand eight hundred and eight, but a Tax or duty may be imposed on such Importation, not exceeding ten dollars for each Person.

The Privilege of the Writ of Habeas Corpus shall not be suspended, unless when in Cases of Rebellion or Invasion the public Safety may require it.

No Bill of Attainder or ex post facto Law shall be passed.

No Capitation, or other direct, Tax shall be laid, unless in Proportion to the Census or enumeration herein before directed to be taken.

No Tax or Duty shall be laid on Articles exported from any State.

No Preference shall be given by any Regulation of Commerce or Revenue to the Ports of one State over those of another; nor shall Vessels bound to, or from, one State, be obliged to enter, clear, or pay Duties in another.

No Money shall be drawn from the Treasury, but in Consequence of Appropriations made by Law; and a regular Statement and Account of the Receipts and Expenditures of all public Money shall be published from time to time.

No Title of Nobility shall be granted by the United States: And no Person holding any Office of Profit or Trust under them, shall, without the Consent of the Congress, accept of any present, Emolument, Office, or Title, of any kind whatever, from any King, Prince, or foreign State.

SECTION 10

No State shall enter into any Treaty, Alliance, or Confederation; grant Letters of Marque and Reprisal; coin Money; emit Bills of Credit; make any Thing but gold and silver Coin a Tender in Payment of Debts; pass any Bill of Attainder, ex post facto Law, or Law impairing the Obligation of Contracts, or grant any Title of Nobility.

No State shall, without the Consent of the Congress, lay any Imposts or Duties on Imports or Exports, except what may be absolutely necessary for executing it's inspection Laws: and the net Produce of all Duties and Imposts, laid by any State on Imports or Exports, shall be for the Use of the Treasury of the United States; and all such Laws shall be subject to the Revision and Control of the Congress.

No State shall, without the Consent of Congress, lay any Duty of Tonnage, keep Troops, or Ships of War in time of Peace, enter into any Agreement or Compact with another State, or with a foreign Power, or engage in War, unless actually invaded, or in such imminent Danger as will not admit of delay.

Article II

SECTION 1

The executive Power shall be vested in a President of the United States of America. He shall hold his Office during the Term of four Years, and, together with the Vice President, chosen for the same Term, be elected, as follows:

Each State shall appoint, in such Manner as the Legislature thereof may direct, a Number of Electors, equal to the whole Number of Senators and Representatives to which the State may be entitled in the Congress: but no Senator or Representative, or Person holding an Office of Trust or Profit under the United States, shall be appointed an Elector.

The Electors shall meet in their respective States, and vote by Ballot for two Persons, of whom one at least shall not be an Inhabitant of the same State with themselves. And they shall make a List of all the Persons voted for, and of the Number of Votes for each; which List they shall sign and certify, and transmit sealed to the Seat of the Government of the United States, directed to the President of the Senate. The President of the Senate shall, in the Presence of the Senate and House of Representatives, open all the Certificates, and the Votes shall then be counted. The Person having the greatest Number of Votes shall be the President, if such Number be a Majority of the whole Number of Electors appointed; and if there be more than one who have such Majority, and have an equal Number of Votes, then the House of Representatives shall immediately choose by Ballot one of them for President; and if no Person have a Majority, then from the five highest on the List the said House shall in like Manner choose the President. But in choosing the President, the Votes shall be taken by States, the Representation from each State having one Vote; A quorum for this purpose shall consist of a Member or Members from two thirds of the States, and a Majority of all the States shall be necessary to a Choice. In every Case, after the Choice of the President, the Person having the greatest Number of Votes of the Electors shall be the Vice President. But if there should remain two or more who have equal Votes, the Senate shall choose from them by Ballot the Vice President.

The Congress may determine the Time of choosing the Electors, and the Day on which they shall give their Votes; which Day shall be the same throughout the United States.

No Person except a natural born Citizen, or a Citizen of the United States, at the time of the Adoption of this Constitution, shall be eligible to the Office of President; neither shall any Person be eligible to that Office who shall not have attained to the Age of thirty five Years, and been fourteen Years a Resident within the United States.

In Case of the Removal of the President from Office, or of his Death, Resignation, or Inability to discharge the Powers and Duties of the said Office, the Same shall devolve on the Vice President, and the Congress may by Law provide for the Case of Removal, Death, Resignation or Inability, both of the President and Vice President, declaring what Officer shall then act as President, and such Officer shall act accordingly, until the Disability be removed, or a President shall be elected.

The President shall, at stated Times, receive for his Services, a Compensation, which shall neither be increased nor diminished during the Period for which he shall have been elected, and he shall not receive within that Period any other Emolument from the United States, or any of them.

Before he enter on the Execution of his Office, he shall take the following Oath or Affirmation:—"I do solemnly swear (or affirm) that I will faithfully execute the Office of President of the United States, and will to the best of my Ability, preserve, protect and defend the Constitution of the United States."

SECTION 2

The President shall be Commander in Chief of the Army and Navy of the United States, and of the Militia of the several States, when called into the actual Service of the United States; he may require the Opinion, in writing, of the principal Officer in each of the executive Departments, upon any Subject relating to the Duties of their respective Offices, and he shall have Power to grant Reprieves and Pardons for Offences against the United States, except in Cases of Impeachment.

He shall have Power, by and with the Advice and Consent of the Senate, to make Treaties, provided two thirds of the Senators present concur; and he shall nominate, and by and with the Advice and Consent of the Senate, shall appoint Ambassadors, other public Ministers and Consuls, Judges of the supreme Court, and all other Officers of the United States, whose Appointments are not herein otherwise provided for, and which shall be established by Law: but the Congress may by Law vest the Appointment of such inferior Officers, as they think proper, in the President alone, in the Courts of Law, or in the Heads of Departments.

The President shall have Power to fill up all Vacancies that may happen during the Recess of the Senate, by granting Commissions which shall expire at the End of their next Session.

SECTION 3

He shall from time to time give to the Congress Information of the State of the Union, and recommend to their Consideration such Measures as he shall judge necessary and expedient; he may, on extraordinary Occasions, convene both Houses, or either of them, and in Case of Disagreement between them, with Respect to the Time of Adjournment, he may adjourn them to such Time as he shall think proper; he shall receive Ambassadors and other public Ministers; he shall take Care that the Laws be faithfully executed, and shall Commission all the Officers of the United States.

SECTION 4

The President, Vice President and all civil Officers of the United States, shall be removed from Office on Impeachment for, and Conviction of, Treason, Bribery, or other high Crimes and Misdemeanors.

Article III

SECTION 1

The judicial Power of the United States shall be vested in one supreme Court, and in such inferior Courts as the Congress may from time to time ordain and establish. The Judges, both of the supreme and inferior Courts, shall hold their Offices during good Behaviour, and shall, at stated Times, receive for their Services a Compensation, which shall not be diminished during their Continuance in Office.

SECTION 2

The judicial Power shall extend to all Cases, in Law and Equity, arising under this Constitution, the Laws of the United States, and Treaties made, or which shall be made, under their Authority;—to all Cases affecting Ambassadors, other public Ministers and Consuls;—to all Cases of admiralty and maritime Jurisdiction;—to Controversies to which the United States shall be a Party;—to Controversies between two or more States;—between a State and Citizens of another State;—between Citizens of different States;—between Citizens of the same State claiming Lands under Grants of different States, and between a State, or the Citizens thereof, and foreign States, Citizens or Subjects.

In all Cases affecting Ambassadors, other public Ministers and Consuls, and those in which a State shall be Party, the supreme Court shall have original Jurisdiction. In all the other Cases before mentioned, the supreme Court shall have appellate Jurisdiction, both as to Law and Fact, with such Exceptions, and under such Regulations as the Congress shall make.

The Trial of all Crimes, except in Cases of Impeachment, shall be by Jury; and such Trial shall be held in the State where the said Crimes shall have been committed; but when not committed within any State, the Trial shall be at such Place or Places as the Congress may by Law have directed.

SECTION 3

Treason against the United States, shall consist only in levying War against them, or in adhering to their Enemies, giving them Aid and Comfort. No Person shall be convicted of Treason unless on the Testimony of two Witnesses to the same overt Act, or on Confession in open Court.

The Congress shall have Power to declare the Punishment of Treason, but no Attainder of Treason shall work Corruption of Blood, or Forfeiture except during the Life of the Person attainted.

Article IV

SECTION 1

Full Faith and Credit shall be given in each State to the public Acts, Records, and judicial Proceedings of every other State. And the Congress may by general Laws prescribe the Manner in which such Acts, Records and Proceedings shall be proved, and the Effect thereof.

SECTION 2

The Citizens of each State shall be entitled to all Privileges and Immunities of Citizens in the several States.

A Person charged in any State with Treason, Felony, or other Crime, who shall flee from Justice, and be found in another State, shall on Demand of the executive Authority of the State from which he fled, be delivered up, to be removed to the State having Jurisdiction of the Crime.

No Person held to Service or Labour in one State, under the Laws thereof, escaping into another, shall, in Consequence of any Law or Regulation therein, be discharged from such Service or Labour, but shall be delivered up on Claim of the Party to whom such Service or Labour may be due.

SECTION 3

New States may be admitted by the Congress into this Union; but no new State shall be formed or erected within the Jurisdiction of any other State; nor any State be formed by the Junction of two or more States, or Parts of States, without the Consent of the Legislatures of the States concerned as well as of the Congress.

The Congress shall have Power to dispose of and make all needful Rules and Regulations respecting the Territory or other Property belonging to the United States; and nothing in this Constitution shall be so construed as to Prejudice any Claims of the United States, or of any particular State.

SECTION 4

The United States shall guarantee to every State in this Union a Republican Form of Government, and shall protect each of them against Invasion; and on Application of the Legislature, or of the Executive (when the Legislature cannot be convened), against domestic Violence.

Article V

The Congress, whenever two thirds of both Houses shall deem it necessary, shall propose Amendments to this Constitution, or, on the Application of the Legislatures of two thirds of the several States, shall call a Convention for proposing Amendments, which, in either Case, shall be valid to all Intents and Purposes, as Part of this Constitution, when ratified by the Legislatures of three fourths of the several States, or by Conventions in three fourths thereof, as the one or the other Mode of Ratification may be proposed by the Congress; Provided that no Amendment which may be made prior to the Year One thousand eight hundred and eight shall in any Manner affect the first and fourth Clauses in the Ninth

Section of the first Article; and that no State, without its Consent, shall be deprived of its equal Suffrage in the Senate.

Article VI

All Debts contracted and Engagements entered into, before the Adoption of this Constitution, shall be as valid against the United States under this Constitution, as under the Confederation.

This Constitution, and the Laws of the United States which shall be made in Pursuance thereof; and all Treaties made, or which shall be made, under the Authority of the United States, shall be the supreme Law of the Land; and the Judges in every State shall be bound thereby, any Thing in the Constitution or Laws of any State to the Contrary notwithstanding.

The Senators and Representatives before mentioned, and the Members of the several State Legislatures, and all executive and judicial Officers, both of the United States and of the several States, shall be bound by Oath or Affirmation, to support this Constitution; but no religious Test shall ever be required as a Qualification to any Office or public Trust under the United States.

Article VII

The Ratification of the Conventions of nine States, shall be sufficient for the Establishment of this Constitution between the States so ratifying the Same.

The Word, "the," being interlined between the seventh and eighth Lines of the first Page, the Word "Thirty" being partly written on an Erazure in the fifteenth Line of the first Page, The Words "is tried" being interlined between the thirty second and thirty third Lines of the first Page and the Word "the" being interlined between the forty third and forty fourth Lines of the second Page.

Attest William Jackson Secretary

Done in Convention by the Unanimous Consent of the States present the Seventeenth Day of September in the Year of our Lord one thousand seven hundred and Eighty seven and of the Independence of the United States of America the Twelfth In witness whereof We have hereunto subscribed our Names,

G°. Washington
Presidt and deputy from Virginia

Delaware
Geo: Read
Gunning Bedford jun
John Dickinson
Richard Bassett
Jaco: Broom

Maryland
James McHenry
Dan of St Thos. Jenifer
Danl. Carroll

Virginia
John Blair
James Madison Jr.

North Carolina
Wm. Blount
Richd. Dobbs Spaight
Hu Williamson

South Carolina
J. Rutledge
Charles Cotesworth Pinckney
Charles Pinckney
Pierce Butler

Georgia
William Few
Abr Baldwin

New Hampshire
John Langdon
Nicholas Gilman

Massachusetts
Nathaniel Gorham
Rufus King

Connecticut
Wm. Saml. Johnson
Roger Sherman

New York
Alexander Hamilton

New Jersey
Wil: Livingston
David Brearley
Wm. Paterson
Jona: Dayton

Pennsylvania

B Franklin

Thomas Mifflin

Robt. Morris

Geo. Clymer

Thos. FitzSimons

Jared Ingersoll

James Wilson

Gouv Morris

Articles

In addition to, and Amendment of the Constitution of the United States of America, proposed by Congress, and ratified by the Legislatures of the several States, pursuant to the fifth Article of the original Constitution.

(The first ten amendments to the U.S. Constitution were ratified December 15, 1791, and form what is known as the "Bill of Rights.")

AMENDMENT I

Congress shall make no law respecting an establishment of religion, or prohibiting the free exercise thereof; or abridging the freedom of speech, or of the press; or the right of the people peaceably to assemble, and to petition the Government for a redress of grievances.

AMENDMENT II

A well regulated Militia, being necessary to the security of a free State, the right of the people to keep and bear Arms, shall not be infringed.

AMENDMENT III

No Soldier shall, in time of peace be quartered in any house, without the consent of the Owner, nor in time of war, but in a manner to be prescribed by law.

AMENDMENT IV

The right of the people to be secure in their persons, houses, papers, and effects, against unreasonable searches and seizures, shall not be violated, and no Warrants shall issue, but upon probable cause, supported by Oath or affirmation, and particularly describing the place to be searched, and the persons or things to be seized.

AMENDMENT V

No person shall be held to answer for a capital, or otherwise infamous crime, unless on a presentment or indictment of a Grand Jury, except in cases arising in the land or naval forces, or in the Militia, when in actual service in time of War or public danger; nor shall any person be subject for the same offence to be twice put in jeopardy of life or limb; nor shall be compelled in any criminal case to be a witness against himself, nor be deprived of life, liberty, or property, without due process of law; nor shall private property be taken for public use, without just compensation.

AMENDMENT VI

In all criminal prosecutions, the accused shall enjoy the right to a speedy and public trial, by an impartial jury of the State and district wherein the crime shall have been committed, which district shall have been previously ascertained by law, and to be informed of the nature and cause of the accusation; to be confronted with the witnesses against him; to have compulsory process for obtaining witnesses in his favor, and to have the Assistance of Counsel for his defence.

AMENDMENT VII

In Suits at common law, where the value in controversy shall exceed twenty dollars, the right of trial by jury shall be preserved, and no fact tried by a jury, shall be otherwise re-examined in any Court of the United States, than according to the rules of the common law.

AMENDMENT VIII

Excessive bail shall not be required, nor excessive fines imposed, nor cruel and unusual punishments inflicted.

AMENDMENT IX

The enumeration in the Constitution, of certain rights, shall not be construed to deny or disparage others retained by the people.

AMENDMENT X

The powers not delegated to the United States by the Constitution, nor prohibited by it to the States, are reserved to the States respectively, or to the people.

AMENDMENT XI

Passed by Congress March 4, 1794. Ratified February 7, 1795.

Note: Article III, Section 2, of the Constitution was modified by Amendment XI. The Judicial power of the United States shall not be construed to extend to any suit in law or equity, commenced or prosecuted against one of the United States by Citizens of another State, or by Citizens or Subjects of any Foreign State.

AMENDMENT XII

Passed by Congress December 9, 1803. Ratified June 15, 1804.

Note: A portion of Article II, Section 1, of the Constitution was superseded by the Twelfth Amendment.

The Electors shall meet in their respective states and vote by ballot for President and Vice-President, one of whom, at least, shall not be an inhabitant of the same state with themselves; they shall name in their ballots the person voted for as President, and in distinct ballots the person voted for as Vice-President, and they shall make distinct lists of all persons voted for as President, and of all persons voted for as Vice-President, and of the number of votes for each, which lists they shall sign and certify, and transmit sealed to the seat of the government of the United States, directed to the President of the Senate;—the President of the Senate shall, in the presence of the Senate and House of Representatives, open all the certificates and the votes shall then be counted;—The person having the greatest number of votes for President, shall be the President, if such number be a majority of the whole number of Electors appointed; and if no person have such majority, then from the persons having the highest numbers not exceeding three on the list of those voted for as President, the House of Representatives shall choose immediately, by ballot, the President. But in choosing the President, the votes shall be taken by states, the representation from each state having one vote; a quorum for this purpose shall consist of a member or members from two-thirds of the states, and a majority of all the states shall be necessary to a choice. [And if the House of Representatives shall not choose a President whenever the right of choice shall devolve upon them, before the fourth day of March next following, then the Vice-President shall act as President, as in case of the death or other constitutional disability of the President.—]* The person having the greatest number of votes as Vice-President, shall be the Vice-President, if such number be a majority of the whole number of Electors appointed, and if no person have a majority, then from the two highest numbers on the list, the Senate shall choose the Vice-President; a quorum for the purpose shall consist of two-thirds of the whole number of Senators, and a majority of the whole number shall be necessary to a choice. But no person constitutionally ineligible to the office of President shall be eligible to that of Vice-President of the United States.

AMENDMENT XIII

Passed by Congress January 31, 1865. Ratified December 6, 1865.

Note: A portion of Article IV, Section 2, of the Constitution was superseded by the Thirteenth Amendment.

*Superseded by Section 3 of the Twentieth Amendment.

Section 1

Neither slavery nor involuntary servitude, except as a punishment for crime whereof the party shall have been duly convicted, shall exist within the United States, or any place subject to their jurisdiction.

Section 2

Congress shall have power to enforce this article by appropriate legislation.

AMENDMENT XIV

Passed by Congress June 13, 1866. Ratified July 9, 1868.

Note: Article I, Section 2, of the Constitution was modified by Section 2 of the Fourteenth Amendment.

Section 1

All persons born or naturalized in the United States, and subject to the jurisdiction thereof, are citizens of the United States and of the State wherein they reside. No State shall make or enforce any law which shall abridge the privileges or immunities of citizens of the United States; nor shall any State deprive any person of life, liberty, or property, without due process of law; nor deny to any person within its jurisdiction the equal protection of the laws.

Section 2

Representatives shall be apportioned among the several States according to their respective numbers, counting the whole number of persons in each State, excluding Indians not taxed. But when the right to vote at any election for the choice of electors for President and Vice-President of the United States, Representatives in Congress, the Executive and Judicial officers of a State, or the members of the Legislature thereof, is denied to any of the male inhabitants of such State, being twenty-one years of age,* and citizens of the United States, or in any way abridged, except for participation in rebellion, or other crime, the basis of representation therein shall be reduced in the proportion which the number of such male citizens shall bear to the whole number of male citizens twenty-one years of age in such State.

Section 3

No person shall be a Senator or Representative in Congress, or elector of President and Vice-President, or hold any office, civil or military, under the United States, or under any State, who, having previously taken an oath, as a member of Congress, or as an officer of the United States, or as a member of any State legislature, or as an executive or judicial officer of any State, to support the Constitution of the United

*Changed by Section 1 of the Twenty-sixth Amendment.

States, shall have engaged in insurrection or rebellion against the same, or given aid or comfort to the enemies thereof. But Congress may by a vote of two-thirds of each House, remove such disability.

Section 4

The validity of the public debt of the United States, authorized by law, including debts incurred for payment of pensions and bounties for services in suppressing insurrection or rebellion, shall not be questioned. But neither the United States nor any State shall assume or pay any debt or obligation incurred in aid of insurrection or rebellion against the United States, or any claim for the loss or emancipation of any slave; but all such debts, obligations and claims shall be held illegal and void.

Section 5

The Congress shall have the power to enforce, by appropriate legislation, the provisions of this article.

AMENDMENT XV

Passed by Congress February 26, 1869. Ratified February 3, 1870.

Section 1

The right of citizens of the United States to vote shall not be denied or abridged by the United States or by any State on account of race, color, or previous condition of servitude.

Section 2

The Congress shall have the power to enforce this article by appropriate legislation.

AMENDMENT XVI

Passed by Congress July 2, 1909. Ratified February 3, 1913.
Note: Article I, Section 9, of the Constitution was modified by Amendment XVI.
The Congress shall have power to lay and collect taxes on incomes, from whatever source derived, without apportionment among the several States, and without regard to any census or enumeration.

AMENDMENT XVII

Passed by Congress May 13, 1912. Ratified April 8, 1913.
Note: Article I, Section 3, of the Constitution was modified by the Seventeenth Amendment.
The Senate of the United States shall be composed of two Senators from each State, elected by the people thereof, for six years; and each Senator shall have one vote.

The electors in each State shall have the qualifications requisite for electors of the most numerous branch of the State legislatures.

When vacancies happen in the representation of any State in the Senate, the executive authority of such State shall issue writs of election to fill such vacancies: Provided, That the legislature of any State may empower the executive thereof to make temporary appointments until the people fill the vacancies by election as the legislature may direct.

This amendment shall not be so construed as to affect the election or term of any Senator chosen before it becomes valid as part of the Constitution.

AMENDMENT XVIII

Passed by Congress December 18, 1917. Ratified January 16, 1919. Repealed by Amendment XXI.

Section 1

After one year from the ratification of this article the manufacture, sale, or transportation of intoxicating liquors within, the importation thereof into, or the exportation thereof from the United States and all territory subject to the jurisdiction thereof for beverage purposes is hereby prohibited.

Section 2

The Congress and the several States shall have concurrent power to enforce this article by appropriate legislation.

Section 3

This article shall be inoperative unless it shall have been ratified as an amendment to the Constitution by the legislatures of the several States, as provided in the Constitution, within seven years from the date of the submission hereof to the States by the Congress.

AMENDMENT XIX

Passed by Congress June 4, 1919. Ratified August 18, 1920.

The right of citizens of the United States to vote shall not be denied or abridged by the United States or by any State on account of sex.

Congress shall have power to enforce this article by appropriate legislation.

AMENDMENT XX

Passed by Congress March 2, 1932. Ratified January 23, 1933.

Note: Article I, Section 4, of the Constitution was modified by Section 2 of this amendment. In addition, a portion of the Twelfth Amendment was superseded by Section 3.

Section 1

The terms of the President and the Vice President shall end at noon on the 20th day of January, and the terms of Senators and Representatives at noon on the 3d day of January, of the years in which such terms would have ended if this article had not been ratified; and the terms of their successors shall then begin.

Section 2

The Congress shall assemble at least once in every year, and such meeting shall begin at noon on the 3d day of January, unless they shall by law appoint a different day.

Section 3

If, at the time fixed for the beginning of the term of the President, the President elect shall have died, the Vice President elect shall become President. If a President shall not have been chosen before the time fixed for the beginning of his term, or if the President elect shall have failed to qualify, then the Vice President elect shall act as President until a President shall have qualified; and the Congress may by law provide for the case wherein neither a President elect nor a Vice President shall have qualified, declaring who shall then act as President, or the manner in which one who is to act shall be selected, and such person shall act accordingly until a President or Vice President shall have qualified.

Section 4

The Congress may by law provide for the case of the death of any of the persons from whom the House of Representatives may choose a President whenever the right of choice shall have devolved upon them, and for the case of the death of any of the persons from whom the Senate may choose a Vice President whenever the right of choice shall have devolved upon them.

Section 5

Sections 1 and 2 shall take effect on the 15th day of October following the ratification of this article.

Section 6

This article shall be inoperative unless it shall have been ratified as an amendment to the Constitution by the legislatures of three-fourths of the several States within seven years from the date of its submission.

AMENDMENT XXI

Passed by Congress February 20, 1933. Ratified December 5, 1933.

Section 1

The eighteenth article of amendment to the Constitution of the United States is hereby repealed.

Section 2

The transportation or importation into any State, Territory, or Possession of the United States for delivery or use therein of intoxicating liquors, in violation of the laws thereof, is hereby prohibited.

Section 3

This article shall be inoperative unless it shall have been ratified as an amendment to the Constitution by conventions in the several States, as provided in the Constitution, within seven years from the date of the submission hereof to the States by the Congress.

AMENDMENT XXII

Passed by Congress March 21, 1947. Ratified February 27, 1951.

Section 1

No person shall be elected to the office of the President more than twice, and no person who has held the office of President, or acted as President, for more than two years of a term to which some other person was elected President shall be elected to the office of President more than once. But this Article shall not apply to any person holding the office of President when this Article was proposed by Congress, and shall not prevent any person who may be holding the office of President, or acting as President, during the term within which this Article becomes operative from holding the office of President or acting as President during the remainder of such term.

Section 2

This article shall be inoperative unless it shall have been ratified as an amendment to the Constitution by the legislatures of three-fourths of the several States within seven years from the date of its submission to the States by the Congress.

AMENDMENT XXIII

Passed by Congress June 16, 1960. Ratified March 29, 1961.

Section 1

The District constituting the seat of Government of the United States shall appoint in such manner as Congress may direct:

A number of electors of President and Vice President equal to the whole number of Senators and Representatives in Congress to which the District would be entitled if it were a State, but in no event more than the least populous State; they shall be in addition to those appointed by the States, but they shall be considered, for the purposes of the election of President and Vice President, to be electors appointed by a State; and they shall meet in the District and perform such duties as provided by the twelfth article of amendment.

Section 2
The Congress shall have power to enforce this article by appropriate legislation.

AMENDMENT XXIV
Passed by Congress August 27, 1962. Ratified January 23, 1964.

Section 1
The right of citizens of the United States to vote in any primary or other election for President or Vice President, for electors for President or Vice President, or for Senator or Representative in Congress, shall not be denied or abridged by the United States or any State by reason of failure to pay poll tax or other tax.

Section 2
The Congress shall have power to enforce this article by appropriate legislation.

AMENDMENT XXV
Passed by Congress July 6, 1965. Ratified February 10, 1967.
Note: Article II, Section 1, of the Constitution was affected by the Twenty-fifth Amendment.

Section 1
In case of the removal of the President from office or of his death or resignation, the Vice President shall become President.

Section 2
Whenever there is a vacancy in the office of the Vice President, the President shall nominate a Vice President who shall take office upon confirmation by a majority vote of both Houses of Congress.

Section 3
Whenever the President transmits to the President pro tempore of the Senate and the Speaker of the House of Representatives his written declaration that he

is unable to discharge the powers and duties of his office, and until he transmits to them a written declaration to the contrary, such powers and duties shall be discharged by the Vice President as Acting President.

Section 4

Whenever the Vice President and a majority of either the principal officers of the executive departments or of such other body as Congress may by law provide, transmit to the President pro tempore of the Senate and the Speaker of the House of Representatives their written declaration that the President is unable to discharge the powers and duties of his office, the Vice President shall immediately assume the powers and duties of the office as Acting President.

Thereafter, when the President transmits to the President pro tempore of the Senate and the Speaker of the House of Representatives his written declaration that no inability exists, he shall resume the powers and duties of his office unless the Vice President and a majority of either the principal officers of the executive department or of such other body as Congress may by law provide, transmit within four days to the President pro tempore of the Senate and the Speaker of the House of Representatives their written declaration that the President is unable to discharge the powers and duties of his office. Thereupon Congress shall decide the issue, assembling within forty-eight hours for that purpose if not in session. If the Congress, within twenty-one days after receipt of the latter written declaration, or, if Congress is not in session, within twenty-one days after Congress is required to assemble, determines by two-thirds vote of both Houses that the President is unable to discharge the powers and duties of his office, the Vice President shall continue to discharge the same as Acting President; otherwise, the President shall resume the powers and duties of his office.

AMENDMENT XXVI

Passed by Congress March 23, 1971. Ratified July 1, 1971.

Note: Amendment XIV, Section 2, of the Constitution was modified by Section 1 of the Twenty-sixth Amendment.

Section 1

The right of citizens of the United States, who are eighteen years of age or older, to vote shall not be denied or abridged by the United States or by any State on account of age.

Section 2

The Congress shall have power to enforce this article by appropriate legislation.

AMENDMENT XXVII

Originally proposed Sept. 25, 1789. Ratified May 7, 1992.

No law, varying the compensation for the services of the Senators and Representatives, shall take effect, until an election of representatives shall have intervened.

Lincoln's Gettysburg Address (1863)

Four score and seven years ago our fathers brought forth on this continent, a new nation, conceived in Liberty, and dedicated to the proposition that all men are created equal.

Now we are engaged in a great civil war, testing whether that nation, or any nation so conceived and so dedicated, can long endure. We are met on a great battle-field of that war. We have come to dedicate a portion of that field, as a final resting place for those who here gave their lives that that nation might live. It is altogether fitting and proper that we should do this.

But, in a larger sense, we can not dedicate—we can not consecrate—we can not hallow—this ground. The brave men, living and dead, who struggled here, have consecrated it, far above our poor power to add or detract. The world will little note, nor long remember what we say here, but it can never forget what they did here. It is for us the living, rather, to be dedicated here to the unfinished work which they who fought here have thus far so nobly advanced. It is rather for us to be here dedicated to the great task remaining before us—that from these honored dead we take increased devotion to that cause for which they gave the last full measure of devotion—that we here highly resolve that these dead shall not have died in vain—that this nation, under God, shall have a new birth of freedom—and that government of the people, by the people, for the people, shall not perish from the earth.

Appendix B
Historical Facts and Data

US Presidents and Vice Presidents

	President	Vice President	Political Party	Term
			Table App B-1 Presidents and Vice Presidents	
1	George Washington	John Adams	No party designation	1789–1797
2	John Adams	Thomas Jefferson	Federalist	1797–1801
3	Thomas Jefferson	Aaron Burr George Clinton	Democratic (Pres.) Republican (VP)	1801–1809
4	James Madison	George Clinton Elbridge Gerry	Democratic (Pres.) Republican (VP)	1809–1817
5	James Monroe	Daniel D. Tompkins	Democratic (Pres.) Republican (VP)	1817–1825
6	John Quincy Adams	John C. Calhoun	National Republican (Pres.) Republican (VP)	1825–1829
7	Andrew Jackson	John C. Calhoun (1829–1832) Martin Van Buren (1833–1837)	Democratic	1829–1837
8	Martin Van Buren	Richard M. Johnson	Democratic	1837–1841
9	William Henry Harrison	John Tyler	Whig	1841
10	John Tyler	None	Whig	1841–1845
11	James Knox Polk	George M. Dallas	Democratic	1845–1849
12	Zachary Taylor	Millard Fillmore	Whig	1849–1850
13	Millard Fillmore	None	Whig	1850–1853
14	Franklin Pierce	William R. King	Democratic	1853–1857
15	James Buchanan	John C. Breckinridge	Democratic	1857–1861
16	Abraham Lincoln	Hannibal Hamlin Andrew Johnson	Republican Democratic	1861–1865
17	Andrew Johnson	None	Democratic	1865–1869

	President	Vice President	Political Party	Term
18	Ulysses Simpson Grant	Schuyler Colfax Henry Wilson	Republican	1869–1877
19	Rutherford Birchard Hayes	William A. Wheeler	Republican	1877–1881
20	James Abram Garfield	Chester Alan Arthur	Republican	1881
21	Chester Alan Arthur	None	Republican	1881–1885
22	Stephen Grover Cleveland	Thomas Hendricks	Democratic	1885–1889
23	Benjamin Harrison	Levi P. Morton	Republican	1889–1893
24	Stephen Grover Cleveland	Adlai E. Stevenson	Democratic	1893–1897
25	William McKinley	Garret A. Hobart Theodore Roosevelt	Republican	1897–1901
26	Theodore Roosevelt	Charles W. Fairbanks (no VP 1901–1905)	Republican	1901–1909
27	William Howard Taft	James S. Sherman	Republican	1909–1913
28	Woodrow Wilson	Thomas R. Marshall	Democratic	1913–1921
29	Warren Gamaliel Harding	Calvin Coolidge	Republican	1921–1923
30	Calvin Coolidge	Charles G. Dawes	Republican	1923–1929
31	Herbert Clark Hoover	Charles Curtis	Republican	1929–1933
32	Franklin Delano Roosevelt	John Nance Garner Henry A. Wallace Harry S. Truman	Democratic	1933–1945
33	Harry S. Truman	Alben W. Barkley (1949–1953)	Democratic	1945–1953
34	Dwight David Eisenhower	Richard Milhous Nixon	Republican	1953–1961
35	John Fitzgerald Kennedy	Lyndon Baines Johnson	Democratic	1961–1963
36	Lyndon Baines Johnson	Hubert Horatio Humphrey (1965–1968)	Democratic	1963–1969
37	Richard Milhous Nixon	Spiro T. Agnew Gerald Rudolph Ford	Republican	1969–1974
38	Gerald Rudolph Ford	Nelson Rockefeller	Republican	1974–1977
39	James Earl Carter Jr.	Walter Mondale	Democratic	1977–1981
40	Ronald Wilson Reagan	George Herbert Walker Bush	Republican	1981–1989
41	George Herbert Walker Bush	J. Danforth Quayle	Republican	1989–1993
42	William Jefferson Clinton	Albert Gore Jr.	Democratic	1993–2001
43	George Walker Bush	Richard Cheney	Republican	2001–2009
44	Barack Hussein Obama	Joseph R. Biden Jr.	Democratic	2009–2017
45	Donald J. Trump	Michael R. Pence	Republican	2017–2021
46	Joseph R. Biden Jr.	Kamala D. Harris	Democratic	2021–

Admission of States into the Union

	Table App B-2 Admission of States into the Union	
	State	**Date of Admission**
1	Delaware	December 7, 1787
2	Pennsylvania	December 12, 1787
3	New Jersey	December 18, 1787
4	Georgia	January 2, 1788
5	Connecticut	January 9, 1788
6	Massachusetts	February 6, 1788
7	Maryland	April 28, 1788
8	South Carolina	May 23, 1788
9	New Hampshire	June 21, 1788
10	Virginia	June 25, 1788
11	New York	July 26, 1788
12	North Carolina	November 21, 1789
13	Rhode Island	May 29, 1790
14	Vermont	March 4, 1791
15	Kentucky	June 1, 1792
16	Tennessee	June 1, 1796
17	Ohio	March 1, 1803
18	Louisiana	April 30, 1812
19	Indiana	December 11, 1816
20	Mississippi	December 10, 1817
21	Illinois	December 3, 1818
22	Alabama	December 14, 1819
23	Maine	March 15, 1820
24	Missouri	August 10, 1821
25	Arkansas	June 15, 1836
26	Michigan	January 26, 1837
27	Florida	March 3, 1845
28	Texas	December 29, 1845
29	Iowa	December 28, 1846
30	Wisconsin	May 29, 1848

	State	Date of Admission
31	California	September 9, 1850
32	Minnesota	May 11, 1858
33	Oregon	February 14, 1859
34	Kansas	January 29, 1861
35	West Virginia	June 20, 1863
36	Nevada	October 31, 1864
37	Nebraska	March 1, 1867
38	Colorado	August 1, 1876
39	North Dakota	November 2, 1889
40	South Dakota	November 2, 1889
41	Montana	November 8, 1889
42	Washington	November 11, 1889
43	Idaho	July 3, 1890
44	Wyoming	July 10, 1890
45	Utah	January 4, 1896
46	Oklahoma	November 16, 1907
47	New Mexico	January 6, 1912
48	Arizona	February 14, 1912
49	Alaska	January 3, 1959
50	Hawaii	August 21, 1959

Credits

Image Credits

Cover and p. iii *(left)*, William James Glackens. Girl in Green Turban, c. 1913. The Barnes Foundation. BF172. Peter Turnley / Contributor; Cover and p. iii *(right)*, © 2023 Wyeth Foundation for American Art / Artists Rights Society (ARS), New York

Chapter 15

P. 608, Courtesy of the Library of Congress; p. 614, Courtesy of the Library of Congress; p. 618, Courtesy of the Library of Congress; p. 620, Courtesy of the Library of Congress; p. 623, Courtesy of the Library of Congress; p. 625, Division of Cultural and Community Life, National Museum of American History, Smithsonian Institution; p. 628, A: National Portrait Gallery, Smithsonian Institution, in memory of Kenneth G. Murphy, B: William T. Sherman Mathew Brady Studio. Glass plate collodion negative. National Portrait Gallery, Smithsonian Institution; Frederick Hill Meserve Collection; p. 634, Courtesy of the Library of Congress; p. 635, Courtesy of the Library of Congress; p. 639, Courtesy of the Library of Congress

Chapter 16

P. 646, National Portrait Gallery, Smithsonian Institution; p. 653, Sarin Images / GRANGER; p. 659, Sarin Images / GRANGER; p. 668, Division of Political and Military History, National Museum of American History, Smithsonian Institution; p. 672, National Portrait Gallery, Smithsonian Institution; p. 674, Sarin Images / GRANGER; p. 677, Sarin Images / GRANGER; p. 680, GRANGER; p. 681, GRANGER

Chapter 17

P. 688, Courtesy of the Library of Congress; p. 694, Andrew J Russell / Wikipedia; p. 695, Division of Political and Military History, National Museum of American History, Smithsonian Institution; p. 702, National Child Labor Committee (Lewis Hine photographs); p. 704, Harry T. Peters "America on Stone" Lithography Collection; p. 705, The Picture Art Collection / Alamy Stock Photo; p. 708, A: National Archives photo NAID: 533791, B: Courtesy of the Library of Congress; p. 712, Courtesy of the Library of Congress; p. 714, Asar Studios / Alamy Stock Photo; p. 715, Sarin Images / GRANGER; p. 719, Division of Political and Military History, National Museum of American History, Smithsonian Institution; p. 722, National Portrait Gallery, Smithsonian Institution; gift of Margaret Carnegie Miller; p. 725, A: From The New York Public Library, B: Historic Collection / Alamy Stock Photo

Chapter 18

P. 732, National Museum of American History; p. 738, Courtesy of the Library of Congress; p. 740, Smithsonian Institution Archives; p. 742, unknown author / Wikipedia; p. 743, M.B. Leiser, engraver / Wikipedia; p. 746, Courtesy of the Library of Congress; p. 747, Courtesy of the Library of Congress; p. 751, Sarin Images / GRANGER; p. 754, Courtesy of the Library of Congress; p. 755, Giuseppe Pellizza da Volpedo, Public domain, via Wikimedia Commons; p. 758, Courtesy of the Library of Congress; p. 760, Wisconsin Historical Society, WHI-3238; p. 764, Courtesy of the Library of Congress; p. 767, Sarin Images / GRANGER

Chapter 19

P. 778, Allen, Gordon, Schroeppel and Redlich, Inc., photographer. "Jane Addams and a group of children at Hull-House," JAMC_0000_0030_0058, Seven Settlement Houses digital image collection, Special Collections and University Archives, University of Illinois at Chicago.; p. 783, Library of Congress, Prints and Photographs Division, National Child Labor Committee Collection, LC-USZ62-108765; p. 784, Preus museum, No restrictions, via Wikimedia Commons; p. 786, Security Pacific National Bank Collection/Los Angeles Public Library; p. 787, Courtesy of the Library of Congress; p. 790, Chicago History Museum, ICHi-004064; p. 791, Courtesy of the Library of Congress; p. 795, Courtesy of the Library of Congress; p. 797, Courtesy of the Library of Congress; p. 800, Courtesy of the Library of Congress; p. 802, George Frederick Keller, Public domain, via Wikimedia Commons; p. 804, Library of Congress, Public domain, via Wikimedia Commons; p. 812, Division of Political and Military History, National Museum of American History, Smithsonian Institution; p. 813, Courtesy of the Library of Congress Institution

Chapter 20

P. 820, Courtesy of the Library of Congress; p. 828, Courtesy of the Library of Congress; p. 830, Courtesy of the Library of Congress; p. 832, National Portrait Gallery, Smithsonian Institution; gift of the Bernice Pauahi Bishop Museum; p. 834, Smithsonian American Art Museum, Gift of Mrs. Theodore J. Richardson; p. 839, From The New York Public Library, NY; p. 843, Courtesy of the Library of Congress; p. 844, National Portrait Gallery, public domain via Wikimedia Commons; p. 847, Northwest Photo Co., Chadron, Neb., Public domain, via Wikimedia Commons; p. 858, Courtesy of the Library of Congress; p. 859, Courtesy of the Library of Congress; p. 849, Courtesy of the Library of Congress; p. 850, Bernhard Gillam, Public domain, via Wikimedia Commons; p. 852, GRANGER; p. 855, Courtesy of the Library of Congress; p. 862, Sarin Images / GRANGER

Chapter 21

P. 868, A: Agence de presse Meurisse, Public domain, via Wikimedia Commons, B: Library of Congress, public domain, via Wikimedia; p. 878, Courtesy of the Library of Congress; p. 879, DAE-10391738: ©DEA PICTURE LIBRARY/De Agostini Editore/agefotostock; p. 882, Courtesy of the Library of Congress; p. 883, Courtesy of the Library of Congress; p. 884, Library of Congress, Prints and Photographs Division, Alfred Bendiner Memorial Collection, LC-USZ62-107709; p. 886, Courtesy of the Library of Congress; p. 887, Library of Congress, Prints and Photographs Division, American National Red Cross Collection, LC-DIG-ppmsca-123456; p. 890, Courtesy of the Library of Congress; p. 893, Division of Political and Military History, National Museum of American History, Smithsonian Institution; p. 898, Rue des Archives / GRANGER; p. 899, Collection of the Smithsonian National Museum of African American History and Culture; p. 902, Collection of the Smithsonian National Museum of African American History and Culture, Gift of Cassandra P. Johnson Smith; p. 906, Courtesy of the Library of Congress; p. 908, Bettmann / Contributor; p. 910, A: 1997.10.19, Washington State Historical Society, Tacoma (Wash.), B: National Archives at College Park - Still Pictures

Chapter 22

P. 918, Everett Collection / Bridgeman Images; p. 925, Image from the Collections of The Henry Ford; p. 927, From Chicago Tribune © 1921 Chicago Tribune. All rights reserved. Used under license; p. 930, Courtesy of the Library of Congress; p. 932, American Photo Archive / Alamy Stock Photo; p. 934, Public domain, via Wikimedia Commons; p. 936, Whitney Museum of American Art, New York; gift of Edith and Milton Lowenthal in memory of Juliana Force; p. 940, Courtesy of the Library of Congress; p. 941, Tango Images / Alamy Stock Photo; p. 942, Division of Political and Military History, National Museum of American History, Smithsonian Institution; p. 947, Courtesy of the Library of Congress; p. 948, A: Courtesy of the Library of Congress,

B: Courtesy of the Library of Congress; p. 949, Uncredited news photographer, Public domain, via Wikimedia Commons; p. 950, Everett Collection / Bridgeman Images

Chapter 23

P. 958, Charles L. Todd and Robert Sonkin migrant workers collection (AFC 1985/001), American Folklife Center, Library of Congress; p. 963, Everett Collection Historical / Alamy Stock Photo; p. 966, Peter Barritt / Alamy Stock Photo; p. 967, UIG-975-05-SOV-C-001: ©Sovfoto/UNIVERSAL IMAGES GROUP/agefotostock; p. 969, Smithsonian American Art Museum, Gift of Mr. and Mrs. Moses Soyer; p. 971, GRANGER; p. 972, Courtesy of the Library of Congress; p. 978, From The New York Public Library; p. 979, Courtesy of the Library of Congress; p. 985, The Print Collector / Alamy Stock Photo; p. 986, agefotostock / Alamy Stock Photo

Chapter 24

P. 998, Sarin Images / GRANGER; p. 1004, Printed by permission of the Norman Rockwell Family Agency Copyright ©1943 the Norman Rockwell Family Entities; p. 1005, A: Image provided by Curtis Licensing, B: Image provided by Curtis Licensing; p. 1014, Unknown (Pseudonym: Hans Stalüter / Horst Schlüter), Public domain, via Wikimedia Commons; p. 1016, A: Courtesy of the Library of Congress, B: Courtesy of the Library of Congress; p. 1018, A: GRANGER, B: GRANGER; p. 1020, Courtesy of the Library of Congress; p. 1022, Courtesy of the Library of Congress; p. 1025, Alpha Stock / Alamy Stock Photo; p. 1027, Agence Roger Viollet / GRANGER; p. 1029, National Archives and Records Administration, public domain, via Wikimedia; p. 1030, Bill Waterson / Alamy Stock Photo; p. 1034, Everett Collection Inc / Alamy Stock Photo

Chapter 25

P. 1040, Public domain / https://www.bonestell .org/Image-Gallery.aspx#images-14; p. 1046, University of Liverpool Faculty of Health & Life Sciences from Liverpool, United Kingdom, CC BY-SA 2.0 <https://creativecommons.org/licenses/by-sa/2.0>, via Wikimedia Commons; p. 1047, Library of Congress, Prints and Photographs Division, NYWT&S Collection, LC-DIG-ppmsca-04642; p. 1048, Index Fototeca / Bridgeman Images; p. 1052, Shawshots / Alamy Stock Photo; p. 1054, Keystone-France / Contributor; p. 1056, Everett Collection Inc / Alamy Stock Photo; p. 1061, Patti McConville / Alamy Stock Photo; p. 1062, Pictorial Press Ltd / Alamy Stock Photo; p. 1063, ClassicStock / Alamy Stock Photo; p. 1064, AP Photo; p. 1066, Everett Collection Inc / Alamy Stock Photo; p. 1068 vint3 / Alamy Stock Photo; p. 1069, Nixon Presidential Library and Museum, Public domain, via Wikimedia Commons; p. 1071, Courtesy of National Archives, photo no. 531373; p. 1076, William J. Eisenlord. City Lights Bookstore, ca. 1959. William J. Eisenlord photographs, 1953-1976. Archives of American Art, Smithsonian Institution.; p. 1077, Division of Culture and the Arts, National Museum of American History, Smithsonian Institution.; p. 1078, Courtesy of the Library of Congress; p. 1079, AP images; p. 1080, Associated Press; p. 1081, Collection of the Smithsonian National Museum of African American History and Culture, Gift of Paxton and Rachel Baker

Chapter 26

P. 1088, By S.Sgt. Albert R. Simpson. Department of Defense. Department of the Army. Office of the Deputy Chief of Staff for Operations. U.S. Army Audiovisual Center., Public domain, via Wikimedia Commons; p. 1096, John F. Kennedy. Flip Schulke 1963. Gelatin silver print. National Portrait Gallery, Smithsonian Institution © 1963 Flip Schulke; p. 1098, Division of Political and Military History, National Museum of American History, Smithsonian Institution; p. 1100, GRANGER; p. 1102, Charles Moore / Contributor; p. 1103, © 1976, Ivan Massar / TakeStock; p. 1105, Yoichi Okamoto, Public domain, via Wikimedia Commons; p. 1107, © 1976, George Ballis / TakeStock; p. 1108, © 1976, Matt Herron / TakeStock; p. 1114, GRANGER; p. 1118, Courtesy of the Library of Congress; p. 1120, Image courtesy of the photographer, Builder Levy; p. 1121, Smithsonian American Art Museum, Museum

Text Credits

Chapter 15

P. 641, Courtesy of the Library of Congress; p. 643, Courtesy of the Library of Congress

Chapter 17

P. 728, Courtesy of the Library of Congress

Chapter 19

P. 816, Oregon Voter, 5 June 1920

Chapter 22

P. 953, Used with Permission of the Long Legacy Project, www.HueyLong.com; p. 955, Principles of the National Union of Social Justice (1936)

Chapter 24

P. 1036, Henry Luce, Life Magazine, February 17, 1941, Springer; Copyright © 1969, Springer

Chapter 25

P. 1984, The Platform of the Progressive Party adopted at the Founding Convention, Philadelphia, July 23–25, 1948

Chapter 27

P. 1180, Philip Kurland, "What Watergate Revealed About Presidential Power in America, 1974 © 2004–2023 Chicago Booth Review; p. 1181, Center for American Progress

Chapter 28

P. 1224, https://www.reaganfoundation.org; p. 1226, National Council on Crime and Delinquency

Index

Note: Tables and figures are indicated by an italic *t* and *f* following the page number.